NORTHERN CALIFORNIA HIKING

ANN MARIE BROWN & FELICIA LEO KEMP

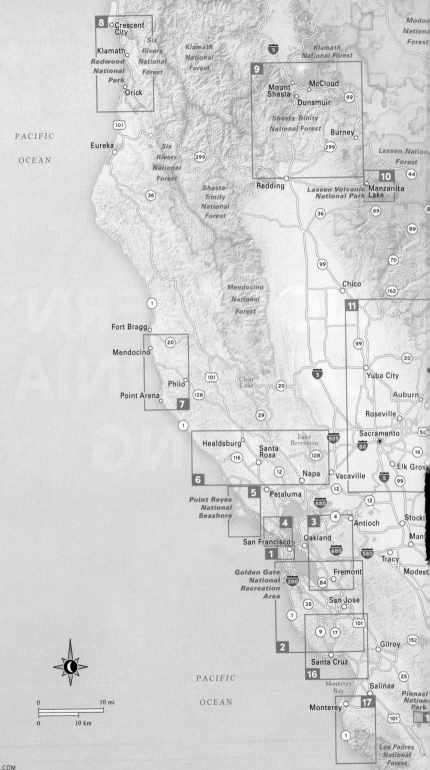

NORTHERN CALIFORNIA HIKING REGIONS

1. San Francisco
2. Peninsula & South Bay
3. East Bay
4. Muir Woods & Mount Tamalpais
5. Point Reyes National Seashore
6. Napa & Sonoma
7. Mendocino
8. North Coast & Redwood Empire
9. Shasta-Trinity National Forest
10. Lassen Volcanic National Park
11. Sacramento & Gold Country
12. Tahoe
13. Yosemite National Park
14. Eastern Sierra
15. Sequoia & Kings Canyon National Parks
16. Santa Cruz
17. Monterey & Big Sur
18. Pinnacles National Park

CONTENTS

NORTHERN
CALIFORNIA HIKING
TOP EXPERIENCES

1 Reveling in the beauty of blankets of flowers in bloom (pages 55, 348, and 394).

2 Witnessing the wintering of thousands of ladybugs (page 78) and monarch butterflies (page 553).

3 Discovering geothermal wonders and the otherworldly terrain of twisted crags and spires (page 190), volcanic rock formations (page 325), and wind caves (page 627).

4 Hiking beneath towering giant redwoods (pages 115 and 256) and seeing the world's largest living thing (page 509).

5 Watching thundering falls hit the sand and pour into the sea (pages 169 and 613).

6 Sauntering along the Pacific Coast, surrounded by wildlife (page 146) and marine life (page 213).

7 Summiting a volcano (page 321).

8 Swimming in invigorating alpine lakes (pages 372 and 381).

9 Climbing to the top of North America's tallest free-falling waterfall (page 424).

10 Walking among flaming-gold aspen groves in autumn (pages 446 and 455).

HIT THE TRAIL

t's the moment you spot migrating whales off the coast or stand in silence at the center of a grove of giant redwoods. When you're treated to panoramic views atop a mountain ridge or feel the mist of a rushing waterfall. The second your eyes fall on wildflower blossoms in a spectrum of colors or smell the aroma of grapes ready for harvest. There are countless natural wonders to take your breath away while hiking in Northern California.

With six national parks, plus dozens of state parks and other green spaces, step in any direction and you'll quickly come across a trail. People travel from around the world to experience what residents have at their doorstep: limitless adventures through rugged canyons and up mountain peaks, over gentle rolling hills and along pristine alpine lakes. Nearly every photo you take while hiking in Northern California could be a postcard.

Every region here brims with vibrance and opportunity for exploration. Wander the terraces of the Ecological Staircase in Mendocino. Hike up granite domes and through the high meadows of Yosemite. Hear the waves crash as you walk the beach to a majestic tide fall in Point Reyes National Seashore. Conquer the summit of Lassen Peak, one of the largest plug dome volcanoes in the world. Roam through vineyard-covered hills in Napa and Sonoma. Look out on Lake Tahoe, the largest alpine lake in North America. The list of awe-inspiring Northern California hiking destinations goes on and on.

By opening this book, you've opened yourself to the possibility of creating amazing lifelong memories on Northern California's trails. With this guide close at hand, you'll be ready to discover all that hiking in Northern California has to offer. Just take your first step.

▼ FOUR FRIENDS HIKE THE PURISIMA LOOP IN THE SAN FRANCISCO BAY AREA.

Camping the Coast

To get the ultimate experience traveling along the world-famous Pacific Coast Highway, you want to sip your morning coffee listening to the crashing waves and watch the last rays of daylight reflect off the Pacific Ocean.

BIG SUR

Pitch your tent along the Big Sur River and under the canopy of redwoods at **Pfeiffer Big Sur State Park.** In the morning, hike **Pfeiffer Falls Loop** to start your day, followed by breakfast at **Café Kevah** and then views of Big Sur's most iconic waterfall, **McWay Falls.** Imagine liquor smugglers sneaking through the tunnel as you hike to the aqua waters of **Partington Cove** and later climb up **Buzzards Roost Trail** for panoramic views from mountains to sea. Grab a tasty meal in the state park at **Big Sur Lodge** and then end your day at **Pfeiffer Beach,** where its **Keyhole Arch** and wisps of purple sand are just as breathtaking as the setting sun.

SONOMA COAST

Sleep at the sandy campground of **Wright's Beach Campground** in **Sonoma Coast State Park,** where you can leisurely whale- and bird-watch from your tent's ocean views. Grab a tea or a latte at **Cafe Aquatica** in Jenner and spend your morning wandering the hills through redwoods and views of the **Russian River** flowing to the ocean on the **Pomo Canyon Trail.** At low tide, wander the tide pools of the many Highway 1 pullouts of Sonoma Coast State Park along the coastline. Snag some clam chowder at **Spud Point Crab Company,** and end your night by campfire in the fire ring at your campsite.

NORTH COAST AND REDWOODS

Spend the night at **Elk Prairie Campground** in **Prairie Creek Redwoods State Park** and you may see massive Roosevelt elk grazing on grasses right outside your tent. You'll also be the first morning hiker on the **James Irvine** and **Miners Ridge Loop** to spectacular **Fern Canyon,** where thousands of graceful ferns cling to 50-foot-high (15-m) walls. Two more top-notch trails lie within a 10-minute drive, including Redwood National Park's **Skunk Cabbage Creek Trail** and Prairie Creek's **Brown Creek, Rhododendron, and South Fork Loop.**

MENDOCINO

Pitch your tent at **Van Damme State Park** so you can walk to the trailhead for **Fern Canyon Trail,** then traipse across 20 wooden footbridges as you skirt alongside **Little River** and enter an enchanting redwood forest. For a scenery contrast, drive five minutes south to the **Spring Ranch**

VAN DAMME STATE PARK, MENDOCINO ▶

Trail, which offers inspiring vistas of the wave-pummeled coast. No matter where you hike on this glorious stretch of coast, be sure to spend a few hours in **Mendocino**'s picture-perfect village, admiring manicured Victorians, browsing come-hither boutiques, and dining at charming bistros.

Eastern Sierra Road Trip: U.S. 395

At every curve on the Eastern Sierra's U.S. 395, wonders appear through your windshield. With the saw-toothed Sierra peaks on one side and the arid Great Basin on the other, this highway is just right for a camping, hiking, and beer-sipping road trip. The places below are arranged south to north.

MAMMOTH LAKES

California's largest ski resort morphs into a hiker's playground in the summer months. Take the kids on the easy trail to **Mammoth Consolidated Gold Mine** and **Heart Lake** for a history lesson and a swim, or hike to the top of 10,797-foot (3,291-m) **Duck Pass** for an aerobic ascent to glacier-carved lakes and a lofty view. Pitch a tent at **Coldwater Campground** and you can walk to these trailheads and visit two breweries in a 10-minute drive: **Mammoth Brewery** and **Distant Brewing.**

JUNE LAKE

Spend the night at **June Lake Campground** so you can swim, kayak, or SUP right from your site and walk to **June Lake Brewing Company** for dinner and a beer. Just a few miles away, the easy hike to **Parker Lake** will delight photographers, anglers, and hikers with swimming on their minds.

LEE VINING

A hike in **Lundy Canyon** offers colorful metamorphic peaks, shimmering aspen groves, and a spectacular waterfall-and-wildflower show in early summer. A few miles away, the **Virginia Lakes Trail** leads to a high-drama mountain pass at 11,130 feet (3,392 m). Camp at **Trumbull Lake Campground** 12 miles (19.3 km) north of town for easy access to hikes and fishing lakes, plus an option to drive to **Tioga Pass** to hike on Yosemite's glorious eastern side.

BRIDGEPORT

There's no better place to catch the Eastern Sierra's fall-color show than on the **Barney Lake (Robinson Creek) Trail** in **Hoover Wilderness.** Just a few

miles south, a wealth of wildflowers and cobalt-blue lakes are tucked in below **Green Creek** canyon's 11,000-foot (3,353-m) peaks. Camp at **Lower Twin Lake,** a five-minute drive to the **Barney Lake Trailhead.** Head into town for liquid refreshment at **Big Meadow Brewery.**

Mount Shasta Excursion

The largest stratovolcano in the Cascade Range, Mount Shasta soars to 14,179 feet (4,322 m) and can be seen from 150 miles (242 km) away on clear days. Its often snowcapped massif dominates the landscape,

◄ HEART LAKE, MAMMOTH LAKES, EASTERN SIERRA

with a base diameter that stretches more than 17 miles (27 km). If you're tempted to summit this mighty monolith, consider hiring a guide for the epic 10-hour trek—it requires not just superior fitness but also thorough knowledge of the mountain's peculiarities.

For campers who don't need a water spigot or a picnic table, dispersed camping is permitted along the paved 15-mile (24-km) Everitt Memorial Highway. Most locations are best for campervans and small RVs, but tent campers can find good spots too. Campfires, wood fires, and charcoal barbecues are strictly prohibited in summer and fall, but you can use a gas camping stove.

If you'd like to try out a few easy to moderate day hikes on the volcano's slopes, try these three top-shelf trails:

BUNNY FLAT TO ALPINE LODGE

Hike to the historic **Sierra Club Alpine Lodge** for an iconic view of Mount Shasta. The stone lodge, which houses exhibits on Mount Shasta and a small library of mountaineering books, was built by the Sierra Club in 1922. For more of a challenge, follow the path from the lodge to **Hidden Valley**'s talus wonderland at 9,200 feet (2,804 m) elevation.

GRAY BUTTE

From the 8,129-foot (2,478-m) summit of **Gray Butte,** Mount Shasta's monumental hulking cone stares you right in the eyes. You'll begin with a brief look at **Panther Meadows'** pristine expanse of grasses and wildflowers, then wind your way uphill through Shasta red firs to the summit's dramatic vista.

SOUTH GATE MEADOWS

This undulating ramble travels through a colorful proliferation of volcanic rocks to a mountain-backed meadow boasting a bounty of summer wildflowers, a glistening waterfall, and a dramatic vista of **Shastarama Point** and Mount Shasta.

BEST BY SEASON

Spring

- **Uvas Canyon Waterfall Loop:** This mountain forest hike is flush with growth when its springs and the past season's rain maximize the abundant waterfalls of Uvas Canyon (page 70).
- **Carson Falls:** This tucked-away waterfall comes to life each spring, providing refuge for one of the few remaining breeding sites for the rare foothill yellow-legged frogs that live here (page 133).
- **Skunk Cabbage Creek and Coastal Trail:** March to May, skunk cabbages bloom in bright yellow flowers, shining like lanterns above the plant's 3- to 5-foot-long (1- to 1.5-m) dark-green leaves (page 252).
- **River Trail to Roaring River Falls and Zumwalt Meadow:** Kings Canyon's most easily accessed waterfall flows with ebullience only during spring snowmelt (page 491).

Summer

- **Point Lobos Perimeter Loop:** At one of the most stunning coastlines in Northern California, watch the summer fog wax and wane through a Monterey cypress grove on the rocks (page 593).
- **Lassen Peak:** The switchback-laden path to the summit of Lassen volcano is only accessible to hikers July to October when the mountain is snow-free (page 321).
- **Lakes Trail to Heather, Aster, Emerald, and Pear Lakes:** June to September, you can visit four of Sequoia National Park's lakes in one day, and each will invite you to swim (page 506).

- **Mount Tallac:** Zealous snow lovers climb Mount Tallac on skis and snowshoes in winter, but casual peak baggers make the strenuous climb during the snow-free months of summer (page 384).

Fall

- **Monarch-Moore Creek Loop:** Each fall, this hike escalates in natural beauty as monarch butterflies migrate here to make the eucalyptus grove their winter habitat (page 553).
- **Lundy Canyon:** In September and October, Lundy Canyon's stands of

quaking aspens turn bright gold and orange, their delicate leaves dancing in the slightest breeze (page 455).

- **Barney Lake:** During autumn, this trail's dense aspen groves show off golden fluttering leaves that shine like stained glass in the low-angled sunlight (page 446).

- **Point Arena-Stornetta Trails:** The Mendocino coast is known for fickle weather—damp in winter, foggy in summer, and windy in spring—but autumn delivers the best chance of calm, sunny days for admiring this trail's sea stacks, arches, and battering waves (page 222).

Winter

- **Año Nuevo Point Trail:** Witness the northern elephant seals come ashore to give birth and mate starting in early December on this family-friendly hike (page 58).

- **Chimney Rock Trail:** Each winter, California gray whales travel over 10,000 miles (16,000 km), right past Chimney Rock and the nearby Point Reyes Lighthouse on their southern migration (page 153).

- **General Grant Tree, North Grove, and Dead Giant:** Nothing compares to seeing giant sequoias crowned with a mantle of snow, and this Grant Grove trail provides easy winter access—but bring your snowshoes just in case (page 494).

- **Point Cabrillo Light Station:** During the cool winter months, this sun-drenched trail to a historic light station delivers chart-topping coastal scenery minus the chilly shade that covers many Mendocino trails, plus a great chance at spotting migrating gray whales (page 207).

CHIMNEY ROCK, POINT REYES NATIONAL SEASHORE ▼

BEST COASTAL HIKES

- **Lands End:** Atop rocky cliffs, stroll through history and classic San Francisco views of the Pacific Ocean, Golden Gate Bridge, and Marin Headlands (page 32).

- **Tennessee Valley Trail:** Traverse the valley to the gorgeous Tennessee Beach, where the engine of the SS *Tennessee* shipwreck, visible at low tide, rests (page 107).

- **Secret Beach:** The farther you go, the fewer people you see, and the more amazing sea stacks, caves, and tide pools there are to explore (page 156).

- **Spring Ranch Trail:** Savor the best of Mendocino on this easy path along the headlands, where you'll linger over vistas of relentless waves, passing gray whales, spring wildflowers, and an ocean blowhole (page 213).

- **Yurok Loop and Coastal Trail to Hidden Beach:** A gentle walk leads to an alluring beach marked by tan sand, jagged boulders rising from the sea, surly waves, and driftwood logs of every shape and size (page 242).

▼ SPRING RANCH TRAIL, MENDOCINO

BEST WATERFALL HIKES

- **Upper Yosemite Fall:** Nothing gets your adrenaline pumping quite like standing on top of North America's tallest free-falling waterfall and watching 2,425 feet (739 m) of white water plummet to the floor of Yosemite Valley (page 424).

- **Vernal and Nevada Falls:** Two of the world's most photographed waterfalls plunge downstream on the frothing Merced River, and you can see them both from one of Yosemite Valley's most popular hikes (page 427).

- **Devils Postpile and Rainbow Falls:** By Northern California standards, Rainbow Falls isn't notably tall, at only 101 feet (31 m), but this crashing cataract punches well above its weight for scenic beauty—especially if you catch the rainbow hovering above its pool (page 471).

- **Tokopah Falls:** An easy trek alongside the Tokopah River leads to Sequoia National Park's tallest waterfall, where the Marble Fork Kaweah River tumbles 1,200 feet (366 m) over polished granite (page 503).

- **Cataract Falls:** The majority of this heart-pumping hike is within view of a wide variety of falls of Mount Tamalpais Watershed (page 129).

- **Alamere Falls:** Likely the Bay Area's most famous waterfall, Alamere Falls plummets off the seaside cliffs onto the beach below (page 169).

VERNAL FALL, YOSEMITE ▾

BEST SWIMMING HOLE HIKES

- **McCloud Falls:** In spring, the McCloud River is a tempestuous watercourse with a swift current, but by midsummer, the river quiets down and the broad pools at Lower and Upper Falls lure swimmers and waders (page 286).

- **Terrace, Shadow, and Cliff Lakes:** Summer days can heat up in Lassen Volcanic National Park, but this trail takes you to three swimmable lakes where you can float in warm water and backstroke away the afternoon (page 318).

- **Vikingsholm Castle and Emerald Point:** Most visitors think Lake Tahoe is unbearably frigid, but Emerald Bay's white sands reflect the summer sun and make Vikingsholm's shallow beach pleasantly warm (page 381).

- **Bear, Silver, Round Lakes Loop:** You could pick almost any body of water in the Lakes Basin and go for a delightful swim, but this trail visits five lakes in one trip, and each is worth a dip (page 372).

▼ TERRACE LAKE, LASSEN VOLCANIC NATIONAL PARK

BEST REDWOOD HIKES

- **Purisima Loop:** Hike the western slopes of the Santa Cruz Mountains with glimpses of Half Moon Bay and towering redwood trees thick with fern and sorrel understory and countless banana slugs (page 52).

- **Fall Creek Loop:** Scramble over, under, and around fallen trees as the trail follows along the creek in this dense forest (page 540).

- **Canopy View Loop:** From the wider giants on the forest floor to the high canopy of the second-growth redwoods closer to the ridge, there's a reason Muir Woods National Monument is visited by so many every year (page 115).

- **Brown Creek, Rhododendron, and South Fork Loop:** You'll find yourself walking slowly and reverently through this cathedral-like grove of leviathan redwoods, where the treetops seem to scrape the sky (page 245).

- **Tall Trees Grove:** Reserve a permit in advance and you can be one of the lucky few who get to hike in the rich alluvial plain next to Redwood Creek, where a secluded grove contains dozens of chart-topping redwoods (page 256).

- **General Sherman Tree and Congress Trail:** No visit to Sequoia National Park is complete without paying homage to the General Sherman, the largest living thing on earth by volume. Other trees are taller or wider, but none has the combined height and width of this sequoia—275 feet (84 m) tall with a 102.6-foot (31.3-m) circumference (page 509).

CANOPY VIEW LOOP, MUIR WOODS ▼

Entering
Muir Woods
National Monument

BEST WILDFLOWER HIKES

- **Russian Ridge Loop:** Every spring the grassy hills put on a show of brilliant colors (page 55).

- **Tomales Point:** It's easy to imagine the working ranch that once operated here as you wander down an island of wildflowers set between the Pacific Ocean and Tomales Bay (page 146).

- **Monterey Bay Coastal Recreation Trail:** There's nothing like the purple carpet of ice plant that blankets the Pacific Grove section of this oceanside urban stroll (page 577).

- **Paradise Meadow:** Explore on your own or join a ranger-led hike to Lassen's Paradise Meadow to see a flower-palooza of lavender fleabane, yellow and blue lupine, red paintbrush, and purple gentian (page 311).

- **Carson Pass to Winnemucca and Round Top Lakes:** Time your trip for peak bloom time (typically mid-July, but it varies) on one of the Sierra's top wildflower trails, and you'll discover a riot of technicolor blossoms lighting up the volcanic slopes (page 394).

- **Mount Dana:** Hike to the summit of Mount Dana at just the right time in late July or early August and you'll be able to see and photograph the highly coveted sky pilot, a purple-blue beauty that blooms among the scree and patches of lingering snow at 13,000 feet (3,962 m) elevation (page 421).

▾ MOUNT DANA, YOSEMITE

BEST KID-FRIENDLY HIKES

- **Carmel Meadows:** Ocean views and sandy beach time await the family on this beautiful and easy hike (page 589).

- **Pioneer Nature Trail Loop:** A peaceful introduction to the redwoods on a soft dirt path is the perfect hike for all ages (page 187).

- **Stream-East Ridge Loop:** Every year from November through February, thousands of wintering ladybugs can be spotted gathering along the trails (page 78).

- **Bowling Ball Beach:** Children can't resist playing on this beach's 100 or more sandstone secretions—which look a lot like large bowling balls. You'll be tempted to join them as they hop from one ball to the next (page 226).

- **Tharp's Log and Log Meadow:** Kids will love seeing this real-life tree house that was built into a fallen sequoia log, where rancher Hale Tharp lived for nearly 30 summers (page 517).

- **Moro Rock:** Kids and adults alike enjoy climbing the 390 carefully engineered stairsteps that lead to Moro Rock's bald granite summit (page 513).

STREAM-EAST RIDGE LOOP, DR. AURELIA REINHARDT REDWOOD REGIONAL PARK ▾

BEST DOG-FRIENDLY HIKES

- **Almaden Quicksilver Loop:** Four-legged friends are welcome on all of the trails within the park, making it highly likely you'll pass many other dog lovers on this hike (page 67).

- **Briones Loop:** While Fido and Fifi are required to be leashed in some areas of this park, in others they can freely hike alongside you if under reliable voice control (page 81).

- **American River Parkway:** This dog-friendly path in the William B. Pond Recreation Area welcomes dogs on leash for the entirety of the hike (page 361).

- **Little Lakes Valley to Gem Lake:** This lake-dotted trail is one of the Eastern Sierra's gentlest pathways, and the abundance of water and the easy grade makes it popular with dog walkers (page 478).

- **Bennettville Mine and Fantail Lake:** Almost every step of this high-elevation trail is near a creek or a lake, so there's no shortage of spots for canines to cool off, drink, and swim (page 458).

- **Parker Lake:** A short hike next to Parker Creek leads to its eponymous lake, where dogs can fetch sticks all afternoon (page 461).

▼ BRIONES LOOP, BRIONES REGIONAL PARK

THE PELICAN INN AT MUIR BEACH ▲

BEST BREW HIKES

- **Presidio Tunnel Tops and Promenade Tour:** A walk through history and views of the bay paired with a beer from Fort Point Beer, the city's largest independent craft brewery, located just down the street, makes for an ideal San Francisco day (page 35).
- **Dias Ridge:** Halfway through this classic Mount Tamalpais hike, stop by The Pelican Inn at Muir Beach for a warm meal and cold on-tap beer to keep you going (page 111).
- **Bonny Doon Beach and Shark Fin Cove:** A fantastic local brew at Santa Cruz Mountain Brewing is the perfect way to continue your day after hiking the sandy bluffs along the coast (page 547).
- **Big Hendy Grove and Hermit Huts:** Hike among Hendy Woods State Park's stately redwoods—the last vestiges of Anderson Valley's ancient forests—before taking a brewery tour, listening to live music, playing 18 holes of disc golf, or just drinking Boont Amber Ale at Anderson Valley Brewing Company, 15 minutes from the trailhead (page 219).
- **Duck Pass:** Nothing says Mammoth Lakes quite like the Mammoth Brewery, where picnic tables are crowded with families, friends, and canine companions who've just finished one of dozens of day hikes in the Mammoth Lakes Basin, like the spectacular summit of Duck Pass (page 467).
- **Crags Trail to Castle Dome:** Completing this strenuous trek is sure to leave you hot and thirsty, so make a beeline for Dunsmuir Brewery Works, only 10 minutes away. Order a Trainspotter IPA, then pat yourself on the back for being such a hardy mountaineer (page 289).

FORT POINT BEER FOR SALE IN THE PRESIDIO

SAN FRANCISCO BAY AREA

SAN FRANCISCO

San Francisco may be less than 50 square miles (130 sq km), but its mild year-round climate, bay and Pacific Ocean coastline, rolling hills, and more than 200 parks provide an abundance of easily accessible outdoor adventure. You can observe American bison in Golden Gate Park, walk along the edge of the continent, break a sweat working your way up San Francisco's seven famous hills, watch migrating birds, and take in panoramic views showcasing the bay, ocean beaches, and bridges that link the city to the rest of the Bay Area.

▲ LANDS END

▲ SAN FRANCISCO NATIONAL CEMETERY

1 Lands End
DISTANCE: 3.3 miles (5.3 km) round-trip
DURATION: 1.5 hours
EFFORT: Easy

2 Presidio Tunnel Tops and Promenade Tour
DISTANCE: 1.9 miles (3.1 km) round-trip
DURATION: 1 hour
EFFORT: Easy

3 Ecology Trail and Lovers' Lane Loop
DISTANCE: 2.2 miles (3.5 km) round-trip
DURATION: 1 hour
EFFORT: Easy

4 Mount Sutro Loop
DISTANCE: 2.5 miles (4 km) round-trip
DURATION: 1 hour
EFFORT: Easy

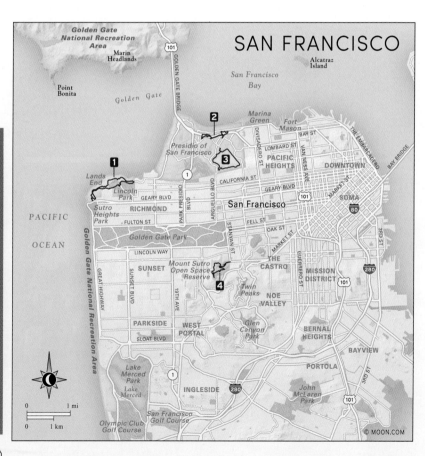

1

Lands End

GOLDEN GATE NATIONAL RECREATION AREA

🦌 🏛 🐾 🚶 🚌

Take in views of the Golden Gate Bridge and the Marin Headlands, look below for hidden shipwrecks in the crashing waves, and let the forest obscure the busy city as you wander through nature and history on this classic San Francisco hike.

BEST: Coastal Hikes
DISTANCE: 3.3 miles (5.3 km) round-trip
DURATION: 1.5 hours
ELEVATION GAIN: 340 feet (104 m)
EFFORT: Easy
TRAIL: Dirt, gravel, single-track, paved
USERS: Hikers, wheelchair users, leashed dogs
SEASON: Year-round
PASSES/FEES: None
MAPS: Lands End Map on the park website
PARK HOURS: 6am to 1 hour after sunset
TRAILHEAD: Lands End Main Parking Lot
FACILITIES: Restrooms and drinking fountain at the Visitor Center
CONTACT: Golden Gate National Recreation Area, 415/561-4700, www.nps. gov/goga

START THE HIKE

▶ **MILE 0-0.4: Parking Lot to USS** *San Francisco* **Memorial**
Begin the hike at the northwest corner of the **Lands End Main Parking Lot,** where you can look over the remains of the **Sutro Baths.** Once an elaborate complex of heated seawater pools, a stadium, restaurants, and entertainment, it drew crowds to Lands End for 70 years before closing permanently in 1966.

Follow the sidewalk as it curves southeast away from the water along the parking lot. Look for stairs to the left (northeast) and a trail marker for Coastal Trail, indicating the USS *San Francisco* Memorial and an overlook are ahead. Go up the stairs, toward the cypress trees.

At 0.3 mile (0.5 km), continue straight on Coastal Trail where it intersects with Lands End Trail. Within 0.1 mile (0.2 km), the views have opened to the water, and if the fog isn't too heavy, you can see the **Golden Gate Bridge** and beyond.

Climb the stairs to your right (southeast) that lead up to the **El Camino Del Mar Trail** and make your way right (south) to the **USS** *San Francisco* **Memorial,** which contains a section of the World War II ship's bridge and commemorates those wounded and killed in the Battle of Guadalcanal in 1942.

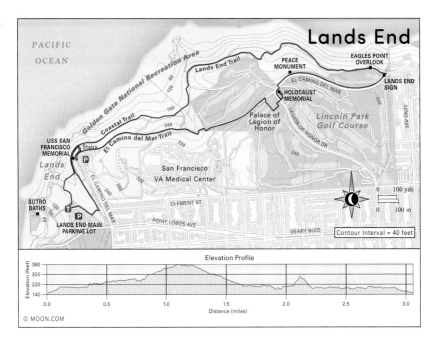

© MOON.COM

▶ **MILE 0.4–1.1: USS *San Francisco* Memorial**
to Palace of the Legion of Honor

Return the way you came, passing the top of the stairs to walk east along the north side of the **El Camino Del Mar Parking Lot.** Continue on the path as it passes where the parking lot turns into a dead-end road.

At 0.6 mile (1 km), the trail becomes single-track through a forested area for just over 0.25 mile (0.4 km). Wander among wildflowers like the red garden nasturtium, then cross a wooden boardwalk and take the stairs back onto **El Camino Del Mar Road.** Arrive at the golf course and stay on the sidewalk. Do not enter the golf course.

At 1.1 miles (1.8 km), you arrive across the street from the impressive **Palace of the Legion of Honor.** The building was built to beautify the city, honor those who fought in World War I, and host art and historical treasures promoting education and culture.

▶ **MILE 1.1–1.8: Palace of the Legion of Honor to Lands End Sign**

Carefully cross El Camino Del Mar Road and head right (southeast) up the sidewalk to the front of the palace and left (northeast) through the lawn toward the traffic-circle fountain. Cautiously cross Legion of Honor Drive to the **Holocaust Memorial** at Palace of the Legion of Honor. Created by artist George Segal and installed in 1984, the juxtaposition of the somber sculpture against the beauty of nature and grandeur of the palace in a busy modern city requires a moment of reflection.

Take care crossing northwest back over El Camino Del Mar Road and continue walking northeast on the sidewalk, where you'll shortly come upon the **Peace Monument,** in recognition of the continued quest for world peace. When you reach the **Lands End sign** at 1.8 miles (2.9 km), turn left (west) toward the water onto the **Coastal Trail-Lands End Trail** and toward **Eagles Point Overlook.**

▶ **MILE 1.8-3.3: Lands End Sign to Parking Lot**
After enjoying the views (fog will determine how much of the Golden Gate Bridge is visible), continue east on the **Coastal Trail** as it winds along the cliffs overlooking the entrance to the bay.

The final stretch of the hike provides an opportunity to watch for migrating whales and shipwrecks along the shore. At 3.1 miles (5 km), you will recognize the stairs to the left (southeast) that lead up to the El Camino Del Mar Trail. Staying on the Coastal Trail, return the way you came to the parking lot.

DIRECTIONS

From San Francisco's Civic Center, go west, just north of Golden Gate Park, on Fulton Street. Turn north (right) onto 42nd Street for 0.5 mile (0.8 km) and turn west (left) onto Point Lobos Avenue. Travel for 0.4 mile (0.6 km) and turn north (right) into the Lands End Main (Merrie Way) Parking Lot.

GPS COORDINATES: 37.7806, −122.5119; 37°46′50.2″ N, 122°30′42.8″ W

BEST NEARBY BITES
Less than 0.5 mile (0.8 km) and four minutes' walk from the trailhead is the **Café at the Butterfly Joint** (4411 Cabrillo St., San Francisco, 415/894-2685, 7:15am-2:30pm Mon.-Fri., 8am-2:30pm Sat.-Sun., $2.50-15). The Butterfly Joint focuses on teaching children how to create beautiful wood projects from reclaimed and repurposed wood using traditional Japanese hand tools. Go early for a hot drink and baked goods, including delicious gluten-free doughnuts, to enjoy as you stroll the trail. The café is south of the trailhead at 45th Avenue and Cabrillo Street.

2

Presidio Tunnel Tops and Promenade Tour

GOLDEN GATE NATIONAL RECREATION AREA

✿ 🏛 ⚇ 🚍🚃

This urban stroll includes views of the Golden Gate Bridge, the opportunity to walk through history and pay respect to those who served, travel over and under U.S. 101, and ample opportunity for all to play.

BEST: Brew Hikes

DISTANCE: 1.9 miles (3.1 km) round-trip

DURATION: 1 hour

ELEVATION GAIN: 140 feet (43 m)

EFFORT: Easy

TRAIL: Gravel, dirt, paved

USERS: Walkers and hikers, bikers, wheelchair users, leashed dogs in some sections

SEASON: Year-round

PASSES/FEES: None

MAPS: Select "Plan Your Visit" and then "Maps" on the website

TRAILHEAD: Presidio Visitor Center

FACILITIES: Restrooms in the parking lot and Field Station

CONTACT: Golden Gate National Recreation Area, 415/561-4323, www.presidio.gov

START THE HIKE

▶ **MILE 0-0.5: Presidio Visitor Center to San Francisco National Cemetery**

From the **Presidio Visitor Center,** follow the path left (west) around the back of the center toward the **Campfire Circle.** No national park is complete without a campfire ring; this one is a central gas fire pit and can seat up to 75 people. Continue on toward the **Lodge at the Presidio** in the Montgomery Street Barracks. Built in 1895-1897 by the U.S. Army, it was used as wartime hospital wards and housed artillery and infantry companies until the 1980s.

Take the multiuse path west (watch out for bikes) between the lodge and the fence along U.S. 101. Following alongside **Lincoln Boulevard,** after 0.1 mile (0.2 km) is the **Korean War Memorial** that pays tribute to the 1 million Koreans and 37,000 Americans who lost their lives during the Korean War from 1950 to 1953.

Just past the memorial, take a moment to enter the **San Francisco National Cemetery.** The combination of cypress trees, white headstones, and bay fog make it a stunning final resting place for 30,000 military veterans and their families.

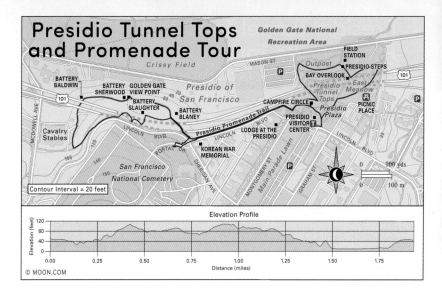

Presidio Tunnel Tops and Promenade Tour

Golden Gate National Recreation Area

Elevation Profile

© MOON.COM

▶ **MILE 0.5-1: San Francisco National Cemetery to Cavalry Stables**
Back outside the cemetery, cross Lincoln Boulevard and head along the paved trail over U.S. 101, the **Presidio Promenade.** Where the trail splits at 0.6 mile (1 km), continue right (northeast) toward **Battery Blaney.** One of four historic gun batteries nestled in the hillside above Crissy Field, these batteries were built by the U.S. Army in 1899-1902 to protect underwater minefields placed in the San Francisco Bay. The batteries are named for soldiers who gave their lives for their country.

On a clear day, the Golden Gate Bridge begins to appear through the cypress trees ahead on the right (northwest). At 0.8 mile (1.3 km) is the **Golden Gate Viewpoint,** then **Battery Sherwood,** and finally **Battery Baldwin.**

The Presidio Promenade descends under U.S. 101. At 1 mile (1.6 km), take the pedestrian walkway left (south), with a view of the brick cavalry stables to the right (west). Built in 1914, each of the five stables could house 102 horses, enough for a cavalry company. Later the buildings were used for a K-9 Corps facility and a veterinary hospital.

▶ **MILE 1-1.5: Cavalry Stables to Lodge at the Presidio**
The pedestrian walkway winds through native plants and reaches the Presidio Promenade and Presidio Promenade Connector **split.** Turn left (east) onto the connector toward the National Cemetery. Take care along the sidewalk here and do not walk in the street, as vehicles can move fast along the curving Lincoln Boulevard. Remain on the sidewalk and follow signs for the Presidio Promenade.

The promenade reaches the final battery, **Battery Slaughter,** then returns to where you first approached Battery Blaney. Retrace your steps back over U.S. 101, to the right (east) and along the sidewalk, passing again the Lodge at the Presidio.

▶ MILE 1.5-1.9: **Lodge at the Presidio to Presidio Visitor Center**
Back at the Presidio Tunnel Tops, turn left (north) and follow the path down the staircase. Pass the **Bluff Walk** area to continue straight (north) until the path curves right (east) to take you to the **Outpost** (9:30am-6pm daily Apr.-Oct., 9:30am-4:30pm daily Nov.-Mar.). This unique playground is designed to promote independence; the level of challenge increases from east to west across natural elements to allow kids to steadily gain confidence.

Continue straight (east) to the **Field Station** (11am-4pm Wed.-Fri., 10am-5pm Sat.-Sun.) where there is an accessible and gender-inclusive restroom. At the Field Station, children can learn more about the Presidio using their senses plus imagination, science, and art.

Walk up the **Presidio Steps** and continue left (east) to the **Bay Overlook,** where you can learn about some of the plants that are indigenous to the Presidio. Follow the path is it curves southwest, past the **East Meadow, Picnic Place,** and **Presidio Plaza** before returning to the visitor center.

DIRECTIONS

From San Francisco Civic Center, take Van Ness Avenue north for 1.8 miles (2.9 km). Turn west (left) onto Lombard Street for 1.1 miles (1.8 km) and then Richardson Avenue onto Presidio Parkway. From Presidio Parkway, take exit 437 and turn left to continue on Girard Road. After 0.4 mile (0.6 km), at the traffic circle, take the first exit onto Lincoln Boulevard to arrive at the parking lot, located at 210 Lincoln Boulevard.

GPS COORDINATES: 37.8016, −122.4569; 37°48'5.8" N, 122°27'24.8" W

BEST NEARBY BITES AND BREWS
On weekends, seasonal food trucks and tents are just steps away from the Presidio Visitor Center, located near the Main Parade Lawn and parking lot. Get a taste of the diversity of San Francisco's culture and cuisine and grab a brew from San Francisco's hometown beer company, **Fort Point Beer** (near 210 Lincoln Blvd., San Francisco, 415/917-7647, 11am-4:30pm Fri. and Sun.).

Ecology Trail and Lovers' Lane Loop

GOLDEN GATE NATIONAL RECREATION AREA

🦌 ❀ 🏛 🐾 🚶 🚌

Disappear from the busy city and into the forest, passing through part of the Tennessee Hollow watershed to panoramic views at Inspiration Point, and stroll down an 18th-century footpath once utilized by missionaries and the military.

DISTANCE: 2.2 miles (3.5 km) round-trip

DURATION: 1 hour

ELEVATION GAIN: 320 feet (98 m)

EFFORT: Easy

TRAIL: Dirt, gravel, sand, paved

USERS: Hikers, bikers in some sections, wheelchair users in some sections, leashed dogs

SEASON: Year-round

PASSES/FEES: None

MAPS: Select "Plan Your Visit" and then "Maps" on the website

TRAILHEAD: Chapel of Our Lady

FACILITIES: Restrooms and drinking fountain at Paul Goode Field

CONTACT: Golden Gate National Recreation Area, 415/561-4323, www. presidio.gov

START THE HIKE

▶ **MILE 0-0.6: Chapel of Our Lady to Upper Ecology Trail**

From the **Chapel of Our Lady,** turn left (southeast) and walk in the direction of the **Inn at the Presidio.** Follow the sidewalk around the east side of the building toward the parking lot behind the inn. Enter the watershed at the south side of the back parking lot and look for the **Ecology Trail** sign.

You're immediately surrounded in a vine-covered forest of redwoods, eucalyptus, pine, and cypress. Head southwest, and where the trail first splits, continue left (south).

Continue straight (southwest) where the trail begins its only ascent, which will get your heart pumping. Take a break on the memorial bench along the way and look for pinecones, acorns, blackberries, and coffeeberry.

At 0.6 mile (1 km), the trail divides into **Upper Ecology Trail** and Lower Ecology Trail. Stay right (west) to continue toward Inspiration Point.

▶ **MILE 0.6-0.7: Upper Ecology Trail to Inspiration Point**

Just 0.1 mile (0.2 km) farther, the spur path to **Inspiration Point** at 0.7 mile (1.1 km) takes you up 150 feet (46 m) on a winding wooden plank staircase onto a sidewalk and the rounded Inspiration Point parking lot. Follow the sidewalk right (north) to the bluestone and sandstone plaza. On a clear

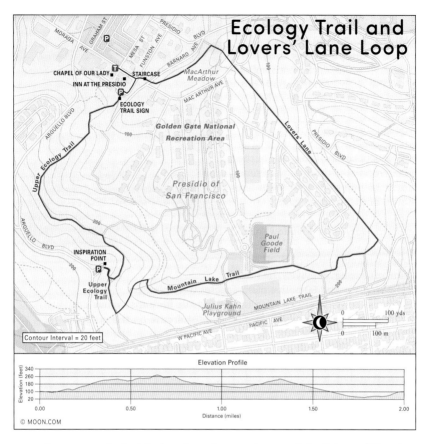

Ecology Trail and Lovers' Lane Loop

Elevation Profile

© MOON.COM

day, you can look right (northeast) to see the top of the Palace of Fine Arts as well as out to the San Francisco Bay, Alcatraz Island, and Angel Island.

▶ MILE 0.7–1.2: Inspiration Point to Paul Goode Field

Retrace your steps down the stairs to the start of the spur trail. At the bottom of the stairs, continue right (south) on Upper Ecology Trail. At 0.8 mile (1.3 km), you reach a junction with **Lower Ecology Trail.** Turn left (northeast) onto Lower Ecology Trail and descend through the pines. As you approach the junction with **Mountain Lake Trail** at 1 mile (1.6 km), the dirt and gravel path becomes sandy and the landscape opens. Here you may see California poppies, coyote brush, honeysuckle, and common yarrow. Watch and listen for the wide variety of birds that frequent the area, including the California scrub jay, hawks, and sparrows. Turn right (south) onto Mountain Lake Trail and follow the trail left (east).

The trail returns to dirt and gravel at 1.1 miles (1.8 km), where those with small children may want to take a detour at the junction that leads right (south) to the **Julius Kahn Playground.** Otherwise, continue straight (east) to **Paul Goode Field,** where you can use the restrooms.

▶ MILE 1.2–2.2: Paul Goode Field to Chapel of Our Lady

Just past the field, the path splits, with the right (south) trail proceeding to West Pacific Avenue. Turn left (northeast) onto the soft wooded dirt path along the wooden fence and into the trees. The path meets **Lovers' Lane,** one of the oldest footpaths through the Presidio, at 1.5 miles (2.4 km). Turn left (north) onto the paved path.

At 1.9 miles (3.1 km), the path leads to **MacArthur Meadow,** once the place where tributaries from three streams converged. Restoration efforts have revived the flow of the streams, and 60 native plant species were planted.

The trail turns left (west) and runs alongside **Barnard Avenue** until just before MacArthur Boulevard. Look for the **staircase** on the other side of Barnard with a trail marker for the Main Post. Head up the stairs, where you arrive at the corner of Funston Avenue and Moraga Avenue, back at the Inn at the Presidio. Cross Funston and follow the sidewalk to return to the front of the Chapel of Our Lady.

DIRECTIONS

From San Francisco Civic Center, take Van Ness Avenue north for 1.8 miles (2.9 km). Turn west (left) onto Lombard Street for 0.4 mile (0.6 km) and turn slight north (right) onto Presidio Boulevard. Stay on Presidio for 0.3 mile (0.5 km), and turn left onto Mesa Street into the Moraga Avenue Parking Lot.

GPS COORDINATES: 37.7978, −122.4587; 37°47′52.1″ N, 122°27′31.3″ W

BEST NEARBY BITES

Just steps from the start of this hike is **Colibri Mexican Bistro** (50 Moraga Ave., San Francisco, 415/678-5170, 11:30am-9pm Mon.-Thurs., 11:30am-10pm Fri., 10:30am-10pm Sat., 10:30am-9pm Sun., $14-35), located at the historic Presidio Officers' Club.

Mount Sutro Loop
MOUNT SUTRO OPEN SPACE RESERVE

✿ 🏛 🐾 🚶 🚌🚆

Escape from bustling city life on an unsuspecting street and into an ethereal forest with fairy houses, history, and beautiful San Francisco Bay views.

DISTANCE: 2.5 miles (4 km) round-trip

DURATION: 1 hour

ELEVATION GAIN: 440 feet (134 m)

EFFORT: Easy

TRAIL: Dirt, gravel, single-track

USERS: Hikers, runners, mountain bikers, leashed dogs

SEASON: Year-round

PASSES/FEES: None

MAPS: On the website find "Mount Sutro Open Space Reserve" and select "Trail Map"

PARK HOURS: 5am-midnight for the San Francisco Recreation and Parks section, sunrise-sunset for the UCSF section

TRAILHEAD: Cole Valley neighborhood, 17th Street and Stanyan Street

FACILITIES: Restrooms and water fountain at the Aldea Community Center

CONTACT: San Francisco Recreation and Parks, 415/831-2700, www.sfrecpark.org, University of California, San Francisco, 415/476-1000, www.ucsf.edu

START THE HIKE

▸ **MILE 0-0.5: Trailhead to Medical Center Way**

From the **Stanyan Street** entrance, head up a wooden stairway between two homes to the **Historic Trail.** Little fairy houses, cute figurines, and knickknacks can be found along tree stumps and rocks on this section of the Historic Trail. Make sure to stop when looking so you don't trip on the sometimes bumpy trail's roots and rocks.

At 0.4 mile (0.6 km), stay right (east) when the trail first splits. At the next junction, with Edgewood Trail, 0.1 mile (0.2 km) later, go left (north) to stay on the Historic Trail, making your way to the crosswalk at **Medical Center Way.**

▸ **MILE 0.5-1.1: Medical Center Way to Gardeners Trail**

Cross the street and stay on Historic Trail by following the path to the right (north), where a wooden fence borders the trail on the street side. The trail contours around the northwest slopes of the hill, overlooking the **University of California, San Francisco, Parnassus Campus.** On a clear enough day, you can see past the campus to Golden Gate Park, the Presidio, and even farther to the Golden Gate Bridge and Alcatraz. Historic Trail continues around Mount Sutro, turning south after 0.1 mile (0.2 km).

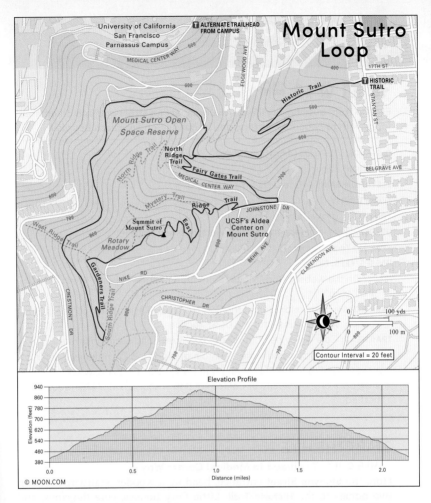

At 0.9 mile (1.4 km), pass the intersection with the very steep West Ridge Trail to stay on Historic Trail and watch for the **South Ridge Trail** at 1.1 miles (1.8 km). Turn left (north) onto South Ridge Trail and immediately look for the unmarked **Gardeners Trail** to the left (west).

▶ MILE 1.1–1.3: Gardeners Trail to Rotary Meadow

Turn onto Gardeners Trail as it curves right (north) toward the summit. The path narrows; watch for poison oak close to the trail.

Stay on Gardeners Trail as you pass another junction with West Ridge Trail at 1.2 miles (1.9 km). Look for a trail marker pointing in the direction of the summit and turn left (northeast), where the trail merges with **Nike Road** and becomes paved and then gravel. An interpretive sign just 0.1 mile (0.2 km) later, at **Rotary Meadow,** explains that during the Cold War, in the 1950s, a Nike missile radar site, SF-89C, was established atop Mount Sutro. Each of these radar sites monitored for enemy planes and was linked to a defensive missile launch site. SF-89C's missile was at SF-89L, about 2 miles (3.2 km) north in the Presidio. Today, the area's grassland habitat has been restored, and some of the native plants include coast buckwheat, California poppies, and purple needle grass.

▶ **MILE 1.3–2.5: Rotary Meadow to Trailhead**
From Rotary Meadow, take the **East Ridge Trail,** on your right (east), to continue to the summit. At 1.4 miles (2.3 km), the **summit of Mount Sutro** (911 ft/278 m) has picnic tables and benches. Look for the trail marker and stay on East Ridge Trail by continuing straight (northeast) as the trail begins to descend. Along the switchbacks downward are views north to the San Francisco Bay and southeast to Sutro Tower and Twin Peaks.

Pass the junction with Mystery Trail at 1.6 miles (2.6 km) and stay on East Ridge Trail until it meets **Johnstone Drive,** 0.1 mile (0.2 km) later. Turn left (east) onto Johnstone Drive, carefully watching for vehicles. Across the street is a sign for **UCSF's Aldea Center on Mount Sutro,** with restrooms and a water fountain. Cross the street and continue east on Johnstone Drive to the sidewalk. Pass the intersection with Medical Center Way, and just prior to the intersection with **Behr Avenue,** find the post with the address "66 Johnstone Drive" and a mailbox, on the north side of the street. Here, cross the street again, and find a trail marker to the left (west) of a "Private Residence" sign, marking where the hike reenters the forest on the dirt path of **Fairy Gates Trail,** at 1.8 miles (2.9 km).

When Fairy Gates Trails intersects with the **North Ridge Trail** at 1.9 miles (3.1 km), turn right (north) onto North Ridge Trail. At 2.1 miles (3.4 km), the trail meets Historic Trail. Turn right (west) onto Historic Trail and retrace your steps to the trailhead.

DIRECTIONS

From San Francisco Civic Center, go southwest on Market Street for 0.7 mile (1.1 km) and take a slight right onto 14th Street. Continue for 0.5 mile (0.8 km) and turn left onto Roosevelt Way. Continue for 0.7 mile (1.1 km) and turn right onto 17th Street. Continue for 0.4 mile (0.6 km).

GPS COORDINATES: 37.7613, −122.4520; 37°45'40.7" N, 122°27'7.2" W

> ### BEST NEARBY BITES
> If you have a sweet tooth, head to the Valencia location of **Dandeli-on Chocolate** (740 Valencia St., San Francisco, 415/349-0942, 10am-9pm Sun.-Thurs., 10am-10pm Fri.-Sat., $3.50-18), just 2 miles (3.2 km) and 11 minutes from the trailhead. With amazing bonbons, frozen hot chocolate, and house-made pastries, get yourself a treat for now and take one for later! Go east on 17th Street past Stanyan Street for 0.8 mile (1.3 km), then turn right when it becomes Eureka Street for just 0.1 mile (0.2 km). Turn left onto 18th Street and continue for 0.9 mile (1.4 km), and then turn right onto Valencia Street for 250 feet (76 m).

NEARBY CAMPGROUNDS

NAME	DESCRIPTION	FACILITIES	SEASON	FEE
Rob Hill	At the highest point of the Presidio above Baker Beach	4 group campsites for up to 30 people each. Each site has a fire ring, large charcoal grill, 4 picnic tables, 2 food storage boxes.	spring-fall	$92 Sun.-Thurs., $140 Fri.-Sat.

Hunter Road, San Francisco, 415/561-5083, www.recreation.gov

PENINSULA & SOUTH BAY

The Peninsula and South Bay extend down the coastline just south of San Francisco to the border of Santa Cruz County and east to Gilroy. Here you'll find everything from gentle shoreline, marshes, rising hills, canyons, and towering redwood forests. You can view hundreds of elephant seals loudly congregate at the shore for their annual mating and birthing rituals, and count dozens of banana slugs while hiking across the ridgeline of the Santa Cruz Mountains.

▲ PURISIMA LOOP

▲ RUSSIAN RIDGE LOOP

1 **Mori Point and Sweeney Ridge**
DISTANCE: 6.8 miles (10.9 km) round-trip
DURATION: 3.5 hours
EFFORT: Moderate-strenuous

2 **Purisima Loop**
DISTANCE: 8.8 miles (14.2 km) round-trip
DURATION: 4.5 hours
EFFORT: Moderate

3 **Russian Ridge Loop**
DISTANCE: 3.4 miles (5.5 km) round-trip
DURATION: 1.5 hours
EFFORT: Easy-moderate

4 **Año Nuevo Point Trail**
DISTANCE: 4.3 miles (6.9 km) round-trip
DURATION: 2 hours
EFFORT: Easy

5 **Hunter's Point Loop**
DISTANCE: 2.9 miles (4.7 km) round-trip
DURATION: 1 hour
EFFORT: Easy

6 **Eagle Rock**
DISTANCE: 2.7 miles (4.3 km) round-trip
DURATION: 1.5 hours
EFFORT: Easy

7 **Almaden Quicksilver Loop**
DISTANCE: 5.9 miles (9.5 km) round-trip
DURATION: 3 hours
EFFORT: Easy-moderate

8 **Uvas Canyon Waterfall Loop**
DISTANCE: 3.5 miles (5.6 km) round-trip
DURATION: 1.5 hours
EFFORT: Easy-moderate

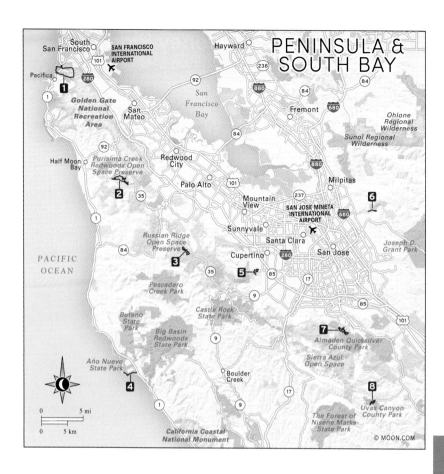

PENINSULA &
SOUTH BAY

South
San Francisco
Pacifica
SAN FRANCISCO
INTERNATIONAL
AIRPORT
Hayward

Golden Gate
National
Recreation
Area

San
Mateo

San
Francisco
Bay

Fremont

Ohlone
Regional
Wilderness

Sunol Regional
Wilderness

Half Moon
Bay

Purisima Creek
Redwoods Open
Space Preserve

Redwood
City

Palo Alto

Mountain
View

Milpitas

PACIFIC
OCEAN

Russian Ridge
Open Space
Preserve

Sunnyvale

Santa Clara

Cupertino

San Jose

SAN JOSE MINETA
INTERNATIONAL
AIRPORT

Joseph D.
Grant Park

Pescadero
Creek Park

Castle Rock
State Park

Butano
State
Park

Big Basin
Redwoods
State Park

Almaden Quicksilver
County Park

Sierra Azul
Open Space

Año Nuevo
State Park

Boulder
Creek

Uvas Canyon
County Park

The Forest of
Nisene Marks
State Park

California Coastal
National Monument

0   5 mi
0   5 km

© MOON.COM

Mori Point and Sweeney Ridge

GOLDEN GATE NATIONAL RECREATION AREA

Take a journey up to Sweeney Ridge for a walk through history, from the first Europeans arriving to the Cold War, with panoramic views of San Francisco Bay and the Pacific Ocean.

DISTANCE: 6.8 miles (10.9 km) round-trip

DURATION: 3.5 hours

ELEVATION GAIN: 1,430 feet (436 m)

EFFORT: Moderate-strenuous

TRAIL: Dirt fire road, gravel, single-track, paved, sidewalk

USERS: Hikers, mountain bikers on part of the trail, horseback riders on part of the trail, leashed dogs

SEASON: Year-round

PASSES/FEES: None

MAPS: Select "Sweeny Ridge Trail Map" on the park website

PARK HOURS: Sunrise-sunset daily

TRAILHEAD: Shelldance Nursery Parking Lot

FACILITIES: Vault toilets at 2.3 miles (3.7 km) on Sweeney Ridge Trail

CONTACT: Golden Gate National Recreation Area, 650/355-4122, www.nps.gov/goga

START THE HIKE

▶ **MILE 0-2.3: Shelldance Nursery Parking Lot to Vault Toilet Station**

From the parking lot at **Shelldance Nursery,** take **Mori Ridge Road** up a dirt and gravel service road through a vehicle gate with a trail marker. Remain on this path, and at 1.2 miles (1.9 km), turn right (southeast) onto **Sweeney Ridge Trail.** In less than 0.5 mile (0.8 km), the path becomes paved and you arrive at the **Nike Site SF-51,** a control station for the Cold War-era Nike antiaircraft missiles at a nearby launch site on Milagra Ridge. Continue south on Sweeney Ridge Trail to the **vault toilet station** at 2.3 miles (3.7 km), at the junction with Sneath Lane Trail.

▶ **MILE 2.3-4: Vault Toilet Station to Farallones Viewpoint**

Back on the dirt and gravel path, just south of the toilets where the Sweeney Ridge Trail splits, stay left (east) to the **Ohlone-Portolá Heritage Site,** where a Spanish expedition accidentally became the first Europeans to see San Francisco Bay, in 1769, when they overshot while trying to find Monterey Bay. According to the National Park Service, even though the Europeans were assisted by Ohlone people, who shared their food and company, the Spanish "discovery" of San Francisco Bay led to the loss of Ohlone lives and land when colonization started seven years later with Mission Dolores.

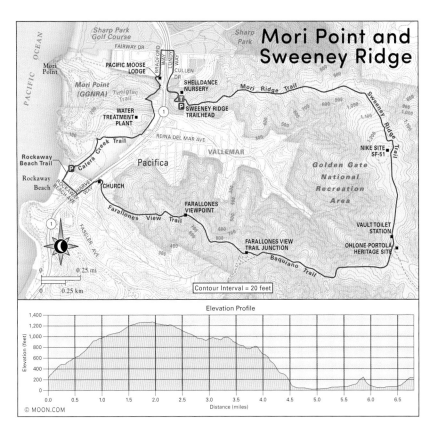

Take a moment to observe the monuments at the site, then proceed south and take the **Baquiano Trail** to the right (southwest) to begin descending. At the **junction** at 3.4 miles (5.5 km), look for the trail marker to continue upon **Farallones View Trail** (sometimes marked as Ahni Trail or Cattle Hill Trail), heading northwest, down toward Cattle Hill (801 ft/244 m).

The trail narrows, and while mountain bikers are not officially permitted on single-track trails in the Golden Gate National Recreation Area, this section has become increasingly popular. The recreation area border ends just past the **Farallones Viewpoint** at 4 miles (6.4 km), at the steepest downhill section of the hike. From the viewpoint, on a clear day you can see out to the Farallones Islands, known as the site of many shipwrecks of those attempting to enter the bay.

▶ MILE 4-5: Farallones Viewpoint to Rockaway Beach

Be extremely cautious on this section for the trail conditions, and stay aware of your surroundings. In less than 1 mile (1.6 km) from the viewpoint, the trail loses 790 feet (241 m) elevation; take your time. In the rainy season, the trail turns into thick mud, and even when it's dry, slips can easily happen. At 4.2 miles (6.8 km), multiple trails intersect; continue left (southwest), as many trails join Farallones View Trail from the right (north).

SWEENEY RIDGE ▲

Highway 1 soon appears below you, and as you get closer to it, the steep descent ends. The slope eventually turns grassy, passing through a small stand of trees behind a **church.** Cross the church's parking lot, being mindful of vehicles, and down to where Highway 1 meets **Harvey Way** at the entrance to the church. Turn left (southwest) onto Harvey Way at 4.8 miles (7.7 km). When you arrive at the **intersection** of Fassler Avenue, Highway 1, and Rockaway Beach Avenue, at the gas station, walk across Fassler Avenue and then Highway 1 to the western sidewalk of Rockaway Beach Avenue.

Take the sidewalk all the way to **Rockaway Beach** at 5 miles (8.1 km) and catch dozens of surfers riding the massive waves.

▸ **MILE 5–6.8: Rockaway Beach to Shelldance Nursery Parking Lot**
Follow the sidewalk right (northeast) on the **Rockaway Beach Trail** between the beach and vacation rentals to the **parking lot** where the trail ends. At the southeast corner of the parking lot, get onto the multiuse **Calera Creek Trail** through the Calera Creek wetlands, south of the creek. At 5.7 miles (9.2 km), the trail arrives at the **Liberty Garden,** created and maintained by a Pacifica resident in memory of those lost in the 9/11 tragedy.

From here, continue on the trail where it turns left (northeast) on a protected path set back from the west side of Highway 1, passing a water treatment plant to the left (west). The trail curves left (northwest). At 6 miles (9.7 km), turn right (northeast) onto **Timigtac Trail.** After less than 0.25 mile (0.4 km), the trail ends at Mori Point Road, near southbound Highway 1. Turn left (northwest) onto Mori Point Road, bearing right (northeast) around the **Pacific Moose Lodge** onto **Bradford Way** and through the residential area to the intersection of **Westport Drive.** Turn right (east) onto Westport Drive, using the crosswalk and signals to safely get to **Lundy Way**

▲ ROCKAWAY BEACH

at 6.4 miles (10.3 km). Turn right (south) onto the residential street and follow it until the road curves left (east) onto **Cullen Road.**

Take this short section of trail to connect to Mori Ridge Road, which you drove up from Highway 1 to get to the trailhead. Turn left (east) onto the winding road for one last push up to the parking lot at Shelldance Nursery.

DIRECTIONS

From San Francisco, take U.S. 101 south to I-280 south toward Daly City. Continue south on Highway 1, following signs for Pacifica. Take Mori Ridge Road to Shelldance Nursery and park near the large Sweeney Ridge Golden Gate National Recreation Area sign.

GPS COORDINATES: 37.6172, −122.4833; 37°37′1.9″ N, 122°28′59.9″ W

BEST NEARBY BITES

A Bay Area favorite, the deliciousness that is Señorita bread at **Star Bread Bakery** (1261 Linda Mar Shopping Center, Pacifica, 650/733-7750, www.starbreadca.com, 7am-7pm daily) is a fantastic post-hike treat just 2.5 miles (4 km) south of the trailhead. The airy rolled bread is sweet and buttery inside and a treasured snack at the traditional midafternoon break (merienda) in the Philippines.

To see a Taco Bell unlike any other, the **Taco Bell Cantina** (5200 Coast Hwy., Pacifica, 650/420-7130, 7am-midnight daily) in Pacifica captures the chain's number-one spot for coolest location. Located directly on the beach and offering local wine, beer, and Twisted Freezes, grab your food and watch surfers take on the waves from the patio or through its large windows.

An enchanting forest envelops you with the sounds of Purisima Creek, the shade of towering redwoods, and views over Half Moon Bay and the Pacific Ocean.

BEST: Redwood Hikes
DISTANCE: 8.8 miles (14.2 km) round-trip
DURATION: 4.5 hours
ELEVATION GAIN: 1,880 feet (573 m)
EFFORT: Moderate
TRAIL: Dirt, gravel, single-track
USERS: Hikers, mountain bikers, horseback riders
SEASON: Year-round
PASSES/FEES: None
MAPS: Select "Download Map" on the park website, at the trailhead
PARK HOURS: 30 minutes before sunrise to 30 minutes after sunset daily
TRAILHEAD: Purisima Creek Parking
FACILITIES: Vault toilets at the trailhead
CONTACT: Midpeninsula Regional Open Space Preserve, 650/691-1200, www.openspace.org

START THE HIKE

▶ **MILE 0-3.5: Purisima Creek Parking to Craig Britton Trail**
Start the hike by proceeding east (the vault toilets are to the right) onto **Purisima Creek Trail.** The dirt path is wide and shaded, bordered by a hillside of ferns to the south and Purisima Creek below, to the north.

Pass the Borden Hatch Mill Trail **junction** to the right (south) side of the trail at 1.6 miles (2.6 km). At 1.9 miles (3.1 km) is the first of several **bridge crossings,** as the path steadily climbs alongside and over the creek. The 3.3-mile (5.3-km) point is the farthest southeastern point of the hike, where the trail U-turns to the northwest over a massive drainage pipe built into the earth. The trail continues uphill, now headed north, away from the creek.

At 3.5 miles (5.6 km), look for the **wooden fence** that marks the entry to **Craig Britton Trail,** tucked into the forest on the north side of Purisima Creek Trail.

▶ **MILE 3.5-6.5: Craig Britton Trail to Harkins Ridge Trail Junction**
Turn left (north) onto Craig Britton Trail. The trail narrows to single-track that's exclusively for hiking—no equestrians or bikers—and the serenity of the forest engulfs you. Once named the Soda Gulch Trail for the ravine it follows, the path was renamed to honor Craig Britton, who is credited with helping to protect this area through preservation. Down the

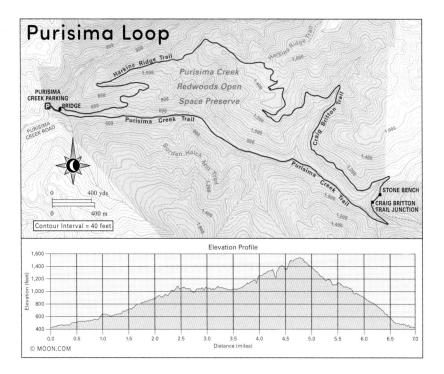

Purisima Loop

Purisima Creek Redwoods Open Space Preserve

Contour Interval = 40 feet

0 400 yds
0 400 m

Elevation Profile

© MOON.COM

trail about 500 feet (152 m) is a commemorative plaque on a curved stone bench that's dedicated to Britton. It's an ideal place to pause and take in the beauty around you.

At 4 miles (6.4 km), the path begins to run parallel to Purisima Creek for approximately 0.5 mile (0.8 km), though you're well above it and not within sight of the water. The trail is narrow and winding with steep drop-offs. Although it's well maintained, downed trees, prominent roots, and the undulation of the path require attention to your footing in this section.

At 6 miles (9.7 km), the trail leaves the forest, entering moss-covered oak woodland and chaparral with bursts of color from wildflowers like the orange bush monkey flower, pink honeysuckle, and yellow coastal bush lupine. The last 0.5 mile (0.8 km) before reaching **Harkins Ridge Trail** junction gains over 250 feet (76 m) elevation, bringing you to the highest point of the route at 1,540 feet (469 m).

▶ MILE 6.5–8.8: Harkins Ridge Trail Junction to Purisima Creek Parking

At the junction with Harkins Ridge Trail, turn left (west). This is a wide multiuse trail, so be mindful of equestrians and bicyclists. Over the next 2.3 miles (3.7 km), you'll quickly descend most of the elevation gained over the previous 6.5 miles (10.5 km), with intermittent shade and lovely views that open on each side of the trail. Some sections of the trail here are very steep, so ensure your shoelaces are securely tied and take your time. Don't forget to look up occasionally: The westward view ahead extends all the way to the Pacific.

The trail descends back into the redwood forest, and at 8.3 miles (13.4 km) the path runs along the north side of Purisima Creek. At 8.5 miles (13.7 km) is a **trail marker** that says only "Trail" with an arrow pointing in the direction you came from. At this **junction** is a trail to the left, but continue straight. The creek will be on the left (south), and you may spot hikers across the way on Purisima Creek Trail.

Just prior to reaching the trailhead, cross a **concrete vehicle bridge** with a trail marker indicating that the Purisima Creek Parking is just 0.1 mile (0.2 km) over the bridge. Even though "Higgins" is used on some signs, follow what's on the official park map.

DIRECTIONS

From San Francisco, take Highway 1 south for 23 miles (37 km) toward Pacifica, passing Half Moon Bay. Turn left onto Verde Road and drive 0.4 mile (0.6 km), then keep left to continue onto Purisima Creek Road for 3.5 miles (5.6 km). Turn right at Higgins Canyon Road to arrive at Purisima Creek Parking.

GPS COORDINATES: 37.4376, −122.3705; 37°26'15.4" N, 122°22'13.8" W

BEST NEARBY BITES

For a meal as rewarding as this hike, travel up Highway 1 just 13 miles (20.9 km) and 23 minutes from the trailhead to **Sam's Chowder House** (64210 N. Cabrillo Hwy., Half Moon Bay, 650/712-0245, www.samschowderhouse.com, 11:30am-8:30pm Mon.-Thurs., 11:30am-9pm Fri., 11am-9pm Sat., 11am-8:30pm Sun., $16-37). In addition to award-wining seafood, this family-friendly restaurant has indoor and outdoor oceanfront dining with a pet-friendly patio and live music on Friday evenings.

3 Russian Ridge Loop

RUSSIAN RIDGE OPEN SPACE PRESERVE

In the spring, this hike is a wildflower stunner with ancient oaks and panoramic rolling hill views of the southern peninsula out to the Pacific Ocean and San Francisco Bay.

BEST: Wildflower Hikes

DISTANCE: 3.4 miles (5.5 km) round-trip

DURATION: 1.5 hours

ELEVATION GAIN: 560 feet (171 m)

EFFORT: Easy-moderate

TRAIL: Gravel fire road, gravel, dirt, single-track

USERS: Hikers, mountain bikers, horseback riders

SEASON: Year-round

PASSES/FEES: None

MAPS: Select "Download Map" on the park website

PARK HOURS: 30 minutes before sunrise to 30 minutes after sunset daily

TRAILHEAD: Skyline Boulevard roadside parking, across from Silicon Valley Vista Point

FACILITIES: None

CONTACT: Midpeninsula Regional Open Space, 650/691-1200, www. openspace.org

START THE HIKE

▸ **MILE 0-2: Ridge Trailhead to Ancient Oaks Trail**

The trailhead is just southwest of the street-side parking, at an **interpretive board** behind the service road gate. Take the **service road,** passing the trail marker sign on the left (east), and turn uphill to the right (west) for **Ridge Trail.** In spring you'll immediately spot the wildflower show, including purple owl's clover, dwarf checker mallow, California poppies, and tidy tips along the exposed path.

At the trail **junction** at 0.7 mile (1.1 km), turn left (west) and descend onto **Hawk Ridge Trail.** Red-tailed hawks, turkey vultures, Cooper's hawks, sharp-shinned hawks, and golden eagles are all known to ride the wind drafts within view above the rolling grasslands that turn golden come summer. The trail hugs the curves of the slope, and you soon approach the first of many steep forested canyons.

Just before the path transitions to **Alder Spring Trail,** at 1.2 miles (1.9 km), is the first shade of the hike. The trail passes in and out of the shade, often with a view of springwater flowing down the inner canyons and sometimes across the trail. The path transitions again into Charquin Trail. Stay right (south) at 1.7 miles (2.7 km), where another section of Charquin

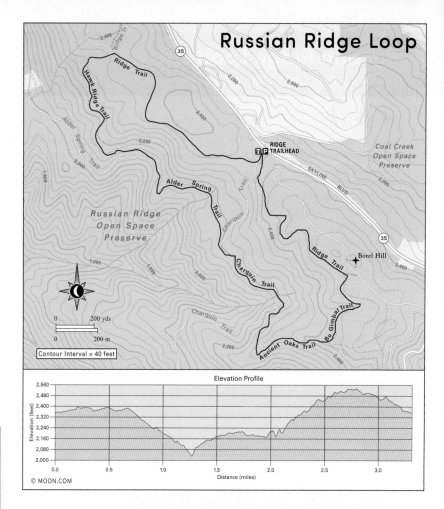

Russian Ridge Loop

Russian Ridge Open Space Preserve

Coal Creek Open Space Preserve

Borel Hill

RIDGE TRAILHEAD

Contour Interval = 40 feet

0   200 yds

0   200 m

Elevation Profile

© MOON.COM

Trail comes in from the north. At 2 miles (3.2 km), stay left (south), ascending into the forest to continue onto **Ancient Oaks Trail.**

▶ **MILE 2-3.4: Ancient Oaks Trail to Ridge Trailhead**
Some of the wide-trunk oaks in this area may be 200 to 300 years old, and among the twisting oaks grow fungi, ferns, moss, and a variety of flowers. The rolling hills and ridgeline views are beautifully framed by the branches of these long-lived trees. At 2.5 miles (4 km), turn left (north) onto **Bo Gimbal Trail,** climbing alongside a wide ravine and arriving at a meadow.

Bo Gimbal ends at a **T junction** with Ridge Trail. Turn left (northwest) onto Ridge Trail, where the remainder of the hike is without tree cover from the sun. Follow the posted trail sign to **Borel Hill.** At 2.9 miles (4.7 km) into the hike, it appears to be just a slight rise in the ridge, but this is the highest named point in San Mateo County, at 2,572 feet (784 m), offering 360-degree views of the Pacific Ocean and San Francisco Bay.

From Borel Hill, begin the gradual descent back to the trailhead by traveling northwest on Ridge Trail, now a gravel service road. At 3.3 miles (5.3

▲ RUSSIAN RIDGE LOOP

km), the trail rejoins the first service road that took you to the beginning of Ridge Trail at the start of the hike. Turning right (north), it leads back to the street-side parking area.

DIRECTIONS

From San Jose, take I-280 to exit 16 for El Monte Road. Keep left at the fork and follow signs for Foothill College, Moody Road, and El Monte, then merge onto El Monte Road. Take Moody Road and Page Mill Road to Highway 35. Turn right and proceed for 1.2 miles (1.9 km). Park on the left side of the road.

GPS COORDINATES: 37.3245, −122.2050; 37°19′28.2″ N, 122°12′18″ W

BEST NEARBY BITES

With breakfast until 2pm and lunch served all day, **Alice's Restaurant** (17288 Skyline Blvd., Woodside, 650/851-0303, 8am-8pm Mon.-Sat., 8am-7pm Sun., $8-35) was built in the early 1900s as a general store to support the logging industry. The porch and grassy lawn provide ample dining space under the cool cover of the redwoods, and the extensive menu promises something for everyone.

4

Año Nuevo Point Trail

AÑO NUEVO STATE PARK

🦌 ❀ 🏛 🚶

Set between the Santa Cruz Mountains and the Pacific Ocean, this hike visits a gorgeous natural habitat for migrating birds, elephant seals, and a variety of other animals and plants.

BEST: Winter Hikes

DISTANCE: 4.3 miles (6.9 km) round-trip

DURATION: 2 hours

ELEVATION GAIN: 200 feet (61 m)

EFFORT: Easy

TRAIL: Dirt, sand fire road, gravel, wooden boardwalk, single-track

USERS: Hikers, wheelchair users on part of the trail

SEASON: Year-round

PASSES/FEES: $10 day-use fee per vehicle, or California State Parks Pass

MAPS: Select "Brochures" then "Park Brochure" on the park website; at the park entrance station

PARK HOURS: 8:30am-sunset daily

TRAILHEAD: Año Nuevo State Park Parking Lot

FACILITIES: Restrooms and drinking fountain at the trailhead, vault toilets at the Staging Area

CONTACT: California State Parks, 650/879-2025, www.parks.ca.gov

START THE HIKE

December to March, reservations are required to visit the preserve, and you can only visit on a guided tour. Tickets typically go on sale in October. When reservations are not required, April to November, a free visitor permit is required to do this hike. See the park website for more information on reservations, tours, and getting a permit.

This hike meets ADA trail standards for the first 1.3 miles (2.1 km), but that part of the trail does not connect with the elephant seal viewing areas. For mobility assistance to view the elephant seals, make a reservation for an Equal Access Tour, described on the park website.

▶ **MILE 0-0.3: Parking Lot to Cove Beach Junction**

Begin hiking **Año Nuevo Point Trail** from the southwest corner of the **parking lot.** When the trail splits at 0.1 mile (0.2 km), continue right (west). At 0.2 mile (0.3 km) is a **junction** with New Years Creek Trail, which goes left (south) along the coast and turns to meet Highway 1. Continue straight to remain on Año Nuevo Point Trail as it runs along the top of an earthen dam that creates an invaluable habitat for endangered species.

As you pass a pond at 0.3 mile (0.5 km), a short turnoff to the left (south) leads down to Cove Beach. From the **junction,** you may see any number of

Año Nuevo Point Trail

Elevation Profile

© MOON.COM

birds enjoying the seashore and the pond, including pelicans, sandpipers, and a variety of gulls.

▶ **MILE 0.3-0.8: Cove Beach Junction to Año Nuevo Coast Natural Preserve**

You'll come back to the beach on the return trip; for now, continue on Año Nuevo Point Trail and cross a wooden **bridge** over the Frijoles fault. The trail briefly turns north, and one of the most scenic spots of the hike is when it curves back toward the coast at 0.4 mile (0.6 km)—take in the views over the pond and have a seat on the bench to see the ridge of the Santa Cruz Mountains.

Turning inland, continue right (west) on Año Nuevo Point Trail as it slightly gains elevation. When you see a small stand of Monterey pines ahead, you've almost arrived at the Staging Area and Natural Preserve Trailhead. The junction is at 0.8 mile (1.3 km), and hikers must present a permit (or proceed with a guide) to enter the **Año Nuevo Coast Natural Preserve** area beyond this point.

▶ **MILE 0.8-1.7: Año Nuevo Coast Natural Preserve to Bight Point Loop**

Look around the exhibit building before continuing straight on Año Nuevo Point Trail, which travels southwest above the coast. At any point when the water is visible, look for elephant seals and other water mammals like otters and sea lions.

After a brief **boardwalk section,** at 1.3 miles (2.1 km) the accessible part of the trail ends and the surface becomes sand. Take the trail split left (south) toward **South Point.** Ropes line the path and brown park signs help keep hikers oriented toward the point and your first views of Año Nuevo Island, with the remains of a 19th-century lighthouse and a fog signal station. Birds like Brandt's cormorants call the island home, and according to one docent, sea lions roam up and down the stairs of the historic keeper's house.

Continue northwest along the coast to the boardwalk junction for **Bight Point Loop** at 1.7 miles (2.7 km). Turn left (west) onto the boardwalk and stay left to begin the loop. Year-round, you can look down the beach toward North Point for lounging elephant seals, or use the boardwalk's binoculars to see farther out to the water and Año Nuevo Island.

▶ **MILE 1.7–4.3: Bight Point Loop to Parking Lot**

After completing the loop, continue west on Año Nuevo Point Trail toward North Point. Cross over a short **bridge,** where the path narrows and the sand deepens. Follow signs for the North Point Viewing Area and stay on trail to protect the fragile dune habitat filled with coastal bush lupine, coast paintbrush, California goldenbush, and coyote brush. At 2.2 miles (3.5 km), you've reached the end of Año Nuevo Point Trail.

Return the way you came, taking a quick detour down to **Cove Beach** at 3.8 miles (6.1 km), just past the stand of pines by the pond. If you choose to explore the beach, beware of high tides. Back on Año Nuevo Point Trail, continue east in the direction of the trailhead. When the trail splits at 4.2 miles (6.8 km), stay right (south) to explore the historic **Cypress Dairy complex** before taking the path north back to the parking lot.

DIRECTIONS

From San Mateo, take Highway 92 to Half Moon Bay, and turn left onto Highway 1 (Cabrillo Hwy.). Continue for 27.6 miles (44 km) and turn right onto New Years Creek Road to enter the park.

GPS COORDINATES: 37.1197, −122.3073; 37°7′10.9″ N, 122°18′26.3″ W

BEST NEARBY BREWS

A quick 5 miles (8.1 km) and 7 minutes up the road is **Highway 1 Brewing Company** (5720 Cabrillo Hwy., Pescadero, 650/879-9243, www.highway1brewing.com, noon–5pm Fri.-Sun.). A "casual coastal sanctuary," the outdoor beer garden is kid- and dog-friendly, and all beers are brewed on-site, sourced with sustainable and local ingredients.

5

Hunter's Point Loop

FREMONT OLDER PRESERVE

This short hike provides enough of a challenge to get your heart pumping, along with the serenity of a dense forest, the delight of wildflowers when in bloom, and wide-open views of the Santa Clara Valley and beyond at the 945-foot (288-m) Hunter's Point hilltop.

DISTANCE: 2.9 miles (4.7 km) round-trip

DURATION: 1 hour

ELEVATION GAIN: 560 feet (171 m)

EFFORT: Easy

TRAIL: Dirt, gravel, single-track

USERS: Hikers, mountain bikers, horseback riders, leashed dogs

SEASON: Year-round

PASSES/FEES: None

MAPS: Select "Download Map" on the park website

PARK HOURS: 30 minutes before sunrise to 30 minutes after sunset daily

TRAILHEAD: Prospect Parking Area

FACILITIES: None

CONTACT: Midpeninsula Regional Open Space, 650/691-1200, www. openspace.org

START THE HIKE

Seven Springs Trail at places is narrow with steep drop-offs. Take care with children and when passing other hikers. As mountain bikers are allowed on all sections of this hike, be alert to the possibility of their approach.

▶ **MILE 0-1.1: Prospect Parking Area to Ranch Road Intersection**
Start this hike at the northwest corner of the **Prospect Parking Area** on **Cora Older Trail.** The dirt path immediately and steadily climbs up a **switchback,** bordered by lush greenery of oak and bay trees, poison oak, toyon, coyote brush, and wildflowers like redstem stork's bill and orange bush monkey flower. In less than 0.5 mile (0.8 km), the trail ascends 200 feet (61 m) into an open grassy hillside.

At the **three-way junction** at 0.4 mile (0.6 km), turn right (northwest) onto **Seven Springs Trail.** The trail continues to rise another 500 feet (152 m) then snakes down under the tree canopy, along the bends of a canyon with steep drop-offs and into the abundant forest, with glimpses of the Diablo Range in the distance. Look for the remnants of an old walnut orchard as the path continues and then runs along a streambed at the floor of the small valley.

At 1.1 miles (1.8 km), the trail reaches an **intersection** with Ranch Road.

PENINSULA & SOUTH BAY

Hunter's Point Loop

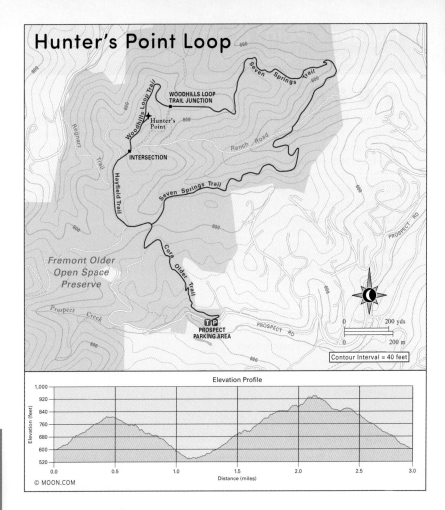

Hunter's Point Loop

Elevation Profile

© MOON.COM

▶ **MILE 1.1–2.1: Ranch Road Intersection to Hunter's Point Spur**

Cross Ranch Road to stay on Seven Springs Trail headed northeast, briefly staying along the valley floor before leaving the shade while climbing the opposite side of the canyon, catching frequent views of the Santa Clara Valley. At 1.3 miles (2.1 km), the trail skirts the park's eastern boundary, passing an electric tower, and then turns left (west) into grasslands.

Just over 0.5 mile (0.8 km) later, Seven Springs Trail turns left (south) when it reaches a **junction** with **Woodhills Loop Trail** at 1.9 miles (3.1 km). Continue straight (west) onto Woodhills Loop Trail and continue farther uphill, arriving at the **spur trail** for **Hunter's Point** at 2.1 miles (3.4 km). Along the way, look for the turkey vultures in the sky and the quail that scurry on the ground.

▶ **MILE 2.1–2.9: Hunter's Point Spur to Prospect Parking Area**

Turn left (northeast) onto the spur for Hunter's Point and finish the climb. You can sit on the park bench with nothing to impede the view. Peer down on the path you've hiked and out to 360-degree views of the San

Francisco Bay Area. Mount Hamilton is in view to the east, to the north Mount Tamalpais, and to the south Mount Umunhum.

From the spur, return to Woodhills Loop Trail and continue left (south) on the loop through the grasslands. At 2.2 miles (3.5 km) is an **intersection** at the confluence of Ranch Road and Seven Springs Trail, where Woodhills Loop Trails joins Hayfield Trail. Stay right (west), continuing on Hayfield Trail, and then straight (south) where Regnart Trail meets Hayfield Trail. Continue to descend and return to the Cora Older Trail-Seven Springs Trail-Hayfield junction at 2.5 miles (4 km).

Take Cora Older Trail right (south) to return the way you came.

DIRECTIONS

From San Jose, take I-280 and then exit 12B onto Highway 85 south toward Gilroy. After 2.7 miles (4.3 km), take the exit for De Anza Boulevard and turn right. Continue for 0.5 mile (0.8 km) and turn right onto Prospect Road. Continue for 0.4 mile (0.6 km) and then turn left to cross the railroad tracks and remain on Prospect Road. In 1.1 miles (1.8 km), turn left again to stay on Prospect Road for less than 0.5 mile (0.8 km) to arrive at the preserve's Prospect Parking Area.

GPS COORDINATES: 37.2860, −122.0553; 37°17'9.6" N, 122°3'19.1" W

BEST NEARBY BREWS

Located in a building considered "heritage architecture," **Off the Rails Brewing** (111 S. Murphy Ave., Sunnyvale, 408/773-9500, www. offtherailsbrewing.com, 11am-10pm Mon.-Fri., 10am-10pm Sat., 10am-9pm Sun.) offers a variety of beers on tap and a full menu, along with patio seating and board game and trivia nights. Eight miles (12.9 km) and 20 minutes from the trailhead, take Highway 85 north to exit 23 for Evelyn Avenue to arrive in Sunnyvale.

6

Eagle Rock

ALUM ROCK PARK

🏛 🚶

This easy, family-friendly hike takes you near the remnants of stone grottos and up along the north rim of the canyon to beautiful views of the South Bay and the valley below.

DISTANCE: 2.7 miles (4.3 km) round-trip
DURATION: 1.5 hours
ELEVATION GAIN: 325 feet (99 m)
EFFORT: Easy
TRAIL: Dirt fire road, gravel, paved
USERS: Hikers, mountain bikers, horseback riders
SEASON: Year-round
PASSES/FEES: $6 per day parking, $10 on holidays
MAPS: Park website
PARK HOURS: 8am to 30 minutes after sunset daily
TRAILHEAD: Alum Rock Visitor Center
FACILITIES: Restrooms at visitor center
CONTACT: City of San José Parks, 408/259-5477, www.sanjoseca.gov

Founded in 1872, Alum Rock is California's oldest municipal park and was once a nationally known health spa. The park was named for a giant boulder once thought to be made of alum, a compound containing aluminum. The rock was later found to be manganese, was mined, and is now gone. Until the 1930s, the Alum Rock Steam Railroad shuttled riders from downtown San Jose to enjoy the park's 27 mineral springs, indoor swimming pool, and tea garden. According to one park ranger, the path where this hike begins was part of the train's route. On the North Rim Trail are remnants of a stone grotto, marking one of the park's mineral springs.

START THE HIKE

The park may close during periods of high fire danger, so call ahead to confirm that the park is open on the day you want to visit. As you're hiking, make sure to listen for bikers calling out that they're passing, and be prepared to yield to equestrians.

▶ **MILE 0-0.4: Visitor Center to North Rim Trail**
From the **visitor center,** take the wide path immediately outside to the east. The creek is on your left, with the parking lot on the other side of it. The path merges onto the **Penitencia Trail** just before passing the **Youth Science Institute's Science and Nature Center** (noon-4pm Wed.-Fri., 10:30am-4:30pm Sat.-Sun.), to the south. The center houses unique artifacts, collections, and resources that connect the public with nature while teaching science. Young and old are welcome to visit and learn.

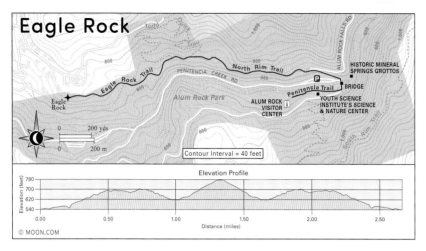

Eagle Rock

Contour Interval = 40 feet

Elevation Profile

© MOON.COM

At 0.2 mile (0.3 km), the trail intersects with the South Rim Trail to the right (south). Continue on the Penitencia Trail as it curves left (north). Look for the first of several **stone grottos** in the area, built into the rock walls along the right (east) side of the trail. Over 20 different mineral springs were identified in 1891 and 1892, and to protect them, tunnels were dug into the hillside and masons created the grottos. You may catch a whiff of the sulfur compounds seeping from the rocks here before you even see the grotto. For kids, you could use the opportunity to introduce the element sulfur and the periodic table.

Cross a small **bridge** left (west) to **Mineral Springs Loop Trail** at 0.4 mile (0.6 km) and immediately turn left (southwest) to meet the **North Rim Trail.**

▶ **MILE 0.4–1.4: North Rim Trail to Eagle Rock**

The North Rim Trail gradually makes its way uphill, hugging the canyon, and intersects with Weather Loop Trail at 0.9 mile (1.4 km); stay straight (west). The trail then descends before crossing with the Weather Loop Trail-Todd Quick Trail at 1 mile (1.6 km). You can take the Todd Quick Trail to add a strenuous mile (1.6 km) to your hike. To the south are continuous clear views down the canyon with oak trees speckled throughout. Kids will enjoy spotting birds riding the wind, and parents will want to keep them on the inside of the wide trail.

At 1.1 miles (1.8 km), North Rim Trail again intersects with the Todd Quick Trail. Stay on North Rim and continue to descend another 0.1 mile (0.2 km).

At 1.2 miles (1.9 km), the trail travels back uphill. Pay close attention to the signs on the right (north) side of the trail and watch for the right-side turnoff to **Eagle Rock Trail** at 1.3 miles (2.1 km). (If you reach Lariat Trail, you've gone too far down North Rim Trail.)

The short final push to **Eagle Rock** rewards hikers with three viewing benches overlooking the South Bay and the opportunity to explore and scramble around the igneous Eagle Rock.

▶ **MILE 1.4–2.7: Eagle Rock to Visitor Center**
Return to the visitor center by hiking back the way you came.

EAGLE ROCK TRAIL ▲

DIRECTIONS

From downtown San Jose, follow East Taylor Street northeast for 3.4 miles (5.5 km) as it turns into Mabury Road. Turn left onto North White Road. After 0.5 mile (0.8 km), turn right onto Penitencia Creek Road to enter the park's main entrance. Follow the road through the park to the visitor center parking lot.

GPS COORDINATES: 37.3971, −121.7987; 37°23'49.6" N, 121°47'55.3" W

BEST NEARBY BREWS

Make your way to **Faultline Brewery** (1235 Oakmead Pkwy., Sunnyvale, 408/736-2739, www.faultlinebrewing.com, 11am-9am Mon.-Fri., 10am-9pm Sat.-Sun.), just 13 miles (20.9 km) and 26 minutes from the trailhead. Situated by a small lake, this brewery and restaurant features gorgeous scenery and four award-winning flagship beers. To get here, hop on U.S. 101 west to Sunnyvale, then take Lawrence Parkway south to Oakmead Parkway.

7

Almaden Quicksilver Loop
ALMADEN QUICKSILVER COUNTY PARK

As you pass through forests and over streams, admire the expansive city views and take in Mount Umunhum and the Diablo Range.

BEST: Dog-Friendly Hikes

DISTANCE: 5.9 miles (9.5 km) round-trip

DURATION: 3 hours

ELEVATION GAIN: 830 feet (253 m)

EFFORT: Easy-moderate

TRAIL: Paved road, dirt, single-track

USERS: Hikers, mountain bikers, horseback riders, leashed dogs

SEASON: Year-round

PASSES/FEES: None

MAPS: Select "Available Documents" then "Almaden Quicksilver County Park Guide Map" on the park website

PARK HOURS: 8am-sunset daily

TRAILHEAD: Webb Canyon trail entry

FACILITIES: None

CONTACT: Santa Clara County Parks, 408/535-4070, https://parks.sccgov.org

START THE HIKE

Do not eat or drink anything from within the park. Sediments that contain mercury have been deposited in some of the local reservoirs and streams, which may have been converted to toxic methyl mercury by naturally occurring bacteria. Stick to what you carry in, and be sure to carry it out.

The Randol Trail can be closed seasonally due to poor trail conditions—check the park's website to make sure it's open before starting this hike.

▶ **MILE 0-1.4: Webb Canyon Trail Entry to Cinnabar Trail**
From the **Webb Canyon trail entry,** walk south through the park gate to remain on **Webb Canyon Road.** Leave the neighborhood behind and head up the paved road to the marker for **Webb Canyon Trail** at 0.2 mile (0.3 km).

Turn right (west) onto Webb Canyon Trail. Continue to climb as the trail curves north, quickly rewarding you with views of the Diablo Range far to the northeast. The trail curves in a broad C shape, first turning west and then south. At 0.6 mile (1 km), Webb Canyon Trail ends where it runs into **New Almaden Trail.** Turn right (west) onto New Almaden. The single-track trail zigzags in and out of canyons and rolls over seasonal streams that dry out by summer, with intermittent views of the city and the mountains.

At 1.4 miles (2.3 km), the trail briefly travels along a wire fence that marks the park border before reaching the trail marker for the intersection with **Cinnabar Trail,** named after the red pigment the Indigenous Ohlone people used for religious ceremonies and as decorative body paint.

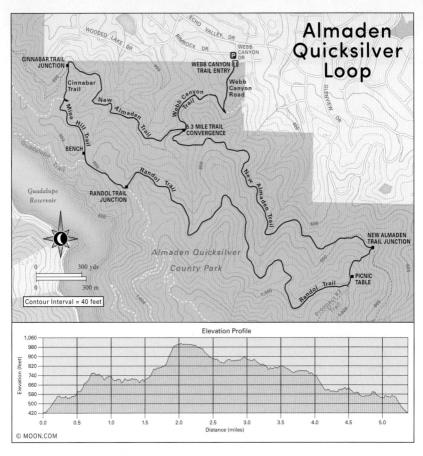

Elevation Profile

© MOON.COM

▸ **MILE 1.4-2.1: Cinnabar Trail to Randol Trail**

Turn left (south) to follow the Cinnabar Trail. Although this connector trail is just 0.1 mile (0.2 km), the exposed 100-foot (30-m) elevation gain up the steep slope is a heart-pumping climb. At the top of Cinnabar Trail, turn left (south) onto **Mine Hill Trail.** This wide dirt and gravel fire road is heavily used by hikers, equestrians, and mountain bikers. Views open up to the west, revealing the beauty of the Guadalupe Reservoir, the foothills of the Santa Cruz Mountains, and Mount Umunhum. At 1.8 miles (2.9 km) into the hike is a **memorial bench** overlooking the reservoir, a perfect spot to rest.

Just past the memorial bench, the Mine Hill Trail intersects with the Guadalupe Trail, which descends west from Mine Hill to follow the northeast portion of the reservoir. Remain on Mine Hill Trail, heading southeast above the reservoir to the junction with the **Randol Trail** at 2.1 miles (3.4 km).

▸ **MILE 2.1-4: Randol Trail to New Almaden Trail**

Turn left (northeast) onto the wide Randol Trail, shared with equestrians and bikers. At 3.7 miles (6 km), Randol Trail intersects with Prospect 3 Trail at the **highest point** of this hike (1,000 ft/305 m). Hike to the lone

picnic table and look left across the grasslands, taking in the panoramic view of San Jose.

From the picnic table, look for the exposed single-track **Prospect 3 Trail** to the west. There is no trail marker here, but the path should be easy to spot. The steep dirt and gravel trail runs north and descends 150 feet (46 m) over 0.2 mile (0.3 km). Watch for the prickly yellow star thistle that borders the narrow path. Prospect 3 Trail meets **New Almaden Trail** at 4 miles (6.4 km).

▶ MILE 4–5.9: New Almaden Trail to Webb Canyon Trail Entry

As you turn left (west) onto New Almaden Trail, you're about 1.25 miles (2 km) east of where you first started the hike. The trail winds along the hillside with slight changes in elevation, and at 4.2 miles (6.8 km) it crosses a seasonal creek. After the crossing, the creek runs parallel to the trail. There are a few bridge crossings until the 4.6-mile (7.4-km) mark, and some tricky roots to navigate on narrower sections of the trail.

Continue downhill to the **convergence** of trails at 5.3 miles (8.5 km), where you turn right (north) at the Webb Canyon trail marker and retrace your earlier route 0.6 mile (1 km) to the Webb Canyon trail entry.

DIRECTIONS

From downtown San Jose, take Almaden Expressway south for 6.7 miles (10.8 km) to Trinidad Drive and turn right. After 0.2 mile (0.3 km), turn left onto Elwood Road for 0.8 mile (1.3 km) and then right onto Echo Valley Drive. Travel for 0.2 mile (0.3 km) to Webb Canyon Drive, which dead-ends at the trailhead and park entrance. Commonly known as the Webb Canyon trail entry, it's not an official entrance; park on neighborhood streets, avoiding driveways and fire lanes.

GPS COORDINATES: 37.2040, −121.8632; 37°12′14.4″ N, 121°51′47.5″ W

BEST NEARBY BREWS

After your hike, grab a beer at **Uproar Brewing Company** (439 S. 1st St., San Jose, 408/673-2266, www.uproarbrewing.com, 4pm-11pm Sun. and Wed.-Thurs., noon-midnight Fri., 4pm-midnight Sat.), just over 11 miles (17.7 km) from the trailhead in downtown San Jose. For something refreshing and light, try their Sofa-King Good Hazy IPA for a melon and citrus taste.

PENINSULA & SOUTH BAY

Almaden Quicksilver Loop

Follow this loop to see multiple waterfalls, immerse yourself in the lush shaded forest, and take in views of Uvas Canyon and the Santa Cruz Mountains.

BEST: Spring Hikes

DISTANCE: 3.5 miles (5.6 km) round-trip

DURATION: 1.5 hours

ELEVATION GAIN: 760 feet (232 m)

EFFORT: Easy-moderate

TRAIL: Paved road, dirt, dirt and gravel fire road, rock, single-track

USERS: Hikers, leashed dogs

SEASON: Year-round

PASSES/FEES: $6 day-use fee per vehicle; advanced parking reservations at www.gooutsideandplay.org

MAPS: Select "Uvas Canyon County Park Guide Map" on the park website; at the park entrance station

PARK HOURS: 8am-sunset daily

TRAILHEAD: Day-use parking lot

FACILITIES: Restrooms at the trailhead

CONTACT: Santa Clara County Parks, 408/779-9232, https://parks.sccgov.org

START THE HIKE

To get to the park, the road passes through Sveadal, a private Swedish cultural heritage site and recreation area belonging to the Swedish American Patriotic League. Respect their privacy and drive slowly, and be ready to back up to share the narrow road with other traffic.

Note that while the park closes at sunset, the majority of this hike is well shaded and within the canyon—the trails get dark earlier than sunset. Be prepared with appropriate gear for creek crossings year-round, and check in at the park gate to confirm trail conditions before starting your hike.

▶ **MILE 0-0.8: Day-Use Parking Lot to Contour Trail**

From the **day-use parking lot** at the park's entrance, take the stairs at the northwest end up to the restrooms. Follow the path southwest (left) past the picnic area and amphitheater to meet the **paved park road.** Turn right (southwest) onto the road, keeping right at the fork, headed in the direction of the campground, not left toward the Black Oak Group Area. Follow the road briefly downhill and look for the trail marker to join the **Waterfall Loop Nature Trail** to the left (south) at 0.14 mile (0.2 km).

The trail goes up **rocky stairs** and passes over a **bridge,** looking down on the 5-foot (1.5-m) **Granuja Falls** that gently flows over the rocks in **Swanson Creek.** Shortly after the bridge at 0.2 mile (0.3 km) is a fork in the trail. Stay

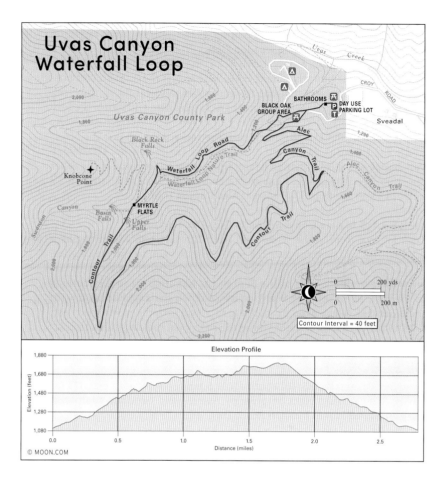

Uvas Canyon Waterfall Loop

right (southwest) and continue onto **Waterfall Loop Road.** The wide path crosses another **bridge** over Swanson Creek and then runs parallel to the creek on the left, steadily leading uphill.

At 0.6 mile (1 km), the trail intersects with the **spur trail** to the 35-foot (11-m) Black Rock Falls. It's 0.6 mile (1 km) out and back if you choose to add it, but the falls typically only flow after the winter rains into spring and dry up by summer. At 0.8 mile (1.3 km), the trail arrives at a picnic table at **Myrtle Flats,** once the site of an early settler's cabin. Here is a multiway **junction,** where the Waterfall Loop Nature Trail U-turns and descends toward the creek. To the right (west) is the Knobcone Trail, a steep 0.4-mile (0.6-km) out-and-back to Knobcone Point. Continue straight (southwest) by crossing the **bridge** where a trail marker indicates the start of the **Contour Trail.**

▶ **MILE 0.8-2.7: Contour Trail to Alec Canyon Trail**
After crossing the bridge, on the left is the unmarked yet impressive **Upper Falls,** and on the right is a **spur trail** for Basin Falls, 0.8 mile (1.3 km) out and back if you choose to add it to your hike. Otherwise, continue straight (southwest) on Contour Trail. As tempting as it is to keep your eyes on the

multilevel Upper Falls, watch your footing, as the trail continues to ascend over the rocky terrain and up wooden steps.

At 1.3 miles (2.1 km), follow the signs to carefully cross the creek. Most people utilize the many boulders; make sure to test them for stability before taking a step. Note that due to seasonal high-water flows, the creek may at times be impassable, and you have to stop here and return the way you came.

If you're able to cross the creek, take the **rocky stairs** up into the forest to the right (south). At the top of the stairs, take the abrupt 180-degree **switchback** to the left. Though a faint trail seems to continue in the other direction, heed the posted signs and remain on the designated trail. At 2.7 miles (4.3 km), Contour Trail ends at **Alec Canyon Trail.**

▶ MILE 2.7–3.5: Alec Canyon Trail to Day-Use Parking Lot

Turn left (west) onto the wide-open Alec Canyon Trail, which begins a 400-foot (122-m) descent over 0.8 mile (1.3 km) back to the parking lot. At 0.1 mile (0.2 km) along Alec Canyon, look for a bench and a picnic table with a stunning view of the Santa Cruz Mountains and the foothills to the east. At 3.3 miles (5.3 km), continue down the **switchbacks** toward the **Black Oak Group Area.** From the group area, take the paved road east, back to the path that brought you to the road, past the amphitheater, picnic area, restrooms, and down the stairs to the parking lot.

DIRECTIONS

From San Jose, take U.S. 101 south for 12.5 miles (20.1 km) to exit 373 for Bailey Avenue. Turn right onto Bailey Avenue and continue southwest for 3 miles (4.8 km) to McKean Road. Turn left onto McKean Road, which becomes Uvas Road after 2.2 miles (3.5 km). Turn right onto Croy Road, which narrows and passes through the private property of Sveadal; stay on the road and drive slowly. After 4.4 miles (7.1 km) on Croy Road is the park's entrance.

GPS COORDINATES: 37.0844, −121.7930; 37°5′3.8″ N, 121°47′34.8″ W

BEST NEARBY BREWS

Inspired by the famed long-distance Camino de Santiago hiking route in Spain, the draft menu at **Camino Brewing Co.** (718 S. 1st St., San Jose, 408/352-5331, www.caminobrewing.com, 5pm–11pm Tues.–Fri., noon–11pm Sat., noon–9pm Sun.) includes a tribute to Spain in its Café con Leche Coffee Milk Stout as well as a nonalcoholic sparkling water made with Lemondrop hops, called Hop Water. From the parking lot at Uvas Canyon, travel 28.2 miles (45 km) or 40 minutes north on U.S. 101, taking exit 384 for downtown San Jose.

NEARBY CAMPGROUNDS

NAME	DESCRIPTION	FACILITIES	SEASON	FEE
Black Mountain Backpack Camp	1.5-mi/2.4-km hike from the Monte Bello Parking Area, with 500 ft/152 m elevation gain	4 single campsites and 1 group site for up to 24 people, nonpotable water, no trash, food lockers, no fires allowed except gas camp stoves in designated areas only	year-round	$2 pp; permit required

Monte Bello Open Space Preserve, Montebello Road, Los Altos, 650/691-1200, www.openspace.org

NAME	DESCRIPTION	FACILITIES	SEASON	FEE
Francis State Beach	Beach access	52 campsites, picnic tables, fire rings, no water or sewer hookups, restrooms, coin-operated hot showers, firewood	year-round	from $35

Half Moon Bay State Park, 800/444-7275, www.reservecalifornia.com

NAME	DESCRIPTION	FACILITIES	SEASON	FEE
Joseph D. Grant County Park	Lake only for fishing; trails access	40 campsites, restrooms, showers, fire rings	year-round	from $34

Santa Clara County Parks, 408/274-6121, https://parks.sccgov.org

EAST BAY

Over the Bay Bridge from San Francisco, the East Bay offers an abundance of easy escapes from its many cities. Containing the vast East Bay Regional Parks' network of nature trails and other green spaces, you can find yourself under the canopy of a redwood forest, at the summit of a mountain, scrambling through wind caves, or hiking around the remnants of a 10-million-year-old volcano, and back in civilization by dinnertime.

▲ MOUNT DIABLO WATERFALLS LOOP

▲ ROCKY RIDGE LOOP

◀ STREAM-EAST RIDGE LOOP

1. Stream-East Ridge Loop
DISTANCE: 3.2 miles (5.2 km) round-trip
DURATION: 1.5 hours
EFFORT: Easy

2. Briones Loop
DISTANCE: 5 miles (8.1 km) round-trip
DURATION: 2 hours
EFFORT: Easy-moderate

3. Mount Diablo Waterfalls Loop
DISTANCE: 5.8 miles (9.3 km) round-trip
DURATION: 3 hours
EFFORT: Moderate

4. Rocky Ridge View-Elderberry Loop
DISTANCE: 5.2 miles (8.4 km) round-trip
DURATION: 2.5 hours
EFFORT: Easy-moderate

5. Mission Peak
DISTANCE: 7.3 miles (11.7 km) round-trip
DURATION: 3.5 hours
EFFORT: Moderate-strenuous

6. Little Yosemite
DISTANCE: 3.1 miles (5 km)
DURATION: 1.5 hours
EFFORT: Easy

ROCKY RIDGE VIEW-ELDERBERRY LOOP ▼

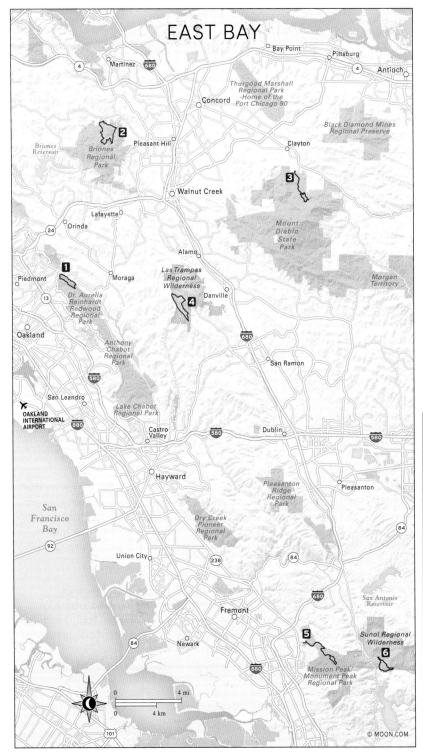

1 Stream-East Ridge Loop

DR. AURELIA REINHARDT REDWOOD REGIONAL PARK

Follow the babbling Redwood Creek as it curves through the redwoods to countless hibernating ladybugs, then climb to the top of the East Ridge for scenic Oakland views.

BEST: Kid-Friendly Hikes

DISTANCE: 3.2 miles (5.2 km) round-trip

DURATION: 1.5 hours

ELEVATION GAIN: 570 feet (174 m)

EFFORT: Easy

TRAIL: Dirt, fire road

USERS: Hikers, dogs, mountain bikers on part of the trail, horseback riders on part of the trail

SEASON: Year-round

PASSES/FEES: $5 day-use fee per vehicle weekends and holidays April-October, $2 per dog, free for guide dogs and service dogs

MAPS: Select "View Map" on the park website

PARK HOURS: 5am-10pm daily

TRAILHEAD: Skyline Gate Staging Area

FACILITIES: Vault toilets at the trailhead

CONTACT: East Bay Regional Park District, 888/327-2757, www.ebparks.org

START THE HIKE

This hike is popular for families and dog owners, with the return on the ridge also popular with mountain bikers. Dogs are required to be on-leash on Stream Trail, as well as within 200 feet (61 m) of any trailhead and in parking areas. Be respectful of others on the trail. If you do this hike November to February, bring along a magnifying glass to get a close-up look of the ladybug loveliness on the Stream Trail.

▶ **MILE 0-1.6: Skyline Gate Staging Area to Prince Trail Junction**

Start the hike on the south end of **Skyline Gate Staging Area** where West Ridge Trail and Stream Trail begin and join the **Stream Trail,** heading southeast. Until this trail reaches Prince Trail, you will gradually descend 500 vertical feet (152 m) into Redwood Creek Canyon.

The wide path winds through redwoods along Redwood Creek, a primary spawning and rearing habitat for rainbow trout and California newts. The shade of creek bank plants such as ferns and huckleberries, plus the canopy of the trees, help keep the water cool with enough oxygen to support aquatic life.

Stream-East Ridge Loop

Elevation Profile

Contour Interval = 20 feet

0   300 yds

0   300 m

© MOON.COM

Composed of soft dirt covered in leaves and needles, the path practically bounces back under your steps, making the 1.6 miles (2.6 km) to Prince Trail go by quickly. At 0.4 mile (0.6 km), pass the junction to **Girls Camp,** a primitive group campsite just south of Stream Trail. After another 0.4 mile (0.6 km), the trail intercepts Eucalyptus Trail to the left (east).

Beginning around this junction, and if you are here during just the right time window between November and February, look for ladybug colonies. Fun fact: A group of ladybugs is called a loveliness, and to stay warm in the colder months, they hibernate in groups. Look for them in the bushes, branches, rock crevices, and fence posts.

Continue your stroll until you arrive at the picnic bench at the **intersection** with **Prince Trail** at 1.6 miles (2.6 km).

▶ **MILE 1.6-3.2: Prince Trail Junction to Skyline Gate Staging Area**
Turn left (north) and begin the ascent up the short 0.4-mile (0.6 km) Prince Trail. As the wide trail climbs, it leaves the redwoods of Redwood Creek behind for a mix of oak, madrone, and bay laurel trees.

Where the trail intersects with **East Ridge Trail** at 2 miles (3.2 km), turn left (west) on this often sunny trail. There may be much more activity than on the previous trails of this hike. Dogs run off-leash, and the multiuse trail is heavily trafficked. The trail continues to ascend; benches along the way are a great place to take a breath and take in the view. Atop the ridge, the trees are mostly pines, but the views include dense redwood forests and, on a clear day, Mount Diablo.

From 2.2 to 3 miles (3.5-4.8 km), the Phillips Loop meets the trail to the left (southwest) at several intersections. This allows some relief, as some hikers leave the East Ridge for these paths. To stay on East Ridge Trail and close the loop, continue straight (northwest).

DIRECTIONS

From Oakland, take I-580 east toward Hayward for 2.6 miles (4.2 km), taking exit 22 for Park Boulevard, merging onto MacArthur Boulevard before turning left onto Park Boulevard. After just 0.1 mile (0.2 km), use the left lane to turn right to stay on Park Boulevard and continue for 2 miles (3.2 km). Use any lane to turn left onto Mountain Boulevard. After 0.2 mile (0.3 km), turn right onto Snake Road, and after another 0.2 mile (0.3 km), continue straight onto Shepherd Canyon Road for 1.5 miles (2.4 km). Turn right onto Aitken Drive, and after 0.2 mile (0.3 km), take a sharp left onto Evergreen Avenue. After 0.2 mile (0.3 km), turn right onto Skyline Boulevard. The parking lot is on the left.

GPS COORDINATES: 37.8316, −122.1854; 37°49′53.8″ N, 122°11′7.4″ W

BEST NEARBY BREWS

Make a point to check out **Hella Coastal** (shared tap room at 420 3rd St., Oakland, www.hellacoastal.com, 2pm-8pm Wed., 2pm-10pm Thurs.-Fri., noon-10pm Sat., noon-8pm Sun.), the first Black-owned brewery in Oakland, where proceeds often benefit social justice organizations. Try the Coconut Stout, inspired by the age-old Puerto Rican holiday drink coquito.

For those seeking to increase their mileage from easy beginner trails, this hike provides a nontechnical yet lovely loop of rolling hills, oak-studded grasslands, and lagoons.

BEST: Dog-Friendly Hikes
DISTANCE: 5 miles (8.1 km) round-trip
DURATION: 2 hours
ELEVATION GAIN: 990 feet (302 m)
EFFORT: Easy-moderate
TRAIL: Dirt, gravel
USERS: Hikers, mountain bikers, horseback riders, leashed dogs
SEASON: Year-round
PASSES/FEES: $3 day-use fee per vehicle, $2 per dog, free for guide dogs and service dogs
MAPS: Select "Download Park Map" on the park website
PARK HOURS: 8am-sunset daily
TRAILHEAD: Alhambra Creek Staging Area
FACILITIES: Vault toilets and drinking fountain near the bridge over Alhambra Creek on Orchard Trail
CONTACT: East Bay Regional Park District, 888/EBPARKS—888/327-2757, www.ebparks.org

START THE HIKE

▸ **MILE 0-0.9: Alhambra Creek Staging Area to Pine Tree Trail Junction**
From the southwest side of **Alhambra Creek Staging Area,** head northwest on a broad fire road through a **gate** with a sign warning that it's illegal to touch or approach baby calves. Just past the gate is an interpretive sign with a trail map posted. Cross the **bridge** over Alhambra Creek and onto **Orchard Trail,** heading straight (northwest) and away from the creek. Pass a picnic area and vault toilets through a **gate** to the right (north) as the path enters the grasslands, under some power lines and intermittent shade.

At 0.6 mile (1 km), go through a **gate** to cross Briones Road toward the cactus patch and a sign for "Rancho Briones Equestrian Facility." While horses are allowed on trails in the park, coming across grazing cattle during this hike is far more common. Brought to California in the late 1700s, grass seed came with the cattle, which rooted and now covers the woodland-dotted hills. Wildflowers like California poppies and buttercups bloom in spring, and as the trail rolls northwest, take a moment to look back to see Mount Diablo.

Orchard Trail continues along the left (west) side of the equestrian facility's fence, and you reach a **junction** with Pine Tree Trail at 0.9 mile (1.4 km).

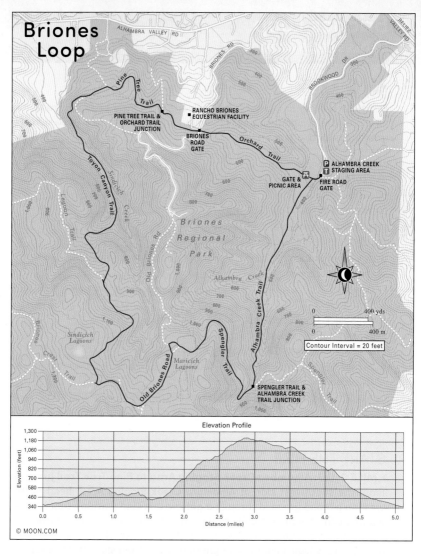

▶ MILE 0.9–3.1: Pine Tree Trail Junction to Sindicich Lagoons

Turn left on **Pine Tree Trail** to continue northwest among the pines and past the first lagoon of the hike, off the trail and on the other side of a barbed-wire fence.

Shortly thereafter, at 1.4 miles (2.3 km), turn off Pine Tree Trail to the right (north), onto **Toyon Canyon Trail,** and enter the beautiful woodland section of the hike. At 1.9 miles (3.1 km), Toyon Canyon Trail begins to climb approximately 500 vertical feet (152 m) in 0.5 mile (0.8 km), with steepening drop-offs.

Toyon Canyon Trail joins **Lagoon Trail** at 2.5 miles (4 km) for a final push to the highest elevation of the hike (1,224 ft/373 m), a gain of 300 feet (91 m) in 0.5 mile (0.8 km) to a hilltop meadow. At 3.1 miles (5 km), turn left (east) onto **Briones Crest Trail** in the **Sindicich Lagoons** area. These lagoons

are among the most popular destinations in Briones Regional Park, naturally formed and then enlarged to serve as stock ponds, where livestock can come to drink. The blue and green of these lagoons pop especially in summer's heat, when the surrounding grasses have turned yellow.

From here, you can see the Carquinez Strait to the north, where Alhambra Creek and its tributaries drain, between the delta to the east and San Francisco to the west.

▶ **MILE 3.1-5: Sindicich Lagoons to Alhambra Creek Staging Area**

Departing the Sindicich Lagoons, Briones Crest Trail joins **Old Briones Road Trail** at 3.3 miles (5.3 km) as it curves left (northeast) toward the **Maricich Lagoons.** As with Sindicich Lagoons, these were naturally formed when landslides dammed gullies and they eventually filled with water.

At 3.6 miles (5.8 km), the road splits—go right (east) onto **Spengler Trail** to descend into a woodland section, and keep left (north) after 0.1 mile (0.2 km) to curve around and arrive at a **junction** with Alhambra Creek Trail at 4.3 miles (6.9 km). Turn left (north) onto **Alhambra Creek Trail** as it takes you along the west side of the creek, back down through rolling grasslands to the trailhead.

DIRECTIONS

From Pleasant Hill's city center, head west on Gregory Lane for 1.2 miles (1.9 km). When it turns into Grayson Road, continue another 0.9 mile (1.4 km). Turn northwest (right) onto Reliez Valley Road for 1.6 miles (2.6 km), and then left onto Brookwood Drive for 1 mile (1.6 km) to arrive at the Alhambra Creek Staging Area parking lot.

GPS COORDINATES: 37.9569, −122.1230; 37°57′24.8″ N, 122°7′22.8″ W

BEST NEARBY BREWS

An "ode to impromptu backyard hangouts," **Side Gate Brewery and Garden** (1822 Grant St., Concord, 925/349-6034, www.sidegate-brewing.com, 3pm-10pm Mon.-Thurs., noon-10pm Fri.-Sat., noon-9pm Sun.) wants you to feel like a friend letting themselves in through the side gate. Family-friendly, including fur babies, Side Gate serves its own craft beer and seltzers brewed on-site. Grab food from a food truck in the parking lot, have food delivered, or bring your own, then grab a board game from the brewery's selection and sit with friends for a laid-back afternoon.

Briones Loop

EAST BAY

Hikers feel far from civilization as they teeter on the steep single-track along the canyon walls of Falls Trail and look for the cascading water tumbling down the mountain.

DISTANCE: 5.8 miles (9.3 km) round-trip
DURATION: 3 hours
ELEVATION GAIN: 1,230 feet (375 m)
EFFORT: Moderate
TRAIL: Dirt fire road, gravel, single-track
USERS: Hikers, mountain bikers, horseback riders
SEASON: Year-round
PASSES/FEES: None
MAPS: Select "Brochures" and "Park Brochure" on the park website
PARK HOURS: 8am-sunset daily
TRAILHEAD: Regency Drive dead end
FACILITIES: None
CONTACT: California State Parks, 925/837-2525, www.parks.ca.gov

START THE HIKE

▶ **MILE 0-2.2: Regency Drive to Falls Trail Junction**

Just before **Regency Drive** dead-ends at the barrier and the state park sign to the right (north) of the street, walk beside the gate marked "11-23," meaning **Contra Costa Fire Trail 11-23,** to begin the hike. Walk down the trail as it passes over Donner Creek to an **intersection** with other trails and turn left (south) onto **Donner Creek Road.** At 0.1 mile (0.2 km), pass through a **park boundary gate** (the Regency Gate). Stay on the wide fire road as it runs alongside the creek, passing junctions for Back Creek Trail and Murchio Road.

At 0.4 mile (0.6 km), at the junction with Clayton Oaks Road, keep right (west) of the creek to remain on Donner Creek Road, ignoring the intersections with other trails. At 1.2 miles (1.9 km), the path begins to ascend more steeply, rising above the creek to better views of the peaks above. Turn left (southeast) at 1.7 miles (2.7 km), where Donner Creek Road ends at the **junction** of Cardient Oaks Road and Meridian Ridge Road. Follow trail markers for **Cardient Oaks Road** to the park boundary.

At about 0.1 mile (0.2 km) on Cardient Oaks Road, the trail briefly descends to cross Donner Creek, requiring a careful rock-hop across the water, before Cardient Oaks Road continues to climb the canyon with a handful of wide **switchbacks** that include the steepest uphill grades of the hike.

Where Cardient Oaks Road intersects with **Falls Trail** at 2.2 miles (3.5 km), leave the road for the single-track rocky path as it climbs right (southeast).

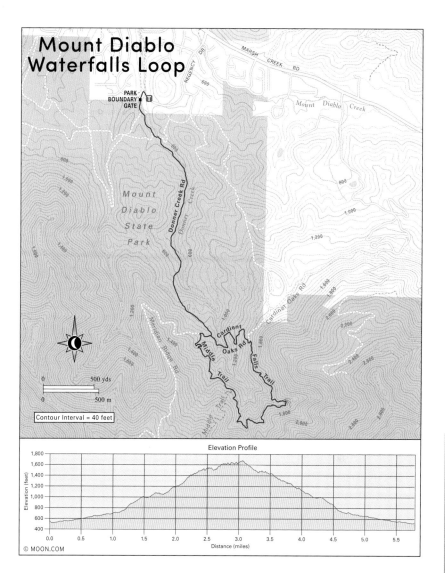

Mount Diablo Waterfalls Loop

Elevation Profile

Contour Interval = 40 feet

© MOON.COM

▶ **MILE 2.2-2.8: Falls Trail Junction to Creek Crossing**

Falls Trail is the crown jewel of this hike, with steep drop-offs and views across and down Wild Oat Canyon. The path passes some high grasslands, and around 2.6 miles (4.2 km), careful observers will spot the first of the waterfalls in the central rocks of the canyon to the south. To the north, fog may fill the canyon from the bay, or you may be able to see past the city of Clayton to Suisun Bay.

In the next 0.1 mile (0.2 km), the trail draws closer to the falls and **splits** on a curve above the water and around rocks. Heading straight (south) provides an additional waterfall vista below your feet but requires a bit of rock scrambling up around the curve, whereas taking the split left (east) is a slightly easier path. Follow the trail left, above the north side of the water, until 2.8 miles (4.5 km), where you turn right (south) to **cross over**

the creek and begin a U-turn around the hike's most central section of the canyon.

▸ MILE 2.8-5.8: Water Crossing to Regency Drive

After you cross the water, the trail gradually rises to the highest elevation of the hike. On the way is an ideal photo spot on a **rocky outcrop** off the trail at 3 miles (4.8 km). To the left (south) is a perfect showcase of the vertical plunge of a waterfall, and to the right (north) awaits stunning views down the center of the canyon. After you reach another **creek crossing** at 3.2 miles (5.2 km), turn left (northwest) and travel down the left (west) side of the bubbling water, with multiple little tributaries crossing the path toward the creek.

You soon reach a small cascade that pools beside the trail amid moss-covered rocks before the trail turns away from the creek and merges into **Middle Trail** at 3.5 miles (5.6 km). Continue straight (northwest) on Middle Trail. Enjoy the stretch of manzanita as you descend, with filtered views of the opposite side of the canyon. At 4.1 miles (6.6 km), Middle Trail meets **Meridian Ridge Road.** Turn right (east) onto the road for the last stretch of new trail for this hike as you continue your descent.

After less than 0.1 mile (0.2 km), the road arrives at **Donner Canyon Road.** Turn left (north) onto Donner Canyon Road and follow the trail marker toward "Regency Gate" to return to the trailhead the way you came.

DIRECTIONS

From Clayton's city center, take Center Street east to Marsh Creek Road and turn south (right) for 0.9 miles (1.4 km). Stay on Marsh Creek Road by turning south (right) again and continue for 0.4 miles (0.6 km). At Regency Drive, turn southwest (right) for 0.6 miles (1 km). Park at the end of the street, after the speed bumps, just before the barricade.

GPS COORDINATES: 37.9220, −121.9270; 37°55′19.2″ N, 121°55′37.2″ W

BEST NEARBY BREWS

For a bit of whimsy at an ethically conscious brewery, check out the taproom and beer garden of **Calicraft Brewing Company** (2700 Mitchell Dr., Walnut Creek, 925/478-8103, www.calicraft.com, 3pm-8pm Mon., 3pm-10pm Tues.-Thurs., noon-10pm Fri.-Sat., noon-8pm Sun.). With over 16 beers on draft, ranging from IPAs, light beers, sours, dark beers, fruit beers, and gluten-free vegan "untraditional" ciders, the gem is under 10 miles (16.1 km) and 20 minutes from the trailhead.

Rocky Ridge is one of the highest points in the East Bay, at just over 2,000 feet (610 m), and provides a commanding vantage point of the rolling hills, mountains, and San Francisco Bay.

DISTANCE: 5.2 miles (8.4 km) round-trip

DURATION: 2.5 hours

ELEVATION GAIN: 1,150 feet (351 m)

EFFORT: Easy-moderate

TRAIL: Dirt, dirt fire road, single-track, paved

USERS: Hikers, mountain bikers on part of the trail, horseback riders, leashed dogs

SEASON: Year-round

PASSES/FEES: None

MAPS: Select "Download Park Map" on the park website

PARK HOURS: From 8am daily; closing time varies—check the park website

TRAILHEAD: Bollinger Staging Area

FACILITIES: Vault toilets at the trailhead

CONTACT: East Bay Regional Park District, 888/EBPARKS—888/327-2757, www.ebparks.org

START THE HIKE

You can see trails on the other side of the fence at the top of Rocky Ridge View Trail, but those are on EBMUD land—for this hike, you do not need to venture onto EBMUD land, for which a permit is required.

▶ **MILE 0-1.1: Bollinger Staging Area to Rock 2**

From the northwest side of the **Bollinger Staging Area,** follow the paved service road through the gate and begin the steep climb of **Rocky Ridge View Trail.** In the first 1.3 miles (2.1 km) of this hike, the trail ascends over 900 vertical feet (274 m), with most of it through the grasslands in the first mile (1.6 km) or so. It's a relief, once at the ridge, to know there aren't significant additional uphill sections ahead, and you can enjoy the view.

The views open on the way up, and it's likely that cows will meander along your way. Look across the canyon to the east and you may spot hikers climbing Bollinger Creek Loop Trail, named for the creek below that formed the canyon. Keep an eye on the antenna tower atop the ridge; you pass under its wires just before the trail curves south at 0.7 mile (1.1 km). At 0.9 mile (1.4 km) and prior to the road entering the signed EBMUD property, continue left (south) onto the **dirt single-track.** At 1.1 miles (1.8 km), you have completed the toughest climb of the hike, and arrive near a spot known as **Rock 2** (2,024 ft/617 m).

Rocky Ridge View-Elderberry Loop

Elevation Profile

© MOON.COM

▶ **MILE 1.1-3: Rock 2 to Elderberry Trail Junction**

At 1.2 miles (1.9 km), you will see a second entry point to cross into EBMUD property through a gate off the trail. It's fun to peek through the fence to look at the landscape, and this is a good place to sit on the rocks if you need a break after ascending to the ridge.

For the next 1.8 miles (2.9 km), the trail takes you along the crests of the ridge, with views in every direction. Along the path, find the unusual rocks that hold remnants of an ancient ocean floor, including imbedded fossilized shells. In spring, look down at the wildflowers and green rolling hills dotted with live oaks and bay laurels. To the east, take in Mount Diablo, and to the west, seek out Mount Tamalpais and the length of San Francisco Bay. In the sky, you might spot birds of prey such as hawks and golden eagles.

A few other trails intersect Rocky Ridge View Trail at 1.7 miles (2.7 km), 2.1 miles (3.4 km), and 2.5 miles (4 km), but for this hike, keep heading southeast on Rocky Ridge Trail. Between the second and third junctions is a nice break in the wind where the trail is below the ridge and the trees briefly top it.

At 3 miles (4.8 km) is a **junction** with Elderberry Trail. Just past the turn onto Elderberry Trail is a bench where you can take a break.

▶ **MILE 3–5.2: Elderberry Trail Junction to Bollinger Staging Area**

Back at the junction, take **Elderberry Trail** to the right (northwest). The path curves north as it immediately descends. While the trail is wide, the start of the descent is steep through grassland, and then hugs the curves of the canyon into intermittent woodland shade. While cattle may be present on the entirety of the hike, other wildlife, such as deer and rabbits, as well as coyotes and bobcats, may be more visible along this trail.

You reach a primitive group campsite, **Corral Camp,** at 4.7 miles (7.6 km), and the path levels. Turn left (northwest) to remain on Elderberry Trail as it runs west along Bollinger Canyon Creek. The path leads through a meadow before returning to the Bollinger Staging Area.

DIRECTIONS

From Oakland, take I-980 east, then follow Highway 24 east and I-680 south to Crow Canyon Road in San Ramon for 24.6 miles (40 km). Take exit 36 to turn right onto Crow Canyon Road for 1.1 miles (1.8 km). Turn right onto Bollinger Canyon Road and continue for 4.4 miles (7.1 km). Where the road turns left and becomes Rocky Ridge Road, the parking lot is on the left in 150 feet (46 m) at 18015 Bollinger Canyon Road, also known as Bollinger Staging Area.

GPS COORDINATES: 37.8160, −122.0496; 37°48′57.6″ N, 122°2′58.6″ W

BEST NEARBY BREWS

Three-time Great American Beer Festival winner **Danville Brewing Company** (200 Railroad Ave., Danville, 925/217-4172, www.danvillebrewing.com, 11:30am-9pm Sun.-Thurs., 11:30am-9:30pm Fri.-Sat., $16-26) will entice you with beer, and pairing it with the food will have you stay a while. Check out "Hoppy Hour," 3pm-6pm Monday-Friday, for $5 DBC beers, $3 off all wines, $6 well drinks, and selected appetizers.

🦌 ❀ 🐾 🚌🚆

Considered a rite of passage for Bay Area outdoor enthusiasts, on a clear day trekking to the peak rewards hikers with 360-degree views of the bay.

DISTANCE: 7.3 miles (11.7 km) round-trip

DURATION: 3.5 hours

ELEVATION GAIN: 2,100 feet (640 m)

EFFORT: Moderate-strenuous

TRAIL: Dirt fire road, gravel, single-track

USERS: Hikers, mountain bikers on part of the trail, horseback riders, leashed dogs

SEASON: Year-round

PASSES/FEES: $4 day-use fee per vehicle Monday-Saturday when Ohlone College is in session, payable at parking lot vending machines; free on holidays, after 5pm Saturday, and Sunday

MAPS: Select "Download Park Map" on the park website

PARK HOURS: 6am-10pm daily

TRAILHEAD: Peak Trail Access Trail

FACILITIES: Vault toilets and drinking water at Ohlone College, vault toilets at the rest area at 2.8 miles (4.5 km)

CONTACT: East Bay Regional Park District, 888/EBPARKS—888/327-2757, www.ebparks.org

B ragging rights are earned over 7 miles (11.3 km) of exposed trail with an elevation gain of over 2,000 feet (610 m) on a mostly nontechnical (except the final stretch) climb, memorialized by most with a photo at the Mission Peeker pole up top.

START THE HIKE

▶ **MILE 0-1.3: Ohlone College Parking Garage to Mill Creek Road Junction**

Exit the **parking garage** at Ohlone College and carefully cross Anza-Pine Street, following the brown regional park sign with an arrow indicating "Mission Peak Trail Access." The trailhead for the Peak Trail Access Trail is a large brown sign for Mission Peak Regional Preserve, with an arrow indicating "Peak Trail Access" near the water fountain and portable toilets, east of the tennis courts. The trail curves southeast, passing through a cattle gate and parallel to the road below (Aquatic Way). Between cattle fences, the dirt path continues to curve east and then north to meet the Peak Trail.

Turn right (southeast) onto **Peak Trail.** You will immediately notice the exposure that persists for most of this hike as the trail rises through grasslands and past a shallow hillside rock cave. Shrubs begin to break up the

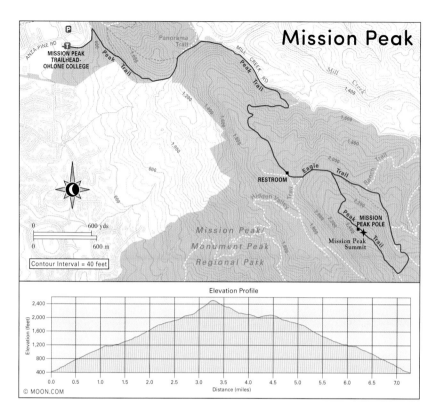

Mission Peak

Elevation Profile

© MOON.COM

scenery, and a few oaks provide brief shade before Peak Trail turns left (northeast) and away from an unmarked trail junction.

At 1 mile (1.6 km), continue right (east) to remain on Peak Trail at the **junction** with Panorama Trail. The wide trail levels out between hills and passes over a cattle guard. The path reaches another **split** at 1.3 miles (2.1 km), where a cattle gate leads to Mill Creek Road, just left (north) of a narrower forested path. A trail marker for Mission Peak indicates hikers should follow the narrow trail up into the shaded woodlands.

▶ MILE 1.3–2.8: Mill Creek Road Junction to Rest Area

Peak Trail curves southeast through the trees, parallel to Mill Creek Road below. Pass over another cattle guard and bear right (south) at 1.8 miles (2.9 km), back into grasslands, as the trail continues to gain elevation.

On this section of the hike, you may see deer leaping across the grasslands, the ever-present cows, and in the spring, wildflowers like California poppies. Look back for views of the rolling hills and distant mountains coming into sight if weather conditions are right. At other times, it feels as if you're surrounded by the mysterious foggy moors of English literature.

At 2.8 miles (4.5 km), you reach an ideal **rest area,** with vault toilets and a picnic table, before the push to the top. At the rest area, several trails intersect, with hikers coming up Hidden Valley Trail from the Stanford Avenue Staging Area (a shorter and steeper route with extremely limited parking) from the right (south), and Eagle Trail from the left (east).

▶ **MILE 2.8-3.4: Rest Area to Mission Peak Summit**

While the Peak Trail remains wide as it briefly joins Eagle Trail heading east, the grade quickly doubles over 0.1 mile (0.2 km) and then decreases back to the previous grade, about 6 percent, for 0.1 mile (0.2 km). Where Peak Trail splits from Eagle Trail at 3 miles (4.8 km), the path narrows and becomes rocky as you climb the summit's ridge, where at times the grade is as steep as 20 percent.

Around 3.4 miles (5.5 km), you reach the famous **Mission Peeker.** Constructed in 1990, the tall pole stands on a rock pile with sighting tubes in all directions. Looking through these tubes pinpoints Bay Area landmarks, but they're often used as hand- or footholds for those posing to snap the social media-worthy accomplishment of reaching the peak. Most visitors don't realize that the true **summit** of Mission Peak is farther east of the pole, atop another rock pile. You can find it by looking for the round survey marker on the ground.

Take in the panoramic view, which on a clear day includes Mount Hamilton to the south, the Santa Cruz Mountains to the west, Mount Tamalpais to the north, and Mount Diablo and the Sierra Nevada to the northeast.

When you've taken it all in, retrace your steps back to the trailhead.

DIRECTIONS

From Fremont's city center, take Freemont Boulevard southeast onto Washington Boulevard, continuing east for 2.2 miles (3.5 km). Turn right onto Mission Boulevard and proceed for 0.5 mile (0.8 km) to Pine Street. Turn left onto Pine Street for 0.4 miles (0.6 km), past the tennis courts on the right, and enter the parking structure to the north, on the left.

GPS COORDINATES: 37.5272, −121.9126; 37°31'37.9" N, 121°54'45.4" W

BEST NEARBY BREWS

Less than 8 miles (12.9 km) and 15 minutes from the trailhead, grab one of the creative brew concoctions at **Jack's Brewing Company** (39176 Argonaut Way, Fremont, 510/796-2036, www.jacksbrewing.com, 11:30am-10pm Mon.-Thurs., 11:30am-11pm Fri., 10:30am-11pm Sat., 10:30am-9pm Sun.). The family-friendly brewery offers food and a wide variety of suds, including the Dark Sexy Cara Wheat, described as having the aroma of coffee and flavors of chocolate, coffee, and hint of vanilla.

Little Yosemite

SUNOL WILDERNESS REGIONAL PRESERVE

This loop is a treat for every hiker: Scramble over rocks along the scenic gorge or see how many types of wildflowers you can spot on the rolling hills.

DISTANCE: 3.1 miles (5 km)

DURATION: 1.5 hours

ELEVATION GAIN: 500 feet (152 m)

EFFORT: Easy

TRAIL: Dirt, dirt fire road, gravel, single-track

USERS: Hikers, mountain bikers, horseback riders

SEASON: Year-round

PASSES/FEES: $5 day-use fee per vehicle on weekends, $2 per dog, free for guide dogs and service dogs

MAPS: Select "Download Park Map" on the park website, at the trailhead

PARK HOURS: 8am-dusk daily

TRAILHEAD: Wooden Footbridge just south of the Old Green Barn Visitor Center

FACILITIES: Vault toilets at the trailhead, Little Yosemite, and parking lots

CONTACT: East Bay Regional Park District, 510/544-3249, www.ebparks.org

START THE HIKE

Little Yosemite is owned by the San Francisco Water Department; obey all the boundary signs. Before your hike, check the park's website for a variety of wildflower-related information and activity ideas, including naturalist guided programs.

▸ **MILE 0-1.5: Trailhead to Little Yosemite**

Start the hike by taking the **wooden footbridge** over **Alameda Creek** and going right (southeast) onto **Canyon View Trail.** The beginning of the trail parallels the creek and passes through a lightly shaded woodland area.

The trail is easy to follow, but there are a couple of trails that intersect it that are not always marked. The first junction is at 0.2 mile (0.3 km) for Indian Joe Creek Trail, which shoots off left to follow Indian Joe Creek.

Continue straight on Canyon View Trail, and at 0.5 mile (0.8 km) the path turns away from the creek and provides the hike's only ascent, gaining 430 vertical feet (131 m) over the next 0.5 mile (0.8 km). In spring the grassland hills are known for their wildflower blooms. Red maids, Johnny-jump-ups, scarlet pimpernel, and blue-eyed grass can be spotted along this section—for kids, it's a great opportunity to play "I Spy."

Prior to reaching the highest point, Canyon View will cross McCorkle Trail at 0.7 mile (1.1 km), which runs east-west. From this junction, continue on Canyon View Trail, limited to hikers (no equestrians or mountain bikers), with gorgeous views of the oak canyon.

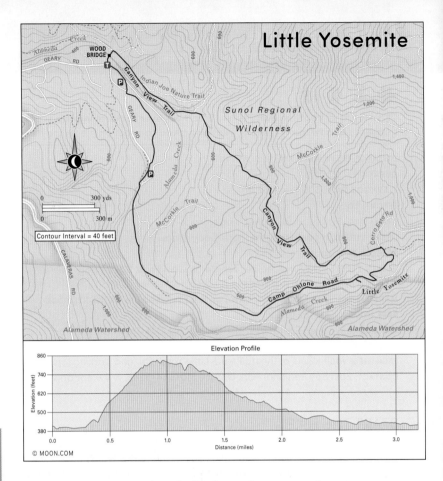

Little Yosemite

Elevation Profile

While the narrow trail gradually descends as you make your way toward Little Yosemite, due to the drop-off of the slope it can be difficult for hikers to pass one another. Those with children should pay attention here and keep them close. As you get closer to the water, beautiful weathered serpentine sandstone juts out from the grassland hills.

At 1.3 miles (2.1 km), the trail meets a junction with **Cerro Este Road.** Turn right (south), and over the next 0.25 mile (0.4 km), descend 100 feet (30 m). Past the picnic table and vault toilet, cross over **Camp Ohlone Road** to arrive at the scenic gorge known as **Little Yosemite.** The story goes that over 100 years ago an article was published in which the writer declared that during the rainy season the falls contained the beauty of those at Yosemite, and the name "Little Yosemite" stuck.

▶ **MILE 1.5-3.1: Little Yosemite to Trailhead**
Follow **Camp Ohlone Road** along Alameda Creek southwest for 0.5 mile (0.8 km). Adults and children alike delight in climbing boulders and tossing rocks into the cascading waterfalls of the gorge in spring. By mid- to late summer, only small pools remain, until springs in winter return the flow of water.

There are multiple access points to the creek from Camp Ohlone Road, but keep in mind that swimming is not allowed, and on the opposite side of Alameda Creek is the preserve boundary, where hikers are prohibited from entering.

After having fun at the creek, complete the loop by continuing on Camp Ohlone Road as it turns north, staying alongside the creek. From the right (east), McCorkle Trail joins Camp Ohlone at 2.4 miles (3.9 km) and 2.6 miles (4.2 km). Continue on Camp Ohlone Road.

The southernmost **parking lot** on Geary Road comes into view at 2.7 miles (4.3 km), where vault toilets are available. At 3 miles (4.8 km), the trail ends, and either side of Geary Road will return you to where you began in 0.1 mile (0.2 km).

DIRECTIONS

From Fremont, travel I-680 toward Sacramento for 4.6 miles (7.4 km) and take the Calaveras Road exit toward Sunol onto Highway 84 west. Turn right onto Calaveras Road and continue for 4.2 miles (6.8 km). Turn left onto Geary Road. If you drive uphill on a narrow winding road, you've missed the Geary Road turnoff. Geary Road leads directly into the park. Park in the first parking area, just past the Old Green Barn Visitor Center and restrooms.

GPS COORDINATES: 37.5158, −121.8299; 37°30'56.9" N, 121°49'47.6" W

BEST NEARBY BITES AND BREWS

Less than 8 miles (12.9 km) and 15 minutes north of the trailhead, **Bosco's Bones & Brew** (11930 Main St., Sunol, 925/862-0821, www.boscosbonesandbrews.com, 8am-8pm Wed.-Sun., $8-16) is a dog-friendly restaurant and bar styled like the 1800s. It honors the first nonhuman mayor in the United States, Bosco Ramos, a rottweiler-black Lab mix. Order a Bosco brew; a Bosco life-size replica will pour beer when his leg is lifted. He's the main tap for the restaurant's microbrew.

NEARBY CAMPGROUNDS

NAME	DESCRIPTION	FACILITIES	SEASON	FEE
Anthony Chabot	1.5 mi/2.4 km above Lake Chabot	78 sites, including 11 RV hookup sites and 7 group sites, showers, potable water, restrooms, picnic tables	year-round	$25–40 plus $8 service fee

East Bay Regional Parks, Castro Valley, 888/327-2757, ext. 4502, www.reserveamerica.com

NAME	DESCRIPTION	FACILITIES	SEASON	FEE
Del Valle	Campsites and cabins	145 sites, including 2 accessible sites, 21 RV hookup sites, 9 group sites, 5 cabins, showers, potable water, restrooms, picnic tables	year-round	$30–45 plus $8 service fee

East Bay Regional Parks, Livermore, 888/327-2757, option 2, www.reserveamerica.com

NAME	DESCRIPTION	FACILITIES	SEASON	FEE
Briones Regional Park	Primitive hike-in group campsites	3 hike-in group sites, 1 accessible site, showers, potable water, restrooms, picnic tables, fire pits	year-round	$75–100 plus $8 service fee

East Bay Regional Parks, Martinez, 888/327-2757, option 2, www.reserveamerica.com

CATARACT FALLS

NORTH BAY

MUIR WOODS & MOUNT TAMALPAIS

Perhaps the Bay Area's best-known spot to gaze up at revered old-growth redwoods, the area of Muir Woods National Monument, neighboring Mount Tamalpais State Park and Mount Tamalpais Watershed, contains a network of trails that allow hikers to experience every kind of topography in Northern California. From just north of San Francisco's Golden Gate Bridge to the peaks of Mount Tamalpais, you'll find deep canyons, rolling hills with ocean views, rushing waterfalls, shady oak forests, and windy beaches.

▲ ANGEL ISLAND

▲ CARSON FALLS TRAIL

1 **Angel Island**
DISTANCE: 5.5 miles (8.9 km) round-trip
DURATION: 3 hours
EFFORT: Moderate

2 **Tennessee Valley Trail**
DISTANCE: 4 miles (6.4 km) round-trip
DURATION: 1.5 hours
ELEVATION GAIN: 250 feet (76 m)
EFFORT: Easy

3 **Dias Ridge**
DISTANCE: 7.2 miles (11.6 km) round-trip
DURATION: 4 hours
EFFORT: Moderate

4 **Canopy View Loop**
DISTANCE: 3.8 miles (6.1 km) round-trip
DURATION: 2 hours
EFFORT: Easy-moderate

5 **Dipsea-Matt Davis Loop**
DISTANCE: 9 miles (14.5 km) round-trip
DURATION: 5 hours
EFFORT: Moderate-strenuous

6 **Mount Tamalpais West Point Loop**
DISTANCE: 4.2 miles (6.8 km) round-trip
DURATION: 2.5 hours
EFFORT: Easy-moderate

7 **East Peak Summit Lookout Loop**
DISTANCE: 1.7 miles (2.7 km) round-trip
DURATION: 1 hour
EFFORT: Easy

8 **Cataract Falls**
DISTANCE: 3 miles (4.8 km) round-trip
DURATION: 2 hours
EFFORT: Easy-moderate

9 **Carson Falls**
DISTANCE: 4.6 miles (7.4 km) round-trip
DURATION: 2 hours
EFFORT: Easy-moderate

10 **Bay View Loop**
DISTANCE: 3.7 miles (6 km) round-trip
DURATION: 1.5 hours
EFFORT: Easy

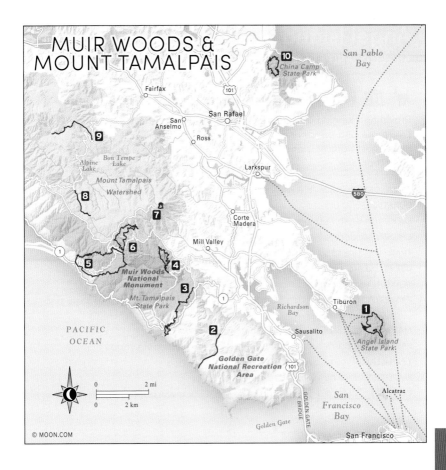

MUIR WOODS &
MOUNT TAMALPAIS

Angel Island
ANGEL ISLAND STATE PARK

Providing stunning 360-degree views of the entire Bay Area atop Mount Livermore and preserving the extensive history of Angel Island, this hike of the largest natural island in San Francisco Bay broadens horizons in more ways than one.

DISTANCE: 5.5 miles (8.9 km) round-trip
DURATION: 3 hours
ELEVATION GAIN: 790 feet (241 m)
EFFORT: Moderate
TRAIL: Dirt fire road, dirt, gravel, single-track, paved, stairs
USERS: Hikers, mountain bikers on part of the trail
SEASON: Year-round
PASSES/FEES: Ferry service from San Francisco or Tiburon includes state park admission
MAPS: Ranger Station in Ayala Cove, www.parks.ca.gov
PARK HOURS: 8am-sunset daily; departure ferry schedule varies
TRAILHEAD: Ayala Cove
FACILITIES: Restrooms in Ayala Cove
CONTACT: California State Parks, 415/435-1915, www.parks.ca.gov

START THE HIKE

▶ **MILE 0-0.9: Ayala Cove to Angel Island Immigration Station**
After disembarking from the ferry in **Ayala Cove,** head left (northeast) from the restrooms and onto **North Ridge Trail,** where you immediately get your heart pumping up the nearly **150 wooden stairs** through pine, toyon, and oak trees, past a **picnic area** about midway, and topping out at **Perimeter Road.** Turn left (northeast).

Follow the road as it curves around the northernmost tip of the island, **Campbell Point,** toward **China Cove.** At 0.9 mile (1.4 km) is the **Angel Island Immigration Station.** Here, interpretive signs explain some of the history of the center; unlike Ellis Island in New York that has the reputation of welcoming newcomers into the United States, Angel Island, opened in 1910, was used to detain and keep immigrants out.

▶ **MILE 0.9-2.5: Angel Island Immigration**
   Station to Mount Livermore Summit
Just after the Immigration Station, turn off Perimeter Road by going right (south), up a graded concrete section of fire road between aged white park buildings. Now gravel, the fire road passes a turnoff to the right (west) and gains elevation, rising above Perimeter Road, which leads to **Fort McDowell-East Garrison,** built in 1899 as a quarantine station to isolate troops exposed to contagious diseases while overseas.

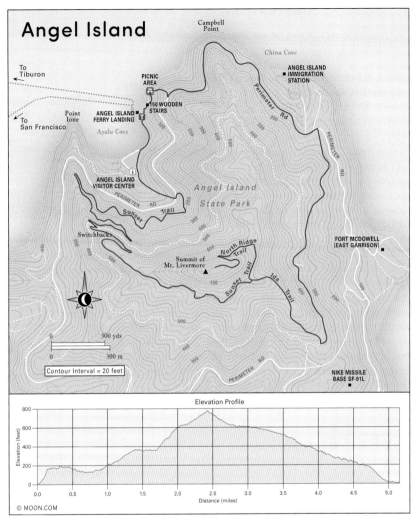

Angel Island

To Tiburon

To San Francisco

Point Ione

Campbell Point

China Cove

ANGEL ISLAND IMMIGRATION STATION

PICNIC AREA

150 WOODEN STAIRS

ANGEL ISLAND FERRY LANDING

Ayala Cove

ANGEL ISLAND VISITOR CENTER

PERIMETER RD

Sunset Trail

Switchbacks

Angel Island State Park

North Ridge Trail

Summit of Mt. Livermore

Sunset Trail

Ida Trail

PERIMETER RD

FORT MCDOWELL (EAST GARRISON)

NIKE MISSILE BASE SF-91L

0   300 yds
0   300 m

Contour Interval = 20 feet

© MOON.COM

Elevation Profile

Elevation (feet) / Distance (miles)

Across the water, the cities and hills of the East Bay come into view. As you proceed, you will see markers for campsites and potable water stations, where you should consider filling up. At 1.7 miles (2.7 km) you reach the southeasternmost point of the hike, the **Nike Missile Site** near **Point Blunt,** but your eyes will be on the horizon and the phenomenal panoramic views that extend to San Francisco, Alcatraz Island, and the Golden Gate Bridge.

Turn right (north) off the fire road and onto the grassy **Ida Trail.** Over the next 0.25 mile (0.4 km), wide northern views continue to open as the trail rises 250 feet (76 m). At 2 miles (3.2 km), Ida Trail ends at a **junction** with North Ridge Trail and Sunset Trail. Turn right (north) onto the narrow single-track of **North Ridge Trail.** After 0.1 mile (0.2 km), the path turns left (west) toward the 788-foot (240-m) **summit** of **Mount Caroline Livermore,** reached at 2.5 miles (4 km). There are a few benches and picnic tables along the top and just off the slopes of the peak to sit and take in the

360-degree views of the entire San Francisco Bay.

▶ **MILE 2.5-5.5: Mount Livermore Summit to Ayala Cove**

Return down to the junction with Sunset Trail and Ida Trail and keep right (west) to continue the hike on **Sunset Trail.** This top section of the trail is exposed but provides excellent views as you descend around the western side of the island, passing a fire road at 3.3 miles (5.3 km). From the trail's vantage point, you can take in the Golden Gate Bridge, the Marin Headlands, and Mount Tamalpais rising above it.

At 3.5 miles (5.6 km) is the beginning of a series of **switchbacks.** After approximately 0.25 mile (0.4 km), cross a fire road and proceed down into the coverage of a forest with coast live oak, pine, buckeye, poison oak, and blackberry. From here, Sunset Trail reaches out toward **Point Ione,** the western point of Ayala Cove, and continues to descend above and parallel with Perimeter Road in an easterly direction, intersecting at 4.9 miles (7.9 km). Cross Perimeter Road and take the service road toward Ayala Cove to the **visitor center.** Once a bachelor officers' quarters, its viewing room shows films on the history and beauty of the island.

Continue on the paved path past the popular beach area, marina, rental stands, and concessions to the ferry benches to depart the island.

DIRECTIONS

To get to Angel Island, you must purchase a round-trip ticket departing San Francisco (Golden Gate Ferry, www.goldengate.org) or Tiburon (Angel Island Tiburon Ferry, www.angelislandferry.com). One-way tickets are not sold on the island. Personal vehicles are not allowed on the island.

Public transportation is available from Mill Valley to Tiburon, or visitors may drive to Tiburon by taking East Blithedale Avenue to Highway 131 (Tiburon Blvd.) east and then finding public parking. The Angel Island Tiburon Ferry website has a parking page detailing the best places to park to catch the ferry.

GPS COORDINATES: 37.8683, −122.4345; 37°52'5. 9" N, 122°26'4.2" W

BEST NEARBY BITES

To grab a bite on the island, the **Angel Island Café and Cantina** (Ayala Cove, 415/435-3392, www.angelisland.com, hours and prices vary) can satisfy your need for a soda, snack, or lunch. Their boxed lunch ($26.50) includes a sandwich, a side salad, a cookie, and a bottle of water and can be picked up at 10:30am or 12:30pm when available. Make sure to check the website before arriving on the island.

🦌 ❀ 🏛 🚶‍♂️

Despite the weekend crowds, this easy and peaceful hike provides gorgeous valley and ocean cove views.

BEST: Coastal Hikes

DISTANCE: 4 miles (6.4 km) round-trip

DURATION: 1.5 hours

ELEVATION GAIN: 250 feet (76 m)

EFFORT: Easy

TRAIL: Dirt fire road, gravel, paved, sand

USERS: Hikers, mountain bikers, horseback riders, wheelchair users on part of the trail

SEASON: Year-round

PASSES/FEES: None

MAPS: Marin Headlands Map on the park website

PARK HOURS: Open 24 hours

TRAILHEAD: Tennessee Valley Parking Lot

FACILITIES: Vault toilets at the trailhead and at 1.7 miles (2.7 km)

CONTACT: Golden Gate National Recreation Area, 415/561-4700, www.nps.gov/goga

START THE HIKE

Tennessee Cove is unsafe for swimming or wading. Be mindful of the posted warnings. If you choose to explore the borders of the cove, be careful not to get trapped by the rising tide. This hike is also exposed and on the coast, which calls for wearing layers and appropriate sun and wind protection.

▶ **MILE 0-0.9: Parking Lot to Upper Tennessee Valley Trail Junction**
At the southwest corner of the Tennessee Valley **parking lot,** just west of the picnic tables, start the **Tennessee Valley Trail** on a wide paved path. The entire trail to Tennessee Cove is used as a service road but is only paved for 0.75 mile (1.2 km).

Pass through the service road gate at the trailhead to proceed. Like many in the area, this valley was cut by an ancient river, developing steep ridges, rolling hills, and a rich habitat for flora and fauna to thrive. In spring, native favorites like lupines and California poppies take over the green hills that turn yellow in summer and then bloom with orange sticky monkey flower and blackberry bushes.

For kids and inquisitive minds, a series of interpretive panels border the trail's western (right) side. Astute observers may notice deer, bobcats, and coyotes on the hills, snakes sunning on rocks (or slithering across the trail!), and a variety of birds in the air like herons, ravens, and sparrows.

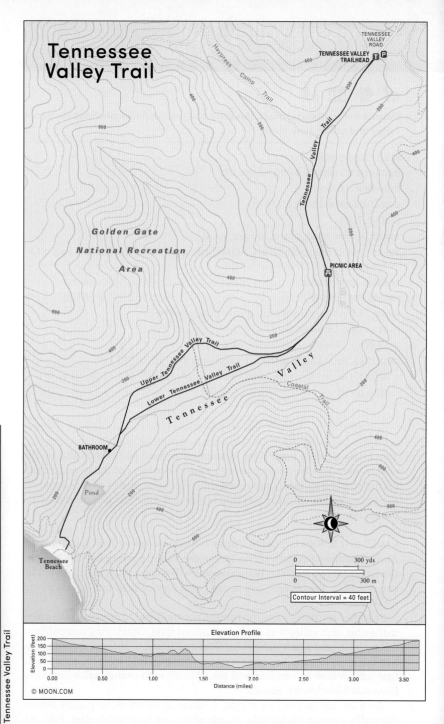

Tennessee Valley Trail

TENNESSEE VALLEY ROAD

TENNESSEE VALLEY TRAILHEAD

Haypress Camp Trail

Tennessee Valley Trail

Golden Gate National Recreation Area

PICNIC AREA

Upper Tennessee Valley Trail

Lower Tennessee Valley Trail

Coastal Trail

Tennessee Valley

BATHROOM

Pond

Tennessee Beach

| 0 | 300 yds |
| 0 | 300 m |

Contour Interval = 40 feet

Elevation Profile

Distance (miles)

© MOON.COM

▲ UPPER TENNESSEE VALLEY TRAIL

When the trail forks at 0.9 mile (1.4 km), continue on the **Upper Tennessee Valley Trail** to the right (north). On the return hike, you will take the other trail.

▶ **MILE 0.9–2: Upper Tennessee Valley Trail Junction to Tennessee Cove**
From the junction, the trail begins its only significant climb, and hikers can begin to see the ocean in the distance between the hills ahead and to the left (southwest) at 1.1 miles (1.8 km). The trail intersects with the Coastal Fire Road 0.1 mile (0.2 km) later, which is the only trail in the area where leashed dogs are allowed. Continue southwest on Upper Tennessee Valley Trail.

At 1.6 miles (2.6 km), Upper Tennessee Valley Trail meets Lower Tennessee Valley Trail at the bottom of the hill. Heading southwest, follow the trail marker directing you to the beach. On the way, you'll pass a vault toilet and **beach TLC station** where you can get a repurposed bag to pick up trash on the beach. Just past the TLC station, look to the left (east) side of the path for a **small 2-acre pond.** Past the pond, the dirt path gradually transitions into **Tennessee Cove**'s sandy beach.

Those who arrive at low tide may be able to spot the namesake of the valley peeking out of the water, the wreckage of steamship SS *Tennessee*, which ran aground here in 1853 on its way to San Francisco. While all passengers and crew made it off safely, the ship was a total loss. The wreckage that can still be seen includes the ship's anchor and parts of the steam engine. According to the National Park Service, you will need to coordinate your visit with low tide and seasonal sand alignments in order to see any of the shipwreck.

MUIR WOODS & MOUNT TAMALPAIS

Tennessee Valley Trail

LOWER TENNESSEE VALLEY TRAIL ▲

▶ **MILE 2-4: Tennessee Cove to Parking Lot**

Once you are ready to go, head back the way you came. At the split for the hill, consider taking the **Lower Tennessee Valley Trail** for variety and a more direct and flatter route. It rejoins the Upper Tennessee Valley Trail at 3 miles (4.8 km). However, the lower trail is not as well-groomed as the upper, and if it has been rainy, it may be muddy. If trail conditions are poor, take the Upper Tennessee Valley Trail to return the same way you came.

DIRECTIONS

From Mill Valley, take Miller Avenue south and continue onto Almonte Boulevard for 0.4 mile (0.6 km). Take Highway 1 south for 0.2 mile (0.3 km) and turn right onto Tennessee Valley Road. Follow the road 1.7 miles (2.7 km) until it dead-ends at the Tennessee Valley Trail parking lot.

GPS COORDINATES: 37.8606, −122.5362; 37°51'38.2" N, 122°32'10.3" W

BEST NEARBY BREWS

Less than 2 miles (3.2 km) (5 minutes) from the trailhead on Highway 1 is **Proof Lab Beer Garden** (254 Shoreline Hwy., Mill Valley, 415/569-4984, www.prooflab.com, 11:30am-9pm daily). Proof Lab's mission is to be the best local surf, skate, and outdoor shop, focused on community-building and connecting people with the outdoors. The beer garden is nestled between the retail stores. Over 40 drinks are on tap, including local beers, ciders, kombuchas, and nonalcoholic beverages.

Dias Ridge

MOUNT TAMALPAIS STATE PARK

From atop a ridgeline down to Muir Beach, this hike presents panoramic views of the Marin Headlands and the Pacific Ocean.

BEST: Brew Hikes

DISTANCE: 7.2 miles (11.6 km) round-trip

DURATION: 4 hours

ELEVATION GAIN: 1,180 feet (360 m)

EFFORT: Moderate

TRAIL: Dirt, gravel, single-track, sand, paved road

USERS: Hikers, mountain bikers, horseback riders

SEASON: Year-round

PASSES/FEES: None

MAPS: Select "Brochures" and "Park Brochure" on the park website

PARK HOURS: 7am–sunset daily

TRAILHEAD: Roadside at Mount Tamalpais State Park sign on Panoramic Highway

FACILITIES: Restrooms and drinking fountain at Muir Beach Parking Area

CONTACT: California State Parks, 415/388-2070, www.parks.ca.gov

START THE HIKE

▶ **MILE 0–1.6: Panoramic Highway Trailhead to Golden Gate National Recreation Area**

On the west side of **Panoramic Highway,** take the gravel path just north of the **Mount Tamalpais State Park sign.** A small trail sign hidden by brush indicates that you are on **Dias Ridge Trail,** with Miwok Trail and Muir Beach ahead. Just a bit farther, you will come to an interpretive sign with a map. Pretty quickly the trail becomes a narrow single-track dirt path through the chaparral.

Where Dias Ridge Trail meets Miwok Trail at 0.4 mile (0.6 km), stay left (south) to continue on Dias Ridge. From here, the trail widens slightly and nears a large boulder that looks out of place, alone in a sea of coastal scrub. Climbers use the western and southern sides of the rock for high ball bouldering practice, so watch for others if you take the **spur trail** to reach it.

After a constant gentle descent from the trailhead, the path climbs 150 feet (46 m) in about 0.5 mile (0.8 km) and under some shade, beginning at 1.2 miles (1.9 km). The views of rolling coastal hills and deep valleys below expand, and at the crest, the trail enters the **Golden Gate National Recreation Area,** at 1.6 miles (2.6 km).

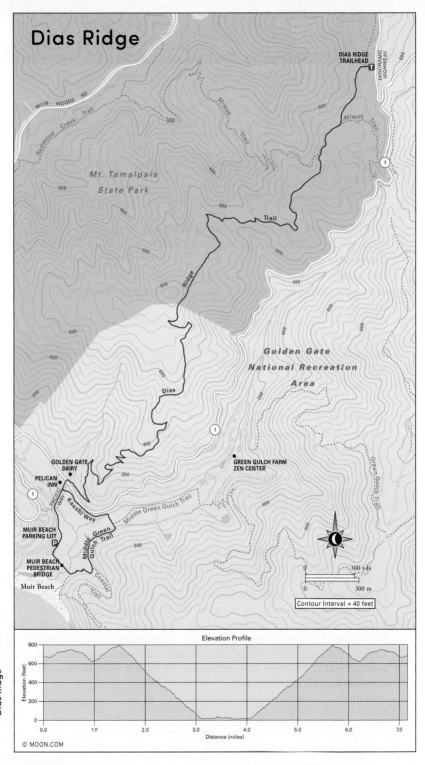

© MOON.COM

▲ DIAS RIDGE

▶ **MILE 1.6–3.2: Golden Gate National Recreation Area to Golden Gate Dairy**

From here, Dias Ridge eagerly drops in elevation as the trail makes its way closer to Highway 1 and the Pacific Ocean. At 2.9 miles (4.7 km), Dias Ridge Trail runs alongside a wooden fence and looks down on the covered livestock stalls of a working ranch, with rocks of the Franciscan Complex Marin Headland Terrane jutting out from the side of the slope beyond. At 3.1 miles (5 km), the path runs beside Highway 1, crosses a **wooden bridge,** and arrives at a **bench** with an interpretive sign just like the one at the trailhead at the top of the ridge. Pass through the wooden fence onto the parking area of the **Golden Gate Dairy** at the intersection of Highway 1 and Pacific Way at 3.2 miles (5.2 km). The historic dairy farm evolved into a horse boarding facility in the 1970s and is now primarily utilized as a trail riding barn.

▶ **MILE 3.2–4: Golden Gate Dairy to Muir Beach**

From Golden Gate Dairy, carefully cross Highway 1 (Shoreline Hwy.) to the left (east) side of Pacific Way and look for the trail marker and start of the service road **Kaashi Way,** to the left (east). The flat path heads southeast and parallel to Highway 1 until 3.4 miles (5.5 km), where it turns right (southeast), past the **junction** with Middle Green Gulch Trail, and then turns right (southwest). Kaashi Way intercepts Coastal Trail at 3.7 miles (6 km). Stay right (south) to continue onto Muir Beach Trail and pass the **pedestrian bridge** to the right (northwest). The dirt trail turns to sand and arrives at **Muir Beach** at 4 miles (6.4 km).

The quiet cove is a favorite of locals, and the Redwood Creek Lagoon and the surrounding riparian area provides critical habitat for coho salmon and red-legged frogs. Wintering monarch butterflies can also sometimes be found gathered in the small grove of Monterey pines at Muir Beach.

MUIR BEACH ▲

▶ MILE 4–7.2: Muir Beach to Panoramic Highway Trailhead

Once you are ready to leave the beach, retrace your steps back to the pedestrian bridge and cross it. The 450-foot-long (137-m) bridge passes over the lagoon and leads to the **parking area, picnic area, and restrooms.** Past the restrooms, turn right (northeast) onto the gravel trail alongside the right (east) side of Pacific Way. Where the road splits, turn right (northeast) over Redwood Creek on **Pacific Way.** Watch for vehicles on the short road. To the left (northwest) is **Pelican Inn,** a whitewashed English 16th-century-style inn, pub, and kitchen. Pass the inn and cross Highway 1 to make your way up Dias Ridge to return to the trailhead.

DIRECTIONS

From Mill Valley, travel southwest on Edgewood Avenue until it turns left and becomes Sequoia Valley Road for 0.7 mile (1.1 km). Turn left onto Panoramic Highway and continue for 0.6 mile (1 km) and look for roadside parking.

GPS COORDINATES: 37.8849, −122.5549; 37°53′5.6″ N, 122°33′17.6″ W

BEST NEARBY BITES AND BREWS

A great way to refuel before heading back up the ridge is timing your hike so you can get a meal and a drink at **The Pelican Inn** (10 Pacific Way, Muir Beach, 415/383-6000, www.pelicaninn.com, 8am-7pm daily, $13-42) at Muir Beach. Whether you are craving something on the lighter side, like an organic mixed greens salad with steelhead paired with a California cider, or hearty beef wellington and an English stout, anything your order here will be fantastic.

Canopy View Loop
MUIR WOODS NATIONAL MONUMENT

Hike through the only old-growth coastal redwood forest in the Bay Area—and one of the last on the planet—on this loop of the highlights of Muir Woods National Monument.

BEST: Redwood Hikes

DISTANCE: 3.8 miles (6.1 km) round-trip

DURATION: 2 hours

ELEVATION GAIN: 680 feet (207 m)

EFFORT: Easy-moderate

TRAIL: Wooden boardwalk, dirt, single-track, paved

USERS: Hikers, wheelchair users on part of the trail

SEASON: Year-round

PASSES/FEES: $15 over age 15, free under age 16, Muir Woods Annual Pass or National Park Pass, mandatory parking reservation ($9 per vehicle) or shuttle reservation ($3.50 over age 15, free under age 16)

MAPS: Select "Maps" and "Muir Woods Trail Map" on the park website

PARK HOURS: 8am-sunset daily

TRAILHEAD: Muir Woods National Monument Sign

FACILITIES: Restrooms and drinking fountain at the main parking lot and at Café & Gift Shop

CONTACT: Muir Woods National Monument, 415/561-2850, www.nps.gov/muwo

START THE HIKE

▶ **MILE 0-0.3: Muir Woods National Monument Sign to Canopy View Trail Junction**

From the often photographed **Muir Woods National Monument Sign,** follow the wooden boardwalk of the **Main Trail,** also known as Redwood Creek Trail, northwest, approaching the stairs and ramp to the right (east) that lead up to the **Café and Gift Shop** as well as restrooms and water fountains. Pass **Bridge 1,** which crosses over Redwood Creek, and continue on the Main Trail.

Ahead you'll see **A Tree for the Ages,** a cross-section of a redwood tree bearing markers of moments in history along the tree rings, from the tree's birth in AD 909 to its fall in 1930. Pass it and continue straight (northwest). Farther along the Main Trail, in **Founder's Grove,** stop by **Pinchot Tree,** dedicated in 1910 in honor of the first chief of the U.S. Forest Service, Gifford Pinchot, and hear one of the 15-minute ranger talks that regularly take place here.

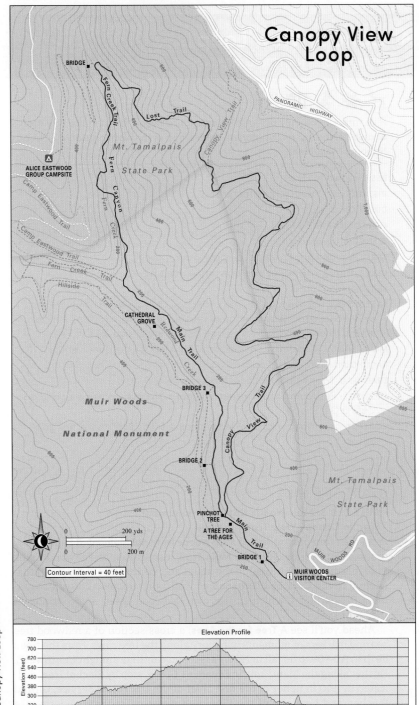

Canopy View Loop

BRIDGE

Fern Creek Trail

Lost Trail

Canopy View Trail

Mt. Tamalpais

State Park

ALICE EASTWOOD
GROUP CAMPSITE

Camp Eastwood Trail

Fern Canyon

Fern Creek

Camp Eastwood Trail

Fern Creek Trail

Hillside Trail

CATHEDRAL GROVE

Redwood Creek

Main Trail

Muir Woods

BRIDGE 3

Canopy View Trail

National Monument

BRIDGE 2

Mt. Tamalpais

State Park

PINCHOT TREE

A TREE FOR THE AGES

Main Trail

BRIDGE 1

MUIR WOODS RD

MUIR WOODS VISITOR CENTER

PANORAMIC HIGHWAY

N

0   200 yds
0   200 m

Contour Interval = 40 feet

Elevation Profile

Elevation (feet) vs Distance (miles)

© MOON.COM

▲ CANOPY VIEW LOOP

Just beyond the grove at 0.3 mile (0.5 km) is the **junction** with **Canopy View Trail,** which ascends a beautiful curving staircase of wood built into the dirt of the canyon wall and bordered by sorrel and ferns.

▶ **MILE 0.3-1.7: Canopy View Trail Junction to Lost Trail Junction**
Head up the curved staircase. Still sometimes referred to as part of what was once Ocean View Trail, Canopy View Trail is a more fitting name, as the path takes you into the canopy of the redwood forest—and there is no view of the ocean from along its narrow path.

As the trail winds along the canyon wall, narrow steep drainage waterfalls may cause small water crossings on the trail, and only in some places are bridges for hikers to cross them, beginning around 0.9 mile (1.4 km). At 1.7 miles (2.7 km) is an open area and a **bench,** signaling that you've reached the highest point of the hike, having gained approximately 600 feet (183 m) elevation from the start. Look for the marker for **Lost Trail** to turn left (northwest) and begin your descent.

▶ **MILE 1.7-3: Lost Trail Junction to Main Trail Junction**
Lost Trail steeply drops into Fern Canyon, which sits outside of the boundaries of Muir Woods National Monument, heading into Mount Tamalpais State Park. In some spots, thick roots can be tricky to navigate, and at others, wooden steps help keep the trail less technical and prevent erosion. The trail leads past moss-covered boulders and descends nearly 500 feet (152 m) in less than 1 mile (1.6 km), with some significant switchbacks as you near Fern Creek Trail.

When Lost Trail meets **Fern Creek Trail** at 2.4 miles (3.9 km), turn left (east) and away from the bridge that leads west toward Camp Alice Eastwood. The wooden fence-lined path takes you down more switchbacks toward the valley floor before traversing multiple wooden bridges over

MUIR WOODS & MOUNT TAMALPAIS

Canopy View Loop

the lush Fern Creek among thick mature redwoods and arriving at a sign indicating you're now re-entering Muir Woods National Monument.

At 3 miles (4.8 km), Fern Creek Trail meets a **three-way junction** with Main Trail and Redwood Creek Trail, where Fern Creek flows into Redwood Creek. Turn left (south-west) onto Main Trail.

▶ MILE 3-3.8: Main Trail Junction to Muir Woods National Monument Sign

Back on the Main Trail, the paved path offers benches to hikers who make it this far into Redwood Canyon. You will reach **Cathedral Grove** at 3.2 miles (5.2 km). Honor the posted request to remain quiet as you enter this section of the forest. The National Park Service describes the grove as a silent preserve and home to the tallest, oldest redwoods at Muir Woods and asks visitors to consider quiet contemplation while in the grove area. Continue straight (southeast), passing **Bridges 3** and **2** to make your way back to Founder's Grove. From Founder's Grove, return to the Muir Woods National Monument Sign the way you came, or wander at your leisure.

DIRECTIONS

From Mill Valley, travel southwest on Edgewood Avenue until it turns left and becomes Sequoia Valley Road for 0.7 mile (1.1 km). Take a slight right onto Muir Woods Road for 1.5 miles (2.4 km) to arrive at the main parking lot, where attendants will assist with parking reservations.

GPS COORDINATES: 37.8927, −122.5725; 37°53′33.7″ N, −122°34′21″ W

BEST NEARBY BITES

Without even needing to get in your vehicle, you can grab a bite to eat at the monument at **Muir Woods Trading Company** (1 Muir Woods Rd., Mill Valley, 415/388-7059, www.muirwoodstradingcompany.com, $7-13). Grab a warm and gooey grilled cheese and a cup of soup to recharge before your next adventure.

Dipsea-Matt Davis Loop
MOUNT TAMALPAIS STATE PARK

Travel the most famous trail in Marin County up Mount Tamalpais with evergreen forest and ocean views, past Pantoll Ranger Station, and back down the mountain on grassy slopes with waterfall ravines.

DISTANCE: 9 miles (14.5 km) round-trip

DURATION: 5 hours

ELEVATION GAIN: 1,867 feet (569 m)

EFFORT: Moderate-strenuous

TRAIL: Dirt fire road, dirt, gravel, single-track, stairs, boardwalk, paved, roots

USERS: Hikers, mountain bikers on part of the trail

SEASON: Year-round

PASSES/FEES: None

MAPS: On the park website

PARK HOURS: 7am-sunset daily

TRAILHEAD: Dipsea Trail Trailhead

FACILITIES: Drinking fountain on Cardiac Hill, restrooms and drinking fountain at Pantoll Ranger Station

CONTACT: California State Parks, 415/388-2070, www.parks.ca.gov

START THE HIKE

▶ **MILE 0-1.6: Dipsea Trail Trailhead to White Gate Junction**

Start the hike where the **Dipsea Trail** meets Highway 1 (Shoreline Hwy.), on its east side, just south of Arenal Drive. Look for the Dipsea Trail sign indicating Muir Woods is 5.1 miles (8.2 km) ahead. Your legs immediately warm up as the trail ascends wooden stairs and then uphill to cross Panoramic Highway. Look both ways before carefully crossing and rejoining the trail on the other side, where another Dipsea Trail sign indicates Steep Ravine Trail is 1.2 miles (1.9 km) ahead.

At 0.3 mile (0.5 km), follow the wooden boardwalk as the trail continues to ascend. The **"Dipsea 7" marked rock** on the right (southwest) side of the trail marks mile 7 for runners on the 7.4-mile (11.9-km) course of the annual Dipsea Trail Race. At 1 mile (1.6 km), the trail intersects with **Hill 640 Fire Road.** Turn right (south) on the fire road and hike for under 0.25 mile (0.4 km) to a nice viewpoint of the coastline at what's known as **Stinson Tree,** a large eucalyptus that stands alone by the ruins of the World War II-era Hill 640 Military Reservation barracks, today just some concrete foundation. From Stinson Tree, retrace your steps to the junction with Dipsea Trail and turn right (east) to reach the **junction** with **White Gate** at 1.6 miles (2.6 km).

▶ **MILE 1.6-4.4: White Gate Junction to Pantoll Ranger Station**

Technically, you were in Stinson Beach Golden Gate National Recreation Area until just past this junction, where you enter into a mixed evergreen

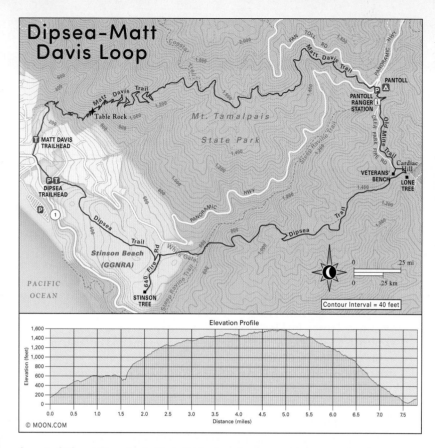

Dipsea-Matt Davis Loop

Elevation Profile

© MOON.COM

forest of Mount Tamalpais State Park. A rocky descent takes you to a **junction** where Steep Ravine Trail briefly merges with Dipsea Trail at an electrical box and pole. Stay left (north) and approach Webb Creek to the right (east) of the path.

A wooden bridge marks the **fork** of the two trails: Steep Ravine Trail continues ahead on the northwest side of the ravine, and Dipsea Trail crosses the bridge to the right (southeast) side of the ravine. Cross the bridge, passing through a doorway of trees, and begin the long climb toward Cardiac Hill. Stairs and more stairs lead from 507 feet (155 m) elevation to 835 feet (255 m) in just over 0.25 mile (0.4 km), with a nice respite from the climb at 2.1 miles (3.4 km).

Dipsea Trail continues east, becoming less damp and more exposed among coastal scrub. At 2.9 miles (4.7 km), a large area near wooden power poles makes a **quick spur viewpoint** to look out at the ocean. Lots of hikers stop here for lunch, and it's a good spot to apply or reapply sun protection. Continuing straight (northeast), you pass the **"Dipsea 5" trail marker** as the trail ascends and becomes increasingly rocky.

At 3.8 miles (6.1 km), you arrive at the often busy and beautiful **Cardiac Hill** (1,360 ft/415 m). A water fountain is available, and you can read the interpretive sign about the history of the trail and the **Lone Tree**. It's also worth it to venture out to the boulders on the knoll to take in the stunning

▲ DIPSEA TRAIL

coastal views. When you're ready to move on, look for the trail sign for **Deer Park Fire Road** toward Pantoll. Follow the road as it goes uphill and northwest, and be aware that bicycles are allowed on fire roads in the park. At 4 miles (6.4 km), take the quick **spur trail** to **Veterans' Bench** to take in the views, then return to the road. Turn left (northwest) onto the road and immediately look for the trail sign for **Old Mine Trail,** toward Pantoll, and cross the road to get on the trail going north.

This short connector section of Old Mine Trail crosses five wooden bridges on the forested path and a sign titled "Denos Claim," with history about this trail. At 4.4 miles (7.1 km), arrive at **Pantoll Ranger Station,** where Old Mine Trail reconnects to Deer Park Fire Road.

▶ **MILE 4.4–6.2: Pantoll Ranger Station to Coastal Trail Junction**
Turn right (north) onto the fire road and pass the water fountains, restrooms, and trash cans. Cross the center of the **parking lot** going left (northwest) from the disabled parking spaces to the handful of steps up to **Panoramic Highway.**

Exercise extreme caution crossing the highway to the trail sign on the other side of the road, for Matt Davis Trail. Take the rock stairs up and arc left (southwest) as the trail runs for about 1 mile (1.6 km) between Pan Toll Road to the right (northwest) and Panoramic Highway to the left (southwest), until pulling away from both at 5.5 miles (8.9 km). Through this section, you have to navigate rocks and roots, encountering waterfalls on the inside of each curve of the mountain slope.

Beginning at 5.8 miles (9.3 km), several trails intersect Matt Davis Trail, providing opportunities to explore the grassy slopes right (north) to O'Rourke's Bench or left (south) to Bare Knoll (1,568 ft/478 m) before the hike begins its descent. At 6.2 miles (10 km), the **Coastal Trail** is the last intersecting path to the right (north).

▶ **MILE 6.2–9: Coastal Trail Junction to Dipsea Trail Trailhead**

Stay on Matt Davis Trail, enjoying the last open views of the Pacific as the path enters the forest for what can seem like endless switchbacks down the mountain.

The path down requires attention to your footing, as there are rocks and roots all along the way, with several wooden steps down at many of the curves. You can glimpse the ocean and then Stinson Beach through the trees and hear the water flowing down the creek you cross on a **wooden bridge** at 8.5 miles (13.7 km). You know you've completed most of the switchbacks when you pass the giant and unmistakable **Table Rock** just as the sound of the rushing water crescendos. Just past Table Rock, a trail marker directs hikers to keep left (southeast). Cross back over the creek on a **wooden bridge,** and the path then remains just to the left (east) of the creek. At 8.8 miles (14.2 km), Matt Davis Trail crosses the creek one final time on another **wooden bridge,** where you can see the trailhead ahead at Belvedere Drive.

Turn left (south) onto **Belvedere Drive** toward Highway 1 (Shoreline Hwy.). To complete the loop, with excessive care, turn left (east) onto Highway 1 and proceed to the Dipsea Trail Trailhead on the east side of the highway, just south of Arenal Drive.

DIRECTIONS

From Mill Valley, take Panoramic Highway northwest from Sequoia Valley Road for 8.1 miles (13 km). Turn north on Highway 1, and the trailhead is in 0.2 mile (0.3 km). Find local parking, being mindful of posted time limits.

GPS COORDINATES: 37.8979, −122.6372; 37°53'52.4" N, 122°38'13.9" W

BEST NEARBY BITES

A three-minute walk southwest on Arenal Drive from the trailhead, **Parkside Snack Bar** (43 Arenal Dr., Stinson Beach, 415/868-1272, www.parksidecafe.com, 11am–8pm daily, $6–13) is the perfect place to order a burger, coconut shrimp, soup, or a sandwich from the window after your hike.

Mount Tamalpais West Point Loop

MOUNT TAMALPAIS STATE PARK

Hike through the natural beauty of Mount Tamalpais and the wonder of history up to the West Point Inn and around to the Mountain Theater.

DISTANCE: 4.2 miles (6.8 km) round-trip

DURATION: 2.5 hours

ELEVATION GAIN: 550 feet (168 m)

EFFORT: Easy-moderate

TRAIL: Paved, gravel, fire road, dirt, single-track

USERS: Hikers, mountain bikers on part of the trail, horseback riders, leashed dogs on part of the trail

SEASON: Year-round

PASSES/FEES: $8 day-use fee per vehicle, cash or check only

MAPS: Select "Brochures" and "Park Brochure" on the park website, Pantoll Visitor Service Kiosk at Pantoll Camping Parking Area

PARK HOURS: 7am-sunset daily

TRAILHEAD: Pantoll Camping Parking Area

FACILITIES: Restrooms and drinking fountain at Pantoll Camping Parking Area, West Point Inn, and Mountain Theater

CONTACT: California State Parks, 415/388-2070, www.parks.ca.gov

START THE HIKE

▶ **MILE 0-2.1: Pantoll Camping Parking Area to West Point Inn**

The trailhead for this hike is near the junction of Panoramic Highway and Pan Toll Road—be extremely cautious when crossing either road from the **Pantoll Camping Parking Area** to begin on **Stagecoach Fire Road** (also called Old Stage Road). Several trails intersect or stem from the road, including Old Mine Trail at 0.1 mile (0.2 km) and Easy Grade Trail at 0.2 mile (0.3 km). Remain on Stagecoach Fire Road, heading straight (north). At 0.3 mile (0.5 km), Stagecoach Fire Road curves left (northwest) and away from Panoramic Highway, and meets Bootjack Trail at a **junction** at 0.5 mile (0.8 km).

From the junction, continue on Stagecoach Fire Road as it turns more west, becoming rocky before curving right (north) and arriving at a **gate** at 0.7 mile (1.1 km), departing Mount Tamalpais State Park as it leads into Marin Municipal Water District land, where a greater population of chaparral plants begins to appear. At 1.7 miles (2.7 km), where Stagecoach Fire Road curves inland toward Spike Buck Creek, you can see West Point Inn across the shallow canyon. Just after a **junction** with Nora Trail to the south, the trail curves north to end at Railroad Grade Fire Road, and you arrive at **West Point Inn** at 2.1 miles (3.4 km).

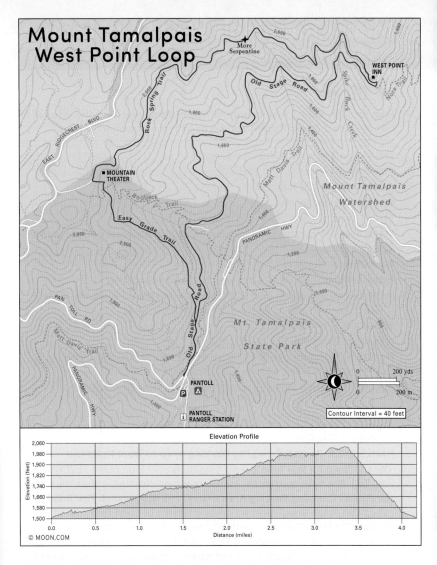

Mount Tamalpais
West Point Loop

MORE
Serpentine

WEST POINT
INN

MOUNTAIN
THEATER

Mount Tamalpais
Watershed

Mt. Tamalpais
State Park

PANTOLL

PANTOLL
RANGER STATION

Contour Interval = 40 feet

0   200 yds
0   200 m

Elevation Profile

Elevation (feet): 2,060 / 1,980 / 1,900 / 1,820 / 1,740 / 1,660 / 1,580 / 1,500

Distance (miles): 0.0   0.5   1.0   1.5   2.0   2.5   3.0   3.5   4.0

© MOON.COM

▶ **MILE 2.1–3.7: West Point Inn to Mountain Theater**

From the inn, continue by following **Railroad Grade Fire Road** northwest, around the building, and look for the trail marker for **Rock Spring Trail**. Unlike the fire road, this narrow trail is exclusive to hikers and leashed dogs. At 2.3 miles (3.7 km), cross a **footbridge** over Spike Buck Creek and take the wooden stairs up to a clearing where you can look back at West Point Inn and down on Stagecoach Fire Road.

You may notice another **footbridge** farther along stamped with "TCC 1999," evidence of the work of the Tamalpais Conservation Club, founded over 100 years ago to preserve and protect the area's natural features. From here, a serpentine section of Rock Spring Trail has panoramic views to the south as the trail continues southwestward through the woods and over

a few more wooden bridges before reentering Mount Tamalpais State Park at 3.6 miles (5.8 km).

Pass the Rock Springs Trail Spur to the right (north) just after reentering the park to stay on Rock Springs Trail. A bench soon comes into view, and then you reach the Sidney B. Cushing Memorial Amphitheatre, commonly known as the **Mountain Theater,** at 3.7 miles (6 km). In a natural amphitheater, a "mountain play" theatrical event has taken place here almost every spring since 1913. In the 1930s, the Civilian Conservation Corps built the stone seating that accommodates approximately 4,000 people.

▸ **MILE 3.7-4.2: Mountain Theater to Pantoll Camping Parking Area**
Walk through the theater seating to the southern side, toward the paved **restroom area.** Look for the interpretive sign with a park map. Begin the hike's descent on the **Easy Grade Trail,** located near the stage. The path almost immediately splits. Continue right (south), past a mysterious locked wooden box and pipes through a forest of Douglas firs and California bays. When you come to a sign directing hikers to Old Mine Trail or Pantoll, continue straight (southeast) toward Pantoll. Soon after, a second trail sign directs you to stay straight to reconnect to Stagecoach Fire Road in 0.1 mile (0.2 km). Follow the path down and over a **wooden bridge** to Stagecoach Fire Road. Turn right (south) onto Stagecoach Fire Road and return to the trailhead the way you came.

DIRECTIONS

From Mill Valley, travel southwest on Edgewood Avenue until it turns left and becomes Sequoia Valley Road for 0.7 mile (1.1 km). Take a sharp right onto Panoramic Highway and continue for 4.5 miles (7.2 km) to the Pantoll Camping Parking Area, on the left, at the junction with Pan Toll Road.

GPS COORDINATES: 37.9041, −122.6041; 37°54′14.8″ N, 122°36′14.8″ W

BEST NEARBY BITES

The **West Point Inn** (100 Old Railroad Grade Fire Rd., Mill Valley, 415/388-9955, www.westpointinn.com) serves a pancake breakfast 9am-1pm every Mother's Day, Father's Day, and the second Sunday of the month May-October (weather permitting). For current pricing or accessibility, check the website or contact the inn. Note that trailhead parking lots fill up early and the line gets long for these special events.

East Peak Summit Lookout Loop

MOUNT TAMALPAIS STATE PARK

🦌 ❀ 🏛 🐾 🚶 ♿

Easily earned sweeping views of the entire Bay Area await hikers at the top of Mount Tamalpais's East Peak, with summit views at 2,571 feet (784 m).

DISTANCE: 1.7 miles (2.7 km) round-trip
DURATION: 1 hour
ELEVATION GAIN: 325 feet (99 m)
EFFORT: Easy
TRAIL: Dirt, gravel, rock, single-track, paved loop, wooden plank
USERS: Hikers, wheelchair users on part of the trail, leashed dogs
SEASON: Year-round
PASSES/FEES: $8 day-use fee per vehicle, cash or check only
MAPS: Select "Brochures" and "Park Brochure" on the park website
PARK HOURS: 7am–sunset daily
TRAILHEAD: East Peak Parking Area
FACILITIES: Restrooms and drinking fountain at the trailhead
CONTACT: California State Parks, 415/388-2070, www.parks.ca.gov

START THE HIKE

▶ **MILE 0-0.5: East Peak Parking Area to Scenic Overlook Spur Trail**
From the east side of the **parking lot,** follow the paved path down past the **visitor center** toward the restrooms. To join the **Verna Dunshee Trail,** take either the stairs by the picnic tables to the south or the ADA-accessible ramp just south of the restrooms, and see the dedication rock honoring the longtime Marin resident, outdoorswoman, and passionate conservationist for whom this section of the hike is named.

An **observation deck** at 0.3 mile (0.5 km) offers views of the entire East Bay, from the Richmond-San Rafael Bridge all the way west to the Pacific Ocean. In 0.1 mile (0.2 km), pass the **junction** with Temelpa Trail that descends to the right (east). Continue on Verna Dunshee Trail and, in another 0.1 mile (0.2 km), arrive at a trail marker for a **spur trail** to a **Scenic Overlook.**

▶ **MILE 0.5-1: Scenic Overlook Spur Trail to Gravity Car Barn Museum**
The gravel trail to the overlook is not accessible and is more technical than the flat paved path of the Verna Dunshee Trail, but it's worth descending the wooden steps that lead to a single-track and slightly overgrown rocky scrambling finish in 400 feet (122 m). From the overlook you get a unique bird's-eye view of the entire San Francisco Bay. While the view from the fire lookout is just as expansive and from a higher elevation, fewer hikers come to this point, and it's possible to enjoy a quiet moment sitting on the rocks to watch turkey vultures ride the wind between you and the slopes of the peak. On your way back up to Verna Dunshee Trail, you can spot the fire lookout rising high above at the peak.

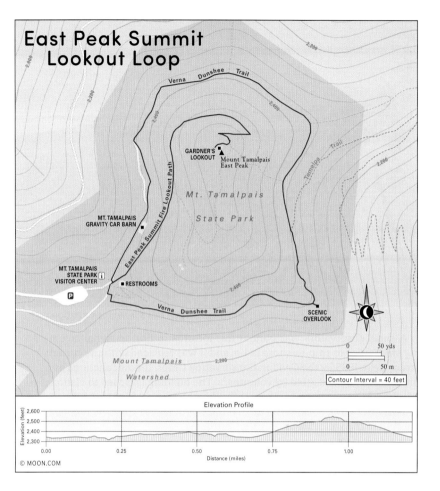

East Peak Summit
Lookout Loop

Elevation Profile

Contour Interval = 40 feet

© MOON.COM

Past the spur trail, Verna Dunshee now curves along the northern side of the peak. At 1 mile (1.6 km) is the **Gravity Car Barn Museum** (noon-4pm Sat.-Sun.), which houses railroad memorabilia and a replica of a gravity car, a small open-air four-wheeler with wooden seats that took passengers down the mountain at a speed of 10 to 12 miles per hour (16-19 km/h).

▶ **MILE 1–1.7: Gravity Car Barn Museum to Gardner Lookout**
You reach the welcome area near the restrooms at 1.1 miles (1.8 km). Make a sharp turn left (east) to start on the **East Peak Summit Fire Lookout Path,** which begins as a wooden plank trail and immediately climbs toward the peak, almost like a long switchback from where you just came. The lookout comes into view, but where the trail turns to gravel and rock, it continues to climb up and around toward the north side of the peak. As you get closer to the lookout, the trail contains more rocky steps as it continues to the eastern side of the peak. Look for the summit marker in the boulders on the right (north) side of the trail. Just after the summit marker, a smooth rock staircase leads you up the final stretch to **Gardner Lookout**'s front door and 1937 dedication plaque.

A small observatory was built at this location in 1901 to signal incoming ships prior to ship-to-shore radio, and it was replaced with the current structure in 1935 by the Civilian Conservation Corps. It now functions as a fire lookout and is staffed by volunteers. The building is closed to visitors, but there is no shortage of views at this height.

To return to the start of the hike, retrace your steps down the fire lookout trail to the welcome area by the restrooms.

DIRECTIONS

From Mill Valley, take Miller Avenue south and turn right onto Montford Avenue for 0.2 mile (0.3 km). Turn right onto Miller Avenue and proceed for 0.4 mile (0.6 km). Continue straight onto Edgewood Avenue for 0.7 mile (1.1 km), which turns left and becomes Sequoia Valley Road. Proceed for 0.7 mile (1.1 km) and make a sharp right onto Panoramic Highway. Stay on the highway for 4.5 miles (7.2 km) to Pantoll Road and turn right. After 1.4 miles (2.3 km), turn right onto East Ridgecrest for 3 miles (4.8 km) to the East Peak parking area.

GPS COORDINATES: 37.9274, −122.5799; 37°55'38.6" N, 122°34'47.6" W

BEST NEARBY BITES

On your way down the mountain, pop into **Mountain Home Inn** (810 Panoramic Hwy., Mill Valley, 415/381-9000, from noon daily, last seating 6:30pm, $18-34) for a meal, just 7 miles (11.3 km) and 20 minutes from the East Peak Parking Area on Panoramic Highway. If it's warm enough, take a seat on the deck to enjoy panoramic mountain views, or look out from inside, through the enormous bay windows.

This hike takes you from the glassy water of Alpine Lake up the stunning cascading falls of Cataract Creek to the base of Cataract Falls.

BEST: Waterfall Hikes

DISTANCE: 3 miles (4.8 km) round-trip

DURATION: 2 hours

ELEVATION GAIN: 1,000 feet (305 m)

EFFORT: Easy-moderate

TRAIL: Dirt, rock, single-track

USERS: Hikers, horseback riders, leashed dogs

SEASON: Year-round

PASSES/FEES: None

MAPS: Select "Visiting Mt. Tam," then "Recreation," and "Double-sided Mount Tamalpais Watershed Visitor Map" on the park website

PARK HOURS: Sunrise-sunset daily

TRAILHEAD: Roadside parking on Fairfax-Bolinas Road near Alpine Lake

FACILITIES: Portable toilets at the trailhead

CONTACT: Marin Municipal Water District, 415/945-1180, www.marinwater.org

START THE HIKE

▶ **MILE 0-0.6: Cataract Falls Trailhead to Falls Crossing Bridge**

This hike starts at the tall wooden **"Cataract Trail" post** to the east of the southernmost curve of Fairfax-Bolinas Road along the west side of Alpine Lake. The beginning of the trail leisurely rolls alongside the lake, with beautiful reflections in the water. At 0.3 miles (0.5 km), cross a **bridge** and come to the first of many stairs of the hike, as the trail leaves the lake behind and continues along the eastern side of Cataract Creek.

Moss covers everything in the moist forest, and the sound of cascading water draws your attention to the series of falls beside the climbing trail. When the water is at its lowest, the falls appear to cross every which way, finding the rocky path of least resistance. At other times, the rushing water fans out, overtaking larger sections of the creek bed. Where you see the steps leading up to a landing before another set of steps curve right (west), know that a breathtaking reward is ahead.

As the grade of the trail increases, the landscape creates dramatically tiered drops for the falls, with water gathering in pools that overflow and stream down to the next pool. Crossing a narrow **wooden bridge** at 0.6 mile (1 km), travel over to the eastern side of the falls, which now spread across a wider expanse and flow around large boulders beneath your feet.

MUIR WOODS & MOUNT TAMALPAIS

Cataract Falls

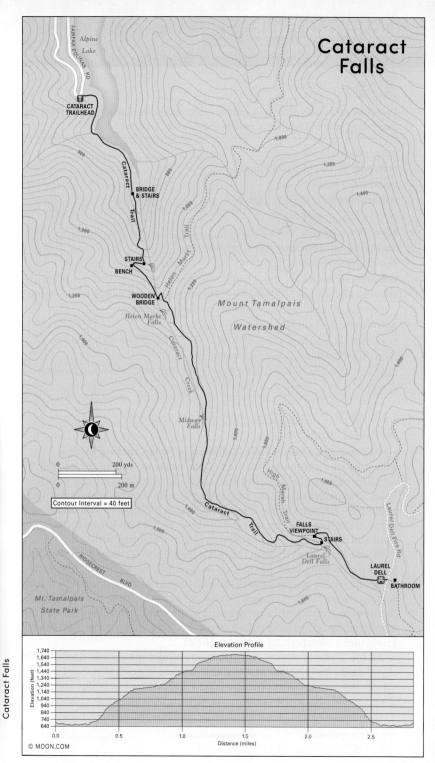

Cataract Falls

Alpine Lake

FAIRFAX-BOLINAS RD.

CATARACT TRAILHEAD

Cataract Trail

BRIDGE & STAIRS

STAIRS

BENCH

WOODEN BRIDGE

Helen Markt Falls

Helen Markt Trail

Cataract Creek

Mount Tamalpais

Watershed

Midway Falls

High Marsh Trail

Laurel Dell Fire Rd.

Cataract Trail

FALLS VIEWPOINT

STAIRS

Laurel Dell Falls

LAUREL DELL

BATHROOM

RIDGECREST BLVD.

Mt. Tamalpais State Park

0   200 yds
0   200 m

Contour Interval = 40 feet

800

1,000

1,000

1,200

1,200

1,400

1,400

1,200

1,400

1,600

1,600

1,800

1,800

Elevation Profile

Elevation (feet): 1,740 / 1,640 / 1,540 / 1,440 / 1,340 / 1,240 / 1,140 / 1,040 / 940 / 840 / 740 / 640

Distance (miles): 0.0 / 0.5 / 1.0 / 1.5 / 2.0 / 2.5

© MOON.COM

▲ CATARACT TRAIL

▶ **MILE 0.6–1.5: Falls Crossing Bridge to Cataract Falls**
The ideal spot for a group photo or a snack stop is after a bit of scrambling up from the base of the bridge, on the rocks just right (west) of the trail, before it intersects with Helen Markt Trail to the left (east). The pool is so large it could be tempting to wade in, but do not get in the water at any point—it's prohibited, as Mount Tamalpais Watershed is a public drinking water supply. The water collects here before spilling to the rocks under the bridge.

Continue uphill on **Cataract Falls Trail,** watching for roots and rocks. The trail slightly eases in grade as some of the creek's small falls glide over rocks to the right (west) before a short and steep scramble up a few boulders. While still gaining elevation, the next section of trail is more serene and less of a challenge, giving you the chance to spot mushrooms, wildflowers, and banana slugs.

The respite concludes with the final approach to the base of **Cataract Falls,** as the trail ascends switchbacks up about 80 stairs away from the water to a **bench.** The path then leads back toward the falls, and at 1.4 miles (2.3 km) is the opportunity to take a few dozen steps down to the rush of the water. When the water is low enough, some visitors boulder hop in the creek to try to capture the best view or snap a selfie. Others simply let the sound of the cascading water add to the relief that the climb is mostly over.

For one final viewpoint of the falls, continue up to a wooden fence at the base of the stairs that lead up to connect High Marsh Trail, coming from the northwest to Cataract Falls Trail as it continues to follow the creek to the southeast. For those who wish to explore just a bit farther, you can climb the steps to continue on Cataract Falls Trail for another 0.2 mile (0.3 km) to reach **Laurel Dell Picnic Area.** The full trail terminates at Rock Spring Trailhead, an additional 1.3 miles (2.1 km) from the picnic area.

MUIR WOODS & MOUNT TAMALPAIS

Cataract Falls

131

▶ **MILE 1.5-3: Cataract Falls to Cataract Falls Trailhead**

When ready, retrace your steps back to the trailhead at Alpine Lake.

DIRECTIONS

From Mill Valley, take Miller Avenue south and turn right onto Montford Avenue for 0.2 mile (0.3 km). Then turn right onto Miller Avenue and proceed for 0.4 mile (0.6 km). Continue straight onto Edgewood Avenue for 0.7 mile (1.1 km), which turns left and becomes Sequoia Valley Road. Proceed for 0.7 mile (1.1 km) and make a sharp right onto Panoramic Highway. Continue for 8.1 miles (13 km) and turn right onto Highway 1 for 4.7 miles (7.6 km). Turn right onto Fairfax-Bolinas Road and proceed for 6.6 miles (10.6 km).

GPS COORDINATES: 37.9366, −122.6380; 37°56'11.8" N, 122°38'16.8" W

BEST NEARBY BITES

A great excuse to head to Stinson Beach, **Breakers Café** (3465 Shoreline Hwy., Stinson Beach, 415/868-2002, www.stinsonbeachbreakerscafe. com, 11am-9pm Thurs.-Mon., $12-36) is 11 miles (17.7 km) and 30 minutes from the trailhead, south down Highway 1. Take your order to go for a beach picnic or grab a drink and hang out on the patio.

In early spring, when the roads are dry and the waterfalls at peak, this short hike leads to a flowing waterfall tucked into a small rocky canyon.

BEST: Spring Hikes

DISTANCE: 4.6 miles (7.4 km) round-trip

DURATION: 2 hours

ELEVATION GAIN: 1,000 feet (305 m)

EFFORT: Easy-moderate

TRAIL: Gravel fire road, dirt, single-track

USERS: Hikers, mountain bikers, horseback riders, leashed dogs

SEASON: Year-round

PASSES/FEES: None

MAPS: Select "Visiting Mt. Tam," then "Recreation," and "Double-sided Mount Tamalpais Watershed Visitor Map" on the park website

PARK HOURS: Sunrise-sunset daily

TRAILHEAD: Roadside parking at Azalea Hill Trailhead

FACILITIES: Portable toilets at the trailhead

CONTACT: Marin Municipal Water District, 415/945-1180, www.marinwater.org

START THE HIKE

The fire roads are shared with mountain bikers. Especially on Pine Mountain Road, they pass at a high rate of speed. Carson Falls can slow to a trickle or vanish in dry seasons, so it's best visited in winter and spring.

▸ **MILE 0-1.3: Azalea Hill Parking Lot to Carson Falls Trail Junction**
After parking roadside at the **Azalea Hill Trailhead,** cross Bolinas-Fairfax Road to **Pine Mountain Road.** Look for interpretive signs to the left (south) before getting started up the exposed rocky fire road. As you climb the road, watch for mountain bikers flying down, and make sure to give room to those slowly making their way up.

Beside the road, shrubs like leather oak, chamise, and musk bush grow. Blooms of morning glory, yellow mariposa lily, sticky *Calycadenia,* and slender clarkia can be spotted, and lizards scurry across the path. As you rise in elevation, wide-open views present rolling foothills, low range ridges, mountain peaks, and valleys. Below is the Meadow Club golf course you drove past to park, and a glimmer of Alpine Lake is visible to the south. Ahead, you may notice where Pine Mountain Road teeters along the ridge, up to the peak of Pine Mountain.

At 1.1 miles (1.8 km), Pine Mountain Road meets Oat Hill Road. Turn left (southwest) onto **Oat Hill Road.** As the road descends, look east to see the three peaks of Mount Tamalpais. Continue straight (southwest) on the

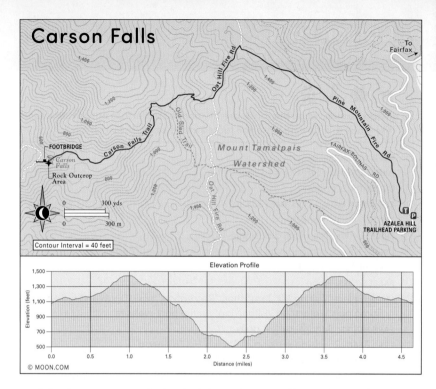

Carson Falls

Elevation Profile

© MOON.COM

road for the next 0.25 mile (0.4 km) through coast silk tassel, manzanita, and buckbrush.

At 1.3 miles (2.1 km) is a **junction** with **Carson Falls Trail.** Turn right (west) off the road and onto the single-track trail.

▶ **MILE 1.3-4.6: Carson Falls Trail Junction to Azalea Hill Parking Lot**
The path leads you into the only shade of the hike, descending into a brief grove of bay laurels, tan oaks, and ferns on a handful of switchbacks before coming out into grasslands. The unsigned Old Sled Road meets the trail from the left (south) at 1.6 miles (2.6 km). Take a moment to look back in the direction you came from on Carson Falls Trail to remember which way to go on your return. Remaining on Carson Falls Trail, it begins to follow the creek, which flows down beyond this hike to the long western arm of Kent Lake.

The trail makes a short split: To the right (north) is a footbridge, and to the left (south), a rocky outcrop. First, head left to the **rock outcrop area** for your first view of the waterfall. There's no one spot to get a great view of the entire series of falls, and from this vantage point you have the unique perspective of looking down from atop the falls. Retrace your steps to the **junction,** and this time, go right to cross the **bridge.**

The trail descends rocky steps and makes a wide curve, providing different viewpoints of the tiers of the falls as they drop and pool. The volume of water cascading down determines whether hikers will see a faint trickle or a roaring deluge, and the volume is entirely dependent on the amount of rain received.

Take care not to disturb the habitat along the creek and falls; this is one of the few remaining areas where foothill yellow-legged frogs breed and lay their eggs. Rarely observed far from the water's edge, the frogs have rough pebbly skin that is generally a camouflage of gray, olive, or brown with yellow shading on the belly and underside of the rear legs.

Where the path seems to head right (west) away from the falls, turn around and return the way you came.

DIRECTIONS

From Fairfax, take Bolinas Road southwest. Continue onto Fairfax-Bolinas Road for 1.3 miles (2.1 km), past the golf course to the left. Look for street-side parking to the left at the Azalea Hill trailhead.

GPS COORDINATES: 37.9636, −122.6250; 37°57'49" N, 122°37'30" W

BEST NEARBY BITES AND BREWS

About 7 miles (11.3 km) and 20 minutes from the trailhead in San Rafael, **The State Room** (1132 4th St., San Rafael, 415/295-7929, www.stateroombrewery.com, 11:30am-9pm Tues.-Sat., 11:30am-8pm Sun.) is a brewery, bar, and kitchen where all brews are made on-site. The extensive dining menu has something for everyone. Try the award-winning Altered State Belgian golden ale, brewed with coriander, and pair it with a hearty State Room Burger.

Bay View Loop
CHINA CAMP STATE PARK

This forested hike along a popular hillside track provides a variety of views of the salt marsh and San Pablo Bay below.

DISTANCE: 3.7 miles (6 km) round-trip
DURATION: 1.5 hours
ELEVATION GAIN: 710 feet (216 m)
EFFORT: Easy
TRAIL: Dirt fire road, gravel, single-track, paved road
USERS: Hikers, mountain bikers, horseback riders
SEASON: Year-round
PASSES/FEES: $5 day-use fee per vehicle
MAPS: Select "Brochures" and "Park Brochure" on the park website
PARK HOURS: 8am-sunset daily
TRAILHEAD: China Camp Group Campsite Parking Area
FACILITIES: Portable toilets at the trailhead, restrooms and drinking fountain at Back Ranch Meadows Campground
CONTACT: California State Parks, 415/456-0766, www.parks.ca.gov

START THE HIKE

▸ **MILE 0-1.1: China Camp Group Campsite Parking Area to Peace Trail Junction**

Begin hiking at the west end of the parking area, passing through the break in the fence onto **Shoreline Trail,** just before the **China Camp Group Campsite.** Turn right (north) onto the gravel path, following Shoreline Trail to the right (east) at a **junction** with Powerline Fire Trail. Continue straight (east) toward a wooden bridge, **Shoreline Trail Bridge 1.** On the trail post here, and throughout the hike, you may notice a marker for the San Francisco Bay Trail, connecting hundreds of miles of trails that circle the bay.

Follow the Shoreline Trail as it leads toward the San Pablo Bay and, at the wooden fence at 0.1 mile (0.2 km), make a sharp U-turn to the left (southwest), onto **Bay View Trail.** The trail gains 110 feet (34 m) in elevation, intersecting with Powerline Fire Road again at 0.4 mile (0.6 km). Look up and you are literally under power lines—follow them to the right (north). It will look like you are briefly using the fire road as a connector to continue on Bay View Trail as it switchbacks left (south) at a wooden bike-repair box on a post.

The hike follows the bends of the hill through madrones, oaks, bays, and toyons, with views of the bay just past the trees and shrubs. At 0.7 mile (1.1 km), the trail begins climbing a **series of switchbacks,** reaching the **intersection with Peace Trail** at 1.1 miles (1.8 km). Despite its name, this area can be less than peaceful; the trail is congested with bikers and hikers on their own routes, so be alert. While trail rules call for bikers to yield

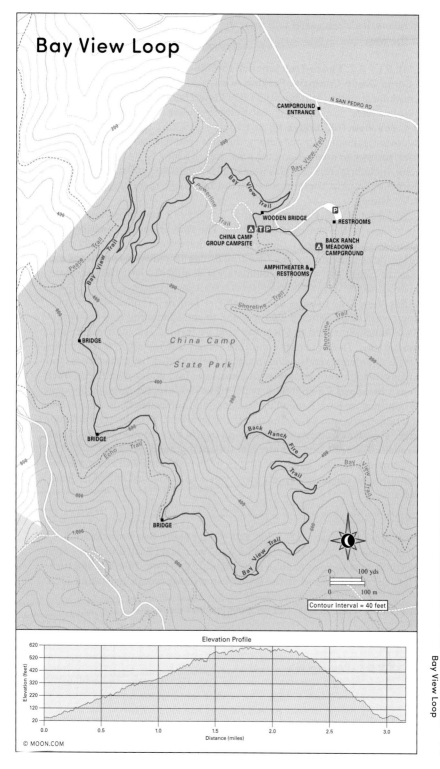

Bay View Loop

N SAN PEDRO RD

CAMPGROUND
ENTRANCE

Bay View Trail

Powerline
Trail

Peace Trail

Bay View Trail

P

WOODEN BRIDGE

RESTROOMS

CHINA CAMP
GROUP CAMPSITE

A T P

BACK RANCH
MEADOWS
CAMPGROUND

AMPHITHEATER &
RESTROOMS

Shoreline Trail

Shoreline Trail

China Camp

State Park

BRIDGE

Back Ranch Fire

Bay View Trail

BRIDGE

Echo Trail

Trail

BRIDGE

Bay View Trail

Bay View Trail

0   100 yds
0   100 m

Contour Interval = 40 feet

Elevation Profile

Elevation (feet)

620
520
420
320
220
120
20

0.0   0.5   1.0   1.5   2.0   2.5   3.0
Distance (miles)

© MOON.COM

to hikers, it's often easier and safer for hikers to find a place to move out of the way.

▶ **MILE 1.1–3.7: Peace Trail Junction to China Camp Group Campsite Parking Area**

Continue straight (southwest) on Bay View Trail. The next section of the hike has steep drop-offs as it peacefully meanders to another bridge crossing, **Bay View Trail Bridge 14,** at 1.4 miles (2.3 km). Here, and especially at other freshwater sources along the hike, you may see wildlife such as deer, turkeys, or quail. Along the hike, you also may be treated to bursts of color, including from Douglas irises, golden yarrows, milkmaids, and California milkworts. Looking out east, the salt marsh that borders the bay is now visible.

At 1.6 miles (2.6 km) and again at 2 miles (3.2 km), cross over wooden bridges as the trail steadily climbs. The **first bridge** is unmarked and rounds a curve, and you'll notice the path thereafter is increasingly rocky. After the second bridge, **Bay View Trail Bridge 12,** redwoods and ferns mix into the forest, and after approximately 0.25 mile (0.4 km), the trail starts to descend.

Bay View Trail reaches **Back Ranch Fire Trail** at 2.7 miles (4.3 km) on a downward slope before a transmission tower. Follow the trail marker for Back Ranch Fire Trail to Shoreline Trail by turning left (northwest) onto the fire road. The wide path continues steeply downward, first with views of the salt marsh and bay and into the forest of oaks, bays, madrones, and toyons, reaching a junction with Shoreline Trail and a gate to the **Back Ranch Meadows Campground** at 3.3 miles (5.3 km). Go through the gate to continue on Back Ranch Fire Trail, passing **campsites 12, 11, 10,** and **9** to the right (east), and follow the trail to the left (west) past the amphitheater area. The trails curves north, crossing over a low wooden bridge, **Camp Grounds Bridge 17,** and you arrive at the **campground restrooms.**

Complete the hike by proceeding past the restrooms, and when the trail splits, follow the driveway left (northwest) up to the east end of the parking area.

DIRECTIONS

From San Rafael, take U.S. 101 to exit 454 for North San Pedro Road. Keep right at the fork, following signs for San Pedro Road East, and merge onto North San Pedro Road to enter China Camp State Park. Take the first turnoff to the right and park in the China Camp Group Campsite Parking Area.

GPS COORDINATES: 38.0060, −122.4972; 38°0′21.6″ N, 122°29′49.9″ W

BEST NEARBY SIGHT

Make the time to head farther into China Camp State Park and visit the **China Camp Village.** The historic center of the park, a Chinese shrimp-fishing village thrived here in the 1800s. Explore the small museum and enjoy the family-friendly swimming beach access and snack shop. More details can be found on the park website.

NEARBY CAMPGROUNDS

NAME	DESCRIPTION	FACILITIES	SEASON	FEE
Pantoll	100 yards/91 m from the parking area on Mount Tamalpais	15 first-come, first-served sites, wheelchair-accessible sites available, potable water, firewood, restrooms with flush toilets, no showers	year-round	$25; pay at Pantoll Ranger Station

Mount Tamalpais State Park, Mill Valley, 415/388-2070, www.reservecalifornia.com

NAME	DESCRIPTION	FACILITIES	SEASON	FEE
Bootjack	about 100 yards/91 m from the parking area on Mount Tamalpais	16 first-come, first-served sites, wheelchair accessible sites available, potable water, firewood, restrooms with flush toilets, no showers	year-round	$25; pay at Pantoll Ranger Station

Mount Tamalpais State Park, Mill Valley, 415/388-2070, www.reservecalifornia.com

NEARBY CAMPGROUNDS (continued)

NAME	DESCRIPTION	FACILITIES	SEASON	FEE
Kirby Cove	nestled at the foot of the craggy Marin Headlands with beach access	5 overnight campsites, 2 accessible sites available, vault toilets, fire pits, barbecues, picnic tables, food lockers	year-round	$40

Fort Barry, Sausalito, 415/331-1540, www.recreation.gov

NAME	DESCRIPTION	FACILITIES	SEASON	FEE
Angel Island State Park	Walk-in or bike-in sites	13 campsites, 1 kayak-only site, 2 group sites, vault toilets, picnic tables, food lockers	year-round	from $30

Angel Island State Park, Tiburon, 415/435-1915, www.reservecalifornia.com

POINT REYES NATIONAL SEASHORE

Point Reyes National Seashore is home to over 1,500 species of plants and animals. Nature lovers can hike to the tip of Tomales Point among the tule elk and wildflowers, watch from a lighthouse as whales migrate along the coast, hear the loud call of northern elephant seals on the many beaches, and even catch a glimpse of leopard sharks and bat rays gliding through these protected waters. Point Reyes's popular Coast Trail, which meanders through creekside habitats and passes wetlands as you approach the ocean, is often used to branch off onto other trails, including this chapter's hikes to Secret Beach and Alamere Falls, a tide fall that flows directly into the Pacific Ocean.

Before exploring the national seashore, ensure that your gas tank is full, as there are no refueling stations within the park. The nearest is as far as 32 miles (52 km) away in Point Reyes Station.

▲ HERON AT ABBOTS LAGOON

▲ VIEW FROM INVERNESS RIDGE

◄ SECRET BEACH

1 **Tomales Point**
DISTANCE: 9.4 miles (15.1 km) round-trip
DURATION: 5 hours
EFFORT: Moderate

2 **Abbotts Lagoon**
DISTANCE: 3.3 miles (5.3 km) round-trip
DURATION: 1.5 hours
EFFORT: Easy

3 **Chimney Rock Trail**
DISTANCE: 1.9 miles (3.1 km)
DURATION: 1 hour
EFFORT: Easy-moderate

4 **Secret Beach**
DISTANCE: 7.6 miles (12.2 km) round-trip
DURATION: 4 hours
EFFORT: Moderate

5 **Inverness Ridge Loop**
DISTANCE: 5.2 miles (8.4 km) round-trip
DURATION: 2.5 hours
EFFORT: Easy-moderate

6 **Mount Wittenberg**
DISTANCE: 5.2 miles (8.4 km) round-trip
DURATION: 2.5 hours
EFFORT: Moderate

7 **Stairstep Falls**
DISTANCE: 2.3 miles (3.7 km) round-trip
DURATION: 1 hour
EFFORT: Easy

8 **Alamere Falls**
DISTANCE: 13.4 miles (21.6 km) round-trip
DURATION: 7 hours
EFFORT: Strenuous

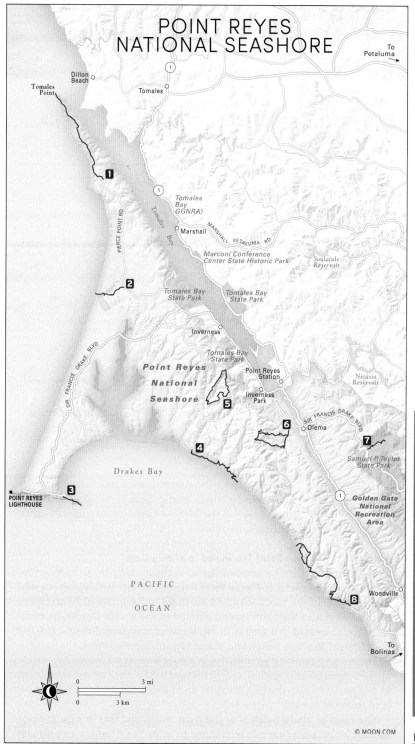

POINT REYES
NATIONAL SEASHORE

POINT REYES NATIONAL SEASHORE

1 Tomales Point

POINT REYES NATIONAL SEASHORE

🦌 ✻ 🏛 🚶

Tomales Point provides some of the best views of the Pacific Coast, Tomales Bay, and Bodega Bay, but the chance to see statuesque tule elk is the biggest draw.

BEST: Wildflower Hikes

DISTANCE: 9.4 miles (15.1 km) round-trip

DURATION: 5 hours

ELEVATION GAIN: 1,180 feet (360 m)

EFFORT: Moderate

TRAIL: Dirt fire road, sand, sea cliffs

USERS: Hikers, horseback riders

SEASON: Year-round

PASSES/FEES: None

MAPS: Tomales Point Map and North District Map, on the park website and at visitor centers

PARK HOURS: 6am-midnight daily

TRAILHEAD: Tomales Point Trailhead

FACILITIES: Vault toilets at McClures Beach parking lot, 0.2 mile (0.3 km) down Pierce Point Road from Tomales Point Trailhead

CONTACT: Point Reyes National Seashore, 415/464-5100, www. nps.gov/pore

START THE HIKE

Make sure to bring both sun and wind protection for this hike. The route is exposed and often extremely windy, particularly at Windy Gap and as you near Tomales Point. Exercise the highest caution along the sea cliffs, particularly as the peninsula narrows.

▶ MILE 0-1: Tomales Point Trailhead to Windy Gap

Find the trailhead at the northwest end of the parking lot at an interpretive display just south of **Pierce Point Ranch.** The dirt path wraps around the west side of the ranch, heading north for just 0.1 mile (0.2 km) before turning west and then continuing parallel to the Pacific Ocean. Immediately you're treated to a variety of wildflowers and coastal views, looking back toward McClure Beach and ahead toward Tomales Point.

There's no mistaking your arrival at **Windy Gap,** as it's incredibly windy at the 1-mile (1.6-km) mark. The trail follows the route of an old ranch road as it dips down into the gap, creating an opening for the wind to gust inland from the ocean.

The head of **White Gulch** is to the right (east), and this is a great place to start looking for tule elk, who come to drink from the ravine's stream

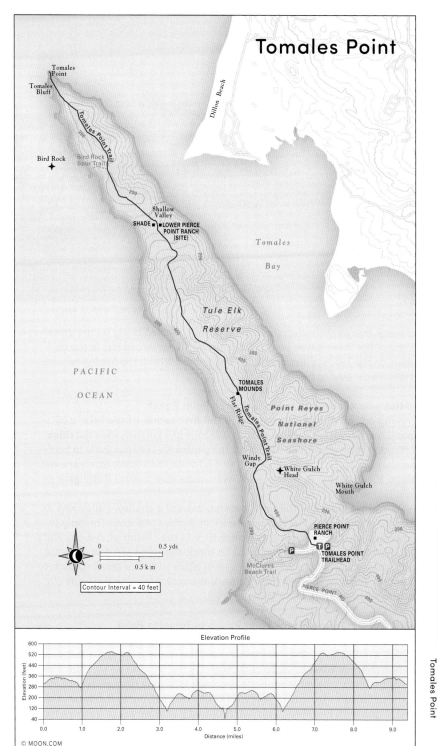

Tomales Point

Tomales Point

Tomales Bluff

Tomales Point Trail

Bird Rock

Bird Rock Spur Trail

Shallow Valley

SHADE ■ LOWER PIERCE POINT RANCH (SITE)

Tomales

Bay

Tule Elk Reserve

PACIFIC

OCEAN

TOMALES MOUNDS

Flat Ridge

Tomales Point Trail

Point Reyes

National

Seashore

Windy Gap

White Gulch Head

White Gulch Mouth

PIERCE POINT RANCH

P

T P

TOMALES POINT TRAILHEAD

McClures Beach Trail

PIERCE POINT RD

0   0.5 yds
0   0.5 km

Contour Interval = 40 feet

Elevation Profile

Elevation (feet)

600
520
440
360
280
200
120
40

0.0   1.0   2.0   3.0   4.0   5.0   6.0   7.0   8.0   9.0

Distance (miles)

© MOON.COM

or water trough. Tule elk, native to California, roamed freely on the grasslands of the Point Reyes peninsula until they were wiped out in the mid-1850s. In the 1970s, a reintroduction began with 10 elk; the herd grew and is now estimated to number over 300.

▸ MILE 1-3: Windy Gap to Lower Pierce Point Ranch

Coming out of Windy Gap, you begin the first ascent of the hike, a 270-foot (82-m) elevation gain over about 0.75 mile (0.8 km) to a wide flat **ridge.** Sprinkled throughout this section of the peninsula are spur trails to boulders, where some hikers choose to sit and view the sunset on clear evenings. If you decide to watch the sunset, make sure to have flashlights or headlamps.

At 2.2 miles (3.5 km) the trail descends toward a shallow valley and to the site of the **Lower Pierce Point Ranch** at 3 miles (4.8 km). The only indication that the settlement was once here is the cluster of cypress and eucalyptus trees that were planted to block the wind. This area is the only shaded part of the hike and an ideal place to take a break. Look for the stock pond on the east (right) side of the trail, which attracts tule elk, birds, and other animals.

▸ MILE 3-4.7: Lower Pierce Point Ranch to Tomales Point

Beyond the Lower Pierce Point Ranch, the trail is unmaintained. It is exposed, windy, sandy, often overgrown, and has many game trails that can be harrowingly close to steep cliff drop-offs. Be mindful as you pick the paths to follow; the most cautious approach is to stay toward the middle of the peninsula. Around 3.8 miles (6.1 km), look west, out to the ocean; the trail aligns with Bird Rock. This avian-dotted island serves as a refuge for seabirds and shorebirds.

▲ TOMALES POINT

Most of the paths on this section of the peninsula reconnect and merge into a single trail along the last 0.5 mile (0.8 km) out to **Tomales Point.** Proceed with caution: The end of the unmaintained portion and tip of the point collapsed in 2017. Additional sections of the cliff may collapse; dangerous areas may be indicated by small cracks in the ground, some several feet from the edge. Take in the views, but do not attempt any cliff scrambling. Standing on the convergence of Tomales Bay and the Pacific Ocean as the wind whips and the waves lap is plenty exhilarating.

Follow the trail back the way you came to return to the parking lot.

DIRECTIONS

From San Francisco, take U.S. 101 north for 18 miles (29 km) to exit 456 for Lucas Valley Road. Stay on Lucas Valley Road as it turns onto Nicasio Valley Road toward Nicasio for about 15 miles (24 km). Turn left onto Point Reyes-Petaluma Road, continue to Highway 1 in 6 miles (9.7 km), and turn left. Follow Highway 1 through Point Reyes Station to Sir Frances Drake Boulevard and turn right (west). After 6.4 miles (10.3 km) on Sir Frances Drake Boulevard, turn left onto Pierce Point Road and continue on the hilly road for 9 miles (14.5 km) to the trailhead parking lot.

GPS COORDINATES: 38.1889, −122.9540; 38°11'20" N, 122°57'14.4" W

BEST NEARBY BITES

If you're a sucker for popovers or are looking for a hearty meal, travel 30 minutes north from the trailhead to grab a seat inside or on the garden patio at **Station House Café** (11180 Hwy. 1, Point Reyes Station, 415/663-1515, 11am-7pm Sun.-Tues., noon-8pm Fri.-Sat., $12-30).

POINT REYES NATIONAL SEASHORE

Tomales Point

This often-overlooked trail offers the serenity of an easy stroll beside a pond and the calming effect of crashing waves on a beach without the crowds.

DISTANCE: 3.3 miles (5.3 km) round-trip
DURATION: 1.5 hours
ELEVATION GAIN: 120 feet (37 m)
EFFORT: Easy
TRAIL: Gravel, dirt, sand
USERS: Hikers, horseback riders
SEASON: Year-round
PASSES/FEES: None
MAPS: North District Map, on the park website and at visitor centers
PARK HOURS: 6am-midnight daily
TRAILHEAD: Abbotts Lagoon parking lot
FACILITIES: Accessible restrooms at the trailhead
CONTACT: Point Reyes National Seashore, 415/464-5100, www.nps.gov/pore

Birdwatchers are drawn to this trail for the variety of birds that flock to the area's three lagoons as well as its proximity to the ocean, marshes, and coastal grasslands. You may see the threatened western snowy plover, blue herons, ducks, quail, and even peregrine falcons, so bring your binoculars! In spring there's the additional joy of wildflowers to accompany the birdsong and brighten the trail.

START THE HIKE

The entirety of this trail is exposed, but you may not realize it with the usual cloud coverage; make sure to have sun protection even on the cloudiest days when visiting Point Reyes National Seashore. Note that after the footbridge the trail is considered unmaintained and there is no clear path. The National Park Service advises you to take note of your surroundings before exploring to ensure you can find the trail again for the return trip. On Abbotts Lagoon Beach, beware of the hazards of sneaker waves and strong currents. It is not safe to play near the water's edge. Note that every year from Memorial Day to Labor Day the beach area between the North Beach parking lot and the mouth of Abbotts Lagoon is closed to all public use on weekends and federal holidays to better ensure the survival of the western snowy plover.

▶ **MILE 0-0.9: Abbotts Lagoon Parking Lot to Footbridge**
The gravel beginning of the trail starts at the trailhead interpretive display on the west side of the **parking lot** and wanders southwest alongside a working ranch to the south. Cows leisurely graze in the pasture. At

Abbotts Lagoon

Point Reyes National Seashore

Elevation Profile

0.2 mile (0.3 km) the trail crosses a **wooden bridge** and proceeds along the ranch's fence line on the left side of the trail. The trail curves west and becomes more dirt than gravel, and the views of the middle lagoon begin to open. The easternmost lagoon, not seen from the trail, is the freshest water of the three, with the final, westernmost lagoon being the saltiest.

At 0.5 mile (0.8 km) is a bench overlooking the **middle lagoon** and an interpretive display titled "Restoration of the Seashore's Dunes." It explains that while the dunes may appear somewhat barren, they are actually teeming with life. Here you can learn some of the impact of when nonnative invasive plants are introduced to a habitat, and the life on the dunes in need of protection, including clover lupine and beach *Layia*.

Just a bit farther, at 0.6 mile (1 km), the trail transitions to a **wooden boardwalk** for 530 feet (162 m) over a marsh, continuing along the fence line, before returning to dirt and gravel. The trail becomes mostly sand, and around the time you notice that, you may start noticing the life of the middle lagoon.

As you approach the **footbridge** at 0.9 mile (1.4 km), watch for river otters playing, herons fishing, and ducks paddling in the water.

▶ **MILE 0.9–1.6: Footbridge to Pacific Ocean**
The footbridge crosses over a stream that connects the westernmost **two lagoons.** From here, the trail enters the Phillip Burton Wilderness, where the trail is considered unmaintained. Stick to following the north side of the lagoon and continue another 0.75 mile (1.2 km) to the **Pacific Ocean.** Look for driftwood that has found its resting place in the sand and the many remnants from birds feeding on small crabs.

When you've had your fill of the sand-scape for the day, return the way you came.

ABBOTTS LAGOON ▲

DIRECTIONS

From San Francisco, take U.S. 101 north for 18 miles (29 km) to exit 456 for Lucas Valley Road. Stay on Lucas Valley Road as it turns onto Nicasio Valley Road toward Nicasio for about 15 miles (24 km). Turn left onto Point Reyes-Petaluma Road, continue to Highway 1 in 6 miles (9.7 km), and turn left. Follow Highway 1 through Point Reyes Station until Sir Frances Drake Boulevard and turn right (west). After 6.4 miles (10.3 km) on Sir Frances Drake Boulevard, turn left onto Pierce Point Road and continue for 3.4 miles (5.5 km) to the Abbotts Lagoon parking lot, on the left side of the road.

GPS COORDINATES: 38.1235, −122.9355; 38°7′24.6″ N, 122°56′7.8″ W

BEST NEARBY BITES AND BREWS

Inverness Park Market & Tap Room (12301 Sir Frances Drake Blvd., Inverness Park, 415/663-1491, https://invernessparkmarket.com) is equally proud of their conservation efforts and their organic, home-made, farm-fresh, locally sourced food. Grab a sandwich, bagel, or burrito from the Market + Deli Kitchen (7am-8am Mon.-Thurs., 7am-9am Fri.-Sat., $5-16) or have a pour of a local brew and try a Tap Room Special in the Tap Room (4pm-9pm Tues.-Sat., $12-21).

🦌 ❀ 🏛 🚶

On the Chimney Rock Trail, hikers are delighted with sights of the area's wildlife: northern elephant seals lounging, common murres nesting, whale sightings, and more.

BEST: Winter Hikes

DISTANCE: 1.9 miles (3.1 km)

DURATION: 1 hour

ELEVATION GAIN: 180 feet (55 m)

EFFORT: Easy-moderate

TRAIL: Dirt

USERS: Hikers, horseback riders

SEASON: Year-round

PASSES/FEES: None

MAPS: Chimney Rock Area Map, on the park website and at visitor centers

PARK HOURS: 6am-midnight daily

TRAILHEAD: Chimney Rock Trailhead

FACILITIES: Vault toilets at the trailhead, accessible restrooms near Point Reyes Lighthouse disabled parking

CONTACT: Point Reyes National Seashore, 415/464-5100, www.nps.gov/pore

START THE HIKE

As with all trails in Point Reyes National Seashore, do not take game trails, obey trail closure signs, and be extremely cautious near any bluffs and cliffs, which may crumble at any time. This area is typically very windy, so bring a windbreaker or jacket, secure loose items, and keep children close.

▶ **MILE 0-0.4: Chimney Rock Trailhead to Lookout Tower Road**

Start this short hike at the southeast end of the **parking lot,** just past the restrooms at the trailhead sign that details the variety of wildflowers that can be found along the trail in spring. To the left (east) stretches Drakes Bay, with fishing docks and elephant seals often lounging on the beach near the historic U.S. Coast Guard Boathouse at the end of Chimney Rock Road. It's not unusual to hear the seals barking before you find them along the coast. To the right (west), the rugged coastline meets the wide-open Pacific Ocean. The National Park Service urges visitors to be cautious for the entirety of this hike, as the cliffs of the Chimney Rock Headlands are likely to crumble and slide, and it is of utmost importance to stay behind fencing and on the main trail through the center of the peninsula.

At 0.4 mile (0.6 km), the trail is at the narrowest section of the peninsula and intersects with **Lookout Tower Road,** which once led to a since-crumbled lookout tower. On the return trip, some hikers take this road down to Chimney Rock Road and continue to the popular **Elephant Seal Overlook;**

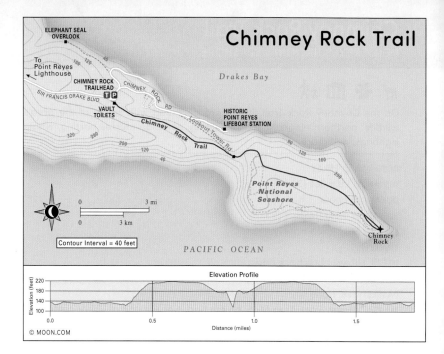

Chimney Rock Trail

ELEPHANT SEAL OVERLOOK

To Point Reyes Lighthouse

CHIMNEY ROCK TRAILHEAD

SIR FRANCIS DRAKE BLVD

VAULT TOILETS

Drakes Bay

CHIMNEY ROCK RD

Chimney Rock Trail

Lookout Tower Rd

HISTORIC POINT REYES LIFEBOAT STATION

Point Reyes National Seashore

Chimney Rock

PACIFIC OCEAN

Contour Interval = 40 feet

0   3 mi
0   3 km

Elevation Profile

© MOON.COM

it's 0.9 mile (1.4 km) from this intersection to the overlook and back to the parking lot.

▶ MILE 0.4-0.9: Lookout Tower Road to Chimney Rock Viewpoint

Pass Lookout Tower Road and remain on the main trail as it briefly leads uphill through sand and brush and then remains relatively level prior to a descent to the viewpoint. You may catch sight of a Point Reyes resident coyote, prairie dogs, or whales migrating along the coast. When you arrive at Chimney Rock Viewpoint, take a seat on one of the benches and look out to watch the seabirds land on the rocks below. Without a map it's hard to tell which one, but one of those rocks was once stacked like a chimney, which gave the trail its name.

To get back to the parking lot, return the way you came.

DIRECTIONS

From San Francisco, take U.S. 101 north for 18 miles (29 km) to exit 456 for Lucas Valley Road. Stay on Lucas Valley Road as it turns onto Nicasio Valley Road toward Nicasio for about 15 miles (24 km). Turn left onto Point Reyes-Petaluma Road, continue to Highway 1 in 6 miles (9.7 km), and turn left. Follow

▲ CHIMNEY ROCK

Highway 1 through Point Reyes Station until Sir Frances Drake Boulevard and turn right (west). Stay on Sir Frances Drake Boulevard for approximately 18 miles (29 km) until you reach the junction with Chimney Rock Road. Turn left and follow Chimney Rock Road 0.9 mile (1.4 km) to the Chimney Rock parking lot. Proceed with caution: Chimney Rock Road is a two-way road, even though it's only about 10 feet (3 m) wide.

GPS COORDINATES: 37.9952, −122.9800; 37°59′42.7″ N, 122°58′48″ W

BEST NEARBY SIGHT

For a fully immersive Point Reyes experience, a visit to the nearby **Point Reyes Lighthouse** is a must. The lighthouse was built in 1870 and retired from service after more than 100 years of warning mariners. Today an automated light is used, but the historic lighthouse continues to welcome visitors to Point Reyes. The accessible Observation Deck is open 6am-9:45pm daily; to reach the lighthouse itself you must hike down and back up 313 stairs—the equivalent of about 30 stories.

The lighthouse visitor center has a wealth of things to learn, including information on the local climate and wildlife and the Fresnel lens. The attached Ocean Exploration Center has a hands-on experience for visitors of all ages.

The short 2.4-mile (3.9-km), 10-minute drive between the parking lots of the lighthouse and Chimney Rock Trail means these two are often visited in tandem. Consider starting with the Point Reyes Lighthouse early, to beat the crowds, and then make your way to the Chimney Rock Trail parking lot.

POINT REYES NATIONAL SEASHORE

Chimney Rock Trail

155

This hike offers panoramic ocean views, the chance to explore tide pools and sea caves, and a showstopping natural amphitheater.

BEST: Coastal Hikes

DISTANCE: 7.6 miles (12.2 km) round-trip

DURATION: 4 hours

ELEVATION GAIN: 600 feet (183 m)

EFFORT: Moderate

TRAIL: Dirt fire road, gravel, sand, rock

USERS: Hikers, beachcombers, mountain bikers on part of the trail, horseback riders on part of the trail, leashed dogs on part of the trail

SEASON: Year-round

PASSES/FEES: None

MAPS: South District Map, on the park website and at visitor centers

PARK HOURS: 6am-midnight daily

TRAILHEAD: Limantour Beach parking lot

FACILITIES: Vault toilets at the trailhead and Coast Campground

CONTACT: Point Reyes National Seashore, 415/464-5100, www.nps.gov/pore

START THE HIKE

Only attempt this hike near a negative tide. Understanding and researching the tide chart for this area is critical, and this hike can be challenging to safely complete at some low tides; it depends on how low. Sneaker waves, rip currents, and hypothermia are very real hazards of visiting Point Reyes beaches.

▶ **MILE 0-1.8: Parking Lot to Coast Campground**

From the southeast corner of the **parking lot,** pass through the wooden fence near the trash receptacles onto a sandy single-track. Just prior to arriving at the beach, a sign indicates the 500-foot (152-m) area that leashed dogs are limited to visit.

Head left (east), with the ocean to your right. Whenever you have a view of the water along this hike is a great opportunity to look for whales, dolphins, seals, and sea lions in the ocean. On land it's not uncommon to see quail and deer.

At 0.6 mile (1 km), turn away from the water toward the **sole pine tree** along the **sand dunes.** There's a break in the sand dunes that leads about 500 feet (152 m) through coastal scrub up to the **Coast Trail.** This section of the Coast Trail is a dirt-and-gravel fire road that rangers routinely use, so be aware that vehicles and bicycles may approach from either direction. Turn right (southeast) onto the trail.

Elevation Profile

© MOON.COM

The trail meanders parallel to the coast, with beach views to the south and rolling hills on the north side. Enter a small coastal valley to arrive at **Coast Campground,** at 1.8 miles (2.9 km), with potable water, vault toilets, and trash bins.

▶ MILE 1.8–3.3: Coast Campground to Sculptured Beach

From the campground, Coast Trail begins to rise at a steeper grade as it weaves alternately toward and away from the ocean over the next mile (1.6 km). At 3.1 miles (5 km), look for a hitching post and trail marker showing you've arrived at the cliffs above **Sculptured Beach,** named for the rocky shoreline that becomes exposed at low tide. Carefully follow the path down the bluff and a wooden staircase 0.2 mile (0.3 km) to the beach. Take extra caution at the base of the stairs, where the ground easily crumbles underfoot. If it is not near low tide when you reach this point, it's strongly advised you not venture beyond the sandy area.

▶ MILE 3.3–3.8: Sculptured Beach to Secret Beach

From Sculptured Beach, head left (south). Staying close to the base of the cliffs, you will find footholds to scramble up the few feet required to continue atop the rocks. An established path hugs the curve of the bluff, first leading out toward the water and then back in, where thousands of mussels appear like a black carpet on the rocks below.

The loose gravel path dead-ends, and scrambling down to the sand requires caution. Stay close to the cliff wall until you can only proceed by passing through an arch to a sandy beach. You've now entered **Secret Beach,** which continues south to Point Resistance. Walk toward the "thumb" sea stack, crossing over a creek running through the sand to the ocean at around 3.7 miles (6 km). Just past the sea stack is the final arch of this hike. Depending on the tide level, you can attempt to go around the ocean side of the rock or through the arch. Either route requires taking calculated steps to avoid treading on mussels and other organisms. Bear in mind that the water can be deeper than it appears, and your feet may sink deep into saturated sand near the water's edge.

▶ **MILE 3.8-7.6: Secret Beach to Parking Lot**
Immediately past the arch, look for the triangle-shaped entrance to the **Point Reyes Amphitheater** to the left (north). The entrance tunnel is no more than 10 feet (3 m) long, but the height can vary based on the amount of sand brought in at high tide. The amphitheater gets its name from its open-air circular shape and high walls, created by erosion. Standing at its center, you can feel the pressure of the limited time this special place has to offer visitors, not unlike the limited time you have before you need to leave, before the tide returns, and go back the way you came.

DIRECTIONS

From San Francisco, take U.S. 101 north for 11.8 miles (19 km) and take exit 450B toward San Anselmo. Merge onto Sir Frances Drake Boulevard and continue northwest for 20.4 miles (33 km) to Highway 1. Turn onto Highway 1 north for just 0.1 mile (0.2 km) before turning left onto Bear Valley Road. Continue on Bear Valley Road for 1.8 miles (2.9 km) before turning left onto Limantour Road. Proceed for 7.5 miles (12.1 km) before turning left onto the spur road that leads to the parking lot. Parking in the main parking lot by turning right adds an additional 0.8 mile (1.3 km) to the hike.

GPS COORDINATES: 38.0262, −122.8769; 38°1'34.3" N, 122°52'36.8" W

BEST NEARBY BITES AND BREWS
At **Palace Market** (11300 Hwy. 1, Point Reyes Station, 415/663-1016, www.palacemarket.com, 8am-8pm daily), you can pull together a meal of your liking at any price point with the array of tasty local specialties, house-made fresh foods, wine and spirits, necessary grocery finds, and the best deal in town—vanilla, chocolate, or swirl soft-serve buffalo milk gelato ($3.50-7).

Witness the majestic fog filling the flanks of the ridge and filtering the sun's light through the trees along this forest loop.

DISTANCE: 5.2 miles (8.4 km) round-trip

DURATION: 2.5 hours

ELEVATION GAIN: 1,050 feet (320 m)

EFFORT: Easy-moderate

TRAIL: Dirt, gravel, paved road

USERS: Hikers, horseback riders, mountain bikers on Inverness Ridge

SEASON: Year-round

PASSES/FEES: None

MAPS: North District Map, on the park website and at visitor centers

PARK HOURS: 6am-midnight daily

TRAILHEAD: Bayview Trailhead

FACILITIES: None

CONTACT: Point Reyes National Seashore, 415/464-5100, www.nps.gov/pore

START THE HIKE

Hikers can take this loop in either direction, but most prefer to take it counterclockwise by starting the loop on the Inverness Ridge Trail, versus the Bayview Trail.

Note that for a portion of Inverness Ridge Trail you are on an in-use paved road, and starting at 1.2 miles (1.9 km), private property stands close to the trail. Be cautious on the road and remain on the trail near the homes and structures.

▶ **MILE 0-1.5: Bayview Trailhead to Drakes View Trail Junction**
Inverness Ridge Trail starts on a fire road beyond the gate at the north end of the parking lot. The trail rolls mildly north along the Inverness Ridge for the first mile (1.6 km), with the view almost immediately opening to the west. On a lightly foggy morning, seeing the fog sit amid the flanks of the ridge is enchanting. When it's clear, you can see out to Drakes Esteros or beyond.

At 0.9 mile (1.4 km), look for the trail marker for Inverness Ridge Trail. The marker also lists Drakes View Trail ahead in 0.8 mile (1.3 km). Following the paved road, look for another trail marker, indicating that Inverness Ridge Trail continues 200 feet (61 m) on the left. At 1 mile (1.6 km), turn off the road and up a dirt path into the forest for some brief shade. Over the next 0.5 mile (0.8 km), the trail gains about 260 feet (79 m) elevation to the hike's highest point (about 1,060 ft/323 m).

Inverness Ridge, sometimes called the backbone of the Point Reyes Peninsula, acts as a wind barrier and blocks the residents of Point Reyes

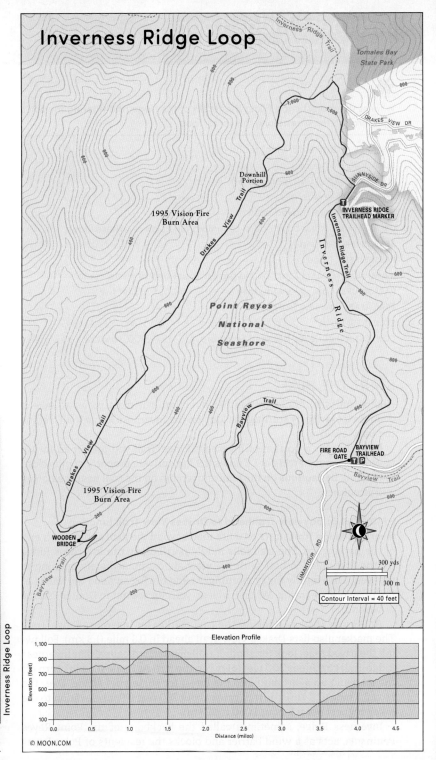

Inverness Ridge Loop

Tomales Bay State Park

DRAKES VIEW DR

SUNNYSIDE DR

INVERNESS RIDGE TRAILHEAD MARKER

Inverness Ridge Trail

Downhill Portion

Drakes View Trail

1995 Vision Fire Burn Area

Inverness Ridge Trail

I n v e r n e s s   R i d g e

Point Reyes

National

Seashore

Bayview Trail

FIRE ROAD GATE

BAYVIEW TRAILHEAD

Bayview Trail

Drakes View Trail

1995 Vision Fire Burn Area

WOODEN BRIDGE

Bayview Trail

LIMANTOUR RD

0   300 yds

0   300 m

Contour Interval = 40 feet

Elevation Profile

Elevation (feet)

1,100 / 900 / 700 / 500 / 300 / 100

0.0   0.5   1.0   1.5   2.0   2.5   3.0   3.5   4.0   4.5

Distance (miles)

▲ INVERNESS RIDGE LOOP

Station from seeing a full sunset. After just under than 0.5 mile (0.8 km) from where you turned off the road is the first of several homes and structures atop the ridge to the right (east). Stay on the trail and look for the monkey flower, with its tubular orange flowers and blossoms that resemble a monkey's face sticking out its tongue. Continue to the **junction** with Drakes View Trail at 1.5 miles (2.4 km).

▶ **MILE 01.5–3.4: Drakes View Trail Junction to Wooden Bridge**

At the junction, you will see the trail marker for Drakes View Trail. Turn left (southwest) onto **Drakes View Trail.** The duration of the hike on Drakes View Trail is downhill, beginning in the intermittent shade of Bishop pines, whose needles soften the path.

Despite the trail name, there are few views beyond the forest on this section of the hike. Throughout the hike's loop you will still see close-up the damage and recovery from the 1995 Vision Fire. A major historical event for the Point Reyes National Seashore and West Marin County, it started from smoldering embers in an illegal campsite and burned over 12,000 acres. Within a couple of years, plantlife was springing back, as found on the trail, including lupines, huckleberries, ceanothus (resembles lilac), and coffeeberry. Starting on Drakes View Trail, you can also find a bounty of white and purple sweet peas.

Beginning at 3.3 miles (5.3 km), the trail has a few **switchbacks** and crosses a **wooden bridge** at 3.4 miles (5.5 km).

▶ **MILE 3.4–5.2: Wooden Bridge to Bayview Trailhead**

After crossing the bridge, look for the trail marker that leads onto **Bayview Trail.** The trail runs south for 0.4 miles (0.6 km) before curving northeast, requiring an uphill finish that gains 620 feet (189 m) elevation over the

POINT REYES NATIONAL SEASHORE

Inverness Ridge Loop

INVERNESS RIDGE LOOP ▲

final 1.8 miles (2.9 km). At 4.9 miles (7.9 km), the trail curves south again, with views of Inverness Ridge through the trees on a sunny day.

The trail turns due east for the last 0.1 mile (0.2 km) to return to the trailhead.

DIRECTIONS

From San Francisco, take U.S. 101 north for 11.8 miles (19 km) and take exit 450B toward San Anselmo. Merge onto Sir Frances Drake Boulevard and continue northwest for 20.4 miles (33 km) to Highway 1. Turn onto Highway 1 north for just 0.1 mile (0.2 km) before turning left onto Bear Valley Road. Continue on Bear Valley Road for 1.8 miles (2.9 km) before turning left onto Limantour Road. Proceed for 4.4 miles (7.1 km) and look for the Bayview Trailhead Parking on the right side of the road.

GPS COORDINATES: 38.0591, −122.8504; 38°3′32.8″ N, 122°51′1.4″ W

BEST NEARBY BITES

From the trailhead, head north 14 miles (22.5 km) to **Tony's Seafood Restaurant** (18863 Shoreline Hwy., Marshall, 415/663-1107, https://hogislandoysters.com, 11am-4pm Mon.-Tues. and Thurs., 11am-7:30pm Fri.-Sun., $16-40, dog-friendly), with both indoor and outdoor seating right on Tomales Bay. Get your fill of fresh oysters or enjoy gluten-free fish-and-chips. The drink menu has local brews on tap and wine from Northern California and around the world.

This loop will take you up through a shaded forest to the highest peak of Point Reyes Peninsula (1,407 ft/429 m) and a bird's-eye view of Drakes Bay.

DISTANCE: 5.2 miles (8.4 km) round-trip

DURATION: 2.5 hours

ELEVATION GAIN: 1,300 feet (396 m)

EFFORT: Moderate

TRAIL: Gravel, dirt

USERS: Hikers, horseback riders

SEASON: Year-round

PASSES/FEES: None

MAPS: South District Map, on the park website and at visitor centers

PARK HOURS: 6am–midnight daily

TRAILHEAD: Bear Valley Trailhead

FACILITIES: Restrooms in Bear Valley Visitor Center, before reaching trailhead parking

CONTACT: Point Reyes National Seashore, 415/464-5100, www.nps.gov/pore

If you're an aspiring peak bagger and summit seeker, you can easily add this one to your list, although it's at low elevation and without a view. It's still fun to find the U.S. Geological Survey marker, and the summit is a great place to take a break for a snack before heading to the middle section of the hike, where you can catch a beautiful coastal view.

START THE HIKE

This hike has a significant elevation gain of 1,300 feet (396 m) over 2 miles (3.2 km), and the Meadow Trail has a 920-foot (280-m) descent over 1.6 miles (2.6 km), so make sure you're prepared. That may mean a slow ascent for some and thick-toed socks and protected toes for the way down.

▶ **MILE 0-1.8: Bear Valley Trailhead to Z Ranch Trail**
Make your way to the **Bear Valley Trailhead** at the southwest corner of the parking lot and what looks like the road continuing beyond the gate. Take the wide gravel path for just 0.2 mile (0.3 km) and turn right (west) away from the crowds and onto **Mount Wittenberg Trail.** The trail immediately leads up into the lush forest. Look down at the dirt path to watch for roots, but don't forget to look around as the trail gently winds up toward the base of Mount Wittenberg. Notice the forest's recovery from past fire damage, and where the trees part just right, you can catch glimpses of Olema Valley to the east. At 1.8 miles (2.9 km) you leave the shade of the forest and enter a meadow, where Mount Wittenberg Trail meets **Z Ranch Trail.**

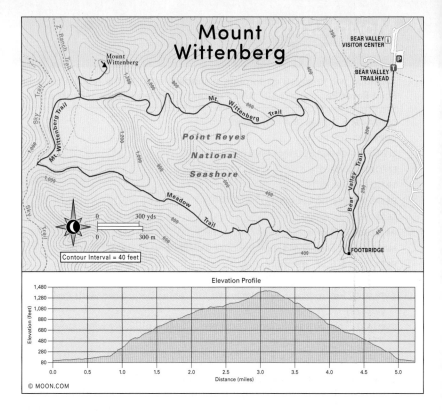

Mount Wittenberg

Point Reyes National Seashore

BEAR VALLEY VISITOR CENTER

BEAR VALLEY TRAILHEAD

FOOTBRIDGE

Contour Interval = 40 feet

0   300 yds
0   300 m

Elevation Profile

© MOON.COM

▶ **MILE 1.8–2.1: Z Ranch Trail to Mount Wittenberg Summit**

Follow the summit trail sign to take the 0.3-mile (0.5-km) path to ascend another 100 feet (30 m) to the **summit** of Mount Wittenberg. At one time the summit provided unobstructed views, until the forest recovery from a mid-1990s fire allowed Douglas fir thickets to grow and envelop the summit. It may look like there is a path that continues beyond the USGS marker, but following it in hopes of a view will lead to disappointment; it quickly splits into game trails running in various directions.

▶ **MILE 2.1–2.8: Mount Wittenberg Summit to Meadow Trail**

Return the way you came to head down the summit and continue on Mount Wittenberg Trail toward Sky Trail for 0.4 mile (0.6 km). This short part of the trail is exposed, but when the skies are clear it provides breathtaking views of the moon-shaped coast of Drakes Bay, including Limantour Spit and the mouth of Drakes Esteros. It's helpful to have the Point Reyes National Seashore official park brochure map for orientation.

At 2.8 miles (4.5 km), look for the trail marker for **Meadow Trail** to the left (east) indicating 1.6 miles (2.6 km) to Bear Valley Trail and 2.4 miles (3.9 km) to the Bear Valley Trailhead.

▶ **MILE 2.8–5.2: Meadow Trail to Bear Valley Trailhead**

Follow Meadow Trail as it descends into the forest and across meadows, with a handful of steep sections, until you reach a **footbridge** crossing the

▲ MOUNT WITTENBERG TRAIL

Bear Valley Creek, which connects Meadow Trail to Bear Valley Trail. Turn left onto **Bear Valley Trail** and follow the relatively flat path along the creek for 0.8 mile (1.3 km) back to the trailhead.

DIRECTIONS

From San Francisco, take U.S. 101 north for 11.8 miles (19 km) and take exit 450B toward San Anselmo. Merge onto Sir Frances Drake Boulevard and continue northwest for 20.4 miles (33 km) to Highway 1. Turn onto Highway 1 north for just 0.1 mile (0.2 km) before turning left onto Bear Valley Road. After 0.5 mile (0.8 km), turn left onto Bear Valley Visitor Center Access Road. Park in the large parking lot past Bear Valley Welcome Center. The trail is where it looks like the road continues past the gate.

GPS COORDINATES: 38.0402, −122.7997; 38°2'24.7" N, 122°47'58.9" W

BEST NEARBY BITES

Less than 10 minutes from the trailhead, **Side Street Kitchen** (60 4th St., Point Reyes Station, 415/663-0303, https://sidestreet-prs.com, 11am-6pm Wed.-Thurs., $8-24) is a great pick for the entire family, with dog-friendly patio seating. Known for their spice-rubbed rotisserie chicken and crispy brussels sprouts, the kind-natured staff here will make you feel at home.

This mostly shaded and fern-filled trail will take you over a salmon-spawning stream and to the gentle 40-foot (12-m) Stairstep Falls of Samuel P. Taylor State Park.

DISTANCE: 2.3 miles (3.7 km) round-trip
DURATION: 1 hour
ELEVATION GAIN: 290 feet (88 m)
EFFORT: Easy
TRAIL: Paved road, dirt, single-track
USERS: Hikers, mountain bikers on Bill's Trail, horseback riders on Bill's Trail
SEASON: Year-round
PASSES/FEES: None
MAPS: "Golden Gate National Recreation Area" by Dave Nalley, "Trails of West Marin" by Pease Press, www.avenzamaps.com
PARK HOURS: 8am-sunset daily
TRAILHEAD: Sir Frances Drake Boulevard
FACILITIES: Vault toilets just past the first Devil's Gulch group campsite, on Devil's Gulch Road, near the start of the hike
CONTACT: Samuel P. Taylor State Park, 415/488-9897, www.parks.ca.gov

START THE HIKE

Since parking is across busy Sir Frances Drake Boulevard, be excessively cautious crossing the winding road and as you begin the hike on Devil's Gulch Road. A 0.5 mile (0.8 km) section of this hike utilizes part of Bill's Trail, and according to the state park website, portions of it close during the rainy season. Make sure to check the park's website or call to check for closures. Once on Stairstep Falls Trail, look out for poison oak along this narrower and slightly overgrown section of the hike.

To get to the vault toilets, either continue on the road to the toilets and then come back on the road to the dirt path, as described below, or proceed on the road past the vault toilets for 0.1 mile (0.2 km), pass horse stalls, and get on the trail just past the campground on the right. This leads down toward the creek in less than 0.1 mile (0.2 km) to the Salmon Crossing Bridge.

▶ **MILE 0-0.3: Devil's Gulch Road Trailhead to Salmon Crossing Bridge**
Start the hike where **Sir Frances Drake Boulevard** intersects with **Devil's Gulch Road.** Devil's Gulch Road is open to vehicles, but the narrow paved road only leads to parking for overnight campers. The Devil's Gulch Creek is on the right (south), and the hike leaves the road at 0.1 mile (0.2 km) onto **Devil's Gulch Trail,** a dirt path that runs between the road and the creek without a trail name sign. Look for the post with signs indicating that no dogs, bikes, or horses are allowed on the trail. Shortly farther along is a

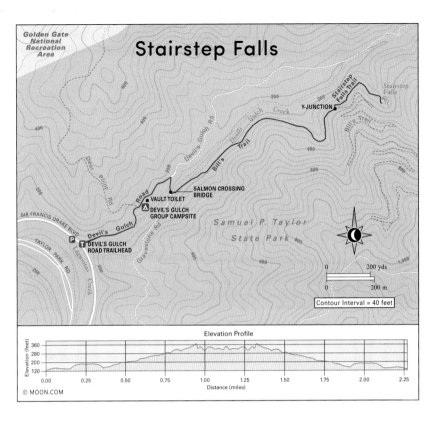

Stairstep Falls

Elevation Profile

faded interpretive display that details the spawning of salmon and steel-head trout in the creek. As you walk, be sure to watch for salmon in the creek.

Continue another 0.2 mile (0.3 km) alongside the creek, crossing a few **footbridges.** Around 0.3 mile (0.5 km) you arrive at a towering redwood, hollowed at its base, on the left. On the right is another faded interpretive display titled "You Are Entering Salmon Country," immediately before you reach a **bridge** decorated with wooden cutouts of salmon painted red and a "salmon crossing" sign. Cross the bridge.

▶ MILE 0.3–1: Salmon Crossing Bridge to Stairstep Falls Trail

On the other side of the bridge, turn left (northeast) to see a trail marker for **Bill's Trail,** with Stairstep Falls Trail listed as 0.6 mile (1 km) ahead. Bill's Trail is a 4-mile (6.4-km) multiuse path frequented by bicyclists, so listen for their approach. As the trail gains elevation with steep drop-offs on the creek side (now on your left), you come across several thick, short stag-gered logs, likely used to help cyclists maintain speed going downhill. Af-ter crossing a few more bridges, at 1 mile (1.6 km) is a narrow **Y-junction,** where **Stairstep Falls Trail** splits down and to the left from Bills Trail.

▶ MILE 1–1.1: Stairstep Falls Trail to Stairstep Falls

Head left (north) on Stairstep Falls Trail. There are no bikes allowed on the trail, which narrows and is overgrown in parts as it gently continues

STAIRSTEP FALLS TRAIL ▲

uphill. The short 0.2-mile (0.3-km) trail ends at **a wooden fence** just past a bench, and **Stairstep Falls** is tucked back in vegetation past the end of the path. From the limited viewing area, it can be difficult to see the falls flow down the narrow steps due to overgrown brush and deadfall, and as a result, it is not a particularly photogenic waterfall. Even so, to sit on the bench and listen to the falls is incredibly soothing and enriches the experience of being surrounded by the forest.

Return the way you came.

DIRECTIONS

From San Francisco, take U.S. 101 north for 11.8 miles (19 km) and take exit 450B toward San Anselmo. Merge onto Sir Frances Drake Boulevard and continue northwest for 16.2 miles (26 km). One mile (1.6 km) after seeing the entrance for Samuel P. Taylor State Park, look for Devil's Gulch Road, on the right. Do not drive onto Devil's Gulch Road, but immediately look for parking on the left side of Sir Frances Drake Boulevard.

GPS COORDINATES: 38.0298, −122.7369; 38°1'47.3" N, 122°44'12.8" W

BEST NEARBY BITES

Olema House Due West Tavern & Market (10005 Coastal Hwy. 1, Olema, 415/663-9000, https://olemahouse.com) is a centrally located market (7am-4pm daily) and sit-down restaurant (4pm-9pm Mon.-Thurs., noon-9pm Fri.-Sat., noon-8pm Sun., $19-39) just 4 miles (6.4 km) north of the trailhead. The market offers a coffee bar and quick-grab beer, wine, and gourmet food. The menu at the tavern is short but packs flavor.

8 Alamere Falls

POINT REYES NATIONAL SEASHORE

A bucket-list hike for many, this strenuous trail traverses towering coastal cliffs overlooking the ocean, past forested lakes, and along crashing waves to the stunning 40-foot (12-m) tide falls known as Alamere Falls.

BEST: Waterfall Hikes

DISTANCE: 13.4 miles (21.6 km) round-trip

DURATION: 7 hours

ELEVATION GAIN: 1,870 feet (570 m)

EFFORT: Strenuous

TRAIL: Dirt fire road, gravel, roots, single-track

USERS: Hikers, runners, horseback riders

SEASON: Year-round

PASSES/FEES: None

MAPS: South District Map and Alamere Falls Map, on the park website and at visitor centers

PARK HOURS: 6am-midnight daily

TRAILHEAD: Palomarin Trailhead

FACILITIES: Vault toilets at the trailhead and Wildcat Campground, potable water at Wildcat Campground

CONTACT: Point Reyes National Seashore, 415/464-5100, www.nps.gov/pore

START THE HIKE

Do not attempt routes to Alamere Falls that are not recommended by the National Park Service. Other routes or shortcuts are not maintained and endanger hikers and their rescuers and can damage the land. Understanding and researching the tide chart for this area is critical (www.usharbors.com/harbor/california/point-reyes-ca/tides). Plan to be on the beach portion of this hike during low tide.

▶ MILE 0-2.8: Palomarin Trailhead to Bass Lake

The **Palomarin Trailhead** is just north of the parking lot, on the other side of the vault toilets. Begin hiking on **Coast Trail,** and at 0.1 mile (0.2 km), pass the spur trail for Palomarin Beach Trail to the left (south), and continue straight.

You reach a **picnic table and hitching post** at 0.4 mile (0.6 km). From here, the trail meanders along near the top of an ocean bluff with steep drop-offs and loose gravel, briefly turning inland at 0.6 mile (1 km) and passing over a **bridge** before curving back toward the ocean.

At 1.1 miles (1.8 km), Coast Trail heads northeast, leaving the ocean views. The trail dips into a ravine and crosses another **bridge** at 1.4 miles

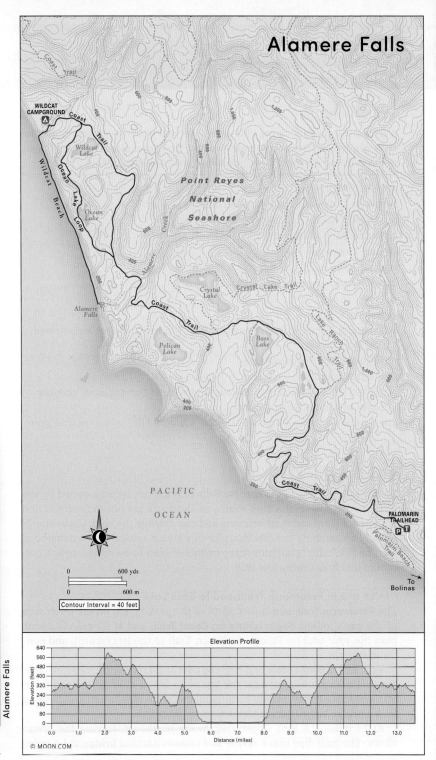

© MOON.COM

▲ ALAMERE FALLS

(2.3 km) before ascending approximately 300 feet (91 m) to the **junction** with Lake Ranch Trail at 2.2 miles (3.5 km). Stay on Coast Trail, and after passing a few small ponds, you reach **Bass Lake** at 2.8 miles (4.5 km).

▸ **MILE 2.8–5.2: Bass Lake to Wildcat Lake**
Passing the northeastern edge of Bass Lake, the trail steadily rises to the 3-mile (4.8-km) mark, then gradually descends as it turns back toward the coast and approaches **Pelican Lake** at 3.4 miles (5.5 km). You can see beyond the lake and dunes to the sea, and in spring you may be surrounded by wildflowers. Before crossing the **bridge** over Alamere Creek, which feeds Alamere Falls, you may see unauthorized rocks made into an arrow or rock cairns with the word "Falls." Ignore these signs and remain on Coast Trail.

At 4.2 miles (6.8 km), you arrive at the **junction** with **Ocean Lake Loop Trail.** Go left (west) onto the narrow Ocean Lake Loop Trail and pass **Ocean Lake** to the right (east). At 4.7 miles (7.6 km), the crumbly trail climbs 200 feet (61 m) over 0.25 mile (0.4 km), and the views from the top are absolutely worth the trek. Sit on the bench and take in your surroundings: Looking back to the south is a bird's-eye view of Ocean Lake and the coast, most notably Alamere Falls itself tucked into the cliffs.

Pass above **Wildcat Lake** through the brush down to the right (east), as the trail curves right (northeast) and inland.

▸ **MILE 5.2–6.8: Wildcat Lake to Alamere Falls**
The route reconnects with Coast Trail at 5.3 miles (8.5 km). Take Coast Trail left (northwest) and steeply descend 0.2 mile (0.3 km), then cross a bridge to **Wildcat Campground.** A potable water tap is near the vault toilets up the hill to the right (north). To continue the hike, turn left (south) at the campground and hike down the bluff to **Wildcat Beach.**

Walk 1.1 miles (1.8 km) south along the beach to **Alamere Falls.** Even when the water flow is light, the 40-foot (12-m) tide fall is stunning as it cascades over the cliff and water carves its way through the sand to join the ocean. While you want to make sure to soak up the experience of making it to the falls, don't lose sight of the changing tide.

▶ **MILE 6.8-13.4: Alamere Falls to Palomarin Trailhead**

Retrace your steps to the campground and get back on Coast Trail. When Coast Trail intersects Ocean Lake Loop Trail at 8.3 miles (13.4 km), instead of returning the way you came, stay straight (east) to remain on Coast Trail, as it heads a bit farther inland through coastal scrub and forest. When it reconnects to Ocean Lake Loop Trail, stay on Coast Trail and return the way you came, back to Palomarin Trailhead.

DIRECTIONS

From San Francisco, take U.S. 101 north for 7.2 miles (11.6 km) to exit 445B for Highway 1 toward Mill Valley and Stinson Beach. Continue north onto Highway 1 for 16.7 miles (27 km). Be prepared to proceed slowly and cautiously as needed. Turn left at Bolinas-Fairfax Road, then turn left onto Olema Bolinas Road and drive 1.2 miles (1.9 km). Take another left to stay on Olema Bolinas Road and proceed for 0.5 mile (0.8 km). Turn right on Mesa Road and continue carefully for 4.6 miles (7.4 km).

GPS COORDINATES: 37.9340, −122.7470; 37°56′2.4″ N, 122°44′49.2″ W

BEST NEARBY BITES

From the trailhead, take Mesa Road for 4.6 miles (7.4 km) and turn right onto Olema Bolinas Road. Continue straight onto Wharf Road and find **Coast Café** (46 Wharf Rd., Bolinas, 415/868-2298, www. coastcafebolinas.com, 11am-3pm and 5pm-8pm Tues.-Thurs. and Sun., 11am-3pm and 5pm-9pm Fri.-Sat., $13-34) ahead on the right. The café focuses on locally grown and caught food, offering brunch, lunch, and dinner.

NEARBY CAMPGROUNDS

NAME	DESCRIPTION	FACILITIES	SEASON	FEE
Wildcat	Backcountry hike in; closest camping to the falls	5 campsites, 3 group campsites, picnic tables, food lockers, potable water, vault toilets	year-round	$30-90

Point Reyes National Seashore, Highway 1, 451/464-5100, www.recreation. gov

NAME	DESCRIPTION	FACILITIES	SEASON	FEE
Samuel P. Taylor State Park	Camping under redwoods, oaks, and bay laurels	59 campsites, 1 group campsite, 2 primitive campsites, 1 primitive equestrian campsite	year-round	$35-225

Sir Francis Drake Boulevard, Lagunitas, 415/488-9897, www. reservecalifornia.com

NAPA & SONOMA

California's Wine Country pulls visitors into its vineyard-covered hills and valleys to indulge in world-famous wines and devour mouthwatering cuisine. Yet the allure of Napa and Sonoma Counties isn't limited to just food and drink. With a temperate climate that's suitable for year-round outdoor discovery, there's no shortage of enticing trails to travel. From the highest point in Napa atop Mount Saint Helena to the rocky shoreline of the Sonoma Coast, all your senses are enchanted when spending time in this region.

▲ FORT ROSS

▲ HOMESTEAD-BLUE RIDGE

◄ PIONEER NATURE TRAIL LOOP

1 Salt Point Trail
DISTANCE: 3.3 miles (5.3 km) round-trip
DURATION: 1.5 hours
EFFORT: Easy

2 Fort Ross Reef Trail
DISTANCE: 2.7 miles (4.3 km) round-trip
DURATION: 1.5 hours
EFFORT: Easy

3 Pomo Canyon Red Hill
DISTANCE: 5.2 miles (8.4 km)
DURATION: 2.5 hours
EFFORT: Easy-moderate

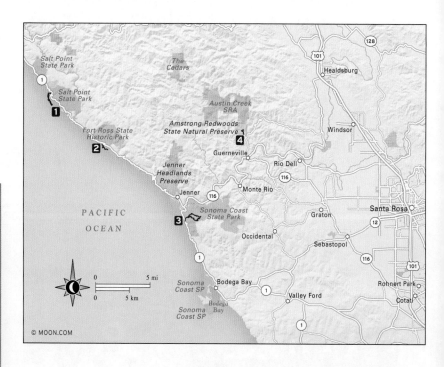

4 Pioneer Nature Trail Loop
DISTANCE: 1.2 miles (1.9 km) round-trip
DURATION: 30 minutes
EFFORT: Easy

5 Table Rock
DISTANCE: 4.2 miles (6.7 km)
DURATION: 3 hours
EFFORT: Moderate

6 Homestead-Blue Ridge
DISTANCE: 5.3 miles (8.5 km)
DURATION: 3 hours
EFFORT: Moderate-strenuous

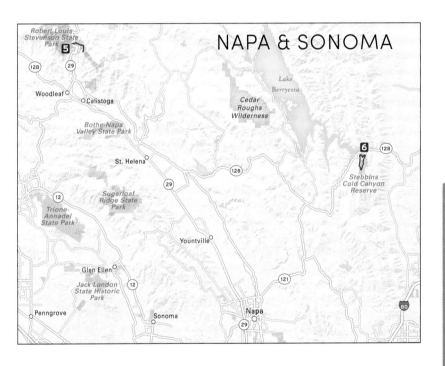

Salt Point Trail

SALT POINT STATE PARK

🦌 ❀ 🚶

This family-friendly hike leisurely takes you along the windy Sonoma Coast among gorgeous wildflowers and the park's honeycomb-weathered rocks to sandy Stump Beach Cove.

DISTANCE: 3.3 miles (5.3 km) round-trip
DURATION: 1.5 hours
ELEVATION GAIN: 200 feet (61 m)
EFFORT: Easy
TRAIL: Paved, dirt, sand, rock
USERS: Hikers
SEASON: Year-round
PASSES/FEES: $8 day-use fee per vehicle, or California State Parks Pass
MAPS: Select "Brochures" and "Park Brochure" on the park website
PARK HOURS: Sunrise-sunset daily
TRAILHEAD: Parking lot
FACILITIES: Vault toilets and drinking fountain at the trailhead
CONTACT: Salt Point State Park, 707/847-3221, www.parks.ca.gov

START THE HIKE

There are a variety of paths to follow from the trailhead to Stump Beach and back, all of which are easy to navigate without more than a few boulders to block your view across the low-lying vegetation out to the ocean. It gets very windy along the coastal bluffs, and hikers should bring appropriate outerwear. Use caution along the cliffs and avoid nearing the edge.

▶ **MILE 0-1.6: Parking Lot to Stump Beach**

This hike begins at the southwest corner of the trailhead **parking lot** and is paved for the first 750 feet (229 m). Go right (north) to continue onto **Salt Point Trail.**

You can choose your own adventure from the multiple footpaths from the grasslands to the bluffs. Staying closest to the jagged shoreline provides the most opportunity for whale watching, typically best December to April. The entire hike is popular for bird watching, typically best March to October. On any given day, hikers may spot ospreys, pelicans, Steller's jays, or orange-billed oyster catchers. Along all sections of the hike are pops of color from the pom-pom pink of sea thrift, yellow bush lupine, purple-fringed red maids, orange-scarlet pimpernel, and white coast range false bindweed. You can also look inland to see vehicles traveling down Highway 1 in the distance.

The most unique features of this hike are the tafoni along the sandstone by the water. Tafoni are small, rounded, smooth-edged openings in a rock surface, sometimes known as honeycomb weathering. This type of

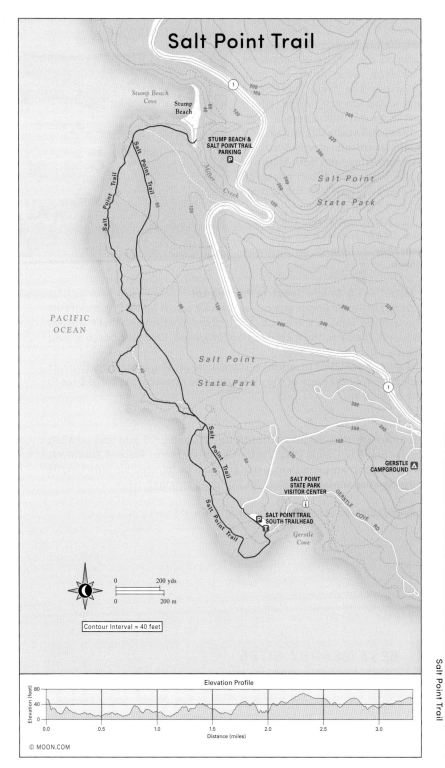

Salt Point Trail

PACIFIC OCEAN

Stump Beach Cove

Stump Beach

Miller Creek

STUMP BEACH & SALT POINT TRAIL PARKING

Salt Point State Park

Salt Point Trail

Salt Point State Park

SALT POINT STATE PARK VISITOR CENTER

SALT POINT TRAIL SOUTH TRAILHEAD

Gerstle Cove

GERSTLE CAMPGROUND

GERSTLE COVE RD

0   200 yds
0   200 m

Contour Interval = 40 feet

Elevation Profile

Elevation (feet)

80
40

0.0   0.5   1.0   1.5   2.0   2.5   3.0

Distance (miles)

© MOON.COM

weathering occurs when salt collects on the surface of permeable rock from ocean water, sea mist, or wind. The water evaporates and leaves the salt behind, which works its way into the rock, crystallizes, and opens up the rock. The openings are then more susceptible to weathering, and with time become noticeable. When occurring in clusters, they give the appearance of a sponge.

If you've followed the coastline, at 1.6 miles (2.6 km) the trail descends 20 feet (6 m) to **Stump Beach.**

▸ MILE 1.6–3.3: Stump Beach to Parking Lot

Arriving at Stump Beach, you can easily walk across Miller Creek as it cuts through the sand to the ocean. You'll discover driftwood that's washed ashore in the cove, and it's fun to wander around. Enjoy the beach at your leisure before heading back.

Retrace your steps to return or, since there are few visual impediments along the way, take one of the alternate more direct inland paths back to the parking lot.

DIRECTIONS

From Jenner, take Highway 1 north for 18.2 miles (29 km) and turn left at the Salt Point State Park Visitor Center entrance. Proceed southwest for 0.6 miles (1 km), continuing straight past the intersection with Gerstle Cove Road on the left, to Salt Point Trailhead parking.

GPS COORDINATES: 38.5666, −123.3318; 38°33′59.8″ N, 123°19′54.5″ W

BEST NEARBY BITES

A chilly day on the coast calls for a cup of tasty clam chowder at **Ocean Cove Bar & Grill** (23255 Coast Hwy., Jenner, 707/847-3089 www.oceancovelodge.com, noon-8pm daily, $8-20), just 2.4 miles (3.9 km) and six minutes from the trailhead, south down Highway 1 and on the left. Enjoy your meal from a seat on the ocean view deck or inside the roomy dining room.

🦌 ❀ 🏛 🚶

Travel back in history to learn about the Kashaya people, pass through a 19th-century Russian fort compound, and walk along the waves at Sandy Cove and on a bluff-top trail to the serenity of a secluded rocky beach on this out-and-back hike.

DISTANCE: 2.7 miles (4.3 km) round-trip

DURATION: 1.5 hours

ELEVATION GAIN: 320 feet (98 m)

EFFORT: Easy

TRAIL: Paved, dirt, rock, sand, gravel road

USERS: Hikers

SEASON: Year-round

PASSES/FEES: $10 day-use fee per vehicle, or California State Parks Pass

MAPS: Select "Brochures" and "Park Brochure" on the park website, at the Visitor Center

PARK HOURS: Sunrise-sunset daily

TRAILHEAD: Visitor Center

FACILITIES: Restrooms inside the Visitor Center, 10am-4:30pm daily

CONTACT: Fort Ross Historic State Park, 19005 Coast Highway 1, Jenner, 707/847-3286, www.parks.ca.gov

START THE HIKE

▶ **MILE 0-0.2: Visitor Center to Fort Ross Loop**

Walk through the **visitor center** to the back of the building and down the stairs to where the path begins. If the visitor center is closed, take the path around the south side of the building. This paved accessible section of the hike is known as the **Fort Trail** and extends to the entrances of the fort, established in 1812 by the Russian American Company, a commercial hunting and trading company that controlled all Russian exploration, trade, and settlement in North America at the time.

Follow the winding path through a small cypress forest, over a wooden bridge, and into a gentle meadow. Pass along the fenced-in **Russian Orchard** to the right (west) of the trail. Ahead is the fort's **northwest blockhouse,** a watchtower intended to be staffed by soldiers with weapons and cannons to protect the compound from external threats.

The trail curves right (southwest) along the western wall of the stockade to a **side entrance,** where you can step inside to tour **Fort Ross.**

▶ **MILE 0.2-0.4: Fort Ross Loop to Fort Entrance**

Pass through the stockade opening and get a glimpse of the early 1800s. The only remaining original Russian-built structure of the fort is to the

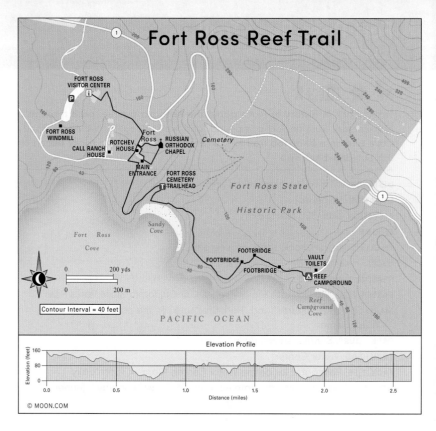

Fort Ross Reef Trail

Elevation Profile

right, the **Rotchev House,** built around 1836 for the last Russian American Company manager of the fort, Alexander Rotchev.

Turning left (north), you'll pass the **Magazin,** which was used as both a company store and warehouse. Past the northwest blockhouse and against the north wall is the **Kuskov House,** a reconstruction of the residence of the founder and first manager of Fort Ross, Ivan Alexandrovich Kuskov.

In the northeast corner is the **chapel,** the first Russian Orthodox structure in North America outside Alaska. Built in the mid-1820s, it was partially damaged in the 1906 earthquake. In 1925 it began to be used for Orthodox religious services that continue today.

Head right (southwest) from the chapel, passing the cannons and the well in the courtyard to the **southeast blockhouse.** Turn right (west) and you'll find picnic tables and the main entrance to the fort to the left (south). Ahead is the **officials' quarters** or barracks.

Loop back to the side entrance where you entered, exiting the fort with Rotchev House on your left (south). Continue on the paved path around the outside of the stockade and look for the **Call Ranch House** to the right (west). Built in 1878 by the Call family, it reflects early California life on the farm during the American ranch period.

The path ends at the paved road. Follow along the walls of the stockade, taking the road east to the **main entrance** of Fort Ross.

▸ **MILE 0.4-1.3: Fort Entrance to Reef Campground Cove**

From the main entrance, the path becomes a gravel road as it leads southwest toward the ocean. At 0.6 mile (1 km) and the edge of the cliffs, enjoy a 360-degree view of the Pacific Ocean, Fort Ross, and Sandy Cove below, to the north. Follow the wide road as it U-turns and leads sharply down into the cove. After descending 70 feet (21 m) over 0.1 mile (0.2 km), you'll reach a picnic table, trash bins, and the option to hike to Fort Ross Cemetery or arc again toward a gate to the beach. Pass through the gate and into **Sandy Cove.**

The stunning beach-scape provides ample room for play, but the water here is not safe to enter due to strong currents and freezing temperatures. During low tide, tide-pooling is possible on the north end of the beach, and you may catch sight of Steller sea lions and a variety of sea birds. Walk onto the beach and look for the **wooden stairs** to the east.

Back up on the bluffs, follow the easy single-track dirt trail as it meanders along the coast. Just past 1 mile (1.6 km) is the first of three wooden footbridges. At 1.2 miles (1.9 km), at the **third wooden footbridge,** the trail splits. Go right (east), staying toward the ocean. (If you go north, the trail will take you to Highway 1.)

Over the next 0.1 mile (0.2 km), the trail heads down 40 feet (12 m), including some wooden steps, to the **Reef Campground** area. Cross the gravel road and follow the trail to the secluded rocky crescent beach of this protected cove.

Return to the visitor center the way you came.

DIRECTIONS

From Jenner, take Highway 1 North for 11.5 miles (18.5 km) and turn west (left) onto Fort Ross Road to enter the state park.

GPS COORDINATES: 38.5164, −123.2465; 38°30'59" N, 123°14'47.4" W

BEST NEARBY BITES

About 25 minutes south of the trailhead, **Cafe Aquatica** (10439 Hwy. 1, Jenner, 707/865-2251, www.cafeaquaticajenner.com, 8am-5pm daily, $3-25) serves a short food and drinks menu and an eyeful of beauty along Highway 1. The café offers fresh vegetarian and vegan options, fantastic avocado toast (try adding a poached egg or smoked salmon), and a creamy yogurt parfait. The outdoor seating looks out on the mouth of the Russian River, and local musicians create the perfect soundtrack to the experience 11am-3pm Saturday-Sunday.

Reach the easy summit of Red Hill, with panoramic views that include the Russian River on its way to the sea as well as the town of Jenner, wildflowers, redwoods, oak woodlands, and grasslands.

DISTANCE: 5.2 miles (8.4 km)
DURATION: 2.5 hours
ELEVATION GAIN: 1,030 feet (314 m)
EFFORT: Easy–moderate
TRAIL: Gravel, dirt, single-track
USERS: Hikers
SEASON: Year-round
PASSES/FEES: $8 day-use fee per vehicle, or California State Parks Pass
MAPS: Select "Brochures" and "Park Brochure" on the park website
PARK HOURS: 8am–dusk daily
TRAILHEAD: Dr. David C. Joseph Memorial Trailhead
FACILITIES: None
CONTACT: Sonoma Coast State Park, 707/875-3483, www.parks.ca.gov

START THE HIKE

▶ **MILE 0-2.5: Kortum Trail Parking Lot to Red Hill Trail**

To reach the trailhead, walk from the **Kortum Trail Parking Lot** across Highway 1, a total distance of just over 500 feet (152 m). Exercise caution and keep in mind that vehicles travel fast along this stretch; pedestrians are not always easy to see. Once on the east side of Highway 1, look for the gravel path, a gate, and a **wooden sign** that reads "Dr. David C. Joseph Memorial Trail" with an arrow pointing left toward the gate and "Pomo Canyon 2.9 miles" (4.7 km). Pass through the gate and begin hiking uphill. As you walk, look for the wooden trail marker posts and in spring, the bright pop of purple irises and lupines, among other wildflowers. At 0.7 mile (1.1 km), continue left (north) to stay on **Pomo Canyon Trail** at the intersection with Red Hill Trail. On your return, you'll come from the right on Red Hill Trail.

Just past the intersection, the trail turns from gravel to dirt and can be muddy in winter and spring. On completing the first mile (1.6 km), take the short 500-foot (152-m) out-and-back **spur trail** to a picnic table to the left (north) of Pomo Canyon Trail. On a clear day it offers wide panoramic views of the winding Russian River and the Pacific Ocean in the distance.

Not far past your return from the spur trail is the first of many **water crossings** on wood planks—sometimes a single board, sometimes wide enough for a vehicle—that lead you through brush and woodland and eventually into an enchanting Douglas fir and redwood forest. Between these crossings, the trail has become a single-track over gently rolling

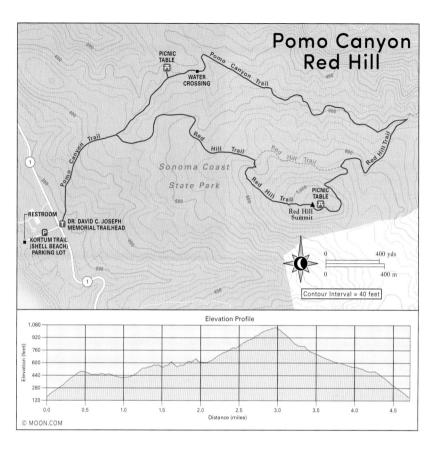

PICNIC
TABLE

Pomo Canyon Trail

WATER
CROSSING

Pomo Canyon Trail

Red

Hill Trail

Sonoma Coast

Red Hill Trail

Red Hill Trail

State Park

Red Hill Trail

PICNIC
TABLE

Red Hill
Summit

RESTROOM

DR. DAVID C. JOSEPH
MEMORIAL TRAILHEAD

P

KORTUM TRAIL
(SHELL BEACH)
PARKING LOT

0   400 yds

0   400 m

Contour Interval = 40 feet

Elevation Profile

slopes, and you'll increasingly be able to see the depth of the wide canyon through the brush and trees as you continue inland. Closer to the trail, notice the variety of wildflowers, including bindweed, coast paintbrush, and monkey flower.

At 2.4 miles (3.9 km), you'll skirt around to the right (east) of a tall **rock outcrop.** Several spur trails lead up to the top of the rocks for those who want to explore more. At 2.5 miles (4 km), look for the Pomo Canyon-Red Hill Trail **junction.** Pomo Canyon Trail continues straight (northeast) toward Pomo Canyon Campground; you split right (southwest) onto **Red Hill Trail.**

▶ **MILE 2.5-4.7: Red Hill Trail to Pomo Canyon Trail**
Red Hill Trail climbs and emerges above the trees with views over the canyon through grasslands, where a variety of flowers unfold in the spring, including California poppies and lupines.

At 3 miles (4.8 km), Red Hill Trail splits. Go left (west) to head up toward the summit of Red Hill. (Going straight will bypass the summit and is a more direct return to the trailhead.) The trail briefly passes through a shady redwood forest, and after about 0.25 mile (0.4 km), a game trail splits off to the right (west). Continue left (southeast) to stay on Red Hill Trail.

You will soon after reach the **Red Hill summit** (1,040 ft/317 m), with a picnic table and beautiful 360-degree views of Bodega Bay and up the jagged Sonoma Coast. The open grasslands on the approach are so lovely that they may inspire you to twirl around as if you're a nun in an alpine meadow.

Continuing past the summit, at 2.9 miles (4.7 km) the trail rejoins the section of Red Hill Trail that split the other direction—make sure to go left (west) to return toward the trailhead.

At 4.7 miles (7.6 km), Red Hill Trail ends back at the junction with Pomo Canyon Trail. You'll recognize the wooden trail marker post that closes the loop of the lollipop.

▶ **MILE 4.7-5.2: Pomo Canyon Trail to Kortum Trail Parking Lot**
Turn left (southwest) onto Pomo Canyon Trail and return the way you came.

DIRECTIONS

From Jenner, go south on Highway 1 for 3 miles (4.8 km). Turn off to the right and park in the Kortum Trail Parking Lot at Shell Beach.

GPS COORDINATES: 38.4190, −123.1019; 38°25'8.4" N, 123°6'6.8" W

BEST NEARBY BITES
From the Kortum Trail Parking Lot, take Highway 1 south for 8.4 miles (13.5 km), a 15-minute drive, to **Spud Point Crab Company** (1910 Westshore Rd., Bodega Bay, www.spudpointcrabco.com, 9am-5pm daily) for outstanding white clam chowder, voted best on the Sonoma Coast. Grab a chowder and a crab sandwich and enjoy the Bodega Harbor as you sit at one of the picnic tables and take in the salt air.

A wide path wanders through a thriving forest of coast redwoods, sorrel, and ferns, offering an education at every turn along this short hike.

BEST: Kid-Friendly Hikes

DISTANCE: 1.2 miles (1.9 km) round-trip

DURATION: 30 minutes

ELEVATION GAIN: 60 feet (18 m)

EFFORT: Easy

TRAIL: Dirt

USERS: Hikers

SEASON: Year-round

PASSES/FEES: $10 day-use fee per vehicle, or California State Parks Pass

MAPS: Select "Brochures" and "Park Brochure" on the park website, at the Visitor Center

PARK HOURS: 8am to 1 hour after sunset

TRAILHEAD: Visitor Center parking lot

FACILITIES: Restrooms at the main parking lot

CONTACT: Armstrong Redwoods State Natural Reserve, 707/869-2015, www. parks.ca.gov

START THE HIKE

The Armstrong Nature Trail section of this loop is not wheelchair accessible. For an accessible route, at the junction of Pioneer Nature Trail with Armstrong Nature Trail, continue on Pioneer Trail for an additional 0.2 mile (0.3 km) to a picnic area, an alternative 1.4-mile (2.3-km) round-trip out-and-back hike.

▶ **MILE 0-0.5: Parking Lot to Icicle Tree**
At the northwest end of the **parking lot** is the **visitor center,** where you pay the day-use fee and can obtain a map. Walk northwest across the road you entered on, behind the admission booth, to the sign for **Pioneer Nature Trail.**

You're immediately consumed by the redwood forest as low-lying fences guide the soft dirt trail gently through the large grove of first-generation redwoods. Just prior to the trail crossing the road, at 0.1 mile (0.2 km), you can look across the road at the **Parson Jones Tree,** the tallest in the grove. Over 310 feet (94 m) in height, it's taller than the Statue of Liberty (305 ft/93 m)! With Parson Jones towering above, it can be difficult to see all the way up through the surrounding treetops from the trail. Instead, look for the cross-section of a redwood tree trunk where historical events are labeled by the rings of the tree, which predates the signing of the Magna Carta (AD 1215).

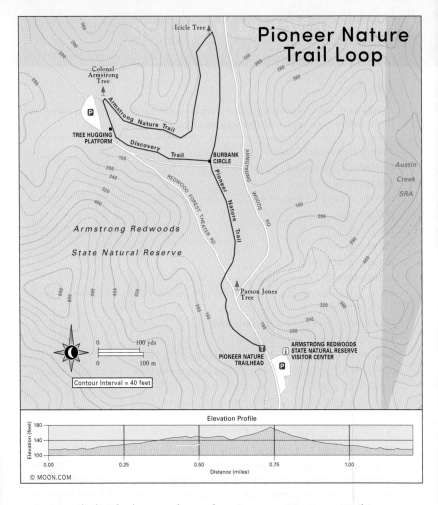

Pioneer Nature Trail Loop

At 0.3 mile (0.5 km), cross the road again to see Discovery Trail intersect Pioneer Nature Trail to the left (west). From the intersection, notice the huge downed redwood tree base and its roots, located in the disabled parking area to the right (east). Redwood tree roots are considered shallow, but a tree's root system can extend over 100 feet (30 m) from the base, intertwining with the roots of other redwoods, helping to increase their stability during strong winds and floods. Remain on the Pioneer Nature Trail, and just past the intersection, look for the **Burbank Circle** to the right (east).

Throughout the grove and whenever hiking amid redwoods, you may notice circles of trees known as "fairy rings." When one redwood is cut down or falls due to wind or fire, new trees will commonly resprout from its roots in a circle. Even in death, the tree continues to care for the next generation by providing a root system in addition to reproducing by seed. In time, the parent tree is no longer visible and what remains is a fairy circle.

At 0.5 miles (0.8 km), the Pioneer Nature Trail intersects with the Armstrong Nature Trail to the left (southwest) at the **Icicle Tree.**

▶ **MILE 0.5–0.8: Icicle Tree to Colonel Armstrong Tree**
Circle the Icicle Tree and examine what remains of its "icicles." These are actually burls, deformed-looking growths that begin to develop on healthy trees when it is just a seedling. In time, the stems within a burl grow and present as knobby formations often seen at the base of the tree, although burls can be found all the way to the canopy. Some burls are rounded and knotty, others are long and resemble icicles, and they can weigh many tons.

From the Icicle Tree, head left (southwest) on **Armstrong Nature Trail,** which continues for 0.3 mile (0.5 km) and leads to the oldest tree in the grove, the **Colonel Armstrong Tree.** This giant, named for Colonel James Boydston Armstrong, who took over ownership of the park in 1875, is over 300 feet (91 m) tall and is estimated to be over 1,400 years old, the oldest tree in the grove.

▶ **MILE 0.8–1.2: Colonel Armstrong Tree to Parking Lot**
From Colonel Armstrong Tree, take **Discovery Trail** southeast. Along this short trail you'll find several braille interpretive panels and a treat for all—a **tree hugging platform.** After just 0.2 mile (0.3 km), the Discovery Trail reconnects to the Pioneer Nature Trail. Turn right (south) and return the way you came.

DIRECTIONS

From downtown Guerneville, travel 2 miles (3.2 km) north on Armstrong Woods Road. The road leads directly into the park and to the Visitor Center parking lot, with entry to the right of the park entrance kiosk.

GPS COORDINATES: 38.5323, −123.0026; 38°31'56.3" N, 123°0'9.4" W

BEST NEARBY BITES

Whether it's before or after a hike, if you love a good biscuit, you must stop at **Big Bottom Market** (6228 Main St., Guerneville, 707/604-7295, www.bigbottommarket.com, $5-14). Just 2.3 miles (3.7 km) from the Visitor Center parking lot, the biscuits here were even named one of Oprah's favorites. Ask about the daily specialty biscuit, or sink your teeth into a delicious biscuit breakfast sandwich.

Pioneer Nature Trail Loop

NAPA & SONOMA

189

5 Table Rock

ROBERT LOUIS STEVENSON STATE PARK

Travel through volcanic formations and past interconnected rock labyrinths to the Bay Area's tallest precipice, where hikers are rewarded with an expansive view of the vineyards, farms, and hills of Napa Valley.

DISTANCE: 4.2 miles (6.7 km)

DURATION: 3 hours

ELEVATION GAIN: 1,310 feet (399 m)

EFFORT: Moderate

TRAIL: Dirt, gravel fire road, gravel, rock, single-track, creek crossing

USERS: Hikers

SEASON: Year-round

PASSES/FEES: None

MAPS: Select "Park trail map" on the park website; Bay Area Ridge Trail website, https://ridgetrail.org

PARK HOURS: Sunrise-sunset daily

TRAILHEAD: Table Rock Trailhead

FACILITIES: None

CONTACT: Napa County Regional Park and Open Space District, 707/942-4575, www.napaoutdoors.org

START THE HIKE

People underestimate the need for hydration on this hike due to its length and forested start. It is primarily exposed and solidly a moderate hike with challenging elevation changes. Beware of the overgrowth as you near Table Rock; it's best to wear full coverage clothing to minimize the potential for contact with poison oak and unwanted ride-along pests such as ticks.

▶ **MILE 0-1: Parking Lot to the Turret**

From the **parking lot,** the trail immediately leads up under the cover of trees for 0.1 mile (0.2 km) to an **old utility road,** where you turn left (east). The path gently climbs to **Bear Rock Overlook** at 0.5 mile (0.8 km), where the view opens. Look for the **bench** to the left (north) of the trail, which offers a great panoramic view, including rolling hills and peaks, with Mount St. Helena (4,342 ft/1,323 m) to the west and Snow Mountain (7,055 ft/2,150 m) farther northwest.

Look for the Table Rock trail marker to continue southeast, as the trail increases in rockiness and the path gradually narrows. The trail continues to steadily climb up to its highest point (2,760 ft/841 m), and what's known as the **turret,** a pointy boulder formation that loosely resembles a small tower atop a corner of an old-world castle.

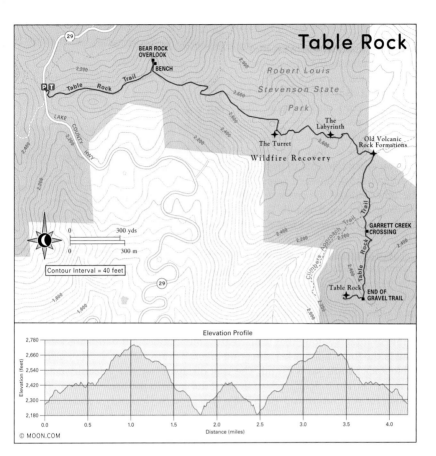

Table Rock

Robert Louis Stevenson State Park

Contour Interval = 40 feet

© MOON.COM

▶ MILE 1-1.3: **The Turret to the Labyrinth**

While it's fun to explore around the turret, note that the hike does not go through the formation. From the approach to the turret, the trail takes a left (west) turn down the rocky eastern slope. Carefully follow the rock and gravel path through the low bushes and down approximately 80 vertical feet (24 m) over 0.1 mile (0.2 km) to a trail marker that confirms you're on the correct path at just about the point you realize you're now walking on sandy gravel. The trail levels out, and at 1.3 miles (2.1 km), you reach a multi-sectioned **labyrinth** to the north of the path.

▶ MILE 1.3-2.1: **The Labyrinth to Table Rock**

After taking a stroll through the swirls of the labyrinth, descend steeply along a rocky path and follow the trail as it curves south at 1.5 miles (2.4 km). Along the remainder of the trail to Table Rock, watch for the trail markers letting you know how much farther it is until you reach the rock; the wooden posts are at 0.7 mile (1.1 km), 0.35 mile (0.6 km), 0.2 mile (0.3 km), and 100 yards (91 m) to Table Rock.

The hike takes you along more **volcanic rock formations** ripe for exploration, but as you continue, the trail becomes increasingly narrow and overgrown in many places; it's clear that fewer hikers explore beyond the

labyrinth. Take caution in exploring this often undisturbed area, watching for poison oak and wildlife.

Crossing **Garrett Creek** at 1.7 miles (2.7 km) almost feels like you've lost your way. The creek can be clogged with tree branches, and the creekside is thick with brush, but you should be able to hop over or utilize those downed trees. On the other side of the creek, follow the faint dirt path uphill, watching for tree roots, rocks, and poison oak.

The 0.2-mile (0.3-km) trail marker directs you to continue straight (south) and scramble up and over volcanic rock formations, the first formation that's actually a part of the trail. Once over the rocks, at 2.1 miles (3.4 km) is the **intersection** with the longer Palisades Trail, marked by a large brown park sign, indicating points of interest along that trail. Nearby, the intersection with Palisades Trail is the final trail marker, directing hikers to turn right (west) to reach Table Rock in 100 yards (91 m). The trail dissipates on the volcanic rock, so make certain to look back to understand how to get back to the trail marker for your return trip. Atop **Table Rock,** you can leisurely wander the rocky crags, peer over the cliff edge, or stare out upon the sweeping views of Calistoga and wine country to the south.

Return the way you came.

DIRECTIONS

From Calistoga, take Highway 29 for 7.5 miles (12.1 km) to the Mount St. Helena trailhead. Park in the dirt parking area on either side of the road. The Table Rock trailhead is on the east side of the road, opposite the Mount St. Helena trailhead.

GPS COORDINATES: 38.6527, −122.5999; 38°39′9.7″ N, 122°35′59.6″ W

Homestead-Blue Ridge
UC DAVIS STEBBINS COLD CANYON RESERVE

Enjoy the thrill of this trail atop the exposed ridgeline of Blue Ridge and look down at Lake Berryessa.

DISTANCE: 5.3 miles (8.5 km)

DURATION: 3 hours

ELEVATION GAIN: 1,450 feet (442 m)

EFFORT: Moderate-strenuous

TRAIL: Dirt, rock, single-track

USERS: Hikers

SEASON: Year-round

PASSES/FEES: $3 donation

MAPS: At the top of the park website

PARK HOURS: Dawn-dusk daily

TRAILHEAD: Homestead-Blue Ridge street-side parking

FACILITIES: Vault toilets at the nearby parking lot

CONTACT: University of California Natural Reserve System, 530/752-1011, https://naturalreserves.ucdavis.edu

START THE HIKE

▶ **MILE 0-0.2: Roadside Parking to Official Trailhead**

From the **street-side trailhead parking,** look for the wooden stairs up and over a dirt and grass dune with a wooden "Trailhead" sign up top, which lead to interpretive signs and maps. From the interpretive signs, go left (east) and look for trail signs leading to half a dozen uneven rocky stairs taking you down to **two drainage tunnels** that pass under Highway 128. When the drainage is dry, pass through one of the two tunnels and follow the trail signs for Homestead Trail; however, do not attempt the crossing when water is flowing, which may be the case after a wet season or recent rain. When the tunnels are impassable, you can dash from the parking lot across Highway 128 to the trailhead instead of going over the dirt and grass dune, but be wary of the dangers of crossing a curving highway.

The **official trailhead** begins at the wooden trail markers beyond the tunnels, pointing straight (south) for "Junction" and left (east) for "Parking," where crossing the highway would lead you. There's a smaller horizontal rectangle pointing straight to Blue Ridge-Homestead Junction in 0.1 mile (0.2 km) with a vertical blue rectangle marker. Look for these vertical blue rectangle markers on the hike when you don't see other trail markers. Continue straight (south) to follow the arrow for Homestead.

▶ **MILE 0.2-2.1: Official Trailhead to Blue Ridge-Annie's Trail Junction**

At 0.4 mile (0.6 km), you've arrived at the entrance of **Stebbins Cold Canyon Reserve,** where you can sign in and leave an optional donation to the

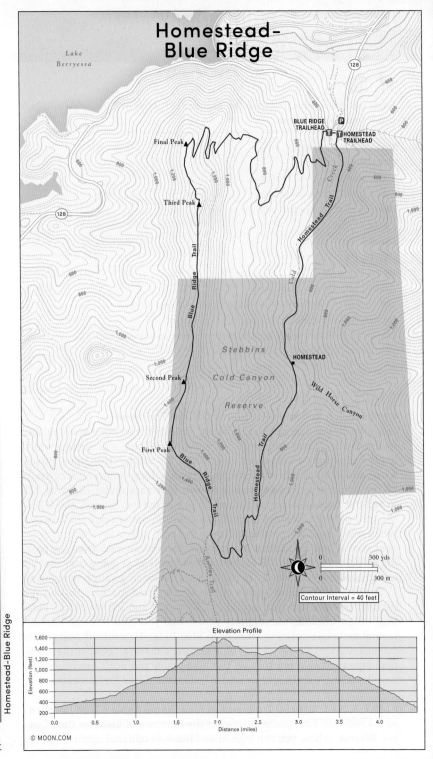

Homestead–Blue Ridge

Lake Berryessa

128

BLUE RIDGE TRAILHEAD

HOMESTEAD TRAILHEAD

P

Final Peak

Third Peak

128

Second Peak

First Peak

Blue Ridge Trail

Homestead Trail

Cold Creek

Stebbins Cold Canyon Reserve

HOMESTEAD

Wild Horse Canyon

Annies Trail

300 yds

300 m

Contour Interval = 40 feet

Elevation Profile

© MOON.COM

▲ HOMESTEAD-BLUE RIDGE

reserve. Signing in provides the most accurate count of visitors and helps inform first responders in case of emergency.

Warm up by ascending and descending two sets of a dozen stairs before rock hopping through the creek bed of **Cold Creek** at 0.7 mile (1.1 km). Shortly after, you'll reach a **junction** with stairs to Annie's Trail to the right (north) and a path to Coolers going straight (south). Go straight (south) and at 1.2 miles (1.9 km), you'll arrive at the **Homestead,** which gives the first portion of the hike its name. You can catch sight of the stone foundation ruins of a cold storage building used for cheese in the early 1900s at the Homestead, commonly referred to as the "Coolers." Look for quail in the brush as you make your way back to the split and up the stairs (now to your left) toward Annie's Trail.

From the start of the stairs, several steady switchbacks take you 590 vertical feet (180 m) up the canyon, and Homestead Trail meets the **junction** of Blue Ridge Trail and Annie's Trail at 2.1 miles (3.4 km).

▶ **MILE 2.1-3.5: Blue Ridge-Annie's Trail Junction to the Fourth Peak**
Turn right (north) to continue onto **Blue Ridge Trail** and immediately ascend to the trail's **first peak** (1,527 ft/465 m). Once over the peak, you can see the winding road far below to the right (northeast)—look for the zigzag of the switchbacks along the slope of the canyon that's part of the final descent of Blue Ridge Trail.

At 2.5 miles (4 km), the **second peak** (1,580 ft/482 m) is the highest of the four on this trail. On the descent on the other side, you'll catch sight of the beautiful aqua-blue water of Lake Berryessa to the left (west), with wider views of the lake revealed as you navigate over and around the rocks along the next mile (1.6 km) of the craggy ridge.

Many hikers mistakenly believe that the dusty scramble up to the **third peak** (1,456 ft/444 m) is the last on the trail; it's just that they can't see

beyond it to the fourth, and fatigue is setting in. Carry on to the **fourth and final peak** (1,365 ft/416 m) of the trail, the lowest elevation of the four. From here you can see where the trail levels out far below as you begin the steady return descent.

▶ MILE 3.5-5.3: Fourth Peak to Roadside Parking

At 3.5 miles (5.6 km), Blue Ridge Trail leads down switchbacks to descend 460 vertical feet (140 m) in about 0.7 mile (1.1 km). Once you reach the junction with the Homestead Trail at 5.2 miles (8.4 km), you've descended a total of 1,050 feet (320 m) from the fourth peak. Turn left (north) onto Homestead Trail and return the way you came.

DIRECTIONS

From Winters, travel west 9.1 miles (14.7 km) on Highway 128 and look for the small strip of roadside parking on the right side of the road. About 0.25 mile (0.4 km) before the roadside parking is a parking lot (also on the west side) with vault toilets. Parking there adds approximately 0.5 mile (0.8 km) to your hike.

GPS COORDINATES: 38.5095, −122.0967; 38°30'34.2" N, 122°5'48.1" W

BEST NEARBY BREWS

Just nine minutes east of the trailhead is **Berryessa Brewing Company** (27260 Hwy. 128, Winters, www.berryessabrewingco.com, 3pm-8pm Thurs.-Fri., noon-6pm Sat.-Sun.). This taproom and 20-barrel craft brewery is in a family- and dog-friendly country setting with outdoor seating. With a regular and seasonal rotation of beers, live music, and often food trucks, be sure to check out their online calendar for details.

NEARBY CAMPGROUNDS

NAME	DESCRIPTION	FACILITIES	SEASON	FEE
Wright's Beach	Adjacent to the beach	27 campsites, no potable water, fire rings, picnic tables, restrooms with flush toilets, running water	year-round	from $35

Sonoma Coast State Park, 800/444-PARK—800/444-7275, www.reservecalifornia.com

NAME	DESCRIPTION	FACILITIES	SEASON	FEE
Bodega Dunes	Camping under redwoods, oaks, and bay laurels	68 campsites, fire rings, picnic tables, token-operated hot showers, restrooms with flush toilets, potable water filling station	year-round	from $35

Sonoma Coast State Park, 800/444-PARK—800/444-7275, www.reservecalifornia.com

NAME	DESCRIPTION	FACILITIES	SEASON	FEE
Gerstle Cove	Camping atop the coastal bluffs on the ocean side of Highway 1	30 campsites	year-round	from $35

Salt Point State Park, 800/444-PARK—800/444-7275, www.reservecalifornia.com

▲ FERN CANYON TRAIL TO RUSSIAN GULCH FALLS

MENDOCINO &
NORTH COAST

MENDOCINO

You can shed life's stresses merely by driving along the Mendocino coast, but this soul-stirring seascape is most compelling when seen on foot. At the mainland's edge, rugged headlands, rocky promontories, and crashing waves vie for your attention. A short distance inland, sunlight wafts through redwood and fir groves, warming the ferns and mosses thriving on the forest floor. Highway 1 twists and turns along the coast, affording easy access to dozens of public lands within a 70-mile (113-km) stretch from Point Arena to Rockport. Since mild temperatures are the norm year-round, the hiking season extends through all 12 months. Best of all, if you're clamoring for a refined meal or a cozy inn to ease you off the trail at the end of the day, the villages of Mendocino, Fort Bragg, and Point Arena offer a wealth of welcoming spots.

◄ POINT CABRILLO LIGHT STATION

◄ POINT ARENA-STORNETTA UNIT OF CALIFORNIA COASTAL NATIONAL MONUMENT

◄ BIG HENDY GROVE

1 Ecological Staircase Nature Trail
DISTANCE: 5.1 miles (8.2 km) round-trip
DURATION: 2.5 hours
EFFORT: Easy-moderate

2 Point Cabrillo Light Station
DISTANCE: 1-2.3 miles (1.6-3.7 km) round-trip
DURATION: 30 minutes-1 hour
EFFORT: Easy

3 Fern Canyon Trail to Russian Gulch Falls
DISTANCE: 6.3 miles (10.1 km) round-trip
DURATION: 3 hours
EFFORT: Easy-moderate

4 Spring Ranch Trail
DISTANCE: 3.6 miles (5.8 km) round-trip
DURATION: 2 hours
EFFORT: Easy

5 Fern Canyon and 20 Bridges Loop
DISTANCE: 8.2 miles (13.2 km) round-trip
DURATION: 4 hours
EFFORT: Easy-moderate

6 Big Hendy Grove and Hermit Huts
DISTANCE: 3.8 miles (6.1 km) round-trip
DURATION: 2 hours
EFFORT: Easy

7 Point Arena-Stornetta Trails
DISTANCE: 5.2 miles (8.4 km) round-trip
DURATION: 2.5 hours
EFFORT: Easy-moderate

8 Bowling Ball Beach
DISTANCE: 1.2 miles (1.9 km) round-trip
DURATION: 1 hour
EFFORT: Easy

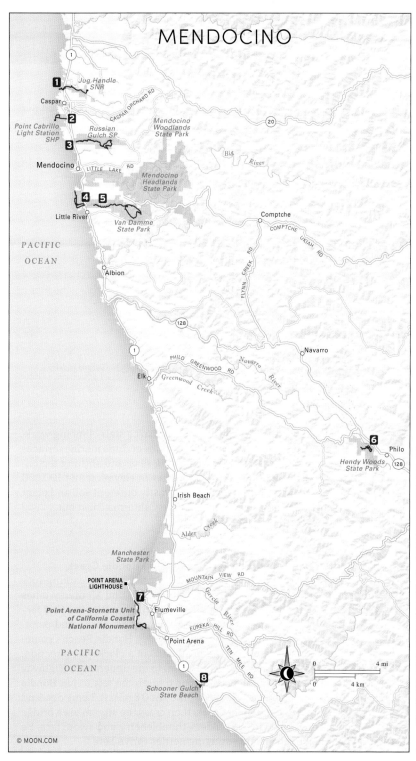

MENDOCINO

PACIFIC OCEAN

PACIFIC OCEAN

1 Jug Handle SNR

Caspar

2

Point Cabrillo Light Station SHP

3 Russian Gulch SP

Mendocino Woodlands State Park

CASPAR ORCHARD RD

Mendocino

LITTLE LAKE RD

Mendocino Headlands State Park

4 **5**

Little River

Van Damme State Park

Albion

Comptche

COMPTCHE UKIAH RD

FLYNN CREEK RD

Big River

128

PHILO GREENWOOD RD

Navarro River

Navarro

Elk

Greenwood Creek

6 Philo

Hendy Woods State Park

128

Irish Beach

Alder Creek

Manchester State Park

POINT ARENA LIGHTHOUSE

7 Flumeville

Point Arena-Stornetta Unit of California Coastal National Monument

MOUNTAIN VIEW RD

Garcia River

EUREKA HILL RD

Point Arena

TEN MILE RD

1

8

Schooner Gulch State Beach

0   4 mi

0   4 km

© MOON.COM

203

MENDOCINO

Witness the geologic evolution of marine terraces beneath your feet on this trek from coastal prairie to a pygmy forest of stunted trees.

DISTANCE: 5.1 miles (8.2 km) round-trip

DURATION: 2.5 hours

ELEVATION GAIN: 320 feet (98 m)

EFFORT: Easy-moderate

TRAIL: Dirt trail, wooden stairs, boardwalk

USERS: Hikers, leashed dogs only on the first 0.2 mile (0.3 km) west of Highway 1

SEASON: Year-round

PASSES/FEES: None

MAPS: Jug Handle State Natural Reserve brochure map and trail guide that corresponds to numbered markers at www.parks.ca.gov

PARK HOURS: Dawn-dusk daily

TRAILHEAD: Jug Handle State Reserve Parking Lot

FACILITIES: Vault toilet

CONTACT: Jug Handle State Natural Reserve, 707/937-5804, www.parks. ca.gov

---

Despite its name, the Ecological Staircase isn't a stair-climbing workout. This trail ascends gently along a series of three marine terraces carved by relentless ocean waves, rising seas, and shifting tectonic plates. Each terrace is 100 feet (30 m) higher in elevation and 100,000 years older than the one below and exhibits vastly different soil and plant life. Terraces like these are common along the California coast but, at Jug Handle, they are plainly on display.

START THE HIKE

▶ **MILE 0-1: Parking Lot to First Terrace and Jug Handle Creek**

Follow the **Ecological Staircase Nature Trail** west from the parking lot's western edge. You'll pass through a grove of bishop and Monterey pines as you head toward the coast and a grassy blufftop prairie, the **first terrace.** Continue past spring-blooming lupine, poppy, sea thrift, and paintbrush to the bluff's edge and gaze northeast to Jug Handle Beach's comely white sands. Your path circles the headlands in a clockwise direction, veering north and then east at 0.6 mile (1 km) to dip underneath Highway 1. (You may be tempted to follow the spur trail on the left to **Jug Handle Beach,** but save it for a picnic after your hike.) At 0.8 mile (1.3 km), descend a wooden staircase to **Jug Handle Creek,** then cross the stream via a bridge and boardwalk enveloped in leafy alders, thimbleberry, and sword fern. Be careful if you touch any plants—stinging nettles thrive here.

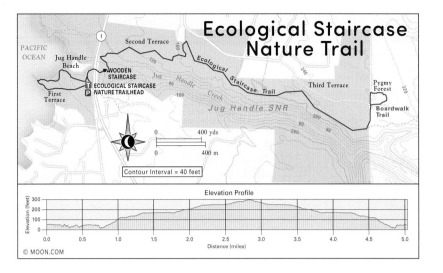

▶ MILE 1-1.8: Jug Handle Creek to Second Terrace

The trail leaves the creek and highway noise behind, gradually ascending to the **second terrace,** where the soil is 100,000 years older than the coastal prairie. The vegetation shifts from Jug Handle's riparian flora to a mixed conifer forest of bishop pine, Douglas fir, western hemlock, and Sitka spruce; the spruce here are at the far southern end of their range, which extends up the Pacific Coast to Alaska. Beneath the tree canopy is a mix of woodland plants—wax myrtle, false lily of the valley, and rhododendron—that nearly obscure the massive stumps from a 1960s logging operation. In the farthest reaches of the second terrace, at mile 1.8, you'll find a great place for a snack break among redwoods and shade-loving ferns, sorrel, and trillium.

▶ MILE 1.8-2.7: Second Terrace to Third Terrace and Pygmy Forest

Continue a mellow ascent through the woods, watching for the approaching **third terrace.** The signs become fairly obvious at about 2 miles (3.2 km), as the conifers gradually diminish in size and the soil appears drier, sandier, and much poorer in nutrients—and no wonder, since this soil is 300,000 years older than the soil near the ocean. At 2.5 miles (4 km), your trail enters the **pygmy forest** of miniaturized pines and cypress. Most are 6 to 15 feet (1.8-4.6 m) tall, but it's mind-boggling to consider that even a 4-foot-high (1.2-m) tree may be more than a century old, its growth stunted by weak soil and poor drainage. Among the scraggly trees are a few rare and endemic Bolander pines, which grow only in the most acidic soils.

At the 2.6-mile (4.2-km) mark, your trail connects with a dirt road skirting the state park boundary. Turn right on a **boardwalk trail** that makes a 0.1-mile (0.2-km) loop through the diminutive trees. Trailside benches invite you to pause and contemplate this fascinating bonsai forest.

Complete the loop, then simply head back the way you came.

ECOLOGICAL STAIRCASE NATURE TRAIL ▲

DIRECTIONS

From Mendocino, drive about 5 miles (8.1 km) north on Highway 1 to the Jug Handle State Natural Reserve parking area. From Fort Bragg, drive 5 miles (8.1 km) south on Highway 1. The Ecological Staircase Nature Trail begins on the west side of the parking lot.

GPS COORDINATES: 39.3751, −123.8165; 39°22'30.4" N, 123°48'59.4" W

BEST NEARBY BREWS

Craft beer pioneers since 1988, North Coast Brewing is ranked as one of the top 50 breweries in the country. At The **Pub at North Coast Brewing** (444 N. Main St., Fort Bragg, 707/964-3400, www. northcoastbrewing.com, 11:30am-8pm Thurs.-Mon.), pair a Red Seal Ale or Scrimshaw Pilsner with fish-and-chips or deep-fried brussels sprouts. From the trailhead, drive 5 miles (8.1 km) north on Highway 1, about 8 minutes.

Point Cabrillo Light Station
POINT CABRILLO LIGHT STATION STATE HISTORIC PARK

🦌 🏛 🐾 🏃 ♿

Meander along grassy coastal bluffs to a dramatic meeting of land and sea, where a 1909 lighthouse stands sentry.

BEST: Winter Hikes

DISTANCE: 1–2.3 miles (1.6–3.7 km) round-trip

DURATION: 30 minutes–1 hour

ELEVATION GAIN: 100 feet (30 m)

EFFORT: Easy

TRAIL: Paved path or dirt trail

USERS: Hikers, wheelchair users on South Trail, leashed dogs

SEASON: Year-round

PASSES/FEES: None

MAPS: Point Cabrillo Light Station State Historic Park brochure map at www. parks.ca.gov

PARK HOURS: Dawn–dusk daily

TRAILHEAD: Point Cabrillo Light Station Parking

FACILITIES: Vault toilet, museum

CONTACT: Point Cabrillo Light Station State Historic Park, 707/937-6123, https://pointcabrillo.org

The Mendocino coast is home to two historic lighthouses: Point Cabrillo Light Station and Point Arena Lighthouse. Both shine their beacons to protect mariners from the treacherous coastline, have museums crammed with fascinating exhibits, and rent cottages for overnight lodging. You can drive right up to Point Arena Lighthouse, but getting to Point Cabrillo requires hiking this lovely path through 300 acres of coastal headlands.

START THE HIKE

▶ **MILE 0-0.8: Parking Lot to Point Cabrillo Light Station**
Two trails lead from the parking lot. The **South Trail** is a paved roadway that travels 0.5 mile (0.8 km) one-way to the light station. It's a straight out-and-back venture that's ideal for wheelchair users. The trail described here is the 2.3-mile (3.7-km) **North Trail,** a dirt trail that winds west through the coastal prairie. These grasslands attract many birds of prey, including northern harriers and white-tailed kites.

Where North Trail forks at 0.4 mile (0.6 km), continue straight and you'll soon spot the lighthouse complex. Turn left (south) toward the buildings at a T junction at 0.6 mile (1 km). If you're expecting a tall skinny lighthouse like the romantic towers in Thomas Kinkade paintings, prepare to be surprised. **Point Cabrillo Light Station** is short and squatty, resembling a red-roofed church. Constructed in 1909, an octagonal tower anchors its

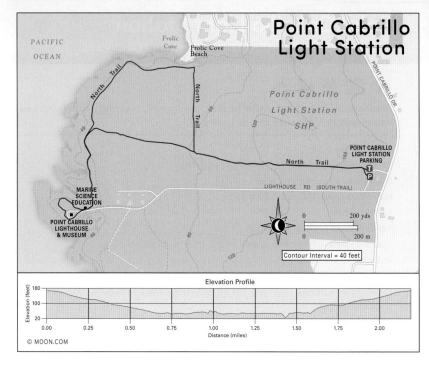

Point Cabrillo Light Station

PACIFIC OCEAN

Frolic Cove · Frolic Cove Beach

Point Cabrillo Light Station SHP

North Trail

POINT CABRILLO LIGHT STATION PARKING

LIGHTHOUSE RD (SOUTH TRAIL)

MARINE SCIENCE EDUCATION

POINT CABRILLO LIGHTHOUSE & MUSEUM

Contour Interval = 40 feet

Elevation Profile

© MOON.COM

eastern end. As you wander the headland on which it stands, notice how the Pacific has cut deep channels into the bluffs, making Point Cabrillo almost an island. Fifty feet (15 m) below the headlands, waves batter the rocky shoreline.

The lighthouse complex's nine buildings are managed by the nonprofit Point Cabrillo Lightkeepers Association. Step into the **lighthouse museum** (11am-4pm daily) to learn about the life and work of 20th-century lighthouse keepers. Then stroll over to the restored blacksmith and carpenter shop, which now houses **marine science exhibits,** including a 240-gallon saltwater aquarium.

▶ **MILE 0.8-1.7: Point Cabrillo Light Station to Frolic Cove Overlook**
Retrace your steps, heading north from the light station, keeping straight at the T junction you visited previously. Take a longer, rambling route back to your car by following the dirt path along the bluffs' edge. You'll have nonstop views of the intertidal reef surrounding Point Cabrillo, which harbors a wealth of marine life. You'll likely hear sea lions barking, and you may see harbor seals resting on offshore rocks. December-April, you may also spot gray whales traversing their long Pacific migration route (scan the sea for telltale "puffs of smoke"—condensed whale breath—rising into the air). In summer and fall, blue and humpback whales make occasional appearances. Your sea-vista path skirts along the southern edge of **Frolic Cove,** named for a San Francisco-bound sailing brig that ran aground here in 1850. The crew escaped in lifeboats, but the ship's cargo was lost. The *Frolic*'s wreck was the impetus for the light station's construction.

▲ POINT CABRILLO LIGHT STATION

▶ **MILE 1.7-2.3: Frolic Cove Overlook to Parking Lot**

At a trail junction and interpretive sign, turn your back on the coast and follow North Trail right (south) and then left (east), circling back to the parking lot.

DIRECTIONS

From Mendocino, drive 2 miles (3.2 km) north on Highway 1 and turn left (west) at the sign for Russian Gulch State Park. Drive straight on Point Cabrillo Drive for 1.3 miles (2.1 km) to the parking lot. From Fort Bragg, drive south on Highway 1 for 4 miles (6.4 km) and turn right on Point Cabrillo Drive. Drive 1.7 miles (2.7 km) to the parking lot.

GPS COORDINATES: 39.3501, −123.8130; 39°21'0.4" N, 123°48'46.8" W

BEST NEARBY BITES

For a family-friendly meal, head to **Frankie's Pizza and Ice Cream** (44951 Ukiah St., Mendocino, 707/937-2436, www.frankiesmendocino. com, noon-8pm Tues.-Sun.). This community-focused spot hosts art exhibitions and sponsors kids' sports teams, so it's a great place to chat with the locals while noshing on cheesy pizza and hearty salads. From the trailhead, drive 3.5 miles (5.6 km) south via Highway 1, about 7 minutes.

3

Fern Canyon Trail to Russian Gulch Falls

RUSSIAN GULCH STATE PARK

Hike along a stream and through a mossy redwood grove to discover a shimmering waterfall plunging into a fern-laden grotto.

DISTANCE: 6.3 miles (10.1 km) round-trip

DURATION: 3 hours

ELEVATION GAIN: 570 feet (174 m)

EFFORT: Easy-moderate

TRAIL: Partially paved path, dirt trail

USERS: Hikers, mountain bikers only on the first 2.1 miles (3.4 km), wheelchair users only on the first mile (1.6 km)

SEASON: Year-round

PASSES/FEES: $8 day-use fee per vehicle

MAPS: Russian Gulch State Park brochure map at www.parks.ca.gov

PARK HOURS: Dawn-dusk daily

TRAILHEAD: Russian Gulch State Park day-use parking area

FACILITIES: Restroom, visitor center

CONTACT: Russian Gulch State Park, 707/937-5804, www.parks.ca.gov

START THE HIKE

The route described here is one of a handful of hiking options to lovely Russian Gulch Falls. This lollipop loop delivers maximum eye candy by combining the Fern Canyon Trail (the lollipop's stick) with Falls Loop Trail (the circle-shaped candy). If you have young kids in tow, consider biking Fern Canyon's initial 2.1 miles (3.4 km) (you can then park it at a bike rack) to ensure everybody has enough stamina to complete the trip.

▶ **MILE 0-2.1: Parking Area to Fern Canyon/Falls Loop Junction**

Fern Canyon Trail begins on the east side of the small parking area. In just a few footsteps, you enter a dense riparian forest filled with second-growth redwoods, western hemlocks, Douglas firs, big-leaf maples, and alders. The partially paved trail surface may not be completely au naturel, but it's so deeply smothered in leaves and fir needles that you won't even notice the asphalt. True to the trail's name, you're accompanied by thousands of ferns waving their delicate fronds as you pass and the pleasing sound and sight of **Russian Gulch Creek**'s flowing waters. In the rainy season (Dec.-Apr.), you might spot coho salmon or steelhead trout swimming upstream to lay their eggs. Blooming trillium, a redwood forest wildflower with three green leaves and three white petals, brightens the forest floor in early spring. If you stray off the pavement, watch where you tread. Stinging nettles and poison oak thrive here. At 2.1 miles (3.4 km), the

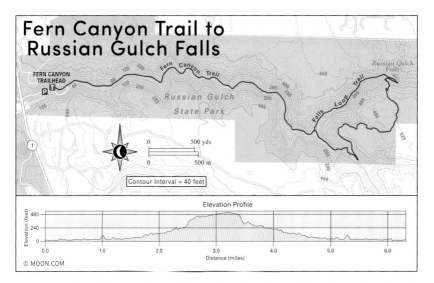

paved treadway ends at a **bike rack** and major **trail junction,** where North Trail comes in on your left, Falls Loop Trail heads off to your right, and Fern Canyon Trail continues straight ahead.

▶ **MILE 2.1-2.9: Fern Canyon-Falls Loop Junction to Russian Gulch Falls**
Stay straight on a much narrower stretch of Fern Canyon Trail for an 0.8-mile (1.3 km) tromp to the waterfall. Up to this point your route has been almost level, so this stretch's ups and downs may surprise you. Wooden stairsteps aid your undulating progress through dense redwoods decked in downy moss. A glimpse of **Russian Gulch Falls** comes into view just before the trail descends to the fall's grotto, where the stream plummets 36 feet (11 m) into a fern-lined pool. The waterfall's flow varies with the seasons: In winter, a rushing torrent spills over a rock face cluttered with fallen tree trunks, while in summer a more delicate cascade trickles over the ledge.

▶ **MILE 2.9-4.1: Russian Gulch Falls to Fern Canyon-Falls Loop Junction**
Ascend the trail on the waterfall's right side to its fern-clad lip. In 0.1 mile (0.2 km), veer right at the junction with East Trail coming in from County Road 409 (some people drive this road for an easy shortcut to the falls). You're now following the dirt **Falls Loop Trail,** where you'll enjoy a little solitude as you climb up and over a redwood-covered ridge, traveling clockwise around the loop. In April or May, bright pink rhododendron bouquets brighten the green understory.

▶ **MILE 4.1-6.3: Fern Canyon-Falls Loop Junction to Parking Area**
Falls Loop Trail leads you right back to the main junction with **Fern Canyon Trail,** where the bike rack is located. Now back on the "stick" of this lollipop loop, simply retrace your steps back to your car.

RUSSIAN GULCH FALLS ▲

DIRECTIONS

From Mendocino, drive 2 miles (3.2 km) north on Highway 1 to the entrance for Russian Gulch State Park on the left (west) side of the highway. Pay your entrance fee at the kiosk, then continue straight, crossing back under the highway to the park's inland side. Drive past the recreation hall and campground to the Fern Canyon Trail parking lot. From Fort Bragg, drive south on Highway 1 for 9 miles (14.5 km) to the Russian Gulch State Park turnoff.

GPS COORDINATES: 39.3306, −123.8015; 39°19'50.2" N, 123°48'5.4" W

BEST NEARBY BREWS

Housed in a modest unassuming building, **Overtime Brewing** (190 Elm St., Fort Bragg, 707/813-7991, www.overtimebrewing.com, 2pm-9pm Tues.-Sat.) is easy to overlook. But if you're thirsty for craft beer and hearty grub fare—burgers, jambalaya, ribs, or chowder—you've found your mecca. From Russian Gulch, drive 10 miles (31 km) north via Highway 1, about 15 minutes, to the brewery.

4 Spring Ranch Trail

VAN DAMME STATE PARK

Savor Pacific views, roiling waves, spring wildflowers, and an ocean blowhole from lofty bluffs perched above a rocky intertidal shelf.

BEST: Coastal Hikes
DISTANCE: 3.6 miles (5.8 km) round-trip
DURATION: 2 hours
ELEVATION GAIN: 100 feet (30 m)
EFFORT: Easy
TRAIL: Dirt trail
USERS: Hikers, leashed dogs
SEASON: Year-round
PASSES/FEES: None
MAPS: Van Damme State Park brochure map at www.parks.ca.gov
PARK HOURS: Dawn–dusk daily
TRAILHEAD: The Inn at the Cobber's Walk
FACILITIES: None
CONTACT: Van Damme State Park, 707/937-0851, www.parks.ca.gov

Spring Ranch's 350 acres of coastal headlands were added to Van Damme State Park in 1996. The level, easy paths on these former dairy ranch lands are ideal for meandering and dawdling in splendid seaside scenery. Bring binoculars to aid in whale-watching and bird identification.

START THE HIKE

▶ **MILE 0-0.7: Parking Area to Coastside Bench**
From the parking area, walk a few steps north on Highway 1 to the north side of **The Inn at the Cobbler's Walk,** where you'll see a trail sign. Start wandering through groves of shore pine and Monterey cypress interspersed with coyote brush, huckleberry, and monkey flower. In shady spots, miner's lettuce grows at your feet—a delicacy for salad lovers, both human and animal. You can't see the ocean on this first woodsy stretch, but at 0.7 mile (1.1 km) you'll step into a clearing and find the vast Pacific spread out before you. A **bench carved from an ancient cypress log** marks the spot. Sit and linger awhile with your eyes trained on the ocean's surface. December-April, you may spot some of the 24,000 Pacific gray whales migrating between their Baja mating and calving waters and Bering Sea feeding grounds. These amazing sea mammals make this 10,000-mile (16,100-km) round-trip every year of their lives.

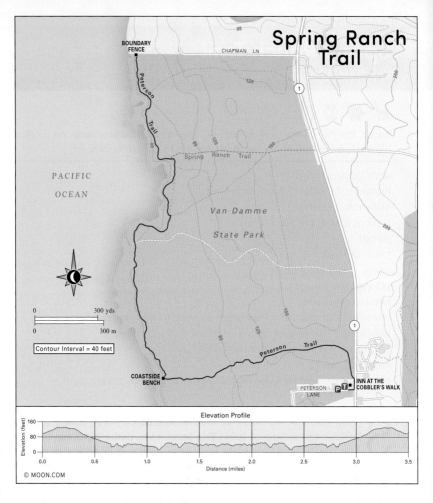

Elevation Profile

© MOON.COM

▶ **MILE 0.7–1.8: Coastside Bench to Boundary Fence**

From the coastside bench, follow the trail north, passing offshore sea stacks pierced by tunnels, arches, and even a blowhole, where surging waves thrust geysers of ocean water into the air. Your trail is just a few feet from the bluffs' edge, an ideal spot for bird-watching. You might see cormorants and oystercatchers roosting on the rocks or a squadron of brown pelicans soaring by at eye level.

A few small pocket beaches may call your name, but the bluffs here are too steep and unstable for safe access; instead, turn your attention to the wide-angle Pacific views and close-up scenery at your feet. In spring, these grasslands are dotted with California poppies, paintbrushes, seaside daisies, and Douglas irises. Alongside the native coastal flowers, you'll also see thick mats of showy pink ice plant, a nonnative.

At 1.3 miles (2.1 km), an unsigned trail heads inland; stay straight and stick to the coast. You'll soon pass by an uplifted sand deposit—it looks like an elevated beach—where it's possible to carefully make your way down to a tiny kelp-strewn cove.

▲ SPRING RANCH TRAIL

The trail reaches an obvious end point at a **boundary fence** at 1.8 miles (2.9 km). To the north lies the southern edge of Mendocino Village, only 1 mile (1.6 km) distant. From this spot, you'll have a clear view of harbor seals bobbing in the waves or hauling their blubbery bodies onto rocks to rest in the sun.

For your return trip, simply retrace your steps and enjoy the coastal scenery from the opposite direction.

DIRECTIONS

From Mendocino, take Highway 1 south for 2.5 miles (4 km). Just south of The Inn at the Cobbler's Walk, turn right on Peterson Lane and park in the small lot that holds only about 10 cars (there's usually space).

GPS COORDINATES: 39.2763, −123.7919; 39°16'34.7" N, 123°47'30.8" W

BEST NEARBY BITES

For a casual dinner, Mendocino Village's **Fog Eater Cafe** (45104 Main St., Mendocino, 707/397-1806, www.fogeatercafe.com, 4pm-8:30pm Wed.-Sat., 10am-2pm Sun.) serves vegetarian and vegan food inspired by the soul-soothing recipes of the Deep South. All produce is organic and sourced locally, and an adjacent retail shop sells local wines and picnic foods. From Spring Ranch, the 2.5-mile (4-km) drive north takes 5 minutes via Highway 1.

🐾 🚶 ♿

Traipse across 20 bridges, skirt alongside Little River's free-flowing waters, and discover an enchanting redwood forest on this multifaceted trek.

DISTANCE: 8.2 miles (13.2 km) round-trip
DURATION: 4 hours
ELEVATION GAIN: 690 feet (210 m)
EFFORT: Easy-moderate
TRAIL: Compacted gravel, dirt trail
USERS: Hikers, mountain bikers only on the first 2.3 miles (3.7 km), wheelchair users only on the first mile (1.6 km)
SEASON: Year-round
PASSES/FEES: $8 day-use fee per vehicle
MAPS: Van Damme State Park brochure map at www.parks.ca.gov
PARK HOURS: Dawn-dusk daily
TRAILHEAD: Fern Canyon Trailhead
FACILITIES: Restroom, visitor center
CONTACT: Van Damme State Park, 707/937-0851, www.parks.ca.gov

There are two Fern Canyon Trails on the Mendocino coast: one in Russian Gulch State Park (also covered in this chapter) and this one in Van Damme State Park. Both are lollipop-shaped trails that show off crystal-clear streams and beautiful forests. While Russian Gulch's Fern Canyon rewards with a glistening waterfall, this Fern Canyon delivers 20 delightful wooden bridges across Little River, a pygmy forest of stunted trees, and a dreamy redwood grove.

START THE HIKE

▶ **MILE 0-2.3: Fern Canyon Trailhead to Old Logging Road and Pygmy Forest Junction**

From the gate across from the parking area, start walking on the gravel-lined **Fern Canyon Trail,** which hugs **Little River**'s melodic flowing water. Your path is bordered by a lush tableau of ferns, red alders, and big-leaf maples. These riparian trees shade the waterway in summer, but in winter, they shed their leaves, allowing a clear view of the creek's deep pools. December-March, you may see coho salmon swimming upstream to spawn. In the first 1.5 miles (2.4 km), the trail sticks closely to the river's edge. You'll cross back and forth across its musical waters via 10 numbered wooden bridges. Past **Bridge 10,** the trail heads slightly uphill and away from the creek, entering a forest of second-growth redwoods where large stumps remain from logging in the late 1800s. At 1.8 miles (2.9 km), you'll pass a few primitive campsites and an outhouse. At 2.3 miles (3.7 km), Fern Canyon Trail dead-ends at a Y-fork signed for "Pygmy Forest."

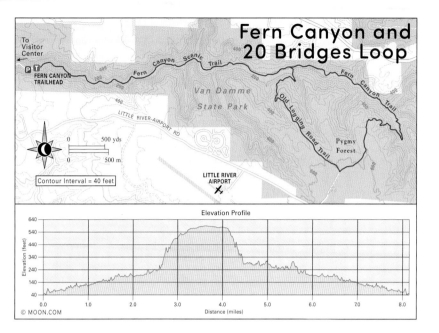

▶ MILE 2.3–3.8: Old Logging Road and Pygmy Forest Junction to Pygmy Forest

Both forks lead to the pygmy forest, but you'll take the right fork on **Old Logging Road** to start a counterclockwise loop. Prepare for a short but noticeably steep climb (a trail sign notes that it's 1.2 mi/1.9 km to the pygmy forest, but it's actually 1.5 mi/2.4 km). This wide dirt road may be the least interesting leg of the trip, but the sharp grade offers a quick cardio workout. You'll gain 650 feet (198 m) over the 1.5 miles (2.4 km) and notice a remarkable change in your surroundings as shady redwoods are replaced by sun-loving pines, rhododendrons, and manzanitas.

▶ MILE 3.8–5.7: Pygmy Forest to Bridges 11– 20 and Fern Canyon Trail Junction

At the ridgetop, the logging road continues straight to a small parking lot on Little River Airport Road; turn left at a sign for **Fern Canyon Trail** and walk through the **pygmy forest** of stunted cypress and pines growing in low-nutrient soil. (To see a larger and more impressive grove of these strange trees, hike the Ecological Staircase Nature Trail at Jug Handle State Natural Reserve, also covered in this chapter.) In 0.25 mile (0.4 km), you'll descend from this arid ridge into dense, shady redwood forest, where every inch of the ground seems blanketed in sorrel, ferns, and gargantuan tree trunks. Cross **Bridges 20 through 11** in descending order over the next 1.5 miles (2.4 km). As you curve around this canyon, the redwoods and sword ferns appear larger with every step. You may find yourself entering a dream-like redwood haze as you zigzag gently downhill on the winding single-track trail, passing a series of behemoth trees and astoundingly large stumps.

▶ **MILE 5.7-8.2: Fern Canyon Trail Junction to Fern Canyon Trailhead**
Too soon, you've closed out the loop. Retrace your steps on Fern Canyon Trail to your car.

DIRECTIONS

From Mendocino, take Highway 1 south 2.8 miles (4.5 km) to the Van Damme State Park entrance. Turn left (east), pay an entrance fee at the kiosk, then continue 0.8 mile (1.3 km) to the Fern Canyon Trailhead, just beyond the upper campground. Start hiking by walking past the gate just beyond the parking area.

GPS COORDINATES: 39.2768, −123.7809; 39°16'36.5" N, 123°46'51.2" W

BEST NEARBY BITES

If you're hankering for a beef, bison, elk, lamb, or vegetarian burger—or the chance to watch a baseball game on a flat-screen TV—head to **Patterson's Pub** (10485 Lansing St., Mendocino, 707/937-4782, www.pattersonspub.com, 11am-9pm daily). This local institution serves lunch and dinner daily and has 26 beers on tap. From Van Damme, drive 2.8 miles (4.5 km) north via Highway 1, about 5 minutes.

6

Big Hendy Grove and Hermit Huts
HENDY WOODS STATE PARK

🏛 🚶 ♿

Find serenity in a grove of venerable old-growth redwoods, then visit the site where a 20th-century hermit made his home in tree stumps.

BEST: Brew Hikes
DISTANCE: 3.8 miles (6.1 km) round-trip
DURATION: 2 hours
ELEVATION GAIN: 250 feet (76 m)
EFFORT: Easy
TRAIL: Dirt trail, paved path, wooden stairs, boardwalk
USERS: Hikers, wheelchair users on the All-Access Trail
SEASON: Year-round
PASSES/FEES: $8 day-use fee per vehicle
MAPS: Hendy Woods State Park brochure map at www.parks.ca.gov
PARK HOURS: Dawn-dusk daily
TRAILHEAD: Hendy Woods Day-Use Area
FACILITIES: Restroom, visitor center
CONTACT: Hendy Woods State Park, 707/895-3537, www.parks.ca.gov

Most people associate massive old-growth redwoods with the coast north of Mendocino, but Hendy Woods State Park is home to venerable giants that are nearly as impressive as the big trees farther north.

START THE HIKE

This hike includes two parts: a loop through one of Hendy Wood's two ancient redwood groves as well as an out-and-back hike to visit the park's "hermit huts."

▶ **MILE 0–1.8: Big Hendy Grove Loop**
From the day-use area parking lot, hop onto the signed **All-Access Trail.** Cross a small wooden bridge at 0.1 mile (0.2 km) and then veer left at the junction, heading southward onto the **Discovery Trail** to begin a clockwise loop through the 80-acre **Big Hendy Grove,** a deep green redwood wonderland. These massive trees—many of them 300 feet (91 m) tall and nearly 1,000 years old—are one of the last vestiges of Anderson Valley's native landscape before extensive logging in the 1860s. As you walk, this primeval forest works its magic on you. The farther you travel from the parking area, the quieter the hush. Patches of sorrel form green clouds at your feet. Soft sunlight filters through the canopy. Black-tailed deer munch on greenery. You'll find yourself stopping every few feet to gaze at the treetops or examine the downy moss carpeting fallen trunks. Follow **Discovery Trail** to **Upper Loop,** but don't turn left to circle back until you reach **Back**

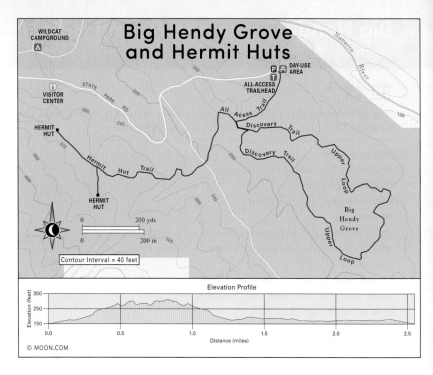

Big Hendy Grove and Hermit Huts

WILDCAT CAMPGROUND

VISITOR CENTER

STATE PARK RD

HERMIT HUT

HERMIT HUT

Hermit Hut Trail

DAY-USE AREA

ALL-ACCESS TRAILHEAD

All Acess Trail

Discovery Trail

Discovery Trail

Upper Loop

Big Hendy Grove

Upper Loop

Navarro River

0   200 yds
0   200 m

Contour Interval = 40 feet

© MOON.COM

Elevation Profile

Elevation (feet)

Distance (miles)

Loop Trail. The myriad trail junctions along the way may raise questions, but just stay straight at each fork until you reach the back of the grove, where there's no alternative but to turn left. This will give you the longest possible tour around this cathedral-like grove of virgin redwoods. Wander as slowly and reverently as you can, because much too soon, your loop will bring you back to where you started.

▶ **MILE 1.8-3.8: All-Access Trail Junction to Hermit Huts**
Back at the junction, follow the **All-Access Trail** west. In 0.1 mile (0.2 km) and a couple of bridge crossings, you'll reach another trail junction. Turn left onto the **Hermit Hut Trail** and climb steadily uphill from the red-wood-lined valley floor into a drier forest of oaks and madrones. The temperature rises as you climb out of the redwoods' dense shade. Cross a fire road and keep ascending gently for 0.8 mile (1.3 km), then turn left onto a spur trail to visit the first of two primitive **"hermit huts,"** a fallen hollowed-out redwood log that housed Russian immigrant Petrov Zailenko for nearly 18 years. Throughout the 1960s and 1970s, Zailenko lived in Hendy Woods, building shelters out of branches, logs, and stumps; eating food he hunted and gathered; and wearing clothing that others discarded. When he died in 1981, his ashes were spread in the park. Back on the main trail, continue 0.1 mile (0.2 km) to a large signboard that displays old newspaper clippings about Zailenko's life. Just behind the signboard is the second of the huts, a massive stump capped with a roof made of branches. Perhaps it's a trick of the light filtering through the tree canopy, but it isn't hard to picture this humble man living in these serene woods. If you're intrigued, you can learn more about him at the park's visitor center.

▲ BIG HENDY GROVE

At 2.8 miles (4.5 km), after visiting Petrov's homesite, simply return the way you came to the day-use parking area.

DIRECTIONS

From Mendocino, drive south 10 miles (16.1 km) on Highway 1 to its junction with Highway 128 at the Navarro Bridge. Head east on Highway 128 for 20 winding miles (32 km) to Philo-Greenwood Road and the sign for Hendy Woods State Park. Turn right on Philo-Greenwood Road and drive 0.5 mile (0.8 km) to the park entrance on the left. Pay your entrance fee at the kiosk, then follow the park road 1.8 miles (2.9 km) to the day-use parking area.

GPS COORDINATES: 39.0742, −123.4662; 39°4'27.1" N, 123°27'58.3" W

BEST NEARBY BREWS

Enjoy craft beer at **Anderson Valley Brewing Company** (17700 Boonville Rd., Boonville, 707/895-2337, www.avbc.com, 11am–6pm Mon.-Thurs., 11am–7pm Fri.-Sat., noon–6pm Sun.). Tour the brewery, listen to live music, or play disc golf at the 30-acre "beer park." Along with the best-selling Boont Amber Ale, Anderson Valley is known for producing fruit-forward goses. From this trailhead, the 12-mile (19.3-km) drive south via Highway 128 takes about 15 minutes.

7

Point Arena-Stornetta Trails

POINT ARENA-STORNETTA UNIT OF CALIFORNIA COASTAL NATIONAL MONUMENT

Wander past continuously evolving sea stacks, arches, sinkholes, and tunnels on this wave-battered parcel of California Coastal National Monument.

BEST: Fall Hikes
DISTANCE: 5.2 miles (8.4 km) round-trip
DURATION: 2.5 hours
ELEVATION GAIN: 230 feet (70 m)
EFFORT: Easy-moderate
TRAIL: Dirt trail
USERS: Hikers, leashed dogs
SEASON: Year-round
PASSES/FEES: None
MAPS: www.blm.gov/visit/point-arena-stornetta-unit
PARK HOURS: Dawn-dusk daily
TRAILHEAD: Bend-in-the-Road Trailhead on Lighthouse Road
FACILITIES: Vault toilet
CONTACT: BLM Ukiah Field Office, 707/468-4000, www.blm.gov

These 1,600 acres of grassy headlands jut to the northwest in a peninsula cut from the shoreline by the Garcia River. This is the only parcel of California Coastal National Monument you can drive to and hike on; the remainder comprises offshore rocks, islands, and exposed reefs.

START THE HIKE

▶ MILE 0-0.7: Bend-in-the-Road Trailhead to Sinkholes

From the **Bend-in-the-Road trailhead,** walk through the livestock gate and follow a clearly delineated path through coastal grasslands. These headlands were once owned by the Stornetta family of dairy ranchers, who donated the land to the federal government. On the peninsula's tip, the monolithic **Point Arena Lighthouse** has warned away ships since 1870.

For now, turn your back on this historic landmark and follow the trail southward. The artist known as Mother Nature has used a heavy hand on this landscape. The headlands have been sliced and diced by wave action, leaving knife-edged coastal shelves and offshore sea stacks large enough to be considered islands. The largest stack, known as **Sea Lion Rocks,** commands your attention—it's marked by a perfect arch formation and a flat top dotted with hundreds of cormorants.

At 0.7 mile (1.1 km), you'll approach several large **sinkholes** that are set back 30 feet (9 m) or more from the bluff's edge. Some are merely large depressions in the ground, and others tunnel through the headlands to the

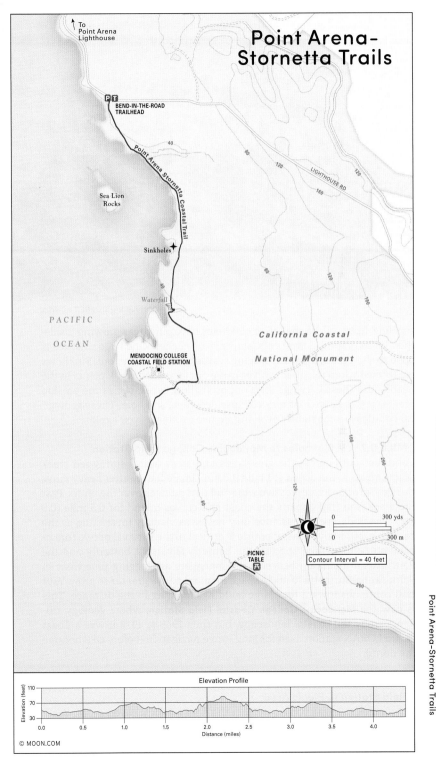

Point Arena-Stornetta Trails

To Point Arena Lighthouse

BEND-IN-THE-ROAD TRAILHEAD

Point Arena Stornetta Coastal Trail

Sea Lion Rocks

Sinkholes

Waterfall

PACIFIC

OCEAN

LIGHTHOUSE RD

California Coastal

National Monument

MENDOCINO COLLEGE COASTAL FIELD STATION

PICNIC TABLE

40

80

120

160

200

Contour Interval = 40 feet

0   300 yds

0   300 m

Elevation Profile

Elevation (feet)

110
70
30

0.0   0.5   1.0   1.5   2.0   2.5   3.0   3.5   4.0

Distance (miles)

© MOON.COM

surf line. Many of the shallower sinkholes have pine trees growing inside, their limbs draped in layers of California lace lichen. One large sinkhole is open to the ocean, allowing surging waves to move in and out. Sinkholes are formed when relentless waves carve out faults and weak points in the headlands. These carvings start out as shallow caves, but as the erosion progresses, the cave roof may collapse, leaving a sinkhole. These geological oddities are constantly evolving, so use caution as you explore.

▶ **MILE 0.7-1.3: Sinkholes to Mendocino College Field Station**
Continue south across the grasslands and cross over a spring-fed creek that tumbles to the ocean at 1 mile (1.6 km). Immediately after heavy rains, this creek forms an impressive **waterfall** that plunges over the bluffs. Past the creek, the trail departs the coast and curves inland for 0.5 mile (0.8 km). The wide-open grasslands may not be as visually interesting as the coastline, but native coastal prairie is critical to the survival of two threatened and endangered species: the Behren's silverspot butterfly and the Point Arena mountain beaver. Land managers are logging pine trees in Point Arena-Stornetta to make space for more native grasses to grow. Your trail continues toward four large buildings looming in the distance. This is now the **Mendocino College Coastal Field Station,** where geology students study the coastal landscape, but from 1945 to 1979 it was a Coast Guard LORAN station used for long-range navigation (before GPS became the norm).

▶ **MILE 1.3-2.6: Mendocino College Coastal Field Station to Picnic Area**
At 1.3 miles (2.1 km), you'll intersect the field station's paved access road. Turn right on the road and follow the trail signs that direct you around the college property and back to the shoreline. Keep to the path, admiring

▲ POINT ARENA-STORNETTA UNIT

more coastal eye-candy until you reach a **picnic table** situated beneath a cluster of tall cypress trees, where you can enjoy your trail snacks.

Return the way you came.

DIRECTIONS

From Point Arena, drive north for 1.6 miles (2.6 km) on Highway 1 and turn left (west) on Lighthouse Road. Drive west for 1.4 miles (2.3 km) to a sharp bend in the road. Park in the pullout on the left near the trailhead sign.

GPS COORDINATES: 38.9403, −123.7299; 38°56'25.1" N, 123°43'47.6" W

BEST NEARBY BITES AND A BONUS
Before departing the area, drive 1 mile (1.6 km) north to visit the national monument's icon, the 115-foot-tall (35-m) **Point Arena Lighthouse** (45500 Lighthouse Rd., Point Arena, www.pointarenalighthouse.com, 10am-3:30pm daily, free). Climb the tower's 145 steps for eye-popping views of the coast. Then, for a special dinner, head to **Bird Cafe and Supper Club** (194-A Main St., Point Arena, 707/882-1600, www.birdcafepa.com, 4:30pm-8pm Thurs.-Sun.) in the historic Point Arena Hotel. Make advance reservations. From the trailhead, the 3-mile (4.8 km) drive south via Lighthouse Road and Highway 1 takes about five minutes.

You don't need to be a geology buff to be awed by this lovely beach and its massive "bowling balls" lined up in the sand.

BEST: Kid-Friendly Hikes
DISTANCE: 1.2 miles (1.9 km) round-trip
DURATION: 1 hour
ELEVATION GAIN: 100 feet (30 m)
EFFORT: Easy
TRAIL: Dirt trail, wooden stairs
USERS: Hikers, leashed dogs
SEASON: Year-round
PASSES/FEES: None
MAPS: USGS topographic map "Point Arena"
PARK HOURS: Dawn-dusk daily
TRAILHEAD: Schooner Gulch State Beach parking pullout alongside Highway 1
FACILITIES: Vault toilet
CONTACT: Schooner Gulch State Beach, 707/937-5804, www.parks.ca.gov

START THE HIKE

Be sure to check a tide table before planning this trek, available at www.usharbors.com. Although Bowling Ball Beach is photogenic at any time of the day or year, its famous "bowling balls" are revealed only during very low or minus tides.

▶ **MILE 0-0.2: Parking Area to Staircase and Beach**

From the Schooner Gulch State Beach parking pullout alongside Highway 1, two trails lead to Bowling Ball Beach, so you might as well make a semi-loop. Start on the unsigned trail located about 50 feet (15 m) north of the trail marked by two yellow posts. Follow this **northern trail** 0.1 mile (0.2 km) across a blufftop meadow, where it meets the southern trail coming in on your left (note this spot for your return trip). Keep right and continue north to the bluff's edge. Descend a series of rustic **wooden stairsteps** to the **beach,** then pick your way across a driftwood **logjam** that bridges a shallow creek.

▶ **MILE 0.2-0.6: Staircase and Beach to Bowling Balls**

Proceed north along the sand for another 0.4 mile (0.6 km). You won't see the **"bowling balls"** until you practically step on them, but there's no mistaking them. Approximately 100 sandstone "balls," some as large as 3 feet (1 m) in diameter, rest in tidy rows in the surf zone sand. This astounding assemblage of rounded rocks was formed by eons of weathering. Technically known as concretions, the spheres are formed in the strata of the

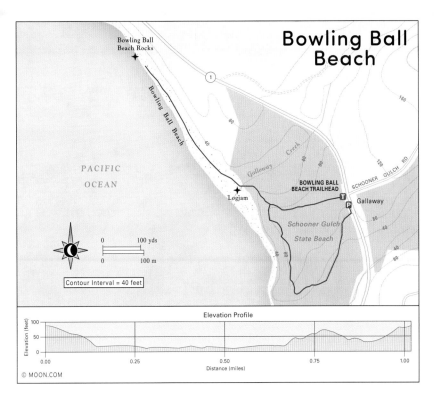

Bowling Ball Beach

beach cliffs. Over millions of years, minerals in these cliffs cement together around grains of sand, gradually expanding into sphere-shaped rock formations. Eventually the cliffs' softer sandstone erodes away, leaving the hard, round balls stranded. Examine the cliffs carefully to discover concretions that are still embedded in the sandstone, waiting for their turn to be set free. Similar formations exist elsewhere in the world, but this beach's concretions are unique for their large size and prodigious

numbers. During almost every low tide, you'll see someone under the age of 12 hopping gleefully from one bowling ball to the next.

▶ MILE 0.6–1.2: **Bowling Balls to Parking Area**

After exploring this remarkable beach, return the way you came to the driftwood-laden creek. Climb the bluff stairs, then follow the trail back to the junction of the northern and southern trails. Stay straight on the **southern trail** as it skirts the bluffs, then descends to the edge of Schooner Gulch State

BOWLING BALL BEACH ▲

Beach (Bowling Ball Beach is technically the southern section of Schooner Gulch State Beach). Extend your beach explorations on this lovely stretch of sand, or just follow the trail that leads past a vault toilet and back up-hill to your parked car.

DIRECTIONS

From Point Arena, drive 3.5 miles (5.6 km) south on Highway 1 to the road-side pullouts for Schooner Gulch State Beach, just north of the highway bridge. Note the signs stating "Park facing south only" and do as they say. There's space for about 12 cars. (If you can't score a spot, you can also hike to Bowling Ball Beach from Moat Creek Beach Access parking lot 1 mi/1.6 km north.)

GPS COORDINATES: 38.8692, −123.6535; 38°52'9.1" N, 123°39'12.6" W

BEST NEARBY BITES

The mother-daughter bakers at **Franny's Cup & Saucer** (213 Main St., Point Arena, 707/882-2500, www.frannyscupandsaucer.com, 8am-2pm Wed.-Sat., 8am-noon Sun.) make luscious pastries, to-die-for cookies, and heavenly cakes. They're so good that there's often a line out the door, so show up at opening time to avoid the crowds. The bakery is 3.5 miles (5.6 km) north of Bowling Ball Beach via Highway 1.

▲ TRILLIUM ON THE ECOLOGICAL STAIRCASE NATURE TRAIL

NEARBY CAMPGROUNDS

NAME	DESCRIPTION	FACILITIES	SEASON	FEE
MacKerricher State Park	Easy access to beaches and tide pools	75 sites for tents or RVs up to 35 ft/10.7 m (no hookups), 37 tent-only sites, 10 walk-in sites, restrooms, drinking water, showers, dump station	year-round	$40–45
Highway 1, Fort Bragg, 707/964-9112, www.parks.ca.gov				
Russian Gulch State Park	Access to hiking and biking trails, redwoods, waterfall, beach	26 sites for tents or RVs up to 24 ft/7.3 m (no hookups), restrooms, drinking water, showers, dump station	May-September	$40–45
Highway 1, Mendocino, 707/937-5804, www.parks.ca.gov				
Van Damme State Park	Access to hiking and biking trails, ocean kayaking and diving, redwoods	63 sites for tents or RVs up to 35 ft/10.7 m (no hookups), 5 tent-only sites, restrooms, drinking water, showers, dump station	year-round	$40–45
Highway 1, Mendocino, 707/937-0851, www.parks.ca.gov				

NEARBY CAMPGROUNDS (continued)

NAME	DESCRIPTION	FACILITIES	SEASON	FEE
Hendy Woods State Park	Access to hiking trails in redwoods, a short drive to Anderson Valley wineries	92 sites for tents or RVs up to 35 ft/10.7 m (no hookups), 4 camping cabins, restrooms, drinking water, showers, dump station	year-round	campsites $40-45, cabins $60-70

Highway 128, Philo, 707/895-3537, www.parks.ca.gov

NAME	DESCRIPTION	FACILITIES	SEASON	FEE
Manchester Beach KOA	Walking distance to Manchester Beach; easy access to Point Arena	43 RV sites with hookups, 57 tent sites, 27 cabins, restrooms, drinking water, showers, dump station	year-round	campsites $60-85, cabins $100-210

Highway 1, Point Arena, 707/882-2375, www.manchesterbeachkoa.com

NORTH COAST & REDWOOD EMPIRE

A day spent in California's ancient redwood forests, where the treetops seem to scrape the sky, puts even 6-foot-plus (1.8-m) humans in their place. With an average lifespan of 500 to 700 years—although many live as long as 2,000 years—coastal redwoods can grow to more than 375 feet (114 m), much taller than the Statue of Liberty.

A cluster of federal and state parklands stretching from Crescent City south to Trinidad protect 45 percent of California's remaining old-growth redwoods. These lands also contain Sitka spruce, western hemlock, Douglas fir, big-leaf and vine maples, huckleberry, and salmonberry. Ferns, lichens, and mosses carpet tree trunks and branches, and redwood sorrel spreads across the forest floor. Mushrooms in an astonishing variety of colors and shapes pop up after every rainfall. America's largest land animal, the Roosevelt elk, grazes in grassy prairies.

With hundreds of miles of trails, this is a place for taking slow-down strolls, communing with venerable trees, and savoring the vast open space between sea and sky.

▲ BOY SCOUT TREE TRAIL

HIDDEN BEACH

1 **Boy Scout Tree Trail to Fern Falls**
DISTANCE: 5.6 miles (9 km) round-trip
DURATION: 3 hours
EFFORT: Easy-moderate

2 **Damnation Creek Trail**
DISTANCE: 4 miles (6.4 km) round-trip
DURATION: 2–3 hours
EFFORT: Moderate

3 **Yurok Loop and Coastal Trail to Hidden Beach**
DISTANCE: 2.3 miles (3.7 km) round-trip
DURATION: 1 hour
EFFORT: Easy

4 **Brown Creek, Rhododendron, and South Fork Loop**
DISTANCE: 3.6 miles (5.8 km) round-trip
DURATION: 2 hours
EFFORT: Easy-moderate

5 **James Irvine and Miners Ridge Loop to Fern Canyon**
DISTANCE: 11.4 miles (18.4 km) round-trip
DURATION: 6-7 hours
EFFORT: Moderate-strenuous

6 **Skunk Cabbage Creek and Coastal Trail**
DISTANCE: 7.6 miles (12.2 km) round-trip
DURATION: 4 hours
EFFORT: Easy-moderate

7 **Tall Trees Grove**
DISTANCE: 3.6 miles (5.8 km) round-trip
DURATION: 2–3 hours
EFFORT: Easy-moderate

8 **Rim Trail**
DISTANCE: 5 miles (8.1 km) round-trip
DURATION: 2.5 hours
EFFORT: Easy-moderate

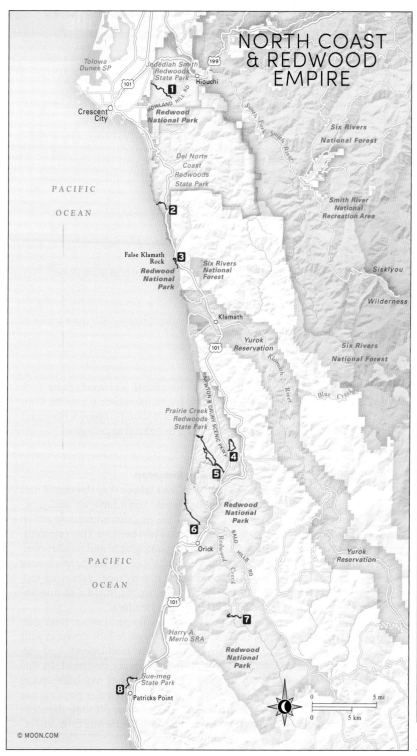

NORTH COAST & REDWOOD EMPIRE

PACIFIC OCEAN

Tolowa Dunes SP

Jedediah Smith Redwoods State Park

Hiouchi

Crescent City

Redwood National Park

Del Norte Coast Redwoods State Park

Six Rivers National Forest

Smith River National Recreation Area

False Klamath Rock

Redwood National Park

Six Rivers National Forest

Siskiyou Wilderness

Klamath

Yurok Reservation

Six Rivers National Forest

Blue Creek

Prairie Creek Redwoods State Park

Redwood National Park

Orick

Yurok Reservation

PACIFIC OCEAN

Harry A. Merlo SRA

Redwood National Park

Sue-meg State Park

Patricks Point

0   5 mi
0   5 km

© MOON.COM

Boy Scout Tree Trail to Fern Falls

JEDEDIAH SMITH REDWOODS STATE PARK

Wander through miles of old-growth redwoods, jumbo-size sword ferns, and clover-like sorrel, culminating with a visit to pretty Fern Falls.

DISTANCE: 5.6 miles (9 km) round-trip

DURATION: 3 hours

ELEVATION GAIN: 650 feet (198 m)

EFFORT: Easy-moderate

TRAIL: Dirt trail

USERS: Hikers only

SEASON: Year-round

PASSES/FEES: None

MAPS: National Geographic Maps "Redwood National and State Parks"

TRAILHEAD: Boy Scout Tree Trailhead

FACILITIES: Restroom

CONTACT: Jedediah Smith Redwoods State Park, 707/464-6101, www.parks. ca.gov or www.nps.gov/redw

This trail leads into the heart of Jedediah Smith Redwoods State Park and one of the densest rainforests found anywhere on earth. Even the drive to the trailhead—a slow cruise along unpaved Howland Hills Road through pristine redwoods—is a delightful experience.

START THE HIKE

▶ MILE 0-1: Boy Scout Tree Trailhead to Ridgetop

From the parking area, the **Boy Scout Tree Trail** takes off to the north, and you'll enjoy a mellow ascent for the first mile. You'll have no trail junctions to concern yourself with, and the trail never gains enough elevation to leave you breathless. Even so, your progress will be slow. This primordial forest of greenery gives you much to see, photograph, and ponder over. You'll find yourself stopping every few feet to gaze at the light shining through the redwood canopy or examine the downy moss carpeting toppled tree trunks. In between the prodigious redwoods, you'll also find impressive specimens of Douglas fir and western hemlock.

As you walk through this ancient forest, you'll spend much time gazing upward at the skyscraping trees. But don't forget to look down at your feet too. The sword ferns, deer ferns, wood ferns, huckleberry, and sorrel at your feet are as oversized as the trees towering overhead. In this forest, plantlife springs forth from every centimeter of available space. Among the never-ending palette of greens, flashy pink color pops appear in the spring months. Every May, rhododendrons show off their flamboyant flower bouquets. The blossoms of red clintonia and white false-lily-of-the-valley embellish the dark forest floor.

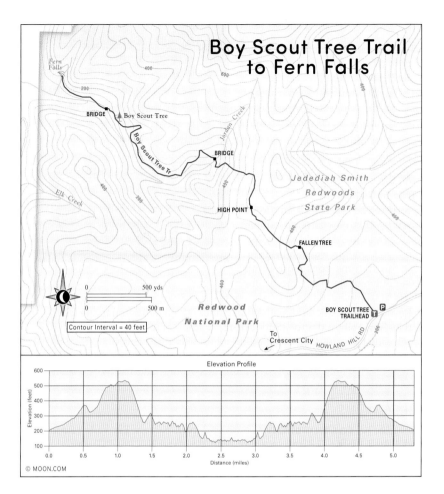

Boy Scout Tree Trail to Fern Falls

Elevation Profile

At 1 mile (1.6 km), you'll gain the top of a ridge and this hike's **high point,** a mere 450 feet (137 m) above sea level. Take a deep breath—the air is full of oxygen from the photosynthesis occurring all around you.

▶ **MILE 1-2.4: Ridgetop to Boy Scout Tree**

The trail's next stretch is a series of **zigzagging switchbacks** into the Jordan Creek drainage. You'll cross the gurgling creek on a **bridge** at 1.4 miles (2.3 km). This creek possesses a special beauty in autumn, when the leaves on streamside vine maples turn gold, copper, and burgundy. Other color-changing plants here include huckleberry and salmonberry. In early fall, these bushes can be thick with berries, which attract hungry bears.

On the bridge's far side, the trail veers west and in 0.4 mile (0.6 km) enters a grove of even bigger redwoods than the ones you've passed so far. One particularly gargantuan tree appears on your right, just inches from the trail.

Your path now parallels Jordan Creek as it tumbles downstream, crossing a **bridge** over a small tributary at 2.2 miles (3.5 km). At 2.4 miles (3.9 km), watch for an **unsigned junction** on your right. Follow the 50-foot-long

(15-m) **spur trail** uphill to see the largest tree in this grove, the **Boy Scout Tree.** More than 300 feet (91 m) tall, this double-trunked tree—technically two intertwined redwoods—was named by its discoverer, Jack Breen, who also founded a Crescent City Boy Scout troop.

▶ MILE 2.4–2.8: Boy Scout Tree to Fern Falls

Return to the main trail and keep pursuing this downstream ramble for 0.2 mile (0.3 km), crossing Jordan Creek on **two wooden bridges.** The forest transitions here—with fewer redwoods present, more light filters in, allowing alders, big-leaf maples, and Sitka spruce to flourish.

Beyond the second bridge, the trail climbs 0.2 mile (0.3 km) to the trail's end at **Fern Falls,** a dainty 35-foot (11-m) cascade on a tributary of Jordan Creek. The twisting rope of sparkling white water carves a sharp S-curve as it tumbles downslope, framed by deep-green sword ferns. Admire the cataract for as long as you wish, then turn around and follow the same lovely path back to your car.

DIRECTIONS

From U.S. 101 on Crescent City's south end, turn east on Elk Valley Road and drive 1.1 miles (1.8 km) to a fork with Howland Hill Road. Turn right and drive 3.7 miles (6 km) to the Boy Scout Tree Trailhead on the left. (Howland Hill Road is not suitable for trailers or motor homes.) The small parking lot usually has space available, but if it's full, park alongside Howland Hill Road.

GPS COORDINATES: 41.7686, −124.1102; 41°46'7" N, 124°6'36.7" W

BEST NEARBY BREWS

A 20-minute drive from this trailhead, **Seaquake Brewing** (400 Front St., Crescent City, 707/465-4444, seaquakebrewing.com, 11:30am-8:30pm daily) cooks up artisan IPAs, coastal pale ales, complex blonde ales, freshly caught rock cod-and-chips, and wood-fired pizzas. Crave-worthy side dishes include fresh cheese curds and parmesan fries. Kids are welcome in this lofty brewery near Battery Point Lighthouse.

This trek tunnels through a forest overflowing with ancient redwoods and Sitka spruce to a seldom-visited beach.

DISTANCE: 4 miles (6.4 km) round-trip

DURATION: 2-3 hours

ELEVATION GAIN: 1,190 feet (363 m)

EFFORT: Moderate

TRAIL: Dirt trail

USERS: Hikers

SEASON: Year-round

PASSES/FEES: None

MAPS: Del Norte Coast Redwoods State Park, available online at www.parks. ca.gov

TRAILHEAD: Damnation Creek Trailhead, by U.S. 101 mile marker 16

FACILITIES: Restroom

CONTACT: Redwood National and State Parks, 707/464-6101, www.nps.gov/ redw

M any trails in Redwood National Park and its adjoining state parks are level, or nearly so; not this one. If you're hungering for an aerobic workout, the Damnation Creek Trail provides it. You'll also enjoy fern-festooned redwood scenery and a high viewpoint above a secluded beach. But know before you go: This is an upside-down hike, with all the elevation gain occurring on the return trip.

START THE HIKE

▶ **MILE 0-0.6: Damnation Creek Trailhead to Coastal Trail Junction**
From the **Damnation Creek Trailhead,** begin with a short but steep northward ascent to the top of a redwood-lined ridge. Enjoy the beauty of the impressively large old-growth trees around you, and the overflowing abundance of sword ferns, huckleberry, salal, and rhododendron growing in their understory.

Top the ridge at 0.2 mile (0.3 km), and prepare for an easygoing zigzagging descent to the sea. At 0.6 mile (1 km), you'll meet up with a section of trail that was once U.S. 101 and is now a part of the 40-mile (64-km) **Coastal Trail.** Turn right (northwest) here; **Damnation Creek Trail** joins this level, paved path for about 40 yards (37 m). Then turn left (west) and exit Coastal Trail to continue along Damnation Creek Trail's downhill course.

▶ **MILE 0.6-1.9: Coastal Trail Junction to Damnation Creek Crossing**
Keep switchbacking downhill through enchanting conifer forest, accompanied by the soundtrack of thundering Pacific waves in the distance. In spring, a profusion of white fairy bells and false-lily-of-the-valley borders the path. If the marine layer isn't smothering the coast, soft sunlight filters

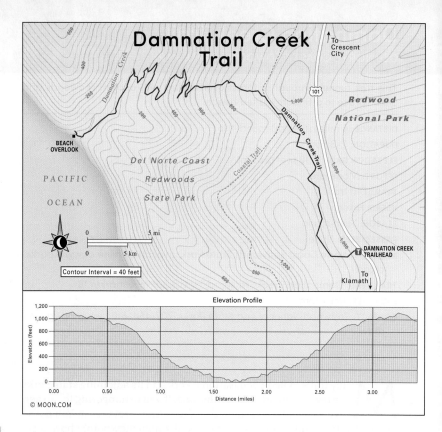

Damnation Creek Trail

To Crescent City

Redwood National Park

BEACH OVERLOOK

Del Norte Coast Redwoods State Park

PACIFIC OCEAN

Coastal Trail

Damnation Creek Trail

101

To Klamath

DAMNATION CREEK TRAILHEAD

Contour Interval = 40 feet

0   5 mi
0   5 km

Elevation Profile

© MOON.COM

through the tree canopy, and you'll catch peekaboo glimpses of the ocean at the 1.6-mile (2.6-km) mark, where the forest transitions from redwoods to Sitka spruce.

Your trail winds downward to the narrow, steep ravine that contains Damnation Creek. At 1.9 miles (3.1 km), you'll cross the creek on **two bridges** in quick succession. The first bridge is a bit rickety but passable. The second bridge is out of order, closed since 2015 due to "structural failure." As of 2023, it hasn't been rebuilt.

If the second bridge is still uncrossable when you visit, you may want to utilize a well-traveled bypass: Just to the right of the broken bridge, clamber down into the streambed and scramble up the opposite slope. A well-worn path and makeshift stepping stones show that many hikers have crossed the stream this way, but do so at your own discretion.

▶ **MILE 1.9-2: Damnation Creek Crossing to Beach Overlook**

Once on Damnation Creek's far side, it's only 0.1 mile (0.2 km) to a **grassy headland** overlooking the ocean and the rocky cove below. A narrow trail leads down these steep cliffs to a small, rocky beach, which has some interesting tide pools at very low tide. But accessing the beach is a risky endeavor: The 50-foot (15-km) descent down the cliffs can be treacherous, especially when it's muddy or slippery. Also, keep in mind that when the

tide is high, there is no beach at all, just treacherous surf. Use your best judgment.

Staying put on this high perch is also a fine choice. You can gaze across the mouth of Damnation Creek as it empties into the ocean, watch the wild surf crash against offshore sea stacks, and perhaps wave your hat at passing gray whales. Open up your pack and pull out some snacks to pair with the frothing Pacific, and let this rugged coast work its magic on you.

▸ **MILE 2-4: Beach Overlook to Damnation Creek Trailhead**

For your trip back to your car, expect a fair amount of heavy breathing on the 1,000-foot (305-m) ascent. The climb is easier than it looks, though, thanks to plentiful shade and an alluring forest that gives you many reasons to stop and catch your breath.

DIRECTIONS

From Crescent City, drive 10 miles (16.1 km) south on U.S. 101 to the Damnation Creek Trailhead by mile marker 16 (at a wide dirt turnout on the highway's southwest side). If you're coming from the south, the trailhead is 5.1 miles (8.2 km) north of Trees of Mystery.

GPS COORDINATES: 41.6478, −124.1129; 41°38'52.1" N, 124°6'46.4" W

BEST NEARBY BITES

Refuel at **Schmidt's House of Jambalaya** (110 Anchor Way, Crescent City Harbor, 707/465-1465, www.jambalaya.house, noon-7pm Thurs.-Sat., 11am-6pm Sun., 11am-7pm Mon.), only 15 minutes from the trailhead. Take your pick from mouthwatering Cajun favorites: shrimp bisque, beer-battered fish-and-chips, crawdad fritters, snapper po'boy, and shrimp-filled jambalaya with peppery andouille sausage. Every meal is served with a side of ocean view.

This easy trek leads to an island-dotted coastline, dramatic waves, and the tan sands of an alluring beach that's hidden from the highway.

BEST: Coastal Hikes

DISTANCE: 2.3 miles (3.7 km) round-trip

DURATION: 1 hour

ELEVATION GAIN: 150 feet (46 m)

EFFORT: Easy

TRAIL: Dirt trail

USERS: Hikers

SEASON: Year-round

PASSES/FEES: None

MAPS: National Geographic Maps "Redwood National and State Parks"

TRAILHEAD: Lagoon Creek parking lot

FACILITIES: Restroom

CONTACT: Redwood National and State Parks, 707/464-6101, www.nps.gov/redw

This trail offers an alternative to this region's many redwood-studded trails. In place of towering trees, you'll find a driftwood-strewn beach, rocky sea stacks, and a placid lagoon. The trail's highlight is westward-facing Hidden Beach, a prime spot for sunset-watching.

START THE HIKE

▸ **MILE 0-1: Lagoon Creek Parking Lot to Hidden Beach**

Begin hiking at the northwest end of the **Lagoon Creek parking lot,** heading north. Ignore the junction with Coastal Trail continuing north at 0.1 mile (0.2 km) on the right; veer left instead and cross a **footbridge** over Lagoon Creek. The rush of U.S. 101's car traffic is quickly replaced by the sound of the Pacific's sonorous waves. You're following the west side of **Yurok Loop,** an ancient Native American pathway that travels along the sea bluffs, alternating between dense thickets of oak, willow, and alder and wide-open meadows.

Yurok Loop soon merges with the **Coastal Trail** heading south. Views of driftwood-laden **False Klamath Cove** to the north and massive **False Klamath Rock** to the west will capture your attention. At 209 feet (64 m) tall, False Klamath Rock dwarfs all the neighboring sea stacks on this stretch of coast. The rock and some of its neighbors are home to thousands of breeding seabirds, including black oystercatchers, Brandt's cormorants, common murres, double-crested cormorants, and tufted puffins. False Klamath Rock was also very important to the Yurok tribe. During low

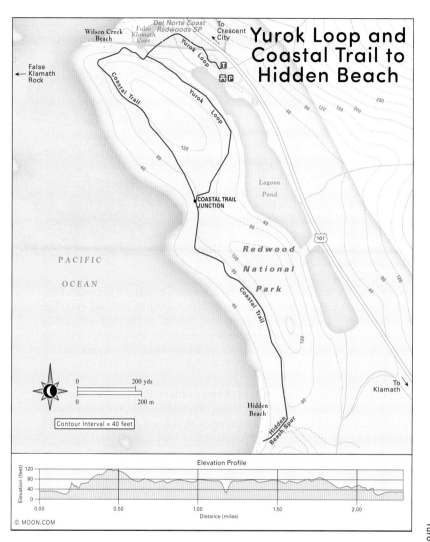

Yurok Loop and Coastal Trail to Hidden Beach

Elevation Profile

tide—when it's possible to walk right up to the rock—the Yurok people dug brodiaea bulbs ("Indian potatoes") at its base.

The long curve of **Wilson Creek Beach,** at the south end of False Klamath Cove, lies to the right. Bleached-white driftwood logs form a barrier at the back of the dark-gray beach, a popular spot for strolling and picnicking.

At a **junction** at 0.4 mile (0.6 km), keep right on Coastal Trail, saving the east side Yurok Loop for your return. Ramble along Coastal Trail for another 0.6 mile (1 km), enjoying a level fern-lined grade and coastal vistas. When you reach the **spur trail to Hidden Beach,** turn right (west) for 100 yards (91 m) to reach a small rugged cove with jagged boulders rising out of the sea, surly waves, and driftwood logs of every shape and size. If you haven't pulled out your binoculars yet, you will now: Seabirds such as cormorants, pigeon guillemots, brown pelicans, and common murres often perch on the sea stacks.

▶ **MILE 1-2.3: Hidden Beach to Lagoon Creek Parking Lot**

For your return from the beach, head back the way you came on Coastal Trail. This time turn right and walk the east side of the Yurok Loop, descending through a tunnel-like canopy of alders and Sitka spruces. Ferns cover the ground and moss clings to the sides of the trees.

When you return to the parking lot, be sure to take a good look at the freshwater pond on Lagoon Creek. A former channel of the Klamath River, this watercourse became the Crescent Plywood Company's millpond in the 1940s. It was enlarged and filled with hundreds of peeled logs, and since that time, it has transitioned into a natural wetland bounded by willows and sedges. Yellow pond lilies bloom on the water's surface in summer, and the pond is a welcome stopover for waterfowl, including ducks, egrets, and herons. You might spot a few trout anglers here too.

DIRECTIONS

From Crescent City, drive 15 miles (24 km) south on U.S. 101 and turn right at the sign for Lagoon Creek Picnic Area. The trail begins on the northwest side of the parking lot. If you're coming from the south, the trailhead is 1 mile (1.6 km) north of Trees of Mystery.

GPS COORDINATES: 41.5942, −124.0990; 41°35'39.1" N, 124°5'56.4" W

BEST NEARBY BREWS

Port O' Pints Brewing (1215 Northcrest Dr., Crescent City, 707/460-1154, www.portopints.com, 1pm-9pm Mon.-Thurs., noon-10:30pm Fri.-Sat., noon-8pm Sun.) is part old-school dive bar, part new wave craft brewery. Chat with the locals while you sample an array of IPAs, porters, stouts, and sours or nosh on pub food. Non-beer-drinkers can sip handcrafted root beer or kombucha. The brewery is a 20-minute drive from this trailhead.

Brown Creek, Rhododendron, and South Fork Loop

PRAIRIE CREEK REDWOODS STATE PARK

This easy loop through towering redwoods is a perfect walk for tree-huggers. If you don't think that describes you, take this walk and you might become a convert.

BEST: Redwood Hikes

DISTANCE: 3.6 miles (5.8 km) round-trip

DURATION: 2 hours

ELEVATION GAIN: 700 feet (213 m)

EFFORT: Easy-moderate

TRAIL: Dirt trail

USERS: Hikers

SEASON: Year-round

PASSES/FEES: None

MAPS: National Geographic Maps "Redwood National and State Parks"

TRAILHEAD: South Fork/Brown Creek Trailhead near Drury Scenic Parkway marker 129

FACILITIES: Restroom

CONTACT: Prairie Creek Redwoods State Park, 707/464-6101, www.parks. ca.gov or www.nps.gov/redw

START THE HIKE

▶ **MILE 0-1: South Fork Trailhead to Schenck Memorial Grove**

Start by following South Fork Trail, passing a **junction** with Foothill Trail on the right at 0.1 mile (0.2 km). Cross Brown Creek on a **footbridge,** then turn left on **Brown Creek Trail,** heading north. (The right fork is South Fork Trail's continuation, where you'll finish out this loop—you'll return to this spot.)

As it meanders alongside charming Brown Creek, the path leads through a spectacular grove of virgin old-growth redwoods accompanied by a jungle of sword ferns and huckleberry bushes. The rippling creek serves as the lifeblood for the majestic trees and supersize shrubs. You may find that your normal walking pace has slowed; many hikers feel an urge to walk slowly and reverently through this cathedral-like forest.

The trail crosses to Brown Creek's western side at a second **footbridge** at 0.4 mile (0.6 km), and the redwoods here appear even larger. Among the still-growing leviathans are giants that have toppled to the forest floor. These fallen trees play a critical role in the redwood forest—their horizontal trunks serve as natural "planters" or nurse logs for ferns, mosses, mushrooms, and sorrels.

At 0.9 mile (1.4 km), a **spur trail** leads off to the right and crosses a **footbridge.** Follow this short path to the **Carl Schenck Memorial Grove,** dedicated to a German forester who operated North America's first forestry

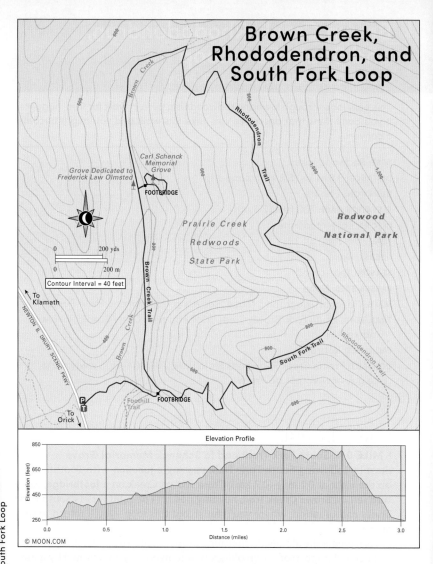

Brown Creek, Rhododendron, and South Fork Loop

Elevation Profile

© MOON.COM

school at the Biltmore Estate in Asheville, North Carolina. Schenck, who taught thousands of students in the early 20th century, was instrumental in protecting these old-growth forests.

▶ MILE 1–2.5: Carl Schenck Memorial Grove to Rhododendron–South Fork Trail Junction

After visiting this lovely grove, backtrack across the bridge and turn right (north) to continue your loop. You'll immediately pass a **grove** on the left dedicated to Frederick Law Olmsted, the landscape architect who designed New York's Central Park and planned the Biltmore Estate's gardens (where Schenck worked). Olmsted was also instrumental in envisioning America's national park system. Both Olmsted and Schenck promoted the idea that forests could be managed sustainably.

Brown Creek Trail meets up with **Rhododendron Trail** at 1.3 miles (2.1 km); turn right (south) on Rhododendron and cross another **bridge** over Brown Creek. You'll face the steepest climb of this trek—still moderate by any standard—as the path traverses the canyon's upper slopes. True to the trail's name, rhododendrons bloom throughout this forest in spring, adding splashes of vibrant pink to the gamut of greenery. Your ascent tops out at 2.5 miles (4 km), where Rhododendron Trail meets up with **South Fork Trail.**

▸ **MILE 2.5-3.6: Rhododendron-South Fork Trail Junction to South Fork Trailhead**

At the **junction,** turn right (west) onto South Fork Trail and finish out the loop with an easy snaking descent. Look for orange leopard lilies, growing as tall as 5 feet (1.5 m), mixed in among the redwoods, huckleberries, and rhododendrons.

When you reach the Brown Creek Trail junction again—the same spot where your loop began—cross the bridge and follow South Fork Trail 0.2 mile (0.3 km) back to your car.

DIRECTIONS

From Orick, drive 5 miles (8.1 km) north on U.S. 101 and take the Newton B. Drury Scenic Parkway exit. Turn left and drive 2.7 miles (4.3 km) to the parking pullout (with about 10 spots) on the east side of the road near mile marker 129. The trail is signed for South Fork Trail and Brown Creek Trail.

GPS COORDINATES: 41.3877, −124.0173; 41°23′15.7″ N, 124°1′2.3″ W

BEST NEARBY BITES

After this hike, drive 45 minutes north to Crescent City for fabulous Thai food at **Kin Khao Eatery** (1270 Front St., Crescent City, 707/460-6611, 11am-9pm Tues.-Sun.). Order popular mainstays like pad thai or pad see ew, or try the local fave, pumpkin salmon curry. For dessert, the mango sticky rice is a winner. Vegetarians will find great options here.

Wander among venerable redwoods and riffling creeks on this day-long trek to Fern Canyon, where a wealth of waving ferns cling to 50-foot-high (15-m) walls.

DISTANCE: 11.4 miles (18.4 km) round-trip

DURATION: 6-7 hours

ELEVATION GAIN: 2,318 feet (706 m)

EFFORT: Moderate-strenuous

TRAIL: Dirt trail

USERS: Hikers

SEASON: Year-round

PASSES/FEES: $8 day-use fee per vehicle

MAPS: Prairie Creek Redwoods State Park, available online at www.parks.ca.gov

TRAILHEAD: Prairie Creek Redwoods State Park visitor center parking lot

FACILITIES: Restroom, visitor center

CONTACT: Prairie Creek Redwoods State Park, 707/488-2039 or 707/488-2171, www.parks.ca.gov

Hikers hoping to visit spectacular Fern Canyon via the short route—from the Davison Road trailhead—must secure an advance permit May 1 to September 30. But if you're willing to take a longer trek, this no-permit-needed route takes you to Fern Canyon with lovely scenery along the way.

START THE HIKE

▶ **MILE 0-3.3: Visitor Center Parking Lot to James Irvine-Clintonia Junction**

From the signboard at the **visitor center parking lot,** head right (east) and cross a **large bridge** over Prairie Creek. Ignore two right turnoffs for Prairie Creek Trail and West Ridge Trail, then cross a **smaller bridge** over Godwood Creek, passing through a mossy grove of big-leaf maples. On the bridge's far side, turn right (north) on **James Irvine Trail** at 0.2 mile (0.3 km). You've just entered a portal into a world in which everything is green and oversize. Moss covers rocks, lichens hang from branches, redwood sorrel carpets the ground, and trees grow to colossal sizes. In late fall, winter, and spring, colorful mushrooms pop from the ground, and banana slugs slime their way through the forest duff.

James Irvine Trail soon switchbacks away from the creek, then at 0.8 mile (1.3 km) reaches a **junction** with the southern end of Miners Ridge Trail on the left. Stay right (north) on James Irvine Trail. Another 2.5 miles

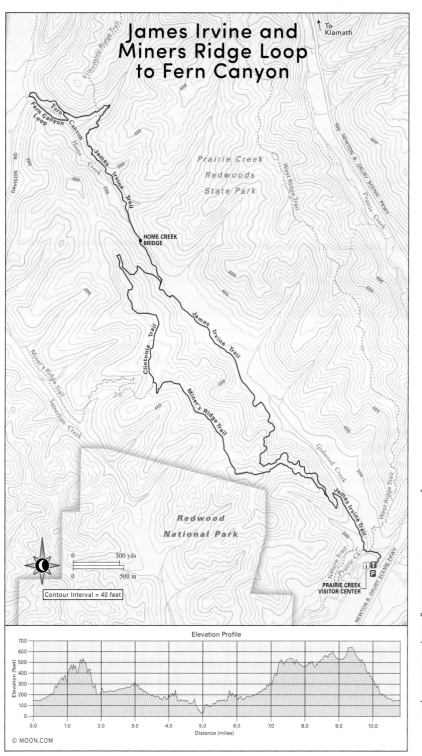

James Irvine and Miners Ridge Loop to Fern Canyon

To Klamath

Fern Canyon Loop

Fern Canyon

Friendship Ridge Trail

DAVISON RD

Home Creek

James Irvine Trail

Prairie Creek Redwoods State Park

West Ridge Trail

NEWTON B. DRURY SCENIC PKWY

Prairie Creek

HOME CREEK BRIDGE

Clintonia Trail

James Irvine Trail

Miner's Ridge Trail

Squashan Creek

Redwood National Park

Godwood Creek

West Ridge Trail

James Irvine Trail

Nature Trail

Prairie Ck

PRAIRIE CREEK VISITOR CENTER

NEWTON B. DRURY SCENIC PKWY

Contour Interval = 40 feet

0   500 yds
0   500 m

© MOON.COM

Elevation Profile

Elevation (feet)

700
600
500
400
300
200
100
0

0.0   1.0   2.0   3.0   4.0   5.0   6.0   7.0   8.0   9.0   10.0

Distance (miles)

(4 km) of moderate climbing past redwoods, Douglas firs, huckleberry, and sword ferns brings you to a **junction** with Clintonia Trail at 3.3 miles (5.3 km). Bear right (northeast) to continue on James Irvine Trail.

▸ **MILE 3.3–5.4: James Irvine–Clintonia Junction to Fern Canyon Loop**
James Irvine Trail descends to a **bridge** over Home Creek, then crosses and recrosses the musical stream for the next 1.3 miles (2.1 km) of easy walking. You've left most of the redwoods behind you, and now you're tunneling through a lush coastal forest of Sitka spruces, western hemlocks, alders, and ferns.

Towering trees along Home Creek filter the sun, creating a shadowy, dreamy effect. At 4.3 miles (6.9 km) you'll spy a delicate 25-foot-high (8-m) **waterfall** that drops into a remarkably narrow side canyon and eventually trickles into Home Creek.

At a **junction** with Friendship Ridge Trail at 4.6 miles (7.4 km), bear left (southwest) on James Irvine Trail to descend into **Fern Canyon.** An easy 0.5-mile (0.8 km) stroll through Sitka spruce forest deposits you at the mouth of this fabled canyon. Turn left on **Fern Canyon Trail** to walk along Home Creek's cobbled streambed, framed by dripping walls of ferns. Don't expect to keep your feet dry; the trail is simply the streambed, so you must hop your way across logs and rocks. Inevitably, at least one shoe will go in the water. Unless you're visiting in the driest, warmest months of summer, it's smart to pack along water sandals for the canyon walk, or at least an extra pair of dry socks to change into.

▶ **MILE 5.4–8.8: Fern Canyon Loop to Clintonia-Miners Ridge Junction**

When you're ready to depart this fern-filled paradise, retrace your steps to the Clintonia Trail junction that you passed earlier, 1.6 miles (2.6 km) away. Turn sharply right (northwest) to follow **Clintonia Trail,** climbing steeply for more than 1 mile (1.6 km). Several memorial groves are located just off the trail, providing convenient rest stops from the steady ascent.

In spring, look near your feet for the trail's namesake—magenta-flowered Andrews' clintonia, a member of the lily family. This pink-red beauty thrives in the redwoods' dense shade. Once the flowers are finished blooming, the plant produces blue berries.

Where Clintonia Trail ends at a junction with Miners Ridge Trail, turn left (east).

▶ **MILE 8.8–11.4: Clintonia-Miners Ridge Junction**
   to Visitor Center Parking Lot

Climb steeply for another 0.3 mile (0.5 km), then begin a long, mellow descent, losing 450 feet (137 m) over 1.5 miles (2.4 km). The redwoods on **Miners Ridge Trail** are as awe-inspiring as those on James Irvine Trail, perhaps even more so because you'll have less company here. Take advantage of benches placed at intervals along the trail; each one offers a place to sit quietly and listen to the forest's silence.

Where Miners Ridge Trail ends at a **junction** with James Irvine Trail, simply turn right (south) and finish out the last 0.8 mile (1.3 km) to the visitor center parking lot.

DIRECTIONS

From Orick, drive 5 miles (8.1 km) north on U.S. 101 and take the Newton B. Drury Scenic Parkway exit. Turn left, following the signs for 1 mile (1.6 km) to the Prairie Creek Redwoods State Park visitor center parking lot. Several trails, including James Irvine Trail, begin at the large signboard on the lot's north side.

GPS COORDINATES: 41.3641, −124.0230; 41°21'50.8" N, 124°1'22.8" W

BEST NEARBY BITES

Less than 10 minutes away from the trailhead is **EdeBee's Snack Shack** (120779 U.S. 101, Orick, 707/951-1777, 11am–5pm Wed.–Sat., 11am–4pm Sun.). You may feel a little funny about ordering the elk burger if you admired some of those magnificent animals today, but it's delicious. The Shack also serves beef burgers, fish-and-chips, milkshakes, and huge portions of fries.

Skunk Cabbage Creek and Coastal Trail

REDWOOD NATIONAL PARK

The magnificent skunk cabbage, with leaves longer than an adult's arm, is the celebrity flora on this trail, which traipses from lush forest to windswept coast.

BEST: Spring Hikes
DISTANCE: 7.6 miles (12.2 km) round-trip
DURATION: 4 hours
ELEVATION GAIN: 1,030 feet (314 m)
EFFORT: Easy-moderate
TRAIL: Dirt trail
USERS: Hikers
SEASON: Year-round
PASSES/FEES: None
MAPS: National Geographic Maps "Redwood National and State Parks"
TRAILHEAD: Coastal Trail Skunk Cabbage Section Trailhead
FACILITIES: Restroom
CONTACT: Redwood National and State Parks, 707/464-6101, www.nps.gov/redw

I f your heart is set on seeing skunk cabbage, hike this trail any time except winter, when the plants lose their remarkably large leaves. Their bright yellow flowers bloom from March to May.

START THE HIKE

▸ **MILE 0-1.4: Skunk Cabbage Trailhead to Skunk Cabbage Creek Bridge**

The **Skunk Cabbage Trail,** a section of Redwood National Park's Coastal Trail, leads deep into Sitka spruce, western hemlock, and red alder forest—a maze of foliage that's so dense you may think you've walked onto the set of a dinosaur movie. This vibrant landscape will capture your imagination, but be forewarned—beyond the **Johnson Creek crossing** at 0.1 mile (0.2 km), you won't see many redwoods. An altogether different flora takes the stage here.

At 0.6 mile (1 km), the trail enters the drainage of Skunk Cabbage Creek, then crosses and recrosses the creek and its tributaries on wooden **footbridges.** Below the trail on your right is a vast swampy bog, where you'll see an astonishing concentration of skunk cabbages growing on both sides of the stream. Hundreds, or perhaps thousands, of these tropical-green plants flourish here. Each plant's leaves may grow up to 5 feet (1.5 m) long and 1 foot (0.3 m) wide. They look like houseplants on steroids.

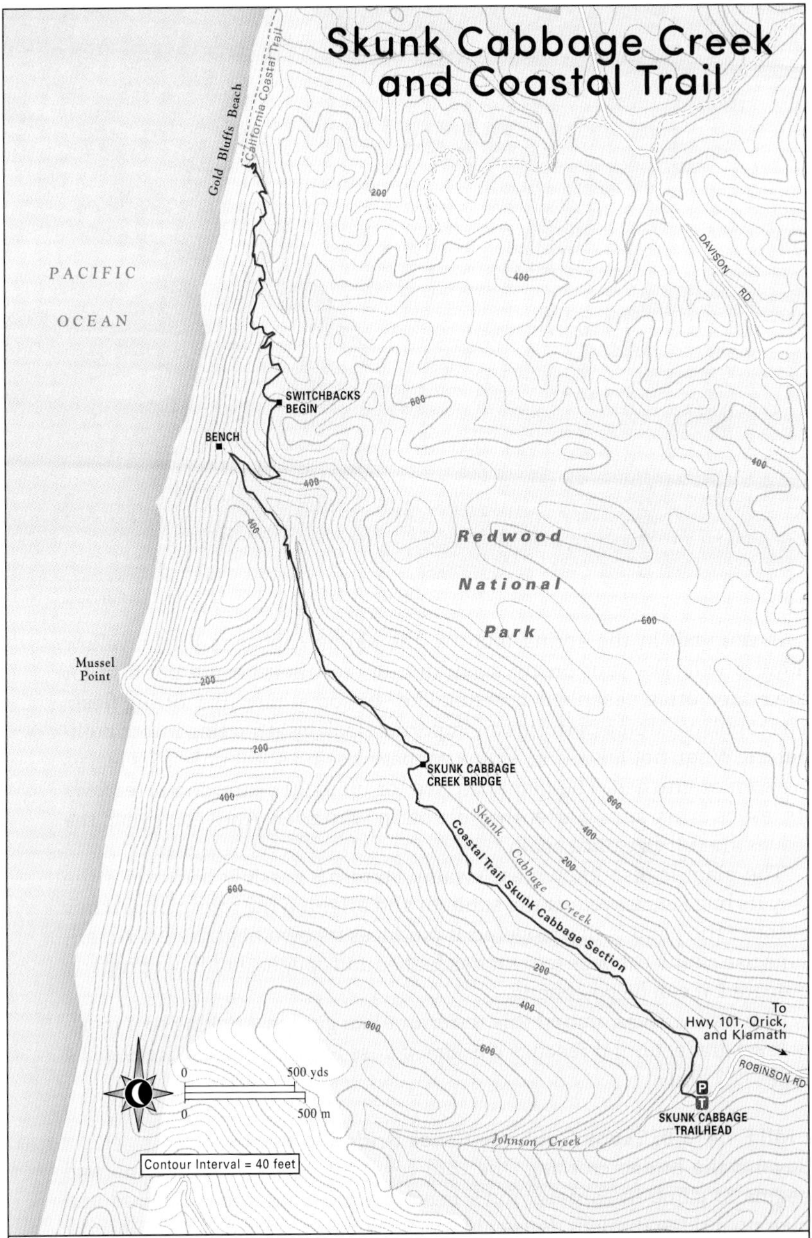

Skunk Cabbage Creek and Coastal Trail

PACIFIC OCEAN

Gold Bluffs Beach

California Coastal Trail

DAVISON RD

200

600

400

SWITCHBACKS BEGIN

BENCH

400

400

Redwood National Park

600

Mussel Point

200

200

400

SKUNK CABBAGE CREEK BRIDGE

Skunk Cabbage Creek

Coastal Trail Skunk Cabbage Section

600

400

200

200

400

600

To Hwy 101, Orick, and Klamath

ROBINSON RD

P T SKUNK CABBAGE TRAILHEAD

Johnson Creek

0   500 yds
0   500 m

Contour Interval = 40 feet

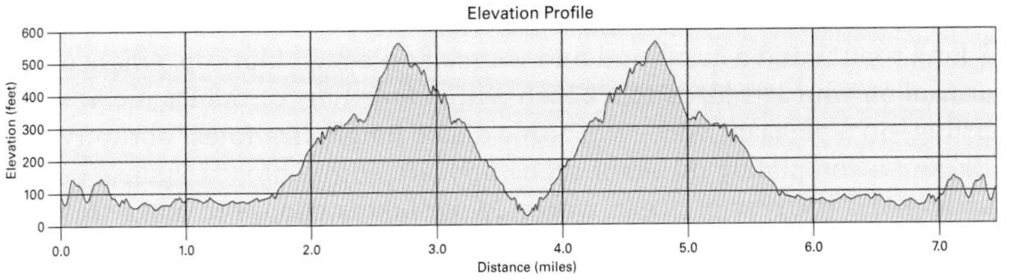

Elevation Profile

Elevation (feet) — 0, 100, 200, 300, 400, 500, 600

Distance (miles) — 0.0, 1.0, 2.0, 3.0, 4.0, 5.0, 6.0, 7.0

© MOON.COM

If you visit in the spring months, the skunk cabbage's bright yellow flowers will take your breath away, not just for their beauty but also for their odor, often described as skunk-like—or sometimes like rotting flesh. The repulsive aroma performs an important task by attracting insect pollinators. When not flowering, skunk cabbage has no scent unless its leaves are torn or crushed. The plant can live for up to 20 years, and it regrows its leaves every spring after they die off in winter. By April each year, the leaves are full size once again.

The plant is also known as "swamp lantern," possibly because of the way its huge leaves reflect the sunlight and brighten the forest, or perhaps because the plant is thermogenic; it produces its own heat. Native Americans use skunk cabbage to treat headaches and coughs, but if not properly prepared, it can be poisonous.

The trail weaves among this terrarium-like garden, sticking to a mostly level grade, until it reaches a **bridge** across Skunk Cabbage Creek at 1.4 miles (2.3 km).

▶ **MILE 1.4–3.8: Skunk Cabbage Creek Bridge to Beach**

Beyond the bridge crossing, the trail ceases its gentle meandering and begins to climb in earnest. You'll leave the coursing stream behind and hike up a ridge through dense alders, reaching the creek's headwaters at 2 miles (3.2 km). Keep tunneling through this forest for another 0.5 mile (0.8 km), then round a curve and find yourself on a high blufftop, where a **spur trail** on your left leads to a **bench** with a fine view of the Pacific. It's startling—in a pleasant way—when this dense jungle-like forest abruptly ends, and a completely different scene appears with a broad expanse of coastline and the roar of ocean waves. Many hikers choose to make this blufftop their turnaround for a 5-mile (8.1-km) round-trip, but if you have energy to spare, return to the main trail for a little more climbing, then a final descent to the ocean.

At 2.7 miles (4.3 km), the path drops downhill in steep **switchbacks,** leading into moss-covered Sitka spruce forest and eventually coastal scrub. The trail's final stint is narrow and often overgrown; watch for poison oak. You're deposited on an alluring, isolated strand of sand about 1.5 miles (2.4 km) south of Gold Bluffs Beach and 1 mile (1.6 km) north of Mussel Point. With luck, the coastal wind won't be howling and you can open up your pack, pull out your charcuterie or peanut butter sandwich, and spend an hour or two savoring sea, sand, and precious solitude.

For your return trip, just turn around and enjoy this scenery all over again.

DIRECTIONS

From Orick, drive 1.1 miles (1.8 km) north on U.S. 101. Shortly past the right turnoff for Bald Hills Road, turn left at the sign for Coastal Trail Skunk Cabbage Section (this is Robinson Road). Drive 0.6 mile (1 km) to the trailhead parking area.

GPS COORDINATES: 41.3075, −124.0568; 41°18′27″ N, 124°3′24.5″ W

BEST NEARBY BREWS

At **Six Rivers Brewery** (1300 Central Ave., McKinleyville, 707/839-7580, www.sixriversbrewery.com, noon-8pm Tues.-Fri., noon-9pm Sat.-Sun.), order a beer flight, house-made pretzels, and beer cheese, then grab a seat on the Pacific-view patio. The brewers concoct intriguing flavor profiles like spicy chili pepper ale, macadamia nut porter, raspberry lambic, and seasonal strawberry wheat. Six Rivers is a 40-minute drive south on U.S. 101 from this trailhead.

7 Tall Trees Grove

REDWOOD NATIONAL PARK

In 1963, this redwood grove boasted the world's tallest tree. Taller redwoods have been discovered since, but this grove's awe factor hasn't waned.

BEST: Redwood Hikes
DISTANCE: 3.6 miles (5.8 km) round-trip
DURATION: 2-3 hours
ELEVATION GAIN: 750 feet (229 m)
EFFORT: Easy-moderate
TRAIL: Dirt trail
USERS: Hikers
SEASON: Year-round
PASSES/FEES: Free permit required; apply online at https://redwoodparksconservancy.org/permits/tall-trees
MAPS: National Geographic Maps "Redwood National and State Parks"
TRAILHEAD: Tall Trees Grove Trailhead on Bald Hills Road and Tall Trees Access Road
FACILITIES: Restroom
CONTACT: Redwood National and State Parks, 707/464-6101, www.nps.gov/redw

Permits for this trail are limited to 65 cars each day. At least 24 hours before your hike, you must apply online for a free permit, which includes a combination for the locked access road gate. (You may apply up to 180 days in advance. During summer, holiday weekends, and other busy times, make sure you reserve a permit at least two weeks in advance.)

START THE HIKE

▶ **MILE 0-1.3: Tall Trees Grove Trailhead to Start of Loop Trail**
At the **Tall Trees Grove Trailhead,** pick up an interpretive brochure at the kiosk and head steeply downhill. You'll pass a **junction** with Emerald Ridge Trail in the first 100 yards; stay right (southwest). The first stretch leads gently downhill through a forest of small redwoods, Douglas firs, and hemlocks intermixed with rhododendrons and 4-foot-tall (1.2-m) sword ferns. You'll see no jumbo-size redwoods yet, but just wait. At 1.3 miles (2.1 km), after descending 750 feet (229 m), your trail bottoms out in the grove's **watershed.** This is a lollipop loop, and you've just completed the "stick." Now head left (west) on the loop trail, circling the grove clockwise.

▶ **MILE 1.3-2.3: Start of Loop Trail to End of Loop**
As you walk along this rich alluvial plain next to Redwood Creek, you'll quickly determine that the trail's name is an understatement. These aren't your average tall trees. Dozens of leviathans exceed 350 feet (107 m), their trunks extending skyward from a ground-carpet of ferns and sorrel.

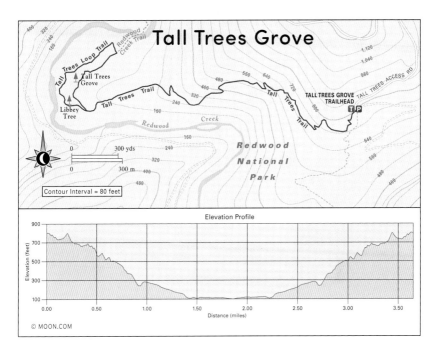

Tall Trees Grove

Elevation Profile

© MOON.COM

In a region that's famous for massively tall trees, these are chart-toppers. As you wander among the behemoths, be sure to follow the short spur trails leading off the loop to the gravel banks of Redwood Creek. The rich soils from the creek's streambed, combined with the foggy and wet coastal climate, help these redwoods to grow to their enormous size. Even the rhododendrons in this grove grow to supersize, as tall as 15 feet (4.5 m). In May and June, they show off flashy pink blooms that light up the redwoods' dark emerald shadows.

The Tall Trees Grove is home to what was once considered the world's tallest tree, the 367-foot-tall (112-m) **Libbey Tree,** which graced the cover of *National Geographic* magazine in July 1964. You'll pass the famous tree, named for the owner of a lumber company, at 1.5 miles (2.4 km). In 1989, the Libbey was downgraded in tall-tree rankings after losing some of its height in a storm—it's now "merely" 362 feet (110 m) tall.

At 0.4 mile (0.6 km) beyond the Libbey Tree, you'll reach a **junction** for Redwood Creek Trail. In the summer months, a bridge is in place here to carry hikers across the creek. Hidden deep in the forest across the creek grows the current tallest tree, 380-foot-tall (116-m) **Hyperion.** There's no trail leading to this record holder. Despite the fact that Hyperion is hard to reach, it's been exploited on social media, and far too many trophy-seeking visitors have trampled its delicate root system. The National Park Service requests that hikers leave the 700-year-old tree to grow in peace.

▸ MILE 2.3–3.6: End of Loop to Tall Trees Grove Trailhead

The loop's far eastern end departs the redwoods and enters a lush grove of maples. You'll wander through this very different forest, which also thrives on nutrients from Redwood Creek, then head back westward into

TALL TREES GROVE ▲

the ancient redwoods. Linger as long as you can among the giants, then rejoin the "stick" of this lollipop to head back uphill to your car.

DIRECTIONS

From Orick, drive 1 mile (1.6 km) north on U.S. 101 and turn right on Bald Hills Road (not recommended for trailers and RVs). Drive 7 miles (11.3 km) to the Tall Trees Access Road on the right, shortly beyond Redwood Creek Overlook. Turn right, stop at the gate, use your permit combination to open it, then drive through and close the gate behind you. Drive 5.8 miles (9.3 km) on the dirt Tall Trees Access Road to the trailhead parking lot.

GPS COORDINATES: 41.2081, −123.9931; 41°12'29.2" N, 123°59'35.2" W

BEST NEARBY BITES

Forty minutes south on U.S. 101, chic seafood spot **Salt Fish House** (835 I St., Arcata, 707/630-5300, www.saltfishhouse.com, 3:30pm-9pm Tues.-Sun.) has put Arcata on the foodie map. Start with Pacific oysters, ceviche tostadas, or smoked steelhead dip, then work your way down the menu to curried mussels and charred octopus with chili jam. Cap off your meal with a chocolate brownie served with two spoons.

Rim Trail
SUE-MEG STATE PARK

Savor vistas of stalwart sea stacks and craggy headlands accompanied by the soundtrack of the Pacific's pounding surf.

DISTANCE: 5 miles (8.1 km) round-trip

DURATION: 2.5 hours

ELEVATION GAIN: 550 feet (168 m)

EFFORT: Easy-moderate

TRAIL: Dirt trail, wooden stairs

USERS: Hikers

SEASON: Year-round

PASSES/FEES: $8 day-use fee per vehicle

MAPS: Sue-meg State Park, available online at www.parks.ca.gov

TRAILHEAD: Palmer's Point parking lot

FACILITIES: Restroom

CONTACT: Sue-meg State Park, 707/677-3570, www.parks.ca.gov

This hike follows Rim Trail across the park's oceanfront headland, but its best treasures lie a short distance off the trail. Don't miss the out-and-back side trips to rugged coastal viewpoints at Rocky Point, Patrick's Point, Wedding Rock, and Mussel Rocks (accessible via spur trails leading off the Rim Trail). If you want to shorten this trek, you can park your car at the day-use lot near Wedding Rock and hike from there instead of completing the entire Rim Trail.

START THE HIKE

▶ **MILE 0-1.5: Palmer's Point Parking Lot to Wedding Rock**

Start on **Rim Trail**'s southern terminus near **Palmer's Point.** You'll immediately enter dense foliage; this forest overflows with Bishop pines, beach pines, and Sitka spruces. You're following an ancient path used by the Yurok people, and it's not difficult to picture this impenetrable forest as it was hundreds of years ago. Lace lichen, sometimes called "old man's beard," hangs from tree branches like a fishing net hanging from a ship. Birds use this soft lichen to line their nests. An understory of salmonberry, thimbleberry, and ferns covers every inch of real estate. If Rim Trail hadn't been carved out of these woods, it would be impossible to pass through.

Cross over **Beach Creek** at 0.4 mile (0.6 km) and **Penn Creek** immediately after. Ignore side trails on your right leading to the park's campgrounds, staying on Rim Trail. In another 0.2 mile (0.3 km), make a detour on the spur trail to **Rocky Point,** where you can gaze over the coast to the north and south and admire dozens of indomitable sea stacks. These tenacious rocks have withstood the Pacific's relentless battering since the Pleistocene era.

Backtrack 0.2 mile (0.3 km) to the Rim Trail and turn left (northeast). The next spur delivers you to a railing-lined overlook at **Patrick's Point,**

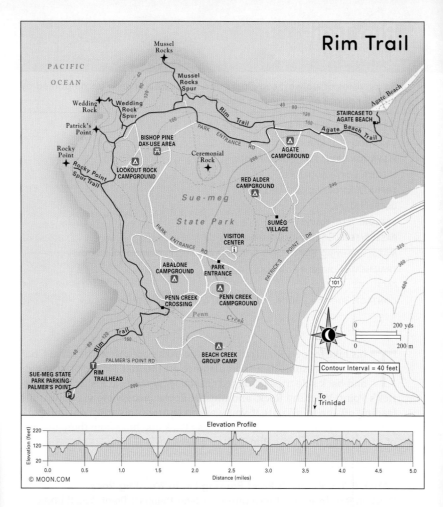

Elevation Profile

© MOON.COM

worth a 50-yard detour to scan the ocean's horizon for migrating California gray whales in late fall and spring. In summer, humpback whales are sometimes seen feeding close to shore.

Back on Rim Trail, reach the spur for turreted **Wedding Rock** at 1.4 miles (2.3 km). This is arguably the park's best viewpoint. In the 1930s, the Civilian Conservation Corps built a masterwork of chiseled rock stairs winding to the top of 140-foot-high (43-m) Wedding Rock. Dotted with shore pines, the castle-like promontory offers head-swiveling views of Rocky Point and Trinidad Head to the south and crashing waves pounding the headlands.

On a clear day, it's hard to leave Wedding Rock, but you might want to explore the rocky **beach** just to the north, particularly if the tide is low. With only a short walk, you can say hello to the tide pool creatures by following the secondary spur trail that forks off Wedding Rock's spur.

▶ **MILE 1.5-2.5: Wedding Rock to Agate Beach**

Backtrack to Rim Trail again, and at 1.8 miles (2.9 km), reach the **Mussel Rocks** spur, where once again you'll make a detour. This path leads to another photogenic stretch of rugged coastline, where you can watch the foaming and frothing Pacific pound away at imposing sea stacks.

Returning to Rim Trail, cross over **Beaver Creek,** then reach Rim Trail's northern terminus near **Agate Campground** at 2 miles (3.2 km). Here, walk along the campground road for a brief stint, then descend a long wooden staircase down to **Agate Beach,** a 2-mile-long (3.2-km) crescent of sand backed by wooded headlands. At low tide, it's possible to find sea-polished agates, moonstones, and other bits of semiprecious stones on the sand. Agate Beach is also a fine spot for a seaside picnic before you retrace your steps back to your car.

DIRECTIONS

From Trinidad, drive 5 miles (8.1 km) north on U.S. 101 and take exit 734 for Patrick's Point Drive. Follow Patrick's Point Drive for 0.4 mile (0.6 km), then turn right on Park Entrance Road. Just beyond the park entrance kiosk, turn left and follow the road to its end at Palmer's Point. Park your car, then backtrack 50 yards (46 m) along the park road to the start of the Rim Trail.

GPS COORDINATES: 41.1296, −124.1633; 41°7′46.6″ N, 124°9′47.9″ W

BEST NEARBY BREWS

A short stroll from Trinidad's harbor and 15 minutes' drive from the trailhead, **Trinidad Bay Eatery & Gallery** (607 Parker St., Trinidad, 707/677-3777, www.trinidadeatery.com, 11am-6pm Mon.-Wed., 9am-8pm Thurs.-Sun.) serves fish-rich cioppino, fresh salmon, and clam chowder in a grilled-on-top bread bowl. Don't forget to order the blackberry cobbler.

NEARBY CAMPGROUNDS

NAME	DESCRIPTION	FACILITIES	SEASON	FEE
Jedediah Smith	On the Smith River in old-growth redwoods; hiking trails, swimming, fishing nearby	86 sites for tents or RVs up to 25 ft/7.6 m, 4 ADA-accessible cabins, restrooms, drinking water, coin showers, dump station	year-round	$35

Jedidiah Smith State Park, 10 miles (16.1 km) east of Crescent City on U.S. 199, 800/444-7275, www.reservecalifornia.com

NAME	DESCRIPTION	FACILITIES	SEASON	FEE
Mill Creek	Sites in a shady mixed forest with access to Mill Creek; hiking trails nearby	145 sites for tents or RVs up to 28 ft/8.5 m, restrooms, drinking water, coin showers, dump station	May 18 to September 30	$35

Del Norte Coast Redwoods State Park, 7 miles (11.3 km) south of Crescent City on U.S. 101, 800/444-7275, www.reservecalifornia.com

NAME	DESCRIPTION	FACILITIES	SEASON	FEE
Elk Prairie	Grazing Roosevelt elk, ancient redwoods, 70 mi/113 km of hiking and biking trails	75 sites for tents or RVs up to 27 ft/8.2 m, restrooms, drinking water, coin showers	year-round	$35

Prairie Creek Redwoods State Park, 6 miles (9.7 km) north of Orick off U.S. 101, 800/444-7275, www.reservecalifornia.com

NAME	DESCRIPTION	FACILITIES	SEASON	FEE
Gold Bluffs Beach	Grazing Roosevelt elk; easy access to a secluded beach, Fern Canyon (access to Davison Road trailhead to Fern Canyon included with campground reservation), and 70 mi/113 km of hiking and biking trails	26 sites for tents or RVs up to 24 ft/7.3 m, 4 ADA-accessible cabins, restrooms, drinking water, solar showers	year-round	$35

Prairie Creek Redwoods State Park, 10 miles (16.1 km) north of Orick on unpaved Davison Road, 800/444-7275, www.reservecalifornia.com

NAME	DESCRIPTION	FACILITIES	SEASON	FEE
Big Lagoon County Park	Waterfront campsites on the lagoon, easy access to the beach, swimming, kayaking, fishing, boat ramp	25 sites for tents or RVs up to 24 ft/7.3 m, restrooms, drinking water, coin showers	year-round	$25

Humboldt County Parks, 7 miles (11.3 km) north of Trinidad off U.S. 101, 707/445-7651, www.humboldtgov.org

NAME	DESCRIPTION	FACILITIES	SEASON	FEE
Clam Beach County Park	Access to beach, clamming, surf fishing, biking on Hammond Trail	15 sites for tents or RVs up to 24 ft/7.3 m, restrooms, drinking water	year-round	$25

Humboldt County Parks, 7.5 miles (12.1 km) north of Arcata off U.S. 101, 707/445-7651, www.humboldtgov.org

▲ GRAY BUTTE

SHASTA CASCADE & LASSEN

SHASTA-TRINITY NATIONAL FOREST

Two hundred miles (322 km) north of Sacramento lies a massive stretch of California that's largely untrammeled. A vast landscape of rugged mountains, steep river canyons, plummeting waterfalls, sparkling lakes, and conifer-covered ridges, this land is where ospreys and eagles soar, black bears roam, and wild trout swim.

Dominating the landscape is Mount Shasta (14,174 ft/4,320 m), a sleeping volcano that can be seen from 150 miles (242 km) away on clear days. Even in summer, it often wears a glistening cap of ice and snow, and runoff from Shasta's eight glaciers feeds dozens of waterways, including the McCloud, Shasta, and Sacramento Rivers. People from around the globe believe that Mount Shasta is the center of a massive energy vortex, and they come here to feel its power.

If you're looking for the ideal environment to hike, fly-fish, swim, bike, or ski, this region is an outdoor enthusiast's dream. The only thing you won't find is a crowd, and that's yet another reason to come here and go for a hike.

▲ McCLOUD FALLS

CASTLE LAKE

1 **Deadfall Lakes and Mount Eddy**
DISTANCE: 10.4 miles (16.7 km) round-trip
DURATION: 6-7 hours
EFFORT: Moderate-strenuous

2 **Bunny Flat to Alpine Lodge and/or Hidden Valley**
DISTANCE: 5.8 miles (9.3 km) round-trip
DURATION: 4 hours
EFFORT: Moderate

3 **Gray Butte**
DISTANCE: 3.2 miles (5.2 km) round-trip
DURATION: 1.5-2 hours
EFFORT: Easy-moderate

4 **South Gate Meadows**
DISTANCE: 3.6 miles (5.8 km) round-trip
DURATION: 2 hours
EFFORT: Easy-moderate

5 **Castle Lake to Heart Lake**
DISTANCE: 2.4 miles (3.9 km) round-trip
DURATION: 1.5 hours
EFFORT: Easy-moderate

6 **McCloud Falls**
DISTANCE: 3.8 miles (6.1 km) round-trip
DURATION: 2 hours
EFFORT: Easy

7 **Crags Trail to Castle Dome**
DISTANCE: 5.4 miles (8.7 km) round-trip
DURATION: 3-4 hours
EFFORT: Moderate-strenuous

8 **Burney Falls, Pacific Crest Trail, and Headwaters Loop**
DISTANCE: 2.7 miles (4.3 km) round-trip
DURATION: 1.5 hours
EFFORT: Easy

9 **James K. Carr Trail to Whiskeytown Falls**
DISTANCE: 3.4 miles (5.5 km) round-trip
DURATION: 2 hours
EFFORT: Easy-moderate

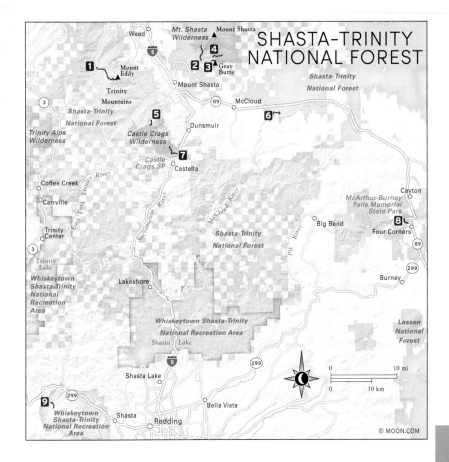

SHASTA-TRINITY
NATIONAL FOREST

1

Deadfall Lakes and Mount Eddy
SHASTA-TRINITY NATIONAL FOREST

Visit two lovely alpine lakes and claim the summit of 9,025-foot (2,751-m) Mount Eddy, the Klamath Mountains' highest peak.

DISTANCE: 10.4 miles (16.7 km) round-trip
DURATION: 6–7 hours
ELEVATION GAIN: 2,123 feet (647 m)
EFFORT: Moderate-strenuous
TRAIL: Dirt trail, talus slopes
USERS: Hikers, leashed dogs
SEASON: June–November
PASSES/FEES: None
MAPS: Download from https://mountshastatrailassociation.org
TRAILHEAD: Parks Creek Trailhead
FACILITIES: Restroom
CONTACT: Mount Shasta Ranger Station, 530/926-4511, www.fs.usda.gov/stnf

START THE HIKE

▶ **MILE 0-2.6: Parks Creek Trailhead to Middle Deadfall Lake**
From **Parks Creek Trailhead,** follow the **Pacific Crest Trail** south, roughly paralleling Forest Road 17 for the first 0.5 mile (0.8 km). The trail soon enters a dense forest of Shasta red fir, white fir, and western white pine. At 0.7 mile (1.1 km), cross a **logging road,** then continue strolling through gradually thinning forest. Soon the grassy expanse of **Deadfall Meadows** appears far downslope on your right, and at 1.7 miles (2.7 km), you'll pass a **trio of springs** pouring across the trail, their streams lined with monkshood and bog orchids in the summer.

The trail gently contours toward the Deadfall Lakes basin, and at 2.5 miles (4 km) you'll reach a major **four-way junction.** Depart the Pacific Crest Trail and bear left on **Sisson-Callahan Trail,** then immediately veer right to detour over to **Middle Deadfall Lake,** which you'll spy about 100 feet (30 m) away. This surprisingly large lake has much to offer: excellent fishing prospects, great backpacking campsites, and a shoreline dotted with shady lodgepole pines. The smaller **Lower Deadfall Lake** lies 150 yards (137 m) to the northwest, and although it's not as alluring as the middle lake, it's worth a look if you're a lake collector.

▶ **MILE 2.6-3.5: Middle Deadfall Lake to Upper Deadfall Lake**
From Middle Deadfall Lake, backtrack to Sisson-Callahan Trail, now heading right (southeast) toward the upper lake. You'll walk through a forest containing five different types of pines—lodgepole, western white, whitebark, foxtail, and Jeffrey. In 0.5 mile (0.8 km), you'll skirt the edge of a large greenish pond that's filled with tadpoles in early summer (on your right),

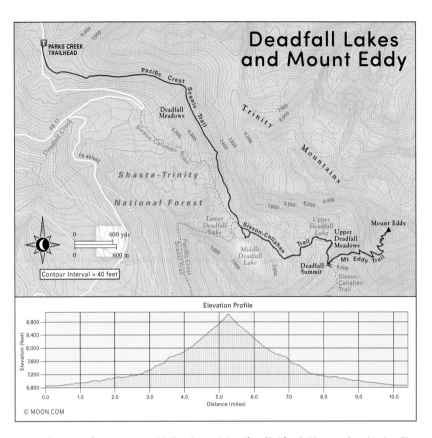

Deadfall Lakes and Mount Eddy

Elevation Profile

then reach **Upper Deadfall Lake** at 3.5 miles (5.6 km). You can't miss it—Sisson-Callahan Trail travels right alongside its southern edge. It's smaller and not as impressive as Middle Deadfall Lake, but you'll want to snap a few photos from its southwest shore, where there's a perfectly framed vista of Mount Eddy towering above, and you can listen to Clark's nutcrackers bickering over whitebark pinecones.

▶ **MILE 3.5-5.2: Upper Deadfall Lake to Mount Eddy Summit**
Continue along the trail as it climbs high above Upper Deadfall Lake. The grade grows noticeably steeper as you pass through **Upper Deadfall Meadows**, then reach a **ridgetop junction** at **Deadfall Summit,** 0.5 mile (0.8 km) from the lakeshore. Turn left (northeast) to ascend Mount Eddy's southern flank. More than a **dozen switchbacks** zigzag up the talus-covered slope, delivering broad views of the wildlands to the southwest. With each winding curve, your perspective changes, and before you know it, you're on top of **Mount Eddy's wide summit,** elevation 9,025 feet (2,751 m), the highest peak west of I-5.

Eddy's summit view will take your breath away; majestic Mount Shasta, often glowing white with snow, seems close enough to touch. Its ever-present sidekick—the nearly symmetrical cone of Black Butte—stands loyally at its eastern side. To the west are Thompson Peak and the Trinity Alps, the Marble Mountains, and Russian Wilderness. Oregon's Mount

Ashland and Mount McLoughlin dominate the northward view.

Scattered around the summit are the concrete and wood remains of an old fire lookout tower and sleeping quarters. Built in 1912, the tower was staffed by an operator whose duty was to spot wildfires throughout the region. Unfortunately, Mount Eddy's summit suffered severe storms, high winds, and lightning strikes, and some operators were struck by lightning and badly injured. Eventually the lookout tower was decommissioned, and the buildings succumbed to wind and weather.

For your return trip, turn around and retrace your steps.

DIRECTIONS

From I-5 north of Weed, take the Edgewood/Gazelle exit (exit 751) and drive west for 0.2 mile (0.3 km). Turn left on Edgewood Road, then turn right almost immediately on Stewart Springs Road. Drive 4 miles (6.4 km), then turn right on Forest Road 17. Drive 9.2 miles (14.8 km) to the Parks Creek Trailhead on the left. The Pacific Crest Trail begins by the restrooms.

GPS COORDINATES: 41.3429, −122.5377; 41°20'34.4" N, 122°32'15.7" W

BEST NEARBY BREWS

A half-hour drive from this trailhead, **Mt. Shasta Brewing Co.** (360 College Ave., Weed, 530/938-2394, https://weedales.com, 11am-9pm daily) has been serving craft brews to thirsty hikers since 1992. Bicycles hang from the ceiling in this fun-loving brewery-bistro, which serves paninis, flatbread pizzas, and beer bratwurst to accompany a wide selection of house-made beers and ciders. For the young ones, there's a special kids' menu.

2

Bunny Flat to Alpine Lodge and/or Hidden Valley

SHASTA-TRINITY NATIONAL FOREST

Hike to the historic Sierra Club Alpine Lodge for an iconic view of the largest stratovolcano in the Cascade Range.

DISTANCE: 5.8 miles (9.3 km) round-trip
DURATION: 4 hours
ELEVATION GAIN: 2,200 feet (671 km)
EFFORT: Moderate
TRAIL: Dirt trail, scree slopes
USERS: Hikers; dogs are not allowed in the Shasta Wilderness
SEASON: Year-round; snowshoes or skis needed in winter
PASSES/FEES: None
MAPS: Tom Harrison Maps "Mount Shasta Wilderness"
TRAILHEAD: Bunny Flat Trailhead
FACILITIES: Restroom
CONTACT: Mount Shasta Ranger Station, 530/926-4511, www.fs.usda.gov/stnf

START THE HIKE

▶ **MILE 0-1.6: Bunny Flat Trailhead to Sierra Club Alpine Lodge**

From the restroom at **Bunny Flat,** hike up the signed **Winter Trail** through the sloping meadow. You won't get far before stopping to gaze at mighty Mount Shasta, which soars to 14,179 feet (4,322 m). Shasta isn't California's highest peak, but it leads the pack in terms of volume. The largest stratovolcano in the Cascade Range, Shasta has a massive base diameter of 17 miles (27 km) and a total volume of 85 cubic miles. As mountains go, it's a hulking beast.

At a **junction** at 0.1 mile (0.2 km), veer left (west) and wave good-bye to the glorious Shasta view. You'll head into a grove of Shasta red firs, pass an old weather gauge tower on your right at 0.8 mile (1.3 km), then reach a **junction** with Sand Flat Trail at 1 mile (1.6 km). Veer right (north) and begin a more energetic climb through Shasta fir forest. Soon you'll enter the **Mount Shasta Wilderness boundary** (dogs are not permitted beyond this point, and it's critical to stay on established trails to protect the fragile high-alpine plantlife).

At 1.6 miles (2.6 km), the trail departs the trees and reaches a large clearing just below the tree line at Horse Camp, where the stately **Sierra Club Alpine Lodge** holds court at 7,880 feet (2,402 m). This lovely stone building, which houses exhibits on Mount Shasta and a small library of mountaineering books, was built by the Sierra Club in 1922. You're welcome to step through its bulky front door and take a look inside. From May through September, the Alpine Lodge is staffed by a knowledgeable caretaker.

Bunny Flat to Alpine Lodge/ Hidden Valley

Mt. Shasta Wilderness

Hidden Valley Trail

Shasta-Trinity

National Forest

SIERRA CLUB
ALPINE LODGE

Avalanche Gulch Climbing Route

Horse Camp Trail

SAND FLAT
TRAIL JUNCTION

Flat Trail

Horse Camp Trail

Sand

Broadway

Bunny Trail

Snow

EVERITT MEMORIAL HWY

WINTER TRAIL
JUNCTION

Winter Trail

RESTROOM

BUNNY FLAT
TRAILHEAD

To
Mount Shasta

| 0 | | 500 yds |
| 0 | | 500 m |

Contour Interval = 40 feet

Elevation Profile

Elevation (feet): 9,300 / 8,820 / 8,340 / 7,860 / 7,380 / 6,900

Distance (miles): 0.0 0.5 1.0 1.5 2.0 2.5 3.0 3.5 4.0 4.5 5.0 5.5

© MOON.COM

▲ SIERRA CLUB ALPINE LODGE AT HORSE CAMP

On the edge of the lodge's stone patio, a natural spring bubbles up from underground. You'll want to fill your water bottles with this delicious cold spring water (there's a spigot for easy bottle-filling). A rock-lined pond next to the spring attracts an abundance of birds and occasional deer.

Like many hikers who wind up at this picturesque spot, you might choose to hang out by the Alpine Lodge and admire its history and scenery, then head back downhill for a 3.2-mile (5.2-km) round-trip. But if you're looking for a little more challenge, continue on this trail's second leg, which leads from the lodge to Hidden Valley.

▶ MILE 1.6–2.9: Sierra Club Alpine Lodge to Hidden Valley

On the Alpine Lodge's northwest side, a path is marked with a **hand-written sign:** "Follow the wands to Hidden Valley." For the uninitiated, "wands" are long, skinny stakes—typically bamboo or metal—that mountaineers use to mark a path in the snow.

Depart the lodge's meadow and its delightful spring and head left (north) into a grove of Shasta red firs. At 0.4 mile (0.6 km) from the lodge, you'll cross over a ridge and reach an open bowl where you're treated to westward vistas of Black Butte, Mount Eddy, and the Trinity Alps and Marble Mountains.

The route steepens considerably as it enters a bleak scree field, where the only plants are a few tenuous grasses and alpine wildflowers. Keep looking uphill for a notch in the ridge. That's your goal. Measure each step carefully, and consider placing a hand on a rock for extra support. A misstep here could result in a long hard fall.

After a final breathless push, you'll top out in the talus wonderland of **Hidden Valley,** elevation 9,200 feet (2,804 m). You'll experience a mind-blowing reveal upon reaching this wide depression on Shasta's western slope. Hidden Valley holds its seclusion tightly right up until you

HIDDEN VALLEY ▲

reach its edge. This austere perch straddles a notch between Mount Shasta and Shastina, Mount Shasta's secondary cone. Like Shasta, Shastina is a popular destination for skilled mountaineers, and this aerie is where they often make camp before making a summit attempt the next day.

For your return trip, retrace your steps to the Sierra Club Alpine Lodge and then back to your car.

DIRECTIONS

From I-5, take the Central Mt. Shasta exit (exit 738) and drive 1.2 miles (1.9 km) east on Lake Street. Stay on Lake Street as it veers left and becomes Everitt Memorial Highway. Follow the highway 11 miles (17.7 km) up the mountain slopes to the large parking area at Bunny Flat, on the left. Start hiking on the trail near the restroom, signed as "Winter Trail."

GPS COORDINATES: 41.3539, −122.2336; 41°21′14″ N, 122°14′1″ W

BEST NEARBY BITES

Yak's Shack (401 N. Mt. Shasta Blvd., Mt. Shasta City, 530/568-8121, www.yaks.com, 7am-8pm daily) is the sibling restaurant of top-rated Yak's on I-5. Order a breakfast sandwich and coconut crème latte to start your day, then come back later for a monster-size burger, mouth-watering garlic fries, or a hearty salad. The Shack bakes a tempting array of cookies and pastries, serves more than a dozen beers on tap, and has an inviting outdoor patio.

3

Gray Butte

SHASTA-TRINITY NATIONAL FOREST

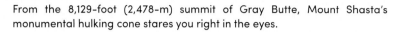

From the 8,129-foot (2,478-m) summit of Gray Butte, Mount Shasta's monumental hulking cone stares you right in the eyes.

DISTANCE: 3.2 miles (5.2 km) round-trip
DURATION: 1.5-2 hours
ELEVATION GAIN: 606 feet (185 m)
EFFORT: Easy-moderate
TRAIL: Dirt trail
USERS: Hikers, leashed dogs
SEASON: May-October (access road closed in winter)
PASSES/FEES: None
MAPS: Tom Harrison Maps "Mount Shasta Wilderness"
TRAILHEAD: Panther Meadows Trailhead
FACILITIES: Restroom
CONTACT: Mount Shasta Ranger Station, 530/926-4511, www.fs.usda.gov/stnf

Newcomers to Mount Shasta are often confused by its abundance of multicolored "butte" trails. Black Butte, Green Butte, Red Butte, and Gray Butte are all popular day-hiking destinations, but if you want easy trailhead access, a well-graded trail with abundant shade, and an unrivaled view of Mount Shasta, Gray Butte is the butte to climb. Bonus for hikers with canine companions: dogs are welcome.

START THE HIKE

▶ **MILE 0-0.6: Panther Meadows Trailhead to Gray Butte Trail Junction**
Follow the obvious trail from the **parking area** to the back of **Panther Meadows Campground.** Beautiful Panther Meadows is an important place in Native American culture; members of the Wintu tribe still perform sacred ceremonies near its pristine spring, as they have done for thousands of years.

Stay straight and stroll across **Lower Panther Meadow,** enjoying the musical rivulets streaming through past tiny sedges and wildflowers. This exquisite, fragile grassland is home to an incredible summer wildflower show, when the meadow is peppered with pink heathers, red paintbrushes, purple asters, and dozens more delicate blossoms. Visit in late July to see the blossoms in their fullest glory.

As you cross the trickling stream, look over your left shoulder for a full-frontal view of snow-streaked Mount Shasta, its white countenance in sharp contrast to the green meadow and blue sky. On the meadow's far side, the trail enters a forest of Shasta red fir, then reaches a **junction** at 0.6 mile (1 km). The left trail heads northeast to South Gate Meadows; veer right (south) on **Gray Butte Trail.**

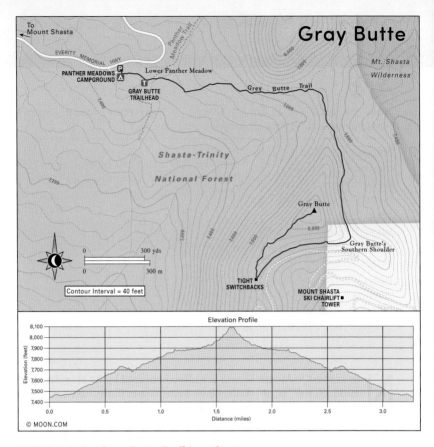

Elevation Profile

© MOON.COM

▶ **MILE 0.6–1.2: Gray Butte Trail Junction to Gray Butte's Southern Shoulder**

The trail ascends gently through old-growth red firs that slowly transition to a grove of hemlocks. Conifers dominate the view on Gray Butte's eastern flank, but at 1 mile (1.6 km), the trail crosses a broad treeless talus slope. Turn around here for an enticing peek at Red Butte and Mount Shasta before heading back into the forest.

At 1.2 mile (1.9 km), your path veers to the right (west) to traverse **Gray Butte's southern shoulder.** You may be surprised to see a **ski chairlift tower** and cables downslope to your left. This is the Gray Butte chairlift at Mount Shasta Ski Resort, constructed in 2022, an addition that greatly expanded the resort's lift-accessed terrain. It was a major gain for the Shasta ski community.

▶ **MILE 1.2–1.6: Gray Butte's Southern Shoulder to Summit**

Beyond the ski lift tower, the trail begins to climb in earnest, navigating a **tight right switchback** to head northeast for the final ascent to Gray Butte's summit. You'll pass a cluster of telecommunications towers visible over your left shoulder, then hike through sparse stunted hemlocks on the final push. The last 0.3 mile (0.5 km) is the steepest of the day.

When you top out on **Gray Butte's summit,** you'll understand why this spot was called Artist's Point in the 19th century. A marvelous mural unfolds: Mount Shasta's south face is in clear view; the hulking volcano stares right at you. If you can take your eyes off its crowned head, it's easy to identify other prominent landmarks, including Thumb Rock, Shastarama Point, Green Butte, and even the top of Shastina, Mount Shasta's secondary cone.

Don't forget to enjoy the other points on the compass. Look west for a fine view of Mount Eddy and the saw-toothed Trinity Alps. To the south lies Lassen Peak, another magnificent Cascade Range volcano and the showpiece of Lassen Volcanic National Park.

Your return trip is all downhill; just retrace your steps.

DIRECTIONS

From I-5, take the Central Mt. Shasta exit (exit 738) and drive 1.2 miles (1.9 km) east on Lake Street. Stay on Lake Street as it veers left and becomes Everitt Memorial Highway. Follow the highway 14 miles (22.5 km) up the mountain slopes to Panther Meadows Campground, on the right.

GPS COORDINATES: 41.3550, −122.2032; 41°21′18″ N, 122°12′11.5″ W

BEST NEARBY BITES

Lily's Restaurant (1013 S. Mt. Shasta Blvd., Mt. Shasta City, 530/926-3372, www.lilysrestaurant.com, 8am-2pm and 4pm-8pm Wed.-Sun.) is the place to go for a delightful farm-to-table meal. Choose from five types of eggs Benedict or a decadent plate of bananas foster. Try french toast for breakfast, wagyu beef or veggie burger for lunch, or meat or fish entrées, plus a wide selection of creative pastas and salads, for dinner.

This undulating ramble travels through a stark, jumbled volcanic landscape to a mountain-backed meadow and a bounty of wildflowers.

DISTANCE: 3.6 miles (5.8 km) round-trip

DURATION: 2 hours

ELEVATION GAIN: 690 feet (210 km)

EFFORT: Easy-moderate

TRAIL: Dirt trail, rock talus and scree

USERS: Hikers; dogs are not allowed in the Shasta Wilderness

SEASON: June-October (access road closed in winter)

PASSES/FEES: None

MAPS: Tom Harrison Maps "Mount Shasta Wilderness"

TRAILHEAD: South Gate Meadows Trailhead

FACILITIES: Restroom

CONTACT: Mount Shasta Ranger Station, 530/926-4511, www.fs.usda.gov/stnf

South Gate Meadows can be accessed from either the South Gate Meadows Trailhead (described in this trip) or the Panther Meadows Trailhead. The two trails can also be combined to make a loop. No matter which trail you take, make sure you're wearing good shoes and sun protection—the terrain is extremely rocky and there's precious little shade.

START THE HIKE

▶ MILE 0-1: South Gate Meadows Trailhead to Panther Meadows- Gray Butte Trail Junction

From the **South Gate Meadows Trailhead,** begin hiking uphill through a stark exposed moonscape of volcanic rocks. In this barren talus field, dusty pink and steel gray are the predominant colors. During the golden hours of dawn and dusk, the rose-hued rocks appear to glow.

Follow the path toward the obvious ridge ahead, climbing steeply. When you need to catch your breath, turn around to gaze over a broad sweep of the Shasta Valley to the south. At 0.6 mile (1 km), you'll

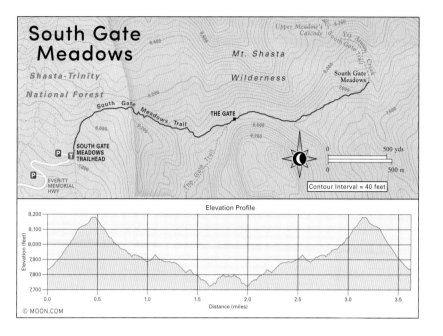

South Gate Meadows

Mt. Shasta Wilderness

Shasta-Trinity National Forest

South Gate Meadows

South Gate Meadows Trail

THE GATE

SOUTH GATE MEADOWS TRAILHEAD

EVERITT MEMORIAL HWY

Upper Meadow's Cascade

500 yds
500 m

Contour Interval = 40 feet

© MOON.COM

Elevation Profile

pass a **Mount Shasta Wilderness sign** (no dogs allowed past this point), then descend into a seemingly barren, sandy, rock-strewn valley punctuated by occasional clumps of alpine grasses. But ignore your initial impression and examine this austere environment more closely. You may find a special plant flourishing here: *Anemone occidentalis,* or western pasque flower, which blooms right after the snow melts.

At 1 mile (1.6 km), reach a **junction** with a trail from Panther Meadows-Gray Butte coming in on your right; keep straight (east).

▶ **MILE 1–1.8: Panther Meadows–Gray Butte Trail Junction to South Gate Meadows**

Just beyond this junction, the South Gate Meadows Trail traces across a rocky squeeze point known as **The Gate,** which lies at the southern tip of Sargents Ridge. This narrow gap is hemmed in to the north by Red Butte, a prominent volcanic dome of red-colored andesite soaring to 8,377 feet (2,553 m). From this divide, the trail descends into a labyrinth of rough-and-tumble boulders and talus. You won't find a scrap of shade here, but you'll be awed by the colorful proliferation of rocks.

At 1.4 miles (2.3 km), the trail heads back into a dense grove of Shasta red firs and whitebark pines, then emerges from the tree cover to a wide vista that evokes reverence and wonder. The emerald expanse of **South Gate Meadows** slopes upward to a dramatic climax that showcases Shastarama Point and Mount Shasta. The tableau includes a glistening waterfall pouring from a complex of springs, the headwaters of Yét Atwam Creek. This watercourse nourishes the meadow and its kaleidoscope of wildflowers. At 1.8 miles (2.9 km), cross the creek with an easy rock-hop to find a clearing or a log to sit on while you gaze at this splendid scene.

Some hikers choose to follow a narrow trail 0.2 mile (0.3 km) to the **up-per meadow's cascade,** but if you do, be extremely careful to stay on the path. You may be tempted to wander through the grasses to admire the wildflowers close-up, but there's one important rule on Mount Shasta: If it's green, don't step on it. Mount Shasta's meadow ecosystems are incredibly fragile and easily destroyed.

This hike is out-and-back, so retrace your steps when ready.

DIRECTIONS

From I-5, take the Central Mt. Shasta exit (exit 738) and drive 1.2 miles (1.9 km) east on Lake Street. Stay on Lake Street as it veers left and becomes Everitt Memorial Highway. Follow the highway 14 miles (22.5 km) up the mountain slopes to the South Gate Meadows trailhead, on the right, just before the road ends at the Old Ski Bowl upper parking lot.

GPS COORDINATES: 41.3612, −122.1997; 41°21'40.3" N, 122°11'58.9" W

BEST NEARBY BITES

Drive 20 minutes down Everitt Memorial Highway to the petite yellow cottage of **Crave Comfort Food** (402 Chestnut St., Mt. Shasta City, 530/918-5276, www.cravefresh.net, 11:30am-8pm Tues.-Sat.) for carne asada, chili verde or Peruvian bean or chicken tacos. All tacos are served street-style with cabbage, cilantro, and onion—just the way you want them. Crave also makes a hearty tri-tip sandwich and oh-so-cheesy enchiladas.

On this easy climb to an Instagram-famous lake, enjoy captivating views of mighty Mount Shasta and its sidekick, Black Butte.

DISTANCE: 2.4 miles (3.9 km) round-trip

DURATION: 1.5 hours

ELEVATION GAIN: 570 feet (174 m)

EFFORT: Easy-moderate

TRAIL: Dirt trail

USERS: Hikers, leashed dogs

SEASON: May-November; may be snowshoe-accessible in winter

PASSES/FEES: None

MAPS: Download map from https://mountshastatrailassociation.org

TRAILHEAD: Castle Lake Parking Lot

FACILITIES: Vault toilets

CONTACT: Mount Shasta Ranger Station, 530/926-4511, www.fs.usda.gov/stnf

Set in a glacial bowl at 5,450 feet (1,661 m) elevation, Castle Lake is clear, cold, and more than 100 feet (30 m) deep. It's also the subject of a Native American legend: The Shasta and Wintu peoples called Castle Lake "Castle of the Devil." They believed an evil spirit lived in the lake and made the eerie echoing sounds heard in winter, a noise that science explains as the expansion and contraction of ice.

START THE HIKE

▶ **MILE 0-0.9: Castle Lake Parking Lot to Heart Lake-Little Castle Lake Junction**

From the **parking lot** at the end of Castle Lake Road and Castle Lake's northern shore, **Little Castle Lake Trail** heads southeast. The first 100 feet (30 m) can be the trickiest: you must boulder-hop across **Castle Lake Creek,** which ranges from 2 feet (0.6 m) wide in midsummer to 25 feet (7.6 m) wide immediately after winter snowmelt and rain.

On the outlet creek's far side, the path laterals above the lake's eastern shore, ascending moderately up a brush-lined slope before entering a shady forest of white firs and Shasta red firs. The vistas of deep-blue Castle Lake keep improving as you climb, culminating at a **high overlook** at 0.7 mile (1.1 km). From here, you can look down about 400 feet (122 m) and pick out stand-up paddleboarders making their way across a cobalt blue canvas.

In another 0.2 mile (0.3 km), your path reaches a **ridgetop saddle,** where two trails converge: The left trail heads to Little Castle Lake and Mount Bradley. You go right for Heart Lake, continuing to climb through a series of easy, brief zigzags.

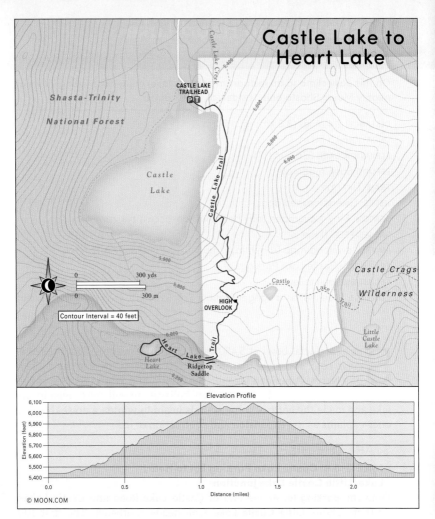

Elevation Profile

© MOON.COM

▸ **MILE 0.9–1.2: Heart Lake–Little Castle Lake Junction to Heart Lake**

Now that you've gained the ridge, Heart Lake is only a short distance farther. Stroll through a meadowy stretch dotted with clumps of sedum, phlox, and pussy paws, then veer around the back side of a rocky knoll. As you traverse this ridgetop, enjoy sublime views of Mount Shasta and Black Butte over your right shoulder. This stretch of trail scores the prize for the most compelling view of Black Butte's conical pyramid. From here, this treeless, volcanic plug dome is dwarfed by neighboring Mount Shasta, which towers 8,000 feet (2,438 m) higher. Even so, Black Butte doesn't shirk from this scene—its remarkable purple-black color and triangular shape give it a commanding presence.

Your trail passes a **Castle Crags Wilderness sign** at 1 mile (1.6 km), then descends through a forested notch to Heart Lake's eastern shore at 1.1 miles (1.8 km). A pint-size pothole tucked into a granite pocket, **Heart Lake** is a social media darling. You'll see why when you veer left and walk around the lake's north side. From this vantage point, you have a perfectly framed

vista of Mount Shasta to the south. In the foreground, Heart Lake's still waters mirror the mighty volcano's majestic visage.

More than a few marriage proposals have occurred at this lake, especially atop the large boulder that juts into the lake, forming the V of the heart. If you're not here to get engaged, consider a swim. Because this lake is small and shallow, it warms up nicely by midsummer.

▶ **MILE 1.2-2.4: Heart Lake to Castle Lake Parking Lot**
When it's time to head back, retrace your steps. This time you'll be facing in the right direction to savor views most of the way.

DIRECTIONS

From I-5 near Mt. Shasta City, take the Central Mt. Shasta exit and drive 0.2 mile (0.3 km) west. Turn left (south) on Old Stage Road. In 0.4 mile (0.6 km), bear right and continue on W. A. Barr Road. Drive 2.3 miles (3.7 km) on W. A. Barr Road to Lake Siskiyou's dam. Cross the dam, then turn left on Castle Lake Road and drive 7.1 miles (11.4 km) to the Castle Lake parking lot. The trailhead is on the south end of the parking lot, near the kayak launch.

GPS COORDINATES: 41.2303, −122.3816; 41°13'49.1" N, 122°22'53.8" W

BEST NEARBY BITES

From Castle Lake, drive 10 miles (16.1 km) and 20 minutes to Mt. Shasta City to nosh on an amazing lamb burger or chicken bánh mì at **Pipeline Craft Taps and Kitchen** (320 N. Mt. Shasta Blvd., Mt. Shasta City, 530/918-6020, www.pipelinecrafttaps.com, 11:30am-8pm Sun.-Thurs., 11:30am-9pm Fri.-Sat.). If you don't feel hungry enough for a big meal, order a good-for-you beet salad or share some cheese curds with your hiking buddy. Everything on this eclectic menu is worth a try.

6

McCloud Falls

SHASTA-TRINITY NATIONAL FOREST

A triumvirate of waterfalls on the McCloud River descend over dark basalt cliffs, creating a misty playground for hikers, swimmers, and anglers.

BEST: Swimming Hole Hikes
DISTANCE: 3.8 miles (6.1 km) round-trip
DURATION: 2 hours
ELEVATION GAIN: 425 feet (130 m)
EFFORT: Easy
TRAIL: Dirt trail, paved path, wooden stairs
USERS: Hikers, wheelchair users between Lower Falls and Fowlers Campground, leashed dogs
SEASON: Spring through fall (access road closed in winter)
PASSES/FEES: None
MAPS: Download from https://mountshastatrailassociation.org
TRAILHEAD: Lower Falls Picnic Area Parking Lot
FACILITIES: Restroom, drinking water
CONTACT: McCloud Ranger Station, 530/964-2184, www.fs.usda.gov/stnf

Many people visit the McCloud River's three waterfalls by driving to three separate parking areas on the McCloud River Loop Road, then strolling a few yards from each parking lot to each waterfall. But it's far more entertaining to leave your car at the Lower Falls parking lot and hike upstream along the river, passing all three waterfalls in succession. You're rewarded with views of the cataracts and also the picturesque forest and flowing waterway in between.

START THE HIKE

▶ **MILE 0-1.3: Lower Falls Picnic Area Parking Lot to Middle Falls**
From the **Lower Falls Picnic Area parking lot,** make your way to the trail signboard and start walking on the paved trail. Within seconds, you arrive at a stone staircase descending to the river's edge at 15-foot-high (4.6-m) **Lower Falls.** You may see people jumping or diving into the river, but this pool is filled with jagged submerged boulders, so it's much safer to wade in. The pool's chilly temperature—often in the low 50s Fahrenheit (10-13°C)—can catch swimmers by surprise, but that's part of the fun.

A standout feature at Lower Falls is the basalt lava rock lining the McCloud River canyon. Shaped by the same volcanic forces that created Mount Shasta, the energetic waterway carved a channel through this deep, erosion-resistant canyon. Where the water couldn't wear away the bands of basalt, it found a way to flow over the top, creating three waterfalls.

From Lower Falls, the paved section of **McCloud River Trail** skirts along the river to busy **Fowlers Campground.** Stick to the pavement as it rolls

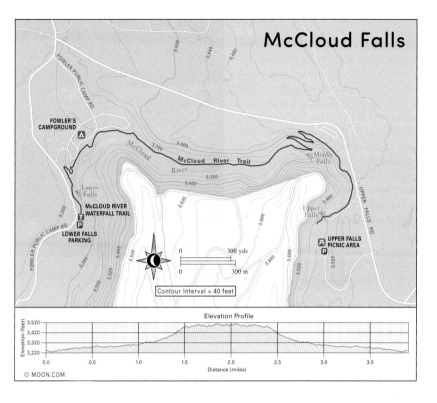

McCloud Falls

Contour Interval = 40 feet

Elevation Profile

© MOON.COM

between the campsites and the waterway. At 0.5 mile (0.8 km), on the camp's east side, the paved trail transitions to dirt. This is the **end of the wheelchair-accessible segment.**

As your trail nears the 1.3-mile (2.1-km) mark, a cacophonous watery roar fills your ears, and soon you're standing just downstream of graceful **Middle Falls,** where a commanding 50-foot (15-m) wall of water plunges over a basalt cliff. This cataract is a scenic blockbuster. Twice as wide as it is tall, its misty showering curtain is divided by a rocky buttress. Swaying ferns and Indian rhubarb cling to every watery foothold.

In summer, Middle McCloud's pool is a popular teenager-hangout spot, but in spring and fall, you have a better chance at solitude here. In any season, you can usually find a fly-fisher or two working the riffles below the falls. The McCloud River is stocked with rainbow, German brown, and brook trout.

▶ MILE 1.3–1.9: Middle Falls to Upper Falls

A series of well-graded **switchbacks and stairsteps** lead you from the wide pool below Middle Falls to its brink (this is a great spot for photography). After this short but steep climb, the path levels and clings to the edge of the canyon wall as it proceeds upriver.

In the next 0.6 mile (1 km), McCloud River Trail makes a very gentle ascent to **Upper Falls.** This cataract is much more secretive than its siblings downriver; you don't get to walk right next to it. Tucked into a rocky gorge of erosion-resistant basalt, Upper Falls is viewed from the trail 80 feet

(24 m) above. Stand on one of two railing-lined overlooks perched on a basalt cliff and watch the river funnel through a narrow chute and plunge 35 feet (11 m) into a circular rock-lined bowl. The frothing falls create clouds of swirling mist that drift downstream across a brilliant aquamarine pool. Although some anglers and photographers make their way down these steep cliffs to the pool, it's a risky proposition (and the U.S. Forest Service discourages it). Instead, savor the mesmerizing view from this high perch, or walk over to take a break at the adjacent **Upper Falls picnic area.**

▸ **MILE 1.9-3.8: Upper Falls to Lower Falls Picnic Area Parking Lot**
You'd think three waterfalls would be all the excitement you could handle on one short trail, but another surprise awaits when you turn around and head back: You'll enjoy an extraordinary view of Mount Shasta, which lurked behind your back on the way in.

DIRECTIONS

From McCloud, drive 5 miles (8.1 km) southeast along Highway 89. Turn right at the sign for Fowlers Campground and Lower Falls; this is the McCloud River Loop Road (Forest Rd. 40N44). Drive 0.7 mile (1.1 km) to a fork shortly before Fowlers Campground. Turn right and drive 0.7 mile (1.1 km) to the end of the road and the Lower Falls day-use parking area. The McCloud River Trail starts at the staircase next to the Lower Falls overlook.

GPS COORDINATES: 41.2404, −122.0250; 41°14′25.4″ N, 122°1′30″ W

BEST NEARBY BREWS

Located 10 minutes from this trailhead, **Siskiyou Brew Works** (110 Squaw Valley Rd., McCloud, 530/925-5894, www.siskiyoubrewworks.com, 4pm-8pm daily) brews with only artesian spring water (from Mount Shasta's glaciers) and GMO-free ingredients. This veteran-owned brewery specializes in German-style kolsches, Bavarian lagers, Belgian ales, and English-style porters and pale ales. A small kitchen cooks pizza and sandwiches.

SHASTA-TRINITY NATIONAL FOREST

McCloud Falls

7

Crags Trail to Castle Dome
CASTLE CRAGS STATE PARK

A thigh-burning climb allows an intimate look at Castle Crags' fistful of jumbled granite spires and monolithic Castle Dome.

BEST: Brew Hikes
DISTANCE: 5.4 miles (8.7 km) round-trip
DURATION: 3-4 hours
ELEVATION GAIN: 2,150 feet (655 m)
EFFORT: Moderate-strenuous
TRAIL: Dirt trail
USERS: Hikers
SEASON: April-November (trail is often snow-covered in winter)
PASSES/FEES: $10 day-use fee per vehicle
MAPS: Castle Crags State Park, available online at www.parks.ca.gov
TRAILHEAD: Vista Point Parking Lot
FACILITIES: Restroom, visitor center
CONTACT: Castle Crags State Park, 530/235-2684, www.parks.ca.gov

I n this Northern California landscape dominated by volcanic features, Castle Crags State Park's glacially carved granite spires are a surreal exception. Most people see these mysterious summits only from far-off I-5, but intrepid hikers tackle this challenging trail that leads to Castle Dome, the largest pinnacle on the Crags' ridgeline.

START THE HIKE

In summer, temperatures can soar to more than 100°F (38°C), so plan to make this trek in the cooler months.

▶ **MILE 0-1.6: Vista Point Parking Lot to Indian Springs Junction**
From the northwest end of the **Vista Point parking lot,** stroll over to **Vista Point** to enjoy impressive views of both Mount Shasta and Castle Crags. Take a minute to admire the light-gray glacially sculpted pinnacles that will be your prize for today's climb.

When you're ready, take the wheelchair-accessible trail from the parking lot. At 0.25 mile (0.4 km), depart the gentle grade of this wheelchair-accessible path and bear left (west) on **Crags Trail.** Cross over the **Pacific Crest Trail** under a set of power lines at 0.4 mile (0.6 km), then proceed on a steady climb up forested **Kettlebelly Ridge.** Ignore the junction with Bob's Hat Trail at 0.7 mile (1.1 km); remain on Crags Trail all the way. Your pathway is mostly smooth and wide, so you don't have to pay much attention to foot placement.

At 1.6 miles (2.6 km), reach a **left fork for Indian Springs.** If it's a warm day and you've already polished off most of your water supply, take a five-minute detour west (0.2 mi/0.3 km), enjoying broad views across forested Castle Creek Canyon. At Indian Springs, refill your bottle with deliciously cold

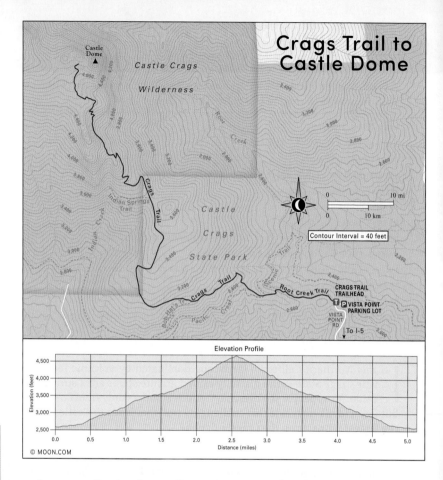

Crags Trail to Castle Dome

Castle Crags Wilderness

Castle Crags State Park

Contour Interval = 40 feet

CRAGS TRAIL TRAILHEAD

VISTA POINT PARKING LOT

VISTA POINT RD

To I-5

Elevation Profile

© MOON.COM

spring water flowing from a fissure in a mossy fern-lined grotto. Then backtrack to this junction and check your motivation level. The day's hardest work lies ahead.

▸ **MILE 1.6-2.7: Indian Springs Junction to Castle Dome and Castle Crags**

You've already completed a substantial amount of climbing—1,000 feet (305 m), to be exact—but Crags Trail's final 1.1 miles (1.8 km) gain another whopping 1,150 feet (351 m) in elevation, a punishing ascent by any measure. Make use of every interesting viewpoint and intriguing rock formation to stop, catch your breath, and drink some water. The path snakes through a labyrinth of sheer slabs and towering pillars, winding and weaving through tight switchbacks to gain the top of a seemingly impassible cliff.

At 2.2 miles (3.5 km), you emerge from this granite garden—breathing hard, most likely—to an exposed bench with an enticing view of monolithic **Castle Dome** and the Sacramento River far below. This scene will convince you to persist with the unrelenting uphill march. The path zooms up a final, nearly vertical pitch in a series of short switchbacks, then reaches

a postage stamp-size meadow just below the granite **Castle Crags** at 2.7 miles (4.3 km).

The maintained trail ends here, but a handful of paths branch off to reach various viewpoints. If you're seeking a greater sense of awe—or perhaps a little humility—follow the path to the right, where a deep cleft between the rocks offers a view of Mount Shasta to the north and a frighteningly steep drop-off to the gorge far below.

Explore around the base of Castle Crags as you please, then retreat to the tiny meadow to admire the full scope of this astounding miniature mountain range, which resembles a line of granite warriors standing guard above the canyon. These castle-like spires were formed nearly 170 million years ago when the Klamath Mountains and the Sierra Nevada Mountains were one contiguous range. The Crags have been revered by Indigenous tribes for thousands of years, so find your own way to honor these geologic marvels, then pull out your well-deserved lunch before trekking back downhill.

DIRECTIONS

From Redding, drive 48 miles (77 km) north on I-5 and take the Castella exit (exit 724). Turn left and drive 0.3 mile (0.5 km) on Castle Creek Road, then turn right at the Castle Crags State Park entrance. Pass the entrance station, then turn right and drive 1.8 miles (2.9 km) to the road's end at the Vista Point parking area, where the Castle Crags Trail begins.

GPS COORDINATES: 41.1596, −122.3061; 41°9′34.6″ N, 122°18′22″ W

BEST NEARBY BREWS

If this strenuous trek has left you feeling hot and thirsty, drive 7 miles (11.3 km) and 10 minutes for a crisp, icy cold one at **Dunsmuir Brewery Works** (5701 Dunsmuir Ave., Dunsmuir, 530/235-1900, www. dunsmuirbreweryworks.com, 11am-10pm daily summer, 11am-9pm Tues.-Sun. winter). Among its many crowd-pleasing beers and ales, the brewery pays tribute to Dunsmuir's railroad heritage with its hoppy Trainspotter IPA. A short but satisfying food menu features beef, elk, and veggie burgers plus beer cheese bread and soft pretzels.

8

Burney Falls, Pacific Crest Trail, and Headwaters Loop

MCARTHUR-BURNEY FALLS MEMORIAL STATE PARK

Visit a spring-fed waterfall that gushes 100 million gallons of water daily, then take a longer tour of its basalt-lined streambanks.

DISTANCE: 2.7 miles (4.3 km) round-trip

DURATION: 1.5 hours

ELEVATION GAIN: 200 feet (61 m)

EFFORT: Easy

TRAIL: Dirt trail, paved path, wooden stairs

USERS: Hikers

SEASON: Year-round

PASSES/FEES: $10 day-use fee per vehicle

MAPS: McArthur-Burney Falls Memorial State Park, available online at www.parks.ca.gov

TRAILHEAD: McArthur-Burney Falls Memorial State Park Day-Use Parking Lot

FACILITIES: Restroom

CONTACT: McArthur-Burney Falls Memorial State Park, 530/335-2777, www.burneyfallspark.org

Burney Falls is nowhere near the tallest waterfall in California, but it ranks high for photogenic beauty and reliable flow. The misty marvel gushes 100 million gallons of turquoise water at nearly the exact same rate every day, regardless of whether it's the dry summer season or wet winter season. Legend has it that President Teddy Roosevelt loved this waterfall; some claim he deemed it "the eighth wonder of the world."

START THE HIKE

▶ **MILE 0-0.2: Day-Use Parking Lot to Burney Falls' Pool**

From the **day-use parking lot,** walk south a few yards to the **overlook** for an inspiring preview of Burney Falls. Light penetrates deep into the clear water, making its milky blue hue appear iridescent. From the overlook, follow the crowds strolling the paved path downhill to Burney Creek's streambanks. A 100-yard (91-m) walk brings you to the 129-foot-tall (39-m) waterfall's **gigantic pool,** where you'll be kissed by a showering veil of spray and mist. A product of the same volcanic region that created Mount Shasta and Mount Lassen, Burney Creek is fed by underground springs and snowmelt stored in its volcanic basalt layers, so these water droplets have recently emerged from deep underground. Burney Falls' pool is a chilly 42°F (6°C) even on the warmest summer days.

As you stand near the base of this gushing white-water deluge, you'll note that much of Burney Falls' flow actually pours *out* of its basalt cliff face—siphoned through tiny basalt crevices—instead of plummeting over

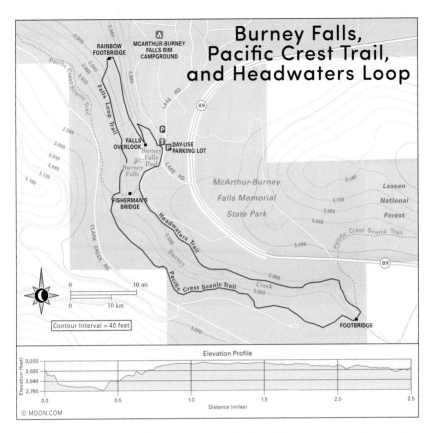

Burney Falls, Pacific Crest Trail, and Headwaters Loop

Elevation Profile

© MOON.COM

its lip. It's easy to relax into a state of delightful watery hypnosis here, but stay poised to spot migratory black swifts, which build their nests on the waterfall's sheer cliffs in early summer.

▸ **MILE 0.2-1.2: Burney Falls' Pool to Pacific Crest Trail Junction**
After feeling suitably awed by Burney Falls, leave the crowds behind and continue hiking upstream on **Falls Loop Trail.** You're walking in the good company of leafy black oaks, Oregon white oaks, and huge Douglas firs and ponderosa pines. The latter is easily identified by its clearly delineated, jigsaw-puzzle bark. At your feet is a jumble of black basalt talus. Most of the rocks are cloaked in thick moss from the waterfall's constant mist.

At a **junction** with Burney Creek Trail at 0.5 mile (0.8 km), turn left to cross the arching **Rainbow Footbridge** (a great place for a family photo), still following Falls Loop Trail but now walking south and upstream along the creek. You'll hike gently uphill on Burney Creek's west side. Surprisingly, the falls sound even louder and more powerful from this angle, although you won't be able to see them from the trail.

Meet up with a **three-way junction** at 1.2 mile (1.9 km), where you could cross **Fisherman's Bridge** on your left and head back to your car—a good choice if you're feeling weary or have young children in tow. To continue on this longer loop, turn right, then immediately left, to join the **Pacific Crest Trail** heading south.

BURNEY FALLS ▲

▶ **MILE 1.2–2.7: Pacific Crest Trail Junction to Day-Use Parking Lot**

Meander south and you'll watch Burney Creek dwindle to a much smaller, quieter waterway. After hiking 0.8 mile (1.3 km) on the Pacific Crest Trail, cross Burney Creek on a small **footbridge.** On its far side, depart the PCT and turn left (northwest) on **Headwaters Trail** to finish out your loop. Headwaters Trail sticks close to the creek for 0.6 mile (1 km), then reaches a trail fork and Fisherman's Bridge on your left (west). Take a quick detour to the bridge for yet another scenic view, or simply keep right and follow Falls Loop on the final uphill tromp back to your car.

DIRECTIONS

From the intersection of Highways 89 and 299 (4.4 mi/7.1 km northeast of Burney), drive north on Highway 89 for 6.4 miles (10.3 km) to the entrance to McArthur-Burney Falls Memorial State Park. Pay at the kiosk, then park in the main day-use lot on the left, just beyond the visitor center. If you're coming from McCloud, take Highway 89 southeast for 41 miles (66 km) to the park entrance.

GPS COORDINATES: 41.0132, −121.6506; 41°0′47.5″ N, 121°39′2.2″ W

BEST NEARBY BITES

Nothing pairs better with one of California's prettiest waterfalls than a meal at the **Alpine Drive Inn** (37148 Hwy. 299, Burney, 530/335-2211, 11am–8pm daily summer, 11am–7pm daily winter), a 15-minute drive from this park. The eatery opened in 1956 and has been pleasing diners with its old-school menu ever since. Munch on the Inn's legendary burgers and tater tots, then follow that up with soft-serve ice cream.

9

James K. Carr Trail to Whiskeytown Falls

WHISKEYTOWN NATIONAL RECREATION AREA

This trek visits Whiskeytown National Recreation Area's tallest waterfall, a triple-tiered cascade on Crystal Creek that plummets 200-plus feet (61 m).

DISTANCE: 3.4 miles (5.5 km) round-trip

DURATION: 2 hours

ELEVATION GAIN: 700 feet (213 m)

EFFORT: Easy-moderate

TRAIL: Dirt trail

USERS: Hikers, leashed dogs

SEASON: Year-round

PASSES/FEES: $25 per vehicle, valid for 7 days

MAPS: Download from www.nps.gov/whis

TRAILHEAD: James K. Carr Trailhead Parking Area

FACILITIES: Vault toilet

CONTACT: Whiskeytown National Recreation Area, 530/242-3400, www.nps.gov/whis

Whiskeytown Falls was somewhat secret until the 21st century. National Park Service officials knew the waterfall existed, but they didn't have the resources to construct and maintain a proper trail to access it, so they decided not to publicize it. Whiskeytown Falls had never appeared on any government map—not even the U.S. Geological Survey topo map. But in 2004, a park biologist heard rumors about the waterfall and began studying aerial photos. After a few bushwhacking expeditions, the waterfall was rediscovered. The James K. Carr Trail to Whiskeytown Falls was constructed and opened in 2006, and the rest is history: This path is now the most popular of Whiskeytown's 50 miles (81 km) of trails.

START THE HIKE

Despite a lengthy list of dire warnings posted at the trailhead, this waterfall trek is doable for almost anyone as long as the weather is cool. Plan your visit for late fall, winter, or spring when the Redding air temperature is comfortable for hiking. In summer, temperatures can soar high above 100°F (38°C), and Whiskeytown Falls dwindles to a trickle.

▸ **MILE 0-1.4: James K. Carr Trailhead Parking Area to Crystal Creek Picnic Area**
From the **parking lot,** the **James K. Carr Trail** descends through a mixed forest of live oaks, ponderosa pines, big-leaf maples, and Douglas firs. At 0.2 mile (0.3 km), cross Crystal Creek on a wooden **footbridge,** then start to

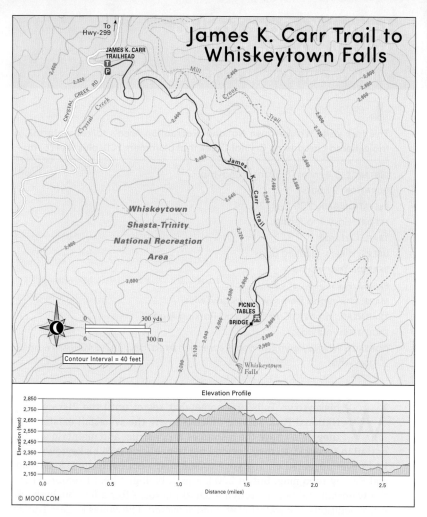

James K. Carr Trail to
Whiskeytown Falls

To Hwy-299

JAMES K. CARR TRAILHEAD

Whiskeytown
Shasta-Trinity
National Recreation
Area

Mill Creek Trail

James K. Carr Trail

PICNIC TABLES
BRIDGE

Whiskeytown Falls

Contour Interval = 40 feet

0   300 yds
0   300 m

Elevation Profile

© MOON.COM

climb uphill on a wide trail (much of this route follows old logging roads). As you walk this wooded stretch, listen for the sound of woodpeckers, who can often be heard drilling the tree trunks in this dense forest.

At a **junction** with Mill Creek Trail at 0.5 mile (0.8 km), go right (southeast) and continue the ascent. The climb is a bit steeper that you'd expect from such a popular, family-friendly trail, but nine benches and several picnic tables are placed at intervals along the route, inviting anyone who feels weary to sit for a spell.

At 1.4 miles (2.3 km), you'll pass a set of **picnic tables** alongside **Crystal Creek.** While you're paused at this enchanting streamside spot, give a salute to the trail's namesake, James K. Carr. The Redding resident was Undersecretary of the Interior during the Kennedy Administration and was instrumental in the protection of Whiskeytown National Recreation Area.

▸ **MILE 1.4–1.7: Crystal Creek Picnic Area to Whiskeytown Falls**
About 50 yards (46 m) from the picnic area, cross the creek on a **picturesque bridge** surrounded by dogwoods. This structure looks surprisingly new because it was rebuilt after the 2018 Carr Fire swept through this area. This trail and its surrounding forest were largely spared, but the footbridges succumbed to flying embers.

Beyond this footbridge, the canyon walls squeeze tighter and the trail moves closer to the creek. The sound of tumbling water will spur you on, and in another 0.3 mile (0.5 km) you're standing at the base of **Whiskeytown Falls.** From this vantage point, you can see only the bottom tier of this triple-tiered fall, a delightful 30-foot (9-m) cataract that's framed by leafy maples. To see the full 220 feet (67 m) of cascading whitewater, you'd have to fly over these dense woods in an airplane. But you can get another perspective by walking up the stone stairsteps on the cataract's left side to see its middle tier. Hold on to the handrail as you go; this stretch can be slippery.

A few feet from the lower cascade's pool, a small metal box is filled with notes from waterfall lovers who felt inspired to pen a few lines. Read some of their messages and you might feel moved to write some pithy words of your own.

For your return trip, just retrace your steps.

DIRECTIONS

From Redding, drive 16 miles (26 km) west on Highway 299 and turn left on Crystal Creek Road (the turnoff is 8.5 mi/13.7 km west of Whiskeytown Visitor Center, where you must stop to buy a 7-day vehicle pass). Drive 3.8 miles (6.1 km) to the Whiskeytown Falls trailhead parking area on the left.

GPS COORDINATES: 40.6383, –122.6761; 40°38'17.9" N, 122°40'34" W

BEST NEARBY BREWS

It's worth driving 20 miles (32 km) east on Highway 299 for an award-winning brew from **Woody's Brewing** (1257 Oregon St., Redding, 530/768-1034, www.woodysbrewing.com, 11am-10pm Tues.-Thurs., 11am-11pm Fri.-Sat., 11am-9pm Sun.). This family-owned brewery offers a full menu of pub food—nachos, wings, fried pickles, and more—plus a rotating selection of 18 ales, stouts, and lagers.

NEARBY CAMPGROUNDS

NAME	DESCRIPTION	FACILITIES	SEASON	FEE
McBride Springs	First-come, first-served sites, easy access to Mount Shasta's trails	12 sites for tents or RVs up to 16 ft/4.9 m, vault toilets, drinking water	late May to late October	$10

Shasta-Trinity National Forest, off Everitt Memorial Highway on Mount Shasta, 530/926-4511, www.fs.usda.gov/stnf

NAME	DESCRIPTION	FACILITIES	SEASON	FEE
Fowlers Camp	On the Upper McCloud River; hiking trails, fishing, waterfalls	40 sites for tents or RVs up to 30 ft/9 m, vault toilets, drinking water	mid-May to mid-November	$15-30

Shasta-Trinity National Forest, off Hwy. 89 near McCloud; 877/444-6777, www.recreation.gov

NAME	DESCRIPTION	FACILITIES	SEASON	FEE
Castle Crags State Park	Hiking trails to glacier-polished crags, fishing on the Sacramento River	76 sites for tents or RVs up to 27 ft/8.2 m, restrooms, drinking water, showers	year-round	$35

Six miles (9.7 km) south of Dunsmuir off I-5, 800/444-7275, www.reservecalifornia.com

NEARBY CAMPGROUNDS (continued)

NAME	DESCRIPTION	FACILITIES	SEASON	FEE
McArthur Burney Falls State Park	Hiking trails, waterfall, kayaking and boating on Lake Britton	128 sites for tents or RVs up to 32 ft/9.8 m, 24 camping cabins, restrooms, drinking water, showers	year-round	$35

Six miles (9.7 km) south of Dunsmuir off I-5, 800/444-7275, www.reservecalifornia.com

NAME	DESCRIPTION	FACILITIES	SEASON	FEE
Oak Bottom	Sites near Whiskeytown Lake, boat rentals, kayaking, hiking, mountain biking	116 sites for tents or RVs up to 32 ft/9.8 m, 24 camping cabins, restrooms, drinking water, showers, dump station	year-round	$20-35

Whiskeytown National Recreation Area, 20 miles (32 km) west of Redding off Hwy. 299, 530/359-2269, www.whiskeytownmarinas.com

LASSEN VOLCANIC NATIONAL PARK

Lassen Peak first blew its top in May 1914, and for the next seven years, the volcanic outbursts continued. The showpiece of Lassen Volcanic National Park, this now quiet volcano rests amid a landscape dotted with otherworldly volcanic features: steaming sulfur vents, belching mud pots, boiling thermal pools, and rumbling fumaroles. Lassen Park also boasts forests of hemlocks, firs, and pines, plus dozens of swimmable lakes.

An astonishing 69 percent of the park burned in the 2021 Dixie Wildfire, when thousands of acres of forests were completely or partially scorched. Fortunately, some of the park's most popular destinations weren't touched by the flames. The National Park Service is actively working to rehabilitate trails within the burn footprint.

Lassen's hiking season is very short, typically mid-May to October. The park's main highway is closed due to snow November to early May, and higher-elevation trails may be snow-covered well into June or July. Near the park's Southwest Entrance, the Kohm Yah-mah-nee Visitor Center is open year-round.

▲ KINGS CREEK FALLS

BUMPASS HELL

◄ TERRACE, SHADOW, AND CLIFF LAKES TRAIL

1 Chaos Crags
DISTANCE: 4.2 miles (6.8 km) round-trip
DURATION: 2-3 hours
EFFORT: Easy-moderate

2 Manzanita Creek Trail
DISTANCE: 6.8 miles (10.9 km) round-trip
DURATION: 3-4 hours
EFFORT: Easy-moderate

3 Paradise Meadow
DISTANCE: 2.8 miles (4.5 km) round-trip
DURATION: 2 hours
EFFORT: Easy-moderate

4 Kings Creek Falls
DISTANCE: 2.5 miles (4 km) round-trip
DURATION: 1.5 hours
EFFORT: Easy-moderate

5 Terrace, Shadow, and Cliff Lakes
DISTANCE: 3.6 miles (5.8 km) round-trip
DURATION: 2 hours
EFFORT: Easy-moderate

6 Lassen Peak
DISTANCE: 4.8 miles (7.7 km) round-trip
DURATION: 3 hours
EFFORT: Moderate

7 Bumpass Hell
DISTANCE: 3.2 miles (5.2 km) round-trip
DURATION: 2 hours
EFFORT: Easy

8 Ridge Lakes
DISTANCE: 2 miles (3.2 km) round-trip
DURATION: 1.5 hours
EFFORT: Easy-moderate

9 Brokeoff Mountain
DISTANCE: 6.9 miles (11.1 km) round-trip
DURATION: 4 hours
EFFORT: Moderate-strenuous

10 Cinder Cone
DISTANCE: 3.8 miles (6.1 km) round-trip
DURATION: 3 hours
EFFORT: Moderate

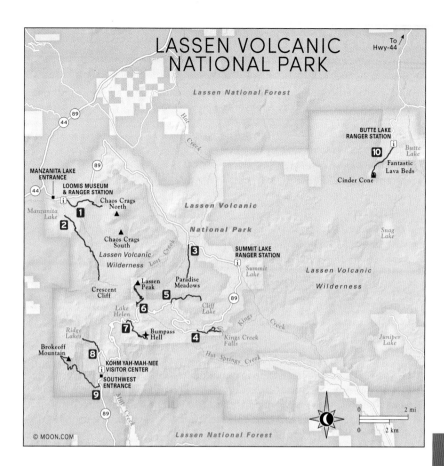

LASSEN VOLCANIC NATIONAL PARK

To
Hwy-44

Lassen National Forest

BUTTE LAKE
RANGER STATION

Butte
Lake

Fantastic
Lava Beds

Cinder Cone

MANZANITA LAKE
ENTRANCE

LOOMIS MUSEUM
& RANGER STATION

Manzanita
Lake

Chaos Crags
North

Lassen Volcanic

National Park

Snag
Lake

Chaos Crags
South

Lassen Volcanic
Wilderness

SUMMIT LAKE
RANGER STATION

Summit
Lake

Lassen Volcanic

Lost Creek

Lassen
Peak

Paradise
Meadows

Wilderness

Crescent
Cliff

Ridge
Lakes

Lake
Helen

Bumpass
Hell

Cliff
Lake

Kings Creek
Falls

Kings Creek

Juniper
Lake

Brokeoff
Mountain

KOHM YAH-MAH-NEE
VISITOR CENTER

SOUTHWEST
ENTRANCE

Hot Springs Creek

Mill Creek

Lassen National Forest

© MOON.COM

0   2 mi

0   2 km

1

Chaos Crags

LASSEN VOLCANIC NATIONAL PARK

Visit a dramatic landscape of stark volcanic cliffs, jumbled talus, and an ephemeral lake created by relatively recent volcanic activity.

DISTANCE: 4.2 miles (6.8 km) round-trip

DURATION: 2-3 hours

ELEVATION GAIN: 877 feet (267 m)

EFFORT: Easy-moderate

TRAIL: Packed dirt and scree

USERS: Hikers

SEASON: June-October; accessible by snowshoes in winter

PASSES/FEES: $30 per vehicle, valid for 7 days

MAPS: On the National Park Service app; National Geographic Maps "Lassen Volcanic National Park"

TRAILHEAD: Chaos Crags Trailhead

FACILITIES: Restroom

CONTACT: Lassen Volcanic National Park, 530/595-4480, www.nps.gov/lavo

L assen's volcanic landscape is remarkably young, and nowhere is that more evident than at Chaos Crags. The six peaks that make up Chaos Crags' massive wall formed about 1,100 years ago, a mere moment in geologic time. This is the park's only trail that gives you a close-up view of the peaks' soaring barren heights.

START THE HIKE

▶ **MILE 0-1.6: Chaos Crags Trailhead to Switchbacks**
The path begins with a gentle climb through an open forest as it roughly parallels Manzanita Creek. You'll see some charred tree trunks on the pines, but the black scars aren't from the 2021 Dixie Fire—they're from park-managed controlled burns. These managed fires are designed to protect this area from large destructive wildfires.

At 0.7 mile (1.1 km), the trail crosses a small stream on a **log bridge,** then continues climbing through gradually thickening forest. Small yellow markers about 8-10 feet (2.4-3 m) high on the tree trunks help snowshoers negotiate this trail in the winter months.

The trail's gradient picks up in the next mile (1.6 km), but still, this pleasant path is far from steep. Hike along in the company of conifers until you reach the first of a handful of short **switchbacks** at 1.6 miles (2.6 km).

▶ **MILE 1.6-2.1: Switchbacks to Chaos Crags Ridgeline**
The switchbacks lead to the **crest of a ridge,** where most of the trees disappear. You're rewarded with a dramatic view of the dusty pink **Chaos Crags** towering 1,600 feet (488 m) above you, Table Mountain looming to the northwest, and forested ridges extending downhill toward the Central Valley.

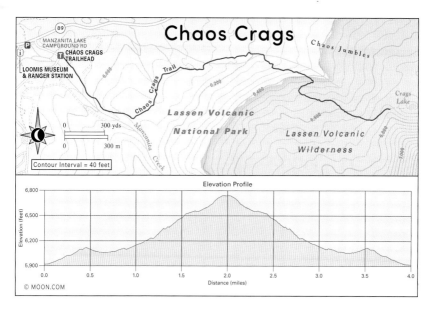

The barren-looking crags are plug-dome volcanoes, much like Lassen Peak, which were formed by viscous lava—so thick that it didn't flow outward, but rather squeezed upward through vents in the earth and then hardened in place.

The trail peters out above the Crags' steep-walled bowl. If you're lucky, the depression at the bowl's base will brim with the blue-green waters of **Crags Lake.** The ephemeral snowmelt-fed lake shows up only after heavy winters, and even then, its waters dry up under the high-elevation sun by late summer. If the lake is present when you visit, you'll find a use trail that leads steeply downhill to its edge.

Lake or no lake, the Crags' massive summits are an impressive sight. Your attention will be turned upward, but don't forget to look down at the soil, where you'll find thousands of glittering pink rocks. This rose-colored dacite sprouted from the earth only 1,100 years ago.

Even more recently, the Crags let loose an avalanche of rock that created the **Chaos Jumbles,** a 2.5-square-mile (6.5-sq-km) debris field that lies to the Crags' northwest. They're the remains of three successive landslides that occurred about 350 years ago (geologists believe around 1660). Most likely instigated by a large earthquake, massive boulders broke off from the Crags' plug-dome volcanoes and tumbled down these slopes at more than 100 miles per hour (161 km/h). The landslides devastated the forest below the Crags and dammed up Manzanita Creek, which led to the formation of Manzanita Lake.

The wreckage isn't finished yet. If you hang around this viewpoint for more than a few minutes, you're likely to witness a cascade of rocks tumbling down the steep flanks of Chaos Crags.

It's hard to find a comfortable seat in this rock-strewn aerie, but pick a large boulder and savor the geologic marvels surrounding you, then head back the way you came.

CRAGS LAKE ▲

DIRECTIONS

From Lassen's Northwest Entrance Station at Manzanita Lake, drive southeast on Highway 89 (Lassen Park Hwy.) for 0.5 mile (0.8 km) to the turnoff for Manzanita Lake Campground (just past the Loomis Museum). Turn right and drive 100 yards (30 m) to the Chaos Crags Trailhead and the small parking area on the left.

GPS COORDINATES: 40.5359, −121.5592; 40°32'9.2" N, 121°33'33.1" W

2

Manzanita Creek Trail

LASSEN VOLCANIC NATIONAL PARK

In Lassen's busy Manzanita Lake region, flower-filled meadows, serene forests, and a fair chance of solitude await on this less-traveled trail.

DISTANCE: 6.8 miles (10.9 km) round-trip

DURATION: 3–4 hours

ELEVATION GAIN: 1,190 feet (363 m)

EFFORT: Easy-moderate

TRAIL: Old dirt road

USERS: Hikers

SEASON: June–October

PASSES/FEES: $30 per vehicle, valid for 7 days

MAPS: On the National Park Service app; National Geographic Maps "Lassen Volcanic National Park"

TRAILHEAD: Manzanita Creek Trailhead, across from campsite 31

FACILITIES: Water spigots, restrooms

CONTACT: Lassen Volcanic National Park, 530/595-4480, www.nps.gov/lavo

START THE HIKE

▶ **MILE 0-2: Manzanita Creek Trailhead to Creek Crossing**

From the **trail sign** across from **campsite 31,** follow the old dirt road past a smattering of tent sites. The moderately ascending trail travels southeast under a canopy of Jeffrey pines, red firs, and white firs. Beneath their boughs grows an understory of dense green-leaf manzanita (larger leaves) and pinemat manzanita (smaller leaves).

After the first mile (1.6 km), the woodland thins out to reveal mature stands of red and white fir, which cast cool shadows along the trail. In spots where the woodland canopy allows the sun to penetrate, you'll find a carpet of gray-leaved, blue-flowered satin lupine punctuated by splashes of scarlet gilia and blue penstemon. You'll also catch occasional glimpses of Lassen Peak's highest reaches.

With few other people around and no junctions to negotiate, you'll be surprised at how easy it is to "tune in" to this forest. In the summer months, mountain chickadees and Steller's jays make cheerful—and often noisy—companions. The calls of these garrulous birds are punctuated by the drilling of woodpeckers.

By the 1.3-mile (2.1-km) mark, you've already gained 550 feet (168 m) on a remarkably steady grade, and now that grade eases up. You're accompanied by Chaos Crags peeking above the trees (look over your left shoulder). Soon you'll hear the aquatic music of Manzanita Creek—the sound is obviously coming from your left, but you can't yet see the stream, which is hemmed in by dense willows and shrubs.

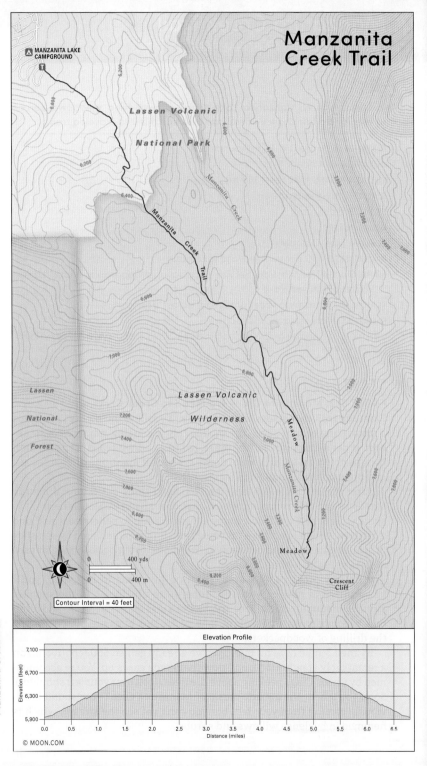

Manzanita Creek Trail

MANZANITA LAKE CAMPGROUND

Lassen Volcanic

National Park

Manzanita Creek

Manzanita Creek Trail

Lassen

National

Forest

Lassen Volcanic

Wilderness

Meadow

Manzanita Creek

Meadow

Crescent Cliff

0   400 yds
0   400 m

Contour Interval = 40 feet

Elevation Profile

Elevation (feet)

Distance (miles)

© MOON.COM

▲ MANZANITA CREEK TRAIL

The watery symphony grows louder over the next 0.5-mile (0.8-km) stretch, then at exactly 2 miles (3.2 km) from the trailhead, your path crosses over it. **Manzanita Creek** is funneled through a culvert, but if you want to cool your toes, just follow a side trail upstream a few feet and dunk your feet in the icy water.

▶ MILE 2-3.4: Creek Crossing to Meadow below Crescent Cliff

Beyond the creek crossing, you're entering this trail's loveliest stretch. Soon you'll gain vistas of Loomis Peak to the southwest, which will keep popping in and out of view for most of the next mile (1.6 km). After a long contour away from the creek, the trail reaches a sloping hillside **meadow** at 2.8 miles (4.5 km). Traipse along its edge and go treasure-hunting for wandering daisies, fireweed, monkshood, pennyroyal, paintbrush, and monkey flower.

In another 0.4 mile (0.6 km), you'll reach a second sloping **meadow,** this one even larger and lusher. A tributary of Manzanita Creek meanders through its center (you'll cross it on a log) amid a colorful canvas of wildflowers. Spend some time near the marshy stream, counting the blooms that pepper the meadow grasses and enjoying impressive views of Loomis Peak.

Many hikers turn around here, but you can push on, following the trail as it narrows to single-track and tunnels through an incredibly dense fir forest—the trees are packed in so tightly that even a deer or coyote couldn't make it through. You'll pop out of this tangle of trees into a wet boggy area, where the trail can be hard to discern. Soon it peters out completely near the pristine headwaters of Manzanita Creek.

You'll find a perfect picnic spot or backpacking site tucked into a copse of firs at the **base of Crescent Cliff,** which forms the headwall of this horseshoe-shaped valley. The creek flows right past, its banks overhung with

willows. Dip your feet or hands in the water; you'll be amazed at just how icy cold it is—this stream springs from deep underground.

When you're ready, retrace your steps to your car.

DIRECTIONS

From Lassen's Northwest Entrance Station at Manzanita Lake, drive southeast on Highway 89 (Lassen Park Hwy.) for 0.5 mile (0.8 km) to the right turnoff for Manzanita Lake Campground (just past the Loomis Museum). Turn right and drive 0.5 mile (0.8 km) to the Manzanita Lake Store. Park there or just beyond the store in the boat ramp lot. Walk up the campground road 0.3 mile (0.5 km) to the D Loop. The trailhead is across from site D31. If you're camping at Manzanita Lake Campground, you can hike from your site.

GPS COORDINATES: 40.5269, −121.5612; 40°31'36.8" N, 121°33'40.3" W

Hike past Hat Creek's whitewater cascades to a serene meadow filled with summer wildflowers.

BEST: Wildflower Hikes

DISTANCE: 2.8 miles (4.5 km) round-trip

DURATION: 2 hours

ELEVATION GAIN: 628 feet (191 m)

EFFORT: Easy-moderate

TRAIL: Packed dirt

USERS: Hikers

SEASON: June-October

PASSES/FEES: $30 per vehicle, valid for 7 days

MAPS: On the National Park Service app; National Geographic Maps "Lassen Volcanic National Park"

TRAILHEAD: Paradise Meadow Trailhead

FACILITIES: Restroom

CONTACT: Lassen Volcanic National Park, 530/595-4480, www.nps.gov/lavo

Spring comes to Lassen Volcanic National Park whenever it feels like it. It might be as early as mid-June, or it might wait till early August. Whenever the season chooses to arrive, it paints Paradise Meadow in a glorious technicolor display of wildflowers. Late July and early August are usually the peak of the blooming bonanza, but every year is slightly different—and that unpredictability is some of this hike's charm.

START THE HIKE

▶ **MILE 0-1.1: Paradise Meadow Trailhead to First Cascade**

The path starts out with easy walking on a level grade, but don't hike so fast that you miss the **giant boulder** on your left, about 100 yards (30 m) in. The gargantuan rock is just a few feet off the trail. Like the Hot Rock that's on display a few miles north on Lassen Park Highway, this 20-ton boulder was one of many that tumbled down in a massive mudflow caused by Lassen Peak's 1915 eruption. Early-20th-century park visitors reported that boulders like this one were still hot to the touch a year after the eruption.

Only a few yards beyond the boulder, you'll tunnel through a gorgeously green forest filled with majestic mountain hemlocks and red firs. The trail's mellow uphill grade and plentiful shade grant you plenty of headspace for appreciating the scenery. Leafy gooseberry bushes grow at your feet. Breaks in the trees allow for peek-a-boo views of Lassen Peak.

At 0.5 mile (0.8 km), the path begins a stiffer ascent, traveling up a narrow ravine bordered by a tributary of the West Fork of Hat Creek. In this

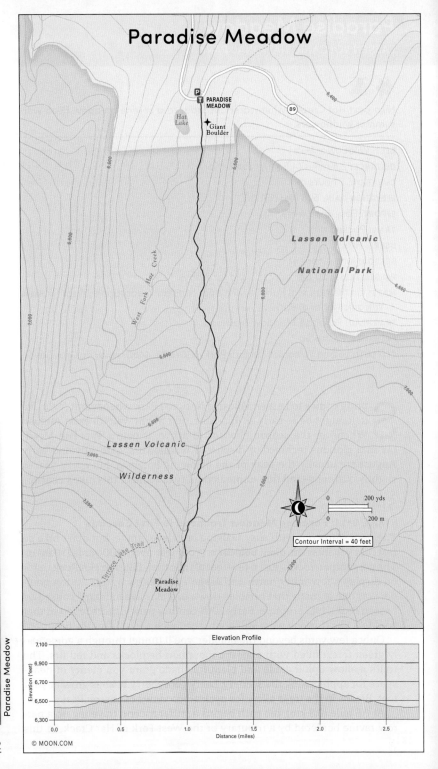

Paradise Meadow

Hat Lake

PARADISE MEADOW

Giant Boulder

89

Lassen Volcanic

National Park

West Fork Hat Creek

Lassen Volcanic

Wilderness

Terrace Lake Trail

Paradise Meadow

0   200 yds
0   200 m

Contour Interval = 40 feet

Elevation Profile

© MOON.COM

▲ WEST FORK OF HAT CREEK

verdant woodland, wildflowers vie for your attention—mariposa lily, scarlet gilia, and spotted coralroot among them.

After crossing two smaller feeder streams on **log bridges,** you'll hear the sound of rushing water up ahead, and at 1.1 mile (1.8 km), you reach the first of two boisterous white-water cascades. This unnamed **cataract** tumbles 15 feet (4.6 m) over multitiered ledges, then braids out in a host of tiny rivulets. Monkshood, bog orchids, and monkey flower cling to watery footholds along the streambank.

▶ MILE 1.1–1.4: First Cascade to Paradise Meadow

Only 0.2 mile (0.3 km) beyond the first cascade is a **second, even lovelier cataract,** where a frothy rush of white water hopscotches down a 20-foot (6-m) drop. A trail signed for Terrace Lake takes off just beyond this waterfall, but you'll stay left (south) for the final stretch to Paradise Meadow. Proceed uphill on one last steep pitch before your path suddenly levels out.

An easy stroll brings you gently to the edge of **Paradise Meadow,** a vast emerald expanse that's larger than a football field and backed by towering rock cliffs. A crystal-clear waterway makes lazy S-turns through the meadow's lush grasses and sedges. During peak bloom time, often starting in late July, this exquisite spot is polka-dotted with lavender fleabane (a.k.a. wandering daisies or asters) and vibrant corn lilies (false hellebore). Scan the meadow for other bloomers, including yellow and blue lupine, paintbrush, clover, and gentian.

If the meadow is blooming, that means it's wet. It may seem tempting to wade through a knee-deep jumble of flowers, but stick to the edges of this fragile and delicate ecosystem. You don't want to crush any of these gorgeous blossoms or tread on even a single blade of grass.

LASSEN VOLCANIC NATIONAL PARK

Paradise Meadow

PARADISE MEADOW ▲

Follow the trail a few yards farther to the meadow's east side, where you'll glimpse a surprising view of mighty Mount Lassen to the west, holding court above the talus-covered cliffs. Pick a spot on a fallen log, pull out that sandwich or trail mix, and gaze over the wonder of Paradise.

When you're ready to return, retrace your steps.

DIRECTIONS

From Lassen's Northwest Entrance Station at Manzanita Lake, drive southeast on Highway 89 (Lassen Park Hwy.) for 9.5 miles (15.3 km) to the Paradise Meadow Trailhead, at a horseshoe curve in the road next to Hat Lake. Park in the large lot on the northeast side of the road, then cross the road to access the trail.

GPS COORDINATES: 40.5094, −121.4649; 40°30'33.8" N, 121°27'53.6" W

LASSEN VOLCANIC NATIONAL PARK

Stretch your legs on this easy hike to fern-fringed Kings Creek Falls, a glistening 50-foot (15-m) cataract.

DISTANCE: 2.5 miles (4 km) round-trip

DURATION: 1.5 hours

ELEVATION GAIN: 400 feet (122 m)

EFFORT: Easy-moderate

TRAIL: Packed dirt, rock stairsteps

USERS: Hikers

SEASON: June-October

PASSES/FEES: $30 per vehicle, valid for 7 days

MAPS: On the National Park Service app; National Geographic Maps "Lassen Volcanic National Park"

TRAILHEAD: Kings Creek Falls Trailhead

FACILITIES: Restroom

CONTACT: Lassen Volcanic National Park, 530/595-4480, www.nps.gov/lavo

Kings Creek Falls is as beautiful as it's been for centuries, but be forewarned: This trail exhibits extensive scars from the 2021 Dixie Fire, especially on the first leg to the waterfall (the return leg is much greener). The hike serves as a fascinating lesson in forest regeneration: Yes, there's devastation, but also abundant beauty.

START THE HIKE

▶ **MILE 0-0.7: Kings Creek Falls Trailhead to Loop Junction**
The **Kings Creek Falls Trail**'s first 0.25 mile (0.4 km) meanders downhill under a canopy of large shady firs that were mostly spared from the Dixie wildfire. Wind onward through this pleasant stretch, then depart the trees for a traverse along the edge of **Lower Kings Creek Meadow,** a dark-green expanse that's awash with corn lilies in early summer. At 0.5 mile (0.8 km), a trail on the right leads to Sifford Lakes; you go left (northeast).

Only 0.2 mile (0.3 km) farther, your path reaches another **junction,** where two trail options are designated as a **one-way loop.** Take the left fork for the descent to the falls, hiking clockwise; you'll return on the right fork.

▶ **MILE 0.7-1.4: Loop Junction to Kings Creek Falls Overlook**
The descending trail travels down-canyon through severely burned forest. You'll notice many large holes in the forest floor from trees that were incinerated all the way down to their underground roots, as well as numerous scorched trunks that remain standing. In the next few years, shrubs, ferns, and ground cover will grow back first, followed by young trees. As

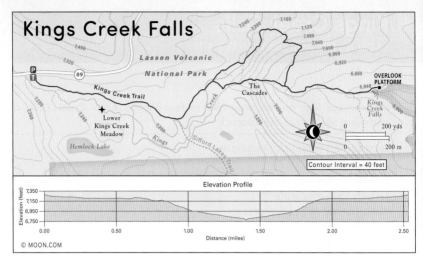

Kings Creek Falls

Lassen Volcanic National Park

Kings Creek Trail

Lower Kings Creek Meadow

Hemlock Lake

The Cascades

Kings Creek Falls

OVERLOOK PLATFORM

Sifford Lakes Trail

Contour Interval = 40 feet

0   200 yds
0   200 m

Elevation Profile

© MOON.COM

devastating as wildfires are, Mother Nature is highly skilled at recovery and regeneration.

The trail makes a long arc northeast and then contours south, offering broad views down-canyon of a vast acreage of burned trees descending all the way to Warner Valley. After 0.5 mile (0.8 km) of walking through blackened forest, you reach a **junction** 0.2 mile (0.3 km) above the waterfall. Take note of this intersection: Your return loop heads upstream here. For now, continue downstream (east).

In a few moments, you step onto **Kings Creek Falls' overlook platform**—reconstructed in summer 2022 from hefty peeled logs—to face a glorious sight: Below your feet, boisterous Kings Creek Falls tumbles 50 feet (15 m) in a joyful shimmer of white water. Although this cataract isn't impressively tall, it boasts a dependable flow even in the driest years. Snowmelt from Lassen Peak seeps into an underground spring that feeds Kings Creek year-round.

A caveat: Kings Creek Falls is beautiful but tricky to photograph. Because the creek canyon is so narrow, the falls are rarely well-lit. To score the best photos, visit early in the morning or when the sky is cloudy.

▶ MILE 1.4-2.5: Kings Creek Falls Overlook to Kings Creek Falls Trailhead

You might expect that Kings Creek Falls packs the biggest punch on this trek, but many hikers find the next stretch of trail is even more wow-worthy. Retrace your steps to the junction you just passed. This time, veer left (west), sticking

CASCADE ON KINGS CREEK ▶

▲ KINGS CREEK

close to the creek upstream of the falls. You're entering the narrow ravine known as **The Cascades**—a stretch of Kings Creek that's highlighted by a series of white-water pools and drops.

Hike up a narrow **stone staircase** that was built just inches from the creek's boisterous cascades. The 0.3-mile (0.5 km) stretch along the Cascades is this trek's steepest pitch, but you won't even notice the stair-climbing workout since every step offers a new view of flirtatious Kings Creek. On this part of the loop, most of the forest is green and thriving, a miraculous contrast to the charred woodland you walked through earlier. Willows and wildflowers cling to rocky footholds along the stream. Amateur botanists will delight in the sight of shrubby mountain ash, which bears bright-red berries in early autumn.

You'll reach the top of the Cascades all too soon. Wave a regretful goodbye as you head back to the loop junction, then veer left (southwest) for the final 0.7 mile (1.1 km) back to your car.

DIRECTIONS

From Lassen's Southwest Entrance Station, drive north on Highway 89 (Lassen Park Hwy.) for 12 miles (19.3 km) to the Kings Creek Falls Trailhead. Park on either side of the road in the large pullouts; the trail begins on the road's south side by the signboard.

GPS COORDINATES: 40.4606, −121.4593; 40°27′38.2″ N, 121°27′33.5″ W

LASSEN VOLCANIC NATIONAL PARK

Kings Creek Falls

A trio of come-hither alpine lakes tempts hikers, swimmers, and picnickers on warm summer days.

BEST: Swimming Hole Hikes
DISTANCE: 3.6 miles (5.8 km) round-trip
DURATION: 2 hours
ELEVATION GAIN: 734 feet (224 m)
EFFORT: Easy-moderate
TRAIL: Packed dirt
USERS: Hikers
SEASON: June-October
PASSES/FEES: $30 per vehicle, valid for 7 days
MAPS: On the National Park Service app; National Geographic Maps "Lassen Volcanic National Park"
TRAILHEAD: Terrace Lake Trailhead
FACILITIES: Restroom
CONTACT: Lassen Volcanic National Park, 530/595-4480, www.nps.gov/lavo

Lassen has so many alluring lakes, it's impossible to choose favorites. But for ease of access and delightful swimming, this trail's three alpine pools deserve a spot on any Top 10 list. Despite the short distance that separates them, each lake is remarkably different.

START THE HIKE

▶ MILE 0-1: Terrace Lake Trailhead to Shadow Lake

This is an upside-down hike: downhill on the way in and uphill on the way back. From **Terrace Lake Trailhead,** it's a remarkably quick and gentle descent to the first lake. Hop on the trail and veer right (east) at a **junction** only 0.2 mile (0.3 km) in (the left fork leads to the Paradise Meadow-Hat Lake Trailhead). Descend about 500 feet (152 m) through a boulder-dotted forest, and in only about 15 minutes, you'll be dipping your toes into **Terrace Lake,** 0.6 mile (1 km) from the start.

Terrace Lake is long and narrow, tucked into a bench below a tall cliff and ringed by scattered hemlocks. Families with young children—or hikers trying to beat the summer heat—may choose to stop right here and cool off in the lake's azure waters. But if you continue onward, the trail skirts 0.1 mile (0.2 km) along Terrace Lake's southern shoreline to a **high bench,** where you can see the tip of Lassen Peak peeking over Terrace's high wall. You can also look downslope to Shadow Lake, this trail's next destination. The path loses another 100 feet (30 m) in 0.3 mile (0.5 km) to reach **Shadow Lake**'s southwestern edge.

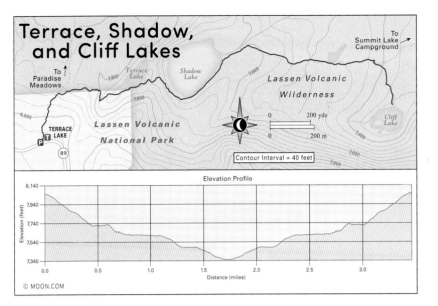

Shadow is the largest of this trail's lakes—a circular-shaped beauty that's three times the size of Terrace, with an open shoreline and very few trees. It makes an ideal destination for hikers with swimming on their minds. The trail clings to the lake's southern shore, so you can easily kick off your shoes and wade in, or wander over to the north shore to claim a more private spot. From the main trail on Shadow's southern shore, you'll enjoy fine views of Lassen Peak towering over the lake.

▶ MILE 1-1.8: Shadow Lake to Cliff Lake

Shadow Lake will tempt you to linger, but there's more to see on this lake-filled trail. The narrow path descends farther, now on a much mellower grade. It enters a small meadow basin bisected by a diminutive stream and dotted by tiny ponds. In late July and early August, a blanket of silverleaf lupine puts on a sky-blue show.

Beyond the meadow, the trail enters a much denser forest than what you've seen so far—lodgepole pines and white firs fill in the gaps between hemlocks. Now that you've lost a few hundred feet, you're in a lower veg-etation zone of open meadows and deeper woods.

At 1.6 miles (2.6 km) from the start, a trail sign points right for Cliff Lake, 0.2 mile (0.3 km) distant. (The left fork leads 1.8 mi/2.9 km to Summit Lake Campground.) Wander through dense woodlands until you reach Cliff Lake's outlet stream, which you'll follow to its shoreline.

Cliff Lake does indeed have a cliff, plus an impressive talus pile of light-colored rocks on its southwest perimeter. Reading Peak rises to the south—the rockslide likely began on its slopes. The lake's waters are shal-low, clear, and blue-green, but because its shoreline is choked with wil-lows and fallen tree snags, you'll have to search around to find a good hangout spot. If you go for a dip, be sure to swim out to the small tree-lined island on the lake's west end.

SHADOW LAKE ▲

Prowl the lakeshore until you reach the lake's inlet, where you'll find an abundance of water-loving wildflowers—wandering daisies, lupine, heather, and corn lilies. Also on the plus side, you'll enjoy much more solitude at this lake than at the first two.

▶ MILE 1.8-3.6: Cliff Lake to Terrace Lake Trailhead

The trip back to your car is all uphill, but since you're now facing west as you walk, you'll enjoy sightings of Lassen Peak that were behind you on the way in. Take time to linger at each lake as you pass it a second time.

DIRECTIONS

From Lassen's Southwest Entrance Station, drive north on Highway 89 (Lassen Park Hwy.) for 8.8 miles (14.2 km) to the Terrace Lake Trailhead (2 mi/3.2 km north of the Lassen Peak Trailhead). Park on either side of the road in the large pullouts; the trail begins on the road's west side.

GPS COORDINATES: 40.4763, −121.4791; 40°28'34.7" N, 121°28'44.8" W

6 Lassen Peak

LASSEN VOLCANIC NATIONAL PARK

A remarkably well-graded trail leads to the 10,457-foot (3,187-m) summit of Lassen Peak, one of the world's largest plug-dome volcanos.

BEST: Summer Hikes
DISTANCE: 4.8 miles (7.7 km) round-trip
DURATION: 3 hours
ELEVATION GAIN: 1,867 feet (569 m)
EFFORT: Moderate
TRAIL: Packed dirt, volcanic gravel, loose scree
USERS: Hikers
SEASON: June-October
PASSES/FEES: $30 per vehicle, valid for 7 days
MAPS: On the National Park Service app; National Geographic Maps "Lassen Volcanic National Park"
TRAILHEAD: Lassen Peak Trailhead
FACILITIES: Restroom
CONTACT: Lassen Volcanic National Park, 530/595-4480, www.nps.gov/lavo

The thrilling ascent to Lassen Peak's volcanic summit is deservedly popular. Make sure you're adequately prepared: Start early in the morning to beat the oppressive alpine sun, wear strong sun protection (there's almost no shade along the trail), and carry plenty of water and a few snacks. If you want to beat the crowds, consider hitting the trail at 5am to catch sunrise from the top of this remarkable volcano.

START THE HIKE

▸ **MILE 0-1.2: Lassen Peak Trailhead to the Tree Line**
From the **parking lot,** the wide sandy path heads steadily uphill under precious little shade, so take advantage of occasional clumps of trees in the trail's first mile (1.6 km). At about 0.5 mile (0.8 km), you've already gained enough elevation along Lassen Peak's south face to have earned a broad perspective on Brokeoff Mountain, Lake Helen, Mount Conard, and Crumbaugh Lake. Lake Almanor is the large body of water to the south, outside of the park. Pretty soon you'll catch a view of the Vulcan's Eye, a conspicuous rock feature on Lassen's south face that resembles an eye. It's a piece of hardened lava that was carried along as Lassen's lava dome rose and expanded.

At 1.2 miles (1.9 km), you rise **above the tree line,** leaving all scraps of shade behind you (except for an occasional large boulder), but with any luck you'll have gained a refreshing breeze at this higher elevation. This trail has no junctions, so you don't have to think about anything besides

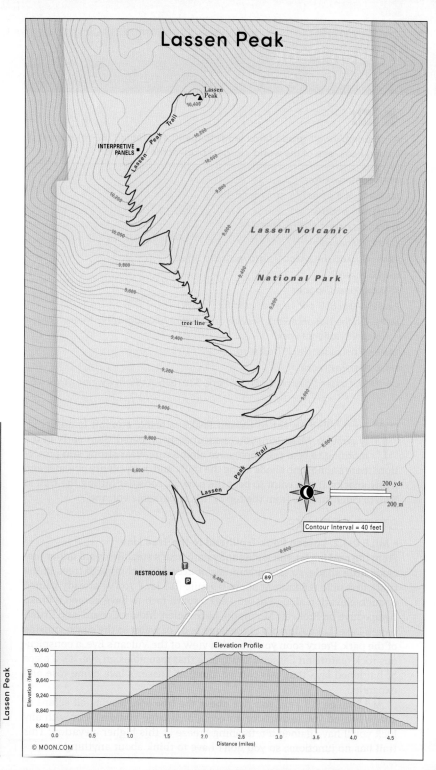

Lassen Peak

Lassen Peak

Lassen Peak Trail

INTERPRETIVE PANELS

Lassen Volcanic

National Park

tree line

Lassen Peak Trail

Lassen

RESTROOMS

Contour Interval = 40 feet

0 — 200 yds
0 — 200 m

89

Elevation Profile

▲ HIKER ASCENDING LASSEN PEAK

climbing—which is fortunate, because the trail steepens for the remaining push to the summit.

▶ **MILE 1.2–2.2: Tree Line to Summit Crater Interpretive Panels**
The trail curves around to the west side of Lassen, offering fantastic views of Brokeoff Mountain and Helen Lake, a prominent feature at the base of the volcano. There's no respite from the sun and little respite from the frequent wind. The setting is pure volcanic as you push on: barren, bleak, yet oh-so-beautiful.

From miles 1.3 to 1.7, you face a daunting series of tight, well-constructed **switchbacks** leading up the scree slope. As your path approaches the summit, it veers eastward, then tops out at a plateau on Lassen's crater, about 75 feet (23 m) below its highest point (2.2 mi/3.5 km from the start). **Four interpretive panels,** anchored in concrete to withstand high winds, describe the flora and fauna on this mountain, such as the millions of orange and black California tortoiseshell butterflies that flit across the summit almost every summer during their annual migration. The number of butterflies and their exact timing is unpredictable, but it's an incredible sight to witness.

It's only another 0.2 mile (0.3 km) to the highest point, but many hikers are content to stop right here. The view from the interpretive display is nearly as expansive as it is on the slightly higher summit, and stopping here saves you a final scramble through loose, sharp scree. If you have young children in tow, it's wise not to push on. A sketchy made-by-use trail ascends to Lassen's highest point, which is fine for sturdy-footed adults, but probably not safe for an excited six-year-old.

SUMMIT OF LASSEN PEAK ▲

▶ **MILE 2.2–2.4: Summit Crater Interpretive Panels to Lassen's Highest Point**

From the crater's interpretive display, follow the trail for another 100 yards (30 m), then begin a rocky scramble to the peak's **highest point.** You'll find a United States Geological Survey marker here and a remarkable vista. Although you've been gazing south, east, and west all the way up the trail, this summit provides a clear view to the north as well—all the way to Mount Shasta and beyond on clear days. You can also peer down the volcano's eastern slopes to observe the furrowed lines left from mud, snow, and water pouring downhill to the aptly named Devastated Area during Lassen's major eruptions.

After enjoying your time on this fabulous summit, retrace your steps.

DIRECTIONS

From Lassen's Southwest Entrance Station, drive north on Highway 89 (Lassen Park Hwy.) for 6.9 miles (11.1 km) to the Lassen Peak trailhead, on the left. The trail begins by the large signboard.

GPS COORDINATES: 40.4748, −121.5057; 40°28′29.3″ N, 121°30′20.5″ W

7 Bumpass Hell

LASSEN VOLCANIC NATIONAL PARK

Hike to an active geothermal wonderland of superheated fumaroles, thumping mud pots, billowing steam, and boiling acidic pools.

DISTANCE: 3.2 miles (5.2 km) round-trip

DURATION: 2 hours

ELEVATION GAIN: 518 feet (158 m)

EFFORT: Easy

TRAIL: Packed gravel and dirt

USERS: Hikers

SEASON: July-October

PASSES/FEES: $30 per vehicle, valid for 7 days

MAPS: On the National Park Service app; National Geographic Maps "Lassen Volcanic National Park"

TRAILHEAD: Bumpass Hell Trailhead

FACILITIES: Restroom

CONTACT: Lassen Volcanic National Park, 530/595-4480, www.nps.gov/lavo

START THE HIKE

▶ MILE 0-1: Bumpass Trailhead to Highest Point

The trail starts at the **large signboard** near the **parking lot entrance.** In the first mile (1.6 km), you travel through a healthy green hemlock forest, with more hemlocks per square acre than you'll see almost anywhere. The trail passes a short **spur to Helen Lake** on the left at 0.3 mile (0.5 km), with Lassen Peak towering over the lake's azure waters. (Some hikers park alongside the highway here to access the Bumpass Hell Trail, especially when the main parking lot is full.) Stay on the main trail; if you wish to visit Helen Lake, you can drive to it later.

In another 0.2 mile (0.3 km), the trail reaches an **overlook** on the right. Signboards name all the volcanic peaks within view: Mount Conard, Diamond Peak, Brokeoff Mountain, Mount Diller, and Pilot Pinnacle. They're all part of ancient Mount Tehama—a volcano that was much bigger than Lassen Peak, measuring 4 miles (6.4 km) across and soaring to 11,000 feet (3,353 m). Lassen Peak was formed from lava flowing from Mount Tehama.

The path travels very gently uphill, and when you reach its **highest point** at 1 mile (1.6 km), you're directly above Bumpass Hell. Trees partially obscure the view, so you still don't have the whole picture. But you will hear the strange-sounding ruckus made by hydrothermal activity—noises that could be described as the rumble of steam or turbine motors, or the whoosh of trucks on a busy freeway.

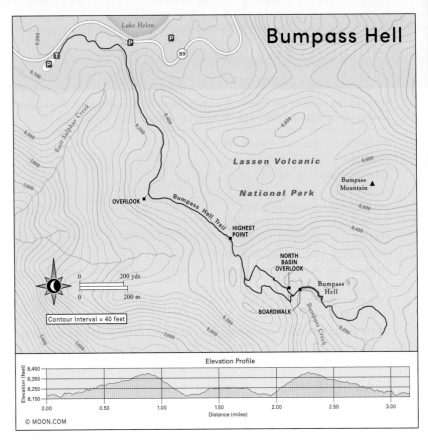

Bumpass Hell

Lake Helen

Lassen Volcanic

National Park

Bumpass Mountain ▲

OVERLOOK ■

Bumpass Hell Trail

HIGHEST POINT

NORTH BASIN OVERLOOK

Bumpass Hell

BOARDWALK

Bumpass Creek

East Sulphur Creek

| 0 | 200 yds |
| 0 | 200 m |

Contour Interval = 40 feet

Elevation Profile

© MOON.COM

▶ **MILE 1-1.7: Highest Point to High Overlook**

Descend 200 feet (61 m) on a path composed of what looks like white chalk dust—it will soon coat your shoes. The soft, powdery soil is what is left of volcanic rock after it has been completely broken down by sulfuric acid and steam. Although you're still enveloped in dense hemlock forest, you're heading for the source of all that noisy commotion—and also the rotten-egg smell that's been tickling your nose. For most visitors, the aroma of hydrogen sulfide (sulfur) makes the biggest impression.

Reach a **junction** with the short loop around the geothermal features at 1.1 miles (1.8 km) from the start. It doesn't matter which way you go; both legs of the loop rejoin, and you'll want to explore every inch of this basin. Your first view of this strange landscape is mind-boggling: Steam from turquoise pools rises to the sky. A milky gray creek meanders through the basin. Clay minerals splash a yellow, orange, and red palette across barren andesite rock.

Wander along the **boardwalk trail,** making sure to obey the signs warning visitors not to stray. The price of stepping off the trail to snap a selfie can be extremely high; the soil is fragile and can't support much weight, and the acidic pools in this geothermal basin reach temperatures of 250°F (121°C). Approximately 75 major fumaroles, acid-sulfate hot springs, and thumping mud pots are found in this 16-acre basin. One major highlight

▲ BUMPASS HELL

is the **Big Boiler,** Lassen's largest super-heated fumarole. The high-velocity steam emitting from the Big Boiler has been measured as hot as 322°F (161°C), making it one of the world's hottest fumaroles.

Once you reach the far end of the boardwalk, follow the signed trail uphill to a **high overlook** on the basin's southeast side. Here you gain a broad overview of the basin's colorful hues: The soil is painted with orange sulfates. Pyrite pools are tinted a brilliant turquoise. Steam vents are dotted with bright-yellow native sulfur.

▶ MILE 1.7-3.2: High Overlook to Bumpass Trailhead

After enjoying the surreal view, retrace your steps back downhill to the boardwalk, stroll past Big Boiler one more time, then take the signed **Alternate Trail** that leads to an **overlook** on the basin's north side, where again you'll be wowed by the colors. The Alternate Trail then travels back uphill to rejoin the main trail. Follow it back to the trailhead, enjoying full-frontal views of Mount Lassen, which were at your back on the way in.

DIRECTIONS

From the Southwest Entrance Station, drive north on Highway 89 (Lassen Park Hwy.) for 5.8 miles (9.3 km) to the Bumpass Hell Trailhead on the right. The trail begins on the northeast side of the parking lot.

GPS COORDINATES: 40.4661, −121.5140; 40°27′58″ N, 121°30′50.4″ W

Only a short but steep mile (1.6 km) from the trailhead, a pair of alluring swimming lakes are nestled in a cliff-backed volcanic basin.

DISTANCE: 2 miles (3.2 km) round-trip
DURATION: 1.5 hours
ELEVATION GAIN: 995 feet (303 m)
EFFORT: Easy-moderate
TRAIL: Packed dirt, rock stairsteps
USERS: Hikers
SEASON: June–October
PASSES/FEES: $30 per vehicle, valid for 7 days
MAPS: On the National Park Service app; National Geographic Maps "Lassen Volcanic National Park"
TRAILHEAD: Ridge Lakes/Sulphur Works Trailhead
FACILITIES: Restroom
CONTACT: Lassen Volcanic National Park, 530/595-4480, www.nps.gov/lavo

Ridge Lakes Trail shares a parking lot with Sulphur Works, Lassen's only geothermal feature that's accessible without hiking. Before heading up to the lakes, take a brief detour to see Sulphur Works' hissing and steaming fumaroles on the park highway, about a 50-yard (46-m) walk from the parking lot. A decade ago, a boardwalk trail wound past these pools and mud pots, but it was destroyed by unstable soil and heavy snows. Now the only way to view the Sulphur Works is from the roadside.

START THE HIKE

▸ **MILE 0-1: Ridge Lakes-Sulphur Works Trailhead to Ridge Lakes**
After surveying the steamy scene at **Sulphur Works,** head uphill on **Ridge Lakes Trail.** The trail traces along a meadowy slope that parallels West Sulphur Creek, the stream that feeds the Sulphur Works' geothermal action. In just a few footsteps, you'll come to two conclusions: The elevation here is high (7,000 ft/2,134 m) and this trail's grade is unusually steep. In a mere 1 mile (1.6 km) to the lakes, you'll gain just under 1,000 feet (305 m), which means this trail averages about a 20 percent grade. Most trails are built with a grade about half that steep or less. Even so, the route is short, and plenty of families with young kids make the trip—they just take their time. Fortunately, there's top-notch scenery every step of the way.

The steep path departs West Sulphur Creek at about 0.5 mile (0.8 km) and follows a tributary that flows out of Ridge Lake. Turn around occasionally to watch the vista to the south grow wider as you gain elevation, taking in Childs Meadow and Mill Creek beyond the park's southern boundary. When you finally **top the ridge** that holds Ridge Lakes at 1 mile

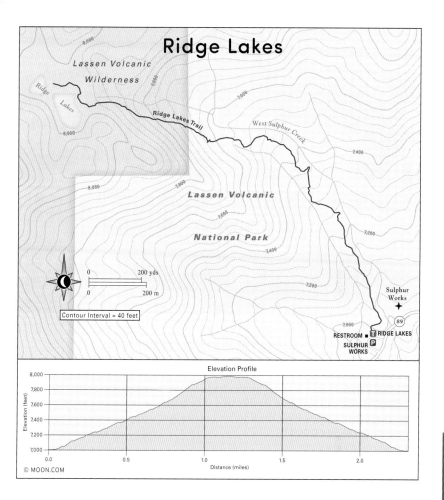

Ridge Lakes

Elevation Profile

(1.6 km), the trail delivers you to a wide-open bowl crowned by three knobby mountains—Brokeoff Mountain, Mount Diller, and Diamond Peak—each a part of the rim of ancient Mount Tehama, a volcano that rose to 11,000 feet (3,353 m) high and eventually collapsed.

Nestled at the base of this rugged ridgeline are the two **Ridge Lakes;** the trail deposits you on the southern shore of the largest one. But there's a seasonal caveat: If you visit in early summer, you may find only one Ridge Lake. In early summer, snowmelt often marries the two lake basins with deep cold water.

Whether it's one lake or two, this turquoise pool is the headwaters for West Sulphur Creek. The lake's open shoreline dotted with big boulders may inspire you to take a swim, but be forewarned that the water is bracingly cold in early summer.

If you aren't feeling the urge to cool off, explore the lakeshore instead. Sure-footed hikers who need to score more elevation gain can climb to the low saddle on the lake's southwest side for broad vistas of Brokeoff Mountain and its meadows. For even more of a challenge, you can head up the ravine on the lake's northwest side (there's no trail, but the route is

RIDGE LAKES ▲

obvious). From the high point of this short steep climb, you can see all the way to Mount Shasta.

Be careful where you step as you explore this basin. In late summer and early fall, you may notice small brown frogs hopping around the shoreline. What looks like the common Pacific tree frog might be the rarer Cascades frog. Their populations have declined in Lassen, but it appears they're still thriving near Ridge Lakes.

▶ **MILE 1–2: Ridge Lakes to Ridge Lakes–Sulphur Works Trailhead**
When you're ready to head back, it's downhill all the way.

DIRECTIONS

From Lassen's Southwest Entrance Station, drive north on Highway 89 (Lassen Park Hwy.) for 1.1 miles (1.8 km) to the Ridge Lake-Sulphur Works Trailhead on the left. The Ridge Lakes Trail begins on the lot's north side.

GPS COORDINATES: 40.4489, –121.5359; 40°26'56" N, 121°32'9.2" W

Tackle the hike to this 9,235-foot (2,815-m) volcanic summit to score a crowd-free vista of Lassen Peak, Chaos Crags, Mount Diller, Mount Shasta, and the Coast Range.

DISTANCE: 6.9 miles (11.1 km) round-trip

DURATION: 4 hours

ELEVATION GAIN: 2,590 feet (789 m)

EFFORT: Moderate-strenuous

TRAIL: Packed dirt

USERS: Hikers

SEASON: July-October

PASSES/FEES: $30 per vehicle, valid for 7 days

MAPS: On the National Park Service app; National Geographic Maps "Lassen Volcanic National Park"

TRAILHEAD: Brokeoff Mountain Trailhead

FACILITIES: Restroom

CONTACT: Lassen Volcanic National Park, 530/595-4480, www.nps.gov/lavo

Just 4 miles (6.4 km) from Lassen Peak lies Lassen's other volcano: Brokeoff Mountain, the remains of ancient Mount Tehama. The park's second highest summit sees a fraction of the Lassen Peak crowds because it's a tougher climb, but that makes it ideal for serious hikers who want to stretch their muscles. The path winds through alluring landscapes—wildflower-filled meadows, hemlock and fir forests, rocky talus slopes—so even if you don't make it to the top, you'll enjoy every footstep.

START THE HIKE

▶ **MILE 0-1.4: Parking Lot to Forest Lake Spur**

From the **parking lot,** cross the road to start on the trail, which begins to climb immediately and maintains a steady, grinding pitch throughout most of the hike. The first stretch ascends past a thicket of willows and alders growing alongside a chortling tributary to Mill Creek. In early summer, this section can be wet and muddy. At 0.3 mile (0.5 km), the warm-up stretch ends; from here on, it's steep all the way.

At 1.3 miles (2.1 km), soon after passing a couple of small ponds (or marshy bogs if the ponds have dried up), the trail bends left to cross the stream on two **log bridges.** Just before the crossing, you'll spot a **spur trail** leading right. This 0.25-mile (0.4-km) spur leads to shallow Forest Lake—a good bailout destination for hikers wearying of the climb. This is not Lassen's most beautiful lake, but it's a quiet, cool spot to rest. If you don't require a bailout, ignore the spur, cross the stream, and keep climbing.

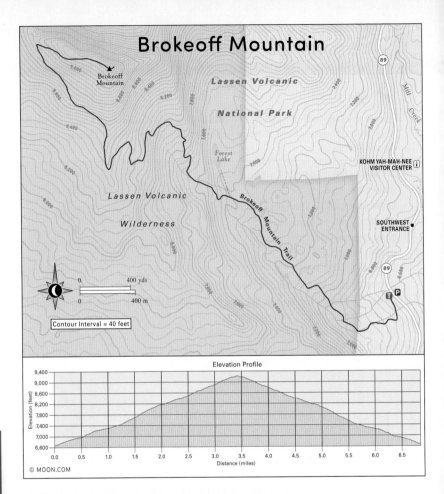

Brokeoff Mountain

Lassen Volcanic

National Park

Lassen Volcanic

Wilderness

Brokeoff
Mountain

Forest
Lake

Brokeoff Mountain Trail

KOHM YAH-MAH-NEE
VISITOR CENTER

SOUTHWEST
ENTRANCE

Contour Interval = 40 feet

0   400 yds
0   400 m

Elevation Profile

© MOON.COM

▶ **MILE 1.4–2.6: Forest Lake Spur to Crest of Ridge**

The higher you ascend, the harder you breathe—this trek is steepest between miles 1.4 and 2.6 as it heads up **Brokeoff's southern ridge.** The trail circles around to Brokeoff's western side, then boomerangs back to the east. You'll notice the landscape becoming increasingly barren and the tree canopy changing from red fir forest to a high-alpine woodland of mountain hemlock. This graceful conifer with its drooping boughs grows slowly, nourished mostly by melting snow, and can live for hundreds of years. As beautiful as it is in summer, it's even lovelier in winter. Hemlocks often stand sentinel on corniced ridges, crusted with windblown snow after each passing storm.

▶ **MILE 2.6–3.5: Crest of Ridge to Brokeoff's Summit**

During your final push to the summit, you'll enjoy almost nonstop vistas. The trees have all but disappeared at this high elevation, and Brokeoff's open ridgeline delivers a different perspective with every few minutes of walking. Where the trail swings far to the northwest, you get a clear view of Mount Shasta—70 miles (113 km) distant—just before the grade eases

▲ VIEW FROM BROKEOFF PEAK

mercifully for the last 0.5 mile (0.8 km) to the top—a welcome surprise after nearly 3 miles (4.8 km) of climbing.

Brokeoff Peak has a surprisingly flat **summit,** and it's worth exploring to take in all the different viewpoints. Lassen Peak dominates the vista to the northeast, with turquoise Helen Lake sparkling at the volcano's base. Vistas to the south include Lake Almanor and Childs Meadow. All the major peaks of the park's western region are visible: Chaos Crags, Diller, and Conard. On clear days, you can even make out the Central Valley and the Coast Range beyond.

Nibble on some trail mix, drink some water, and pat yourself on the back for being such a hardy mountaineer. When you're ready, retrace your steps back downhill.

DIRECTIONS

From Lassen's Southwest Entrance Station, drive south on Highway 89 (Lassen Park Hwy.) for 0.3 mile (0.5 km) to the trailhead parking pullout on the east side of the road. The trail begins on the west side of the road. This trailhead is south of the park entrance station, but you still need to pay the entrance fee and display the receipt on your vehicle dashboard.

GPS COORDINATES: 40.4309, −121.5360; 40°25′51.2″ N, 121°32′9.6″ W

LASSEN VOLCANIC NATIONAL PARK

Brokeoff Mountain

Hike to the top of a cinder cone that erupted about 350 years ago—not just once, but twice—on a trail that adds new meaning to the word *steep*.

DISTANCE: 3.8 miles (6.1 km) round-trip

DURATION: 3 hours

ELEVATION GAIN: 774 feet (236 m)

EFFORT: Moderate

TRAIL: Packed dirt, loose cinders and gravel

USERS: Hikers

SEASON: June–October

PASSES/FEES: $30 per vehicle, valid for 7 days

MAPS: On the National Park Service app; National Geographic Maps "Lassen Volcanic National Park"

TRAILHEAD: Butte Lake boat ramp, by the parking lot

FACILITIES: Restroom

CONTACT: Lassen Volcanic National Park, 530/595-4480, www.nps.gov/lavo

START THE HIKE

Cinder Cone is located in Lassen's far eastern reaches, accessible via Butte Lake Road, a 6-mile-long (9.7-km) bumpy dirt road that's graded to accommodate most passenger cars. It's a long, slow drive—plan on an hour from Manzanita Lake or two hours from the Southwest Entrance Station. Note that Butte Lake Road travels through severely burned forest, but once you reach the trailhead, you've left behind most of the wildfire damage.

The trail's grade is brutally steep, and poor footing in the volcanic ash and gravel increases the difficulty factor. It's hard to get much purchase in the shifting black, brown, and gray cinders, which range 1-2 inches (25-50 mm) in size. Trekking poles are a huge help. You can use them to "dig in" ahead of your feet.

▶ MILE 0-1.3: Butte Lake Trailhead to Base of Cinder Cone

From the trailhead near the edge of **Butte Lake**—just beyond the boat ramp—start walking on the **Cinder Cone Trail,** a wide dirt track with a fascinating history. It's a section of the Nobles Emigrant Trail, a path traveled by several thousand 19th-century migrants en route from Oregon to the Sacramento Valley. Still wide enough for a wagon train, the trail cuts a straight line through a sparse Jeffrey pine forest, which provides a modicum of shade unless you're hiking at high noon.

Except for a few sandy sections, which are a bit like walking on the beach, this first mile (1.6 km) is deceptively easy. Your attention will be drawn to the **Fantastic Lava Beds** on your left—strange piles of black basalt rubble that were formed by a lava flow that spewed from the base of Cinder Cone. At 0.5 mile (0.8 km), you'll pass a **junction** on the right with a narrow trail to Prospect Peak. Ignore it and continue straight ahead.

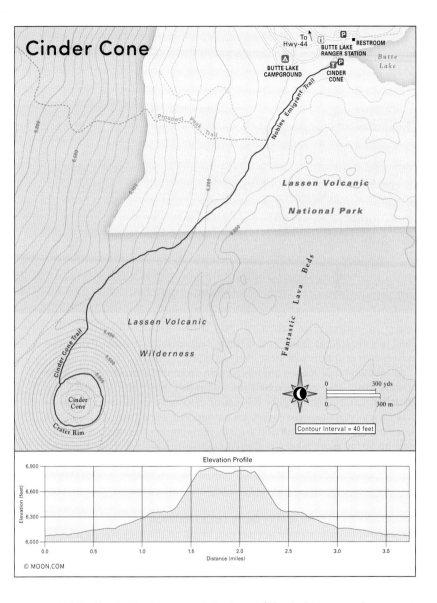

Cinder Cone

To Hwy-44

ℹ️ BUTTE LAKE RANGER STATION
🅿️ RESTROOM

Butte Lake

🏕️ BUTTE LAKE CAMPGROUND

CINDER CONE 🅿️

Prospect Peak Trail

Nobles Emigrant Trail

Lassen Volcanic

National Park

Fantastic Lava Beds

Lassen Volcanic

Wilderness

Cinder Cone Trail

Cinder Cone

Crater Rim

0 — 300 yds
0 — 300 m

Contour Interval = 40 feet

© MOON.COM

Elevation Profile

Elevation (feet): 6,900 / 6,600 / 6,300 / 6,000
Distance (miles): 0.0 / 0.5 / 1.0 / 1.5 / 2.0 / 2.5 / 3.0 / 3.5

At 1.3 miles (2.1 km), you reach the base of the dark-gray nearly symmetrical **Cinder Cone.** You can clearly make out the trail to the top, and it looks a bit daunting. Not bothering with switchbacks, the path shoots upward at a menacing grade, climbing 700 feet (213 m) up a gravelly slope. Make sure your water bottle is full before beginning your ascent.

▶ **MILE 1.3-1.8: Base of Cinder Cone to Crater Rim**
Proceed up Cinder Cone's north flank. After forging your way to the top, you'll feel a flood of relief that's quickly followed by a rush of amazed wonder. You can't help gaping at the mind-boggling **crater.** Two visible rims indicate at least two separate eruptions. Scientists estimate that Cinder

CINDER CONE ▲

Cone has erupted as many as five times, beginning in the mid-1500s. The most recent eruption was most likely in 1851.

An obvious trail makes a double circle around the crater. You'll want to walk every step of the **cone's rim** and relish every hard-earned vista. Whether you circumnavigate the crater clockwise or counterclockwise doesn't really matter—the views are astounding either way. Lassen Peak dominates the western horizon with its massive cone shape, but the coveted prize for most hikers is the Painted Dunes, visible from the rim's southern and eastern edges. A swirling watercolor landscape of orange and gray pumice fields, the Painted Dunes were formed by the oxidation of volcanic ash from the 700-foot-tall (213-m) cinder cone.

▶ MILE 2.3-3.8: Crater Rim to Butte Lake Trailhead

For your return trip, simply retrace your steps on the very steep path you just climbed. It's ridiculously easy going downhill—so easy, in fact, some hikers try galloping down the path.

DIRECTIONS

From Old Station, drive 16 miles (26 km) east on Highway 44 to the signed turnoff for Butte Lake. Drive 6.5 miles (10.5 km) on a graded but bumpy dirt road to the Butte Lake Ranger Station, campground, and trailhead parking lot. The Cinder Cone Trail begins by the boat ramp, on the west side of the parking lot.

GPS COORDINATES: 40.5638, −121.3022; 40°33'49.7" N, 121°18'7.9" W

BEST NEARBY BITES

Lassen Volcanic National Park has very limited food service, so if you don't have a fully stocked cooler in your vehicle, you'll probably need to exit the park to find serious sustenance.

WITHIN THE PARK

On the park's north side—closest to the first three hikes in this chapter—the **Manzanita Lake Camper Store** (Manzanita Lake Campground Rd., www.lassenlodging.com, 8am-8pm daily late May-mid-Oct. hours reduced mid-Sept.-mid-Oct.) offers a minimal supply of groceries and a selection of deli sandwiches, plus soft-serve ice cream cones.

On the park's south side—closest to hikes 4 to 9 in this chapter—the **Lassen Café and Gift Shop** (530/595-3555, www.lassenlodging.com, 9am-5pm daily late May-mid-Oct., 11am-2pm Sat.-Sun. Dec.-mid-May) is located in the Kohm Yah-mah-nee Visitor Center near the Southwest Entrance Station. The café-shop stocks more trinkets and souvenirs than food, but you can usually score an ice cream sandwich, a beverage, or a packaged burrito, breakfast sandwich, or pastry that you can heat up in a self-serve microwave.

In Warner Valley, the historic **Drakesbad Guest Ranch** (530/230-3901 or 877/622-0221) offers dinner by reservation only for park visitors who aren't staying at the ranch. Phone to see if you can secure a spot at the ranch's dinner table. Drakesbad was closed due to Dixie Fire damage in 2022 but will likely reopen in 2024.

NORTH OF THE PARK

Hikers needing calorie-replacement on Lassen's north side can drive to **JJ's Café** (13385 Hwy. 89, Old Station, 530/335-7225, www.jjscafeoldstation.com, 8am-2pm Thurs.-Sun.) in Old Station. This small family-run café, 15 miles (24 km) north of Lassen's Manzanita Lake, serves mountain-size breakfasts—eggs, scrambles, pancakes, and hashes—and tasty burgers and hot sandwiches for lunch.

DRAKESBAD GUEST RANCH ▾

For dinner, you'll need to drive farther afield. In Shingletown, 20 miles (32 km) west of Manzanita Lake on Highway 44, you'll find the saloon-style **Pioneer Hillside Pizza** (31232 Hwy. 44, Shingletown, 530/474-4007, noon-8pm Wed.-Thurs. and Sun., noon-9pm Fri.-Sat.), which serves pizza, pastas, hot sandwiches, and fried appetizers galore.

SOUTH OF THE PARK

If you've just summited Lassen Peak or strolled through Bumpass Hell, the closest place to get a solid meal is in the tiny hamlet of Mineral or its equally diminutive neighbor, Mill Creek. The **Lassen Mineral Lodge Restaurant** (38348 Hwy. 36 E., Mineral, 530/595-4422, www.minerallodge.com, 8am-8pm daily summer, hours vary in winter) is only 10 miles (16.1 km) and 15 minutes from the Southwest Entrance Station. The restaurant has indoor and patio seating and serves a satisfying menu of burgers, steaks, and salads, plus a big selection of local beers. Breakfast attracts a lot of customers—especially fans of big waffles and biscuits and gravy.

In Mill Creek (10 mi/16.1 km and 15 minutes from the Southwest Entrance Station), **Highlands Ranch Resort** (41515 Hwy. 36, Mill Creek, 530/595-3388, www.highlandsranchresort.com, 11am-9pm daily late May-late Oct., 11am-9pm Fri.-Sun. Nov.-Apr.) is a luxurious spot for lunch or dinner, either in its rustic-chic dining room or on its outdoor deck overlooking beautiful Childs Meadow. The menu includes classic American favorites like steak, salmon, scampi, and lamb shank.

Also in Mill Creek is the woodsy, folksy **Mill Creek Resort** (40271 Hwy. 172, Mill Creek, 530/595-4449, www.millcreekresort.net, 11am-8pm daily May-Sept.), where you'll find burgers, hot and cold sandwiches, beer on tap, and silky-creamy milkshakes.

If you need to do a major stock-up on groceries, you can always drive to the "big city" of Chester, 30 miles (48 km) and 45 minutes southeast on Highways 89 and 36, which has a large supermarket.

▼ KOHM YAH-MAH-NEE VISITOR CENTER

NEARBY CAMPGROUNDS

NAME	DESCRIPTION	FACILITIES	SEASON	FEE
Manzanita Lake	Cabins and sites near Manzanita Lake, Loomis Museum, and hiking trails	179 sites for tents or RVs up to 40 ft/12 m, 20 camping cabins, showers, restrooms, drinking water, dump station	late May to mid-October	campsites $26, cabins $76-149

Near Lassen's Northwest Entrance Station, 877/444-6777, www.recreation.gov

NAME	DESCRIPTION	FACILITIES	SEASON	FEE
Summit Lake	Mid-park location near Summit Lake and hiking trails	46 sites for tents or RVs up to 35 ft/10.7 m, restrooms, drinking water	July 1 to mid-September	$24

Midpoint on Lassen Park Highway, 877/444-6777, www.recreation.gov

NAME	DESCRIPTION	FACILITIES	SEASON	FEE
Butte Lake	Near Cinder Cone, swimming and boating on Butte Lake	101 sites for tents or RVs up to 35 ft/10.7 m, vault toilets, drinking water	early June to early September	$22 ($15 when no water is available)

Off Butte Lake Road on Lassen's northeast side, 877/444-6777, www.recreation.gov

NEARBY CAMPGROUNDS (continued)

NAME	DESCRIPTION	FACILITIES	SEASON	FEE
Juniper Lake	Swimming and boating on Juniper Lake, primitive camp with first-come, first-served sites	18 sites for tents only, vault toilets	July to September	$22

Off Juniper Lake Road on Lassen's south side, 530/595-4480, www.nps.gov/lavo

NAME	DESCRIPTION	FACILITIES	SEASON	FEE
Hat Creek	Trophy trout fishing, Subway Cave, first-come, first-served sites	72 sites for tents or RVs up to 40 ft/12 m, restrooms, drinking water	April to October	$16

South of Highway 44-Highway 89 junction in Old Station, 530/336-5521, www.fs.usda.gov

▲ BEAR, SILVER, ROUND LAKES LOOP

SACRAMENTO & TAHOE

SACRAMENTO & GOLD COUNTRY

From the Sacramento Valley to the Sierra Nevada Foothills, there's a bit of gold rush mining history tied to pretty much every hiking area in this region. Many beloved trails in this area focus on rivers, waterfalls, and lakes, where you'll often find locals, once temperatures rise, splashing around, and in some places even panning for gold. While summer can get brutally hot midday, there is the opportunity for year-round hiking, with morning temperatures cool enough most every day.

▲ FAIRY FALLS TRAIL

▲ PHANTOM FALLS TRAIL

1 Phantom Falls Overlook
DISTANCE: 4.5 miles (7.2 km) round-trip
DURATION: 2.5 hours
EFFORT: Easy-moderate

2 Fairy Falls
DISTANCE: 5 miles (8 km) round-trip
DURATION: 2 hours
EFFORT: Easy

3 Stevens Trail
DISTANCE: 7.4 miles (11.9 km) round-trip
DURATION: 3.5 hours
EFFORT: Moderate

4 Hidden Falls Loop
DISTANCE: 4.4 miles (7.1 km) round-trip
DURATION: 2 hours
EFFORT: Easy

5 American River Parkway (Jedediah Smith Memorial Trail)
DISTANCE: 3 miles (4.8 km) round-trip
DURATION: 1.5 hours
EFFORT: Easy

6 Cosumnes Nature Loop
DISTANCE: 4 miles (6.4 km) round-trip
DURATION: 2 hours
EFFORT: Easy

COSUMNES NATURE LOOP ▾

SACRAMENTO & GOLD COUNTRY

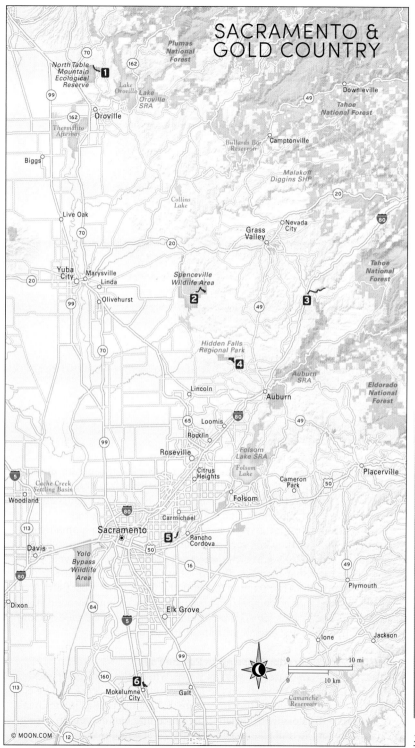

SACRAMENTO & GOLD COUNTRY

SACRAMENTO & GOLD COUNTRY

1 Phantom Falls Overlook
NORTH TABLE MOUNTAIN ECOLOGICAL RESERVE

Travel atop a basalt mesa created by ancient lava flows, where wildflowers and waterfalls come to life each spring.

DISTANCE: 4.5 miles (7.2 km) round-trip

DURATION: 2.5 hours

ELEVATION GAIN: 530 feet (162 m)

EFFORT: Easy-moderate

TRAIL: Mostly wide dirt and rocky sections, loose rocks, creek crossing

USERS: Hikers, hunters, leashed dogs

SEASON: Year-round

PASSES/FEES: Daily or annual California Department of Fish and Wildlife Lands Pass, or California hunting or fishing license

MAPS: "Chico Topo Bundle (39121NW)" by BaseImage Publishing

PARK HOURS: Dawn-dusk daily

TRAILHEAD: Parking lot on Cherokee Road

FACILITIES: Vault toilets at the trailhead

CONTACT: California Department of Fish and Wildlife, 916/445-0411, https://wildlife.ca.gov

START THE HIKE

▶ **MILE 0-0.8: Parking Lot to Stream Crossing**

Look for the wooden entry gate at the northwest end of the **parking lot.** Once through, follow the well-worn dirt path as it curves left (west) through a cow pasture. Make sure to leave at least 300 feet (91 m) between you and any grazing bovines, and watch out for the cow patties!

With the parking lot at your back, continue alongside a small creek sprinkled with wildflowers, such as California goldfields and purple owl's clover. At 0.2 mile (0.3 km) is a **barbed-wire fence** marking private property and a sign that instructs you to follow the fence line north (right) for Phantom Falls. After 0.1 mile (0.2 km), the fence turns west (left). Stay alongside the fence as you begin a gradual descent over and around small basalt rock formations for 0.5 mile (0.8 km). Just prior to 0.8 mile (1.3 km) into the hike, you will encounter a small **stream crossing.**

▶ **MILE 0.8-1.9: Stream Crossing to Ravine Falls**

After crossing the stream, you may see where the trail once passed through the private property on the left. Sometimes the fence will be cut here, but it is not an invitation to explore. Follow the trail as it continues right and to the northwest, leaving the fence line behind you. In spring, this section of the trail displays an abundance of wildflowers.

Phantom Falls Overlook

Elevation Profile

At 1.2 miles (1.9 km) into the hike, take the **left path** where the trail splits, following the sign directing you to Ravine Falls and Phantom Falls. Farther down the trail is another sign, guiding hikers to stay right (north) to continue to Ravine Falls and Phantom Falls.

At 1.4 miles (2.3 km), the trail starts down through a forested ravine into the best shade of the hike. The path narrows to a single-track, and it can be difficult passing others. Look for mushrooms growing on the base of trees, and listen for the sparrow's song. After hiking 100 feet (30 m) down to the base of the ravine, at 1.6 miles (2.6 km) a sign points to the short detour to Ravine Falls. Follow the sign to the base of **Ravine Falls,** where you'll see Ravine Creek flowing into the ravine from a height of 76 feet (23 m). Return to the sign for a total detour of 0.3 miles (0.5 km).

▶ **MILE 1.9–2.3: Ravine Falls to Phantom Falls Overlook**
At this point, the trail gradually ascends the opposite side of the ravine. Watch out for an old barbed-wire fence near the top, somewhat camouflaged in the vegetation on the right side of the trail. Go through the gate at the top, proceeding straight ahead. Note that when you return this way, the reflective sign here will help you find the trail.

When you reach the 2-mile (3.2-km) mark, stay left at the **split** in the trail and follow the path as it curves to the left (west). At 2.2 miles (3.5 km), continue straight (north) at the **final trail marker** to Phantom Falls, as

the trail rolls through lupines, California poppies, and other wildflowers. You'll also likely see low-range mountain birds floating on gusts of wind. The views from the **Phantom Falls overlook** are best in early spring. Here you'll see Gold Run Creek dramatically spill 164 feet (50 m) down into Coal Canyon over flat basalt rock. The waterfall gets its name from its appearance, gradually fading to a trickle of a wisp and sometimes disappearing altogether in drier months.

Return the way you came.

DIRECTIONS

Take I-5 north from downtown Sacramento. After 6 miles (9.7 km), take exit 525B for Highway 99 north toward Yuba City and Marysville. Take Highway 99 for 11.8 miles (19 km). Use the right lane to take the Highway 70 ramp to Marysville and Oroville. Drive 21.4 miles (34 km) on Highway 70 and take exit 48 for Grand Avenue. Turn right onto Grand Avenue and drive for 1 mile (1.6 km). Take a left on Table Mountain Boulevard, and then in 0.1 mile (0.2 km), turn right on Cherokee Road. Continue 6.3 miles (10.1 km) north to the reserve. Drive slowly up Cherokee Road, as there are some steep drop-offs and narrow sections; honk as you approach tight curves to alert oncoming cars. Look for the parking lot on the left side.

GPS COORDINATES: 39.5957, −121.5415; 39°35′44.5″ N, 121°32′29.4″ W

BEST NEARBY BREWS

Just 30 minutes north of the trailhead, the city of Chico is home to several Northern California breweries, including **Sierra Nevada Brewing** (1075 E. 20th St., 530/345-2739, www.sierranevada.com, 11am-9pm Sun.-Thurs., 11am-10pm Fri.-Sat., kid-friendly), **Secret Trail Brewing Company** (132 Myers St., Chico, 530/487-8151, www.secrettrailbrewing.com, 3pm-9pm Mon.-Thurs., noon-9pm Fri.-Sat., noon-7pm Sun., kid- and dog-friendly), and **Mulberry Station Brewing Company** (175 E. 20th St., Chico, 530/809-5616, www.mulberrystationbrewery.com, 3pm-9pm Tues.-Thurs., 11am-10pm Fri.-Sat., 11am-9pm Sun.).

Fairy Falls
SPENCEVILLE WILDLIFE AREA

This family-friendly trail travels over gentle hills and through a woodland forest to the stunning Fairy Falls, also known as Shingle Falls or Beale Falls.

DISTANCE: 5 miles (8 km) round-trip

DURATION: 2 hours

ELEVATION GAIN: 500 feet (152 m)

EFFORT: Easy

TRAIL: Dirt road, dirt path

USERS: Hikers, mountain bikers, horseback riders, hunters, leashed dogs

SEASON: Year-round

PASSES/FEES: None

MAPS: "Yuba City Topo Bundle (39121SE)" by BaseImage Publishing

PARK HOURS: 1.5 hours before sunrise to 1 hour after sunset

TRAILHEAD: Parking lot

FACILITIES: None

CONTACT: California Department of Fish and Wildlife, North Central Region, 916/358-2900, https://wildlife.ca.gov

START THE HIKE

▶ MILE 0-1.6 TRAILHEAD TO LOWER LOOP TRAIL JUNCTION

At the north end of the parking lot, cross the **bridge** over Dry Creek to come to wide dirt **Spenceville Road,** where the trail begins. The land across the road is fenced off and has a sign marked "Falls" with an arrow pointing right. Turn right (east) and continue down the road, with Dry Creek on your right. At 0.5 mile (0.8 km), the road turns north, away from the creek. You'll see scattered oak trees and cows grazing as you slowly gain elevation up gently rolling hills. At 1.2 miles (1.9 km), the road curves to the right. Go through the **pedestrian gate** to the right of the vehicle gate and enter a pasture. At 1.6 miles (2.6 km), the road **splits into three paths.** The left fork heads toward the upper falls and the right goes along the river below the falls. For this hike, take the middle path, also known as **Lower Loop Trail,** which leads through a woodland forest toward the lower falls.

▶ MILE 1.6-2.6: Lower Loop Trail Junction to Upper Fairy Falls

Lower Loop Trail provides a brief, partly shaded respite from the wide-open exposure of most of this hike. The trail winds through the trees, with the occasional need to duck under or step over branches. At 2.1 miles (3.4 km), the three paths reconnect at Dry Creek. Around this area are lots of nice spots to stop for a picnic along the water. Turn left (east) where the trails reconnect to take in the falls from the bottom up. If you're looking to dip a toe into the creek, go right to find calmer waters. Beginning at 2.3 miles (3.7 km), a few trails split off to the right (east) and closer to the falls,

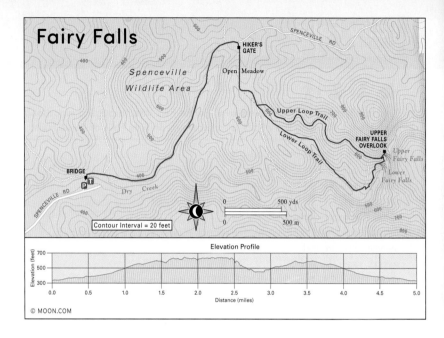

Fairy Falls

which is the best, albeit riskier, way to see the full falls, including the **lower falls.** All paths gain around 150 feet (46 m) elevation over the next 0.25 mile (0.4 km), and you'll notice the falls grow in intensity and height as you ascend.

Look for the California poppies that tend to cluster along these trails in the spring as all the paths lead you to Upper Fairy Falls, with varying distance from the steep drop-offs. **Upper Fairy Falls** is the most photographed section of this hike. The water cascades 100 feet (30 m) into a pool that can be accessed by rock-scrambling at the far south end of the pool. Explore all these areas with caution; the fencing around the upper falls is for your safety. A metal memorial cross bolted to a tree marks the top of the falls.

▶ **MILE 1.6-5: Upper Fairy Falls to Trailhead**
For a slightly different return trip, follow the **Upper Loop Trail** northwest from Upper Fairy Falls, keeping north and away from the path you took to the upper falls. The trail hugs the curve of the hills and remains at approximately the same elevation. After 1 mile (1.6 km), you'll return to the dirt road where the three paths first split.

Retrace your steps through the pasture to the gate, continuing south on the dirt road and back over the bridge to the trailhead.

DIRECTIONS

Take I-5 north from Sacramento for 5.8 miles (9.3 km) and take exit 525B for Highway 99. Take Highway 99 north for 11.8 miles (19 km) and take the ramp for Highway 70 north. After 6.8 miles (10.9 km), exit Highway 70 at Kempton Road. Turn right onto Kempton Road, then left onto 4th Avenue. In 0.5 mile (0.8 km), turn right onto Rio Oso Road and head east for 1.2 miles (1.9 km). Turn left onto Swanson Road. After 0.7 mile (1.1 km),

▲ FAIRY FALLS

veer right onto Bear River Drive. In 1.6 miles (2.6 km), turn left onto Pleasant Grove Road and continue for 0.8 mile (1.3 km). Make a slight right onto Wheatland Road and continue for approximately 3.8 miles (6.1 km). After Wheatland Road turns into 1st Street for two blocks, turn right onto D Street, then left onto Main Street. In 0.5 mile (0.8 km), Main Street turns right and becomes Spenceville Road. Continue for 5.1 miles (8.2 km). At the sign for "Spenceville Wildlife Area," turn right onto Far West Road. In 2.6 miles (4.2 km), this becomes Camp Far West Road. Turn left and continue 5.6 miles (9 km). Turn right onto Spenceville Road. The parking lot is on the left after 1.7 miles (2.7 km).

GPS COORDINATES: 39.1138, −121.2709; 39°6'49.7" N, 121°16'15.2" W

BEST NEARBY BREWS

Relax at dog-friendly **Bullmastiff Brewing** (10183 Commercial Ave., Penn Valley, 530/802-0099, www.bullmastiffbrews.com, 3pm-8pm Wed.-Thurs., noon-10pm Fri.-Sat., noon-8pm Sun.), named for the owners' beloved bullmastiff dogs. Come for the $5 pours on Wednesday, and check out the schedule for live-music nights. From the trailhead, it's a 25-minute drive via Waldo Road, Chuck Yeager Road (Smartsville Rd.), and Highway 20. The brewery is in the farthest corner of the parking lot at the end of a cul-de-sac.

✳ 🎿 🏛 🐾

From varying elevations, this trail provides rewarding canyon views of the North Fork American River, a wooden tepee, an abandoned mine site, and waterfalls along the way down to the rocky river's edge.

DISTANCE: 7.4 miles (11.9 km) round-trip

DURATION: 3.5 hours

ELEVATION GAIN: 1,200 feet (366 m)

EFFORT: Moderate

TRAIL: Dirt, rock, single-track

USERS: Hikers, mountain bikers, horseback riders, hunters, dogs

SEASON: Year-round

PASSES/FEES: None

MAPS: "Stevens Trail," Meadow Vista Trails Association, www.mvtrails.org

TRAILHEAD: Parking lot

FACILITIES: Vault toilets at the trailhead

CONTACT: Bureau of Land Management, 916/941-3101, www.blm.gov

START THE HIKE

▶ **MILE 0-0.7 PARKING LOT TO TEPEE**

The hike begins immediately from the north end of the **parking lot** with a northeast descent. After walking 0.7 mile (1.1 km) and crossing a few streams, the last of which has a wooden beam to balance on, look for the wooden sign stating "Trail" with a yellow arrow pointing to the right. Just behind the sign is a **tepee,** made of thin log poles, that's over 10 feet (3 m) tall.

▶ **MILE 0.7-1.3: Tepee to Robbers Ravine**

After checking out the tepee, continue briefly on the dirt logging road. Over the next 0.25 mile (0.4 km) there is a 100-foot (30-m) ascent as you continue traveling southeast, and the trail splits from the road. At 1.2 miles (1.9 km), look for the marker instructing hikers to stay left (the northern path) and bikers right. Listen for the waterfall as the trail now descends and you navigate through rocky outcroppings. This area is known as

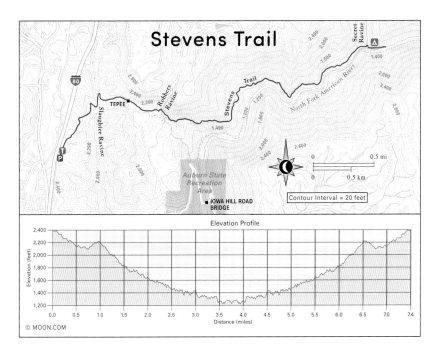

Robbers Ravine, and the rocky path narrows. Extra caution is necessary to cross this midsection of the waterfall as it hugs and wets the rocks on its way down. This is the most technical section of the hike, and after heavy rainfall, the waterfall may make this section impassable.

▸ **MILE 1.3-1.7: Robbers Ravine to Abandoned Mine**
Past the waterfall the view opens, and the remainder of the trail down showcases the **canyon, Iowa Hill Bridge,** and the **North Fork American River** from slightly different angles and elevations. At 1.7 miles (2.7 km) into the hike, you'll find an **abandoned mine** on the left. Resist the temptation to enter; while an interesting historic point, the abandoned mine poses significant safety risks. For those not looking to hike all the way down to the river and its challenging return, this is an ideal turnaround spot. Otherwise, continue onward.

▸ **MILE 1.7-3.6: Abandoned Mine to Secret Ravine**
From the abandoned mine, in spring enjoy an array of wildflowers, the most abundant being lupines and poppies, among a variety of colors, as you continue to descend into the canyon. The **trail splits** at 3 miles (4.8 km). Take the **higher trail,** on the left, to continue. This section of the trail is extremely exposed but easy to enjoy in the morning as you steadily make your way down the canyon, closer and closer to the river.

Before reaching the river, the trail abruptly drops down into the **Secret Ravine** for some brief shade and the opportunity to sit on boulders and dip your feet into the cold **Secret Town Stream** at the crossing. From here, you can see the rushing river more closely where the stream is consumed by the river. Beginning in this area and around the river you might spot areas of bedrock mortars, where Native Americans once gathered to grind food plants. The ravine is an ideal place to sit for a snack after exploring the river shore and before heading back up through the canyon under the sun's rays.

▶ MILE 3.6–7.4: Secret Ravine to Trailhead

Until crossing Secret Town Stream, the route has been mostly parallel to the river. It now begins to turn right (south) toward the river, and a small **dispersed campsite** (no facilities) is just before you reach the rocky **river shore.** Depending on the water level, you can explore up and down the water's edge. Look across the river to see if you can spot where the original path once continued on to Iowa Hill. Exercise caution: The river's flow is often incredibly fast, and the water's freezing temperature can make it unsafe to enter.

When you've had your fill of the shore, return the way you came.

DIRECTIONS

From Sacramento, follow I-80 east for 47 miles (76 km) toward the town of Colfax and take exit 135 for North Canyon Way. Keep left at the fork to continue toward Canyon Court. Take a quick left onto North Canyon Way (Stevens Trail). Continue for 0.6 mile (1 km), passing the Colfax Cemetery. The trailhead parking is on the left.

GPS COORDINATES: 39.1056, −120.9472; 39°6'20.2" N, 120°56'49.9" W

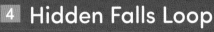

4 | Hidden Falls Loop
HIDDEN FALLS REGIONAL PARK

On this quintessential family hike, journey to the waterfalls flowing through the canyons of Hidden Falls Regional Park.

DISTANCE: 4.4 miles (7.1 km) round-trip

DURATION: 2 hours

ELEVATION GAIN: 610 feet (186 m)

EFFORT: Easy

TRAIL: Dirt, single-track, rocks

USERS: Hikers, mountain bikers, horseback riders, leashed dogs

SEASON: Year-round

PASSES/FEES: Advance vehicle reservations ($4-8) required on weekends and high-usage days

MAPS: On the park website

PARK HOURS: Sunrise-sunset daily; specific times posted daily on the park website and at the trailhead

TRAILHEAD: Parking lot

FACILITIES: Portable toilets at the trailhead and just after Whiskey Diggens Bridge

CONTACT: Placer County Department of Parks and Open Space, 530/886-4901, www.placer.ca.gov

START THE HIKE

Parking reservations are needed for all weekends and for other busy days as determined by the park; check the website for specific dates. Opt for a full-day pass, valid sunrise-sunset ($8) or a partial-day pass, valid sunrise-9:30am or 2:30pm-sunset ($4). Call or visit the website to check on specific opening and closing times before departing. The park closes during extreme fire weather; closure notices are posted online, but you can also call the park to check.

▸ **MILE 0-0.9: Parking Lot to Blue Oak Loop**
At the northeast end of the **parking lot,** find the trailhead and look for the **County of Placer Park User Information sign.** The sign notes the park hours for the day and starts you on a dirt road north, officially marked as **South Legacy Way.** The path gently descends for 0.3 mile (0.5 km) to **Whiskey Diggens Bridge,** crossing over Deadman Creek. On the other side of the bridge, the trail splits in multiple directions near a portable toilet; turn right (north) onto the east portion of **Blue Oak Loop.** The Hidden Falls Access Trail is one of the options at this junction, but following the described route provides a peaceful and less trafficked tour through the park.

SACRAMENTO & GOLD COUNTRY

Hidden Falls Loop

357

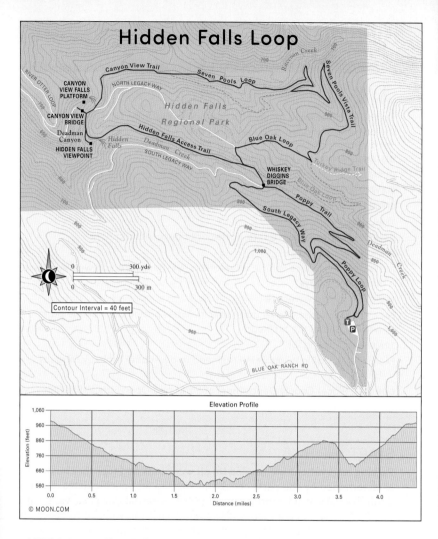

Hidden Falls Loop

Elevation Profile

Contour Interval = 40 feet

© MOON.COM

▶ **MILE 0.9-1.8: Blue Oak Loop to Racoon Creek Canyon View**

Continue on Blue Oak Loop for 0.5 mile (0.8 km) until it meets a **junction** with Turkey Ridge Trail on the right and Seven Pools Vista Trail ahead. Leave the Blue Oak Loop trail, which continues to the left, and head straight (northeast) onto the narrower **Seven Pools Vista Trail.** Seven Pools Vista leads to a **rocky outcropping** after 0.4 mile (0.6 km) that makes for a great snack break with a view of **Racoon Creek Canyon.**

▶ **MILE 1.8-3.2: Racoon Creek Canyon View to North Legacy Way**

Continue west on Seven Pools Vista Trail for a short distance. At 1.9 miles (3.1 km), the trail connects to **Seven Pools Loop.** Go right (northwest) onto Seven Pools Loop and continue along the canyon as Racoon Creek serenely cascades down through seven pools below to your right (north). Horses are permitted anywhere in the park; watch for equestrians on this narrow path and be prepared to yield. After just over 0.5 mile (0.8 km), continue

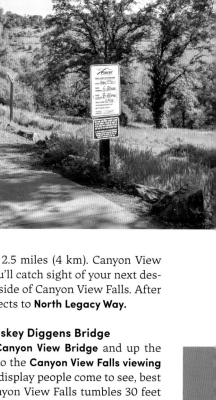

▲ HIDDEN FALLS LOOP

straight (west) onto **Canyon View Trail** at 2.5 miles (4 km). Canyon View Trail leads to **Deadman Canyon,** where you'll catch sight of your next destination: a viewing platform on the other side of Canyon View Falls. After 0.5 mile (0.8 km), Canyon View Trail connects to **North Legacy Way.**

▶ **MILE 3.2–4.1: North Legacy Way to Whiskey Diggens Bridge**
Take North Legacy Way west over the **Canyon View Bridge** and up the short and steep trail on the right (north) to the **Canyon View Falls viewing platform.** This is the impressive waterfall display people come to see, best viewed in late winter or early spring. Canyon View Falls tumbles 30 feet (9 m) down the rocks at this junction of Coon Creek and Deadman Creek. A long shaded bench on the viewing platform is where many people stop to take in the view before heading back toward the trailhead. During drier seasons, some hikers go down to the riverbed boulders to sit by the water.

When finished at the viewing platform, cross back over Canyon View Bridge to North Legacy Way and look right for a sign for Hidden Falls. After walking less than 0.25 mile (0.4 km) on the **Hidden Falls Access Trail,** look for the spur trail for the **Hidden Falls viewpoint.** It's a short 0.1-mile (0.2-km) side trip to a smaller viewing platform, worth the time when the falls' water levels are high. Hidden Falls isn't as dramatic as Canyon View Falls, so this tranquil cascade is sometimes overlooked. Back on the Hidden Falls Access Trail, the path follows above and along Deadman Creek on the right all the way to **Whiskey Diggens Bridge.**

▶ **MILE 4.1–4.4: Whiskey Diggens Bridge to Parking Lot**
After you cross the bridge, turn left (southeast) onto **Poppy Trail,** with the creek on your left (northeast). The trail provides a lovely alternative to returning the same way you first came. It runs parallel to the creek for 0.3 mile (0.5 km) before switchbacks begin, steadily rising in elevation. After

the switchbacks, Poppy Trail runs parallel to the dirt road and leads back to the trailhead.

DIRECTIONS

From Sacramento, take I-80 east for 28 miles (45 km) and take exit 116 onto Highway 193, west toward Lincoln. Immediately exit Highway 193 onto Ophir Road and continue for 0.3 mile (0.5 km), then turn left onto Lozanos Road. Follow Lozanos Road for 1 mile (1.6 km), and then turn right onto Bald Hill Road. Follow signs to remain on Bald Hill Road for approximately 2.3 miles (3.7 km), then turn left onto Mount Vernon Road. Follow signs to remain on Mount Vernon Road for 3.7 miles (6 km). Turn right onto Mears Drive and follow it for 0.6 mile (1 km) before turning right onto Mears Place. After 0.3 mile (0.5 km) is the parking lot.

GPS COORDINATES: 38.9588, −121.1640; 38°57′31.7″ N, 121°9′50.4″ W

BEST NEARBY BITES

A good spot to grab a local craft brew, burger, and fries (or fried pickles!) and sit on the patio is **Local Heroes** (1120 High St., Auburn, 530/820-3030, 11am-8pm Mon.-Sat., 11am-4pm Sun., $6-10), where many of the burgers are named after local trails. From the trailhead, make your way toward downtown Auburn following Mount Vernon Road for 8 miles (12.9 km). Local Heroes is at the intersection of Lincoln Way and High Street.

American River Parkway (Jedediah Smith Memorial Trail)

WILLIAM B. POND RECREATION AREA

✿ 🐾 🚶

This beloved portion of the American River Parkway offers views and access to the namesake waterway, a fun and easy outing for families.

BEST: Dog-Friendly Hikes
DISTANCE: 3 miles (4.8 km) round-trip
DURATION: 1.5 hours
ELEVATION GAIN: 100 feet (30 m)
EFFORT: Easy
TRAIL: Dirt, sand, paved
USERS: Hikers, cyclists on part of the trail, horseback riders on part of the trail, wheelchair users on part of the trail, dogs
SEASON: Year-round
PASSES/FEES: $6 day-use fee per vehicle, or Sacramento County Regional Parks pass
MAPS: On the park website
PARK HOURS: Sunrise–sunset daily
TRAILHEAD: Harrington Way parking lot
FACILITIES: Restrooms at the trailhead and at picnic areas
CONTACT: Sacramento County Regional Parks, 916/875-6961, https://regionalparks.saccounty.gov

The William B. Pond Recreation Area is part of the 32-mile (52-km) American River Parkway, also known as Jedediah Smith Memorial Trail. There are many parking lots and places to get on the parkway. This section of the parkway traverses the north-northwest side of the river as it passes through the Carmichael area of greater Sacramento. Obey all signage, such as pedestrians staying on the left side of bike trails and facing oncoming cycling traffic.

START THE HIKE

▶ **MILE 0-0.6: Harrington Way Parking Lot to Covered Picnic Area**
Starting from the restrooms in the **Harrington Way parking lot,** walk past the vehicle turnaround and toward the water. Kids like to throw rocks in the American River at this spot.

Start the hike here and take the sandy path to the east, with the river on your right. In spring there are blooms along the rolling trail, including lupines, California poppies, and California buckeye. At a few points the trail splits; these all continue in the correct direction and reconnect. You may not immediately realize you're now beside an artificial pond because the American River flows around the opposite side of it. Beginning around 0.3

American River Parkway (Jedediah Smith Memorial Trail)

SACRAMENTO & GOLD COUNTRY

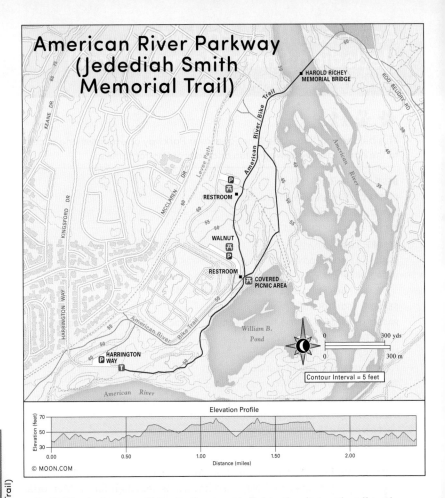

American River Parkway
(Jedediah Smith Memorial Trail)

Elevation Profile

© MOON.COM

---

mile (0.5 km), the paved bike trail runs parallel to the dirt path. All trails convene at a **covered picnic area** at 0.6 mile (1 km).

▶ **MILE 0.6-1.3: Covered Picnic Area to Harold Richey Memorial Bridge**
At the picnic area, an accessible ramp and pier are on the right, where anglers gather to fish the stocked pond for trout, catfish, bass, bluegill, and tule perch. A **parking lot and restrooms** are on the other side of the paved bike trail. Be extremely careful crossing the paved bike trail, as cyclists tend to travel fast.

Continue past the picnic area on the dirt path. After about 500 feet (152 m), the path crosses under power lines and over what looks like a paved sidewalk. Curve left (north) onto the dirt path that is as wide as a road. Stay on this path for about 0.5 mile (0.8 km), heading north, until it intersects with the paved bike trail. Turn right (northeast) onto the **paved bike trail.** Note that pedestrians are to walk on the left side of the trail, facing oncoming cyclists, and on the shoulder when possible. This area of the park tends to be more densely populated with families having picnics, dog walkers, runners, and cyclists. Follow the paved bike trail for 0.25 mile

(0.4 km) to approach the start of the **Harold Richey Memorial Bridge.**

▸ **MILE 1.3-3: Harold Richey Memorial Bridge to Harrington Way Parking Lot**
Spanning 0.25 mile (0.4 km) over the **American River,** the bridge was named for Harold Richey, a man locally known as "Mr. Bike Trail" because of his healthy bike-riding habits and volunteer stewardship that became a model for American River Parkway protection. The bridge is intended to be used by all those on foot, paw, bike, wheelchair, or horse. Cross the bridge, keeping close to the left side, taking in views of the American River. You may catch sight of kayakers and will likely see waterfowl. At the end of the bridge, turn around and retrace your steps, this time on the right side of the bridge path. Once back on land, stay on the bike trail for 0.5 mile (0.8 km) back to the covered picnic area.

Back at the covered picnic area, return the way you originally came to the area, now with the water to your left. Do not attempt stay on the paved bike trail, as it does not run closely parallel to the dirt path back to the parking lot.

DIRECTIONS

From Sacramento, take U.S. 50 east for 6 miles (9.7 km) and take exit 11 for Watt Avenue northbound. Use the left two lanes to turn left onto Watt Avenue. After 0.7 mile (1.1 km), take the American River Drive exit. Follow American River Drive for 2.4 miles (3.9 km), then turn right on Harrington Way and continue 0.3 mile (0.5 km) to the parking lot.

GPS COORDINATES: 38.5816, −121.3439; 38°34'53.8" N, 121°20'38" W

BEST NEARBY BREWS

Check out neighborhood favorite **19 Handles Pub & Grill** (4235 Arden Way, Sacramento, 916/487-4979, https://19handlespub.com, 11am-10pm Tues.-Fri., 9am-10pm Sat., 9am-9pm Sun.) for what they call "fully loaded 19 handles of bliss," plus wines, seltzers, kombucha, and food. 19 Handles Pub & Grill serves 17 local beers on tap, plus two other favorites, making 19, and is just 2.5 miles (4 km) from the Harrington Way parking lot via Kingsford Drive and Arden Way.

American River Parkway (Jedediah Smith Memorial Trail)

SACRAMENTO & GOLD COUNTRY

6 Cosumnes Nature Loop

COSUMNES RIVER PRESERVE

The trails at Cosumnes River Preserve offers hikers of all capabilities the chance to observe over 250 species of bird as well as reptiles, amphibians, fish, and other animals. Don't forget your binoculars!

DISTANCE: 4 miles (6.4 km) round-trip

DURATION: 2 hours

ELEVATION GAIN: 50 feet (15 m)

EFFORT: Easy

TRAIL: Pavement, dirt

USERS: Hikers, wheelchair users on Wetlands Walk and Boardwalk Trail

SEASON: Part of the trail open year-round; floodwaters may overtake large sections in winter

PASSES/FEES: None

MAPS: On the park website, at the visitor center

PARK HOURS: 8am–5pm daily

TRAILHEAD: Cosumnes Visitor Center

FACILITIES: Restrooms at the visitor center

CONTACT: Cosumnes River Preserve, 916/684-2816, www.cosumnes.org

START THE HIKE

▶ MILE 0-0.1: Visitor Center to River Walk Trail Junction

Park in the lot at the **visitor center,** taking time to view the interpretive exhibits displayed inside and outside the building. Afterward, walk north onto the ramp out front of the visitor center, which marks the start of the **River Walk Trail.** After 0.1 mile (0.2 km), cross the **bridge** over Willow Slough, a river channel with no outlet. During high water flows, this area provides an important habitat to juvenile salmon. When you come to the managed wetlands, the trail splits. Turn right (south) onto the **River Walk Trail.**

▶ MILE 0.1-1.6: River Walk Trail Junction to the Point

The River Walk Trail runs alongside another river channel, **Middle Slough.** In addition to birds and amphibians, mammals like deer, rabbits, and raccoons are often spotted on this part of the hike. Just 0.4 mile (0.6 km) past the junction, you cross a wide unmarked path to the left (east). You can turn left here and connect back to the far side of the River Walk Trail for a shorter hike.

Continue straight (south) on the River Walk Trail until you reach the **second wide path** coming from the left (east) at 0.6 mile (1 km). This is the continuation of the River Walk Trail; turn left and continue 0.2 mile (0.3 km) until you face the railroad tracks. Turn right (southeast). As the trail heads into a clearing, it splits in three directions. Go left (east) under the

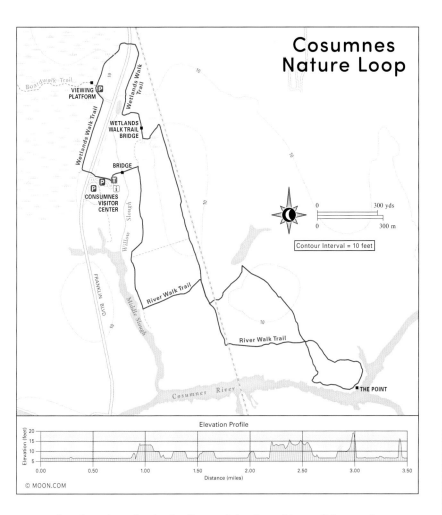

Cosumnes Nature Loop

Contour Interval = 10 feet

Elevation Profile

© MOON.COM

railroad tracks to begin the figure eight-shaped loop of the southernmost part of this hike. The trail then takes you into an oak savannah that's a great spot to see grazing deer.

At 1.3 miles (2.1 km), when the figure eight crosses back on itself, stay left (southeast) and walk 0.3 mile (0.5 km) to get to the farthest point, referred to by locals as **The Point.** Here you can sit on benches and watch the waters of the Consumes River and entrance to Tihuechemne Slough. You may see great blue herons and egrets roosting and feeding in this practically private spot.

▸ **MILE 1.6–3.1: The Point to Franklin Boulevard**
From the Point, complete the figure-eight loop by turning left (west) at the **junction** at 1.8 miles (2.9 km). Continue west on the River Walk Trail for 0.5 mile (0.8 km) to cross under the railroad tracks. Turn north, with the railroad tracks on your right, passing all unmarked paths on your left. After the trail curves left (southwest), at 2.8 miles (4.5 km) turn right (north)

onto the paved **Wetlands Walk Trail** and cross over a bridge. After 0.3 mile (0.5 km), the trail crosses **Franklin Boulevard.**

▸ MILE 3.1-3.8: Franklin Boulevard to Boardwalk Trail

When crossing Franklin Boulevard, be sure to keep a close eye on children, as vehicles may not slow down. The trail turns southwest, and you approach a small **parking lot and restrooms** at 3.3 miles (5.3 km) into the hike. From here, venture right (west) on the wooden **Boardwalk Trail.** The boardwalk leads to a **viewing platform,** where you can get a closer look at a variety of shorebirds. It's 0.5 mile (0.8 km) round-trip to the viewing platform and back. In the fall and winter, this area floods and become a roosting area for sandhill cranes. Look for the ash-gray birds with long bills as they wade in the waters to hunt for insects and frogs.

▸ MILE 3.8-4: Boardwalk Trail to Parking Lot

After completing the Boardwalk Trail, continue south on the Wetlands Walk Trail. At sunset, people line up on this part of the trail to watch the last rays of light dance on the water. If you plan to stay until dark, make sure to have a flashlight and wear reflective clothing. When you're ready, take in the view one last time at the bench at the end of the Wetlands Walk Trail before turning left (east) toward Franklin Boulevard. The visitor center parking lot is visible from the road crossing.

DIRECTIONS

Take I-5 south from Sacramento for 19 miles (31 km) and exit at Twin Cities Road. Go east over the I-5 overpass. Drive 1 mile (1.6 km) to Franklin Boulevard and turn right just before the train tracks. Drive 1.7 miles (2.7 km) to the parking lot, on your left, the location of both the visitor center and the trailhead.

GPS COORDINATES: 38.2659, −121.4401; 38°15′57.2″ N, 121°26′24.4″ W

BEST NEARBY BREWS

Grab a pint at Galt's original brewery and homebrew store, **River Rock Brewery** (608 N. Lincoln Way, Galt, 209/331-6071, www.river-rockbrewery.com, 3pm-8pm Tues.-Wed., 3pm-9pm Fri., noon-9pm Sat., noon-6pm Sun.), owned and operated by lifelong Galt residents. Bring the family and Fido and try the award-winning amber ale, Bern Yur Butt, which is infused with fresh jalapeños. From the trailhead, it's a 15-minute drive via Franklin Boulevard, Twin Cities Road, and Stockton Boulevard.

NEARBY CAMPGROUNDS

NAME	DESCRIPTION	FACILITIES	SEASON	FEE
Beal's Point	Popular with visitors and locals, north of Folsom Dam on Folsom Lake	69 family campsites, 19 full-hookup sites, restrooms, showers, piped drinking water, dump station	year-round	$29 plus $8 reservation fee

Folsom Lake State Recreation Area, Auburn Folsom Road, Granite Bay, 916/988-0205, www.parks.ca.gov

NAME	DESCRIPTION	FACILITIES	SEASON	FEE
Bidwell Canyon	On Lake Oroville, good for picnicking and water activities	75 full-hookup sites, restrooms, token-operated showers	year-round	$45 plus $7 reservation fee

Lake Oroville State Recreation Area, Bidwell Canyon Road, Oroville, 530/538-2218, www.parks.ca.gov

NAME	DESCRIPTION	FACILITIES	SEASON	FEE
Rancho Seco Recreation Area	On Rancho Seco Lake, adjacent to the wildlife sanctuary	32 campsites, 21 RV campsites, fire pits, restrooms, drinking water, dog park, dump station	year-round	from $25 plus $8 reservation fee

Twin Cities Road, Herald, 209/748-2318, www.smud.org

TAHOE

With millions of acres of national forest and state parks laced by hundreds of miles of trails, there's more to explore in Tahoe than you could accomplish in a lifetime of summers. Subalpine and alpine forests, granite-bound lakes, towering peaks, and wildflower-filled meadows offer a multitude of worthy hiking destinations.

The Sierra Nevada's beauty extends north and south of Lake Tahoe too. The Lakes Basin Recreation Area, north of Truckee, has gleaming granite, dozens of lakes, and weather-sculpted pines, firs, and junipers. Carson Pass and the Mokelumne Wilderness, south of South Lake Tahoe, is a volcanic landscape graced by craggy summits and dotted with summer wildflowers. Wherever you go, remember that this part of the Sierra sees a lot of foot traffic, so tread as lightly as possible to help protect its fragile alpine landscape.

▲ BEAR, SILVER, ROUND LAKES LOOP

▲ GLEN ALPINE TRAIL TO SUSIE LAKE

◄ MOUNT TALLAC

1 **Bear, Silver, Round Lakes Loop**
DISTANCE: 4.7 miles (7.6 km) round-trip
DURATION: 2.5 hours
EFFORT: Easy-moderate

2 **Sierra Buttes Lookout**
DISTANCE: 4.6 miles (7.4 km) round-trip
DURATION: 3 hours
EFFORT: Moderate

3 **Five Lakes**
DISTANCE: 4.6 miles (7.4 km) round-trip
DURATION: 2.5 hours
EFFORT: Easy-moderate

4 **Vikingsholm Castle and Emerald Point**
DISTANCE: 4.4 miles (7.1 km) round-trip
DURATION: 2 hours
EFFORT: Easy

5 **Mount Tallac**
DISTANCE: 9.8 miles (15.8 km) round-trip
DURATION: 6 hours
EFFORT: Strenuous

6 **Glen Alpine Trail to Susie Lake**
DISTANCE: 8.4 miles (13.5 km) round-trip
DURATION: 5 hours
EFFORT: Moderate

7 **Echo Lakes to Tamarack and Ralston Lakes**
DISTANCE: 8.1 miles (13 km) round-trip
DURATION: 5 hours
EFFORT: Easy-moderate

8 **Carson Pass to Winnemucca and Round Top Lakes**
DISTANCE: 6.8 miles (10.9 km) round-trip
DURATION: 3 hours
EFFORT: Easy-moderate

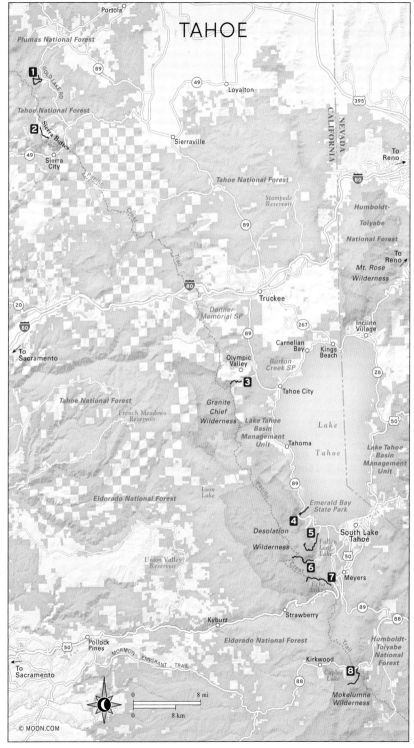

TAHOE

1 Bear, Silver, Round Lakes Loop

PLUMAS NATIONAL FOREST

✤ 🏛 🐾 🚶

A hike through the heart of the Lakes Basin delivers you to the shore of five swimmable lakes in less than 5 miles (8.1 km).

BEST: Swimming Hole Hikes
DISTANCE: 4.7 miles (7.6 km) round-trip
DURATION: 2.5 hours
STARTING ELEVATION: 6,340 feet (1,932 m)
ELEVATION GAIN: 580 feet (177 m)
EFFORT: Easy-moderate
TRAIL: Dirt and rock trail
USERS: Hikers, leashed dogs
SEASON: June-October
PASSES/FEES: None
MAPS: USGS topographic map "Gold Lake"
TRAILHEAD: Long Lake/Bear Lakes Trailhead near Elwell Lodge
FACILITIES: Vault toilet
CONTACT: Beckwourth Ranger District, 530/836-2575, www.fs.usda.gov/plumas

START THE HIKE

▸ **MILE 0-0.6: Long Lake/Bear Lakes Trailhead to Bear Lakes Loop**
Many hikers visit the lovely Bear Lakes from the Round Lake Trailhead near Gold Lake Lodge, but this lollipop loop trail starts at the **Long Lake/Bear Lakes Trailhead** near Elwell Lodge. Two paths begin from this trailhead: Long Lake Trail starts from the west side of the parking lot (Long Lake is one of the largest lakes in the basin and definitely worth a separate trip), but you'll take the southward trail that's signed for Big Bear Lake.

Hike in the good company of lodgepole pines, western white pines, and red firs for 0.6 mile (1 km) until you reach a major **junction** just before Big Bear Lake. You've just completed the "stick" of the lollipop **Bear Lakes Loop,** and your next move is to circle counterclockwise around the "candy." Get ready for sweet surprises in the form of sparkling alpine lakes.

▸ **MILE 0.6-1.6: Bear Lakes Loop to Silver Lake**
Go right (west) on **Bear Lakes Loop,** and in another 30 feet (9 m), you'll skirt **Big Bear Lake's** northern shoreline. Shimmering in the sunlight, this 50-foot-deep (15-m) lake is a conifer-ringed jewel. You can prowl the shoreline to find a spot for the day's first swim, or simply stick to the main trail and stroll the lake's long curvy shoreline. In another 0.25 mile (0.4

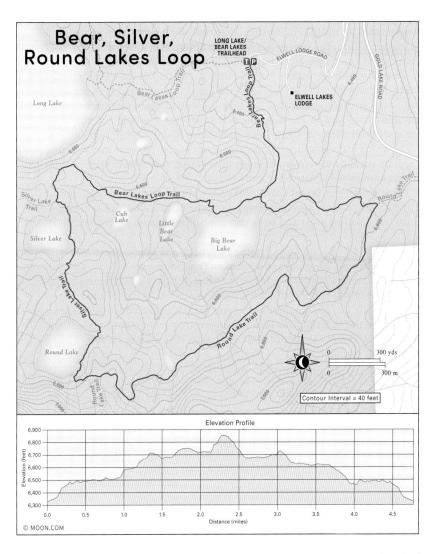

Bear, Silver, Round Lakes Loop

Elevation Profile

km), you'll pass by **Little Bear Lake,** and then **Cub Lake** 0.25 mile (0.4 km) farther. At all three lakes, you'll probably see an angler or two trying their luck for stocked rainbow trout. As you might expect, Little Bear and Cub are much smaller than Big Bear Lake.

In another 0.3 mile (0.5 km), you reach a **T junction** a short distance from Long Lake, which is hidden from view by a forested ridge. Turn left (southwest), then left again at a second **junction** 0.2 mile (0.3 km) farther. You'll arrive at the eastern shore of what is arguably one of this trek's prettiest lakes. Deep, sprawling **Silver Lake** is set in a perfect glacial cirque, and its sparking water will beckon you with a siren call: "Jump in and swim."

▶ **MILE 1.6-3.5: Silver Lake to Round Lake Trailhead Junction**
After a refreshing backstroke session—or at least a toe-cooling session— wave a sad good-bye to Silver Lake, then proceed on a nearly level grade to

Round Lake, 0.6 mile (1 km) farther. Your trail skirts its eastern shore, then leads uphill from the lake to the ruins of a **stamp mill,** where there's an old foundation, an engine block, and assorted bric-a-brac.

From the mill site, follow the old mining road trail in a generally northeastern traverse to the Round Lake Trailhead (ignore a left fork connecting to the Pacific Crest Trail). The next 1.5-mile (2.4-km) stretch has more climbing than you've faced on the rest of this gentle trek, but the work pays off with views of Long Lake and Mount Elwell (again, two destinations worth hiking to on another trip). Even bigger rewards await during the July wildflower season: This leg travels past several wet seeps where bright orange-red alpine lilies grow as tall as 3 feet (1 m).

As you near the **Round Lake Trailhead,** watch for a fork on the left that appears just as you spy Gray Eagle Lodge's buildings across a meadow. Turn left, heading west and back into pine-filled woods.

▸ MILE 3.5-4.7: Round Lake Trailhead Junction to Big Bear Lake and Long Lake/Bear Lakes Trailhead

An easy 0.5 mile (0.8 km) of forested strolling brings you back to the northeast shore of Big Bear Lake, where you'll rejoin the "stick" of the lollipop to head back to your car. But before you rush off, take advantage of your second chance to visit to Big Bear Lake. Now that you've spent a few hours on this sun-kissed Sierra trail, Big Bear Lake's chilly waters will feel like a swimmer's paradise.

DIRECTIONS

From Sierraville at the junction of Highways 89 and 49, drive north on Highway 49 for 18 miles (29 km) to Bassetts and the start of the Gold Lake Highway. Turn north on Gold Lake Highway and drive 8.8 miles (14.2 km) to the left turnoff for Elwell Lodge. Turn left, drive 0.6 mile (1 km), then turn left again and drive 0.3 mile (0.5 km) to the Long Lake/Bear Lakes Loop trailhead at the road's end (beyond Elwell Lodge).

GPS COORDINATES: 39.6987, −120.6670; 39°41′55.3″ N, 120°40′1.2″ W

BEST NEARBY BREWS

A 20-minute drive north on Gold Lake Highway will bring you to **Ronin Fermentation Project** (601 Graeagle Johnsville Rd., Graeagle, no phone, https://roninfermentationproject.com, 2pm-7pm Thurs.-Fri., noon-7pm Sat., noon-5pm Sun.), which makes innovative wild-fermented ales. Try The Multiverse Lives koji beer, which won a silver medal at the 2022 World Beer Cup. Ronin is the only brewery in the world that uses this particular koji brewing process, a fusion of Eastern and Western styles of brewing.

This unforgettable trek offers celestial scenery, a fear-tinged staircase climb, and a 360-degree panorama of the Lakes Basin.

DISTANCE: 4.6 miles (7.4 km) round-trip

DURATION: 3 hours

STARTING ELEVATION: 7,010 feet (2,137 m)

ELEVATION GAIN: 1,470 feet (448 m)

EFFORT: Moderate

TRAIL: Dirt trail, metal stairs and catwalk

USERS: Hikers, leashed dogs

SEASON: June-October

PASSES/FEES: None

MAPS: USGS topographic map "Sierra City"

TRAILHEAD: Sierra Buttes Trailhead, near Packer Saddle

FACILITIES: Vault toilet

CONTACT: Yuba Ranger District, 530/478-6253, www.fs.usda.gov/tahoe

START THE HIKE

▶ **MILE 0-0.9: Sierra Buttes Trailhead to Pacific Crest Trail Junction**

From the **green metal gate** at the trailhead, the trail starts out as an old Jeep road and begins to climb immediately, the wide road quickly narrowing to single-track. You'll catch your breath once you reach the 0.5-mile (0.8-km) mark, where the trail settles into a level southward meander along a ridgetop dotted with summer wildflowers.

At 0.9 mile (1.4 km) is a **junction** where the Pacific Crest Trail crosses your route; stay straight (south).

▶ **MILE 0.9-1.9: Pacific Crest Trail Junction to Summit Dirt Road**

Although the grade has been fairly moderate so far, the ascent steepens considerably in the next 0.7 mile (1.1 km). After an initial exposed stretch, the trail tunnels into a dense hemlock forest, which will shade you from the relentless alpine sun. The route winds uphill through this lovely grove, which is dotted with car-size boulders.

You'll emerge at a clearing on the ridge at 1.6 miles (2.6 km). To the left of the trail, among the boulders scattered on the ridgeline, is a ledge with a precipitous drop-off and a mesmerizing view north and east. Peer over the edge and you'll see Young America Lake hiding in plain sight directly below you, perched in a granite pocket. Farther in the distance, the blue tarns of Upper and Lower Sardine Lakes look like they belong on a High Sierra postcard.

Just a few yards farther along the trail, you'll reach a spider's web of off-highway-vehicle trails. Avoid those side trails and stay on the clearly

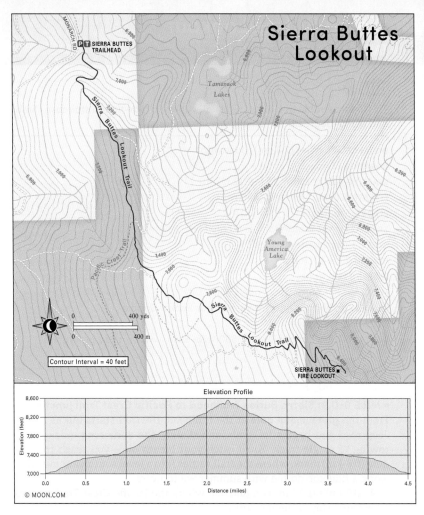

Sierra Buttes Lookout

Elevation Profile

© MOON.COM

signed hiker's path that heads uphill (no OHVs permitted). The next 0.3 mile (0.5 km) is mercilessly steep, but just keep putting one foot in front of the other. As you near the tree line, your narrow trail climbs up a few stair-steps to join a wide **dirt road** to the summit.

▶ **MILE 1.9–2.3: Summit Dirt Road to Fire Lookout Tower**

Turn left (north) on the rocky dirt road; you have 0.4 mile (0.6 km) to go. Sweeping vistas of the valley to the west and north provide the fuel you need to keep climbing. Look north for a view of the Lassen Peak volcano, often capped with snow in early summer.

After one last bend in the rock-strewn road, you're suddenly face-to-face with the highest pinnacle of the Sierra Buttes, **the lookout tower,** and its three aluminum staircases that seem like part of a Rube Goldberg machine. Steady your nerves before you start the climb, and in a minute or two, you'll be summiting the third and final staircase that carries you to the catwalk surrounding the lookout tower's square cupola.

Some people find the catwalk to be a bit more nerve-racking than the stairs because of its grated surface—you can see right through it to the empty air below. Put your faith in its engineering and walk around all four sides of the building to fully savor the astounding 360-degree panorama.

▶ **MILE 2.3-4.6: Fire Lookout Tower to Sierra Buttes Trailhead**
Many hikers discover that going down the staircases is spookier than going up, but just hold on tight to the railings and you'll be fine. On your way back down the Sierra Buttes' dirt road, don't get so lost in your Sierra reverie that you miss the right turnoff for the single-track trail. If you come to a metal gate on the dirt road, you missed it, and you'll need to backtrack.

DIRECTIONS

From Sierraville at the junction of Highways 89 and 49, drive north on Highway 49 for 18 miles (29 km) to Bassetts and the start of the Gold Lake Highway. Turn north on Gold Lake Highway and drive 1.3 miles (2.1 km) to Sardine Lake/Packer Lake Road. Turn left, and in 0.1 mile (0.2 km), veer right to stay on Packer Lake Road. Drive past Packsaddle Campground and the Packer Lake Lodge turnoff, continuing for a total of 4.8 miles (7.7 km) to Packer Saddle. Turn left at the saddle and drive 0.3 mile (0.5 km) (now on a dirt road) to the Sierra Buttes Trailhead on the left. The trail begins at a green steel gate. This parking lot holds about 15 cars. If the lot is full, backtrack to the larger lot at Packer Saddle and begin hiking there; you'll add 0.4 mile (0.6 km) to your round-trip mileage.

GPS COORDINATES: 39.6117, −120.6654; 39°36′42.1″ N, 120°39′55.4″ W

BEST NEARBY BREWS

It's a 40-minute drive from this trailhead, but **The Brewing Lair** (67007 Hwy. 70, Blairsden, 530/394-0940, www.thebrewinglair. com, noon-7pm daily) is worth the trip. This laid-back 15-barrel brewpub offers great beer and fun pastimes—a nine-hole disc golf course, slack line, Ping-Pong tables, fire pits, and more. Sample the blonde ale, black IPA, and seasonal sours, and be sure to take the self-guided brewery tour.

Visit an alpine basin filled with petite, picturesque lakes on this wildflower-filled route.

DISTANCE: 4.6 miles (7.4 km) round-trip

DURATION: 2.5 hours

STARTING ELEVATION: 6,600 feet (2,012 m)

ELEVATION GAIN: 1,035 feet (315 m)

EFFORT: Easy-moderate

TRAIL: Dirt and rock trail

USERS: Hikers, leashed dogs

SEASON: June–October

PASSES/FEES: None

MAPS: USGS topographic maps "Tahoe City" and "Granite Chief"

TRAILHEAD: Five Lakes Trailhead on Alpine Meadows Road

FACILITIES: Vault toilet

CONTACT: Truckee Ranger District, 530/587-3558, www.fs.usda.gov/tahoe

START THE HIKE

▶ **MILE 0-1.6: Five Lakes Trailhead to Granite Chief Wilderness Boundary**

From the trailhead alongside the road to Alpine Meadows Ski Area, start hiking on **Five Lakes Trail,** the obvious path by the signboard. The trail begins with an immediate climb as it cuts across a sun-drenched south-facing slope that's cloaked in hardy sun-loving shrubs, especially manzanita, huckleberry oak, and whitethorn.

In late summer, this initial stretch can seem a bit hot and monotonous, with only occasional shade from Jeffrey pines. But during the July wildflower bloom, when a treasure trove of blossoms brightens the rocky slopes, it's delightful. Standout flowers include bright yellow mule's ears, pink-red scarlet gilia, mint-scented pennyroyal, yellow buckwheat, and orange paintbrush.

Five Lakes Trail quickly ascends out of this brushy swale and makes its way across open slopes below a fascinating cluster of volcanic outcrops. Most are gray andesite, but others give off a rosy pink glow (they're most likely rhyolite). If you have kids hiking with you, ask them what shapes they see in these rugged knobs, spires, and pinnacles. Young imaginations will often spot dogs, bears, or other critters in the rocks.

Gain high views of the Alpine Meadow Ski Area as you switchback your way up this ridge, with occasional Jeffrey pines and western white pines providing a respite from the alpine sun. These twisted, gnarled trees serve as reminders of how severe the winter is here.

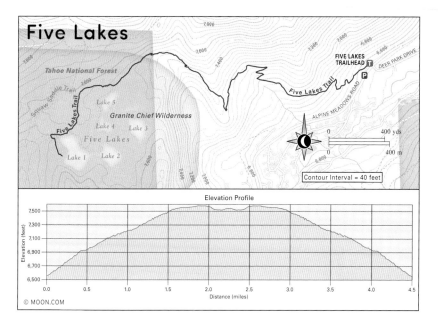

Five Lakes

After crossing over a large basalt outcrop at 1.4 miles (2.3 km), the hardest work is behind you. The volcanic terrain is also finished; now you're entering a landscape of glacier-chiseled granite, the Sierra crest's hallmark rock. At 1.6 miles (2.6 km), you'll reach a sign for **Granite Chief Wilderness.**

▶ **MILE 1.6–2.3: Granite Chief Wilderness Boundary to Lake No. 1**
Just as you cross the wilderness boundary, you'll also enter a magnificent forest of venerable red firs. Many are cloaked in fluorescent green staghorn lichen (it's not a moss, although many hikers call it that). The ridge you've been climbing has topped out, and you'll enjoy an easy level stretch among the firs and a smattering of granite boulders.

In 0.2 mile (0.3 km), you reach a knotted tangle of made-by-use trails. The first of these narrow paths branches off to one of the tiniest of the Five Lakes, but stay on the main Five Lakes Trail for now. (Note this junction in case you choose to loop around the entire basin—this is where your loop will end and you'll rejoin the main trail.)

Continue straight ahead to a second **junction** at 2 miles (3.2 km), where the main trail continues to Whiskey Creek's overnight campsites. Since you're day hiking, turn left here to follow Five Lakes Trail south 0.2 mile (0.3 km). The path deposits you on the north shore of **Lake No. 1,** the largest and westernmost lake in this basin. This picturesque tarn is framed by graceful mountain hemlocks and western white pines. Most hikers will be happy to hang out at a cozy spot along its forested granite-kissed shoreline.

Except in extreme drought years, this lake adjoins the **second-largest and southernmost lake**—the two bodies of water are connected by a narrow strait. Both lakes boast plentiful wildflowers and granite slabs where you can set up a picnic, and both are shallow enough to warm up nicely for swimming by July.

FIVE LAKES TRAIL ▲

From these two lakes, you can simply backtrack for a 4.6-mile (7.4-km) round-trip and a spectacular easy day. But if you're feeling ambitious, follow a made-by-use trail east from Lake No. 2 (the smaller of the connected lakes). This meandering path will lead you to **three even smaller lakes,** which in dry years look more like grass-lined ponds. Good route-finding skills—in other words, not letting yourself get lost in a spiderweb of informal paths—will allow you to visit all three lakes and then circle back to the first junction you passed as you entered the basin.

DIRECTIONS

From Tahoe City, drive 4 miles (6.4 km) north on Highway 89 to Alpine Meadows Road. Turn left (west) and drive 2.1 miles (3.4 km) to the trailhead on the road's north side. Park alongside the road's shoulder. If you're driving from the north, Alpine Meadows Road is 10 miles (16.1 km) south of Truckee.

GPS COORDINATES: 39.1793, −120.2297; 39°10'45.5" N, 120°13'46.9" W

BEST NEARBY BREWS

Just a 10-minute drive away, **Alibi Ale Works' Truckee Public House** (10069 Bridge St., Truckee, 530/536-5029, www.alibialeworks.com, noon-9pm Sun.-Thurs., noon-10pm Fri.-Sat.) is a happening spot all year-round, but especially on summer weekends when live bands play on the patio. Order a lamb burger or a soft pretzel and pair it with just about any of Alibi's pale ales, stouts, IPAs, or sours.

4 Vikingsholm Castle and Emerald Point

EMERALD BAY STATE PARK

✳ 🏛 🚶

Hike along the shoreline of sparkling Emerald Bay and visit its historic landmark castle.

BEST: Swimming Hole Hikes
DISTANCE: 4.4 miles (7.1 km) round-trip
DURATION: 2 hours
STARTING ELEVATION: 6,640 feet (2,024 m)
ELEVATION GAIN: 515 feet (157 m)
EFFORT: Easy
TRAIL: Dirt and rock
USERS: Hikers
SEASON: April-October
PASSES/FEES: $10 day-use fee per vehicle
MAPS: Download from www.parks.ca.gov
TRAILHEAD: Vikingsholm/Emerald Bay State Park parking area
FACILITIES: Restroom
CONTACT: Emerald Bay State Park, 530/525-3384 or 530/525-7232, www.parks.ca.gov

START THE HIKE

▶ **MILE 0-0.8: Parking Lot to Vikingsholm**

From the signboard on the east side of the **parking lot,** take a quick 50-

yard (46-m) detour to your right (southeast), where a large stone-lined **overlook** offers a dazzling view of Emerald Bay and Fannette Island. An early-morning start ensures you can snap stunning photos—or just enjoy this world-class view—without having to fight off the crowds that gather during the busiest hours of the day.

When you're ready, start hiking on **Vikingsholm Trail,** a wide service road that descends 500 feet (152 m). You'll need to regain that elevation on your return trip, but two long switchbacks make both the ascent

◀ EMERALD BAY AND FANNETTE ISLAND

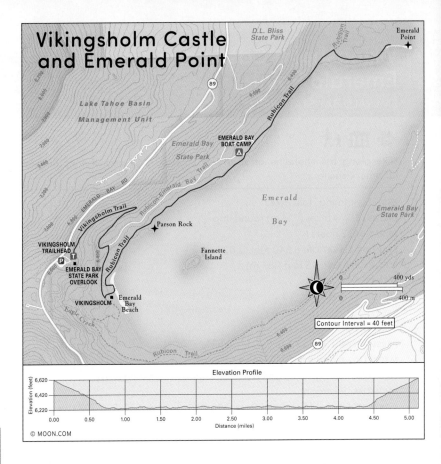

Vikingsholm Castle and Emerald Point

D.L. Bliss
State Park

Emerald
Point

89

Lake Tahoe Basin
Management Unit

Rubicon Trail

EMERALD BAY
BOAT CAMP

Emerald Bay
State Park

EMERALD BAY RD.

Vikingsholm Trail

Rubicon-Emerald Bay Trail

Emerald

Bay

Emerald Bay
State Park

Rubicon Trail

Parson Rock

Fannette
Island

VIKINGSHOLM
TRAILHEAD

P

EMERALD BAY
STATE PARK
OVERLOOK

Eagle Creek

VIKINGSHOLM

Emerald
Bay
Beach

0   400 yds

0   400 m

Contour Interval = 40 feet

Rubicon   Trail

89

Elevation Profile

Elevation (feet)

6,620
6,420
6,220

0.00   0.50   1.00   1.50   2.00   2.50   3.00   3.50   4.00   4.50   5.00
Distance (miles)

© MOON.COM

and descent very manageable, especially if you remembered to wear a sun hat and carry full water bottles.

The road deposits you on Emerald Bay's beautiful **beach.** Veer right for 0.1 mile (0.2 km) to pay a visit to **Vikingsholm,** a glorious stone-and-timber mansion that's one of North America's finest examples of Scandinavian architecture.

In 1929, Lora Josephine Knight hired workers to construct this magnificent 38-room structure that replicates the style of a 1,200-year-old Viking castle in exacting detail. The structure was built out of native stone and timber without disturbing any of the property's existing trees. Crowned by turrets, towers, and a green sod roof, the mansion served as Knight's beloved summer home for 16 years.

Tours of the castle's interior, which is filled with handmade Scandinavian furnishings and museum-replica art, are available during the summer months (purchase tickets at www.vikingsholm.org), but you can walk around its exterior for free.

Knight also built a stone teahouse on the highest point on Fannette Island, Lake Tahoe's only island, where the ruins of the teahouse still stand. On summer days, you can rent a kayak on Emerald Bay's beach, then paddle to the island and climb up 150 feet (46 m) to the ruins' head-turning viewpoint.

▶ MILE 0.8-2.2: Vikingsholm to Emerald Point

After you've visited the mansion or paddled a kayak to Fannette Island, set off on this trip's second leg, which contours along Emerald Bay's northern shoreline. Starting from the beach, head northeast on **Rubicon Trail,** leaving most of the crowds behind you. You'll cross several boardwalks and bridges over small creeks as you wander through this conifer-shaded stretch. A lovely mix of trees accompanies you—Jeffrey pines, incense cedars, white firs, sugar pines—plus a nonstop parade of beautiful water views.

Stop to admire the vista of Fannette Island from **Parson Rock,** a granite pillar that's favored by bold lake jumpers and divers, then keep strolling along the shoreline to Emerald Bay State Park's boat-in **campground.** It's difficult to score a camping reservation here, but worth it. More than 1,000 boats enter the bay daily during the summer, but at night, campers have this glorious place all to themselves.

Beyond the campground, Rubicon Trail heads into a wet, willowy stretch of shoreline. Watch for an unsigned informal path that veers right (southeast) and head through the marshlands to the bay's edge at **Emerald Point.** This is the spot where Emerald Bay and Lake Tahoe meet and shake hands. If Lake Tahoe's water level is low, a small beach will be exposed. If the water level is high, trees and willows will cover every inch of dry ground. Either way, find a seat somewhere and admire the stunning cobalt-blue water.

▶ MILE 2.2-4.4: Emerald Point to Parking Lot

For your return trip, retrace your steps, but make sure you stop for a swim at Emerald Bay's beach before hiking back uphill to your car.

DIRECTIONS

From South Lake Tahoe, drive north on Highway 89 for 10 miles (16.1 km) to the Vikingsholm/Emerald Bay State Park parking area on the right side of the road (just beyond the Eagle Falls/Eagle Lake parking area on the left). If the Emerald Bay State Park lot is full, you'll need to park in the Eagle Falls/Eagle Lake lot and walk carefully alongside Highway 89 to the trailhead.

GPS COORDINATES: 38.9544, −120.1105; 38°57'15.8" N, 120°6'37.8" W

BEST NEARBY BREWS

After this hike, drive 20 minutes south to **The Hangar** (2401 Lake Tahoe Blvd., South Lake Tahoe, 530/578-0089, www.thehangar-laketahoe.com, noon-10pm daily summer, shorter hours in winter). This outdoor playground of picnic tables, string lights, and food trucks offers 30-plus beers on tap—enough choices to please any beer aficionado. Kids and well-behaved dogs are welcome, and on weekends, you can catch some live music.

Mount Tallac

DESOLATION WILDERNESS

Mount Tallac's hulking summit offers unequalled views of Lake Tahoe and the granite mecca of Desolation Wilderness.

BEST: Summer Hikes

DISTANCE: 9.8 miles (15.8 km) round-trip

DURATION: 6 hours

STARTING ELEVATION: 6,470 feet (1,972 m)

ELEVATION GAIN: 3,470 feet (1,057 m)

EFFORT: Strenuous

TRAIL: Dirt, talus, scree

USERS: Hikers, leashed dogs

SEASON: June–October

PASSES/FEES: Fill out a free self-service permit at the trailhead

MAPS: Tom Harrison Maps "Desolation Wilderness"

TRAILHEAD: Mount Tallac Trailhead

FACILITIES: Restroom

CONTACT: Lake Tahoe Basin Management Unit, 530/543-2600, www.fs.usda.gov/ltbmu

START THE HIKE

This route is an out-and-back, but if you can arrange a car shuttle, a great option is to go uphill from the Mount Tallac Trailhead, then come back down the mountain's western slopes to end at the Glen Alpine Trailhead at Fallen Leaf Lake. The shuttle hike is about 2 miles (3.2 km) longer, but worth it. No matter how you do it, try to avoid the heaviest crowds on this popular trip by hiking on a week-day or getting an early morning start.

▶ **MILE 0-2.6: Mount Tallac Trailhead to Cathedral Lake**
The first 0.7 mile (1.1 km) of the **Mount Tallac Trail** rises quickly up a slope covered in sagebrush, man-zanita, and Jeffrey pine to gain the top of an astounding geological feature—the ridgeline of **Fallen Leaf Lake's lateral moraine.** Deposited by long-departed glaciers, this rocky debris pile gives you a high

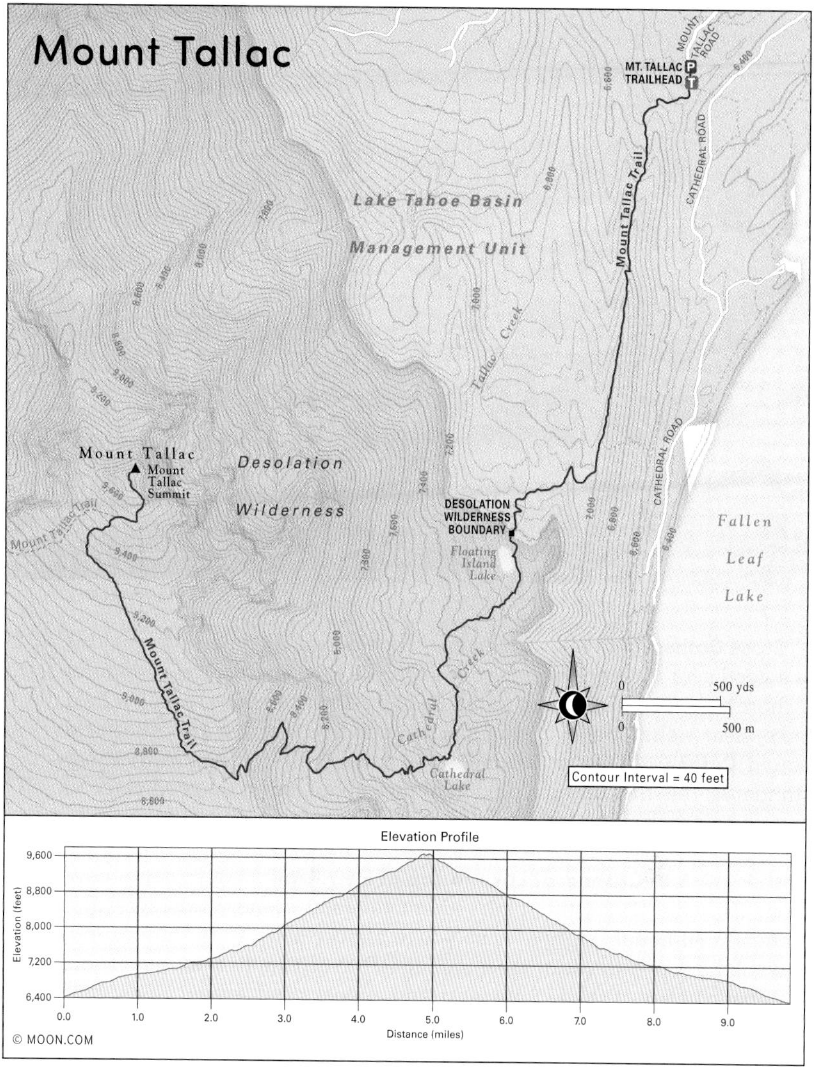

Mount Tallac

Elevation Profile

© MOON.COM

vantage point straight across beautiful Fallen Leaf Lake to the vast blue outline of Lake Tahoe.

Enjoy level walking along the moraine's crest for about 0.3 mile (0.5 km), then drop down its west side into deeper woods, before climbing again to reach the **Desolation Wilderness** boundary and the eastern shore of tiny pond-like **Floating Island Lake,** 1.6 miles (2.6 km) from the start. The serene grass-edged lake occasionally has a mat of soil and grass floating around its surface, but the "floating island" is often absent.

Mount Tallac Trail parallels the lake's shoreline, then moves off and heads uphill through thick forest, passing springs and rivulets where water-loving wildflowers like monkshood and larkspur thrive. Occasionally the trees thin out to swaths of rocky scree, but for the most part, you're hiking in a shady red fir and lodgepole pine woodland.

MOUNT TALLAC ▲

Cross **Cathedral Creek** with an easy rock-hop at 2.3 miles (3.7 km); this is a good spot to filter water if your supply is low. Then at the summit of a short but steep climb, pass a trail heading downhill (left) to Fallen Leaf Lake. Bear right (south) at this **junction** and you'll arrive at petite rock-bound **Cathedral Lake** at 2.6 miles (4.2 km). By Desolation Wilderness standards, this tiny tarn isn't much to rave about, but it's a good place to rest up before the next leg, which is much steeper than the first.

▶ **MILE 2.6-3.8: Cathedral Lake to Top of Headwall**
From Cathedral Lake, this path's character—and scenery—changes dramatically. Although mileage-wise you're almost halfway to the summit, you still have two-thirds of the climbing left to accomplish. Except for occasional patches of shade from western hemlocks and Jeffrey pines, your next mile (1.6 km) is a shadeless march through exposed switchbacks that cut across a scree-lined slope. An open bowl near the ridgeline holds snow well into July in some years, sometimes obscuring the trail.

As you slowly grind your way up the canyon's **headwall,** heading toward the ridge about 1 mile (1.6 km) south of Tallac's summit, don't forget to look behind you. A never-ending banquet of views unfolds as you climb, giving you plenty of reasons to pause, turn around, and catch your breath in this punishing stretch.

▶ **MILE 3.8-4.9: Top of Headwall to Tallac Summit**
It's a relief when you gain the crest, but your work is not done yet. The trail winds around to the mountain's less-steep southwest flank, then proceeds northwest through a windswept meadow. Eventually the path finds some cover in scrubby hemlocks and western white pines. At 4.4 miles (7.1 km), you'll pass a trail on the left heading downhill to Gilmore Lake; if you've opted to do the shuttle hike, you'll follow this trail on your descent.

For now, veer right (northwest) and continue the uphill push. The last few hundred feet seem to take forever, but finally you ascend the jumbled pile of talus that marks the summit. Many hikers choose to use their hands for balance on this rocky stretch.

Tallac's summit block is huge and wide. No matter which way you face, you'll feel Tallac's "wow" factor. The summit's 360-degree panorama is sublime. To the east is Lake Tahoe, Emerald Bay, Fallen Leaf Lake, and the city of South Lake Tahoe. To the west and south are the lake-dotted basins of Desolation Wilderness, backed by glacially sculpted Ralston and Pyramid Peaks. Pick the perspective you like best, and find a comfy place to sit among the rocks. You won't want to give up this hard-earned summit any time soon.

DIRECTIONS

From the Y junction of U.S. 50 and Highway 89 in South Lake Tahoe, drive 3.5 miles (5.6 km) northwest on Highway 89 to the left turnoff for the Mount Tallac Trailhead and Camp Shelly (across from the Baldwin Beach entrance). Turn left and drive 0.4 mile (0.6 km), then turn left and drive 0.6 mile (1 km) to the signed trailhead. Day hikers must fill out a self-serve wilderness permit at the trailhead.

GPS COORDINATES: 38.9214, −120.0682; 38°55'17" N, 120°4'5.5" W

BEST NEARBY BREWS

At Lake Tahoe AleWorx, you're in charge of the taps. Get in line, get an electronic bracelet, and pull your own pints from a choice of two dozen-plus craft libations. At this indoor-outdoor compound, bands take the stage on the patio while chefs bake up thin-crust pizzas in a wood-fired oven. AleWorx has two locations, but the closest one to this trailhead is at the Y junction in South Lake Tahoe (2050 Lake Tahoe Blvd., 530/600-0442, http://laketahoealeworx.com, 11am-9pm daily).

This rock-strewn path carves a historic route into the lake-dotted mecca of Desolation Wilderness.

DISTANCE: 8.4 miles (13.5 km) round-trip
DURATION: 5 hours
STARTING ELEVATION: 6,575 feet (2,004 m)
ELEVATION GAIN: 1,527 feet (465 km)
EFFORT: Moderate
TRAIL: Dirt and rock
USERS: Hikers, leashed dogs
SEASON: June–October
PASSES/FEES: Fill out a free self-service permit at the trailhead
MAPS: Tom Harrison Maps "Desolation Wilderness"
TRAILHEAD: Glen Alpine Trailhead at the end of Fallen Leaf Lake Road
FACILITIES: Restroom
CONTACT: Lake Tahoe Basin Management Unit, 530/543-2600, www.fs.usda.gov/ltbmu

START THE HIKE

▶ **MILE 0-1: Glen Alpine Trailhead to Glen Alpine Springs Resort**
At the trailhead, fill out a free self-serve permit at the signboard, then start walking on the gated road next to it. A moderate climb up this rocky, cobble-lined track leads past a few rustic cabins and lovely **Modjeska Falls** on Glen Alpine Creek. The 35-foot-high (11-m) cataract is named for Helena Modjeska, a famous late-1800s actor who performed at the remote lodge you'll soon pass.

Only 1 mile (1.6 km) from the start, the **Glen Alpine Trail** reaches the historic buildings of **Glen Alpine Springs Resort.** Although the resort is no longer operating, a "curative" mineral spring made this rustic spot a popular getaway from the late 1800s until the 1930s. A few interpretive signs explain Glen Alpine's history. Volunteers occasionally staff the resort's social hall, which was designed by famed architect Bernard Maybeck, who also designed San Francisco's Palace of Fine Arts. Next to the social hall, an iron-rich carbonated spring bubbles up from the ground.

▶ **MILE 1-3.2: Glen Alpine Springs Resort to Creek Crossing**
Only 0.1 mile (0.2 km) past the resort buildings, the path narrows to a single-track trail and climbs up **granite stairsteps.** You'll ascend gently but steadily to the **Desolation Wilderness** boundary at 1.6 miles (1.9 km), and then 0.1 mile (0.2 km) farther, note a left fork leading to Grass Lake. Keep this short easy hike in mind for your next visit—it's only 1 mile (1.6 km) to the edge of lovely Grass Lake, where swimming is a popular pastime.

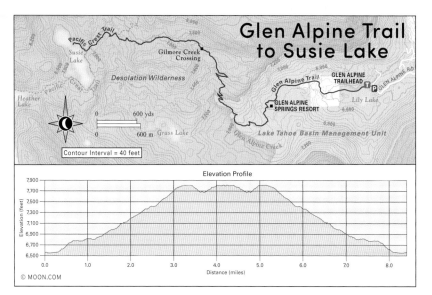

Glen Alpine Trail to Susie Lake

For now, bypass the **Grass Lake spur** and bear right (north) on the main trail; hike in the direction dictated by the wooden post engraved with "Mount Tallac." You'll stroll through a delightfully dense forest of Jeffrey and lodgepole pines alongside a tributary to Glen Alpine Creek, then switchback up a steep granite-lined grade. This is the trail's first sustained ascent. The trail dips in and out of forest as it ascends the north wall of a narrow canyon. Pass a monumental sawed-off tree trunk at 2.7 miles (4.3 km), where you might want to pause to let your heart rate slow down.

At 3.2 miles (5.2 km) from the start, **Gilmore Lake's outlet creek** presents a watery obstacle that may be 10 feet (3 m) wide in early summer or much less than a trickle by late summer. Whether the water is flowing energetically or languidly, you'll cross it on well-placed rocks.

▶ **MILE 3.2–4.2: Creek Crossing to Susie Lake**
On the creek's far side, the Gilmore Lake Trail heads right, but you continue straight (west). Bear left (west) at the **engraved signpost** for Aloha, Susie, and Heather Lakes, then pass a few small ponds. After a pleasant level stretch through forest and meadows, the trail dips downhill, and at 3.8 miles (6.1 km), you reach a **junction** with yet another path to Gilmore Lake. Go left (west) again, now following a stretch of the **Pacific Crest Trail.** You'll travel along the edge of a flower- and fern-filled meadow, then make a quick climb to the multihued rock basin that hems in **Susie Lake,** reaching its eastern shoreline at 4.2 miles (6.8 km).

You could just plop down anywhere you see fit, but it's worth following the trail as it bends left to curve over to Susie's southern shoreline. There you're granted an exceptional view of the dark grey metamorphic rock of 9,735-foot (2,967-m) Mount Tallac, which guards the northeast horizon.

If you have extra energy to burn, consider the 1-mile (1.6-km) trek from Susie Lake to **Heather Lake,** a dramatic, treeless, granite-bound beauty. The additional ascent is minimal and much of the walk is a leisurely stroll along Susie's southwestern shore. If you add on this side-trip, your

SUSIE LAKE ▲

round-trip trek will increase to 11 miles (17.7 km). This is an out-and-back hike, so retrace your steps back to your car.

DIRECTIONS

From the Y junction of U.S. 50 and Highway 89 in South Lake Tahoe, drive 3 miles (4.8 km) northwest on Highway 89 to Fallen Leaf Lake Road on the left (1 mi/1.6 km past Camp Richardson). Turn left and drive 5.4 miles (8.7 km) to the end of the road and the Glen Alpine Trailhead. Be sure to drive very slowly along this busy, extremely narrow road, which has barely enough room for cyclists and pedestrians, let alone cars.

GPS COORDINATES: 38.8771, −120.0805; 38°52′37.6″ N, 120°4′49.8″ W

BEST NEARBY BREWS

After this long hike, drive across town to **South of North Brewing Company** (932 Stateline Ave., South Lake Tahoe, 530/494-9805, www.southofnorthbeer.com, noon-10pm Sat.-Sun., 2pm-10pm Mon.-Fri.). This ultracasual brewery attached to Basecamp Hotel has an outdoor garden decked out with fire pits and string lights. Don't miss the blueberry ale and the hot honey brussels sprouts.

Echo Lakes to Tamarack and Ralston Lakes

DESOLATION WILDERNESS

An undulating hike through granite and fir forest leads to two swimmer-beckoning lakes.

DISTANCE: 8.1 miles (13 km) round-trip
DURATION: 5 hours
STARTING ELEVATION: 7,460 feet (2,274 m)
ELEVATION GAIN: 960 feet (293 m)
EFFORT: Easy-moderate
TRAIL: Dirt and rock
USERS: Hikers, leashed dogs
SEASON: June-October
PASSES/FEES: Fill out a free self-service permit at the trailhead
MAPS: Tom Harrison Maps "Desolation Wilderness"
TRAILHEAD: Echo Lake's causeway
FACILITIES: Restroom
CONTACT: Lake Tahoe Basin Management Unit, 530/543-2600, www.fs.usda.gov/ltbmu

START THE HIKE

Whether or not you utilize the Echo Lakes **boat taxi** (530/659-7207, www.echochalet.net, $20 pp one-way, $7 dogs one-way) will determine the exact distance and difficulty of this out-and-back hike. Taking the boat taxi in both directions makes this trek a mere 3.6 miles (5.8 km), but done entirely on foot, the hike is 8.4 miles (13.5 km). Many hikers split the difference and ride the boat in one direction only for a 5.5-mile (8.9-km) trek.

▶ **MILE 0-3.1: Lower Echo Lake Trailhead to Triangle Lake Junction**
Set out across the causeway on top of **Echo Lake's dam,** located to the left of the **Echo Lakes store.** A trail signboard on the causeway's far side informs you that you're getting on the **Pacific Crest Trail (PCT).** If you're shortening this trip with a boat taxi ride, skip this part and head straight to the boat dock to purchase tickets.

The PCT rises upward immediately to deliver a surprising view of Lake Tahoe to the east. The path then switchbacks to the west and rolls along a manzanita-lined slope, holding steady on an elevation line about 200 feet (61 m) above Lower Echo Lake's cabin-dotted shoreline. The PCT undulates along, not losing or gaining much in the way of elevation, until it reaches a **junction** at 2.6 miles (4.2 km) where a path on the left leads down to the **boat dock** on **Upper Echo Lake.** If you rode the boat taxi, you'll disembark from the boat and join the main trail here.

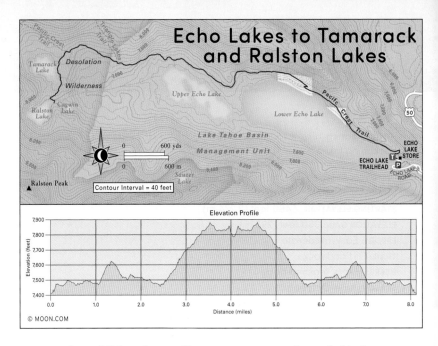

Leave the paddleboarders and happy summer vacationers behind you—now the only other people you'll see are hikers and backpackers. Jeffrey pines and Sierra junipers edge your rocky pathway, which starts to climb with a bit more vigor. At 3.1 miles (5 km), you'll pass a **wilderness boundary sign** and a trail on your right signed for **Triangle Lake.** Stay straight (west) on the PCT, following the sign for Lake Aloha.

▸ MILE 3.1–4: Triangle Lake Junction to Tamarack and Ralston Lakes

The Pacific Crest Trail cuts through a stark glaciated landscape with very few trees and a whole lot of rock. Turn around occasionally to look back downhill at the twin Echo Lakes, which look even more alluring from a distance. In 0.5 mile (0.8 km), watch for the left turnoff for Tamarack Lake; it's marked by a signed wooden post, but many hikers zoom right past it.

The rock-strewn spur to the lake is only 0.2 mile (0.3 km), but you might need to look for trail cairns to help you find the way through this wilderness of rock. Your first glimpse of sparkling **Tamarack Lake,** hemmed in by Jeffrey pines and mountain hemlocks, incites an enthusiastic "wow." The deep-blue conifer-clad lake is gussied up with a tree-covered island.

As lovely as Tamarack Lake is, keep exploring for another 0.3 mile (0.5 km). A made-by-use trail travels along Tamarack's eastern shore, then follows its southern shore (the path bends to the right as it crosses Tamarack's outlet). With a quick ascent up and over a small granite hillock, you'll spy gorgeous **Ralston Lake,** which sits in a glacially carved bowl below the steep walls of 9,235-foot (2,815-m) Ralston Peak. Much smaller than Tamarack Lake, Ralston Lake punches well above its weight class for alpine scenery. With Ralston Peak lording over this gray-and-blue tableau, you'll have a hard time choosing a spot for lunch and a swim. Expert tip: Any spot you choose will be exactly the right spot.

▲ RALSTON LAKE

DIRECTIONS

From the Y junction of U.S. 50 and Highway 89 in South Lake Tahoe, drive 9.8 miles (15.8 km) southwest on U.S. 50 to the Echo Lakes/Berkeley Camp turnoff on the right; this is Johnson Pass Road. Turn right and drive 0.6 mile (1 km) to Echo Lakes Road. Turn left and drive 1 mile (1.6 km) to the Echo Lakes hikers parking lot, perched on a hill above the Echo Lake Resort store and its boat ramp. If the lot is full, find a space along the shoulder of the road. Follow the path downhill from the parking lot to the resort store. The trail begins at Echo Lake's dam and causeway, located between the boat ramp and the store.

GPS COORDINATES: 38.8347, −120.0442; 38°50'4.9" N, 120°2'39.1" W

BEST NEARBY BREWS

A mere 20 minutes' drive from this trailhead, try some of 16 beers on tap in the lofty warehouse space of **South Lake Brewing Company** (1920 Lake Tahoe Blvd., South Lake Tahoe, 530/578-0087, www. southlakebeer.com, noon-9pm daily). This kid- and dog-friendly gathering spot makes tasty pale ales, IPAs, and German lagers and offers a wealth of entertainment—corn hole, board games, trivia games, and more.

8 Carson Pass to Winnemucca and Round Top Lakes

MOKELUMNE WILDERNESS, ELDORADO NATIONAL FOREST

A colorful riot of blossoms awaits on one of the Sierra Nevada's premier wildflower hikes.

BEST: Wildflower Hikes
DISTANCE: 6.8 miles (10.9 km) round-trip
DURATION: 3 hours
STARTING ELEVATION: 8,600 feet (2,621 m)
ELEVATION GAIN: 920 feet (280 m)
EFFORT: Easy–moderate
TRAIL: Dirt and rock
USERS: Hikers, leashed dogs
SEASON: June–October; accessible by snowshoes in winter
PASSES/FEES: $5 day-use fee per vehicle
MAPS: USGS topographic map "Carson Pass"
TRAILHEAD: Carson Pass Information Station
FACILITIES: Visitor center, vault toilet
CONTACT: Amador Ranger District, 209/295-4251, www.fs.usda.gov/eldorado

START THE HIKE

As is true for most hikes in the Carson Pass area, this trail is incredibly popular all summer, but especially during the peak of the wildflower bloom, which typically occurs in late July. During the flower-palooza, as many as 300 people per day hike this trail's first leg to Winnemucca Lake. If you want to avoid most of the crowds, show up on a weekday and time your trip for early morning or very late afternoon.

▶ **MILE 0-2.4: Carson Pass Trailhead to Winnemucca Lake**
The path starts at the **Carson Pass Information Station**—a log cabin staffed by volunteers—at the top of 8,600-foot (2,621-m) Carson Pass. The path wanders 0.4 mile (0.6 km) through a dense grove of lodgepole pines, their trunks contorted from the heavy snow load faced every winter. A bit farther, the trail breaks out to sagebrush-covered slopes, passing a left fork for **Frog Lake** at 1 mile (1.6 km). This shallow lake, about 50 yards (46 m) off the trail, is a popular stopover for dog walkers. Although it's nowhere near as scenic as Winnemucca or Round Top lakes, it offers a botanical bonus in early summer. On Frog Lake's east end is a huge patch of wild irises that bloom for two to three weeks. If you time your visit just right, consider yourself one lucky hiker.

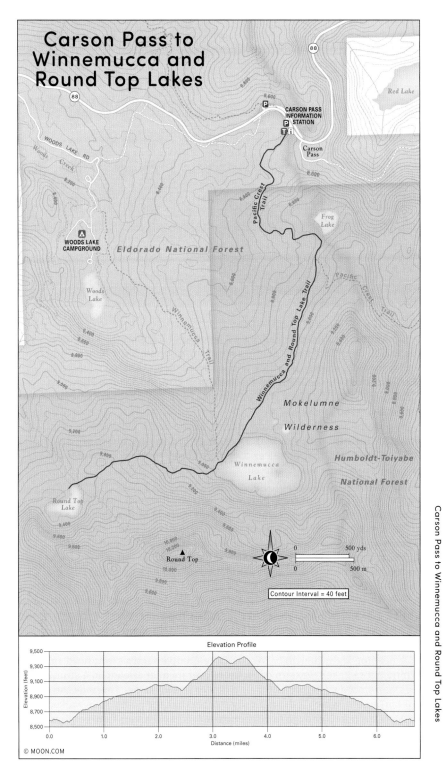

Carson Pass to Winnemucca and Round Top Lakes

88

88

Red Lake

P

CARSON PASS INFORMATION STATION

P

T **i**

Carson Pass

WOODS LAKE RD

Woods Creek

8,200

8,400

8,400

8,600

8,600

8,600

8,800

Pacific Crest Trail

Frog Lake

Pacific Crest Trail

WOODS LAKE CAMPGROUND

Eldorado National Forest

Woods Lake

8,400

8,600

8,800

9,000

Winnemucca Trail

Winnemucca and Round Top Lake Trail

8,800

8,800

9,000

9,200

9,400

9,000

9,200

8,800

8,600

Mokelumne

Wilderness

9,200

9,400

Humboldt-Toiyabe

National Forest

9,000

Winnemucca Lake

9,200

9,400

9,500

Round Top Lake

9,400

9,600

9,800

10,000

10,200

Round Top

10,000

9,800

9,600

9,200

9,400

9,600

9,800

0   500 yds

0   500 m

Contour Interval = 40 feet

Elevation Profile

9,500

9,300

9,100

8,900

8,700

8,500

Elevation (feet)

0.0   1.0   2.0   3.0   4.0   5.0   6.0

Distance (miles)

© MOON.COM

WINNEMUCCA LAKE ▲

Continuing on the main trail, pass a **junction** at 1.2 miles (1.9 km) where the Pacific Crest Trail heads southeast toward Yosemite. Bear right (south) for Winnemucca Lake and enjoy unobstructed views of Round Top Peak. You'll walk directly beneath the fascinating volcanic formation known as Elephants Back. This black cinder "mound" is an ancient lava dome that tops out at 9,580 feet (2,920 m).

During the wildflower season, expect to see some high-octane petal power in the next mile (1.6 km). These high-country meadows are lined with volcanic soil that produces a vibrant flower tapestry of scarlet gilia, paintbrush, blue flax, Sierra lilies, and many other species. Where tiny streams flow across the path, lupine, columbine, and monkey flower grow in profusion. Even if botany isn't your jam, you'll swoon over bountiful blue lupine bouquets and seemingly endless acres of mule's ears.

The dreamy flower wonderland continues to the northern shoreline of **Winnemucca Lake,** a blue-green gem set directly below Round Top Peak. A few spur trails, marked by numbered posts, lead to designated backpacking sites. In July, the sagebrush-dotted meadows edging the lake are ablaze with colorful flowers.

▶ MILE 2.4–3.4: Winnemucca Lake to Round Top Lake

It's tough to leave Winnemucca Lake's bewitching shoreline, but your trek continues west for another mile (1.6 km) to Round Top Lake. Pass a trail heading right (north) to Woods Lake Campground as you head for Winnemucca Lake's western edge. Cross over its inlet stream on a sturdy log, then start a sustained climb up a flower-strewn slope. This mile-long (1.6-km) ascent, which is dramatically steeper than the path you've walked so far, is strenuous enough to discourage most casual hikers from continuing. But some huffing and puffing is a small price to pay for the chance to admire the deeply carved volcanic cliffs that frame Round Top Lake.

▲ WINNEMUCCA LAKE

The climb tops out at 3.3 miles (5.3 km), and a 0.1-mile (0.2-km) descent leads to a **junction** with another trail to Woods Lake Campground, then a short stroll to **Round Top's edge.** About half the size of Winnemucca, this lovely lake is hemmed in by willows and stands of whitebark pines, which offer shade for picnickers. High-alpine flowers thrive in this lofty setting at 9,350 feet (2,850 m) elevation, but the lake's water feels achingly cold even in July and August.

DIRECTIONS

From South Lake Tahoe, drive 13 miles (20.9 km) south on Highway 89 to its junction with Highway 88. Turn right (west) on Highway 88 and drive 8.7 miles (14 km) to the summit of Carson Pass. Park in the large parking lot on the left, next to the log cabin visitor center.

GPS COORDINATES: 38.6951, −119.9894; 38°41'42.4" N, 119°59'21.8" W

BEST NEARBY BREWS

Serving hungry travelers since 1864, the **Kirkwood Inn and Saloon** (Hwy. 88, across from Kirkwood Ski Resort, 209/258-7304, www. kirkwood.com, 3pm-9pm Tues.-Sun.) is housed in a vintage log cabin just 10 minutes' drive west of the trailhead. Order a beer and see if you can spot the bullet holes in the walls from Prohibition days. The kitchen serves up hearty salads, burgers, barbecued ribs, and hot sandwiches.

NEARBY CAMPGROUNDS

NAME	DESCRIPTION	FACILITIES	SEASON	FEE
Lakes Basin	Near Gold Lake, hiking trails, fishing, swimming	24 sites for tents or RVs up to 28 ft/8.5 m, vault toilets, drinking water	mid-May to mid-October	$32
Plumas National Forest, off Gold Lake Highway near Graeagle, 877/444-6777, www.recreation.gov				
Donner Memorial State Park	On the shore of Donner Lake; near hiking trails, fishing, swimming	154 sites for tents or RVs up to 28 ft/8.5 m, restrooms, drinking water, showers	late May to early September	$35
Off I-80 near Truckee, 800/444-7275, www.reservecalifornia.com				
D. L. Bliss State Park	On Lake Tahoe, water sports, swimming, hiking trails	165 sites for tents or RVs up to 18 ft/5.5 m, restrooms, drinking water, showers, dump station	late May to early September	$35-45
Off Highway 89 south of Tahoe City, 800/444-7275, www.reservecalifornia.com				

NEARBY CAMPGROUNDS (continued)

NAME	DESCRIPTION	FACILITIES	SEASON	FEE
Emerald Bay State Park	On Lake Tahoe, water sports, swimming, hiking trails, waterfalls	89 sites for tents or RVs up to 28 ft/8.5 m, restrooms, drinking water, showers	late May to early September	$35

Off Highway 89 north of South Lake Tahoe, 800/444-7275, www.reservecalifornia.com

NAME	DESCRIPTION	FACILITIES	SEASON	FEE
Fallen Leaf Lake	Walk to Fallen Leaf Lake; boat rentals, kayaking, hiking, mountain biking, swimming	206 sites for tents or RVs up to 32 ft/9.8 m, 6 yurts, restrooms, drinking water, showers, dump station	mid-May to mid-October	$41 (yurts $110)

Tahoe National Forest, off Highway 89, South Lake Tahoe, 877/444-6777, www.recreation.gov

▲ UPPER YOSEMITE FALL

SIERRA NEVADA

YOSEMITE NATIONAL PARK

From plunging waterfalls and alpine lakes to granite domes and glistening meadows, Yosemite National Park is a hiker's paradise with more than 800 miles (1,288 km) of trails. Yosemite is nearly the size of Rhode Island at 1,169 square miles (3,028 sq km), but too many visitors don't explore beyond Yosemite Valley, a mere 1 percent of the park's acreage. The 7-mile-long (11.3-km) valley is an incomparable natural wonder, but sublime scenery is also found in the high country of Tioga Pass Road, and alongside Tuolumne Meadows' subalpine expanse. In the park's northwest reaches lies Hetch Hetchy, a reservoir in a valley considered a twin of Yosemite Valley. To the south lies Glacier Point, famous for its postcard vistas. Every region provides a wealth of world-class trails to explore.

▲ HETCH HETCHY RESERVOIR

▲ McGURK MEADOW

◄ VERNAL FALL

1 **Wapama Falls and Hetch Hetchy Reservoir**
DISTANCE: 5 miles (8.1 km) round-trip
DURATION: 2.5 hours
EFFORT: Easy-moderate

2 **May Lake and Mount Hoffmann**
DISTANCE: 5.8 miles (9.3 km) round-trip
DURATION: 4 hours
EFFORT: Moderate

3 **Cathedral Lakes**
DISTANCE: 9.6 miles (15.4 km) round-trip
DURATION: 5-6 hours
EFFORT: Moderate

4 **Lembert Dome and Dog Lake**
DISTANCE: 5 miles (8.1 km) round-trip
DURATION: 3 hours
EFFORT: Easy-moderate

5 **Middle and Upper Gaylor Lakes**
DISTANCE: 3.8 miles (6.1 km) round-trip
DURATION: 2.5 hours
EFFORT: Moderate

6 **Mount Dana**
DISTANCE: 5.6 miles (9 km) round-trip
DURATION: 4 hours
EFFORT: Strenuous

7 **Upper Yosemite Fall**
DISTANCE: 6.4 miles (10.3 km) round-trip
DURATION: 5 hours
EFFORT: Moderate-strenuous

8 **Vernal and Nevada Falls**
DISTANCE: 6 miles (9.7 km) round-trip
DURATION: 4 hours
EFFORT: Moderate

9 **McGurk Meadow and Dewey Point**
DISTANCE: 7.6 miles (12.2 km) round-trip
DURATION: 4 hours
EFFORT: Moderate

10 **Sentinel Dome and Taft Point**
DISTANCE: 4.5 miles (7.2 km) round-trip
DURATION: 2.5 hours
EFFORT: Easy-moderate

11 **Chilnualna Falls**
DISTANCE: 7.7 miles (12.4 km) round-trip
DURATION: 4.5 hours
EFFORT: Moderate

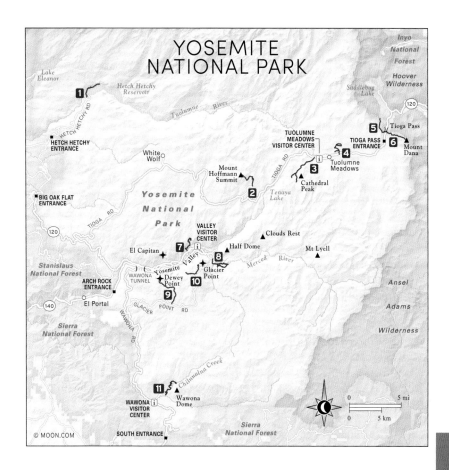

YOSEMITE NATIONAL PARK

1

HETCH HETCHY
ENTRANCE

Lake
Eleanor

Hetch Hetchy
Reservoir

White
Wolf

BIG OAK FLAT
ENTRANCE

Tuolumne River

TUOLUMNE
MEADOWS VISITOR CENTER

Mount
Hoffmann
Summit

2

TIOGA RD

Tenaya
Lake

3

4

Tuolumne
Meadows

Cathedral
Peak

Inyo
National
Forest

Hoover
Wilderness

Saddlebag
Lake

5 Tioga Pass

TIOGA PASS
ENTRANCE

6 Mount
Dana

Yosemite
National
Park

Clouds Rest

Mt Lyell

VALLEY
VISITOR
CENTER

El Capitan

7

Half Dome

8

Glacier
Point

Merced River

Yosemite Valley

WAWONA
TUNNEL

Dewey
Point

9

10

GLACIER   POINT   RD

Ansel

Adams

Wilderness

ARCH ROCK
ENTRANCE

El Portal

WAWONA RD

Stanislaus
National Forest

Sierra
National
Forest

Chilnualna Creek

11

WAWONA
VISITOR
CENTER

Wawona
Dome

SOUTH ENTRANCE

Sierra
National Forest

© MOON.COM

0   5 mi

0   5 km

Wapama Falls and Hetch Hetchy Reservoir

YOSEMITE NATIONAL PARK

A smaller twin to Yosemite Valley, Hetch Hetchy boasts tumbling waterfalls, stark granite cliffs and domes, and meadows exploding with colorful spring wildflowers.

DISTANCE: 5 miles (8.1 km) round-trip

DURATION: 2.5 hours

ELEVATION GAIN: 538 feet (164 m)

EFFORT: Easy-moderate

TRAIL: Concrete dam, tunnel, packed dirt

USERS: Hikers

SEASON: Year-round; road sometimes closes due to snowfall

PASSES/FEES: $35 per vehicle, valid for 7 days

MAPS: On the National Park Service app, or Tom Harrison or National Geographic maps of Yosemite National Park

TRAILHEAD: O'Shaughnessy Dam

FACILITIES: Restroom

CONTACT: Yosemite National Park, 209/372-0200, www.nps.gov/yose

Wildflower and waterfall fans will find plenty to love at Hetch Hetchy, as long as their timing is right. For the best blossom and water show, visit between March and May. By June, flowers and cataracts wither in Hetch Hetchy's intense summer heat. Also check the time of day: Although other Yosemite entrances are open 24 hours daily, the Hetch Hetchy Entrance is open only 8am to 5pm.

START THE HIKE

▶ **MILE 0-1.6: O'Shaughnessy Dam to Tueeulala Falls**

Start by crossing the **O'Shaughnessy Dam,** an astonishing feat of engineering that was completed in 1914. Interpretive plaques explain the building of Hetch Hetchy Reservoir and its critical role in supplying water to the city of San Francisco and its environs. As you admire the deep blue lake and its surrounding granite walls, look for a plume of white water flowing down the northern wall—that's Wapama Falls, this trail's final destination.

On the dam's far side 0.2 mile (0.3 km) in, you'll enter a dimly lit, 500-foot-long (152-m) **tunnel,** where the walls and ceiling often drip with water from recent rains. Kids especially enjoy this spooky-fun stroll through semidarkness. The tunnel opens out to a forest of leafy black oak, ponderosa pine, and incense cedar along the edge of the lake, and you'll hear the pleasant sound of water lapping along the shoreline.

You've now traveled 0.4 mile (0.6 km), and from this point, your trail skirts the northern edge of this 400-foot-deep (122-m) lake that stores the

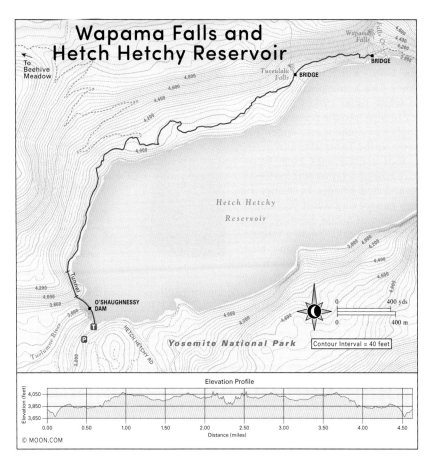

Wapama Falls and Hetch Hetchy Reservoir

To Beehive Meadow

Wapama Falls

Falls Cr.

BRIDGE

Tueeulala Falls

BRIDGE

Hetch Hetchy Reservoir

Tunnel

O'SHAUGHNESSY DAM

HETCH HETCHY RD.

Yosemite National Park

Tuolumne River

0   400 yds

0   400 m

Contour Interval = 40 feet

Elevation Profile

Elevation (feet)

4,050
3,850
3,650

0.00   0.50   1.00   1.50   2.00   2.50   3.00   3.50   4.00   4.50

Distance (miles)

© MOON.COM

Tuolumne River's water. At a **junction** at 1.2 miles (1.9 km), a trail heads left and uphill to Beehive Meadow. Bear right (east) and continue along the water's edge.

In another 0.4 mile (0.6 km), you reach a set of **trail bridges** that carry you across the typically wispy flow of **Tueeulala Falls.** These sturdy bridges will seem like overkill if Tueeulala isn't in full flood mode. If the creek's small watershed isn't continuously fed by snowmelt or heavy rain, the waterfall diminishes quickly. But catch it at just the right time, and you'll see a dazzling sheet of water dropping 1,000 feet (305 m) to the reservoir's surface.

▸ MILE 1.6-2.5: Tueeulala Falls to Wapama Falls
This trail's celebrity waterfall is just under 1 mile (1.6 km) farther, and what a lovely mile it is, highlighted by petite meadows, broad granite slabs, and grand views of the reservoir's granite cliffs. Because your trail ascends ever so gently, your wide-angle views of the reservoir keep growing wider. Here the lake is dramatically edged by slate-gray boulders and forest-green pines, making its deep waters appear sapphire blue. On sunny days, the afternoon sunlight creates a twinkling show on its surface.

At 2.4 miles (3.9 km), you round a corner and reach the base of **Wapama Falls,** which drops on Falls Creek. This horsetail-shaped plume of white water makes a thundering plunge into the reservoir, and it holds its volume much longer than neighboring Tueeulala Falls.

Your trail crosses over Wapama's flow on a series of three wooden and steel bridges. In spring, you may get soaking wet if you stop to snap photos while crossing these bridges—the falls create a tremendous amount of spray and mist. During peak snowmelt, which can occur any time March to early May, Wapama Falls sometimes gushes so furiously that its pounding flow floods these bridges, and the National Park Service closes this part of the trail.

On a warm sunny day, you might be tempted to stick your toes in the lake, but Hetch Hetchy is a drinking water reservoir, so the rules are strict: No swimming, no boating, no contact with the water. Fishing is permitted, however, and you may see a few anglers tossing in a line from the shore. This is an out-and-back trip, so retrace your steps when you're ready.

DIRECTIONS

From Groveland, drive east on Highway 120 for 22.5 miles (36 km) to the Evergreen Road turnoff, signed for Hetch Hetchy Reservoir; it's 1 mile (1.6 km) west of the Yosemite's Big Oak Flat/Highway 120 Entrance Station. Drive north on Evergreen Road for 7.4 miles (11.9 km), then turn right onto Hetch Hetchy Road. Drive 9 miles (14.5 km) to the dam and trailhead.

GPS COORDINATES: 37.9454, −119.7883; 37°56'43.4" N, 119°47'17.9" W

BEST NEARBY BITES

You'll drive right by **Evergreen Lodge** (33160 Evergreen Rd., Groveland, 209/379-2606 or 800/935-6343, www.evergreenlodge.com, noon-10pm daily summer, shorter hours in winter) on the way to Hetch Hetchy (it's 20 minutes from the trailhead). In addition to a small store where you can pick up picnic supplies, the lodge's tavern serves elk chili, kale salad, and hearty burgers, plus beer and wine.

2

May Lake and Mount Hoffmann
YOSEMITE NATIONAL PARK

Gem-like May Lake is nestled in a granite pocket below 10,850-foot (3,307-m) Mount Hoffmann, a commanding precipice that guards the exact geographical center of Yosemite National Park.

DISTANCE: 5.8 miles (9.3 km) round-trip

DURATION: 4 hours

STARTING ELEVATION: 8,846 feet (2,696 m)

ELEVATION GAIN: 1,912 feet (583 m)

EFFORT: Moderate

TRAIL: Packed dirt, rock scrambling

USERS: Hikers

SEASON: July–October; Tioga Pass Road is closed November–June

PASSES/FEES: $35 per vehicle, valid for 7 days

MAPS: On the National Park Service app, or Tom Harrison or National Geographic maps of Yosemite National Park

TRAILHEAD: May Lake/Snow Flat Parking Area

FACILITIES: Restroom

CONTACT: Yosemite National Park, 209/372-0200, www.nps.gov/yose

START THE HIKE

▶ MILE 0-1.2: Parking Area to May Lake

The trail begins at the **May Lake/Snow Flat parking area,** a scenic 2-mile (3.2-km) drive from Tioga Pass Road. From the trail sign on the northwest side of the parking lot, you'll hike uphill beneath the scattered shade of red firs and lodgepole pines, but there's still plenty of sun exposure on this south-facing trail. The path ascends moderately, climbing past large granite boulders and venerable old trees, and as you gain elevation, you also gain views to the east of Tenaya Canyon and the Cathedral Range (look over your right shoulder). Ahead of you—to the north—you'll spot the granite wall that backs May Lake. It's easy to see where your path is heading.

In only 1 mile (1.6 km) and 500 feet (152 m) of elevation gain, you'll pass a **backpackers' campground** and find yourself on the southern shore of the round cobalt-blue lake at 9,329 feet (2,843 m) elevation. **May Lake** is lovely enough on its own, but its towering granite cirque seals the deal. Wandering along this scenic granite-ringed shoreline is a pleasant way to spend the afternoon.

In the summer months, you'll notice a stone structure and 20 tent cabins on the lake's east side—this is the **May Lake High Sierra Camp.** Hikers who were savvy enough to reserve months in advance spend the night at this rustic camp and enjoy hearty homemade meals.

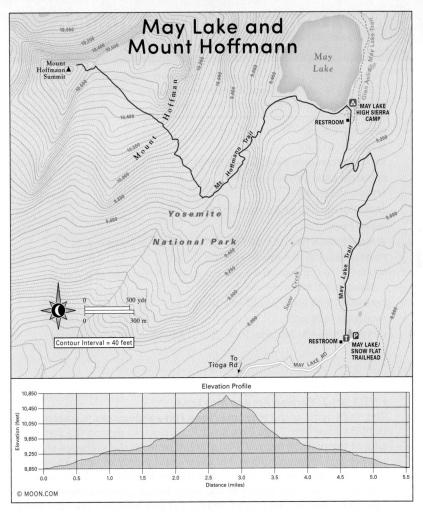

May Lake and Mount Hoffmann

Elevation Profile

▶ **MILE 1.2–2.9: May Lake to Mount Hoffmann's Summit**

Less ambitious hikers in your group may be content to hang out on May Lake's beautiful shoreline, but if you're in a peak-bagging mood, push on to Mount Hoffmann's summit, another 1,500 feet (457 m) higher than where you stand.

Follow the trail leading west (to your left as you face the lake). You'll follow the contour around May Lake's southwest shoreline, then begin to climb high above its western edge. The trail is easy to follow for the first mile (1.6 km) beyond the lake, but it becomes more indistinct as you progress. In the last 0.5 mile (0.8 km), look for rock cairns to help you find the way. For the final summit push, you'll need to focus on your footing and employ safe scrambling skills—use your hands for balance on the boulder-strewn climb.

Mount Hoffmann's summit ridgeline, while not astoundingly high at 10,850 feet (3,307 m), offers one of the park's most sublime views. It's situated in Yosemite's exact geographical center, providing a 360-degree

▲ HIKERS ASCENDING MOUNT HOFFMANN

panorama that takes in many obvious landmarks, including Half Dome, Clouds Rest, Tenaya Lake, and May Lake. The peak has two main summits; the one topped by a weather station is the highest. Explore the entire ridgeline, and visit both summits for different perspectives on this astounding view.

While you're up here so close to the heavens, give a nod to the peak's namesake, topographer Charles F. Hoffmann. He explored and mapped much of the Sierra Nevada Mountains in the 1860s and 1870s.

For your return trip, retrace your steps.

DIRECTIONS

From the Big Oak Flat Entrance Station on Highway 120, drive southeast 7.7 miles (12.4 km) to Crane Flat, and then turn left to stay on Highway 120 (Tioga Pass Rd.). Drive 26.6 miles (43 km) to the May Lake Road turnoff, on the left near mile marker T-21. Turn left and drive 2 miles (3.2 km) to the May Lake/Snow Flat trailhead.

GPS COORDINATES: 37.8325, −119.4910; 37°49'57" N, 119°29'27.6" W

BEST NEARBY BITES

After your hike, drive 15 minutes to **White Wolf Lodge** (Tioga Pass Rd., 209/372-8416, www.travelyosemite.com, 7:30am-9:30am and 6pm-8pm daily summer), a high-country eatery next to White Wolf Campground. The dinner menu typically includes New York steak, chicken, a vegetarian entrée, and hamburgers. The wine list is more extensive than you'd expect in the high country, and the setting can't be beat. It's best to call ahead to secure a spot—especially at dinnertime.

3

Cathedral Lakes
YOSEMITE NATIONAL PARK

Two alpine lakes tucked beneath the jagged peaks of the Cathedral Range are coveted destinations for Tuolumne Meadows hikers.

DISTANCE: 9.6 miles (15.4 km) round-trip

DURATION: 5-6 hours

STARTING ELEVATION: 8,580 feet (2,615 m)

ELEVATION GAIN: 1,648 feet (502 m)

EFFORT: Moderate

TRAIL: Packed dirt

USERS: Hikers

SEASON: July-October; Tioga Pass Road is closed November-June

PASSES/FEES: $35 per vehicle, valid for 7 days

MAPS: On the National Park Service app, or Tom Harrison or National Geographic maps of Yosemite National Park

TRAILHEAD: Cathedral Lakes Trailhead

FACILITIES: Restroom

CONTACT: Yosemite National Park, 209/372-0200, www.nps.gov/yose

W ith its unparalleled alpine scenery, Cathedral Lakes has long been one of Tuolumne Meadow's top day-hiking and backpacking destinations. As a result, this heavily trafficked path has suffered from erosion and overuse issues. In 2021, the Yosemite Conservancy started a multiyear project to relocate parts of the trail, fill in human-made ruts, protect native plants, and restore disturbed meadows. Do your part by obeying all trail signs during and after this major restoration project.

START THE HIKE

▶ **MILE 0-3.2: Cathedral Lakes Trailhead to Lower Cathedral Lake**

Starting from the Cathedral Lakes Trailhead, follow the Cathedral Lakes Trail west for 0.5 mile on a mostly level grade. Cross Budd Creek on a footbridge, then turn left to join the **John Muir Trail.** The initial climb will get your heart beating quickly, both from the high elevation and the steep grade. You'll gain about 600 feet (183 m) in the first 0.8 mile (1.3 km). Although the trail starts out with a fair amount of exposure, you'll soon enter a dense

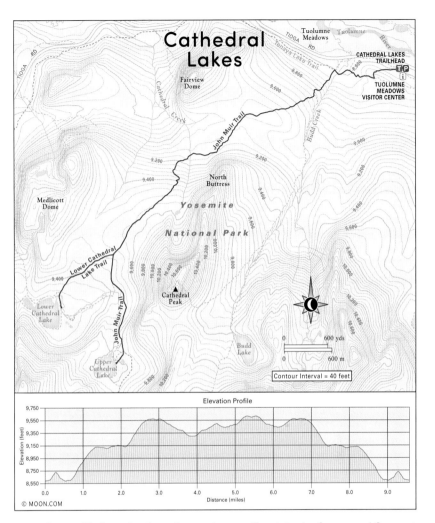

forest of lodgepole pines. Soon other conifers join the forest—red firs, sugar pines, and whitebark pines.

The trail levels out for 0.25 mile (0.4 km), giving you a short breather, and then the steepest stretch occurs between the first and second mile (1.6-3.2 km) as you curve around the west side of the **North Buttress,** an outlier of Cathedral Peak. The granite monolith is a harbinger of more glacially sculpted marvels to come. If you're hiking in July, you may still find patches of snow on this shady north-facing slope.

At 1.8 miles (2.9 km), you'll break out of the conifers to have nonstop views of the highest turrets of 10,940-foot (3,334-m) **Cathedral Peak.** With every few steps, you get a different perspective on "The Great Cathedral," as John Muir called it. If you've admired the peak's soaring white-granite spires from Tioga Road or Tuolumne Meadows, you'll be surprised at how different the formation looks from close up.

At 2.5 miles (4 km), you reach the **turnoff** for Lower Cathedral Lake, a new trail that was constructed in 2021. Turn right (west), depart the John

Muir Trail, and reach **Lower Cathedral Lake**'s northeast shore in 0.7 mile (1.1 km). Set in a classic glacial cirque at 9,300 feet (2,835 m), the lake is a dreamlike tableau of blue water and polished granite. You're surrounded by peaks and spires that were carved by glaciers: Tressider Peak, Echo Peaks, and the twin towers of Cathedral Peak. If you wander a bit around the north shore, you'll find an intriguing vista that overlooks Tenaya Lake. Swimming in Lower Cathedral Lake is frigid but exhilarating.

▶ **MILE 3.2-5: Lower Cathedral Lake to Upper Cathedral Lake**
Plenty of hikers call it a day at Lower Cathedral Lake, but since you've already completely most of the elevation gain, it's worth visiting **Upper Cathedral Lake** as well. Backtrack along the Lower Cathedral Lake spur trail, then rejoin the John Muir Trail and head right (south). You'll have a delightfully easy stroll through flower-strewn alpine meadows to reach the smaller upper lake at 9,600 feet (2,926 m) elevation. From its shoreline, Cathedral Peak is even closer and more alluring. Everywhere you look, you can see evidence of the great rivers of ice that created this glacial wonderland.

▶ **MILE 5-9.6: Upper Cathedral Lake to Cathedral Lakes Trailhead**
It's hard to tear yourself away from all this alpine beauty, but when it's time to head back, follow the John Muir Trail north, all the way back to your car.

DIRECTIONS

From Yosemite's Big Oak Flat Entrance Station on Highway 120, drive southeast 7.7 miles (12.4 km) to Crane Flat, then turn left to stay on Highway 120. Drive 37.5 miles (60 km) to Tuolumne Meadows and the right turnoff signed for Cathedral Lakes (near the Tuolumne Meadows Visitor Center). Park in the large parking lot and follow the signed trail from its southwest edge.

GPS COORDINATES: 37.8734, −119.3827; 37°52'24.2" N, 119°22'57.7" W

BEST NEARBY BITES
Drive 5 miles (8.1 km) to the **Tuolumne Meadows Lodge Dining Room** (Tioga Pass Rd., 209/372-8413, https://travelyosemite.com, 7am-9am and 5:30pm-8pm daily summer). In a large canvas tent right next to the Tuolumne River, you'll sit down to a dinner of trout, chicken, or steak and share trail-talk with your neighbors at the table. If you aren't staying at Tuolumne Meadows Lodge, it's wise to call ahead for a dinner reservation.

Lembert Dome and Dog Lake

YOSEMITE NATIONAL PARK

Hike to the top of an 800-foot-high (244-m) granite dome that lords over Tuolumne Meadows, then picnic at a tranquil lake.

DISTANCE: 5 miles (8.1 km) round-trip

DURATION: 3 hours

STARTING ELEVATION: 8,720 feet (2,652 m)

ELEVATION GAIN: 915 feet (279 m)

EFFORT: Easy-moderate

TRAIL: Packed dirt, steep-sided granite dome

USERS: Hikers

SEASON: July-October; Tioga Pass Road is closed November-June

PASSES/FEES: $35 per vehicle, valid for 7 days

MAPS: On the National Park Service app, or Tom Harrison or National Geographic maps of Yosemite National Park

TRAILHEAD: Dog Lake Trailhead

FACILITIES: Restroom

CONTACT: Yosemite National Park, 209/372-0200, www.nps.gov/yose

START THE HIKE

▶ MILE 0-0.8: Dog Lake Trailhead to Lembert Dome

From the **Dog Lake Trailhead,** the hike starts unceremoniously with a quick uphill tromp through piney woods for 0.1 mile (0.2 km), then a cautious crossing of **Tioga Pass Road** (look both ways!). With that out of the way, the aerobic workout begins: A series of switchbacks lead steeply uphill through a lodgepole pine forest. Most hikers will feel the altitude as they climb this hill—you're starting out at 8,720 feet (2,658 m). At a **junction** at 0.5 mile (0.8 km), you'll see a trail sign directing you left for Lembert Dome. Depart the main trail here and follow this path westward through pines and firs for 0.2 mile (0.3 km), then depart the trees and take your first steps on **Lembert Dome's** exposed granite summit.

If you've never walked on polished granite before, your feet will enjoy a new experience. Lembert's granite is remarkably "grippy"—it's much less slippery than it looks. Make your way up the dome's slope any way you please—there's no formal trail here, so just pick a route that looks good to you.

Granite domes, a common geological feature in the Sierra, are essentially large, rounded rocks formed by the creation of slowly expanding granite. As the granite expands, cracks form, creating individual layers of rock near the surface. Over time, exfoliation occurs—the outer layers of rock break apart and fall off, removing sharp corners and angles from the rock and leaving a smooth round dome. Lembert Dome is a special kind of dome called a roche moutonnée, a French geologic term that designates a dome with one sheer side and one sloping side. Rock climbers tackle

YOSEMITE NATIONAL PARK

Lembert Dome and Dog Lake

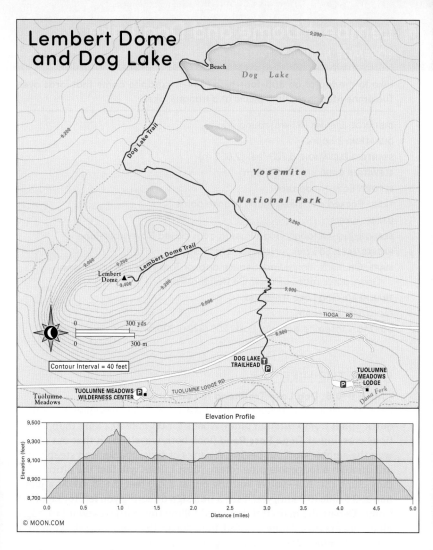

Lembert Dome and Dog Lake

Dog Lake

Beach

Yosemite National Park

Dog Lake Trail

Lembert Dome Trail

Lembert Dome ▲ 9,406

0   300 yds
0   300 m

Contour Interval = 40 feet

TIOGA   RD

DOG LAKE TRAILHEAD

TUOLUMNE MEADOWS LODGE

TUOLUMNE MEADOWS WILDERNESS CENTER

TUOLUMNE LODGE RD

Tuolumne Meadows

Dana Fork

Elevation Profile

© MOON.COM

Lembert Dome's sheer western escarpment; hikers simply hoof it up the sloping eastern side.

When you reach the summit at 9,450 feet (2,880 m) elevation, your reward is an astounding view of Tuolumne Meadows' broad grassy expanse extending 2 miles (3.2 km) alongside the snaking Tuolumne River, plus a wonderland of granite domes and peaks in Yosemite's high country. With the exception of Tioga Pass Road's ribbon of asphalt, the vista you see here today is the same as what Jean-Baptiste Lembert saw in the mid-1880s. The dome's namesake was a Canadian sheepherder who homesteaded in Tuolumne Meadows.

▶ MILE 0.8-2.2: Lembert Dome to Dog Lake's Western Edge

After tearing yourself away from Lembert Dome's summit view, backtrack down the dome to the main trail you recently departed. You could turn right here and return to your car, but Dog Lake is remarkably close by, and you've already completed all the elevation gain required. Turn left (north) and wander 0.3 mile (0.5 km) on a very mellow grade through lodgepole pines and white firs to a **T junction.** Turn right (northeast) and reach a second **junction** in another 0.3 mile (0.5 km), where the main trail heads left (north) to Young Lakes. Go right (northeast) again, and in a few footsteps you're standing on **Dog Lake**'s western edge.

▸ MILE 2.2–3.4: Dog Lake Loop
Set at 9,170 feet (2,795 m) elevation and framed by the mighty profiles of Mount Dana and Mount Gibbs, Dog Lake is wide, shallow, and deeply blue. Some hikers choose a swimming or picnicking spot right here, but instead, take a leisurely 1-mile (1.6-km) stroll around the lake's perimeter. On the lake's eastern edge is a sandy swimming **beach** that's worth the extra walk. Keep your eyes peeled for bald eagles, which are often seen diving for trout.

▸ MILE 3.4–5: Dog Lake's Western Edge to Dog Lake Trailhead
Now that you've explored both Dog Lake and Lembert Dome, retrace your steps back downhill to your car.

DIRECTIONS
From Yosemite's Big Oak Flat Entrance Station on Highway 120, drive southeast 7.7 miles (12.4 km) to Crane Flat, then turn left to stay on Highway 120. Drive 39.5 miles (64 km) to the eastern edge of Tuolumne Meadows and the signed right turnoff for Wilderness Permits and Tuolumne Meadow Lodge. Turn right and drive 0.4 mile (0.6 km) toward Tuolumne Lodge, then park in the lot on your left signed for Dog Lake and John Muir Trail. The trail begins on the north side of the parking lot.

GPS COORDINATES: 37.8784, −119.3389; 37°52'42.2" N, 119°20'20" W

BEST NEARBY BITES
Only 1 mile (1.6 km) from this trailhead is the **Tuolumne Meadows Grill** (Tioga Pass Rd., next to the Tuolumne Meadows Store, 209/372-8426, www.travelyosemite.com, 8am–5pm daily summer), a Yosemite institution that knows how to refuel hungry hikers. The grill produces delicious breakfasts (buckwheat pancakes, biscuit sandwiches, crisp bacon) and hearty lunches (hamburgers, veggie burgers, chicken sandwiches, and veggie chili). Soft-serve ice cream cones are a big hit on warm summer days.

Start climbing at nearly 10,000 feet (3,048 m) elevation and discover a high-alpine landscape dotted with relics from Yosemite's mining past.

DISTANCE: 3.8 miles (6.1 km) round-trip

DURATION: 2.5 hours

STARTING ELEVATION: 9,960 feet (3,036 m)

ELEVATION GAIN: 1,227 feet (374 m)

EFFORT: Moderate

TRAIL: Packed dirt

USERS: Hikers

SEASON: July–October; Tioga Pass Road is closed November–June

PASSES/FEES: $35 per vehicle, valid for 7 days

MAPS: On the National Park Service app, or Tom Harrison or National Geographic maps of Yosemite National Park

TRAILHEAD: Gaylor Lakes Trailhead

FACILITIES: Restroom

CONTACT: Yosemite National Park, 209/372-0200, www.nps.gov/yose

START THE HIKE

▶ **MILE 0-1: Gaylor Lakes Trailhead to Middle Gaylor Lake**

Beginning near **Tioga Pass,** just shy of 10,000 feet (3,048 m), this trail makes a butt-kicking high-altitude ascent that starts on the north side of the parking lot and doesn't relent for the first 0.7 mile (1.1 km). There's no opportunity for a warm-up; prepare to start breathing hard right away. As you make your way up this 600-foot (183-m) elevation gain, pause as often as necessary to slow down your racing heart and admire views of austere-looking 13,061-foot (3,981-m) Mount Dana to the south.

When your aching legs gain the **ridgetop saddle** at 0.9 mile (1.4 km), you can see down the north side to Middle Gaylor Lake, elevation 10,335 feet (3,150 m), a sparkling blue tarn that's the size of a couple of football fields. This alluring vision will remind you why you tackled this relentless grade. Make the 200-foot (61-m) descent over 0.1 mile (0.2 km) to **Middle Gaylor's shoreline,** where you'll likely see a few anglers vying for the attention of dinner-size trout.

▶ **MILE 1-1.5: Middle Gaylor Lake to Upper Gaylor Lake**

From where the trail deposits you on the lakeshore, head to your right (east). The path skirts the lake's eastern edge for 0.3 mile (0.5 km), then turns east, following the course of its inlet creek. You'll hike gently uphill through a high-alpine meadow. You'll know for certain that you're in the rarified landscape of Yosemite's highest country when you see a fat

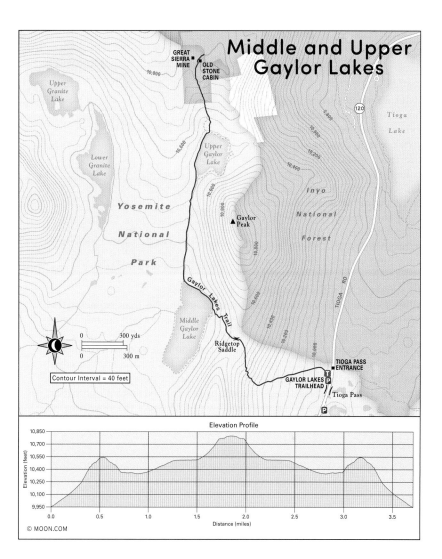

Elevation Profile

© MOON.COM

marmot perched on top of a boulder or a tiny pika scampering among the grasses.

One mile (1.6 km) of this easy rambling through flower-filled grasslands brings you to **Upper Gaylor Lake,** elevation 10,480 feet (3,194 m). Smaller and shallower than the middle lake, Upper Gaylor is backed by conical-shaped Gaylor Peak.

‣ MILE 1.5–1.9: Upper Gaylor Lake to Great Sierra Mine Site

After admiring this beautiful spot, follow the trail as it veers left (northeast) to the upper lake's northern edge, then departs the lake and heads steeply uphill for 0.2 mile (0.3 km). You'll arrive at the walls of an old **stone cabin,** a relic from Yosemite's 1880s silver mining era. Although the cabin's roof is long gone, its 3-foot-thick (1-m) walls remain. The walls were constructed with carefully stacked rock slabs. There's no evidence of mortar

between the rocks, so the wind must have whistled through those walls.

It's a fun exercise to imagine the life of the miners who braved this extreme landscape to pursue their strike-it-rich dreams. Uphill from the cabin you'll find a half-dozen collapsed rubble-filled mine shafts. This spot was known as "Tioga Hill," site of the **Great Sierra Mine,** but like so many High Sierra mining operations, the mine turned out to be not so great. The mining company built a small town here in anticipation of the massive riches to be extracted from the Sheepherder silver lode, but the precious metal was more elusive than expected. No ore was produced, and after only a few years, the town and the mine were abandoned in 1884.

As fascinating as these relics are, your vision will be drawn to the vista of Upper Gaylor Lake and Gaylor Peak from this high crest. You could easily argue that the sought-after riches are right here in plain sight: a hauntingly beautiful landscape marked by red-colored metamorphic rock, high-alpine wildflowers, and precious few people. Savor the view, then retrace your steps back to your car.

DIRECTIONS

From Yosemite's Big Oak Flat Entrance Station on Highway 120, drive southeast 7.7 miles (12.4 km) to Crane Flat, then turn left to stay on Highway 120. Drive 46 miles (74 km) to the Gaylor Lakes parking lot on the road's north side, just before the Tioga Pass Entrance Station.

GPS COORDINATES: 37.9101, −119.2581; 37°54′36.4″ N, 119°15′29.2″ W

BEST NEARBY BITES

A 12-mile (19.3-km) drive down Tioga Pass brings you to the **Tioga Gas Mart,** which is both a gas station and the home of the **Whoa Nellie Deli** (Hwy. 120 and U.S. 395, Lee Vining, 760/647-1088, www.whoanelliedeli.com, 6:30am-9pm daily summer, closed winter). Order the veggie chili, buffalo meatloaf, or World Famous Fish Tacos—perfectly fried and served with lots of crunchy cabbage. The deli also makes sandwiches, veggie burgers, hamburgers, hot dogs, and pizza by the slice.

Earn bragging rights by conquering Yosemite's second-highest summit at 13,061 feet (3,981 m).

BEST: Wildflower Hikes

DISTANCE: 5.6 miles (9 km) round-trip

DURATION: 4 hours

STARTING ELEVATION: 9,960 feet (3,036 m)

ELEVATION GAIN: 3,100 feet (945 m)

EFFORT: Strenuous

TRAIL: Packed dirt, loose talus and scree

USERS: Hikers

SEASON: July–October; Tioga Pass Road is closed November–June

PASSES/FEES: $35 per vehicle, valid for 7 days

MAPS: On the National Park Service app, or Tom Harrison or National Geographic maps of Yosemite National Park

TRAILHEAD: Gaylor Lakes Trailhead

FACILITIES: Restroom

CONTACT: Yosemite National Park, 209/372-0200, www.nps.gov/yose

D
espite the short mileage, this is a grueling hike. A whopping 3,100 feet (945 m) of elevation gain is packed into less than 3 miles (4.8 km), and there's no maintained trail to the summit, just a web of made-by-use trails crisscrossing the upper mountain's scree slopes. Add in the high-altitude factor and you're facing a butt-kicking grind. Even so, hardy hikers summit this peak every summer day. Best advice: Hike much slower than your normal pace, drink a ton of water before and during the climb, and if you start to feel a headache or nausea coming on, head back downhill immediately.

START THE HIKE

▶ **MILE 0-1.8: Gaylor Lakes Trailhead to Rocky Plateau**
Start at the **Gaylor Lakes Trailhead** next to the **Tioga Pass** Entrance Station. Cross to the south side of Tioga Pass Road and begin hiking southeast on the unsigned but obvious trail that starts by the station's small employee parking lot. The trip begins as a pleasant ramble through Dana Meadows, heading due east and very gently uphill past two large ponds. This is your warm-up.

Beyond the meadow, you'll enter a lodgepole and whitebark pine forest, then head into a series of **rocky switchbacks** at 0.5 mile (0.8 km). The grade quickly intensifies, but this first stretch of climbing comes with a spectacular distraction: an alpine wildflower show that usually peaks in late July. Lupine, larkspur, paintbrush, senecio, monkey flower, columbine, corn

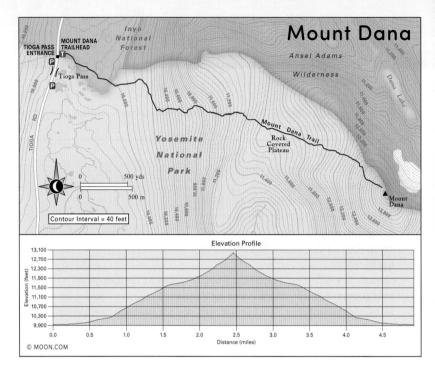

Mount Dana

Inyo National Forest

TIOGA PASS ENTRANCE

MOUNT DANA TRAILHEAD

Tioga Pass

Ansel Adams Wilderness

Dana Lake

TIOGA RD

Yosemite National Park

Mount Dana Trail

Rock Covered Plateau

▲ Mount Dana

0   500 yds
0   500 m

Contour Interval = 40 feet

Elevation Profile

Elevation (feet)

13,100
12,700
12,300
11,900
11,500
11,100
10,700
10,300
9,900

0.0   0.5   1.0   1.5   2.0   2.5   3.0   3.5   4.0   4.5

Distance (miles)

© MOON.COM

lily—they're all here and showing off their brilliant colors. The climbing gets tougher as you depart the flower fields and climb above the tree line at 1 mile (1.6 km). From here on, you won't find a lick of shade.

The trail continues its relentless uphill grind to the 11,700-foot (3,566-m) mark, where a 4-foot-high (1.2-m) trail cairn marks a large **rock-covered plateau** at 1.8 miles (2.9 km). This is a good place to rest and check on your physical and mental state. Although the summit may look like it's fairly close, you still have a long hard mile (1.6 km) to go.

▸ **MILE 1.8-2.8: Rocky Plateau to Mount Dana's Summit**

Two fairly obvious paths head east and uphill from this plateau; pick either one and continue onward, zigzagging your way up the shale-covered slope. In the final mile (1.6 km), you must gain 1,300 feet (396 m), and to call it "slow going" would be a major understatement. There's no shade, but there's often a fierce wind, plenty of loose rock underfoot, and the breathtakingly thin air of high altitude. (Note that your mileage may vary here; it's 1 mile (1.6 km) if you take the most direct route, but plenty of hikers opt to decrease the grade by adding in more zigs and zags.)

If you're extremely fortunate, your timing will coincide with the two-to three-week period when purple-blue sky pilot blooms among the scree and patches of lingering snow on Dana's upper flanks. You'll only find this exquisite flower at the Sierra's highest elevations. Its bloom time is typically late July, although every year is slightly different.

When you finally reach **Dana's summit,** you'll witness one of the finest views in the Sierra. Your field of vision encompasses Mono Lake, Ellery and Saddlebag Lakes, Glacier Canyon, Tuolumne Meadows, Lembert

▲ ROCK CAIRN AT THE HALFWAY POINT UP MOUNT DANA

Dome, and an untold wealth of peaks and precipices. Bring a map so you can identify all you survey, or forget the map and just take in the majesty of it all.

You may find the downhill return on the same trail to be almost as strenuous as the uphill journey—use your hiking poles to take the pressure off your knees and hips.

DIRECTIONS

From Yosemite's Big Oak Flat Entrance station on Highway 120, drive southeast 7.7 miles (12.4 km) to Crane Flat, then turn left to stay on Highway 120. Drive 46 miles (74 km) to the Gaylor Lakes parking lot, on the road's north side, just before the Tioga Pass Entrance station.

GPS COORDINATES: 37.9101, −119.2581; 37°54'36.4" N, 119°15'29.2" W

BEST NEARBY BITES

A 13-mile (20.9-km) drive down Tioga Pass brings you into town, where **The Basin Café** (349 Lee Vining Ave., Lee Vining, 760/914-4224, 7am-7pm Wed.-Sun. May-Oct.) is tucked into the back parking lot of the Lakeview Lodge. Burgers, hot sandwiches, pastas, and salads are on the menu. Wine and beer are available, and you can eat outdoors among the flowers or indoors in the colorful café.

7 Upper Yosemite Fall

YOSEMITE NATIONAL PARK

Trek to the top of the tallest waterfall in North America and fifth highest in the world.

BEST: Waterfall Hikes

DISTANCE: 6.4 miles (10.3 km) round-trip

DURATION: 5 hours

ELEVATION GAIN: 3,018 feet (920 m)

EFFORT: Moderate-strenuous

TRAIL: Packed dirt, granite

USERS: Hikers

SEASON: Year-round; trail may be icy in winter

PASSES/FEES: $35 per vehicle, valid for 7 days

MAPS: On the National Park Service app, or Tom Harrison or National Geographic maps of Yosemite National Park

TRAILHEAD: Upper Yosemite Fall Trailhead

FACILITIES: Restroom

CONTACT: Yosemite National Park, 209/372-0200, www.nps.gov/yose

There's no feeling quite like standing at Yosemite Falls' brink and peering down at its stream plunging 2,425 feet (739 m) to Yosemite Valley's floor. It's so exhilarating that hundreds of park visitors hike this strenuous trail every day in spring and early summer. But check the calendar before you go: April, May, and June are the peak water flow months. Yosemite Falls usually dwindles to a trickle by midsummer.

START THE HIKE

Before you start walking, be forewarned: This trail has more than 100 switchbacks, gains more than 3,000 feet (914 m), and climbs a south-facing slope with several sunny exposed sections. Bring plenty of water and lots of trail snacks, and start early in the day.

▶ **MILE 0-1.2: Upper Yosemite Fall Trailhead to Columbia Rock**

From the **Upper Yosemite Fall Trailhead** in Camp 4, the route begins climbing immediately, switch-backing uphill through a dense forest of black oaks and manzanita. At 1.2 miles (1.9 km) and 1,200 feet (366 m) above your starting point, you reach a spectacular viewpoint atop **Columbia Rock** (sometimes called Columbia Point), which offers a magnificent vista over Yosemite Valley and east toward Half Dome. You'll want to pause here—both to admire the view and catch your breath. Some hikers who are already feeling daunted by the ascent will make this high perch their

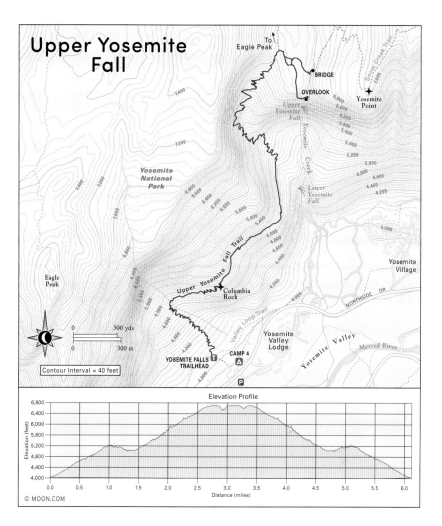

Upper Yosemite Fall

Elevation Profile

turnaround, but if you're determined to get to the top of North America's tallest waterfall, push on.

▶ MILE 1.2–2.8: Columbia Rock to Eagle Peak Trail Junction

The trail levels out for a brief stretch, then makes a dismaying descent between 1.3 and 1.6 miles (2.1-2.6 km); you'll need to gain back that lost elevation. But at the 1.6-mile (2.6-km) mark, you're suddenly rewarded with a surprising look at the colossal plume of **Upper Yosemite Fall.** That view will sustain you over the next mile (1.6 km) of ascent, and you'll hike close enough to the thundering cataract to feel its tremendous energy. Your skin will cool from the chill of windblown spray and mist.

The trail keeps climbing through multiple switchbacks, then departs the trees and enters a cleft in the cliffs just beneath the valley's north rim at 2.3 miles (3.7 km). This rockbound erosion-prone ravine is the recipient of frequent rockfalls and avalanches, and park crews often have to repair or rebuild the trail here. The most destructive slide, which killed 3 hikers and injured 19 others, occurred in 1980.

Your quadriceps will complain about the merciless grade for the last 0.5 mile (0.8 km) to the Valley's north rim, but the unobstructed views of Yosemite Valley will spur you onward. Soon after gaining the rim, you reach a **junction** with the trail to Eagle Peak heading left. You're at 6,700 feet (2,042 m), this trail's highest point.

▶ **MILE 2.8-3.2: Eagle Peak Trail Junction to Yosemite Falls Viewpoint and Creek**

With all the hard work behind you, veer right (southeast) at the Eagle Peak junction and walk another 150 yards (137 m) to a right **turnoff** signed simply as **"Overlook."** Follow this 0.2-mile (0.3-km) spur trail down a set of narrow granite stairsteps to score the day's biggest thrill: You'll stand next to roaring **Yosemite Creek** on a ledge above the lip of Upper Yosemite Fall. It's wise to hold on to the metal railing that's in place here while you admire the waterfall's dizzying drop to the floor of Yosemite Valley.

Once your adrenaline settles down, backtrack 0.2 mile (0.3 km) to the main trail and continue another 100 yards (91 m) to a sturdy **bridge** over Yosemite Creek. Near the bridge are plenty of level creekside spots where you can kick back with a sandwich and savor the day's rewards.

DIRECTIONS

From Yosemite Village, drive west on Northside Drive 0.75 mile (1.2 km) to the Yosemite Valley Lodge parking lot, on the left. Park on the lot's far west side and walk across the road to Camp 4. If these spaces are full, park near the Lower Yosemite Fall Trailhead, on the east side of Yosemite Valley Lodge. You can also ride the Yosemite Valley shuttle bus to stop 7 at Yosemite Valley Lodge.

GPS COORDINATES: 37.7428, −119.6032; 37°44'34.1" N, 119°36'11.5" W

BEST NEARBY BITES

You can walk straight off this trail into Yosemite Valley Lodge, where you'll find comfy seating in the ultra-casual **Mountain Room Lounge** (4pm-9pm daily). This spacious cocktail lounge has an open-sided Swedish-style fireplace, TVs broadcasting sports, beer and wine, and a short but satisfying menu of chili, soup, sandwiches, and salads. In a separate building about 50 feet (15 m) away is the **Mountain Room Restaurant,** a more formal dining room with large windows and a view of Yosemite Falls. The restaurant serves a crowd-pleasing menu of steaks, burgers, trout, and french onion soup.

The loop trail visits two of the world's most photographed waterfalls and traverses a steep granite staircase alongside the frothing Merced River.

BEST: Waterfall Hikes

DISTANCE: 6 miles (9.7 km) round-trip

DURATION: 4 hours

ELEVATION GAIN: 2,162 feet (659 m)

EFFORT: Moderate

TRAIL: Granite stairsteps, packed dirt

USERS: Hikers

SEASON: Year-round; the lower portion of Mist Trail may be closed due to ice and snow in winter

PASSES/FEES: $35 per vehicle, valid for 7 days

MAPS: On the National Park Service app, or Tom Harrison or National Geographic maps of Yosemite National Park

TRAILHEAD: Happy Isles Trailhead

FACILITIES: Restroom, drinking water

CONTACT: Yosemite National Park, 209/372-0200, www.nps.gov/yose

This spectacular loop follows the granite-lined Mist Trail to the tops of Vernal and Nevada Falls, then descends on the vista-filled John Muir Trail. It's an incredibly popular trail, so make your trip more enjoyable by starting early in the morning to get ahead of the inevitable hordes.

START THE HIKE

▶ **MILE 0-0.8: Happy Isles Trailhead to Vernal Fall Footbridge**
Begin your trip at **Happy Isles Trailhead,** following a paved treadway for 0.8 mile (1.3 km) to a sturdy **footbridge** across the Merced River a few hundred feet below Vernal Fall. The bridge offers a view of the voluminous 317-foot-high (97-m) block of falling water that's formed where the Merced River drops over vertically jointed rock.

▶ **MILE 0.8-1.2: Vernal Fall Footbridge to Top of Vernal Fall**
On the far side of the footbridge, you'll find restrooms and a drinking fountain. A trail **junction** lies 0.1 mile (0.2 km) farther—John Muir Trail heads right, but you'll bear left (east) to join **Mist Trail,** sticking close to the Merced River.

The next stretch is one of the West's most remarkable feats of trail-building. Mist Trail's famous **granite stairway** ascends 0.3 mile (0.5 km) to the top of Vernal Fall on 600 stone stairsteps constructed right next to the river's roiling plunge. From April to early June, when snowmelt reaches its

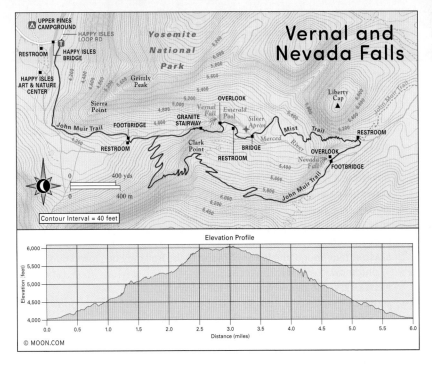

Vernal and Nevada Falls

peak, hikers are often completely drenched by Vernal Fall's mist and spray. As you climb, hold on to the railings and watch your footing carefully—the wet granite can be very slippery, and the gorgeous waterfall view is a constant distraction.

When you reach the 317-foot-high (97-m) **fall's brink,** take a turn standing at the metal railing to watch the dizzying flow of rushing white water as it plummets downward. At peak flow, Vernal Fall can be as wide as 80 feet (24 m). At the fall's base, you can see a voluminous cloud of swirling mist.

▶ **MILE 1.2–2.7: Top of Vernal Fall to Top of Nevada Fall**
After a brief rest at Vernal Fall's overlook, continue on Mist Trail along the Merced River's edge, passing a gorgeous stretch of quieter water known as the **Emerald Pool.** The path continues above the pool to the turbulent **Silver Apron,** a granite "waterslide." Don't even think of entering the water here—the current is much stronger and more hazardous than it appears.

At 1.5 miles (2.4 km), the path crosses to the far side of the river on another sturdy **bridge** and then makes a steep ascent to the brink of horse-tail-shaped **Nevada Fall,** named with the Spanish word for "snow-covered." This final mile (1.6 km) of steep rocky switchbacks is a butt-kicker, but there are dozens of fantastic photography and resting spots along the way. All your effort is repaid when you reach the top and stand above Nevada Fall's dramatic brink. Make sure you follow the short right spur trail to the **waterfall overlook** and get a spot along the railing. Nevada Fall drops 594 feet (181 m) like a liquid avalanche—a seemingly endless plume of white thundering water. It's a heart-pounding experience to peer over

the lip of the waterfall and gaze at the fall's churning tumble.

▶ **MILE 2.7-6: Top of Nevada Fall to Happy Isles Trailhead**

For your return trip, cross the footbridge and follow **John Muir Trail** to loop back. As you descend, turn around often to check out the picture-perfect view of Nevada Fall framed by the majestic granite of **Liberty Cap.** Pause to score amazing photos of this classic Yosemite scene before zigzagging your way back down John Muir Trail.

Note that you have two options for the last stretch of your return trip: You can stay on John Muir Trail all the way—it has a gentler grade, but it's mostly forested and doesn't provide close-up views of the river—or you can cut over to the Mist Trail at **Clark Point,** just above Vernal Fall. Doing so means you get a second chance to see Vernal Fall and hike the Mist Trail's granite staircase. But let your knees decide—plenty of hikers don't want to face those stairsteps a second time, especially in the downhill direction.

DIRECTIONS

From Yosemite's Arch Rock Entrance station on Highway 140, drive 11.6 miles (18.7 km) east to the Curry Village day-use parking lot. Board the free Yosemite Valley shuttle bus to Happy Isles, stop 16. In winter, when the shuttle does not run, you must hike from Curry Village, adding 2 miles (3.2 km) to your round-trip.

GPS COORDINATES: 37.7328, −119.5577; 37°43′58.1″ N, 119°33′27.7″ W

✳

Wander among wildflowers in a mile-long (1.6-km) meadow, then gaze at the view from a lofty promontory above Yosemite Valley.

DISTANCE: 7.6 miles (12.2 km) round-trip

DURATION: 4 hours

STARTING ELEVATION: 7,050 feet (2,149 m)

ELEVATION GAIN: 1,265 feet (386 m)

EFFORT: Moderate

TRAIL: Packed dirt

USERS: Hikers

SEASON: June–October; Glacier Point Road is closed November–May

PASSES/FEES: $35 per vehicle, valid for 7 days

MAPS: On the National Park Service app, or Tom Harrison or National Geographic maps of Yosemite National Park

TRAILHEAD: McGurk Meadow Trailhead on Glacier Point Road

FACILITIES: Restroom

CONTACT: Yosemite National Park, 209/372-0200, www.nps.gov/yose

START THE HIKE

▶ **MILE 0–1: McGurk Meadow Trailhead to McGurk Meadow**

From the trailhead on **Glacier Point Road,** head north on **McGurk Meadow Trail,** which makes a gentle descent through a dense forest of lodgepole pines. Only 0.8 mile (1.3 km) from the trailhead, you'll come across a dilapidated **log cabin**—or what's left of it—that belonged to rancher John McGurk from 1895 to 1897. Listed on the National Register of Historic Places, this rustic shack is a remnant of bygone days when sheep and cattle ranchers grazed their stock in Yosemite. It appears to have been used only in summer—its front door is so low that it would be obstructed by snow in winter.

Beyond the cabin, a few more footsteps take you to a small **footbridge** at the edge of verdant **McGurk Meadow,** where a trail sign notes that Dewey Point is 3 miles (4.8 km) distant. The mile-long (1.6-km) meadow is bisected by a small stream that makes long narrow *S* marks through the tall grass. For a

LOG CABIN ON McGURK MEADOW TRAIL ▶

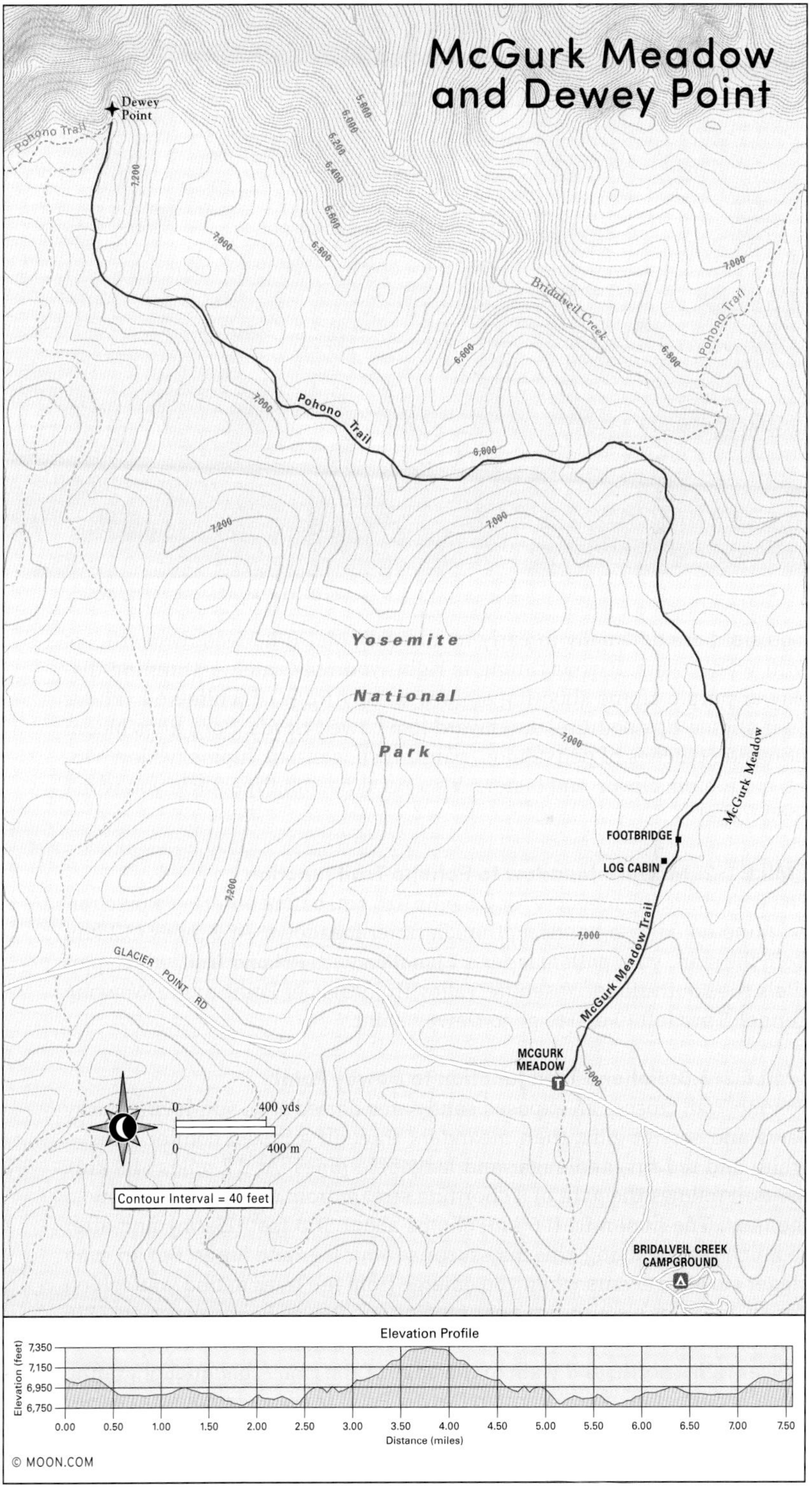

McGurk Meadow
and Dewey Point

Dewey Point

Pohono Trail

7,200

6,800

6,400

6,600

7,000

Bridalveil Creek

Pohono Trail

7,000

7,000

Pohono Trail

6,000

7,000

7,200

Yosemite

National

7,000

Park

7,000

FOOTBRIDGE

McGurk Meadow

LOG CABIN

7,200

McGurk Meadow Trail

7,000

GLACIER POINT RD

McGURK
MEADOW

7,000

| 0 | 400 yds |
| 0 | 400 m |

Contour Interval = 40 feet

BRIDALVEIL CREEK
CAMPGROUND

Elevation Profile

| Distance (miles) | 0.00 | 0.50 | 1.00 | 1.50 | 2.00 | 2.50 | 3.00 | 3.50 | 4.00 | 4.50 | 5.00 | 5.50 | 6.00 | 6.50 | 7.00 | 7.50 |

Elevation (feet): 7,350 / 7,150 / 6,950 / 6,750

© MOON.COM

too-brief period, usually in early to mid-July, McGurk Meadow overflows with wildflowers. If your timing is right, you may catch a stunning display of purple alpine shooting stars with tiny rings of white and yellow, their stigma tips pointing downward like bowed heads. Corn lilies bloom alongside patches of penstemon, paintbrush, gentian, lupine, yellow violet, cinquefoil, clover, and bistort. It's a petal-peeping spectacle you won't soon forget.

▸ MILE 1–2: McGurk Meadow to Pohono Trail Junction

The trail skirts the meadow for 0.5 mile (0.8 km) before entering a pine forest punctuated by a handful of much tinier meadows. At 2 miles (3.2 km) from the start, your path reaches a **T junction** with **Pohono Trail,** which parallels the south rim of Yosemite Valley from Glacier Point to the Wawona Tunnel. Turn left (west) to go to Dewey Point.

▸ MILE 2–3.8: Pohono Trail Junction to Dewey Point

Pohono Trail crosses an exposed sandy area dotted with sun-loving pussy paws and scarlet gilia, then meanders through a mixed conifer forest—white and red firs, and sugar and lodgepole pines. At 2.7 miles (4.3 km), the trail follows the path of a chortling stream from one small meadow to the next. The final mile (1.6 km) climbs about 500 feet (152 m), and after so much level walking, this may surprise your legs and lungs. But an even bigger surprise awaits when you emerge from the trees to find yourself on Yosemite Valley's south rim near precipitous **Dewey Point,** elevation 7,316 feet (2,230 m).

Veer right (north) and walk to the edge of the rim. A banquet of granite spreads out before you. Although Dewey Point is not as famous as Glacier Point or even Taft Point, its position to the west of most major valley landmarks gives it a remarkable wide-angle perspective. Because you're so far west, El Capitan is especially prominent, seeming almost close enough to touch. You'll also see Bridalveil Fall from an unusual angle—you're almost directly on top of it. If you dare, climb out to the highest rock and take in all you survey, from the tiny cars traveling along the Valley floor 3,000 feet (914 m) below to the imposing granite monolith of Half Dome, guarding the Valley's east end.

Before you leave this monumental perch, imagine what it would be like to visit here in winter when the valley rim is covered in snow. Bookmark that image for the future, then plan to snowshoe or cross-country ski here from Yosemite's Badger Pass Ski Area next winter.

To get back to your car, retrace your steps.

DIRECTIONS

From Yosemite's South Entrance, drive 17.3 miles (28 km) north on Highway 41 to Glacier Point Road. From Yosemite Valley, take Highway 41 for 9 miles (14.5 km) to Glacier Point Road. Turn east on Glacier Point Road and drive 7.5 miles (12.1 km) to the signed McGurk Meadow Trailhead.

GPS COORDINATES: 37.6703, −119.6281; 37°40′13.1″ N, 119°37′41.2″ W

BEST NEARBY BREWS

It's a bit of a drive (35 mi/56 km and 1 hour), but if you're craving a beer, head to **South Gate Brewing Company** (40233 Enterprise Dr., Oakhurst, 559/692-2739, www.southgatebrewco.com, noon-8pm Mon.-Thurs., 11am-8:30pm Fri.-Sun.). South Gate prides itself on its house brews—Tenaya Red IPA, Glacier Point Pale Ale, Deadwood Porter, and Gold Diggin' Blonde Lager—but plenty of non-beer-drinkers frequent this spot for brick-oven pizzas and grass-fed beef burgers served with a massive pile of fries.

This family-friendly trek offers two vastly different perspectives on Yosemite Valley's mind-boggling vistas.

DISTANCE: 4.5 miles (7.2 km) round-trip

DURATION: 2.5 hours

STARTING ELEVATION: 7,700 feet (2,347 m)

ELEVATION GAIN: 690 feet (210 m)

EFFORT: Easy-moderate

TRAIL: Packed dirt, granite slope

USERS: Hikers

SEASON: June-October; Glacier Point Road is closed November-May

PASSES/FEES: $35 per vehicle, valid for 7 days

MAPS: On the National Park Service app, or Tom Harrison or National Geographic maps of Yosemite National Park

TRAILHEAD: Taft Point Trailhead

FACILITIES: Restroom

CONTACT: Yosemite National Park, 209/372-0200, www.nps.gov/yose

START THE HIKE

▶ MILE 0-1.1: Parking Lot to Sentinel Dome

From the **parking lot,** hike to your right (east) toward Sentinel Dome. You'll enter a grove of old-growth fir trees at 0.7 mile (1.1 km) and then approach Sentinel Dome from the southeast side. At 0.8 mile (1.3 km), your trail meets up with an **old paved road,** which leads around the east side of the dome to its northern flank. Stay left at two junctions and you'll be deposited at the base of **Sentinel Dome.** The walking is deceptively easy until the last 0.2 mile (0.3 km), when you gain nearly 300 feet (91 m) walking up the sloping granite monolith. There's no official trail on the exposed granite, but the route is obvious since the summit is in sight. With only a few minutes of heavy breathing, you're on top.

Sentinel Dome's bald pate at 8,122 feet (2,475 m) elevation is 1 mile (1.6 km) west and 1,000 feet (305 m) higher than Glacier Point—which means its vistas are transcendent. You're treated to a full 360-degree panorama, so spend some time wandering around the summit's broad expanse to take it all in. The breathtaking scene includes both Lower and Upper Yosemite Falls, plus the Middle Cascades between them. Half Dome is easy to spot, and just to its left are two twin domes, Basket Dome and North Dome. Behind Half Dome is Quarter Dome, situated at the head of deep forested Tenaya Canyon. In front of Half Dome is Liberty Cap and Nevada Falls, and farther to the right is Bunnell Cascade, which slides straight down to Bunnell Point.

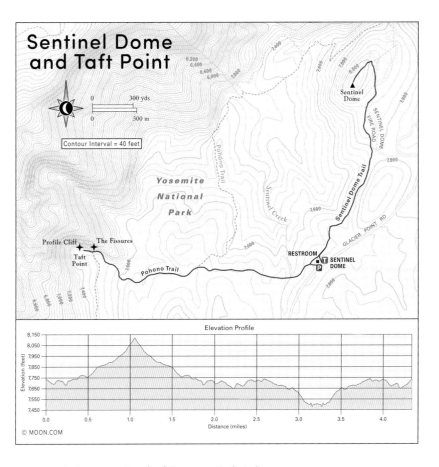

Sentinel Dome and Taft Point

Yosemite National Park

Contour Interval = 40 feet

Profile Cliff · The Fissures
Taft Point
Pohono Trail

Sentinel Creek

Sentinel Dome Trail

SENTINEL DOME FIRE ROAD

Sentinel Dome

GLACIER POINT RD

RESTROOM
SENTINEL DOME

Pohono Trail

© MOON.COM

Elevation Profile

Elevation (feet)

Distance (miles)

▶ **MILE 1.1–3.2: Sentinel Dome to Taft Point**

After enjoying the dome's stupendous view, head back downhill and retrace your steps almost all the way back to your car. When you near the parking lot, veer right (west) to stay on the path to Taft Point. The path tunnels through the forest and crosses a couple of tiny creeks, including one that is surrounded by dense corn lilies and grasses. Soon enough, the trees disappear and you begin to descend along a rocky slope. The trail vanishes on the granite; just head toward the obvious abyss that is Yosemite Valley. In a few hundred feet, you reach the cliff's edge. Nothing can prepare you for how far down it is.

Follow the path a few hundred feet farther along the contours of the rim. You'll pass **The Fissures,** wide-open cracks in the granite that plunge straight down to the valley below. One of the Fissures has a couple of large granite boulders captured in its cleft; they're stuck waiting for the next big earthquake or ice age to set them free.

Make your way to the metal railing that's plainly visibly on top of **Profile Cliff.** This railing—a meager piece of metal pipe—performs an important psychological job: It relieves a bit of the fear that comes with peering 3,000 feet (914 m) straight down to the valley floor. Clutch that railing

tightly while you gawk at the view. If you have kids with you, be sure to keep a firm hand on them.

At 7,503 feet (2,287 m) elevation, Profile Cliff is approximately the same height as 7,569-foot (2,307-m) El Capitan, directly across from you. If you happen to be at Taft Point at sunset, you may notice flashes of light on El Cap's vertical face; those are the headlamps of rock climbers preparing to bed down for the night on tiny rock ledges. Also in view is Upper Yosemite Fall, across the valley; the Merced River cutting in front of El Capitan; and tiny cars parked near the meadow by its side.

Another 100 yards (91 m) west of the metal railing is **Taft Point** proper, which has even better views of El Capitan. There is no railing here, but the cliff top is broad enough that you can find a safe view-filled picnic spot—if you dare.

▶ MILE 3.2–4.5: Taft Point to Parking Lot

Now that you've had your socks knocked off, put them back on your feet and retrace your steps to your car.

DIRECTIONS

From Yosemite's South Entrance, drive 17.3 miles (28 km) north on Highway 41 to Glacier Point Road. From Yosemite Valley, take Highway 41 for 9 miles (14.5 km) to Glacier Point Road. Turn east on Glacier Point Road and drive 13.2 miles (21.3 km) to the signed Sentinel Dome Trailhead on the left.

GPS COORDINATES: 37.7124, −119.5863; 37°42′44.6″ N, 119°35′10.7″ W

BEST NEARBY BITES

After you've finished this hike, drive 10 minutes east to the **Glacier Point Snack Stand** (at Glacier Point, www.travelyosemite.com, 10am–5pm daily summer), order a dog in a bun or a packaged sandwich, and then polish it off with an ice cream sandwich. Is this the best food you've ever eaten? Probably not, but the view of Half Dome and its granite neighbors can't be beat.

Chilnualna Falls

YOSEMITE NATIONAL PARK

A springtime hike in southern Yosemite leads to a shimmering cataract and broad views of the South Fork Merced River canyon.

DISTANCE: 7.7 miles (12.4 km) round-trip

DURATION: 4.5 hours

ELEVATION GAIN: 2,084 feet (635 m)

EFFORT: Moderate

TRAIL: Packed dirt

USERS: Hikers

SEASON: Year-round; the road sometimes closes due to snowfall

PASSES/FEES: $35 per vehicle, valid for 7 days

MAPS: On the National Park Service app, or Tom Harrison or National Geographic maps of Yosemite National Park

TRAILHEAD: Chilnualna Falls Parking Lot

FACILITIES: Restroom

CONTACT: Yosemite National Park, 209/372-0200, www.nps.gov/yose

Yosemite Valley's towering waterfalls get all the glory and also the crowds. For a more secluded waterfall hike, head to Wawona in the park's southern reaches and follow the well-graded trail to Chilnualna Falls. You'll need to climb more than 2,000 feet (610 m), so get an early morning start to beat the day's heat—these steep dry slopes can be hot in the afternoon.

START THE HIKE

▶ **MILE 0-1.9: Parking Lot to South Fork Merced River Canyon Viewpoint**

From the **Chilnualna Falls parking lot,** walk up the road about 20 yards (18 m) to find the start of the signed single-track trail. Expect a lot of company on the first 0.5 mile (0.8 km) of trail, which leads to **Lower Chilnualna Falls,** a prime destination for casual walkers. During the weeks of peak snowmelt, the stream rushes furiously over room-size boulders, creating a deafening noise.

This first stretch has a surprisingly steep grade, but after you ascend a set of stairsteps that carry you above the lower falls, the trail's grade mellows out. You'll pass a stock trail coming in from the left at 0.3 mile (0.5 km). You'll head right (northwest), continuing uphill on fairly gentle switchbacks. You'll walking through a low-elevation forest of manzanita, mountain misery, ceanothus, black oaks, ponderosa pines, and incense cedars.

At 1.9 miles (3.1 km) from the start—just under an hour if you've kept a solid pace—you reach a large **granite outcrop** with a big view over the

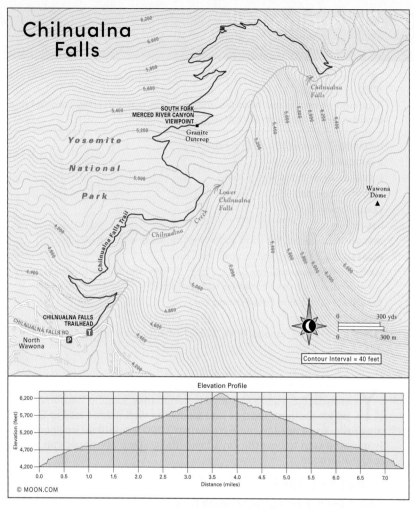

South Fork Merced River canyon. Directly across from you is Wawona Dome, elevation 6,906 feet (2,105 m), its bald granite pate standing guard over the Wawona area.

This outcrop is also the halfway point, so it's an ideal spot to take a break, have a snack, and pat yourself on the back for having already climbed 1,000 feet (305 m).

▶ MILE 1.9-3.8: South Fork Merced River Canyon Viewpoint to Chilnualna Falls

Keep ascending through this lovely forest, zigzagging your way up multiple switchbacks. The roar of flowing water—heard but not yet seen—will spur you onward. At 2.7 miles (4.3 km), you get your first view of the falls about 0.5 mile (0.8 km) across the canyon as the crow flies. Immediately beyond this inspiring peek, you'll cross a creek on mossy rocks, then enter into a much shadier forest of incense cedars and sugar pines.

The trail picks its way across a rock slope on the canyon rim, then laterals across a ledge that's been blasted from the rock. The final 0.6 mile (1 km) is the most exciting stretch—you'll have almost non-stop views of the falls. During its peak flow, you'll also hear the water's roar. Over your right shoulder are more views of the South Fork Merced River canyon.

At 3.6 miles (5.8 km), you're standing on a slope just above the falls' brink, admiring an awesome view above and below you. The series of cascades that make up **Chilnualna Falls** tumble hundreds of feet, separated by a few nearly level stretches where the stream glides over granite slabs. Many hikers stop as soon as they near the water's edge, find a creekside perch, and pull out their picnic lunches, but if you have the energy, keep following the trail and granite stairsteps another 0.25 mile (0.4 km) farther, passing one lovely cascade after another. Retrace your steps to return to your car.

DIRECTIONS

From the Wawona/South Entrance to Yosemite National Park, drive north on Highway 41 for 7.5 miles (12.1 km) to Wawona. Turn right on Chilnualna Falls Road and drive 1.7 miles (2.7 km) east. Park in the large lot on the right side of the road, just before the road makes a hairpin turn. Walk 20 yards (18 m) farther east on Chilnualna Falls Road to find the signed trail on the right side.

GPS COORDINATES: 37.5481, −119.6346; 37°32′53.2″ N, 119°38′4.6″ W

BEST NEARBY BITES

From this trailhead, drive 10 minutes to the Victorian **Wawona Hotel Dining Room** (8308 Wawona Rd., 209/375-6556 or 888/413-8869, www.travelyosemite.com, 7am-10am, 11:30am-2pm, and 5:30pm-9pm daily Apr.-Dec., closed Jan.-Mar.). The restaurant is not especially formal, but it has a grand old-school ambience with high ceilings and big windows overlooking the hotel lawn. The menu focuses on American classics, and the signature burger and vegan three-bean chili are crowd pleasers.

NEARBY CAMPGROUNDS

NAME	DESCRIPTION	FACILITIES	SEASON	FEE
North Pines	In the heart of Yosemite Valley, walking distance to trails, sights, and Merced River	81 sites for tents or RVs up to 40 ft/12 m, restrooms, drinking water, dump station	mid-April to late October	$36

Yosemite National Park, Highway 140 in Yosemite Valley; 877/444-6777, www.recreation.gov

NAME	DESCRIPTION	FACILITIES	SEASON	FEE
Wawona	On the South Fork Merced River; near Mariposa Grove and Glacier Point	93 sites for tents or RVs up to 35 ft/10.7 m, restrooms, drinking water	year-round	$36

Yosemite National Park, Highway 41 near Wawona in southern Yosemite, 877/444-6777, www.recreation.gov

NAME	DESCRIPTION	FACILITIES	SEASON	FEE
Bridalveil Creek	At 7,200 ft/2,194 m near Glacier Point Road trails and sights	110 sites for tents or RVs up to 35 ft/10.7 m, restrooms, drinking water	mid-July to late September	$36

Yosemite National Park, Glacier Point Road, 877/444-6777, www.recreation.gov

NAME	DESCRIPTION	FACILITIES	SEASON	FEE
Crane Flat	Shady, forested sites midway between Yosemite Valley and Tuolumne Meadows	166 sites for tents or RVs up to 35 ft/10.7 m, restrooms, drinking water	mid-July to October 30	$36

Yosemite National Park, Highway 120, near Big Oak Flat Entrance in northwest Yosemite, 877/444-6777, www.recreation.gov

NEARBY CAMPGROUNDS (continued)

NAME	DESCRIPTION	FACILITIES	SEASON	FEE
White Wolf	In a lodgepole pine forest at 8,000 ft/2,438 m; trails lead right from camp	74 sites for tents or RVs up to 27 ft/8.2 m, restrooms, drinking water	mid-July to early September	$30

Yosemite National Park, Highway 120, between Crane Flat and Tioga Pass in northern Yosemite, 877/444-6777, www.recreation.gov

NAME	DESCRIPTION	FACILITIES	SEASON	FEE
Porcupine Flat	First-come, first-served sites near Tioga Pass trails and sights	52 sites for tents, vault toilets	mid-July to mid-October	$20

Yosemite National Park, Highway 120, between Tuolumne Meadows and Tioga Pass, 877/444-6777, www.recreation.gov

NAME	DESCRIPTION	FACILITIES	SEASON	FEE
Tuolumne Meadows	At 8,600 ft/2,621 m in Tuolumne Meadows; walking distance to Tuolumne Grill, store, and dozens of hiking trails	304 sites for tents or RVs up to 35 ft/10.7 m, restrooms, drinking water	mid-July to early September	$36

Yosemite National Park, Highway 120, at Tuolumne Meadows in northern Yosemite, 877/444-6777, www.recreation.gov

EASTERN SIERRA

On California's eastern edge, desert and mountain environments join in a marriage of unparalleled beauty. Due to a spectacularly diverse landscape and easy access via U.S. 395, which runs north to south through the region, the Sierra's eastern escarpment has become one of California's busiest year-round outdoor playgrounds.

The region boasts two popular ski resorts, Mammoth Lakes and June Lake, plus a host of unusual natural and constructed features, including California's largest ghost town at Bodie State Historic Park, the 700,000-year-old saline waters of Mono Lake, dozens of silver and gold mining sites, barren volcanic craters, steaming hot springs, and 60-foot-high (18-m) basalt columns at Devils Postpile National Monument. Hikers can explore all these wonders plus hundreds of alpine lakes, lush meadows, rushing waterways, sagebrush and wildflower-dotted plains, and skyscraping summits.

▲ BENNETTVILLE

▲ LUNDY CANYON

1 **Barney Lake**
DISTANCE: 8 miles (12.9 km) round-trip
DURATION: 5 hours
EFFORT: Moderate

2 **Green Creek Trail to East Lake**
DISTANCE: 9 miles (14.5 km) round-trip
DURATION: 5 hours
EFFORT: Moderate

3 **Virginia Lakes to Summit/Burro Pass**
DISTANCE: 5.8 miles (9.3 km) round-trip
DURATION: 3-4 hours
EFFORT: Moderate

4 **Lundy Canyon**
DISTANCE: 3.5 miles (5.6 km) round-trip
DURATION: 2.5 hours
EFFORT: Easy-moderate

5 **Bennettville Mine and Fantail Lake**
DISTANCE: 4.4 miles (7.1 km) round-trip
DURATION: 2 hours
EFFORT: Easy-moderate

6 **Parker Lake**
DISTANCE: 3.8 miles (6.1 km) round-trip
DURATION: 2 hours
EFFORT: Easy-moderate

7 **Mammoth Consolidated Gold Mine and Heart Lake**
DISTANCE: 3 miles (4.8 km) round-trip
DURATION: 2 hours
EFFORT: Easy-moderate

8 **Duck Pass**
DISTANCE: 7.4 miles (11.9 km) round-trip
DURATION: 4 hours
EFFORT: Moderate

9 **Devils Postpile and Rainbow Falls**
DISTANCE: 5.2 miles (8.4 km) round-trip
DURATION: 3 hours
EFFORT: Easy-moderate

10 **Convict Lake Loop**
DISTANCE: 2.5 miles (4 km) round-trip
DURATION: 1.5 hours
EFFORT: Easy

11 **Little Lakes Valley to Gem Lake**
DISTANCE: 7.2 miles (11.6 km) round-trip
DURATION: 4-5 hours
EFFORT: Moderate

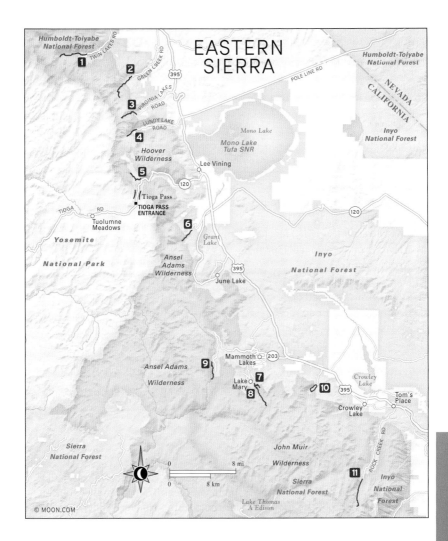

EASTERN SIERRA

1 Barney Lake

HOOVER WILDERNESS, HUMBOLDT-TOIYABE NATIONAL FOREST

This crowd-pleasing trek is a study in contrasts—you'll hike through high-desert sagebrush to an awe-inspiring alpine lake.

BEST: Fall Hikes
DISTANCE: 8 miles (12.9 km) round-trip
DURATION: 5 hours
STARTING ELEVATION: 7,130 feet (2,173 m)
ELEVATION GAIN: 1,204 feet (367 m)
EFFORT: Moderate
TRAIL: Packed dirt
USERS: Hikers, leashed dogs, horses
SEASON: June–October; road is not plowed in winter
PASSES/FEES: None
MAPS: Tom Harrison Maps "Hoover Wilderness"
TRAILHEAD: Upper Twin Lake Boat Ramp
FACILITIES: Restroom, café, store
CONTACT: Bridgeport Ranger Station, 760/932-7070, www.fs.usda.gov/htnf

This trail goes by two names: Most people call it the Barney Lake Trail, but its official name is Robinson Creek Trail. Whatever you call it, it's one of the most popular trails in the Hoover Wilderness because of its relatively easy grade and knock-your-socks-off scenery.

START THE HIKE

▶ **MILE 0–1.1: Upper Twin Lake Boat Ramp to Hoover Wilderness Boundary**

Park by the **boat ramp** and restaurant at **Upper Twin Lake**, then walk 0.25 mile (0.4 km) due west through the massive "RV city" of **Mono Village Campground** to the trail's beginning. At the camp's western edge, join a gated dirt road and leave the campground chaos behind you. You'll skirt the edge of a large meadow, then just as the road veers left to cross a **bridge** over **Robinson Creek,** turn right (west) on the **signed trail for Barney Lake** (you're now 0.5 mi/0.8 km from your car). Pass a **trail signboard** 0.3 mile (0.5 km) farther that spells out backcountry camping rules, and 0.3 mile (0.5 km) beyond that, enter the **Hoover Wilderness.** All signs of civilization are now behind you, and you'll have no more junctions to worry about for the next 3 miles (4.8 km) to Barney Lake.

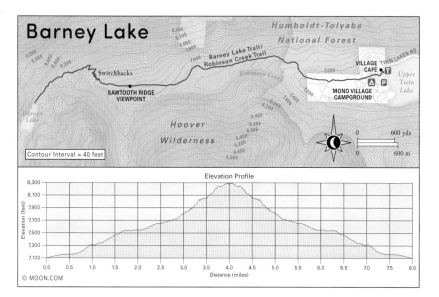

Barney Lake

Humboldt-Toiyabe National Forest

Barney Lake Trail/Robinson Creek Trail

VILLAGE CAFÉ

MONO VILLAGE CAMPGROUND

Upper Twin Lake

TWIN LAKES RD

Robinson Creek

Switchbacks

SAWTOOTH RIDGE VIEWPOINT

Barney Lake

Hoover Wilderness

Contour Interval = 40 feet

600 yds

600 m

Elevation Profile

Elevation (feet)

Distance (miles)

© MOON.COM

▸ **MILE 1.1–2.1: Hoover Wilderness Boundary to Sawtooth Ridge Viewpoint**

The next mile (1.6 km) is a leisurely stroll through a broad sagebrush-lined valley punctuated by vast stands of aspens and backed by a banquet of distant peaks. Robinson, Victoria, and Hunewill peaks loom to the north, over your right shoulder. The path travels westward through sagebrush and rabbitbrush dotted by an array of summer wildflowers—mule ears, lupine, paintbrush, and other sun-loving blossoms. In the autumn months, you'll be wowed by trail stretches that tunnel through aspen groves. When the sunlight hits these trees' golden leaves, they seem to glow like stained glass.

At 2 miles (3.2 km), your attention is drawn to the south, where a cleft in the ridge known as Little Slide Canyon reveals the crenelated peaks of **Sawtooth Ridge,** a knife-edged 3-mile-wide (4.8-km) granite crown. A primitive climbing route heads up the canyon to that wall of rock.

▸ **MILE 2.1–4: Sawtooth Ridge Viewpoint to Barney Lake**

After savoring the Sawtooth view, prepare for your first significant ascent of the day. The next mile (1.6 km) of trail sticks closely to the banks of Robinson Creek, then briefly veers away to climb a series of moderate **switchbacks.** The zigzagging path crosses small tributary streams where water-loving wildflowers like larkspur and monkshood bloom with abandon in July. Large elderberry bushes line the trail—in September, look for their blue-purple berries, which make delicious jams and wine.

As you gain elevation from the valley floor, your views of this canyon's steep slopes and the aspen stands that adorn them are a visual feast. With most of the switchbacks behind you at 3.5 miles (5.6 km), you'll walk through dense tunnels of green fluttering leaves in summer or golden fluttering leaves in autumn. At any point where the trail departs the trees, look behind you to admire views of the broad valley all the way down the hill to Twin Lakes.

BARNEY LAKE ▲

The trail goes completely level in the last 0.25 mile (0.4 km) before **Barney Lake's northeast shore,** elevation 8,260 feet (2,518 m). A small, sandy beach here makes a great spot to drop your pack and enjoy a postcard-like view of 11,346-foot (3,458-m) Crown Point, lording over the far shoreline. While you munch on some trail mix, consider a frigid swim in Barney Lake, a nap on its beach, or a climb up the massive granite outcrop on its southeast shore. This high perch offers an eagle's-eye vista of the lake backed by Crown Point.

There's only one way to get back to your car—turn around and retrace your footsteps.

DIRECTIONS

From Bridgeport, on U.S. 395, drive west on Twin Lakes Road for 13.2 miles (21.3 km) to the signed parking area near Mono Village Campground, on the west end of the upper lake. Park near the boat ramp and walk through the campground to reach the start of the trail.

GPS COORDINATES: 38.1475, −119.3775; 38°8'51" N, 119°22'39" W

BEST NEARBY BREWS

When only a red ale or a mango wheat beer will do, head to **Big Meadow Brewery** (241 Main St., Bridgeport, 951/265-4553, 2pm-7pm Tues.-Sat.), just 15 minutes from the trailhead in downtown Bridgeport. If you're hungry, neighboring Growlers Eatery shares the same outdoor patio and makes awesome barbecue ribs, burgers, and tater tots.

Green Creek Trail to East Lake

HOOVER WILDERNESS, HUMBOLDT-TOIYABE NATIONAL FOREST

A wealth of wildflowers and fascinating mining history await in Green Creek canyon, home to multiple lakes tucked below 11,000-foot (3,353-m) peaks.

DISTANCE: 9 miles (14.5 km) round-trip

DURATION: 5 hours

STARTING ELEVATION: 8,015 feet (2,443 m)

ELEVATION GAIN: 1,505 feet (459 m)

EFFORT: Moderate

TRAIL: Packed dirt, rocky trail

USERS: Hikers, leashed dogs, horses

SEASON: June–October; road is not plowed in winter

PASSES/FEES: None

MAPS: Tom Harrison Maps "Hoover Wilderness"

TRAILHEAD: Green Creek Trailhead

FACILITIES: Vault toilets

CONTACT: Bridgeport Ranger Station, 760/932-7070, www.fs.usda.gov/htnf

START THE HIKE

▶ **MILE 0-2.8: Green Creek Trailhead to Green-East-West Lake Junction**

After a long bumpy drive to the trailhead, you'll be happy to see the **Green Creek Trailhead** sign on the west side of the parking lot. Pick up the trail near the restroom and traipse through a Jeffrey pine forest, warming up your legs and lungs on a mellow ascent. Your route parallels the tumbling cascades of West Fork Green Creek, often heard but not always seen.

At 1.7 miles (2.7 km), pass a **Hoover Wilderness boundary sign,** then continue up a densely vegetated draw alongside the energetic creek. Beyond the wilderness sign, the climb steepens as the path ascends a **rocky ridge.** When it breaks out of the forest at 2 miles (3.2 km), turn around to see an inspiring view down the canyon, which illustrates how much elevation you've already gained.

The ascent continues with little relief, but you'll enjoy views of mighty Gabbro Peak at the head of this canyon. Gabbro and all its neighboring peaks are metamorphic summits with slopes painted in a canvas of reds, grays, and greens. Distant views of these colorful mountains combined with close-up summer wildflowers in boggy wet ravines offer plenty of reasons to stop and catch your breath.

At the 2.8-mile (4.5-km) mark, you reach an important **junction.** The right fork heads to West Lake and the left fork heads to Green and East Lakes—go left (southwest).

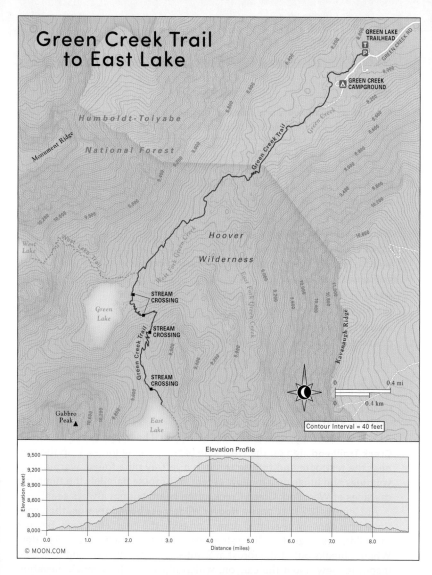

Green Creek Trail to East Lake

GREEN LAKE TRAILHEAD

GREEN CREEK RD

GREEN CREEK CAMPGROUND

Humboldt-Toiyabe

National Forest

Monument Ridge

Green Creek Trail

Green Creek

Hoover

Wilderness

West Lake Trail

West Lake

West Fork Green Creek

East Fork Green Creek

Kavanaugh Ridge

STREAM CROSSING

STREAM CROSSING

STREAM CROSSING

Green Lake

Green Creek Trail

Gabbro Peak ▲

East Lake

0   0.4 mi

0   0.4 km

Contour Interval = 40 feet

Elevation Profile

Elevation (feet)

9,500
9,200
8,900
8,600
8,300
8,000

0.0   1.0   2.0   3.0   4.0   5.0   6.0   7.0   8.0

Distance (miles)

© MOON.COM

▶ MILE 2.8–4.5: **Green-East-West Lake Junction to East Lake**

In 0.2 mile (0.3 km) from the junction, you'll come to a major **stream crossing** of Green Lake's outlet stream. Depending on how high the water is running when you visit, you'll need to exercise either a modicum of caution or an excessive dose. Attempting to ford it is a bad idea. Instead, look for a large piled-up logjam slightly downstream from your trail, and use it as a bridge. On the creek's far side, pause to enjoy the view of seductive **Green Lake** off to the right, about 200 feet (61 m) away. You might want to make a quick side-trip to its shoreline now, or save if for your return trip from East Lake. If you're weary of climbing, Green Lake is a great place for a rest.

Continuing onward, you face a 500-foot (152-m) switchbacking climb in the next mile (1.6 km), but it's worth every bit of huffing and puffing. After the moderate grade of the first 2.8 miles (4.5 km), this steeper stretch may come as an unpleasant surprise, but it tunnels through a shady forest and past a trailside extravaganza of July wildflowers, especially lupine, columbine, and larkspur. You'll have three more **stream crossings**—at 3.4 miles (5.5 km), 3.7 miles (6 km), and 4.2 miles (6.8 km)—but well-placed rocks will keep your feet dry. The trail levels out for the final stint to **East Lake**'s northern edge, elevation 9,458 feet (2,883 m).

East Lake is such a beauty that you'll be tempted to plop down at the first shoreline spot you see, but follow the trail a bit father—it sticks closely to the water—until you have an unobstructed view across the water to Gabbro Peak, Page Peaks, and Epidote Peak. It's hard to believe, but enterprising miners dug holes all over these steep escarpments in the late 1800s. Some gold was mined, but most of it remains buried deep in these hillsides.

Today East Lake's riches are found in its 2-mile-long (3.2-km) shoreline, in the hungry trout that leap in delight at the sight of your fly, and in the cold clear waters that beckon you for a frigid swim. When you've had your fill of this delightful spot, turn around and retrace your steps to your car.

DIRECTIONS

From Bridgeport, drive south on U.S. 395 for 4.5 miles (7.2 km) to dirt-surfaced Green Creek Road. Turn west and drive 8.2 miles (13.2 km) to the signed trailhead parking area, shortly before Green Creek Campground. The road is passable for most passenger cars, but not for a low-slung vehicle.

GPS COORDINATES: 38.1122, −119.2753; 38°6'43.9" N, 119°16'31.1" W

BEST NEARBY BITES

About 25 minutes' drive from the trailhead is the **Burger Barn** (152 Main St., Bridgeport, 760/932-7775, 9am-7pm daily). At this no-fuss walk-up spot, choose from Angus beef burgers, chicken sandwiches, tacos, burritos, and sweet potato or regular fries. Dessert is found right next door at Jolly Kone, where you can score a soft-serve cone, a sundae, or a shake.

Virginia Lakes to Summit/Burro Pass

HOOVER WILDERNESS, HUMBOLDT-TOIYABE NATIONAL FOREST

This high-payoff hike leads through a dramatic timberline basin to multiple lakes and an ice-sculpted mountain pass at 11,130 feet (3,392 m).

DISTANCE: 5.8 miles (9.3 km) round-trip

DURATION: 3–4 hours

STARTING ELEVATION: 9,795 feet (2,985 m)

ELEVATION GAIN: 1,275 feet (389 m)

EFFORT: Moderate

TRAIL: Packed dirt, talus slopes

USERS: Hikers, leashed dogs, horses

SEASON: June–October; road is not plowed in winter

PASSES/FEES: None

MAPS: Tom Harrison Maps "Hoover Wilderness"

TRAILHEAD: Big Virginia Lake Day-Use Area

FACILITIES: Restroom

CONTACT: Bridgeport Ranger Station, 760/932-7070, www.fs.usda.gov/htnf

This lake-dotted trail leads to the high pass at the top of Virginia Lakes Canyon. Some maps don't label this 11,130-foot (3,392-m) pass, while others give it the misleading name "Burro Pass." The real Burro Pass lies to the northwest near Matterhorn Peak. Local hikers simply call it "Summit Pass" because the pass sits above Summit Lake. To avoid confusion, we're calling it Summit/Burro Pass.

START THE HIKE

▶ **MILE 0-1.2: Parking Lot to Cooney Lake**

From the large signboard by the **Big Virginia Lake day-use area parking lot,** follow the path that climbs a small sagebrush-covered ridge. In about 100 yards (91 m), this path drops down the ridge's far side and joins the **main canyon trail.** Turn left (west) and head into the canyon.

You'll pass a **Hoover Wilderness sign** at 0.2 mile (0.3 km), then climb west along the terra-cotta-colored talus slopes alongside mesmerizing **Blue Lake.** This deep triangle-shaped gem, perched on the lip of a rocky bench, boasts an unusual cobalt hue. Be sure to check out the view from the high rock ledge above its western shore (the ledge is just 20 ft/6 m off the trail). Then push on; there's much more to discover ahead.

A steep tromp uphill to the 1.1-mile (1.8-km) mark leads you to a **sturdy cabin,** the home of an 1870s miner named Cooney. A few more steps past stands of whitebark pines brings you to beguiling **Cooney Lake,** its shores peppered with sprays of 3-inch-high (8-cm) alpine flowers, including hikers' gentian, elephant heads, meadow penstemon, and Lemmon's paintbrush.

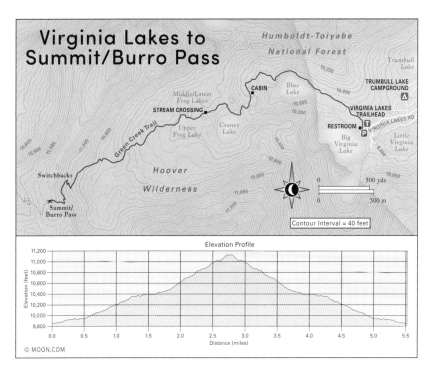

Virginia Lakes to Summit/Burro Pass

Humboldt-Toiyabe National Forest

Hoover Wilderness

Green Creek Trail

Contour Interval = 40 feet

© MOON.COM

Elevation Profile

▶ **MILE 1.2–1.6: Cooney Lake to Upper Frog Lake**

As you wind along Cooney Lake's delightful shoreline at 10,250 feet (3,124 m) elevation, watch carefully for a **tricky junction** at 1.4 miles (2.3 km), just before a **stream crossing.** Here, the main trail appears to veer right to an alluring tarn a short distance northward—it's one of the trio of Frog Lakes—but that's actually an out-and-back spur trail. If you take this short side-trip by accident or on purpose, you'll need to backtrack to the main trail, which crosses the wide shallow creek. Pick the largest, sturdiest rocks to step across.

On the stream's far side, ascend a small ridge to reach **Upper Frog Lake** at 10,400 feet (3,170 m) elevation, then follow the level trail along its charming northwest shoreline.

▶ **MILE 1.6–2.9: Frog Lakes to Summit/Burro Pass**

Beyond Frog Lakes, the trail now starts climbing in earnest, gaining another 700 feet (213 m) in 1.3 miles (2.1 km) to **Summit/Burro Pass.** The landscape in this upper part of the canyon is windswept, barren, and bewitching. As you gain elevation, more alpine scenery unfolds. Snake along a half-dozen **switchbacks** through colorful talus and scree. Keep heading for the canyon's headwall and the saddle sitting high atop the pass.

Once you "bag" this broad **summit** at a breathtaking 11,130 feet (3,392 m), you'll want to wander a bit to take in all the views. Take a five-minute stroll to the top of the rocky slope on your right, where the scene looking north and west doesn't skimp on drama. Enjoy a wide-open vista of the Sierra Crest's rim of mountains, Hoover Lake, and Green Creek Canyon. Also in view is long and narrow Summit Lake, wedged between Camiaca Peak

(11,739 ft/3,578 m) to the north and Excelsior Mountain (12,446 ft/3,793 m) to the south. Summit Lake is the "back door" to Yosemite National Park, lying on the park's northeast boundary.

▶ **MILE 2.9–5.8: Summit/Burro Pass to Parking Lot**

On your way back, pay close attention as you near the trailhead. Once you pass the Hoover Wilderness sign, walk another 0.1 mile (0.2 km) and watch for a **right turn off the main trail**—the junction isn't obvious. This spur takes you back to the parking lot while the main trail continues east to Trumbull Lake Campground. Many blissed-out hikers miss the turn-off and wander all the way back to the campground, necessitating an unwanted backtrack.

DIRECTIONS

From Bridgeport, drive 13.5 miles (21.7 km) south on U.S. 395 to Conway Summit, or from Lee Vining, drive 12 miles (19.3 km) north on U.S. 395 to Conway Summit. Turn west on Virginia Lakes Road and drive 6.5 miles (10.5 km) to the trailhead at the Big Virginia Lake day-use area.

GPS COORDINATES: 38.0479, −119.2631; 38°2'52.4" N, 119°15'47.2" W

BEST NEARBY BITES

From this trailhead, you can stroll over to **Virginia Lakes Resort** (end of Virginia Lakes Rd., Bridgeport, 760/647-6484, www.virginialakes-resort.com, 7am-5pm daily summer only), then grab a seat at the counter and bite into a patty melt, BLT, grilled cheese, chili dog, bacon cheeseburger, or garden burger. Whatever you order, don't forget the chili fries.

4 Lundy Canyon

HOOVER WILDERNESS, INYO NATIONAL FOREST

Colorful metamorphic peaks frame an aspen-filled, flower-blessed canyon that cradles one of the Sierra's loveliest creeks and photogenic beaver ponds.

BEST: Fall Hikes

DISTANCE: 3.5 miles (5.6 km) round-trip

DURATION: 2.5 hours

STARTING ELEVATION: 8,150 feet (2,484 m)

ELEVATION GAIN: 602 feet (183 m)

EFFORT: Easy-moderate

TRAIL: Packed dirt, scree

USERS: Hikers, leashed dogs

SEASON: June-October; road is not plowed in winter

PASSES/FEES: None

MAPS: Tom Harrison Maps "Hoover Wilderness"

TRAILHEAD: Lundy Canyon Trailhead

FACILITIES: Vault toilets

CONTACT: Mono Basin Scenic Area Visitor Center, 760/647-3044, www.fs.usda.gov/inyo

One of the best months to hike here is October, when Lundy Canyon's stands of quaking aspen turn bright gold and orange, their delicate leaves shimmying in the breeze. The canyon's wildflower display, which typically peaks in July, is also worth a special trip.

START THE HIKE

▶ MILE 0-0.75: Lundy Canyon Trailhead to Beaver Ponds

The **Lundy Canyon Trail** begins about 2 miles (3.2 km) west of **Lundy Lake,** a popular trout fishing destination. The gently ascending trail begins in dense aspens near a series of shallow beaver ponds, where Mill Creek has been dammed by the industrious rodents. You'll see more of the beavers' engineering work as you travel upcanyon.

The trail undulates up and over a series of short rises in the first 0.25 mile (0.4 km). These "bumps" are the result of a mudslide that occurred after a torrential rain in July 2018. This stretch of trail was completely rebuilt after the slide washed out the original trail. You'll notice that some aspens withstood the onslaught and others were flattered by it.

The next short stretch is exposed, rocky, and steep, leading you high above the horseshoe-shaped canyon to a **talus bench** at 0.5 mile (0.8 km), where you're granted an inspiring view. Lundy Canyon's colorful cliffs are composed of rust, gold, and red-colored metamorphic rock, a stark

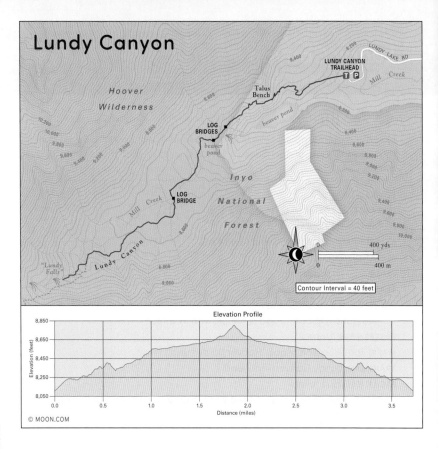

Lundy Canyon

Elevation Profile

© MOON.COM

contrast to the familiar gray and white granite that makes up much of the Sierra. The rugged canyon walls make a fine picture frame for Mill Creek's waterfall, the centerpiece of this magnificent scene. The gleaming white cascade is informally known as Lundy Falls.

Cross over two small tributary creeks on **log bridges** in the next 0.3 mile (0.5 km), then reach the edge of another large **beaver pond.** You're surrounded by chewed aspen trunks and stumps, the telltale signs of beaver activity. It may seem counterintuitive, but the beavers' pervasive tree-cutting and dam-building actually are beneficial for streamside vegetation and wildlife. North American beavers were long considered invasive species in the Sierra Nevada, but recent evidence has shown that these mammals are indigenous to the region, and they do important work.

As you stand on the pond's edge, look uphill over your right shoulder to see a boisterous waterfall flowing up high on the canyon's north side. It's the outlet creek for seldom-visited Burro Lake.

▶ MILE 0.75-1.75: Beaver Ponds to Waterfalls

After crossing the stream on a third **log bridge** near the beaver ponds, you'll climb steeply for 0.25 mile (0.4 km), then head back into a dense aspen forest. The trail flattens out, and in 1.1 miles (1.8 km), you'll cross a **broad sturdy log** over a sometimes raging, sometimes completely dry section of Mill

Creek. The creek goes underground here in the dry summer months, but soon after spring snowmelt, it can flood 12 feet (3.6 m) wide and 6 feet (1.8 m) deep. On the creek's far side, you'll see the dilapidated remains of an **old log cabin.** Continue strolling through the aspens until the 1.5-mile (2.4-km) mark.

You may be sad to leave this leafy and lovely grove, but in the final trail stretch, you're rewarded with grand views of the red, gray, and black talus decorating the canyon walls. In another 0.25 mile (0.4 km), the first of several side trails delivers you to the base of Mill Creek's energetic cascades. Take time to wander and admire the **waterfalls'** lower, middle, and upper tiers. They're all different in appearance and character, and they offer a cooling spray on warm summer days.

When you've lingered long enough by this watery spectacle, retrace your steps back to your car.

DIRECTIONS

From Lee Vining, drive north on U.S. 395 for 7 miles (11.3 km) to Lundy Lake Road. Turn west on Lundy Lake Road and drive 5 miles (8.1 km) on the paved road to Lundy Lake. Continue beyond the lake and Lundy Lake Resort, driving 2 miles (3.2 km) farther on a dirt road that ends at the trailhead. Start hiking on the narrow trail by the signboard.

GPS COORDINATES: 38.0224, −119.2618; 38°1'20.6" N, 119°15'42.5" W

BEST NEARBY BITES

At the **Mono Cone** in downtown Lee Vining (51508 U.S. 395, Lee Vining, 760/647-6606, 10am-7pm daily summer only), you can select from a dizzying array of burgers, then pair it with french fries, onion rings, tater tots, or whatever crispy-fried side that floats your boat. The Mono Cone's big crowd-pleaser is ice cream, available in cones, cups, and a huge array of milkshakes and malts.

In the rarified air at 10,000 feet (3,048 m) elevation, see relics of Tioga Pass Road's silver mining history and follow a winding waterway to three sparking lakes.

BEST: Dog-Friendly Hikes

DISTANCE: 4.4 miles (7.1 km) round-trip

DURATION: 2 hours

STARTING ELEVATION: 9,560 feet (2,914 m)

ELEVATION GAIN: 372 feet (113 m)

EFFORT: Easy–moderate

TRAIL: Packed dirt

USERS: Hikers, leashed dogs

SEASON: June–October; Tioga Pass Road is closed November–May

PASSES/FEES: None

MAPS: Tom Harrison Maps "Yosemite High Country"

TRAILHEAD: Junction Campground

FACILITIES: Restroom

CONTACT: Mono Basin Scenic Area Visitor Center, 760/647-3044, www. fs.usda.gov/inyo

START THE HIKE

▶ **MILE 0–1: Junction Campground to Bennettville Buildings and Mine Site**

The trail starts near the entrance to **Junction Campground,** then makes a moderate ascent through classic High Sierra scenery, first alongside the froth-flecked waters of Mine Creek, then across red talus slopes dotted with lodgepole and whitebark pines. This initial stretch has the steepest climb (really the only climb) of this trip, but the eye-candy scenery will distract you from the high-altitude workout. When you need to catch your breath, make a stop by Mine Creek's small cascade, which fans out over mineral-laden rock.

At 0.8 mile (1.3 km), the trail ascends to a knoll, where two **weathered-wood buildings** stand as testament to Bennettville's heyday. The **mining camp**'s small assay office and larger barn-bunkhouse enjoy a truly majestic backdrop—the soaring ramparts of 13,061-foot (3,981-m) Mount Dana on Yosemite National Park's border. If the buildings' doors are unlocked, take a peek inside, but exercise caution if you choose to enter. Although the structures have been restored, the wood is weak from the harsh conditions at this 10,000-foot (3,048-m) elevation.

After admiring these relics from days long past, follow the trail another 50 yards (46 m), then veer left (south) to cross Mine Creek on a **sturdy log.** A spur trail leads you 0.2 mile (0.3 km) to colorful cliffs 100 yards (91

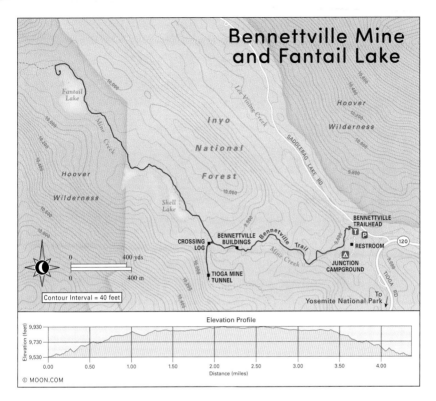

Bennettville Mine and Fantail Lake

Fantail Lake

Hoover

Lee Vining Creek

Inyo

National

SADDLEBAG LAKE RD

Hoover

Forest

Wilderness

Hoover

Wilderness

Shell Lake

BENNETTVILLE TRAILHEAD

CROSSING LOG

BENNETTVILLE BUILDINGS

Bennettville Trail

RESTROOM

120

JUNCTION CAMPGROUND

Mine Creek

TIOGA RD

TIOGA MINE TUNNEL

To Yosemite National Park

0 ___ 400 yds

0 ___ 400 m

Contour Interval = 40 feet

Elevation Profile

Elevation (feet)

9,930
9,730
9,530

0.00   0.50   1.00   1.50   2.00   2.50   3.00   3.50   4.00

Distance (miles)

© MOON.COM

m) south of the buildings, where the **Tioga Mine's tunnel** was bored into the mountain. Stand on a massive pile of mine tailings and peer into the 7-foot-high (2-m) tunnel, now gated off. A small stream trickles through it. Outside the tunnel's mouth, pieces of abandoned mining equipment have been rusting here since the 1880s, including a well-preserved engine boiler and pieces of railcar tracks and iron pipes.

▸ **MILE 1-2.2: Bennettville Buildings and Mine Site to Fantail Lake**
Spend a while pondering the tenacity of those who worked and dreamed at this remote site, then backtrack 0.2 mile (0.3 km) from the tunnel, re-cross Mine Creek, and veer left (northwest) on the **main trail** (don't head back to the buildings). In another 0.2 mile (0.3 km), you'll stand on the edge of beautiful **Shell Lake.** White Mountain towers over the lake's north-west edge, its face reflected in the water's surface.

Keep on the trail for another 0.2 mile (0.3 km) to a second, **unnamed lake,** a shallow tarn edged with verdant grasses. Look south from its shoreline for a perfectly framed view of Mount Dana. In the lakeside meadows, you may see tenacious High Sierra wildflowers blossoming. In July, high-alpine lupine, cinquefoil, and Lemmon's paintbrush brighten the grasses, but once August arrives, you'll find late-summer species like Sierra gentian and hiker's gentian.

Your final destination is **Fantail Lake,** largest and deepest of this trail's lakes. Follow the trail all the way to Fantail's northern edge to enjoy unobstructed views of Mount Conness and North Peak. These 12,000-foot

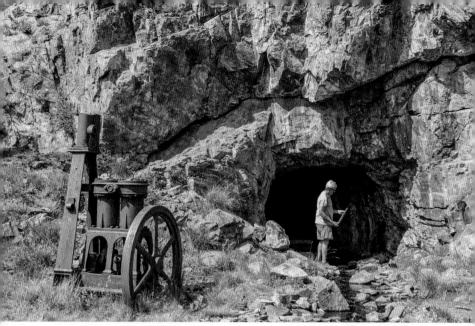

(3,657-m) peaks stand guard at the canyon's headwall. You'll likely hear the noisy chatter of Clark's nutcrackers, a large gray-and-white bird that's fond of the seeds from whitebark pine cones.

The trail continues for another mile (1.6 km), then peters out at a **high bench** below Mount Conness. Keep exploring if you wish, but the scene at Fantail Lake is as lovely as you'll find anywhere. Most hikers are content to choose a lakeside boulder or a cozy spot beneath a whitebark pine, then indulge in a little high-alpine reverie.

For your trip back to your car, just retrace your steps.

DIRECTIONS

From Lee Vining at U.S. 395, drive 12 miles (19.3 km) up Tioga Pass Road and turn right at the sign for Saddlebag Lake, then immediately turn left. Park in the small day-use parking lot outside Junction Campground. Walk up the camp road about 100 feet (30 m) to the Bennettville trailhead sign on the right, just before the first campsite. Don't walk into the campground.

GPS COORDINATES: 37.9386, −119.2503; 37°56′19″ N, 119°15′1.1″ W

BEST NEARBY BITES

From this trailhead, drive 20 minutes down Highway 120 to Lee Vining and **Bodie Mike's** (51357 U.S. 395, Lee Vining, 760/647-6432, www.leevining.com, 11:30am-10pm daily summer only). Nab a table on the outdoor deck and order a slab of beef or pork ribs, barbecued chicken, or beer-battered onion rings.

Follow chortling Parker Creek through sagebrush-covered plains and aspen groves to a glacial lake framed by Parker Peak's imposing backdrop.

BEST: Dog-Friendly Hikes

DISTANCE: 3.8 miles (6.1 km) round-trip

DURATION: 2 hours

STARTING ELEVATION: 7,760 feet (2,365 m)

ELEVATION GAIN: 510 feet (155 m)

EFFORT: Easy-moderate

TRAIL: Packed dirt

USERS: Hikers, leashed dogs, horses

SEASON: June-October

PASSES/FEES: None

MAPS: Tom Harrison Maps "Mammoth High Country"

TRAILHEAD: Parker Lake Trailhead

FACILITIES: Restroom

CONTACT: Mono Basin Scenic Area Visitor Center, 760/647-3044, www.fs.usda.gov/inyo

The Parker Lake Trail in the Ansel Adams Wilderness is a study in contrasts. The trek's first stretch traverses expansive sagebrush plains, the second part winds through a streamside aspen forest, and the third visits a glacial lake.

START THE HIKE

▸ **MILE 0-1: Parking Lot to Aspen Grove**

From the west side of the **parking lot,** this trail's 510-foot (155-m) elevation gain begins right away, allowing no opportunity for a warm-up. Your heart rate will soar for the first half of this trip, but the second half is much easier.

As you ascend, you may get buzzed by a cicada, a noisy grasshopper-like insect that makes its home in sagebrush, bitterbrush, and piñon pines. In early summer, yellow mule ears brighten the gray-green slopes. Another prominent shrub is mountain mahogany, a plant that bears single-seeded fruits with a feathery plume. The plume dries into a curlicue shape, like a silky corkscrew, which makes this plant easy to identify.

After the initial 0.8-mile (1.3-km) grind, you'll top a **sage-covered bench,** from which you can see Parker Creek tumbling energetically downstream, bounded by stands of willows, black cottonwoods, and aspens. Be sure to turn around and look down the canyon at distant views of Mono Lake, the Eastern Sierra's most famous landmark. This 700,000-year-old saline lake is a critical stopping place for millions of migrating birds.

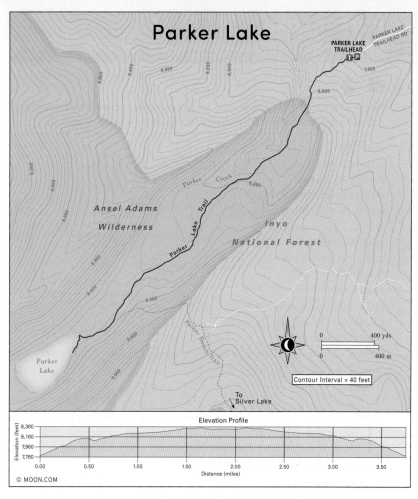

© MOON.COM

You'll be relieved to discover that the trail's grade diminishes over the next 0.2 mile (0.3 km), then levels out completely. At the 1-mile (1.6-km) mark, as you enter a **stand of white-barked aspens,** their leaves dancing in the slightest breeze, enjoy easy walking in close proximity to gurgling Parker Creek.

▶ MILE 1–1.9: Aspen Grove to Parker Lake

Early summer wildflowers thrive on this stretch—look for yellow alpine butterweed, lavender Hooker's onion, dark blue irises, orange paintbrush, dark blue brewer's lupine, and white mariposa lilies.

The raging stream you saw at the beginning of your hike is now tamed and quieted into placid riffles and crystal-clear pools. Be sure to follow each side path that leads to a curve or turn in the winding watercourse. Parker Creek features several tranquil "rooms" or grottos—short stretches where the stream spreads wide over smooth, colorful stones. Each grotto has its own special beauty.

In another 0.5 mile (0.8 km), your surroundings change again. The trail passes a few immense Jeffrey pines interspersed with tall, skinny lodgepole pines. At 1.8 miles (2.9 km), a trail from Silver Lake comes in on your left, and with a few more easy footsteps on the main trail, you're standing on the shoreline of **Parker Lake,** a picturesque glacial tarn set below imposing peaks—most notably 12,861-foot-high (3,920-m) Parker Peak. Duck families often float on its blue-green surface, and ospreys circle high above, hunting for trophy trout.

On the lake's far side, a dense aspen grove makes a perfect horseshoe-shaped curve along the shoreline. On windless summer days, Parker Lake can be so still that its mountain backdrop is duplicated in exact detail—but upside-down—on its mirror-like surface. Of course, the wind isn't always quiet. On some days, cold gusts blow down from Parker Peak and ricochet off the lake surface, sending hikers scrambling for shelter.

Because this hike is so short and easy, you might want to walk the trail circling the lake, adding another mile (1.6 km) to the round-trip mileage shown above. But then again, you might be too slack-jawed by this dazzling lake-and-peak tableau to walk another step. If so, simply claim a seat on a log and soak in the beauty.

When you're ready to turn back, just retrace your steps.

DIRECTIONS

From Lee Vining, drive 5 miles (8.1 km) south on U.S. 395 to the Highway 158 turnoff (this is the north side of the June Lake Loop). Turn right and drive 1.3 miles (2.1 km), then turn right on a dirt road signed for Parker and Walker Lakes. Drive 2.4 miles (3.9 km) to the Parker Lake trailhead at the end of the road, staying straight at all junctions. The dirt road is very bumpy but usually suitable for passenger cars.

GPS COORDINATES: 37.8530, −119.1345; 37°51'10.8" N, 119°8'4.2" W

BEST NEARBY BREWS

At the **June Lake Brewing Company** (131 S. Crawford Ave., June Lake, 760/616-4399, www.junelakebrewing.com, noon-8pm daily) in June Lake Village, there's always a happy crowd gathered at the outdoor picnic tables drinking locally brewed ales, stouts, and hard seltzers. Balance out the alcohol with a Hawaiian-inspired meal from Ohana's 395 food truck—poke bowls, Honolulu noodles, kalua pork, ahi tuna tacos, and burritos.

🏛 🐾 👫

Walk into history at the Mammoth Consolidated Gold Mine, then hike to heart-shaped Heart Lake and savor vistas of the Minaret Range.

DISTANCE: 3 miles (4.8 km) round-trip

DURATION: 2 hours

STARTING ELEVATION: 9,126 feet (2,781 m)

ELEVATION GAIN: 509 feet (155 m)

EFFORT: Easy-moderate

TRAIL: Packed dirt

USERS: Hikers, leashed dogs

SEASON: June-October; road to the trailhead is not plowed in winter

PASSES/FEES: None

MAPS: Tom Harrison Maps "Mammoth High Country"

TRAILHEAD: Coldwater Campground

FACILITIES: Restroom

CONTACT: Mammoth Ranger Station, 760/924-5500, www.fs.usda.gov/inyo

One of the first Mammoth trails to become snow-free each spring, this easy hike travels through aspen groves and along sagebrush-covered slopes to an aptly named heart-shaped lake. Kids will love seeing the historic gold mining camp near the trail's start, and they'll also enjoy swimming, fishing, and exploring at tiny Heart Lake.

START THE HIKE

Three different trails lead from Coldwater Campground; be sure to start on the trail signed for Mammoth Consolidated Gold Mine, 0.2 mile (0.3 km) north of the Duck Lake Pass Trailhead.

▸ **MILE 0-0.7: Parking Lot to Mammoth Consolidated Gold Mine**

From the **parking lot,** cross a **bridge** and stop at the large information signboard that explains the history of this gold mining site. Then continue about 200 feet (61 m) to a

MAMMOTH CONSOLIDATED GOLD MINE BUILDINGS ▸

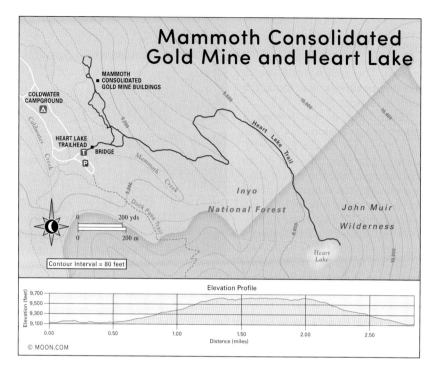

Elevation Profile

© MOON.COM

junction, where you'll see the Heart Lake Trail leading up the hillside to your right. Save that for later. For now, head left (north) to go on a meandering exploration of the **Mammoth Consolidated Gold Mine** buildings, remnants of a camp that served the mine on colorful Red Mountain. These buildings, which stand in various states of disrepair, date from a mining operation that lasted from 1927 to 1933. Although they're slowly succumbing to Mammoth's harsh winters, several bunkhouses, the assay office, and superintendent's office still stand, and you can also see the remains of the cookhouse, mine office, and diesel-powered ore-processing mill. Another intriguing sight is the lower adit, or mine tunnel—you'll see the upper adit on the second part of this hike. The two tunnels were connected by a vertical shaft dug into the mountain. The mine produced about $100,000 worth of gold in the early 20th century, which wasn't enough to make the operation profitable.

▸ **MILE 0.7–1.5: Mammoth Consolidated Gold Mine to Heart Lake**
After a tour of the mine relics, head uphill on **Heart Lake Trail,** gradually ascending the slope of Red Mountain. You're following an old dirt road that led to the mine's upper adit, which you can see quite clearly on your way back downhill; it's not as obvious from this direction.

Pass through a shimmering aspen grove as you huff and puff your way upslope, heading southeast, then depart the trees and traverse a sagebrush-covered slope dotted with bright yellow mule ears in June and July. As the trail curves to the northwest, you're treated to your first broad views of Mammoth Crest and the jagged Minaret Range. The trail levels out at about 9,600 feet (2,926 m) and heads southeast again. After a pleasant

forested stretch, you'll enter the small basin where **Heart Lake** is cradled. The path delivers you to the tiny peninsula that forms the top V of its heart shape.

Heart Lake is not Mammoth Lakes' most dramatic or scenic lake—there are far too many others vying for that title—but it's an inviting spot, and the lake is shallow enough that it heats up nicely for swimming in July and August. It takes only 20 minutes for a pleasant stroll around the lake's perimeter, if the mood strikes. Some hiker-anglers toss a line in the water, and if you do, you might catch a small trout or two.

▶ **MILE 1.5–3: Heart Lake to Parking Lot**

An easy ramble back to the parking lot—descending all the way—offers the best vistas of the day. You'll get a clear view of the second adit, high on Red Mountain's hillside and surrounded by wooden scaffolding. But even better, you're treated to a nonstop parade of mountain skyline vistas: Mammoth Crest, Banner and Ritter peaks, Mammoth Mountain, and the saw-toothed outline of the Minaret Range are all in view.

DIRECTIONS

From the Mammoth Lakes junction on U.S. 395, turn west on Highway 203 and drive 4 miles (6.4 km) through the town of Mammoth Lakes to the junction of Minaret Road (Hwy. 203) and Lake Mary Road. Continue straight on Lake Mary Road and drive 3.5 miles (5.6 km) to a fork just before Lake Mary. Turn left and drive 0.6 mile (1 km) to the Coldwater Campground turnoff, on the left. Turn left and drive 0.9 mile (1.4 km) through the camp to the Mammoth Consolidated Gold Mine trailhead at the farthest parking lot.

GPS COORDINATES: 37.5918, −118.9894; 37°35′30.5″ N, 118°59′21.8″ W

BEST NEARBY BREWS

Nab a seat on the parking lot patio at **Distant Brewing** (568 Old Mammoth Rd., Mammoth Lakes, 760/266-5023, www.distantbeer. com, noon-9pm Sun.-Thurs., noon-10pm Fri.-Sat.), and join the Mammoth locals sipping whatever hazy IPAs, amber ales, or sours are currently in rotation. Located in a commercial center, the ultra-casual brewery also serves grilled paninis, flatbreads, salads, soups, and soft pretzels.

EASTERN SIERRA Mammoth Consolidated Gold Mine and Heart Lake

8

Duck Pass

JOHN MUIR WILDERNESS, INYO NATIONAL FOREST

🏛 🐾 🚶

Enjoy ample rewards for minimal effort on this gently ascending trail through a glacier-carved, lake-filled canyon.

BEST: Brew Hikes

DISTANCE: 7.4 miles (11.9 km) round-trip

DURATION: 4 hours

STARTING ELEVATION: 9,130 feet (2,783 m)

ELEVATION GAIN: 1,633 feet (498 m)

EFFORT: Moderate

TRAIL: Packed dirt

USERS: Hikers, leashed dogs, horses

SEASON: June–October; Mammoth Lakes Basin roads are not plowed in winter

PASSES/FEES: None

MAPS: Tom Harrison Maps "Mammoth High Country"

TRAILHEAD: Coldwater Campground

FACILITIES: Restroom

CONTACT: Mammoth Ranger Station, 760/924-5500, www.fs.usda.gov/inyo

START THE HIKE

▶ MILE 0–2.6: Duck Pass Trailhead to Barney Lake

From the trailhead, the first mile (1.6 km) climbs gently through lodgepole and western white pine forest to the **spur trail** for **Arrowhead Lake** at 1 mile (1.6 km), on your left. If you don't follow the spur, you'll catch only peekaboo glimpses of the lake through the trees—it's about 100 feet (30 m)

below the main trail in a steep canyon. This delightful tarn warms up just enough for a refreshing swim on warm summer days.

Make the moderate climb on a rock-lined trail to the 1.6-mile (2.6-km) mark, then note a **left turnoff** leading to the northwest shore of **Skelton Lake,** as yet unseen. Follow this short spur if you want, or stay on the main trail for another 0.1 mile (0.2 km), where you'll traipse along Skelton's southwest shore. Tall granite cliffs frame its southern edge, beckoning you to stop for

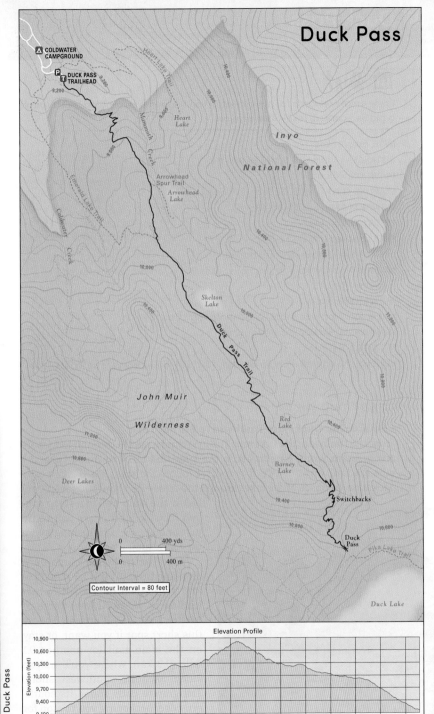

Duck Pass

COLDWATER CAMPGROUND

DUCK PASS TRAILHEAD

Heart Lake Trail

Mammoth Creek

Heart Lake

9,200

Inyo

National Forest

Emerald Lake Trail

Arrowhead Spur Trail

Arrowhead Lake

Coldwater Creek

10,000

10,400

Skelton Lake

Duck Pass Trail

John Muir

Wilderness

11,200

10,800

Deer Lakes

Red Lake

Barney Lake

10,400

10,800

Switchbacks

Duck Pass

Pika Lake Trail

Duck Lake

0   400 yds
0   400 m

Contour Interval = 80 feet

Elevation Profile

© MOON.COM

▲ BARNEY LAKE ON DUCK PASS TRAIL

a picnic. Anglers drop their lines in the glistening waters, and you might find yourself tempted to toe-dip.

Climb more vigorously for another 0.4 mile (0.6 km) to an alpine garden overflowing with summer wildflowers—gentian, lupine, ranger buttons, and more. A bit more climbing leads to a knoll overlooking greenish Barney Lake, an alluring bathtub held in place by a rim of soaring cliffs. The trail starts to descend, then crosses the lake's outlet stream on well-placed rocks. At 2.6 miles (4.2 km) from the trailhead, you'll walk along **Barney's eastern shore.** Unlike the two lakes you passed earlier, which are hugged by a modicum of trees, this lake is more barren and exposed. Its rockbound edges are dotted with a few clumps of willows and mountain hemlocks. Backpackers camp among stunted whitebark pines on its northwest side.

▶ **MILE 2.6-3.7: Barney Lake to Duck Pass**
Most casual hikers go no farther than Barney Lake, so expect less company for the remainder of your trek. You're up against a much steeper grade as you climb another 500 feet (152 m) to the pass, so prepare to perspire. As you snake upward through multiple **switchbacks** that were carved out of the talus-covered slope, your complaints will be diverted by an array of wildflowers at your feet, including alpine columbine, rock fringe, and alpine gentian. Pause often to catch your breath, not only to slow your heart rate but also to gaze down the canyon at the steadily widening view. You can pick out the lakes you just visited, as well as lofty Mount Banner and the Minaret Range, Red Mountain, and ski trail-laced Mammoth Mountain.

When you finally top **Duck Pass,** elevation 10,797 feet (3,291 m), pat yourself on the back for being such a fine mountaineer and enjoy views of Mount Ritter and Banner Peak to the northwest. Then continue another 100 feet (30 m) to an obvious viewpoint looking south. This is one of those knock-your-socks-off vistas that photos can't fully convey. The huge body of water sprawling at your feet is **Duck Lake**—it's one of the largest natural lakes in the Eastern Sierra. **Pika** is the smaller lake on its east side. Both lakes are ringed by a banquet of skyscraping peaks.

The trail continues over the pass, dropping 300 feet (91 m) to reach Duck Lake. It's a fine side trip if you have the time and inclination, and it's easy enough to make your way from Duck to Pika Lake, 0.5 mile (0.8 km) distant. But most hikers will be more than satisfied with the spectacular view from this aerie, so open up your pack and select some snacks to pair with the scenery. When you're ready to head back, retrace your steps.

DIRECTIONS

From the Mammoth Lakes junction on U.S. 395, turn west on Highway 203 and drive 4 miles (6.4 km) through the town of Mammoth Lakes to the junction of Minaret Road (Hwy. 203) and Lake Mary Road. Continue straight on Lake Mary Road and drive 3.5 miles (4.6 km) to a fork just before Lake Mary. Turn left and drive 0.6 mile (1 km) to the Coldwater Campground turnoff, on the left. Turn left and drive 0.8 mile (1.3 km) through the camp to the Duck Pass Trailhead, on the south side of the largest parking lot.

GPS COORDINATES: 37.5913, −118.9892; 37°35′28.7″ N, 118°59′21.1″ W

BEST NEARBY BREWS

During the hiking season, the outdoor picnic tables at **Mammoth Brewery** (18 Lake Mary Rd., Mammoth Lakes, 760/934-7141, www.mammothbrewingco.com, 10am-10pm daily) are some of the busiest spots in town. Grab a seat and gulp down a Golden Trout Pilsner or a 395 IPA, then order food from in-house restaurant The EATery. Top picks: the Damn Good Burger, waffle fries, and Irish caesar salad, made with kale rather than romaine.

9

Devils Postpile and Rainbow Falls

DEVILS POSTPILE NATIONAL MONUMENT

This easy trek boasts three Sierra showstoppers: the free-flowing waters of the San Joaquin River, Rainbow Falls' crashing cataract, and one of the world's finest examples of columnar basalt.

BEST: Waterfall Hikes
DISTANCE: 5.2 miles (8.4 km) round-trip
DURATION: 3 hours
STARTING ELEVATION: 7,615 feet (2,321 m)
ELEVATION GAIN: 527 feet (161 m)
EFFORT: Easy-moderate
TRAIL: Packed dirt
USERS: Hikers, leashed dogs
SEASON: June–September; Devils Postpile Road is closed October–May
PASSES/FEES: Shuttle bus ticket or permit required ($15 adults, $7 ages 3-15)
MAPS: Download at www.nps.gov/depo
TRAILHEAD: Devils Postpile Ranger Station
FACILITIES: Ranger station, restroom
CONTACT: Devils Postpile National Monument, 760/934-2289, www.nps.gov/depo

START THE HIKE

▶ **MILE 0-0.8: Ranger Station to Devils Postpile Summit**
The **Devils Postpile Trail** begins by the **ranger station,** where the shuttle bus drops you off (or where you park if you've driven into the monument). Follow the trail as it travels through a verdant meadow. If you time your trip for July, you'll be wowed by a spectacle of blooming paintbrush and shooting stars.

In a mere 0.4 mile (0.6 km) on a mostly level path, you'll reach the base of the **Devils Postpile.** This surreal-looking cluster of 60-foot-high (18-m) basalt columns—or posts, if you prefer—was formed by lava that was forced up from the earth's core. Less than 100,000 years ago, lava filled this river valley more than 400 feet (122 m) deep. As the lava began to cool from the airflow on top, it simultaneously cooled from the hard granite bedrock below.

◀ DEVILS POSTPILE

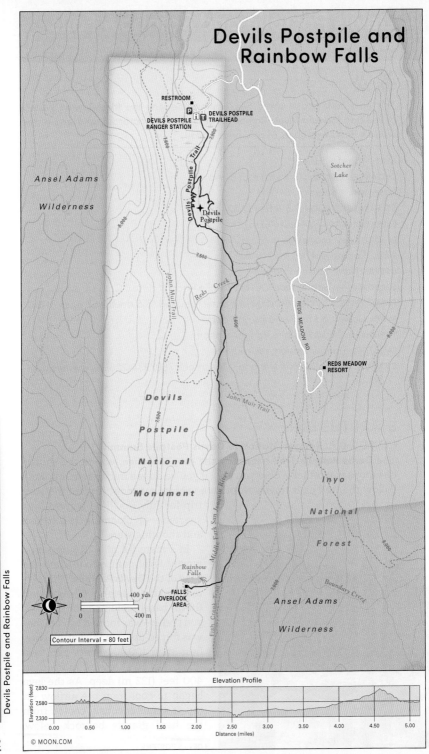

Devils Postpile and Rainbow Falls

RESTROOM

P

DEVILS POSTPILE TRAILHEAD

DEVILS POSTPILE RANGER STATION

Devils Postpile Trail

Ansel Adams

Wilderness

Devils Postpile

John Muir Trail

Reds Creek

Sotcher Lake

REDS MEADOW RD

REDS MEADOW RESORT

Devils

Postpile

National

Monument

John Muir Trail

Middle Fork San Joaquin River

Inyo

National

Forest

Rainbow Falls

FALLS OVERLOOK AREA

Fish Creek Trail

Boundary Creek

Ansel Adams

Wilderness

0   400 yds
0   400 m

Contour Interval = 80 feet

Elevation Profile

Elevation (feet)

7,830
7,580
7,330

0.00   0.50   1.00   1.50   2.00   2.50   3.00   3.50   4.00   4.50   5.00

Distance (miles)

© MOON.COM

<small>▲ RAINBOW FALLS</small>

This caused the lava to harden and crack into tall, narrow pieces, forming nearly perfect columns or posts. Although basalt columns are found elsewhere in the world, Devils Postpile is considered the finest example—its columns are remarkably uniform in size and hexagonal in shape. Most are almost perfectly straight, while others curve like tall candles that have been left out in the sun. At the base of the standing columns is a huge pile of rubble, the crumbled remains of collapsed columns.

On both sides of the Postpile, short paths lead to the **summit** of the lava formation. Follow either path to the top of the columns, which look a lot like honeycomb or six-sided tiles that have been laid side by side. From this high perch, you'll also enjoy a lofty view of the rushing San Joaquin River.

▶ MILE 0.8–2.6: Devils Postpile Summit to Rainbow Falls

Return to the base of the Postpile and continue along the well-marked trail to Rainbow Falls. You'll skirt in and out of the monument boundary and Inyo National Forest as the trail descends gently through lodgepole pines. The sound of the San Joaquin River is always apparent—your trail parallels its downstream course—but you'll see it only where the forest thins out. Pass by two junctions with trails heading toward the river to join the **John Muir Trail.** Your mission is to stay straight at every intersection.

The trees diminish considerably as you near Rainbow Falls and pass another **junction** at 2.4 miles (3.9 km). The left fork heads to Reds Meadow Resort; you should stay straight (south). In another 100 yards (91 m), you'll hear the cataract's roar, and in a few more footsteps, you'll reach the first of **three overlooks.** From this granite-lined viewpoint, you can watch **Rainbow Falls** make a grand entrance as it plunges 101 feet (31 m) over a rhyodacite lip. If you're here in the late morning on a sunny day, you may get to see Rainbow Falls' ephemeral namesake—two colorful rainbows arcing over the falls' mist. The angle of the midday sun on the water droplets creates the perfect recipe for this light-and-color show.

After snapping photos here, continue 50 yards (46 m) to the next viewpoint. Enjoy the waterfall view from a slightly different angle, then follow a short path down granite stairsteps to the falls' base, where your skin will be kissed by Rainbow Falls' spray and mist.

▶ **MILE 2.6-5.2: Rainbow Falls to Ranger Station**
To return to the ranger station and trailhead, retrace your steps. Most of the work on this trail occurs on your return trip. You'll have to gain back the 500 feet (152 m) you lost on your downstream ramble.

DIRECTIONS

From Mammoth Lakes near U.S. 395, take Highway 203 west for 4 miles (6.4 km), then turn right on Minaret Road. Drive 4.5 miles (7.2 km) to the Devils Postpile bus stop, across from Mammoth Mountain Ski Area. Purchase an access pass at the Mammoth Mountain Adventure Center ($15 adults, $7 ages 3-15) and board the bus; disembark at the Devils Postpile Ranger Station. If you arrive before 7am or after 7pm, you may drive your own car into the monument ($10 per vehicle).

GPS COORDINATES: 37.6300, −119.0846; 37°37'48" N, 119°5'4.6" W

BEST NEARBY BITES

If you're in the mood for Mexican food or a margarita, **Gomez's** (Mammoth Village Plaza, 100 Canyon Blvd., Mammoth Lakes, 760/924-2693, www.gomezs.com, 11:30am-9pm daily) fits the bill. This popular spot serves burritos, nachos, chile rellenos, and enchiladas—plus an abundance of fun-loving summer vibes on its huge outdoor patio. Bonus points go to Gomez's for its 500 varieties of tequila.

10

Convict Lake Loop

INYO NATIONAL FOREST

🏛 🐾 🚶

This easy jaunt delivers colorful vistas of metamorphic cliffs and opportunities for picnicking, swimming, fishing, or dawdling along the lakeshore.

DISTANCE: 2.5 miles (4 km) round-trip

DURATION: 1.5 hours

STARTING ELEVATION: 7,612 feet (2,320 m)

ELEVATION GAIN: 56 feet (17 m)

EFFORT: Easy

TRAIL: Packed dirt

USERS: Hikers, leashed dogs

SEASON: June–October

PASSES/FEES: None

MAPS: Tom Harrison Maps "Mammoth High Country"

TRAILHEAD: Convict Lake Day-Use Picnic Area

FACILITIES: Restroom

CONTACT: Mammoth Ranger Station, 760/924-5500, www.fs.usda.gov/inyo

onvict Lake and its creek were named for six convicts who escaped from a Carson City jail in 1871 and fled 200 miles (322 km) south to hide out in this canyon. They were hunted down by a citizen posse, which resulted in a shootout. Two members of the posse were killed, a county sheriff named Robert Morrison and a Paiute guide named Mono Jim. Local residents named the lofty 12,241-foot (3,731-m) peak, southwest of Convict Lake, as Mount Morrison, and the 10,858-foot (3,309-m) peak next to it as Mono Jim Peak. The lake was renamed from its Paiute name, Wutsunupa, which means "lake in a dent in the ground."

START THE HIKE

▶ **MILE 0-1.2: Convict Lake Trailhead to Mildred/Dorothy Lakes Junction**

At the **day-use area,** start walking at the trailhead sign; you'll head clockwise around the lake. Almost immediately, you'll experience the wow factor of deep blue **Convict Lake** and its western backdrop: a palette of reds and grays arrayed in stripes and swirls. The multihued cliffs that frame Convict Lake contain some of the oldest rocks in the Sierra Nevada Mountains, and their kaleidoscopic colors are a photographer's gold mine. Every lake in the Eastern Sierra is a beauty, but most are dominated by light-colored granite. This canyon boasts technicolor rocks, especially the rust, bronze, and gray stripes of 11,812-foot (3,600-m) Laurel Mountain and the Sevehah Cliff.

At 0.8 mile (1.3 km), you'll lose your westward mountain-backdrop views but enter an enchanting grove of quaking aspen and black cottonwood on

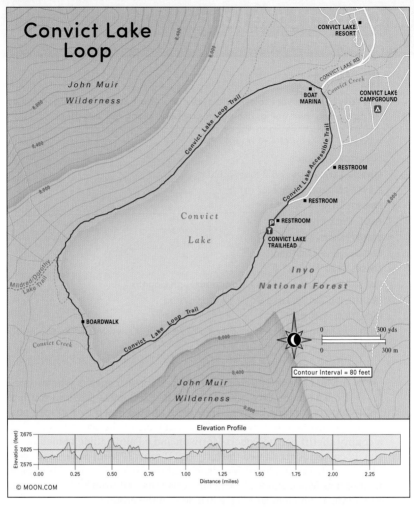

Convict Lake Loop

CONVICT LAKE RESORT

John Muir Wilderness

CONVICT LAKE RD

Convict Creek

BOAT MARINA

CONVICT LAKE CAMPGROUND

RESTROOM

RESTROOM

RESTROOM

CONVICT LAKE TRAILHEAD

Convict Lake Loop Trail

Convict Lake Accessible Trail

Convict Lake

Mildred/Dorothy Lake Trail

Inyo National Forest

BOARDWALK

Convict Creek

Convict Lake Loop Trail

John Muir Wilderness

0   300 yds
0   300 m

Contour Interval = 80 feet

Elevation Profile

Elevation (feet)

7,675
7,625
7,575

0.00   0.25   0.50   0.75   1.00   1.25   1.50   1.75   2.00   2.25

Distance (miles)

© MOON.COM

the lake's southwestern edge. In September and October, these deciduous trees turn brilliant gold—another jackpot for photographers—but even in the summer, when their leaves are green, this riparian corridor is a delight. The trees have their feet in the waters of **Convict Creek,** the lake's inlet, which braids into a half-dozen rivulets before pouring into the lake. The U.S. Forest Service built a 0.2-mile (0.3 km) **boardwalk trail** to transport hikers through this section without the need to ford the creek. At several points, the boardwalk is more like a bridge—it's 5 feet (1.5 m) off the ground to accommodate the torrent that sometimes rushes through here. Kids will love this hobbit-like forest and the sandy beach on the boardwalk's far side, just a few feet off the trail.

At 1.2 miles (1.9 km), you reach a **junction.** The trail to Mildred and Dorothy Lakes heads off to the left; you veer right (northeast) on the trail running along the lakeshore. On the loop's second leg, you'll traverse the lake's northwest edge, where your surroundings metamorphize.

▶ **MILE 1.2–2.5: Mildred/ Dorothy Lakes Junction to Convict Lake Trailhead**

You'll leave the dense, shady, riparian forest behind and enter a xeric landscape. You'll walk among mountain mahogany (look for its silky curlicues), gray-green sagebrush, bitterbrush, and western junipers, plus the occasional mighty Jeffrey pine. From this side of the lake, you'll have the best view of Mount Morrison and neighboring peaks in the Sherwin Range—keep turning around to admire their starkly contrasting colors.

The trail deposits you near the lake's **boat ramp** at 2 miles (3.2 km). You'll need to walk through the small marina's **parking lot** before rejoining a recently constructed section of **wheelchair-accessible trail** right on the lakeshore. This 0.3-mile (0.5-km) paved path accesses dramatic lake-and-cliff vistas and an accessible fishing platform. Where the trail ends, walk along the road for the last short stretch back to your car.

DIRECTIONS

From the Mammoth Lakes junction of U.S. 395 and Highway 203, drive 6 miles (9.7 km) south on U.S. 395 to Convict Lake Road. Turn right (west) and drive 2.4 miles (3.9 km), passing Convict Lake Resort, to the end of the road on Convict Lake's southeast shore. Park in the day-use spots near the road's end. If these are full, park in the day-use lot near Convict Lake Campground.

GPS COORDINATES: 37.5893, −118.8542; 37°35′21.5″ N, 118°51′15.1″ W

BEST NEARBY BREWS

Hikers can find great meals at Convict Lake Resort's **Aspen Grill** (2000 Convict Lake Rd., Mammoth Lakes, 760/934-3800, www.convictlake.com, 7am-1:30pm Thurs.-Tues. summer), an outdoor spot with a food truck and a cluster of picnic tables. Play a few lawn games while you munch on fish tacos, tri-tip sandwiches, pulled pork sliders, and the popular "mountain of fries."

11

Little Lakes Valley to Gem Lake

JOHN MUIR WILDERNESS, INYO NATIONAL FOREST

🏛 🐾 🧍

Savor epic Eastern Sierra scenery by following this old mining road through a glacier-carved, lake-dotted canyon.

BEST: Dog-Friendly Hikes
DISTANCE: 7.2 miles (11.6 km) round-trip
DURATION: 4-5 hours
STARTING ELEVATION: 10,260 feet (3,127 m)
ELEVATION GAIN: 696 feet (212 m)
EFFORT: Moderate
TRAIL: Packed dirt
USERS: Hikers, leashed dogs, horses
SEASON: June-October
PASSES/FEES: None
MAPS: Tom Harrison Maps "Mono Divide High Country"
TRAILHEAD: Parking lot
FACILITIES: Restroom
CONTACT: Mammoth Ranger Station, 760/924-5500, www.fs.usda.gov/inyo

START THE HIKE

▶ MILE 0-2.2: Parking Lot to Long Lake

From the large **parking lot,** the path—a closed-off dirt road—leads south on a remarkably mellow grade. You'll pass an entry sign for the **John Muir Wilderness** in the first 0.3 mile (0.5 km), then remain on a southern beeline for most of the trip. This rapidly narrowing trail was built in the 1920s as a commuting route for workers heading to the tungsten mines at Pine Creek, beyond Morgan Pass. The mine prospered until the 1940s; this route was closed to vehicles in the 1950s.

On this mostly shadeless trek, you'll enjoy wide panoramas almost every step of the way. The only trees that can survive in this canyon are high-elevation species—whitebark pine, limber pine, and mountain hemlock, mostly found in clusters along the lakeshores. With an absence of tree cover to obscure the views, you're almost always walking "into the postcard," becoming part of Little

EASTERN SIERRA

Little Lakes Valley to Gem Lake

LITTLE LAKES VALLEY ▶

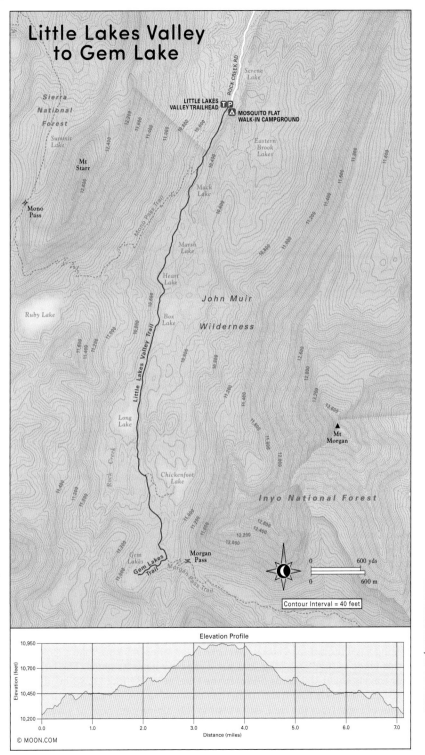

Little Lakes Valley to Gem Lake

Sierra National Forest

Summit Lake

Mt Starr

Mono Pass

Ruby Lake

LITTLE LAKES VALLEY TRAILHEAD

MOSQUITO FLAT WALK-IN CAMPGROUND

ROCK CREEK RD

Serena Lake

Eastern Brook Lakes

Mack Lake

Marsh Lake

Heart Lake

Box Lake

John Muir Wilderness

Long Lake

Rock Creek

Chickenfoot Lake

Mt Morgan

Inyo National Forest

Gem Lakes

Morgan Pass

Mono Pass Trail

Little Lakes Valley Trail

Gem Lakes Trail

Morgan Pass Trail

| 0 | | 600 yds |
| 0 | | 600 m |

Contour Interval = 40 feet

Elevation Profile

Elevation (feet)

10,950
10,700
10,450
10,200

0.0   1.0   2.0   3.0   4.0   5.0   6.0   7.0

Distance (miles)

© MOON.COM

Lake Valley's grand vistas. Several 13,000-foot (3,962-m) peaks are in view, including Mount Morgan, Mount Dade, Mount Abbot, and Bear Creek Spire.

The trail ascends gently for the first 0.5 mile (0.8 km) to a **junction** where the Mono Pass Trail heads right. You'll head left (southwest) into the alpine tableau ahead, passing by four lakes on your left side: **Mack** at 0.7 mile (1.1 km), **Marsh** at 1 mile (1.6 km), **Heart** at 1.2 miles (1.9 km), and **Box** at 1.7 miles (2.7 km). Tucked into granite pockets, each of the four small tarns is worth a stop. Anglers can fish for brook, brown, or rainbow trout. Flower fans can hunt for colorful high-alpine flowers along the lakeshores.

For those who keep walking, 0.3 mile (0.5 km) beyond Box Lake is one of the largest and deepest lakes on this trail, aptly named **Long Lake.** It takes about 15 minutes to walk the level trail stretch along its rocky eastern shore, but only if you don't stop to take dozens of blue-water photos and admire clumps of white Sierra columbine flourishing among the talus. If you pause at every scenic viewpoint, this level 0.2-mile (0.3-km) stroll could easily take upward of an hour. Backed by a canvas of craggy peaks, Long Lake is so appealing that many hikers choose a picnic or fishing spot and while away the day right here—and what a satisfying day it will be.

▶ **MILE 2.2-3.6: Long Lake to Gem Lakes**

Hikers with high-altitude stamina should continue along the main trail, passing a **left turnoff** for **Chickenfoot Lake** at 2.7 miles (4.3 km). Take a look at this lake's outline on a map, and you'll see how it got its name. The left spur travels about 100 yards (91 m) to the lake, at 10,789-foot (3,288-m) elevation. It sees less foot traffic than the lakes you've already passed since it's out of sight from the trail. Pay a visit to this alpine gem now, or save it for the return trip.

Continuing along the main trail, a mostly level meander leads past meadows filled with pink Lemmon's paintbrush and blue Brewer's lupine. Before long, you'll reach the edge of **Gem Lakes' outlet stream** (a.k.a. Rock Creek), a wide and shallow brook that you'll cross on rocks. Enjoy an easier climb and more scenery-ogling, and soon you'll find yourself at the **Morgan Pass-Gem Lakes junction,** 3.3 miles (5.3 km) from the trailhead. Turn right (west) here and follow the undulating path for a final 0.3 mile (0.5 km) to **Gem Lakes.** Don't stop at the first two tiny tarns—you want to visit the largest, upper Gem Lake, perched at just shy of 11,000 feet (3,353 m) elevation. Deep, sprawling, and framed by stark granite ramparts, this lake is the loveliest of the day, despite a lot of stiff competition. Pick a rock slab to lounge on, then gaze at the grandeur of this alpine jewel before retracing your steps to your car.

DIRECTIONS

From the Mammoth Lakes junction of U.S. 395 and Highway 203, drive south on U.S. 395 for 15 miles (24 km) to Tom's Place and the Rock Creek Road turnoff, on the right. The Rock Creek Road turnoff is 24 miles (39 km) north of Bishop. Follow Rock Creek Road southwest for 10.5 miles (16.9 km) to its end at the Mosquito Flat parking area.

GPS COORDINATES: 37.4352, −118.7471; 37°26'6.7" N, 118°44'49.6" W

BEST NEARBY BITES

After your hike, drive 10 minutes back down Rock Creek Road and treat yourself to some tasty barbecue at **Rock Creek Lakes Resort** (1 Upper Rock Creek Rd., Bishop, 760/935-4311, www.rockcreeklakesresort.com, 7am-3pm daily summer). Their lunch menu features smoked meats, homemade sausages, grass-fed Angus burgers, and lentil cauliflower burgers. Top pick: Try the brisket sandwich topped with barbecue sauce that's brewed and bottled right here.

NEARBY CAMPGROUNDS

NAME	DESCRIPTION	FACILITIES	SEASON	FEE
Convict Lake	Easy access to Convict Lake, hiking trails, trout fishing, horseback riding	85 sites for tents or RVs up to 40 ft/12 m, restrooms, drinking water, coin showers, dump station	late April to late October	$30

Inyo National Forest, U.S. 395, south of Mammoth Lakes, 877/444-6777, www.recreation.gov

NAME	DESCRIPTION	FACILITIES	SEASON	FEE
Coldwater	Hiking and biking trails; fishing and boat rentals on nearby Lake Mary	77 sites for tents or RVs up to 40 ft/12 m, restrooms, drinking water	late May to late September	$29

Inyo National Forest, in the Mammoth Lakes Basin, 877/444-6777, www.recreation.gov

NAME	DESCRIPTION	FACILITIES	SEASON	FEE
June Lake	Sites on the lake, easy access to boat rentals, kayaking, SUP, hiking trails	28 sites for tents or RVs up to 28 ft/8.5 m, restrooms, drinking water	late April to mid-October	$28

Inyo National Forest, on the June Lake Loop (Hwy. 158), 877/444-6777, www.recreation.gov

NAME	DESCRIPTION	FACILITIES	SEASON	FEE
Aspen	First-come, first-served sites in aspen forest, easy access to Tioga Pass trails	45 sites for tents or RVs up to 40 ft/12 m, vault toilets, drinking water	late May to late September	$14

Inyo National Forest, on Lee Vining Creek, off Highway 120, 760/647-3044, www.fs.usda.gov/inyo

NAME	DESCRIPTION	FACILITIES	SEASON	FEE
Trumbull Lake	Camp at 9,980-ft/3,042 m elevation near hiking trails, fishing in Trumbull and Virginia Lakes	43 sites for tents or RVs up to 40 ft/12 m, restrooms, drinking water	early June to early September	$28

Humboldt-Toiyabe National Forest, near Virginia Lakes, north of Lee Vining, 877/444-6777, www.recreation.gov

NAME	DESCRIPTION	FACILITIES	SEASON	FEE
Lower Twin Lake	Sites on the lake, near hiking trails, boat rentals, trout fishing	15 sites for tents or RVs up to 35 ft/10.7 m, restrooms, drinking water	late April to early October	$26-28

Humboldt-Toiyabe National Forest, west of Bridgeport, 877/444-6777, www.recreation.gov

Nearby Campgrounds

EASTERN SIERRA

SEQUOIA & KINGS CANYON NATIONAL PARKS

These two side-by-side parks on the western slope of the Sierra Nevada Mountains are famous for their giant sequoia groves, imposing granite cliffs, steep-and-deep canyons, and spectacular hiking trails. Both offer stellar alpine scenery and an impressive list of superlatives: Within the parks' borders are Mount Whitney, the highest point in the contiguous United States at 14,495 feet (4,418 m), and the Kings River Canyon, one of the world's deepest canyons. But what most people want to see are the parks' supersize sequoias, including the General Sherman and General Grant, the two largest trees on earth measured by volume.

Timing matters when you visit these parks: The Kings Canyon Scenic Byway, which travels into the heart of Kings Canyon at Cedar Grove, is usually closed mid-November to late April. The Generals Highway, which travels between Grant Grove and Giant Forest, may be closed any time January to March due to heavy snowfall. Moro Rock-Crescent Meadow Road also closes due to snow. Check for updates online (www.nps.gov/seki) before your visit.

▲ KINGS RIVER

▲ MORO ROCK

◄ ROARING RIVER FALLS

1 Mist Falls
DISTANCE: 7.8-8.2 miles (12.6-13.2 km) round-trip
DURATION: 5-5.5 hours
EFFORT: Easy-moderate

2 River Trail to Roaring River Falls and Zumwalt Meadow
DISTANCE: 5.3 miles (8.5 km) round-trip
DURATION: 3 hours
EFFORT: Easy

3 General Grant Tree, North Grove, and Dead Giant
DISTANCE: 3.4 miles (5.5 km) round-trip
DURATION: 2 hours
EFFORT: Easy-moderate

4 Mitchell Peak
DISTANCE: 6.4 miles (10.3 km) round-trip
DURATION: 4 hours
EFFORT: Moderate-strenuous

5 Little Baldy
DISTANCE: 3.4 miles (5.5 km) round-trip
DURATION: 1.5 hours
EFFORT: Easy-moderate

6 Tokopah Falls
DISTANCE: 4.2 miles (6.8 km) round-trip
DURATION: 2 hours
EFFORT: Easy-moderate

7 Lakes Trail to Heather, Aster, Emerald, and Pear Lakes
DISTANCE: 8-12 miles (12.9-19.3 km) round-trip
DURATION: 5-7 hours
EFFORT: Strenuous

8 General Sherman Tree and Congress Trail
DISTANCE: 2.9 miles (4.7 km) round-trip
DURATION: 1.5 hours
EFFORT: Easy

9 Moro Rock from Giant Forest Museum
DISTANCE: 3.6 miles (5.8 km) round-trip
DURATION: 2 hours
EFFORT: Easy-moderate

10 Tharp's Log and Log Meadow
DISTANCE: 4 miles (6.4 km) round-trip
DURATION: 2 hours
EFFORT: Easy

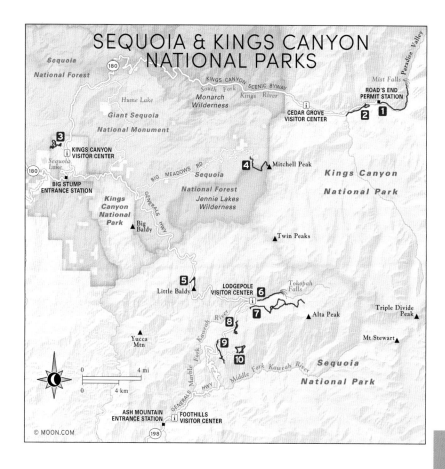

SEQUOIA & KINGS CANYON NATIONAL PARKS

A mist-spraying waterfall on the South Fork Kings River attracts legions of hikers looking for a riverside spot to cool off.

DISTANCE: 7.8–8.2 miles (12.6–13.2 km) round-trip

DURATION: 5–5.5 hours

ELEVATION GAIN: 690 feet (210 m)

EFFORT: Easy-moderate

TRAIL: Packed dirt, rocky

USERS: Hikers

SEASON: May-October; accessible only when the road to Cedar Grove is open

PASSES/FEES: $35 per vehicle, valid for 7 days

MAPS: On the National Park Service app, or Tom Harrison or National Geographic maps of Sequoia and Kings Canyon National Parks

TRAILHEAD: Roads End Trailhead

FACILITIES: Restroom

CONTACT: Kings Canyon National Park, 559/565-3341, www.nps.gov/seki

START THE HIKE

▶ **MILE 0-2: Roads End Trailhead to Bubbs Creek Junction**

Beginning on the **parking lot's eastern side, Mist Falls/Paradise Valley Trail** starts out level and stays that way for the first 2 miles (3.2 km). In your first few steps, you'll cross several small forks of **Copper Creek,** then stroll through a broad sandy stretch with sparse shade from scattered oaks, pines, and incense cedars. You'll pass massive boulders that look like the scattered remains of a bowl-ing match played by giants. Many of these rocks tumbled down from the Grand Sentinel, which towers 3,500 feet (1,067 m) above the val-ley floor. Although you can't always see it, the South Fork Kings River parallels your trail.

At 2 miles (3.2 km), you'll reach a **junction** with Bubbs Creek Trail heading right. Bear left (north) on Paradise Valley Trail to Mist Falls.

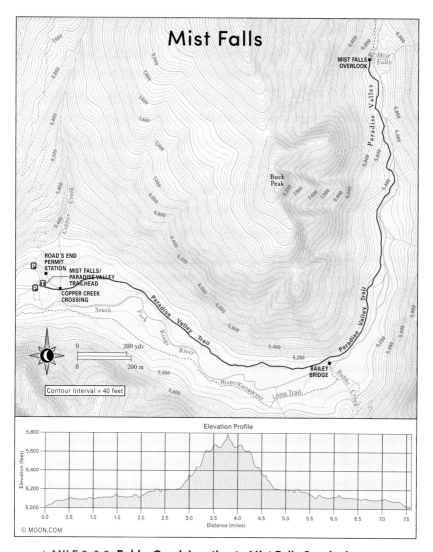

Mist Falls

Elevation Profile

▸ **MILE 2-3.9: Bubbs Creek Junction to Mist Falls Overlook**

Your trail begins to rise above the river, and you'll tackle the first notice-able ascent of this trip. As you enter the higher granite country, views of the Kings River Canyon expand. The river is much closer to the trail here, so it's easy to pause and cool your feet. At 3 miles (4.6 km), be sure to turn around and check out the vista of the Kings River Canyon, framed by 9,000-foot (2,743-m) peaks on all sides. The epitome of classic Sierra drama is the odd-shaped silhouette of **The Sphinx**—it was named by John Muir, who believed the double-pointed granite summit looked something like Egypt's Great Sphinx. Alongside it, 10,079-foot (3,072-m) **Avalanche Peak** stands guard.

At 3.9 miles (6.3 km) from the start—after a few sun-exposed switch-backs and some huffing and puffing—you reach a **signed overlook for Mist Falls.** During the spring snowmelt season, you'll witness a torrent of white water and a billowing cloud of mist. In summer, the river current mellows, so you'll likely see a more delicate waterfall that flares out over a wide granite ledge and crashes into a boulder-lined pool. At any time of year, the cataract is about 40 feet (12 m) high and almost equally wide—but the veracity of its flow varies greatly.

Multiple paths lead from the overlook down to the river's edge, but use plenty of caution here, especially if you have children with you. The rocks can be very slippery and the current is often much stronger than it appears. In late summer, when the flow is greatly reduced, hikers wade into the water below the falls. Use your best judgment if you join them.

▶ MILE 3.9-8.2: Mist Falls Overlook to Roads End Trailhead

For your journey back to the trailhead, you can simply backtrack all the way to your car for a 7.8-mile (12.6-km) round-trip, or you can follow this alternate, less traveled route through piney woods, verdant meadows, and flowing waterways, adding only 0.4 mile (0.6 km) and a negligible elevation gain to your trip. First, retrace your steps for 2 miles (3.2 km) to the Bubbs Creek Junction. Turn left (south) on **Bubbs Creek Trail.** In 200 feet (61 m), you'll cross the remarkably engineered **Bailey Bridge** over the South Fork Kings River.

Watch for a second **junction** 0.2 mile (0.3 km) beyond the bridge: Bubbs Creek Trail heads left and River/Kanawyer Trail heads right. The sign says "River Trail" but the park recently renamed it Kanawyer in honor of a late-1800s pioneering family in Cedar Grove.

Go right (west) on **River/Kanawyer Trail,** now walking on the Kings River's south side (you started the day on the river's opposite side). Stick to River/Kanawyer Trail until you reach a **modern steel bridge** about 50 yards (46 m) downstream of the Roads End parking lot. Simply cross the bridge and head back upstream to your car.

DIRECTIONS

From the Big Stump/Highway 180 Entrance Station at Kings Canyon National Park, drive 1.5 miles (2.4 km) north and turn left to stay on Highway 180 (Kings Canyon Scenic Byway), heading toward Grant Grove and Cedar Grove. Drive 38 miles (61 km)—6 miles (9.7 km) past Cedar Grove Village—to Roads End. Mist Falls/Paradise Valley Trail begins by the ranger station at the eastern end of the Roads End parking lot.

GPS COORDINATES: 36.7948, −118.5829; 36°47'41.3" N, 118°34'58.4" W

2

River Trail to Roaring River Falls and Zumwalt Meadow

KINGS CANYON NATIONAL PARK

Ramble along the River Trail in two directions and savor sparkling Kings River vistas, a boisterous waterfall, and a serene meadow framed by nearly vertical cliffs.

BEST: Spring Hikes

DISTANCE: 5.3 miles (8.5 km) round-trip

DURATION: 3 hours

STARTING ELEVATION: 5,020 feet (1,530 m)

ELEVATION GAIN: 320 feet (98 m)

EFFORT: Easy

TRAIL: Packed dirt

USERS: Hikers; wheelchair users can access Roaring River Falls via a separate trail

SEASON: May-October; accessible only when the road to Cedar Grove is open

PASSES/FEES: $35 per vehicle, valid for 7 days

MAPS: On the National Park Service app, or Tom Harrison or National Geographic maps of Sequoia and Kings Canyon National Parks

TRAILHEAD: Zumwalt Meadow Trailhead

FACILITIES: Restroom

CONTACT: Kings Canyon National Park, 559/565-3341, www.nps.gov/seki

START THE HIKE

This mellow jaunt begins at a midpoint in Cedar Grove's River Trail and heads out and back in two opposite directions along the wildly frothing, or gently flowing—depending on the time of year—Kings River. Of course, you could choose to start on either end of the trail, but the large Zumwalt Meadow parking lot has plenty of room for cars and easy access for picnic spots by the river before or after your hike.

▸ **MILE 0-1.6: Zumwalt Meadow Trailhead to Roaring River Falls**
From the **large signboard** at the trailhead, follow the **Zumwalt Meadow Trail** downstream (west) along the riverbank for about 100 yards (91 m) to a steel-and-wood **suspension bridge** over the greenish-blue Kings River. On the bridge's far side, turn right (west) on **River Trail** toward Roaring River Falls. You'll return to this spot and follow River Trail east to Zumwalt Meadow in an hour or so.

Enjoy an easy, level stroll through the forest. Sometimes you're very close to the river and other times you move away from it, heading deeper into the forest. At 1.7 miles (2.7 km), your dirt pathway (River Trail)

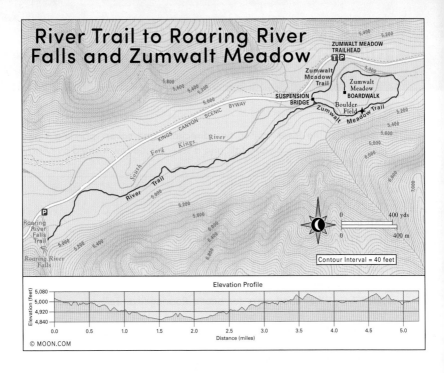

River Trail to Roaring River Falls and Zumwalt Meadow

Elevation Profile

© MOON.COM

meets the paved wheelchair-accessible **Roaring River Falls Trail.** Turn left (southwest) and walk 30 feet (9 m) to the trail's end at the waterfall's boulder-lined pool.

You might think that **Roaring River Falls** is the name of a waterfall that makes a lot of noise, but no—Roaring River Falls is a cataract on the Roaring River. The boisterous river funnels through a narrow rock gorge and pounds into a dark gray rock bowl. The waterfall plummets hundreds of feet down a narrow ravine, but only the lower cascades are visible from your vantage point. The white-water plunge is perfectly framed between huge Jeffrey pines and red firs.

▶ **MILE 1.6-4.2: Roaring River Falls to Zumwalt Meadow Boardwalk**
After admiring the waterfall, retrace your steps—first on pavement and then on the level dirt trail—back to the suspension bridge. Don't cross the bridge and return to your car just yet; you have more lovely riverside walking ahead. Stay on River Trail and pass the bridge, keeping the river on your left and heading upstream toward Zumwalt Meadow.

At 0.2 mile (0.3 km) east of the suspension bridge, you'll cross a **boulder field** of jumbled rocks, the result of a powerful rockslide. The trail is cut right through the talus and boulders, which tumbled down from the Grand Sentinel, the 8,504-foot (2,592-m) peak on your right. Look to the canyon's north side (your left) for impressive vistas of 8,717-foot (2,657-m) North Dome.

Once you exit the rockslide, you'll reach **Zumwalt Meadow,** its edges cloaked in a waist-high forest of bracken ferns. These gorgeous delicate ferns are easy to identify because they grow so tall. If you're visiting in the

▲ RIVER TRAIL TO ROARING RIVER FALLS AND ZUMWALT MEADOW

cool morning or evening, you might come across a mule deer standing up to its neck in the ferns, nearly hidden from view. The trail curves around to the river's edge, then follows its flow downstream through a fragrant forest of incense cedars and pines. Your path ends at a **boardwalk** at 4.2 miles (6.8 km), where a wooden overlook platform with two benches offers a fine view of the meadow.

▶ MILE 4.2–5.3: Zumwalt Meadow Boardwalk to Zumwalt Meadow Trailhead

For many years, you could loop back to the suspension bridge from this spot, but a massive 2019 flood washed away sections of the trail, and the final leg of the loop no longer exists. Retrace your steps through the meadow and forest back to the suspension bridge, cross it, and turn right to return your car. After your hike, indulge in Cedar Grove's best pastime—sitting by the free-flowing Kings River to watch the water roll by.

DIRECTIONS

From the Big Stump/Highway 180 Entrance Station at Kings Canyon National Park, drive 1.5 miles (2.4 km) north and turn left to stay on Highway 180 (Kings Canyon Scenic Byway), heading toward Grant Grove and Cedar Grove. Drive 36 miles (58 km)—past Cedar Grove Village—to the parking area for Zumwalt Meadow, on the right side of the road.

GPS COORDINATES: 36.7937, −118.5985; 36°47'37.3" N, 118°35'54.6" W

3

General Grant Tree, North Grove, and Dead Giant

KINGS CANYON NATIONAL PARK

No visit to Kings Canyon National Park would be complete without paying homage to the General Grant Tree, the world's second-largest tree.

BEST: Winter Hikes

DISTANCE: 3.4 miles (5.5 km) round-trip

DURATION: 2 hours

STARTING ELEVATION: 6,400 feet (1,951 m)

ELEVATION GAIN: 590 feet (180 m)

EFFORT: Easy-moderate

TRAIL: Paved path, dirt trail; wheelchair accessible from parking lot to General Grant Tree

USERS: Hikers, wheelchair users on General Grant Tree Loop only

SEASON: Year-round; snowshoes may be needed in winter

PASSES/FEES: $35 per vehicle, valid for 7 days

MAPS: On the National Park Service app, or Tom Harrison or National Geographic maps of Sequoia and Kings Canyon National Parks

TRAILHEAD: General Grant Tree Trailhead

FACILITIES: Restroom

CONTACT: Kings Canyon National Park, 559/565-3341, www.nps.gov/seki

This trek combines two trails—the extremely popular General Grant Tree Loop and the lesser traveled North Grove and Dead Giant Loop. Both paths begin from the General Grant Tree parking lot; the General Grant Tree Loop starts at the upper end and the North Grove and Dead Giant Loop starts at the lower end.

START THE HIKE

▶ **MILE 0-0.6: General Grant Tree Trailhead to North Grove/Dead Giant Trailhead**

Start by heading right (east) on the paved path from the **Grant Grove signboard.** A gentle uphill leads to the showstopping **General Grant Tree,** only 0.3 mile (0.5 km) away. Estimated to be about 1,650 years old—not extremely ancient for a supersize sequoia, which might live for 3,000 years—the General Grant is 268.1 feet (81.7 m) tall and 107.5 feet (32.8 m) in circumference.

Pay your respects to this legendary sequoia, then continue counterclockwise on the paved trail (ignore all the junctions with dirt trails—stick to the pavement for this part of the trip). At 0.2 mile (0.3 km), stop by the **Gamlin Cabin,** a log cabin built in 1872 by Canadian lumbermen Thomas and Israel Gamlin, who hoped to establish squatters' rights on these 160 acres of giant sequoias. Proceed another 0.2 mile (0.3 km) to the

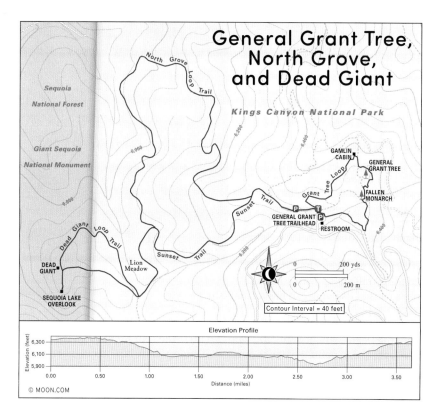

General Grant Tree, North Grove, and Dead Giant

Elevation Profile

© MOON.COM

Fallen Monarch, a fire-hollowed tree with a varied résumé—its broad trunk served as a saloon, park employee camp, and stable for 32 U.S. Cavalry horses.

You'll pass even more gargantuan sequoias as you finish out the short paved loop. Most of the big trees are protected by split-rail fences around their bases. It feels a bit disconcerting to see these ancient behemoths fenced in like animals in a zoo, but the sequoias' fragile root systems need protection from foot traffic.

After completing the **General Grant Loop,** return to the main parking area and walk downhill 200 feet (61 m) to the lower parking lot and the **Dead Giant/North Grove Loop Trailhead.**

▶ **MILE 0.6-2.5: North Grove/Dead Giant Trailhead to Dead Giant**
Follow the dirt-road trail signed for North Grove and Dead Giant, two connected loop trails with a combined distance of 2.5 miles (4 km)—2 miles (3.2 km) for North Grove and 0.5 mile (0.8 km) for Dead Giant. Start by heading downhill through a mixed forest of sequoia, sugar pine, ponderosa pine, white fir, and western dogwood—a delightful tree that turns bright crimson in October and bears beautiful flowering bracts in May. Compared to the paved trail you just completed, you'll find far fewer giant sequoias here.

Keep to the right at the first **junction** at 0.1 mile (0.2 km) from the lower parking lot to follow the **North Grove Loop** counterclockwise. After hiking

downhill on the wide trail for 1 mile (1.6 km), you'll pass an obscure **junction** with an 1890s wagon road that was used to take logged sequoias to the mill town of Millwood. Stay on the main trail and ascend 0.5 mile (0.8 km) back uphill to a **junction.** Turn sharply right (south) and walk 0.25 mile (0.4 km) downhill to lush **Lion Meadow.** Leave the wide trail behind and turn right (north) on the narrow **Dead Giant Loop,** circling counterclockwise to the **Dead Giant.** This nearly hollow, long-dead sequoia has not succumbed to gravity and somehow remains standing tall. It appears that humans caused its demise; it has ax marks in its side.

▶ **MILE 2.5-3.4: Dead Giant to General Grant Tree Trailhead**

From the Dead Giant, it's only 100 yards (91 m) to the spur for **Sequoia Lake Overlook,** a high point that looks down on a large private lake in neighboring Sequoia National Forest, home to a YMCA Camp. The lake was formed in 1889 when the Sanger Lumber Company dammed what was previously a meadow to create a mill pond. The company then built a flume that traveled 54 miles (87 km) from their mill to the railroads in the San Joaquin Valley. Filled with water supplied from the mill pond, the flume was capable of carrying 250,000 board feet of lumber per day.

From Sequoia Lake Overlook, backtrack a few yards, then turn right (east) to finish out the Dead Giant Loop. When you return to the dirt road, turn right (northeast) and head uphill. This last leg is the only truly aerobic stretch of this hike—you'll gain 350 feet (107 m) on your return to the parking lot.

DIRECTIONS

From the Big Stump/Highway 180 Entrance Station at Kings Canyon National Park, drive 1.5 miles (2.4 km) north and turn left to stay on Highway 180 (Kings Canyon Scenic Byway), heading toward Grant Grove. Drive 2 miles (3.2 km), passing Grant Grove Village, to the left turnoff for the General Grant Tree Trailhead. Turn left and drive 0.7 mile (1.1 km) to the upper parking lot.

GPS COORDINATES: 36.7471, −118.9731; 36°44'49.6" N, 118°58'23.2" W

Bag the highest summit in the Jennie Lakes Wilderness and earn a 360-degree vista of High Sierra peaks and precipices.

DISTANCE: 6.4 miles (10.3 km) round-trip

DURATION: 4 hours

STARTING ELEVATION: 8,480 feet (2,585 m)

ELEVATION GAIN: 2,280 feet (695 m)

EFFORT: Moderate-strenuous

TRAIL: Packed dirt, rocky

USERS: Hikers and leashed dogs

SEASON: May-October; only accessible when roads are open

PASSES/FEES: $35 per vehicle, valid for 7 days

MAPS: On the National Park Service app, or Tom Harrison or National Geographic maps of Sequoia and Kings Canyon National Parks

TRAILHEAD: Marvin Pass Trailhead

FACILITIES: Restroom

CONTACT: Kings Canyon National Park, 559/565-3341, www.nps.gov/seki

START THE HIKE

▶ **MILE 0-1.5: Marvin Pass Trailhead to Marvin Pass**

You'll be happy to hit the trail after the bone-rattling drive to the trailhead. The **Marvin Pass Trail** climbs moderately right from the start, ascending a hillside carpeted with pinemat manzanita, then tops a low ridge at 0.3 mile (0.5 km). Enjoy a short stretch of level meandering through two small meadows dotted with shooting stars and corn lilies in early summer. This trek doles out a little bit of beauty at a time, slowly rising to a scenic crescendo at Mitchell Peak's summit.

Beyond the meadows, the switchbacks begin in earnest for the remaining 1.1 miles (1.8 km) to Marvin Pass (9,110 ft/2,777 m) and the boundary of the Jennie Lakes Wilderness. Expect some huffing and puffing as you make your way up the 600-foot (183-m) gain, but thankfully the path is largely shaded by red firs, western white pines, and lodgepole pines.

At **Marvin Pass,** you're joined by a trail from Rowell Meadow coming in on your right. Bear left (east) toward Kanawyer Gap and Mitchell Peak, and get your mind set on more climbing.

▶ **MILE 1.5-3.2: Marvin Pass to Mitchell Peak Summit**

From Marvin Pass, your trail ascends more gradually through forest and flower-dotted meadows for another 0.9 mile (1.4 km) to a **junction,** where the main trail continues straight for Kanawyer Gap. Turn left (north) for Mitchell Peak. You'll face another 0.8 mile (1.3 km) of ascent as your trail curves around to the peak's north side.

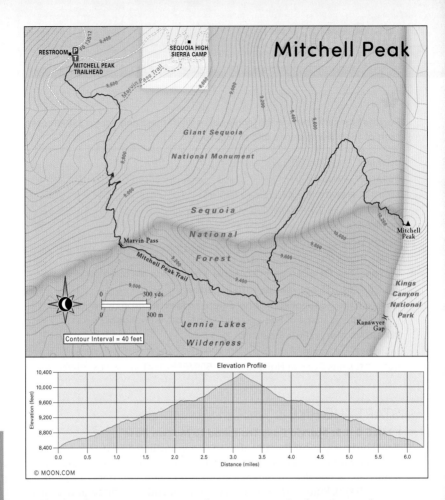

Mitchell Peak

The conifers seem to grow even larger as you gain elevation, and soon the lodgepole pines and red firs are joined by stately foxtail pines—a harbinger of the high country. Just below the summit, you'll leave even these high-elevation trees behind you. The trail dissipates at the base of the talus-covered summit. You only have about 100 feet (30 m) to go, so just pick your own path and scramble your way up the rocks to summit victory.

Atop **Mitchell Peak,** catch your breath and savor the inspiring 360-degree view. While the 10,365-foot (3,159-m) elevation may not seem wildly impressive by High Sierra standards, the peak's standout location—set off on its own, topographically isolated from the Sierra Crest—gives it an unequalled perspective. That broad unobstructed vista was the reason a fire lookout tower was constructed atop Mitchell Peak in 1962. Staffed throughout the summer and fall months, the tower was one of the three highest-elevation fire lookouts in California. But by the late 1970s, the federal government was losing interest in human-staffed towers. As funding dried up, the tower fell into disrepair and was eventually destroyed.

What remains is the tower's concrete slab foundation, plus a stunning view of the Great Western Divide and Kings Canyon high country,

Mitchell Peak

▲ MITCHELL PEAK

including Spanish Mountain and Mount Clarence King. Just below your high perch is Williams Meadow, and Comanche Meadow lies just south of it. Other prominent landmarks include Sugarloaf Dome and the forested terrain of Sugarloaf Valley. To the north, North Palisade dominates the scene at a whopping 14,250 feet (4,343 m) high, the Sierra Nevada's third-highest peak.

▸ **MILE 3.2-6.4: Mitchell Peak Summit to Marvin Pass Trailhead**
Linger as long as possible on the summit, then simply return the way you came.

DIRECTIONS

From the Big Stump/Highway 180 Entrance Station at Kings Canyon National Park, drive 1.5 miles (2.4 km) north and turn right on the Generals Highway, heading toward Sequoia National Park. Drive 7 miles (11.3 km) and turn left on Forest Road 14S11, signed for Big Meadows and Horse Corral. Drive 4 miles (6.4 km) to Big Meadows Campground, then continue 6.7 miles (10.8 km) farther to Horse Corral Meadow. Turn right on Forest Road 13S12 and drive 3.5 miles (5.6 km) to the Marvin Pass Trailhead (drive slowly on this rutted and narrow dirt road). Note that if you're staying at the nearby Sequoia High Sierra Camp, you can hike directly from its property.

GPS COORDINATES: 36.7408, −118.7381; 36°44′26.9″ N, 118°44′17.2″ W

Mitchell Peak

This gently graded hike leads to the top of a bald granite dome with a knock-your-socks-off vista of the Great Western Divide.

DISTANCE: 3.4 miles (5.5 km) round-trip
DURATION: 1.5 hours
STARTING ELEVATION: 7,450 feet (2,271 m)
ELEVATION GAIN: 620 feet (189 m)
EFFORT: Easy-moderate
TRAIL: Packed dirt
USERS: Hikers
SEASON: Year-round; snowshoes may be needed in winter
PASSES/FEES: $35 per vehicle, valid for 7 days
MAPS: On the National Park Service app, or Tom Harrison or National Geographic maps of Sequoia and Kings Canyon National Parks
TRAILHEAD: Little Baldy Saddle Trailhead
FACILITIES: None
CONTACT: Sequoia National Park, 559/565-3341, www.nps.gov/seki

L ittle Baldy's grand vista may be the best panorama in Sequoia National Park that's attainable with an easy day hike. Pick a clear day for this short but sweet trek, or for an extra-memorable trip, start before dawn so you can watch the sunrise from the summit.

START THE HIKE

▶ **MILE 0-0.3: Little Baldy Saddle Trailhead to Big Baldy Viewpoint**
The trail starts at **Little Baldy Saddle** right alongside the Generals Highway. That means you'll hear the murmur of road noise for the first 20 minutes of your hike, but you'll quickly get distracted by the giant red firs and leafy ferns bordering the path as it climbs up and away from the road. In midsummer, you'll see clumps of broadleaf lupine brightening the forest floor.

This initial climb will get your heart rate up, but your lungs catch a break at 0.3 mile (0.5 km) where the trail reaches a **plateau.** Here you're rewarded with a spectacular view of **Big Baldy** across the highway to the west (look over your left shoulder). Big Baldy is a larger version of the same type of granite dome that you're standing on. The smooth rounded shape of these formations makes them relatively easy to ascend, especially with the help of well-constructed switchbacks.

▶ **MILE 0.3-1.7: Big Baldy Viewpoint to Little Baldy Summit**
Continuing your ascent, you'll depart the shady firs and enter a more exposed Jeffrey pine and manzanita forest. The gently graded trail undulates along the ridgeline, passing some burn scars from the 2021 KNP Complex

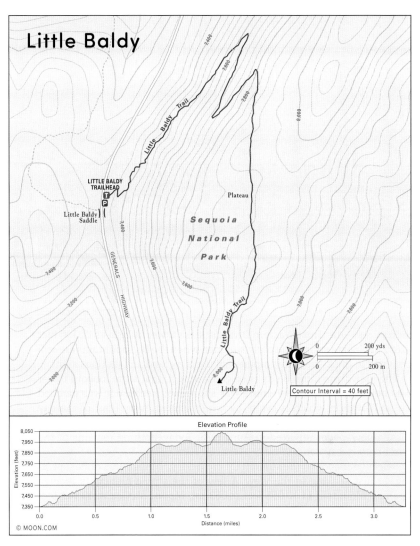

Little Baldy

LITTLE BALDY TRAILHEAD

Little Baldy
Saddle

Plateau

Sequoia

National

Park

GENERALS HIGHWAY

Little Baldy Trail

Little Baldy

0   200 yds

0   200 m

Contour Interval = 40 feet

Elevation Profile

Elevation (feet)

8,050
7,950
7,850
7,750
7,650
7,550
7,450
7,350

0.0   0.5   1.0   1.5   2.0   2.5   3.0

Distance (miles)

© MOON.COM

Fire, which just barely singed this trail but did far more extensive damage to trails and forests across the highway.

The higher you go, the trees decrease and the bare granite increases, expanding your views of distant peaks to the north and east. You might come across a furry marmot or a western fence lizard scurrying along the rocks, or spot a mule deer browsing the greenery. If you hear a strange sound like the beating of a drum—whump, whump, whump—you'll know that a male blue grouse is sounding his mating call nearby.

In short order, you crest **Little Baldy's summit,** where your vistas open wide. Stroll around on the summit's broad treeless expanse and marvel at Little Baldy's 360-degree perspective on Sequoia and Kings Canyon's most notable landmarks. Look for the jagged spires of Castle Rocks to the southeast, and the massive Silliman Crest and Great Western Divide to the north and east. The latter is a prominent ridge of mountains that parallels the

LITTLE BALDY TRAIL ▲

Sierra Crest—the Great Western Divide's peaks tower as high as 12,000 feet (3,657 m). In late spring and early summer, when the big mountains are still crowned in thick snow, this alpine tableau is a grand and glorious sight.

The view from Little Baldy is so good, in fact, that a fire lookout tower was built here in 1934. Its tenure was short-lived because it was perched "at an elevation which is swept by winds almost every hour of the day and night, making observations difficult and living disagreeable," as the Visalia newspaper reported in April 1938. Today, nothing remains of the wind-battered structure.

Select your spot on the summit for picnicking, sunbathing, philosophizing, or just soaking in the view. A few of the alpine highlights include Spanish Mountain at 10,051 feet (3,063 m), Mount McGee at 12,969 feet (3,953 m), Mount Goddard at 13,568 feet (4,135 m), Kettle Dome at 9,446 feet (2,879 m), and Finger Peak at 12,404 feet (3,781 m). Tokopah Valley lies slightly southeast, and farther south is Mineral King, marked by the distinctively pointy shape of Sawtooth Peak.

▶ **MILE 1.7-3.4: Little Baldy Summit to Little Baldy Saddle Trailhead**
Wave good-bye to this epic Sierra Nevada panorama, then retrace your steps to the trailhead.

DIRECTIONS

From the Big Stump/Highway 180 Entrance Station at Kings Canyon National Park, drive 1.5 miles (2.4 km) north and turn right on the Generals Highway, heading toward Sequoia National Park. Drive 18 miles (29 km) to the Little Baldy Trailhead at Little Baldy Saddle, 1.3 miles (2.1 km) south of Dorst Campground. The trail begins on the left (east) side of the road.

GPS COORDINATES: 36.6200, −118.8092; 36°37'12" N, 118°48'33.1" W

Tokopah Falls
SEQUOIA NATIONAL PARK

A riverside ramble leads to the tallest waterfall in Sequoia National Park, where the Marble Fork Kaweah River tumbles 1,200 feet (366 m) over polished granite.

BEST: Waterfall Hikes
DISTANCE: 4.2 miles (6.8 km) round-trip
DURATION: 2 hours
STARTING ELEVATION: 6,770 feet (2,063 m)
ELEVATION GAIN: 604 feet (184 km)
EFFORT: Easy-moderate
TRAIL: Packed dirt
USERS: Hikers
SEASON: Year-round; snowshoes may be needed in winter
PASSES/FEES: $35 per vehicle, valid for 7 days
MAPS: On the National Park Service app, or Tom Harrison or National Geographic maps of Sequoia and Kings Canyon National Parks
TRAILHEAD: Lodgepole Trailhead
FACILITIES: Restroom
CONTACT: Sequoia National Park, 559/565-3341, www.nps.gov/seki

This hike to Tokopah Falls' showering spectacle earns high marks with hikers and nonhikers alike. It's remarkably scenic, easy enough for young children, and culminates at the base of a showstopping 1,200-foot-high (366-m) waterfall. Not surprisingly, the trail attracts a crowd, so show up early in the morning or late in the day so you can enjoy this walk without too much companionship.

START THE HIKE

▶ **MILE 0-1.4: Lodgepole Parking Lot to Horse Creek Footbridge**
The hardest part of the trip is locating the trail's starting point. If you're not camping at **Lodgepole Campground,** you'll need to park outside the camp in the expansive paved trailhead lot. From there, walk to the campground **access road bridge** that crosses the Marble Fork Kaweah River, cross it, then locate the trail on the far side, to your right. The mileage shown here reflects the 0.2-mile (0.3-km) stretch from the parking lot to the trailhead.

Start walking on the wide, smooth, level path, accompanied by the sight and sound of the graceful Marble Fork. The path climbs ever so slightly as it heads into Tokopah Valley, a U-shaped valley that's similar in geological type and appearance to Yosemite Valley. Like Yosemite, it was sculpted by the grinding passage of slow-moving glaciers and the river carving through its center.

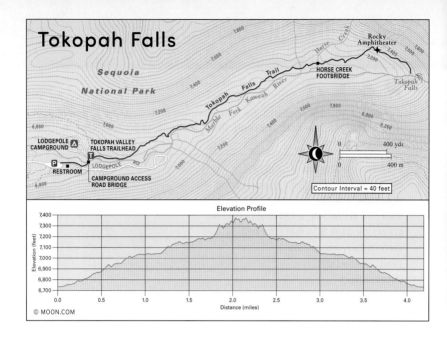

Your trail traces a nearly imperceptible incline as it parallels the Marble Fork and tunnels through a forest of shady firs, pines, incense cedars, and leafy black oaks. The trail surface alternates among a forest floor lined with soft conifer needles, small wooden bridges that cross tiny feeder creeks, and damp meadowy stretches overflowing with ferns, monkey flower, lupine, and columbine. If you're hiking in the early morning or early evening when people are scarce, you're likely to see mule deer meandering through the woods and marmots scrambling over boulders. At periodic gaps in the forest canopy, you'll spot the dramatic presence of the Watchtower, a 1,700-foot (518-m) glacially carved cliff on Tokopah Valley's south side (you can hike to the top of the Watchtower on Lakes Trail; see the hike following this one).

At 1.4 miles (2.3 km), cross Horse Creek on a **small footbridge.**

▶ MILE 1.4-2.1: Horse Creek Footbridge to Tokopah Valley Falls

After crossing the creek, you exit the forest and enter into a **rocky amphitheater** that grants unobstructed views of Tokopah Falls' 1,200-foot (366-m) cascade plummeting down the steep fractured granite of the valley's headwall. The trail's final stretch traverses a boulder field remaining from an ancient rockslide, zigzagging through a tunnel of granite rubble. In one spot, you'll have to duck your head to pass underneath the ledge of a massive boulder.

Beyond the rockslide, you arrive at the waterfall's base, where a sign pronounces the trail's end. From this vantage point, you can see only the lower 200 feet (61 m) of **Tokopah Falls,** but during snowmelt season—typically April to June—or after summer thunderstorms, when the water peaks at maximal flow, the falls' powerful thunder can drown out human conversation. In late summer and fall, the cascade is much less ebullient.

▲ TOKOPAH FALLS

Whether it's a cacophony of gushing water or a gentle trickle, you'll want to find a rock to sit on and admire the show.

▶ **MILE 2.1–4.2: Tokopah Valley Falls to Lodgepole Parking Lot**
Retrace your steps back to your car and enjoy this stunning riverside scenery all over again.

DIRECTIONS

From the Big Stump/Highway 180 Entrance Station at Kings Canyon National Park, drive 1.5 miles (2.4 km) north and turn right on the Generals Highway, heading toward Sequoia National Park. Drive 24 miles (39 km) to the left turnoff for Lodgepole Campground. Turn left and drive 0.75 mile (1.2 km) to the large parking area just before the bridge over the Marble Fork Kaweah River. Walk across the bridge to access the trailhead on the far side.

GPS COORDINATES: 36.6044, −118.7257; 36°36′15.8″ N, 118°43′32.5″ W

SEQUOIA & KINGS CANYON NATIONAL PARKS

Tokopah Falls

A daylong saunter through subalpine high country leads to dramatic granite cliffs, stately fir forests, and four gem-like lakes.

BEST: Summer Hikes

DISTANCE: 8-12 miles (12.9-19.3 km) round-trip

DURATION: 5-7 hours

STARTING ELEVATION: 7,315 feet (2,230 m)

ELEVATION GAIN: 3,720 feet (1,134 m)

EFFORT: Strenuous

TRAIL: Packed dirt, granite ledge

USERS: Hikers

SEASON: Year-round; snowshoes may be needed in winter

PASSES/FEES: $35 per vehicle, valid for 7 days

MAPS: On the National Park Service app, or Tom Harrison or National Geographic maps of Sequoia and Kings Canyon National Parks

TRAILHEAD: Wolverton Trailhead

FACILITIES: Restroom

CONTACT: Sequoia National Park, 559/565-3341, www.nps.gov/seki

START THE HIKE

▸ **MILE 0-2.1: Wolverton Trailhead to Watchtower/Hump Split**

At the **Wolverton Trailhead, Lakes Trail** begins in a shady red fir forest. Ignore two junctions in the first 0.3 mile (0.5 km) of trail—just stay straight and head uphill through the impressively large conifers. You'll climb moderately but steadily through forest and a peaceful meadow to a **junction** with Panther Gap Trail at 1.8 miles (2.9 km). Bear left (north), then ascend more gradually to another **junction** 0.3 mile (0.5 km) farther. The Lakes Trail splits into two paths here: One path traverses a ledge trail blasted into a sheer cliff towering above the Marble Fork of the Kaweah River and visits the Watchtower, a 1,700-foot-high (518-m) granite promontory. The other climbs up and over the Hump—a steep ridge—on a forested path that gets the job done quickly but can't compete with the Watchtower's visual drama.

▸ **MILE 2.1-4: Watchtower-Hump Split to Heather Lake (via Hump Route)**

For the sake of variety, this trek follows the slightly shorter **Hump route** out to the lakes and the Watchtower route on the return. Bear right (east) for the Hump and begin a relentless but shaded climb through lodgepole pine and fir forest. When you finally top the ridge at a **viewpoint** at 3.5 miles

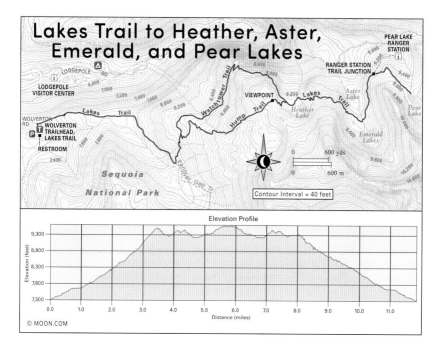

(5.6 km), your hard work is over. Now it's an easy 0.2-mile (0.3-km) march downhill into the lake basin, where you'll note the Watchtower Trail coming in on your left (that will be your return leg). For now, bear right (east), and in just a few minutes you'll be stripping off your socks and shoes and plunging your feet into cold alpine water. Pretty **Heather Lake** (elevation 9,280 ft/2,828 m) has a steep granite backdrop, a smattering of lodgepole pines, red firs, and willows, and rocky ledges for sunbathing or picnicking.

▶ MILE 4-5.1: Heather Lake to Aster and Emerald Lakes

For a better chance at solitude than you'll have at Heather Lake, put your shoes back on and continue along Lakes Trail. There's only about 200 feet (61 m) of climbing over the next 0.9 mile (1.4 km) to Aster Lake, which lies on the far side of a small ridge, off the trail to your left (north). You'll see the lake from the trail; to get there, watch for a **spur trail** heading 0.1 mile (0.2 km) north across granite slabs. Take a peek at rockbound **Aster Lake,** which differs little from other glacially carved Sierra lakes, which is to say it's completely lovely in every way. Or simply push on to arguably lovelier **Emerald Lake** (elevation 9,230 ft/2,813 m), tucked into a rocky basin on the main trail's right (south) side. Emerald Lake's sheer granite wall rises straight up for a few thousand feet, creating an austerely beautiful amphitheater.

▶ MILE 5.1-6.1: Aster and Emerald Lakes to Pear Lake

If you still have some energy to burn, beautiful Pear Lake lies another mile (1.6 km) beyond the spur trails to Aster and Emerald Lake and 400 feet (122 m) higher. At 0.5 mile (0.8 km) beyond Emerald Lake, a **spur trail** heads left to the **Pear Lake Ranger Station;** keep right (southeast) for another 0.5 mile

(0.8 km) to reach **Pear Lake**'s northern edge. Larger than the three other lakes combined, Pear Lake is an alpine stunner at 9,550 feet (2,911 m) elevation that's set directly below Alta Peak (11,204 ft/3,415 m). Once you arrive, you'll find it difficult to tear yourself away from this photogenic landscape of polished granite, cobalt-blue water, and sun-kissed Sierra sky.

▶ **MILE 6.1–12: Pear Lake to Wolverton Trailhead (via Watchtower Route)**

When you're ready to return, retrace your steps past Emerald, Aster, and Heather Lakes to the Watchtower-Hump trail junction 0.2 mile (0.3 km) west of Heather Lake, then veer right (northwest) on **Watchtower Trail.** The route climbs out of the basin, then creeps along a granite ledge more than 1,000 feet (305 m) above Tokopah Valley. Once you glimpse the cliff's near-vertical drop-offs, you'll understand why this route is closed in the icy-snowy season.

The rock-blasted Watchtower Trail offers an astounding perspective on **Tokopah Falls** flowing down the back of its U-shaped valley. From your high perch, you have a dizzying view of the entire 1,200-foot-high (366-m) cascade—a perspective you can't get from the valley floor.

Keep marching along this view-filled ledge until you reach the **Watchtower** itself, an enormous granite pinnacle that's just barely attached to the valley rim. Take some time to carefully explore its summit, but exercise extreme caution around the precipitous drop-offs.

Beyond the Watchtower, the route back to the trailhead is a gradual descent through dense firs and pines, so enjoy some easy, pleasant walking to finish out this superb alpine day.

DIRECTIONS

From the Big Stump/Highway 180 Entrance Station at Kings Canyon National Park, drive 1.5 miles (2.4 km) north and turn right on the Generals Highway, heading toward Sequoia National Park. Drive 27 miles (43 km), past Wuksachi Lodge and Lodgepole Campground, to the Wolverton turnoff on the left (east) side of the road. Turn left on Wolverton Road and drive 1.5 miles (2.4 km) to the parking area and trailhead, on the left. If you are entering the parks from the Ash Mountain Entrance, drive 19 miles (31 km) north to the Wolverton Road turnoff and turn right.

GPS COORDINATES: 36.5965, −118.7343; 36°35'47.4" N, 118°44'3.5" W

8 General Sherman Tree and Congress Trail

SEQUOIA NATIONAL PARK

Giant Forest's gargantuan giant sequoia trees have been growing since before King Arthur's knights gathered at the Round Table. See the biggest of them all on this easy family-friendly walk.

BEST: Redwood Hikes

DISTANCE: 2.9 miles (4.7 km) round-trip

DURATION: 1.5 hours

STARTING ELEVATION: 7,149 feet (2,179 m)

ELEVATION GAIN: 265 feet (81 m)

EFFORT: Easy

TRAIL: Paved trail, dirt trail; wheelchair users can access the General Sherman via a separate trailhead

USERS: Hikers

SEASON: Year-round; snowshoes may be needed in winter

PASSES/FEES: $35 per vehicle, valid for 7 days

MAPS: On the National Park Service app, or Tom Harrison or National Geographic maps of Sequoia and Kings Canyon National Parks

TRAILHEAD: Sherman Tree Trailhead

FACILITIES: Restroom

CONTACT: Sequoia National Park, 559/565-3341, www.nps.gov/seki

START THE HIKE

▶ **MILE 0-0.4: Sherman Tree Trailhead to General Sherman Tree**

The trek to the base of the General Sherman begins in highly civilized fashion at a **huge signboard,** which marks the start of an 8-foot-wide (2.4-km) paved trail. With concrete stairsteps, handrails, and beautifully designed benches, this "designer" trail looks more like the entrance to an art museum or sports arena than a forest footpath—and the number of people around you will support this idea.

At 0.3 mile (0.5 km), stop at an **overlook** for a full view of the General Sherman, your first inspiring glimpse at the colossal tree. In another 100 yards (91 m), you reach a **signboard and junction;** the trail on the right leads to the Sherman Tree, and left is the Congress Trail. Go right (north) and you'll reach the **General Sherman Tree** in another 50 feet (15 m). From close up, there's no denying this sequoia is a doozy.

▶ **MILE 0.4-1.8: General Sherman Tree to McKinley Tree**

Backtrack to the signboard that you passed a few minutes ago, then follow the sign for **Congress Trail.** You'll walk the upper leg of the loop first,

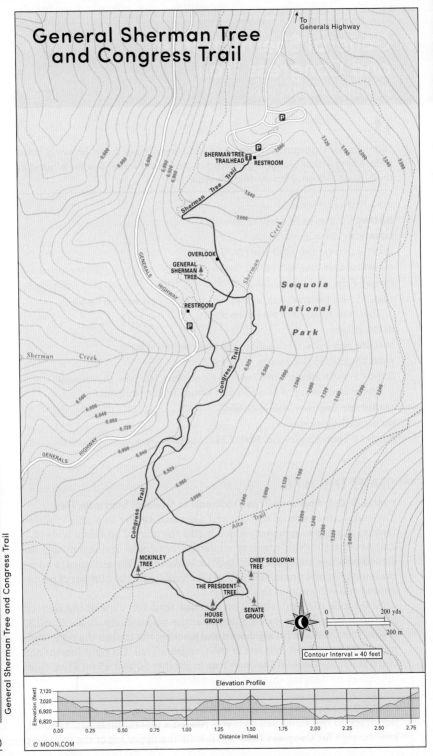

General Sherman Tree and Congress Trail

To Generals Highway

SHERMAN TREE TRAILHEAD
RESTROOM

Sherman Tree Trail

7,040
7,000

OVERLOOK
GENERAL SHERMAN TREE
RESTROOM

Sherman Creek

Sequoia

National

Park

Congress Trail

6,920
6,960
7,000
7,040
7,080
7,120
7,160
7,200
7,240

Sherman Creek

6,560
6,600
6,640
6,680
6,720
6,760
6,800

GENERALS HIGHWAY

6,520
6,960
7,000

Congress Trail

7,040
7,080
7,120
7,160
7,200
7,240
7,280
7,320
7,400

Alta Trail

MCKINLEY TREE

CHIEF SEQUOYAH TREE

THE PRESIDENT TREE

HOUSE GROUP

SENATE GROUP

0   200 yds
0   200 m

Contour Interval = 40 feet

Elevation Profile

© MOON.COM

▲ SEQUOIAS ALONG THE CONGRESS TRAIL

traveling clockwise. Almost immediately you'll stroll past several sequoias with diameters the size of most living rooms. Some trees have name plates and others do not, but each one is awe-worthy—these giants have seen a lot in their 20-century-plus lifetimes. The trees are so incomprehensibly large that they seem to belong to a forest of a dream world, not the real world.

At a **junction** with Alta Trail 0.9 mile (1.4 km) from the General Sherman, veer right (southwest) to stay on Congress Trail and proceed another 0.3 mile (0.5 km) to the **President Tree,** currently the world's third-largest tree by volume, after General Sherman and General Grant. The President Tree and the Grant Tree trade places on the Top 3 list every few years. Both trees are still growing, storms can knock off branches, and lightning and wildfires happen, so the contest isn't over, but the President always wins in the age category. The venerable tree is presumed to be 3,300 years old; the Grant Tree is only half that age.

Compare that to the duration of your own fleeting existence, then take a look at the President's neighbor, the **Chief Sequoyah Tree,** named for the Cherokee chief who created the Cherokee alphabet. Then proceed a few yards farther to marvel at the **Senate Group,** a cluster of nearly a dozen massive sequoias growing in proximity, like a close-knit family.

You might think the big tree show can't get any better than this, but only 0.2 mile (0.3 km) farther—just as the Congress Trail begins to circle back—you'll come up the **House Group,** an even denser collection of close-proximity sequoias. You might have to sit down for a moment so your brain can process what you're seeing. If you're feeling small and humble, you're not alone.

One hundred feet (30 m) beyond lies a **major junction of trails.** Go right (north) on Congress Trail to pay homage to the **McKinley Tree,** which

SEQUOIAS IN THE CONGRESS TRAIL'S "HOUSE" CLUSTER ▲

measures 291 feet (89 m) tall—taller than the General Sherman, but not nearly as wide.

▶ MILE 1.8-2.9: McKinley Tree to Sherman Tree Trailhead

Finish out the Congress Trail loop, then turn left (northwest) to visit the General Sherman a second time, or simply turn right (north) to head back uphill to your car. The final 0.4-mile (0.6-km) stretch to the parking lot climbs nearly 200 feet (61 m), so you'll see plenty of people taking advantage of the trail's "designer" benches.

DIRECTIONS

From the Big Stump/Highway 180 Entrance Station at Kings Canyon National Park, drive 1.5 miles (2.4 km) north and turn right on the Generals Highway, heading toward Sequoia National Park. Drive 27 miles (43 km), past Wuksachi Lodge and Lodgepole Campground, to the Wolverton turn-off, on the left (east) side of the road. Turn left on Wolverton Road and drive 0.6 mile (1 km), then turn right. Drive another 0.6 mile (1 km) and turn right again, following the signs to Sherman Tree Parking. If you are entering the parks from the Ash Mountain Entrance, drive 19 miles (31 km) north to the Wolverton Road turnoff and turn right.

GPS COORDINATES: 36.5847, −118.7498; 36°35'4.9" N, 118°44'59.3" W

9

Moro Rock from Giant Forest Museum

SEQUOIA NATIONAL PARK

Earn that souvenir T-shirt proclaiming "I climbed Moro Rock!" on this sequoia-filled stroll that culminates with an ascent of Sequoia National Park's most famous granite dome.

BEST: Kid-Friendly Hikes

DISTANCE: 3.6 miles (5.8 km) round-trip

DURATION: 2 hours

STARTING ELEVATION: 6,409 feet (1,953 m)

ELEVATION GAIN: 554 feet (169 m)

EFFORT: Easy-moderate

TRAIL: Packed dirt, granite stairsteps

USERS: Hikers

SEASON: Year-round; Moro Rock stairs may be closed in winter due to ice or snow

PASSES/FEES: $35 per vehicle, valid for 7 days

MAPS: On the National Park Service app, or Tom Harrison or National Geographic maps of Sequoia and Kings Canyon National Parks

TRAILHEAD: Giant Forest Museum

FACILITIES: Restroom, visitor center-museum

CONTACT: Sequoia National Park, 559/565-3341, www.nps.gov/seki

START THE HIKE

▶ **MILE 0-1.4: Giant Forest Museum to Hanging Rock**

From the log cabin that houses the **Giant Forest Museum,** start walking on **Moro Rock-Crescent Meadow Road.** In less than 50 yards (46 m), you'll

see the **Moro Rock Trail** sign on the right side of the road. Follow this meandering dirt trail through the forest, passing one supersize sequoia tree after another. The sequoias are joined by sugar pines, red and white firs, and incense cedars, but you'll hardly notice the other conifers because the massive sequoias steal the limelight.

At 0.7 mile (1.1 km) from the start, you'll pass the **Booker T. Washington Tree,** a giant sequoia named for the Black educator, author, and community leader of the late 1800s and early 1900s. At the **junction** in

SEQUOIA & KINGS CANYON NATIONAL PARKS

Moro Rock from Giant Forest Museum

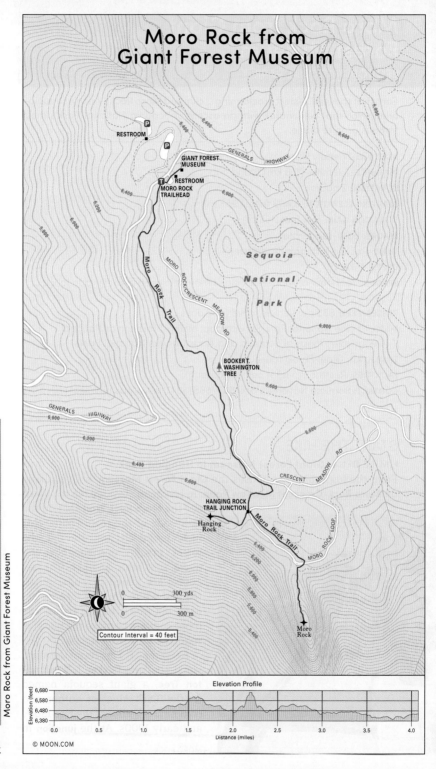

Moro Rock from Giant Forest Museum

RESTROOM

GIANT FOREST MUSEUM

RESTROOM

MORO ROCK TRAILHEAD

Moro Rock Trail

MORO ROCK/CRESCENT MEADOW RD

Sequoia National Park

GENERALS HIGHWAY

BOOKER T. WASHINGTON TREE

GENERALS HIGHWAY

CRESCENT MEADOW RD

HANGING ROCK TRAIL JUNCTION

Hanging Rock

Moro Rock Trail

MORO ROCK LOOP

Moro Rock

0 300 yds
0 300 m

Contour Interval = 40 feet

Elevation Profile

Elevation (feet)

6,680
6,580
6,480
6,380

0.0   0.5   1.0   1.5   2.0   2.5   3.0   3.5   4.0

Distance (miles)

© MOON.COM

▲ MORO ROCK

another 0.6 mile (1 km), ignore the left fork that leads to the paved road to Moro Rock; instead, bear right (south) for **Hanging Rock,** just 100 yards (91 m) farther and a quick tromp uphill. Hanging Rock, like Moro Rock, is a rounded granite dome—a geologic formation created by a process known as exfoliation. The dome is well named: The monolith appears to "hang" precariously from the cliff edge you're standing on.

From this exposed granite perch, you have a clear view of neighboring Moro Rock, and you can also gaze west down the weaving curves of the Generals Highway to the Middle Fork Kaweah River canyon.

▸ **MILE 1.4-2: Hanging Rock to Moro Rock Summit**
Backtrack from Hanging Rock to the turnoff for Moro Rock you passed earlier. This time, bear right (southeast) for Moro Rock and follow the road 0.1 mile (0.2 km) downhill to the **Moro Rock parking lot.** Check out the interpretive sign that describes the 1931 construction of this complex granite-blasted trail. Imagine what it was like to climb Moro Rock in the 1920s, when rickety wooden stairs led to the top.

Now your "rock climbing" commences—but it's more like a stair-climbing workout. You'll reach **Moro Rock's summit** in 0.3 mile (0.5 km) by ascending concrete ramps and granite stairsteps etched into the dome—390 steps, to be exact. Handrails line the rock-blasted trail, and gripping them will ensure you don't fall off the near-vertical escarpment. If you have small children with you, keep a grip on them too.

The path is steep enough to get you panting, but the views will take your breath away. On a clear day you can see all the way to the Coast Range, 100 miles (161 km) west. In closer focus is the Middle Fork Kaweah River gorge, 4,000 feet (1,219 m) below, plus the zigzagging Generals Highway snaking downhill through the foothills to Three Rivers.

Once you reach the dome's relatively broad 6,725-foot (2,050-m) summit, hold on to the railing and admire the view of the massive Great Western Divide, a saw-toothed skyline of alpine cirques and glacier-carved peaks. Of dozens of landmarks, you can easily pick out Castle Rocks at 9,180 feet (2,798 m), Triple Divide Peak at 12,634 feet (3,851 m), and Mount Stewart at 12,205 feet (3,720 m).

There's one Sierra summit that's missing from this knock-your-socks-off vista, and it's the biggest of them all. Mount Whitney, the tallest peak in the contiguous United States at 14,495 feet (4,418 m), is practically due east from Moro Rock and only about 60 miles (97 km) distant, but you can't see it over the high peaks of the Great Western Divide.

▶ MILE 2-3.6: Moro Rock Summit to Giant Forest Museum

To return to your car, simply retrace your steps, and if you skip the short side trip to Hanging Rock, you'll return to Giant Forest Museum after logging 3.6 miles (5.8 km).

DIRECTIONS

From the Big Stump/Highway 180 Entrance Station at Kings Canyon National Park, drive 1.5 miles (2.4 km) north and turn right on the Generals Highway, heading toward Sequoia National Park. Drive 32 miles (52 km) to Giant Forest and park in the Big Trees Trail parking lot, across from the Giant Forest Museum. If you're entering the parks from the Ash Mountain Entrance, drive north on the Generals Highway for 16.5 miles (27 km) to Giant Forest.

GPS COORDINATES: 36.5645, -118.7731; 36°33′52.2″ N, 118°46′23.2″ W

10

Tharp's Log and Log Meadow
SEQUOIA NATIONAL PARK

✿ 🏛 🧍🚶

Stroll past two of Giant Forest's pristine meadows, their green expanses bounded by centuries-old sequoias, and visit the hollowed-log abode of an 1860s rancher.

BEST: Kid-Friendly Hikes
DISTANCE: 4 miles (6.4 km) round-trip
DURATION: 2 hours
STARTING ELEVATION: 6,776 feet (2,065 m)
ELEVATION GAIN: 444 feet (135 m)
EFFORT: Easy
TRAIL: Packed dirt; neighboring Crescent Meadow Trail is wheelchair-accessible
USERS: Hikers
SEASON: April-October, or any time Crescent Meadow Road is snow-free and open
PASSES/FEES: $35 per vehicle, valid for 7 days
MAPS: On the National Park Service app, or Tom Harrison or National Geographic maps of Sequoia and Kings Canyon National Parks
TRAILHEAD: Crescent Meadow Trailhead
FACILITIES: Restroom
CONTACT: Sequoia National Park, 559/565-3341, www.nps.gov/seki

START THE HIKE

▸ **MILE 0-1.1: Crescent Meadow Trailhead to Tharp's Log**

Start hiking from the **Crescent Meadow parking lot**'s north side at the trail sign for Chimney Tree, to the left of the restrooms. Stroll along Crescent Meadow's west side, then turn right (east) at a **four-way junction** at 0.5 mile (0.8 km) and head gently uphill through a forest of sequoias and incense cedars. You'll reach a **spur trail** to the **Chimney Tree** on the left at 0.8 mile (1.3 km). Walk the 20-yard (18-m) spur to the base of this remarkable sequoia, which was killed by a fire in 1919. Its sturdy skeleton remains standing.

Backtrack on the Chimney Tree spur and continue on the main trail toward **Tharp's Log.** In another 0.3 mile (0.5 km), you're standing on **Log Meadow**'s northwest edge, where rancher Hale Tharp lived in a fallen sequoia log for nearly 30 summers, from 1861 to 1890. Tharp fashioned his cozy rustic home from a hollowed fire-scarred sequoia trunk that found its final resting place on the meadow's edge. You can't enter the log, but you can peek inside the windows and door to see his simple dining room table, fireplace chimney, front door, and window shutters with hinges made from horseshoes.

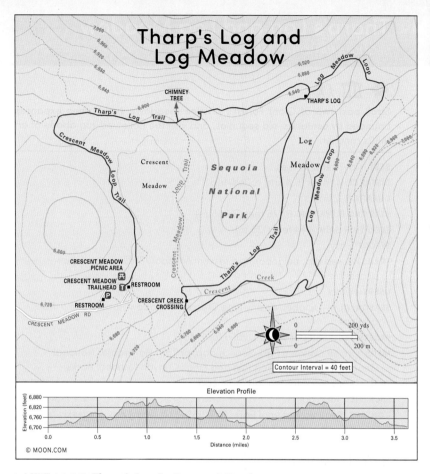

Tharp's Log and Log Meadow

Contour Interval = 40 feet

Elevation Profile

© MOON.COM

▶ **MILE 1.1–1.9: Tharp's Log to Crescent Creek**

From Tharp's log, turn right (south) and ramble along Log Meadow's western edge, now following a paved pathway. Both Log Meadow and its beautiful neighbor, Crescent Meadow, extend for more than 0.5 mile (0.8 km), so circumnavigating them is a slow proposition. But you won't want to hurry. Giant bracken ferns line the path, and massive sequoias stand guard at the meadow's edges, their trunks glowing cinnamon-red in the filtered sunlight. Even if you've seen sequoias in dozens of other places, these trees will take your breath away. It's impossible to feel jaded when you're near these behemoths.

Curve around the meadow's west side, then meet up with **Crescent Creek** on its south side. You're now 0.8 mile (1.3 km) from Tharp's Log.

▶ **MILE 1.9–2.9: Crescent Creek to Tharp's Log**

You could easily head back to your car from this point—it's only about 100 yards (91 m) away—but instead, cross the creek and skirt Crescent Meadow's southern edge, then make a sharp left (north) on **Log Meadow Loop Trail.** Leave Crescent Creek and its meadow behind and ascend the hillside, heading deeper into the forest.

▲ THARP'S LOG

Your trail parallels the creek for 0.2 mile (0.3 km) before descending to the southern edge of Log Meadow, then traces along its eastern edge for 1 mile (1.6 km) back to Tharp's Log. It's hard to pick a favorite, but this might be the loveliest stretch of this trip. You may spot deer browsing in the carpet of sedges, corn lilies, lupine, and other wildflowers in Log Meadow. You'll certainly see many massive living sequoias with no fences around them and no name plates at their bases. Dozens of fallen giants are strewn across the meadow, some with root balls as large as small houses. It's a special experience to see giant sequoias in their "natural" environment, minus the trappings of the park's more manicured groves. This exquisite place evokes reverence, so linger, wander, and worship as you please.

▶ MILE 2.9–4: Tharp's Log to Crescent Meadow Trailhead

Once you return to Tharp's Log, turn left (west) to retrace your steps past the Chimney Tree to your car.

DIRECTIONS

From the Big Stump/Highway 180 Entrance Station at Kings Canyon National Park, drive 1.5 miles (2.4 km) north and turn right on the Generals Highway, heading toward Sequoia National Park. Drive 32 miles (52 km) to Giant Forest, and check at the Giant Forest Museum to see if Crescent Meadow Road is open to private vehicles, or if you must ride the shuttle bus. If the road is open, proceed 3.5 miles (5.6 km) on Crescent Meadow Road to the Crescent Meadow parking area. If you're entering the parks from the Ash Mountain Entrance, drive north on the Generals Highway for 16.5 miles (27 km) to Giant Forest.

GPS COORDINATES: 36.5549, −118.7488; 36°33′17.6″ N, 118°44′55.7″ W

SEQUOIA & KINGS CANYON NATIONAL PARKS

Tharp's Log and Log Meadow

BEST NEARBY BITES

Sequoia and Kings Canyon National Parks encompass a vast mountainous area that's separated from the closest population centers by circuitous mountain roads. If you're on a hiking trip in either park, your best bet is to eat and sleep here too—it will save you a lot of driving time and gasoline. This dining guide will help you find the closest meal to each trailhead in this chapter:

NEAR CEDAR GROVE, KINGS CANYON
Nearby Hikes: No. 1 Mist Falls; No. 2 River Trail to Roaring River Falls and Zumwalt Meadow

In the remote Cedar Grove region of Kings Canyon National Park, it's wise to pack your car with plenty of snacks and water. Within an hour's drive, the only spot for a meal is **Cedar Grove Grill at Cedar Grove Lodge** (off Hwy. 180, Cedar Grove Village, no phone, www.visitsequoia.com, lunch 11am-3pm daily, dinner 4pm-8pm daily Memorial Day-late Sept., dates vary). This order-at-the-counter eatery serves a simple menu of beef burgers, veggie burgers, and hot sandwiches, plus hearty bowls of chili. If the grill is closed, you can pick up snacks at the neighboring **Cedar Grove Market** (7am-9pm daily summer). Both the grill and market are located in Cedar Grove Village.

NEAR GRANT GROVE, KINGS CANYON
Nearby Hikes: No. 3 General Grant Tree, North Grove, and Dead Giant; No. 4 Mitchell Peak

For breakfast, lunch, or dinner, head to **Grant Grove Restaurant and Court-yard** (Hwy. 180, Grant Grove Village, no phone, www.visitsequoia.com, breakfast 7:30am-10am, lunch 11am-3pm, dinner 4pm-8pm daily). The park concessionaire-run restaurant has a large outdoor courtyard seating area and a 100-seat indoor dining room (as of this book's press time, indoor dining is closed). For breakfast, choose from omelets, pancakes, and breakfast burritos. Lunch and dinner options include salads, soups, grilled sandwiches, burgers, and individual-size pizzas. Best of all, there's fruit pie for dessert.

Twenty minutes south of Grant Grove in Sequoia National Forest, **Mon-tecito-Sequoia Lodge** (800/843-8677 or 559/565-3388, www.mslodge.com, hours and availability vary) serves a buffet-style breakfast, lunch, and dinner that is sometimes open to nonguests, but not usually in the summer months. Nearby **Stony Creek Lodge** (877/828-1440, www.sequoia-kingscanyon.com) has a café that serves pizza on summer weekends, plus a small grocery store (8am-8pm daily May-early Oct.).

NEAR GIANT FOREST, WOLVERTON, AND LODGEPOLE AREAS, SEQUOIA
Nearby Hikes: No. 5 Little Baldy, No. 6 Tokopah Falls, No. 7 Lakes Trail to Heather, Aster, Emerald, and Pear Lakes, No. 8 General Sherman Tree and Congress Trail, No. 9 Moro Rock from Giant Forest Museum, No. 10 Tharp's Log and Log Meadow

In this central region of Sequoia National Park, your best place for a pleasant sit-down meal is at the Wuksachi Lodge's **The Peaks Restaurant** (Generals

Hwy., 7 mi/11.3 km north of Giant Forest, no phone, www.visitsequoia.com, breakfast 7am-10am, lunch 11:30am-3:30pm, dinner 5pm-8:30pm year-round). The Peaks serves breakfast and dinner in its dining room overlooking the Silliman Crest; you can also order pizza and salads outdoors on the Wuksachi Pizza Deck at lunch and dinner.

For takeout food or groceries, swing by **Lodgepole Market and Deli** (adjacent to Lodgepole Campground, mid-Apr.-mid-Oct.), 2.5 miles (4 km) south of Wuksachi Lodge and 4.5 miles (7.2 km) north of Giant Forest.

OUTSIDE THE PARKS

When you're hungry, you may not want to drive 30 to 60 minutes outside of the park boundaries, but if you do, you'll find good dining options in three gateway towns—Three Rivers, Miramonte, and Dunlap.

Twenty-five circuitous miles (40 km) south of Giant Forest (plan on a one-hour drive from the General Sherman Tree), charming Three Rivers is the largest gateway town and has a half-dozen casual restaurants and food trucks. In the latter category, **Quesadilla Gorilla** (41119 Sierra Dr., Three Rivers, 559/602-6329; www.quesadillagorilla.com, 11am-8pm Sat.-Mon.) is a perennial favorite for—you guessed it—quesadillas with a variety of fillings, from veggie to chili verde and bacon.

If it's beer you're craving, head to **Three Rivers Brewing Company** (41763 Sierra Dr., Three Rivers, 559/909-5483, www.threeriversbrewingco.com, 11am-9pm Sun.-Mon., 11am-10pm Thurs.-Sat.). Try a red rye or a blue raspberry seltzer, and pair it with a pupusa or two from the Salvadoran food truck **Pupusas la Sabrosa** (41763 Sierra Dr., Three Rivers, 559/661-6263, 11am-7pm Thurs.-Mon.) that's parked outside.

For a sit-down meal of new wave California diner food, nosh on fried brussels sprouts and vegan burgers at the picnic tables alongside the Kaweah River at **Ol Buckaroo** (41695 Sierra Dr., Three Rivers, 559/465-5088, www.oldbuckaroo.com, 5pm-9pm Thurs.-Sat., 10am-1pm Sun.).

Closest to Grant Grove (plan on a 30-minute drive from the General Grant Tree) is the **Pinehurst Lodge** (53783 N. Hwy. 245, Miramonte, 559/336-2603, noon-9pm daily), famous for its rustic barn-style ambience, burgers, and jalapeño poppers.

Or follow Highway 180 west to Dunlap, about 27 miles (43 km) and 45 minutes from Grant Grove, and use a pile of napkins eating pulled pork and tri-tip at **Twin Valleys Smoky Mountain Barbecue** (39316 Dunlap Rd., Dunlap, 559/338-0160, 11am-8pm Tues.-Sun.).

NEARBY CAMPGROUNDS

NAME	DESCRIPTION	FACILITIES	SEASON	FEE
Azalea	Shady conifer forest near General Grant Tree and hiking trails	110 sites for tents or RVs up to 47 ft/14.3 m, restrooms, drinking water	year-round	$22

Sequoia National Park, Highway 180, in Grant Grove Village, 877/444-6777, www.recreation.gov

NAME	DESCRIPTION	FACILITIES	SEASON	FEE
Lodgepole	On the Marble Fork Kaweah River, near Giant Forest hiking trails	214 sites for tents or RVs up to 40 ft/12 m, restrooms, drinking water, dump station	late May to late November	$22

Sequoia National Park, Generals Highway near Giant Forest, 877/444-6777, www.recreation.gov

NAME	DESCRIPTION	FACILITIES	SEASON	FEE
Princess	Hiking trails, sequoias, meadow, 3 mi/4.8 km from Hume Lake	88 sites for tents or RVs up to 35 ft/10.7 m, vault toilets, drinking water, dump station	mid-May to mid-September	$32

Sequoia National Forest, Highway 180, at the Hume Lake Junction, 877/444-6777, www.recreation.gov

NEARBY CAMPGROUNDS (continued)

NAME	DESCRIPTION	FACILITIES	SEASON	FEE
Stony Creek	Stony Creek runs through camp, near Giant Forest hiking trails	50 sites for tents or RVs up to 35 ft/10.7 m, vault toilets, drinking water	mid-May to mid-September	$32

Sequoia National Forest, Generals Highway, near Giant Forest, 877/444-6777, www.recreation.gov

NAME	DESCRIPTION	FACILITIES	SEASON	FEE
Moraine	On the South Fork Kings River, near Cedar Grove hiking trails	121 sites for tents or RVs up to 35 ft/10.7 m, restrooms, drinking water	late May to mid-September	$22

Kings Canyon National Park, Highway 180 in Cedar Grove Village, 877/444-6777, www.recreation.gov

SANTA CRUZ, MONTEREY & BIG SUR

SANTA CRUZ

With coastal redwoods, 14 state parks and beaches, waterfalls, vibrant wildlife, and mountains, plus well-regarded local breweries, farm-to-table meals, and a colorful community unlike anywhere else, Santa Cruz County offers a bit of everything you'd seek from an adventure in Northern California. It will delight you with thousands of monarch butterflies at the Monarch Butterfly Nature Preserve and its beautiful trails and vistas from mountains to sea.

▲ QUAIL HOLLOW LOOP

▲ OLD COVE LANDING TRAIL

◄ FALL CREEK LOOP

1 **Saratoga Gap and Ridge Trail**
DISTANCE: 4.9 miles (7.9 km) round-trip
DURATION: 3 hours
EFFORT: Moderate

2 **Ocean View Summit**
DISTANCE: 3.3 miles (5.3 km) round-trip
DURATION: 1.5 hours
EFFORT: Easy-moderate

3 **Quail Hollow Loop**
DISTANCE: 3 miles (4.8 km) round-trip
DURATION: 1.5 hours
EFFORT: Easy

4 **Fall Creek Loop**
DISTANCE: 3.3 miles (5.3 km) round-trip
DURATION: 1.5 hours
EFFORT: Easy

5 **Henry Cowell Observation Deck Loop**
DISTANCE: 5.3 miles (8.5 km) round-trip
DURATION: 2.5 hours
EFFORT: Easy-moderate

6 **Bonny Doon Beach and Shark Fin Cove**
DISTANCE: 2.4 miles (3.9 km) round-trip
DURATION: 1 hour
EFFORT: Easy

7 **Old Cove Landing Trail**
DISTANCE: 2.4 miles (3.9 km) round-trip
DURATION: 1 hour
EFFORT: Easy

8 **Monarch-Moore Creek Loop**
DISTANCE: 1.5 miles (2.4 km) round-trip
DURATION: 1 hour
EFFORT: Easy

9 **West Cliff Drive**
DISTANCE: 4 miles (6.4 km) round-trip
DURATION: 1.5 hours
EFFORT: Easy

10 **Maple Falls**
DISTANCE: 6 miles (10 km) round-trip
DURATION: 2 hours
EFFORT: Moderate

11 **Aptos Creek Loop**
DISTANCE: 2.9 miles (4.7 km) round-trip
DURATION: 1.5 hours
EFFORT: Easy

12 **South Marsh Loop**
DISTANCE: 2.2 miles (3.5 km) round-trip
DURATION: 1 hour
EFFORT: Easy

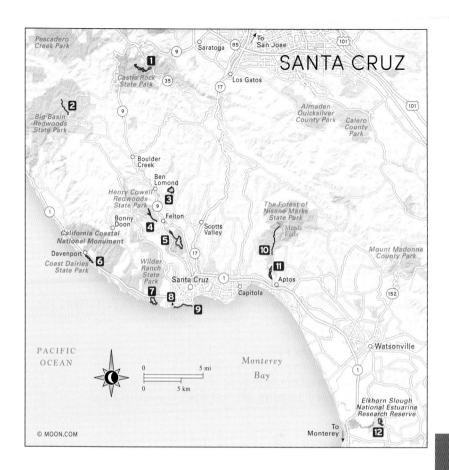

PACIFIC
OCEAN

*Monterey
Bay*

0 — 5 mi
0 — 5 km

© MOON.COM

Saratoga Gap and Ridge Trail

CASTLE ROCK STATE PARK

Thrill-seekers will relish the opportunity to so easily reach panoramic views of the Santa Cruz Mountains and the San Lorenzo River Valley down to Monterey Bay, teeter along the rocks of the cables section, and watch the rush of water flow over Castle Falls.

DISTANCE: 4.9 miles (7.9 km) round-trip

DURATION: 3 hours

ELEVATION GAIN: 1,000 feet (305 m)

EFFORT: Moderate

TRAIL: Dirt, rocks, tree roots, gravel, paved, single-track

USERS: Hikers

SEASON: Year-round

PASSES/FEES: $10 day-use fee per vehicle, or California State Parks Pass

MAPS: On the park website select "Brochures" and "Park Brochure," at the trailhead Ranger's Station

PARK HOURS: 6am-sunset daily

TRAILHEAD: Kirkland Entrance Ranger's Station

FACILITIES: Restrooms, drinking fountain at the trailhead

CONTACT: California State Parks, 408/868-9540, www.parks.ca.gov

START THE HIKE

▶ **MILE 0-0.9: Kirkland Entrance Ranger's Station to Goat Rock**

At the **Ranger's Station** on the southwest side of **Castle Rock State Park's Kirkland Entrance,** begin hiking on the paved path that leads southwest from the interpretive sign with a map. Follow park signs for the **Waterfall Connector Trail,** as the path changes from paved to gravel and approaches an interpretive sign with benches.

The trail descends into a forest of mixed evergreens, down a quick switchback, and follows alongside the southeast side of Kings Creek. Follow moss-covered boulders and trees to a **wooden bridge crossing** at 0.3 mile (0.5 km), where the path splits. Turn right (west), heading down the wooden stairs onto **Saratoga Gap Trail** to continue heading southwest along the babbling creek. The path crosses the creek on a **wooden bridge** and splits again at 0.5 mile (0.8 km). Pass the trail

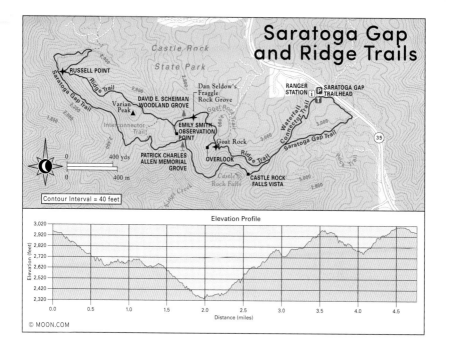

Saratoga Gap and Ridge Trails

Contour Interval = 40 feet

Elevation Profile

© MOON.COM

marked "Saratoga Gap to Castle Rock Falls" and take the second trail to the left (southwest), marked **"Ridge Trail to Goat Rock."** Climb the rocky steps as **Ridge Trail** gains elevation.

Continuing, Goat Rock is easily spotted ahead to the west, often with rock climbers on its flat face. To pass the top of Goat Rock, you must scramble up tree roots between boulders, hike up a series of rocks, past a huge boulder of pitted Vaqueros sandstone, and head up a wooden staircase past the rock's base. You arrive at the top of **Goat Rock** at 0.9 mile (1.4 km).

▶ **MILE 0.9-2.6: Goat Rock to Saratoga Gap Trail Junction**
Pass the trail marker for "Goat Rock Trail to Interpretive Center" and "Ridge Trail to Castle Rock Trail Camp" to the right (north). Follow along the wooden fence to a **stunning overlook** area with benches and an interpretive sign that illustrates points of interest within your view, including a sliver of the waters of Monterey Bay on the far left (west) and the Butano Ridge to the right (east).

Return from the overlook and follow the trail marker for Ridge Trail to Castle Rock Trail Camp to the left (north). The path winds inland, passing another junction with Goat Rock Trail at 1.2 miles (1.9 km). Stay on Ridge Trail as it curves southwest past **Dan Seldow's Fraggle Rock Grove** and **David E. Scheiman Woodland Grove.** Take the spur trail for the **Emily Smith Observation Point** at 1.4 miles (2.3 km). Through the trees, the view extends to the Pacific Ocean, and you can look for hawks and vultures riding the wind currents.

Back on Ridge Trail, continue past a **junction** with Interconnector Trail to the left (south) at 1.6 miles (2.6 km), where some hikers choose to loop down to Saratoga Gap Trail to avoid the cables section of the hike. Stay on

SARATOGA GAP AND RIDGE TRAIL ▲

Ridge Trail as it rises in elevation ever so slightly past **Varian Peak** (2,864 ft/873 m). The trail emerges from the forest and aside a cliff drop-off to the left (south) as it approaches **Russell Point** for another amazing panoramic view at 2.2 miles (3.5 km), before turning inland and northeast downhill toward Castle Rock Trail Camp to meet the **Saratoga Gap Trail** at 2.6 miles (4.2 km).

▸ **MILE 2.6–3.3: Saratoga Gap Trail Junction**
   to Interconnector Trail Junction

Turn left (southeast) onto Saratoga Gap Trail and you'll immediately see a post with a number 13 on it, followed by numbers in ascending order to 18. These are spots along the **Danny Hanavan Nature Trail,** developed in memory of a local 12-year-old Boy Scout. A laminated copy of the nature trail guide is available for reference near the viewpoint at number 18 before the hike begins a gradual continuous ascent all the way back to the trailhead.

The following section of the hike is the most technical, with rock scrambles and cables to assist on narrow single-person rock cliff passages. Stunning wide views are all along the path, with a handful of rocky outcrops to sit on to take a break. At 3.2 miles (5.2 km), climb on a large flat rock to get around smaller rounded boulders. The technical section ends at 3.3 miles (5.3 km), as you reach a **junction** with Interconnector Trail.

▸ **MILE 3.3–4.9: Interconnector Trail to Kirkland**
   Entrance Ranger's Station

Stay on Saratoga Gap Trail heading right (east) as it continues into the inner ridges, where ferns and moss retake the path. At 3.6 miles (5.8 km), a **wooden footbridge** takes you over a **waterfall** cascading down boulders and then past the **Patrick Charles Allen Memorial Grove** of redwoods. There is one final rock scramble before the last panoramic views of the

▲ KINGS CREEK

trail; the path then winds through the forest past more Vaqueros sandstone and over tree roots and rocks.

At 4.2 miles (6.8 km), the trail arrives at the wooden platform for **Castle Rock Falls.** On the far-left corner of the platform, look directly below to see the crest of the falls careen approximately 75 feet (23 m) down into Kings Creek. The trail follows along the north side of the creek until reaching the junction with the Ridge Trail at a footbridge. Cross the footbridge to the right (east) and return to the trailhead the way you came.

DIRECTIONS

From Santa Cruz, take Highway 17 north to the exit for Bear Creek Road and turn right onto Bear Creek Road/Gillian Cichowski Memorial Overcrossing. Turn right at the first cross street, Montevina Road, for 0.3 mile (0.5 km), then turn right onto Black Road. Black Road is narrow and at times a one-lane road for 4.5 miles (7.2 km). At Highway 35 turn right and continue for 4 miles (6.4 km) to the Kirkwood Entrance.

GPS COORDINATES: 37.2321, −122.0988; 37°13'55.6" N, 122°5'55.7" W

BEST NEARBY BREWS

Under 12 miles (19.3 km) from the trailhead, **Hapa's Brewing Company** (114 S. Santa Cruz Ave., Los Gatos, 408/963-3942, 3pm-9pm Tues.-Thurs., noon-9pm Fri., 11am-9pm Sat., 11am-8pm Sun.) in Los Gatos was a winner of "Best Microbrew" and "Best Craft Brewer" by *Metro Silicon Valley.* From their Polar Night imperial stout to their Summer Crush Watermelon Seltzer, there's something satisfying for every hiker.

Saratoga Gap and Ridge Trail

Hike up through a redwood forest in recovery to Ocean View Summit, with views over West Waddell Creek State Wilderness to the west and down to the Pacific Ocean.

DISTANCE: 3.3 miles (5.3 km) round-trip
DURATION: 1.5 hours
ELEVATION GAIN: 660 feet (201 m)
EFFORT: Easy-moderate
TRAIL: Dirt fire road, gravel, sand, single-track
USERS: Hikers, mountain bikers on part of the trail, horseback riders on part of the trail
SEASON: Year-round
PASSES/FEES: $6 day-use fee per vehicle, or California State Parks Pass
MAPS: On the park website select "Brochures" and "Park Map"
PARK HOURS: 8am-sunset daily
TRAILHEAD: Parking Lot
FACILITIES: Restrooms, drinking fountain at the trailhead
CONTACT: California State Parks, 831/338-8860, www.parks.ca.gov

Big Basin Redwoods State Park is California's first state park, established in 1902. In the heart of the Santa Cruz Mountains, some of the park's redwoods are more than 1,000 years old. Most of the park was impacted by the August 2020 CZU Lightning Complex Fire, but the forest is in recovery. The redwoods still stand tall but they're only starting to regain the fullness of branches to shade the understory, which is also creeping back, the brightness of green regrowth popping in contrast to the charred bark of the trees. This hike provides a firsthand opportunity to see the process taking place, but as with all areas where there are changing conditions, check your route with rangers prior to hiking.

START THE HIKE

▸ **MILE 0-0.2: Parking Lot to Dool Trail**
From the west end of the **parking lot,** cross over the bridge and head right (north) along Opal Creek to begin the hike on **Skyline to the Sea Trail.** The full trail, a longtime three-day backpacking route, stretches 30 miles (48 km) from Castle Rock State Park, through Big Basin Redwoods State Park, and ends at Waddell State Beach. As with all trails in California, the impacts of weather and fire events require flexibility, and sections of the trail—or even the full trail—may be closed at various times.

This section of the trail runs along Opal Creek and over a small footbridge, passing some downed trees as sorrel, evergreen huckleberry, and

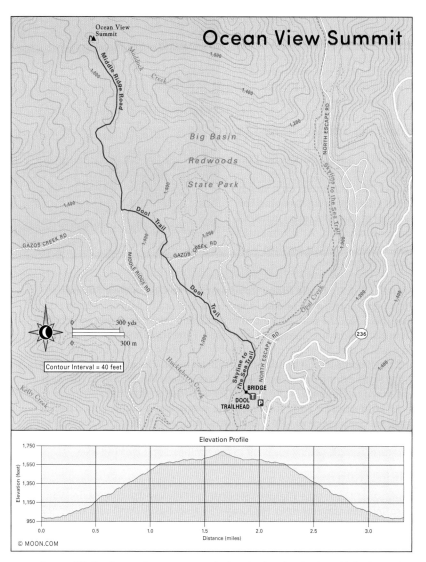

Ocean View Summit

Contour Interval = 40 feet

Elevation Profile

© MOON.COM

fern refill the forest floor. At 0.2 mile (0.3 km), take the handful of wooden steps to your left (northwest) up to meet **Dool Trail**.

▶ MILE 0.2-0.9: Dool Trail to Middle Ridge Road Junction

Turning away from the creek, remain on Dool Trail when passing Sunset Trail to the left (south) at 0.2 mile (0.3 km). The single-track path crosses through rocks and tree stumps, gradually rising among thin redwoods that almost look like matchsticks reaching for the sky with clumps of new green life. The regrowth on some trees looks like fuzzy green leg warmers. Redwoods that are farther along in recovery have short young branches sticking out in different directions, perhaps the model for those cell phone towers made to look like trees. Patches of yellow blooms of prickly

lettuce and redwood violet line the trail, and you'll walk between two sides of a sliced downed redwood.

The trail widens as it approaches **an intersection** with Gazos Creek Road at 0.6 mile (1 km). A trail marker indicates crossing the road for the trail, and on the other side of the road is a trail marker for Dool Trail.

Dool Trail continues on a steady uphill grade, passing Creeping Forest Trail to the right (east) just after the road crossing. At 0.9 mile (1.4 km), you'll come to a **junction** with Middle Ridge Road.

▶ **MILE 0.9-1.7: Middle Ridge Road Junction to Ocean View Summit**
Turn right (north) onto **Middle Ridge Road.** It steadily gains elevation and, atop the ridge, the path continues to climb and becomes sandy. Watch for mountain bikers on the wide service road. Here there are fewer trees, and on a warm day, it can be uncomfortably hot. Look for madrone and pine and the blooms of bull thistle and roughleaf aster. The views from Middle Ridge Road extend over West Waddell Creek State Wilderness to the west and down to glimpses of the Pacific Ocean between the ridges.

At 1.6 miles (2.6 km), you reach the unmarked summit area. Several small footpaths take you up a small knoll to the right (east) of the trail to get to the top of the 1,690-foot (515-m) **Ocean View Summit.** When it is time to return, retrace your steps back to the trailhead and parking area.

DIRECTIONS

From Santa Cruz, take Highway 9 north to Highway 236 (Big Basin Way). Turn left (northwest) onto Highway 236 (Big Basin Way) and drive 9.2 miles (14.8 km) to enter the park, on the left.

GPS COORDINATES: 37.1730, −122.2229; 37°10'22.8" N, 122°13'22.4" W

BEST NEARBY BREWS

The **Sawmill Restaurant and Ale House** (15520 Hwy. 9, Boulder Creek, 831/610-8196, www.thesawmillbc.com, 11am-8:30pm Sun.-Tues. and Thurs., 4pm-8:30pm Wed., 11am-9pm Fri.-Sat.), 30 minutes from the trailhead in Boulder Creek, serves up local craft beers (on tap and bottle), with American fare and outdoor picnic tables under the redwoods.

3

Quail Hollow Loop

QUAIL HOLLOW RANCH COUNTY PARK

❀ 🏛 ⚐

This short hike displays a multitude of habitats found in Santa Cruz County with serene panoramic views, wildflowers, and a 15-million-year-old history.

DISTANCE: 3 miles (4.8 km) round-trip
DURATION: 1.5 hours
ELEVATION GAIN: 560 feet (171 m)
EFFORT: Easy
TRAIL: Dirt, gravel, sand, single-track
USERS: Hikers, horseback riders (some sections)
SEASON: Year-round
PASSES/FEES: None
MAPS: On the park website select "Trails" and "Quail Hollow Ranch Trail Map"
PARK HOURS: Sunrise-sunset daily
TRAILHEAD: Visitor center parking lot
FACILITIES: Restrooms at visitor center, portable toilets outside visitor center
CONTACT: Santa Cruz County Parks, 831/454-7901, www.scparks.com

START THE HIKE

▸ **MILE 0-0.6: Parking Lot to Woodrat Vista Point**
From the southeast corner of the **parking lot,** take the paved road over the cattle crossing. Follow the **"All Trails" sign** to turn left (north) where the road splits, coming around the yard of the **visitor center.** Look for the fence line ahead, with interpretive signs that include a map and trail descriptions. From here, you'll see a wooden trail marker, pointing left (west) for Lower Chaparral Trail and right (east) **"To other trails"**—go right. Shortly

thereafter, at 0.1 mile (0.2 km), the path **splits,** where a wooden trail marker points hikers to the Italian Trail, Chaparral Trail, and Sunset Trail to the left and **Woodrat Trail** to the right. Go right and began ascending into the forest, crossing a wooden stile labeled with the trail's name.

The single-track trail starts bordered by ferns and a barbed-wire fence to the left (northwest), marking the boundary of the **Quail Hollow Ecological Reserve.** As the trail ascends, so does a steep drop-off on the left (west), while views open

Quail Hollow Loop

SANTA CRUZ

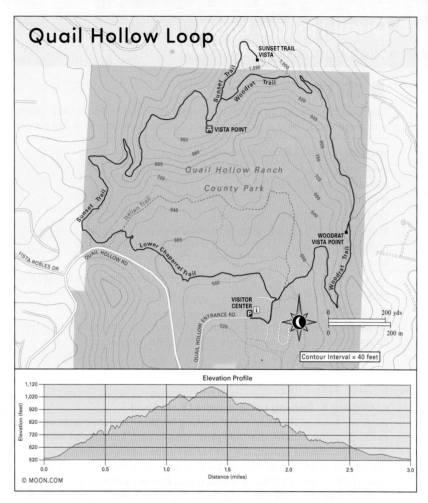

Quail Hollow Loop

SUNSET TRAIL VISTA

Quail Hollow Ranch County Park

VISTA POINT

Sunset Trail

Woodrat Trail

Italian Trail

Lower Chaparral Trail

VISTA ROBLES DR

QUAIL HOLLOW RD

WOODRAT VISTA POINT

Woodrat Trail

VISITOR CENTER

QUAIL HOLLOW ENTRANCE RD

Contour Interval = 40 feet

200 yds
200 m

Elevation Profile

© MOON.COM

through the trees and across the valley. Follow the trail signs to continue toward Sunset Trail, and at 0.6 mile (1 km), take the turnoff to the left (west), looping back at the sign for "To Vista." At the **Woodrat Vista Point,** enjoy a break on the bench and take in the view. To the southwest you'll see a quarry, and all around you the Santa Cruz Mountains.

▶ MILE 0.6-1.4: Woodrat Vista Point to Sunset Trail Vista

Back on the main trail, continue to follow signs for Sunset Trail, following along the ridge. At 0.8 mile (1.3 km), continue straight (northwest) where the path meets with a trail junction that leaves the park to the right (east). Remain on Woodrat Trail and watch for roots, as the path sometimes gets quite narrow, and they can be a tripping hazard.

At 1.2 miles (1.9 km), exit the Woodrat Trail through a fence, like the one you crossed at the beginning of the trail, onto the **Sunset Trail.** Take the 0.4-mile (0.6-km) round-trip spur trail to the right (northeast) 130 feet (40 m) to the **Sunset Trail Vista.** This is the highest point of the hike and provides a bench with a relaxing southern-facing view.

▶ MILE 1.4-3: Sunset Trail Vista to Parking Lot

Back down from the Sunset Trail Vista, continue right (southwest) on the Sunset Trail, and at 1.7 miles (2.7 km), take the short detour left (south) for another vista point and the perfect stop for a shaded picnic. Grab a seat at one of the two picnic tables or sit on the bench overlooking the valley below.

After the vista point, the hike begins its descent. If hiking in the winter, a variety of mushrooms can be found along the trail among the oak woodland and redwoods. The path changes from dirt to deep sand as it leads down and around an exposed Santa Cruz Sandhill at 2.4 miles (3.9 km), with pops of wildflower color in the spring, including Ben Lomond spineflower, Santa Cruz wallflower, and snapdragon.

At 2.5 miles (4 km), keep left (north) to stay on Sunset Trail when the trail passes a junction that leads to the road. The path will continue parallel to the road for a short distance before bending left (northeast) away from the road until the **junction** with Italian Trail. Stay on what is now **Lower Chaparral Trail** as it the path continues southeast. Along Lower Chaparral, look for wildflowers, especially lupine in yellow and blue.

The trail returns to the fence line with interpretive signs where you previously went east, following the "To other trails" sign to begin on the Woodrat Trail. Turn right (east) to return to the road around the visitor center and back to the parking lot.

DIRECTIONS

From Santa Cruz, take Graham Hill Road 6.6 miles (10.6 km) north to East Zayante Road in Felton. Turn right on East Zayante Road, continuing for 1.9 miles (3.1 km). Turn left onto Quail Hollow Road, drive 0.7 mile (1.1 km), and then make a slight turn right onto Entrance Road. Proceed to the parking lot in 0.3 mile (0.5 km).

GPS COORDINATES: 37.0835, −122.0608; 37°5′0.6″ N, 122°3′38.9″ W

BEST NEARBY BITES

For your morning brew (coffee), stop in **The White Raven** (6253 Hwy. 9, Felton, 6:30am-4:30pm Mon.-Fri., 7am-4:30pm Sat.-Sun., $3-8) in Felton, 3.5 miles (5.6 km) south of the trailhead on Highway 9. Before your hike, you grab your latte or tea, and don't pass up the perfect slice of coffee cake.

4

Fall Creek Loop

HENRY COWELL REDWOODS STATE PARK

Follow Fall Creek under the canopy of redwoods and see into the past as the trail leads by remnants of the days of lime processing in the old-growth redwoods a century ago.

BEST: Redwood Hikes

DISTANCE: 3.3 miles (5.3 km) round-trip

DURATION: 1.5 hours

ELEVATION GAIN: 500 feet (152 m)

EFFORT: Easy

TRAIL: Dirt, fire road, single-track, roots

USERS: Hikers

SEASON: Year-round

PASSES/FEES: $10 day-use fee per vehicle, or California State Parks Pass

MAPS: On the park website select "Brochures" and "Park Brochure"

PARK HOURS: Sunrise-sunset daily

TRAILHEAD: Fall Creek Parking Area

FACILITIES: None

CONTACT: Henry Cowell Redwoods State Park, 831/335-7077, www.parks. ca.gov

At its highest demand, 80 percent of the state's lime came from Santa Cruz County, and in the late 1800s nearly a third of the state's supply came from kilns built on Fall Creek Trail. Limestone was cooked to remove carbon dioxide from the rock, leaving behind calcium oxide, or lime.

START THE HIKE

Some of the most dangerous mushrooms grow in this forest. Picking them can result in citation and consuming them can end in death. This hike also requires multiple creek crossings, and conditions may be muddy.

▶ **MILE 0-0.8: Parking Lot to North Fork Trail**

The trailhead for this hike begins at the interpretive signs and trail marker at the northeast end of the **parking lot.** Head straight (north) on **Bennett Creek Trail,** with switchbacks that lead to **Fall Creek Trail** at 0.2 mile (0.3 km).

Under the cover of the forest, you will traverse a mix of second-growth redwoods, firs, oaks, and maples, with groundcover of sorrel and ferns. Fog can gather and remain in this place where creeks travel to the ocean from the slopes of Ben Lomond Mountain. They provide an ideal habitat for moisture-loving life, including banana slugs and mushrooms.

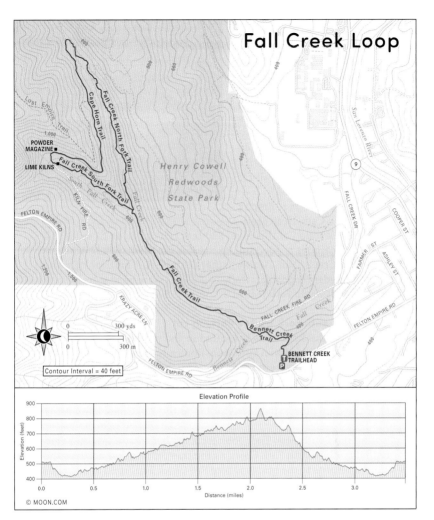

Fall Creek Loop

Elevation Profile

For most of the hike, you will need to navigate roots and rocks, sometimes over narrow single-track sections. Keep to the left (southwest) of Fall Creek; you won't cross the creek until you've passed the junction with South Fork Trail.

At 0.8 mile (1.3 km), cross a wooden bridge to come to the split of the South Fork (left) and North Fork (right) Trail. Follow to the right and continue onto the **North Fork Trail.**

▶ MILE 0.8-2.2: North Fork Trail to South Fork Trail

Just 0.2 mile (0.3 km) past the junction is the first of multiple creek crossings over the next mile (1.6 km) of the hike. While some have wooden bridges or planks, others require rock-hopping or careful use of logs in the creek. Proceed with caution.

At 1.5 miles (2.4 km), depart from the North Fork Trail and turn left (south) onto the old wagon and logging road, **Cape Horn Trail.** This section of the hike gradually rises up the side of the canyon, away from the creek below.

Prior to the **junction** with Lost Empire Trail at 1.7 miles (2.7 km) to the right (west), notice the huge hollowed-out stump of an old-growth redwood on the outside edge of the trail, on your left—it's the perfect hiding place to wait for any stragglers in your group. Continue straight past Lost Empire Trail to remain on Cape Horn Trail.

The highest elevation of this hike, 820 feet (250 m), is at 2.1 miles (3.4 km), and the remainder is downhill, except for the brief switchbacks uphill on Bennett Creek Trail. After another 0.1 mile (0.2 km), look for the well-marked **Powder Magazine,** where explosives were once stored.

The path meets **South Fork Trail** at 2.2 miles (3.5 km).

▶ **MILE 2.2-3.3: South Fork Trail to Parking Lot**

What remains of the lime kilns is located at the junction of South Fork Trail, Cape Horn Trail, and Kiln Fire Road. Ironically, these structures have become faded gray bricks, being swallowed by the forest they once overtook. Storage barrels and logs to keep the kiln fires burning drove deforestation of the old-growth forest, but more efficient oil-fired kilns and the decline of the lime processing industry led to the Fall Creek kilns being closed in 1919.

Following the South Fork Trail, look for a log bench at a low and gentle waterfall on the South Fork Creek as the trail follows just north of the creek until it returns to the bridge where Fall Creek Trail split, at 2.5 miles (4 km).

Cross the bridge and return the way you came.

DIRECTIONS

From Santa Cruz, take Graham Hill Road for 5.7 miles (9.2 km) north to Felton Empire Road. Continue on Felton Empire Road for 0.6 mile (1 km) and turn right into the small parking lot.

GPS COORDINATES: 37.0495, −122.0833; 37°2'58.2" N, 122°4'59.9" W

BEST NEARBY BITES

Less than 1 mile (1.6 km) east on Felton Empire Road is **Humble Sea Tavern** (6256 Hwy. 9, Felton, 831/704-2150, www.humblesea.com, 3pm-8pm Mon.-Tues., 11am-9pm Wed.-Fri., 10am-9pm Sat.-Sun., $11-31). Grab a bite, a beer, or the oat milk soft-serve after your hike. This spot is as old as the ruins in the forest: The redwood building was completed in 1876 as a hotel for logging laborers and is the oldest structure in downtown Felton.

5

Henry Cowell Observation Deck Loop

HENRY COWELL REDWOODS STATE PARK

Go beyond the crowds of the redwoods and the river to the sandy landscape of the Santa Cruz sandhills and an observation deck with 360-degree views.

DISTANCE: 5.3 miles (8.5 km) round-trip

DURATION: 2.5 hours

ELEVATION GAIN: 700 feet (213 m)

EFFORT: Easy-moderate

TRAIL: Dirt, sand, fire road, gravel, single-track, paved

USERS: Hikers; on portions mountain bikers, horseback riders, wheelchair users, leashed dogs

SEASON: Year-round

PASSES/FEES: $10 day-use fee per vehicle, or California State Parks pass

MAPS: On the park website select "Brochures" and "Park Brochure"

PARK HOURS: Sunrise-sunset daily

TRAILHEAD: Henry Cowell Redwoods State Park Visitor Center

FACILITIES: Restrooms at the parking lot and near the Freemont Tree

CONTACT: Henry Cowell Redwoods State Park, 831/335-7077, www.parks.ca.gov

START THE HIKE

▶ **MILE 0-0.4: Visitor Center to The Giant**

From the **visitor center,** follow the trail right (southeast), the counterclockwise direction of the **Redwood Grove Loop Trail.** At 0.4 mile (0.6 km) is **The Giant.** While the trail guide reports this tree is 270 feet (82 m) tall, in 2022 it was measured at 282 feet (86 m). Of all the redwoods of this forest, this is easily the most photographed, so you may have to wait a moment to get your favorite shot.

▶ **MILE 0.4-1.5: The Giant to Ridge Road**

From the Giant, go right (southeast) past **The Fremont Tree** and its picnic area, toward the wooden fence ahead. There is a trail marker where you can walk through the fence marked "To River Trail." Head left (southeast) from the fence to take **Pipeline Road,** a multiuse paved road often busy with mountain bikers, runners, and strollers. Stay on the road to pass under the railroad bridge. Just past the bridge, Pipeline Road intersects with River Trail. At 0.6 mile (1 km), the paths run beside each other for a short distance before Pipeline Road veers east, away from San Lorenzo River. Keep right (west) on **River Trail,** which continues alongside the river, with easy access to the water before the trail slightly ascends. At 0.8 mile (1.3 km), follow the trail marker signed for **River Trail to Eagle Creek Trail.** Just

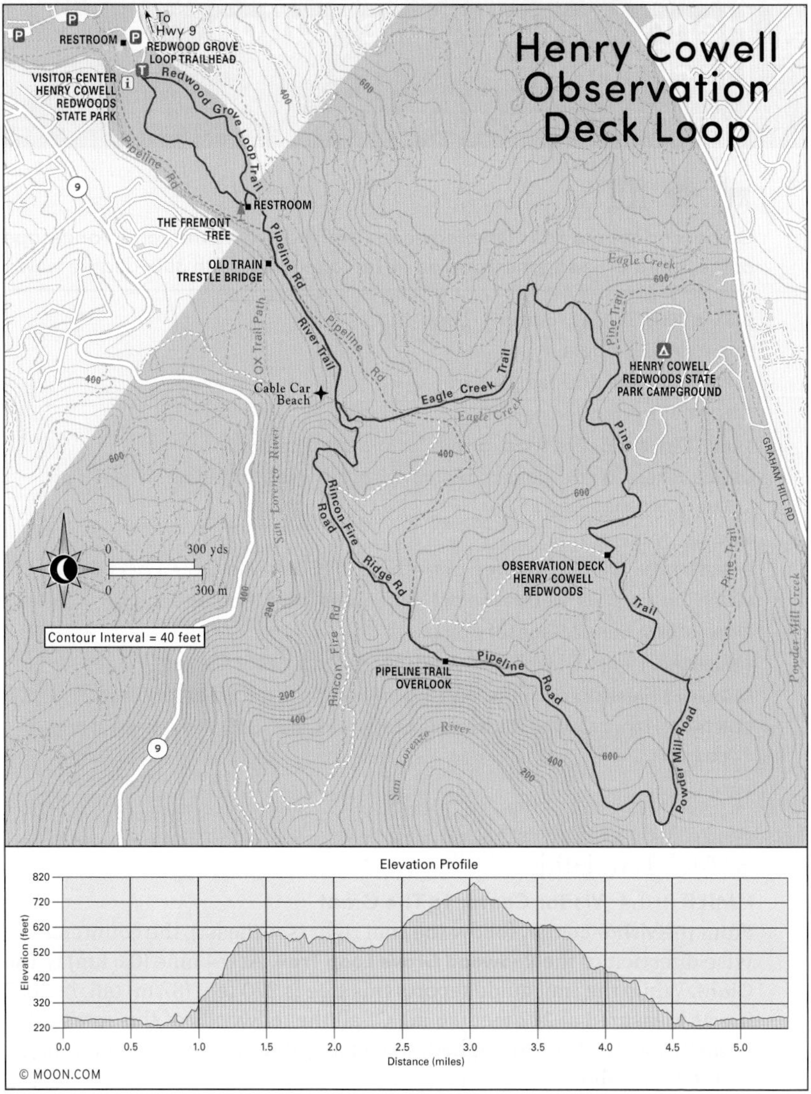
Henry Cowell Observation Deck Loop
To Hwy 9
RESTROOM
REDWOOD GROVE LOOP TRAILHEAD
VISITOR CENTER HENRY COWELL REDWOODS STATE PARK
Redwood Grove Loop Trail
Pipeline Rd
9
RESTROOM
THE FREMONT TREE
Pipeline Rd
OLD TRAIN TRESTLE BRIDGE
OX Trail Path
River Trail
Pipeline Rd
Cable Car Beach
Eagle Creek Trail
Eagle Creek
Eagle Creek
Pine Trail
HENRY COWELL REDWOODS STATE PARK CAMPGROUND
Pine
GRAHAM HILL RD
San Lorenzo River
Rincon Fire Road
Ridge Rd
OBSERVATION DECK HENRY COWELL REDWOODS
Trail
Pine Trail
Powder Mill Creek
0
300 yds
0
300 m
Contour Interval = 40 feet
Rincon Fire Rd
PIPELINE TRAIL OVERLOOK
Pipeline Road
Powder Mill Road
San Lorenzo River
9
400
600
200
Elevation Profile
Elevation (feet)
820
720
620
520
420
320
220
0.0
0.5
1.0
1.5
2.0
2.5
3.0
3.5
4.0
4.5
5.0
Distance (miles)
© MOON.COM

0.1 mile (0.2 km) farther, you arrive at **Cable Car Beach,** a well-loved area where groups gather in the shade and play in the river. Follow the trail through the wooden fence and keep right (west) to stay on River Trail; do not ascend the stairs to the left, marked as Eagle Creek Trail.

Over the next 0.5 mile (0.8 km), the trail rises about 400 feet (122 m) into the lush forest and over a few wooden bridges, joining **Rincon Fire Trail** at 1.3 miles (2.1 km) and staying straight (south) until the trail meets the **junction** of Big Rock Hole Trail and Ridge Fire Road at 1.5 miles (2.4 km). A large park sign indicates the distances to multiple destinations. Look for the trail marker stating "Ridge Road to Pipeline" and turn left (southeast) onto **Ridge Road.**

▶ **MILE 1.5-3.2: Ridge Road to Observation Deck**

Here the trail levels out, acting as a connector back to Pipeline Road at 1.6 miles (2.6 km). Turn right (south) onto Pipeline Road. At 1.8 miles (2.9 km), you reach an **observation bench** with forest views across the San Lorenzo River gorge. Just before the bench, a better framed view is seen through the trees toward the east, where you can spot Monterey Bay in the distance and the mountains of the Santa Lucia Range on the far side of the bay.

At 2.3 miles, the path begins to ascend slightly, and at 2.5 miles is another trail **junction.** Look for a park sign indicating the distances to multiple destinations and take the U-turn bend in the path to proceed onto **Powder Mill Road.** This begins the final ascent, with an elevation gain of about 270 feet (82 m) over the next 0.75 mile (1.2 km). When you reach **Pine Trail** at 2.8 miles (4.5 km), turn left (west).

Follow the trail marker "To Observation Deck" at 3.1 miles (5 km), after which the deck will become visible ahead. At 3.2 miles (5.2 km), you reach the **Observation Deck,** the highest point in Henry Cowell Redwoods State Park, at 805 feet (245 m) elevation. The reward here is the views out to Monterey Bay in one direction and the ridges and valleys of the Santa Cruz Mountains in another.

▶ **MILE 3.2-5.1: Observation Deck to Redwood Grove Trail**

From the base of the stairs at the Observation Deck, pass the picnic area and continue left (north) on Pine Trail. At 3.5 miles (5.6 km), continue on Pine Trail by staying straight at a **junction** that splits right (east) to the park's campground, which Pine Trail will skirt until the **junction** with Eagle Creek Trail at 3.8 miles (6.1 km). Turn left (northwest) onto **Eagle Creek Trail** and stay left again in 0.1 mile (0.2 km), where the trail intercepts a different section of Pine Trail. The trail crosses a couple of wooden bridges as it weaves along the creek, bringing you back into the more populated area of the park and crossing over Pipeline Road to rejoin River Trail at 4.7 miles (7.6 km).

Turn right (north) onto River Trail and arrive back at Cable Car Beach. From the beach, return the way you came by following the River Trail north to the junction with Pipeline Road, just before the railway bridge. Return to the Pipeline Road at 5 miles (8.1 km) by turning slightly right (north) and then pass through the wooden fence to emerge on **Redwood Grove Trail.**

HENRY COWELL OBSERVATION DECK LOOP ▲

▶ **MILE 5.1–5.3: Redwood Grove Trail to Visitor Center**
At 5.1 miles (8.2 km), you pass the Fremont Tree and vault toilets. Enjoy the remainder of the Redwood Grove Trail by heading right (north) as the loop ends back at the visitor center.

DIRECTIONS

From Santa Cruz, take Highway 9 (River St.) north for 5.8 miles (9.3 km) and turn right onto North Big Trees Park Road to enter the park.

GPS COORDINATES: 37.0391, −122.0635; 37°2′20.8″ N, 122°3′48.6″ W

BEST NEARBY BITES
If you're looking for a brunch or lunch place that feels more like home than a tourist spot, check out **Zachary's** (819 Pacific Ave., Santa Cruz, 831/427-0646, www.zacharyssantacruz.com, 7am-2:30pm Tues.-Sun., $6-16). Sample one of their three house-made breads (oatmeal-molasses, sour white, and dark rye) and enjoy one of their brunch specials like Zachary's "Old Fashioned" poached egg meal.

6

Bonny Doon Beach and Shark Fin Cove

COAST DAIRIES STATE PARK

The shark fin rock formation, stream crossing, beach play or lounging, and crashing waves of the coast make this an entertaining and easy hike.

BEST: Brew Hikes
DISTANCE: 2.4 miles (3.9 km) round-trip
DURATION: 1 hour
ELEVATION GAIN: 380 feet (116 m)
EFFORT: Easy
TRAIL: Dirt, gravel, sand
USERS: Hikers, mountain bikers
SEASON: Year-round
PASSES/FEES: None
MAPS: National Geographic Maps "Big Basin, Santa Cruz" bundle, www.avenzamaps.com
PARK HOURS: Sunrise–sunset daily
TRAILHEAD: Bonny Doon Beach roadside parking
FACILITIES: None
CONTACT: California State Parks, 831/335-6318, www.parks.ca.gov

Prior to becoming part of a state park, Bonny Doon Beach was long considered clothing-optional. Today, nude sunbathers gather on the north end of the beach, on the other side of the big flat-topped rock that acts as a natural screen from the families that now frequent the beach. Note that swimming here can be dangerous due to rip currents.

START THE HIKE

Parking along Highway 1 with anything visible in your vehicle is always a risk. Don't bring valuables, or keep them on you, and lock your vehicle.

Be prepared to get sandy and maybe get your feet wet on this coastal trail. As with any hike along coastal bluffs, there can be strong winds and crumbling cliffs. Bring appropriate sun and wind protection, avoid bringing items that can easily fly away, and keep away from the drop-offs.

▸ **MILE 0-0.8: Parking Lot to Shark Fin Cove**
Starting from the **parking lot,** make your way about 50 feet (15 m) down the big sand dune, between the coastal shrubs and bright yellow lupines, to cross Liddell Creek as it snakes through the sand from a pipe up the beach.

Bonny Doon Beach is wide, with plenty of spots to stop and enjoy. To continue the hike, after crossing the creek walk north along the cliffside with the ocean to the left (west). Just past the point where the creek enters the beach, at 0.2 mile (0.3 km), look to pick up the trail heading up the

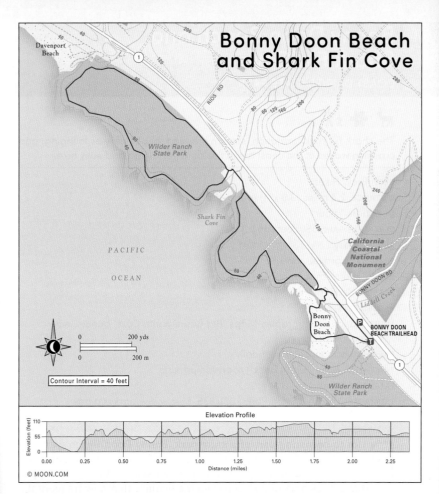

Elevation Profile

© MOON.COM

rocks. The ascent here is the quick route off the beach. There are a few splits in the trail, but any of them will take you up to the main path along the railroad tracks. Alternatively, you can go back up the sand dune and connect to the railroad tracks there.

Where the trail splits at 0.3 mile (0.5 km), go left (west) as the path hugs the coast. At 0.6 mile (1 km), the trail follows the contours of the cliffs on the south side of **Shark Fin Cove,** and the unusual rock formation giving the cove its name is revealed. If you're here in spring, you've likely already noticed the wildflowers, including woolly sunflowers, seaside daisies, coast paintbrushes, and California poppies that cover the cliff tops.

At 0.8 mile (1.3 km), the trail takes you left (northwest), back on the railroad tracks, where photographers, painters, and sketch artists park themselves to capture the best-known view of the rock.

▶ MILE 0.8-2.4: Shark Fin Cove to Parking Lot

You can take the steep trail down to the cove to explore at your leisure. Back on the main trail, continue north where the trail splits and go left (southwest) as the path hugs the coast. Now on the north side of Shark

Fin Cove, the path curves right (northwest) and travel alongside the coast for the next 0.5 mile (0.8 km). Take a moment to study the waves—you might catch sight of sea lions, seals, otters, or even migrating whales in the distance. The Northern California coastline also hosts a wide variety of birds that may be in flight or gathering on the cliffs and rocks below.

The trail turns inland at 1.4 miles (2.3 km) and runs parallel to the Davenport Crack, a narrow crack in the rocks, just to the north, that seawater rushes into. It extends from the edge of the beach to the ocean. You may spot other adventure seekers on the other side of the crack.

When the path turns right (southeast) after 0.1 mile (0.2 km), follow the trail looking down on the railroad tracks in the small ravine below. White calla lilies dot the opposite side of the ravine as the trail leads back to the roadside parking.

DIRECTIONS

From Santa Cruz, drive north on Highway 1 for 9.5 miles (15.3 km) and park at the Bonny Doon Beach parking, on the west side of the highway. If that parking area is full, park at the Shark Fin Cove roadside parking, on the west side of the highway, 0.5 mile (0.8 km) past the Bonny Doon Beach parking.

GPS COORDINATES: 37.0, −122.1799; 37°0'0" N, 122°10'47.6" W

BEST NEARBY BREWS

After your hike, grab a beer at **Santa Cruz Mountain Brewing** (402 Ingalls St., Suite 27, Santa Cruz, 831/425-4900, www.scmbrew. com, noon-10pm Sat.-Thurs., noon-9pm Fri.), just 10 minutes from the trailhead. In addition to their tasty organic brews on tap, SCMB offers local hard ciders, hard kombucha, local wine, house-made Chavela, frosé, and tiki slushies, plus nonalcoholic options including a variety of 0% ABV beverages and house-brewed Alden's Radical Redwood Root Beer.

Bonny Doon Beach and Shark Fin Cove

SANTA CRUZ

🦌 ❀ 🏛 🚶

This family-friendly path is a great spot for wildlife viewing as it hugs the bluffs between brussels sprouts fields and the crashing waves of the Pacific Ocean.

DISTANCE: 2.4 miles (3.9 km) round-trip

DURATION: 1 hour

ELEVATION GAIN: 100 feet (30 m)

EFFORT: Easy

TRAIL: Dirt, gravel

USERS: Hikers, mountain bikers

SEASON: Year-round

PASSES/FEES: $10 day-use fee per vehicle, or California State Parks Pass

MAPS: On the park website select "Brochures" and "Park Brochure"

PARK HOURS: 8am-sunset daily

TRAILHEAD: Wilder Dairy Cultural Preserve

FACILITIES: Restrooms at the trailhead

CONTACT: Wilder Ranch State Park, 1401 Coast Rd., Santa Cruz, 831/423-9703, www.parks.ca.gov

START THE HIKE

This hike takes you past a working farm; be respectful and stay on trail so as not to disrupt the crops or the working community.

▶ **MILE 0-0.7: Wilder Dairy Cultural Preserve to Wilder Beach**

At the large "Welcome to Wilder Ranch" sign, begin the hike by going right (south). Behind the sign you'll see the white picket fence of the **Wilder Dairy Cultural Preserve.** Just before the sign is a trail marker that indicates the Coastal Bluff Trails, to the right. Take the gravel and dirt trail as it crosses by a brussels sprouts field, to the right (west) and an over old railroad track. The trail winds through coastal shrubs.

As the trail curves left (southeast), enjoy the wildflower blooms, including wild radish and lupine. Kids will love looking for rabbits hopping across the wide trail, and

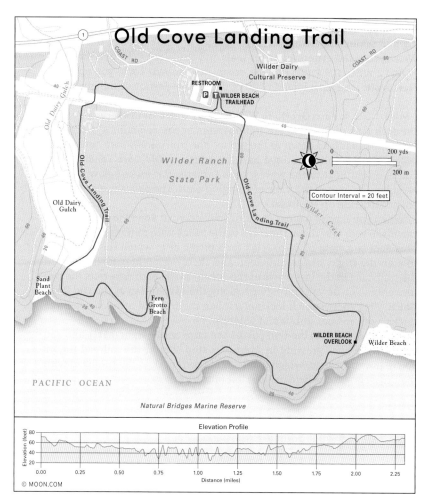

Old Cove Landing Trail

Elevation Profile

© MOON.COM

you might notice **Wilder Creek** to the east, following the same direction as the trail.

Continuing along, you approach views of the **Wilder Beach Natural Preserve,** closed to public exploration to protect the population of snowy plovers, a sparrow-size shorebird that nests in the area. The best views open at 0.7 mile (1.1 km), where you can watch the powerful waves to the south (ahead) crashing into the bluffs and **Wilder Beach.**

▶ MILE 0.7-1.2: Wilder Beach to Fern Grotto

Now at the coastline, you'll see single-track spur trails leading farther out onto the cliffs; these are not kid-friendly. There is an abundance of beautiful views on this hike without venturing out to peer over steep drop-offs. The bluffs can be unstable and crumble at any time. Even at points on the main trail, make sure you stay back from the edge; in places the cliffs are roped off for your safety. Keep children on the inland side of the trail.

Beyond the cliffs, you're looking at the **Natural Bridges State Marine Reserve,** which extends from Four-Mile Beach at the most northern edge of

Wilder Ranch State Park to Natural Bridges State Beach in the south. Fishing and taking any living marine resources are prohibited in the reserve. These protected waters allow for seals and otters to be close to shore.

At 1.2 miles (1.9 km), with the ocean now at your back, you approach **Fern Grotto,** the most inland point of the coastal portion of the hike.

▶ **MILE 1.2-2.4: Fern Grotto to Wilder Dairy Cultural Preserve**
On each side of the path are trail markers at the sometimes overgrown spur trails that lead down to the grotto. The trail curves back toward the ocean. For this hike, continue past the grotto on **Old Cove Landing Trail,** and back out next to the waves. Look for large flat rocks below and you will likely be treated to a view of lounging seals. The pelicans also seem to enjoy gathering on the rocks.

When you reach 1.6 miles (2.6 km), look down at **Sand Plant Beach.** You can make your way down the rocks to the beach with minimal scrambling. This spot is a great place to relax for a picnic or to watch the sunset, although the frigid surf is turbulent, and there are no lifeguards. Back on the trail, take in the last views of the ocean, as the path now puts the water behind you as you travel north along the eastern top of the **Old Dairy Gulch.** This short stretch looks much like the trail did after crossing the tracks, with coastal shrubs and wildflowers.

At 2 miles (3.2 km) the trail passes the farm on the right (east), and you reach white lilies growing in front of a stop sign at the railroad tracks. You're now on a road, which bends right (east) back to the trailhead with the brussels sprouts field on your left (north).

DIRECTIONS

From Santa Cruz, head north on Highway 1 for 3.8 miles (6.1 km). Turn left onto Coast Road and continue to the parking lot.

GPS COORDINATES: 36.9603, −122.0856; 36°57'37.1" N, 122°5'8.2" W

BEST NEARBY BITES AND BREWS
Just five minutes from the trailhead on Highway 1 is **West End Tap and Kitchen** (334 Ingalls St., Santa Cruz, 831/471-8115, www.westendtap. com, noon-9pm daily, $15-36), a family- and dog-friendly restaurant and tap house with a heated patio and an open kitchen. The flatbreads and desserts are delicious, but don't overlook the rest of the menu, especially the local drinks on tap, including beers, cider, and wine.

8 Monarch-Moore Creek Loop

NATURAL BRIDGES STATE PARK

🦌 🚶 ♿ 🚌

See thousands of overwintering monarchs make the eucalyptus trees home in a gently sloping canyon and stand on the sand in the presence of the ocean waves crashing on the last remaining arch of Natural Bridges.

BEST: Fall Hikes

DISTANCE: 1.5 miles (2.4 km) round-trip

DURATION: 1 hour

ELEVATION GAIN: 70 feet (21 m)

EFFORT: Easy

TRAIL: Dirt, sand, single-track, paved, wooden boardwalk

USERS: Hikers, wheelchair users on part of the trail

SEASON: Year-round

PASSES/FEES: $10 day-use fee per vehicle, or California State Parks Pass

MAPS: On the park website select "Brochures" and "Park Map," at the visitor center

PARK HOURS: 8am-sunset daily

TRAILHEAD: Natural Bridges State Park Visitor Center

FACILITIES: Restrooms at the visitor center and the southwest corner of the parking lot

CONTACT: California State Parks, 831/423-4609, www.parks.ca.gov

The Monarch Butterfly Natural Preserve is the only state monarch preserve in California, protecting the delicate butterflies and their winter habitat. The optimal time for this hike is at low tide in November, once there's confirmation that Natural Bridges State Park has welcomed back the monarchs to their winter home and the tide is far enough out to complete the hike's loop.

START THE HIKE

A wooden boardwalk runs 500 feet (152 m) from the visitor center to the monarch viewing platform, and it is both wheelchair and stroller accessible, unlike the remainder of this hike. Bring binoculars or a telephoto lens to ensure you'll be able to observe the monarchs, which

Monarch-Moore Creek Loop

SANTA CRUZ

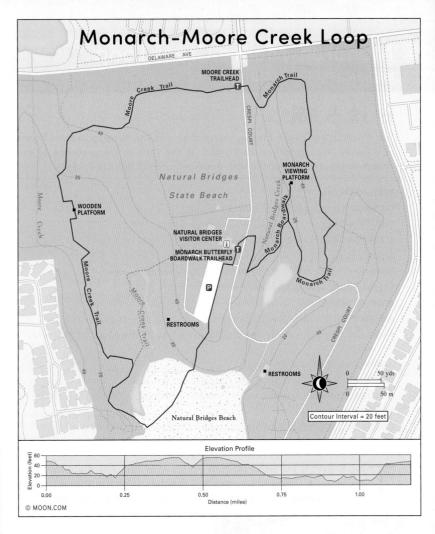

Monarch–Moore Creek Loop

Elevation Profile

Contour Interval = 20 feet

© MOON.COM

congregate in the trees high above the viewing platform. Drinks, food, and pets are strictly prohibited in this protected habitat.

▶ MILE 0–0.1: Visitor Center to Monarch Viewing Platform

Begin this hike at the flagpole east of the **visitor center** entrance. Follow the pavement northeast and walk across a park road to get on the **Monarch Butterfly Boardwalk.**

Under the canopy of eucalyptus trees, the path zigzags and crosses Natural Bridges Creek. As you approach the **viewing platform,** be quiet—keep in mind that the monarchs are overwintering, having migrated to this location and nestled together for survival. On warmer days, you may see some fluttering high above the platform and through the trees.

▶ **MILE 0.1-0.7: Monarch Viewing Platform to Moore Creek Trail**
Leaving the viewing platform, follow the trail marker for **Monarch Trail** onto a dirt path. The trail proceeds south and around the opposite side of the northern section of the pond before looping north, leading through more eucalyptus trees. At 0.4 mile (0.6 km), an unmarked trail makes its way through the meadow to intersect with Monarch Trail, and a trail marker guides hikers to continue on Monarch Trail (north). Just 0.1 mile (0.2 km) farther, a faint spur trail comes off the path to the left (west), toward the canyon. Taking the brief side trail provides the opportunity to get a different vantage point of the monarch butterflies; you can look down at the viewing platform below and straight out into the eucalyptus where they often gather.

At 0.7 mile (1.1 km), Monarch Trail curves west, crossing a bridge over Natural Bridges Creek to a park road at an interpretive board that explains the history of the park. Cross the park road toward the wetland and onto **Moore Creek Trail.**

▶ **MILE 0.7-1.5: Moore Creek Trail to Visitor Center**
Moore Creek Trail heads westward, and the exposed first section doesn't immediately indicate the hike is headed toward the wetlands. At 0.9 mile (1.4 km), keep right (north) at an **unmarked trail junction.** Shortly after the junction, the trail bends south, and an interpretive sign greets you with information about what makes a wetland sanctuary.

A series of wooden boardwalks are all that keep the plant life from taking over the path as it runs along the left (east) side of Moore Creek. At 1 mile (1.6 km), take the narrow **wooden platform** right (west) over the creek and continue on the narrow dirt path. At 1.2 miles (1.9 km), continue straight (south) toward the beach. After rain or close to high tide, this section of salt marsh may qualify as a water crossing. Stay close to the low rocky cliffs that line the right (west) side of the trail or scramble across the rocks to the beach on the other side. Exercise caution when deciding whether to proceed through this section.

Once across, you are now on **Natural Bridges Beach.** Moore Creek pours into the sea, and atop the rocks is an interpretive sign explaining the tide pool zone. Turning left (northeast), look for the path that leads off the beach and up to a picnic area and restrooms. Cross the sand and take the path, which leads up to the parking lot, with the visitor center at the northeast corner.

MONARCH-MOORE CREEK LOOP ▲

DIRECTIONS

From Santa Cruz, take Highway 1 north to Delaware Avenue and turn right. Drive 0.4 mile (0.6 km) and turn left onto Swanton Boulevard. Drive 0.4 mile (0.6 km) and turn right onto West Cliff Drive to enter the park. Follow the road through the park to the visitor center parking lot.

GPS COORDINATES: 36.9524, −122.0570; 36°57'8.6" N, 122°3'25.2" W

BEST NEARBY BITES

Just 20 minutes from the trailhead, the original **Marianne's Ice Cream** (1020 Ocean St., Santa Cruz, 831/458-1447, www.mariannesicecream. com, 10am-10pm Sun.-Thurs., 10am-11pm Fri.-Sat.) is a Santa Cruz institution, beloved for their variety of 150 handcrafted ice cream flavors. The flavor board inside only lists the names, so if you want to know what some of the flavors are, like "2AM Truffle" (vanilla ice cream with chocolate swirl and blackberry swirl), prep ahead of time by checking out the website. The parking lot is tiny, and street parking rules are strictly enforced, but the servings are generous.

SANTA CRUZ

Monarch-Moore Creek Loop

West Cliff Drive

CITY OF SANTA CRUZ

🦌 🌸 🏛 👫 🕴 ♿ 🚌

This urban hike offers stunning views from the coastal bluffs between Lighthouse Field State Park and Natural Bridges State Beach, accessible to all and with benches throughout to stop and enjoy the view.

DISTANCE: 4 miles (6.4 km) round-trip
DURATION: 1.5 hours
ELEVATION GAIN: 70 feet (21 m)
EFFORT: Easy
TRAIL: Gravel, paved
USERS: Hikers, bikers, wheelchair users, leashed dogs
SEASON: Year-round
PASSES/FEES: Metered street parking, paid parking in lots
MAPS: City of Santa Cruz website
TRAILHEAD: Steamer Lane
FACILITIES: Restrooms at Natural Bridges State Park and Lighthouse Field State Park
CONTACT: City of Santa Cruz, 831/420-5030, www.cityofsantacruz.com

On this path you have the chance to see surfers and sea lions, cypress and eucalyptus trees, wildflowers and natural bridges. You can dog-walk or people-watch, observe the variety of architecture of the homes along the drive, and never get lost.

START THE HIKE

West Cliff Drive along the coast expands from where West Cliff Drive and Beach Street merge to the Natural Bridges State Park Visitor Center, walking this stretch adds 2 miles (3.2 km) round-trip. As with any hike along coastal bluffs, there can be strong winds and crumbling cliffs. Bring appropriate sun and wind protection, avoid bringing items that can easily blow away, and keep away from the drop-offs. There are sections along this path that are purposefully blocked off for your safety.

▶ **MILE 0-0.9: Steamer Lane to Mitchell's Cove Beach**
For this hike, begin at **Steamer Lane,** an internationally renowned surfing hot spot, where you're just as likely to see sea lions as surfers riding the waves. Known as Point Santa Cruz, this is the northern boundary of Monterey Bay.

Heading west, pass the brick **Mark Abbott Memorial Lighthouse** at Lighthouse Point, which houses California's first surfing museum, the Santa Cruz Surf Museum. Signs warn to stay back from the cliff edge; don't go beyond the railings.

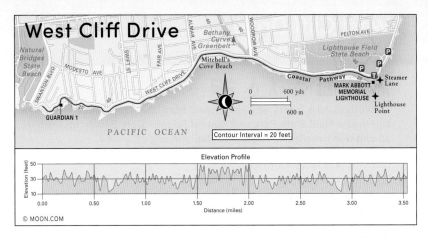

West Cliff Drive

Natural Bridges State Beach · BETHANY Curve Greenbelt · Mitchell's Cove Beach · Lighthouse Field State Beach · Coastal Pathway · Steamer Lane · MARK ABBOTT MEMORIAL LIGHTHOUSE · Lighthouse Point · GUARDIAN 1

ALMAR AVE · SWIFT ST · FAIR AVE · MODESTO AVE · SWANTON BLVD · WEST CLIFF DRIVE · WOODROW AVE · PELTON AVE

PACIFIC OCEAN

Contour Interval = 20 feet

0 — 600 yds
0 — 600 m

Elevation Profile

Elevation (feet) · Distance (miles)

© MOON.COM

Staying on the path above **Its Beach,** you can look over the cliffs to watch dogs enjoying the surf's edge or running under the sandstone arch when the tide is low. While dogs are technically only allowed on leash at this beach, it's clearly a dog's beach paradise.

At 0.7 mile (1.1 km), look inland at the intersection of Woodrow Avenue to see the **Bethany Curve** greenbelt, which provides pedestrian and bicycle access to West Cliff Drive along a peaceful trail. Where the greenbelt meets West Cliff Drive, you can read an interpretive sign explaining the historic streetcars of Santa Cruz.

You will arrive at **Mitchell's Cove Beach** at 0.9 mile (1.4 km). The beach is leashed dog-friendly all the time, with off-leash hours before 10am and after 4pm.

▶ **MILE 0.9-2: Mitchell's Cove Beach to Natural Bridges State Park**

From the start of the hike, you've likely noticed a variety of flowers, including California poppies, lavender, and beach primrose, in addition to the ice plants that line the drive. While abundant along Northern California's coast, ice plant is an invasive succulent shrub that's native to the coast of South Africa. It was introduced as an erosion stabilization tool. If you look carefully along the trail, you'll see how the wind and water has battered the coast, with the faint remains of older paths and benches now crumbled into the eroded cliff-side and buried by the ice plants.

At 1.8 miles (2.9 km) you arrive at **Guardian I,** the triangular steel sculpture that stands nearly 10 feet (3 m) tall in a field of ice plants. Crafted by artist and architect Alan Burrus, it's the oldest public sculpture in Santa Cruz, erected in 1986.

MARK ABBOTT MEMORIAL LIGHTHOUSE ▶

▲ WEST CLIFF DRIVE TRAIL

In this same area, listen for and spot the blowhole, where water surges up into the sky from what remains of a contraption known as a wave motor, built over 100 years ago to harness the ocean's power.

Continue along the path to the 20-minute parking loop just before the entry kiosk for **Natural Bridges State Park.**

▶ **MILE 2-4: Natural Bridges State Park to Steamer Lane**

When you arrive at the 20-minute parking loop, turn around and return the way you came.

DIRECTIONS

From Santa Cruz's city center, go south on Center Street for 0.7 miles (1.1 km). At the traffic circle, take the second exit onto West Cliff Drive. Continue south on West Cliff Drive and find parking in a lot or metered parking before or around Lighthouse Field State Beach, where this hike begins.

GPS COORDINATES: 36.9518, −122.0261; 36°57'6.5" N, 122°1'34" W

BEST NEARBY BITES

After your urban stroll, make your way to **Copal** (1203 Mission St., Santa Cruz, 831/201-4418, 11:30am-8pm Wed.-Thurs. and Sun., 11:30am-9pm Fri.-Sat., $16-30). While more upscale than a burger joint, casual attire and families are welcome at this flavorful Oaxacan restaurant. Their mole and mezcal offerings are the highlight of any meal.

Hike into a dense redwood forest, past historic logging sites and through muddy creek beds to the cascading Maple Falls.

DISTANCE: 6 miles (10 km) round-trip
DURATION: 2 hours
ELEVATION GAIN: 680 feet (207 m)
EFFORT: Moderate
TRAIL: Dirt, rock, single-track, creek
USERS: Hikers, mountain bikers on part of the trail, leashed dogs on part of the trail
SEASON: Year-round
PASSES/FEES: $8 day-use fee per vehicle
MAPS: On the park website select "Brochures" and "Park Brochure"
PARK HOURS: Sunrise-sunset daily
TRAILHEAD: Porter Family Picnic Area parking lot
FACILITIES: Vault toilets at the trailhead
CONTACT: California State Parks, 831/763-7063, www.parks.ca.gov

START THE HIKE

▶ **MILE 0-1.1: Porter Family Picnic Area Parking Lot to Bridge Creek Trail Junction**

From the **Porter Family Picnic Area Parking Lot,** walk northwest and through the gate onto **Aptos Creek Fire Road.** Bikes and leashed dogs are allowed only on the section of the hike on the fire road. At 0.2 mile (0.3 km), go up the incline to the left (west) onto **Loma Preieta Grade Trail** and look down at Margaret's Bridge on Aptos Creek Fire Road before the trail curves northwest, away from the road. The path narrows as it briefly comes out from under the trees, and power lines are visible above. Cross a **bridge** at 0.4 mile (0.6 km), where the trail curves right (northeast).

At 0.8 mile (1.3 km) is the **Porter House Site,** named for the secretary of the Loma Prieta Lumber Company, Warren Porter, who became California's lieutenant governor in 1907. Take the slight detour out and back to the right (east), where

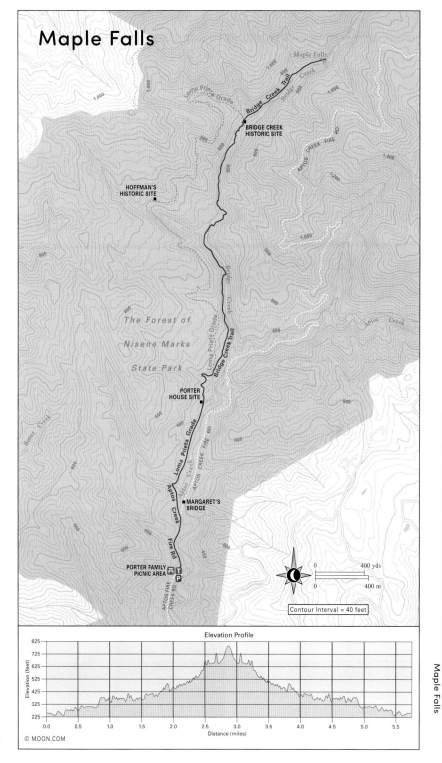

Maple Falls

The Forest of Nisene Marks State Park

Maple Falls

Bridge Creek Trail

BRIDGE CREEK HISTORIC SITE

HOFFMAN'S HISTORIC SITE

Loma Prieta Grade

Bridge Creek

PORTER HOUSE SITE

Loma Prieta Grade

Aptos Creek

Bates Creek

MARGARET'S BRIDGE

Aptos Creek Fire Rd

PORTER FAMILY PICNIC AREA

Aptos Creek Fire Rd

Bridge Creek

Aptos Creek Fire Rd

Aptos Creek

0   400 yds
0   400 m

Contour Interval = 40 feet

Elevation Profile

Elevation (feet)

825
725
625
525
425
325
225

0.0   0.5   1.0   1.5   2.0   2.5   3.0   3.5   4.0   4.5   5.0   5.5

Distance (miles)

© MOON.COM

MAPLE FALLS TRAIL ▲

there's a bench and an interpretive sign with information on the area's logging history. Continue on Loma Prieta Grade Trail to the left (west) of the site, toward **Hoffman's Historic Site.**

Switchbacks take you down and over a bridge, and the path briefly drops steeply to the right (south). Planks reinforce the trail against an earthen wall as the trail curves left (northeast). When you reach the split with Bridge Creek Trail at 1.1 miles (1.8 km), veer right (northwest) onto **Bridge Creek Trail.**

▶ MILE 1.1–2.6: Bridge Creek Trail Junction to Bridge Creek Historic Site

The trail takes you on a hillside, up and down the root-covered western side of the creek, toward a seasonal waterfall that flows over the trail at 1.5 miles (2.4 km). For the remainder of the trail to Maple Falls, the path continues gaining elevation and grows increasingly technical, leading over, under, and around moss-covered trees, roots, rock overhangs, and boulders, often through the creek or along steep drop-offs.

At 2.6 miles (4.1 km), you've arrived at the **Bridge Creek Historic Site.** Here on the banks where Big Stump Gulch enters Bridge Creek are what remains of the buildings

SANTA CRUZ

Maple Falls

and railroad of a large lumber camp from around 1918 to 1920, the tail end of a 40-year logging frenzy that took over Aptos Canyon. With each passing year, the forest reclaims more and recovers with the help of forest regeneration and preservation efforts.

▶ **MILE 2.6-3: Bridge Creek Historic Site to Maple Falls**
From the historic site, it is only 0.5 mile (0.8 km) to Maple Falls, but it is the most technical section of the hike. Some sections are overgrown, and reaching the falls requires repeatedly crossing from bank to bank of Bridge Creek. Depending on the water level, there may not be rocks or downed trees to use for crossing, and those that are visible are likely slippery. Proceed with caution as the canyon narrows. At the point where a logjam appears in the creek, many hikers use tree roots on the left (northern) wall of the creek to pull themselves up, using the ground between roots as footholds.

Just before reaching Maple Falls, at 3 miles (4.8 km), the trail is engulfed in lush forest plants, and after a tight turn on a narrow section, the falls are revealed. Use the rope on the left (north) side of the trail to help you down to the small dirt or mud beach that surrounds **Maple Falls.** Logs and rocks avail themselves as seats for those seeking to rest their feet and take in the view. Make sure not to miss the maple trees for which the falls are named.

When you're ready to return, retrace your steps back to the trailhead.

DIRECTIONS

From Santa Cruz, take Highway 1 south to exit 435 for State Park Drive. Turn left onto State Park Drive and continue 0.3 mile (0.5 km), then turn right onto Soquel Drive. Continue 0.5 mile (0.8 km) to Aptos Creek Fire Road and turn left to enter the park. Proceed for 2.9 miles (4.7 km) to reach the Porter Family Picnic Area parking lot.

GPS COORDINATES: 37.0145, −121.9053; 37°0'52.2" N, 121°54'19.1" W

BEST NEARBY BREWS
After your hike, head to **New Bohemia Brewing Company** (1030 41st Ave., Santa Cruz, 831/350-0253, www.nubobrew.com, 4pm-9pm Mon.-Thurs., noon-9pm Fri.-Sun.). New Bohemia takes pride in its house yeast coming from České Budějovice, in the heart of the Czech Republic's Bohemia, to give their lagers the crisp yet rich flavors found in the Old World.

11

Aptos Creek Loop

THE FOREST OF NISENE MARKS STATE PARK

Enjoy the sound of the water flowing in Apotos Creek and wander through the redwoods and ferns that sometimes feel like a forest walk in prehistoric times.

DISTANCE: 2.9 miles (4.7 km) round-trip
DURATION: 1.5 hours
ELEVATION GAIN: 305 feet (93 m)
EFFORT: Easy
TRAIL: Dirt, single-track
USERS: Hikers, mountain bikers, horseback riders, leashed dogs
SEASON: Year-round
PASSES/FEES: $8 day-use fee per vehicle, or California State Parks pass
MAPS: On the park website select "Brochures" and "Park Brochure," BaseImage Maps "San Jose Topo Bundle," https://store.avenza.com
PARK HOURS: Sunrise-sunset daily
TRAILHEAD: George's Picnic Area
FACILITIES: Vault toilets and drinking fountain at the park entrance parking lot
CONTACT: The Forest of Nisene Marks, 831/763-7063, www.parks.ca.gov

START THE HIKE

▶ **MILE 0-1.3: George's Picnic Area to Park Entrance Parking Lot**
From **George's Picnic Area,** cross Aptos Creek Road to enter the trails at the park sign for Rancho Aptos Trail. Keep left (south) where the trail splits several times over a short distance. Follow the fern-lined path to an open area and look for the trail marker for "Vienna Woods Trail to Mesa Grande Road" at the western side. The path leads along Aptos Creek.

At 1.1 miles (1.8 km), you arrive at the peaceful **Waggoner Overlook,** a fenced-in deck with a picnic table that is intended to overlook Aptos Creek but is mostly just a nice place to take a break. You can follow the trail marker to either continue on Aptos Rancho Trail to Spilt Stuff Trail, or turn left (east) onto Waggoner Overlook Trail. Take the short 0.2-mile (0.3-km) **Waggoner Overlook Trail,** which is wheelchair accessible and the most direct route to the vault toilets at the park's entrance.

At 1.3 miles (2.1 km), the trail ends at the **park entrance parking lot,** where there's a larger picnic area, an interpretive sign with a map (it does not include all the trails), the vault toilets, and a ranger's station.

▶ **MILE 1.3-1.7: Park Entrance Parking Lot to Twisted Grove**
Beyond the vault toilets, follow signs to go north on **Split Stuff Trail.** When you get to the park sign for Aptos Rancho Trail, at 1.4 miles (2.3 km), follow the arrow to go left (southwest) onto **Old Growth Loop.**

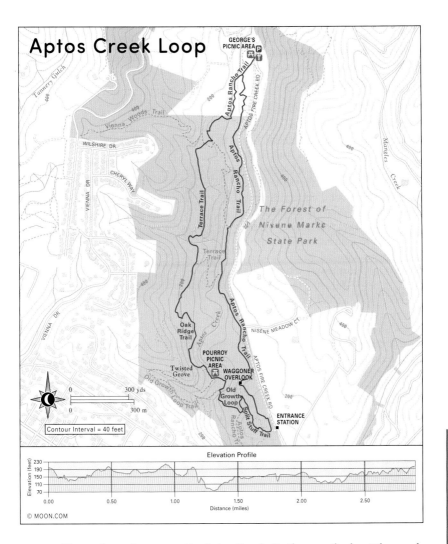

Aptos Creek Loop

Elevation Profile

The trail continues west to Aptos Creek. Farther south along the creek, you may be treated to a swing that hangs from an old downed redwood that crosses the creek from the hill on the other side. Some visitors are tempted to walk across on the top of the tree, but it's not a good idea. The drop from the highest point is higher than a two-story building.

For the first time on this hike, the trail crosses Aptos Creek, at 1.6 miles (2.6 km). A seasonal bridge is in place May to October, but fording the stream is required in other months. On the other side of the bridge is a park sign for **Pourroy Picnic Area.** Inspect the picnic area's filled-in square stone fire pit and the short wall of roots that would make an excellent backdrop for a dramatic performance.

Follow the park sign to continue toward Twisted Grove. The path will begin the hike's steepest ascent, and after the trail marker for the grove indicates to stay right (east), you reach **Twisted Grove** at 1.7 miles (2.7 km), on a bluff overlooking the creek, where the trees bend and twirl like ballerinas reaching to the sky.

▶ **MILE 1.7-2.9: Twisted Grove to George's Picnic Area**

On the other side of the grove, the trail becomes **Oak Ridge Trail.** Take the path right (north) to continue the ascent, with 180 feet (55 m) elevation gain over 1 mile (1.6 km), from just past Pourroy Picnic Area to just past Twisted Grove. Where it appears to split again, follow the trail marker labeled "trail" to continue right (northeast). This is the most densely forested section of the hike, with a thick ground cover mix that includes a variety of ferns, sorrel, thimbleberry, Pacific trillium, and western Solomon's plume.

At 2 miles (3.2 km), continue right (north) onto a connector trail and straight onto **Terrace Trail.** At 2.2 miles (3.5 km), the path crosses a tributary of the creek, and where the trail splits soon after, follow it down toward the creek, to the right (east). When you get to the trail marker for **Vienna Woods Trail** to Aptos Creek Road, follow it north, and at 2.7 miles (4.3 km), it will take you to the bridge over Aptos Creek from the beginning of the hike.

After crossing the bridge, take Terrace Trail left (north) to return the way you came.

DIRECTIONS

From Santa Cruz, head south on Highway 1 to exit 435 for State Park Drive and turn left. Turn right onto Soquel Drive and continue for 0.5 mile (0.8 km), then turn left onto Aptos Creek Road. Follow the road through the entrance ranger station to park at George's Picnic Area.

GPS COORDINATES: 37.0009, −121.9056; 37°0'3.2" N, 121°54'20.2" W

BEST NEARBY BITES

Red Apple Café (783 Rio Del Mar Blvd., Suite 15, Aptos, 831/685-1224, www.redappleaptos.com, 7am-3pm daily, $8-19) is less than 10 minutes away from the park and is an adorable and casual café with a great outdoor patio. The menu is full of breakfast favorites, sandwiches, and salad options.

South Marsh Loop

ELKHORN SLOUGH NATIONAL ESTUARINE RESEARCH RESERVE

Learn the cultural and natural history of this delicate habitat and the importance of its restoration on this relaxed and family-friendly hike.

DISTANCE: 2.2 miles (3.5 km) round-trip

DURATION: 1 hour

ELEVATION GAIN: 130 feet (39 m)

EFFORT: Easy

TRAIL: Dirt, gravel, sand

USERS: Hikers, wheelchair users

SEASON: Year-round

PASSES/FEES: None

MAPS: On the park website select "Visit," "Reserve Visitor Information," and "See the trail map for more," at the visitor center

PARK HOURS: 9am–5pm Wed.–Sun., closed Mon.–Tues.

TRAILHEAD: Elkhorn Slough Reserve Visitor Center

FACILITIES: Restrooms at visitor center and Big Barn

CONTACT: Elkhorn Slough National Estuarine Research Reserve, 831/728-2822, www.elkhornslough.org

START THE HIKE

Visitors are required to check in at the visitor center prior to hiking. During the highest tides of the year, part of the trail becomes impassible, with much of the bridge past the Big Barn covered in water. Call ahead to confirm conditions.

▶ **MILE 0–0.4: Visitor Center to Big Barn**

From the **visitor center,** follow the path that leads southwest past the picnic table area on the right (north). Heading west, the exposed trail gradually descends and intersects with the Long Valley Loop Trail and the Five Fingers Loop Trail before arriving at the **Elkhorn Slough Viewpoint** at 0.2 mile (0.3 km). Take a moment to look through the binocular viewers—you may see anything from a roaming black-tailed deer to an otter on his back in the marsh. Both local

◀ SOUTH MARSH LOOP

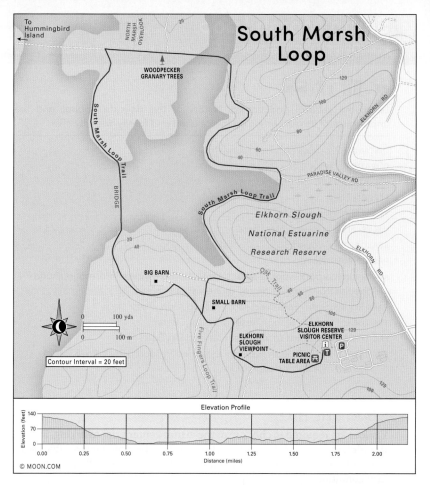

and migratory birds can be seen; the reserve is identified as a Globally Important Bird Area by the American Birding Conservancy. Some nesting birds here include the white-tailed kite, red-shouldered hawk, and barn owl.

Back on the path, continue straight and follow trail sign for **South Marsh Loop Trail.** The trail more steeply descends toward the first barn, and you will pass native coyote brush and invasive plants such as poison hemlock (look for bunches of delicate white flowers) and wild radish—both of which do well in disturbed areas. It is believed they arrived with cattle when a dairy farm took over this land a hundred years ago. At 0.3 mile (0.5 km), pass to the left (west) of the **Small Barn** and arrive at the **Big Barn** at 0.4 mile (0.6 km).

▶ MILE 0.4-1: Big Barn to Woodpecker Granary Trees

At the Big Barn there are two owl boxes and an exterior restroom. The barn was once used to shelter cattle. Look inside the barn and you may get to see great horned or barn owls nesting.

Follow the trail around the left (west) side of the Big Barn, and you will soon come to the **bridge** over tidal mudflats, at 0.5 mile (0.8 km). On the other side of the bridge, continue straight (north) until the path splits. To the left (west) is the option to take the **Hummingbird Island extension.** This addition adds over 1 mile (1.6 km) to the hike, and the path is narrow, passes an active railroad track, and requires climbing steep stairs leading to the crest of the island. At the top is a large trellis for native hummingbird-friendly plants as well as a structure resembling an Ohlone midden overlooking a small pond. The extension is not recommended for young children.

Turning right (east), you pass the **junction** for the North Marsh Overlook extension and then approach **woodpecker granary trees** on the right (south) side of the trail. Woodpeckers reuse these trees over generations to store their winter food supply. Storing the acorns this way keeps them dry. There can be thousands of acorns in a single granary.

▶ **MILE 1-2.2: Woodpecker Granary Trees to Visitor Center**
Enjoy the long-awaited shade as the trail is now in an oak woodland and begins to wind south. At 1.2 miles (1.9 km), keep right (west) to stay on the trail; don't turn east onto the service road. Keep right again at 1.5 miles (2.4 km). To the right (west) of the trail, the mudflats may be obvious at low tide or filled with water at high tide. This zone is a primary feeding area for migrating shorebirds when they stop over. When the tide is low, look for birds foraging for invertebrate species that live at or beneath the surface of the mud.

The trail intersects with the Oak Trail to the left (east) at 1.7 miles (2.7 km). Continue south on South Marsh Trail, and where the path splits again, stay left (south) toward the Small Barn. The path begins to ascend, and after 0.1 mile (0.2 km), return to the visitor center the way you came.

DIRECTIONS

From Santa Cruz, follow Highway 1 south for 19 miles (31 km) and take exit 423 for Salinas Road. Keep right to stay on Werner Road, then turn right onto Elkhorn Road. Continue for 5 miles (8.1 km) and turn right into the reserve at 1700 Elkhorn Road.

GPS COORDINATES: 36.8170, −121.7298; 36°49'1.2" N, 121°43'47.3" W

BEST NEARBY BITES
For the freshest seafood around, make your way south to Castroville to **Phil's Fish Market** (10700 Merritt St., Castroville, 831/633-2152, https://philsfishmarket.com, 10am-7pm Sun.-Wed., 10am-8pm Thurs.-Sat.), just nine minutes from the trailhead. Enjoy some of Mama Nina's Cioppino.

NEARBY CAMPGROUNDS

NAME	DESCRIPTION	FACILITIES	SEASON	FEE
Henry Cowell Redwoods State Park	Campsites in pine and oak forest	113 campsites with potable water, restrooms with flush toilets, showers, picnic table, firewood, fire pit	year-round	$35

2591 Graham Hill Rd., Scotts Valley, 831/438-2396, www.reservecalifornia.com

NAME	DESCRIPTION	FACILITIES	SEASON	FEE
Seacliff State Park Beach	Beachfront	RV sites only (no tent sites), 26 full hookup sites, 37 without hookups, potable water, restrooms with flush toilets, showers, picnic tables, fire pits	year-round	from $35

201 State Park Dr., Aptos, 831/685-6500, www.reservecalifornia.com

NAME	DESCRIPTION	FACILITIES	SEASON	FEE
New Brighton State Park Beach	Beachfront camping	100 developed campsites, including 11 RV hookup sites, potable water, restrooms with flush toilets, showers, picnic tables, fire pits	year-round	from $35

1500 Park Ave., Capitola, 831/464-6329, www.reservecalifornia.com

MONTEREY & BIG SUR

When people dream of driving the Pacific Coast Highway in Northern California, visions of Bixby Bridge, McWay Falls, and the winding rugged cliffs of Big Sur are in their minds. Big Sur has some of the most undeveloped acreage along this roughly 90-mile-long (145-km) stretch of California's famous throughway, tempting even novice hikers to get out to explore its coastal trails and tide pools and climb into its canyons and forests. As you continue north, you approach the villages, towns, and cities of Monterey County, where you will find more people but no less natural splendor. From the bird's-eye view of Monterey Bay atop Ollason Peak to the kelp forest of the bay itself, there is a bounty of delights for outdoors lovers.

▲ CARMEL MEADOWS

▲ REDWOOD CANYON-TERRACE LOOP

1 **Pacific Grove Ocean View**
DISTANCE: 4.4 miles (7.1 km)
round-trip
DURATION: 2.5 hours
EFFORT: Easy

2 **Monterey Bay Coastal Recreation Trail**
DISTANCE: 4.5 miles (7.2 km)
round-trip
DURATION: 2.5 hours
EFFORT: Easy-moderate

3 **Fort Ord National Monument Loop**
DISTANCE: 4 miles (6.4 km)
round-trip
DURATION: 2 hours
EFFORT: Easy

4 **Ollason Peak and Valley View**
DISTANCE: 7.8 miles (12.6 km)
round-trip
DURATION: 4.5 hours
EFFORT: Moderate

5 **Carmel Meadows**
DISTANCE: 1.8 miles (2.9 km)
round-trip
DURATION: 1 hour
EFFORT: Easy

6 **Point Lobos Perimeter Loop**
DISTANCE: 5.2 miles (8.4 km)
round-trip
DURATION: 3 hours
EFFORT: Easy-moderate

7 **Redwood Canyon-Terrace Loop**
DISTANCE: 3.6 miles (5.8 km)
round-trip
DURATION: 2 hours
EFFORT: Easy-moderate

8 **Soberanes Canyon Trail**
DISTANCE: 2.8 miles (4.5 km)
round-trip
DURATION: 1.5 hours
EFFORT: Easy-moderate

9 **Andrew Molera State Park Loop**
DISTANCE: 8 miles (12.9 km)
round-trip
DURATION: 4 hours
EFFORT: Moderate

10 **Pfeiffer Falls**
DISTANCE: 1.6 miles (2.6 km)
round-trip
DURATION: 1 hour
EFFORT: Easy

11 **Buzzards Roost Trail**
DISTANCE: 3 miles (4.8 km)
round-trip
DURATION: 1.5 hours
EFFORT: Easy-moderate

12 **McWay Falls Overlook**
DISTANCE: 0.7 mile (1.1 km)
round-trip
DURATION: 0.5 hours
EFFORT: Easy

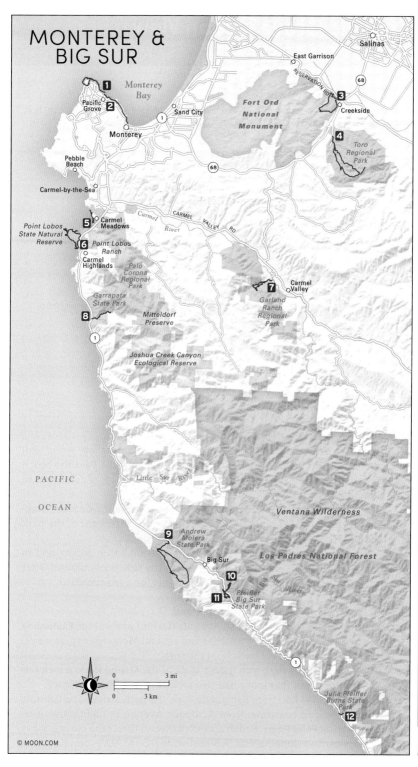

MONTEREY & BIG SUR

Salinas

East Garrison

Monterey Bay

1

Pacific Grove

2

Sand City

Monterey

Fort Ord National Monument

3 Creekside

68

4 Toro Regional Park

Pebble Beach

Carmel-by-the-Sea

Carmel River CARMEL VALLEY RD

Carmel Meadows **5**

Point Lobos State Natural Reserve

6 Point Lobos Ranch

Carmel Highlands

Palo Corona Regional Park

Carmel Valley

7 Garland Ranch Regional Park

Garrapata State Park

8

Mitteldorf Preserve

1

Joshua Creek Canyon Ecological Reserve

Little Sur River

PACIFIC

OCEAN

Ventana Wilderness

Los Padres National Forest

9 Andrew Molera State Park

Big Sur

10

11 Pfeiffer Big Sur State Park

Big Sur River

1

Julia Pfeiffer Burns State Park

12

0   3 mi

0   3 km

© MOON.COM

Pacific Grove Ocean View
PACIFIC GROVE, CALIFORNIA

🦌 ❀ 🏛 😾 🚶 ♿ 🚌

Walk along the world-famous Pacific Grove Magic Carpet, explore tide pools, and pass by the Point Pinos Lighthouse on the northernmost tip of the Monterey Peninsula.

DISTANCE: 4.4 miles (7.1 km) round-trip
DURATION: 2.5 hours
ELEVATION GAIN: 130 feet (40 m)
EFFORT: Easy
TRAIL: Dirt, gravel, sand, boardwalk, decomposed granite
USERS: Hikers, bikers, runners, wheelchair users, leashed dogs
SEASON: Year-round
PASSES/FEES: None
MAPS: Select "Our City," "About the City," "Parking Information," and then "City of Pacific Grove Neighborhoods Map" on City of Pacific Grove website
TRAILHEAD: Lovers Point
FACILITIES: Restrooms on the south side of Lovers Point Beach Café; Crespi Pond restrooms at 1.6 miles (2.6 km)
CONTACT: City of Pacific Grove, 831/648-3100, www.cityofpacificgrove.org

START THE HIKE

▶ **MILE 0-0.7: Lovers Point to Otter Point**

From **Lovers Point,** follow the coastline northwest, with a low stone wall between you and the beach below and to the right (north). Pass the beach access staircase and take the pedestrian walkway. This is a great spot to look for black oystercatchers on the rocky shoreline.

The path takes you into **Perkins Park,** known as Pacific Grove's "Magic Carpet" for its pinkish-purple blooms that cover 90 percent of the park and attract thousands of visitors April through August.

At 0.6 mile (1 km), multiple sets of stairs provide beach access, and in 500 feet (152 m), you arrive at **Otter Point.** In the tide pools around Otter Point you can find sea stars, mussels, anemones, and sea urchins.

▶ **MILE 0.7-1.6: Otter Point to Crespi Pond**

Continue walking along the coast. At 1 mile (1.6 km) you will see **Esplanade Park** across the street, where benches and several Monterey cypresses offer a lovely open space set back from the surf.

After you pass the park, you'll get a view of the **Kissing Rock,** a rock formation in the ocean that looks like two rocks in a perpetual embrace.

At 0.25 mile (0.4 km) from Esplanade Park, the path arrives at a 0.8-mile (1.3-km) stretch of coastline, from Acropolis Avenue to Lighthouse Avenue, known as **Point Pinos.** Beach access pathways direct the crowds away from the sensitive dune habitat. A 5-foot-wide (1.5-m) ADA-compliant trail

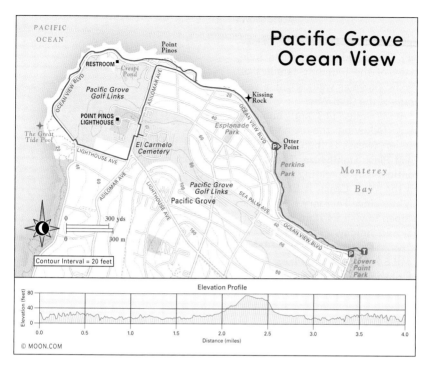

extends to the Great Tide Pool site near Asilomar Beach, ahead. Across the street at 1.6 miles (2.6 km) is **Pacific Grove Municipal Golf Course,** which holds **Crespi Pond,** a brackish-freshwater pond known for the wide variety of birds that visit.

▸ **MILE 1.6–2.7: Crespi Pond to Point Pinos Lighthouse**
Continue on the path past the pond to arrive at the **Great Tide Pool** site. Pass more stairs to the tide pools, parking spots, and views of the lighthouse as the path rounds the northern tip of the peninsula and heads southwest.

Take the path through the dunes or cross the street to the gravel path by the golf course's wooden fence until you arrive at the **junction** of Ocean View Boulevard, Lighthouse Avenue, and Sunset Drive, at 2.4 miles (3.9 km). Turn left (southeast) onto the gravel walkway on the left (north) side of **Lighthouse Avenue.** At the next intersection, turn left (northeast) onto **Asilomar Avenue** and follow the fence line of the golf course. To the

BEST NEARBY SIGHTS

Most visitors to Monterey County can't pass up the **17 Mile Drive,** which provides stunning views along the coast, a drive through the famous Pebble Beach Golf Links area, and the inspiring Lone Cypress. For $11.25 per vehicle, the drive allows visitors to get out at certain points along the route and is extremely popular at sunset. The gates are open sunrise-sunset daily. Use the address for The Lodge at Pebble Beach, 1700 17-Mile Drive, to arrive at the Pebble Beach gate.

right (east) is **El Carmelo Ceme-tery.** Those laid to rest here include many of the founding families of Pacific Grove as well as Union veterans of the Civil War.

At 2.7 miles (4.3 km), immediately following the cemetery to the left (west), is the entrance for **Point Pinos Lighthouse.** The oldest continuously operating lighthouse on the West Coast, it has flashed nightly since February 1, 1855, and is open to visitors 11am-3pm Saturday and Sunday.

▶ **MILE 2.7-4.4: Point Pinos Lighthouse to Lovers Point**

From the lighthouse, continue along the gravel path alongside the golf course on Asilomar Avenue and cross the street to rejoin the path on Ocean View Boulevard at 3 miles (4.8 km). Turn right (southeast) onto the path and retrace your steps back to Lovers Point.

DIRECTIONS

From Monterey city center, head north on Lighthouse Avenue. Continue onto Central Avenue, and then turn right on 3rd Street. Turn left on Ocean View Boulevard and continue for 0.8 mile (1.3 km). Look for street parking, being mindful of posted signs.

GPS COORDINATES: 36.6265, −121.9162; 36°37'35.4" N, 121°54'58.3" W

BEST NEARBY BITES

Five minutes from Lovers Lane is the local institution **Lucy's On Lighthouse** (1120 Lighthouse Ave., Pacific Grove, 831/920-2006, www.lucyspg.com, 11am-7pm Fri.-Sun., $6-13). Serving award-winning all-beef, veggie, and Polish sausage hot dogs, tots, balsamic brussels sprouts, homemade chili, and mac-and-cheese along with Marianne's ice cream, beer, bubbles, coffee, and wine to wash it down! Try the Lovers Point, a bacon wrapped dog with guacamole, tomatoes, jalapeños, green onion, and Lucy's sauce.

2

Monterey Bay Coastal Recreation Trail

MONTEREY, CALIFORNIA

🦌 ❀ 🏛 🐾 🚶 ♿ 🚆

Feel the ocean's mist kiss your face, spot marine life and seabirds, and learn the long history of the peninsula along this entertaining urban hike.

BEST: Wildflower Hikes
DISTANCE: 4.5 miles (7.2 km) round-trip
DURATION: 1.5 hours
ELEVATION GAIN: 50 feet (15 m)
EFFORT: Easy-moderate
TRAIL: Dirt, gravel, paved
USERS: Hikers, bikers, runners, skaters, wheelchair users, leashed dogs
SEASON: Year-round
PASSES/FEES: None
MAPS: Select "Resources" on www.seemonterey.com
TRAILHEAD: Lovers Point
FACILITIES: Restrooms on south side of Lovers Point Beach Café, restrooms on Wave Street at 1.5 miles (2.4 km)
CONTACT: City of Monterey, 831/646-3799, www.monterey.org

The entire Monterey Bay Coastal Recreation Trail is 18 miles (29 km), stretching from Castroville down the coast to Pacific Grove. It follows the former Southern Pacific Railroad line, much of it on the same route where the track once transferred goods between this historic fishing area and the rest of Northern California.

START THE HIKE

▶ **MILE 0-0.4: Lovers Point to Berwick Park**
From **Lovers Point,** follow the coastline southeast, past the picnic area, Lovers Point Beach Café, and sand volleyball courts. Join the **Monterey Bay Coastal Recreation Trail** at the "Lovers Point Pacific Grove, CA" sign, keeping to the paved right lane.

Beginning at 0.4 mile (0.6 km), the four-panel **Pacific Grove Historical Mural,** painted by John Tonn in 1988, decorate the walls along

SIGN ON THE MONTEREY BAY
◀ COASTAL RECREATION TRAIL

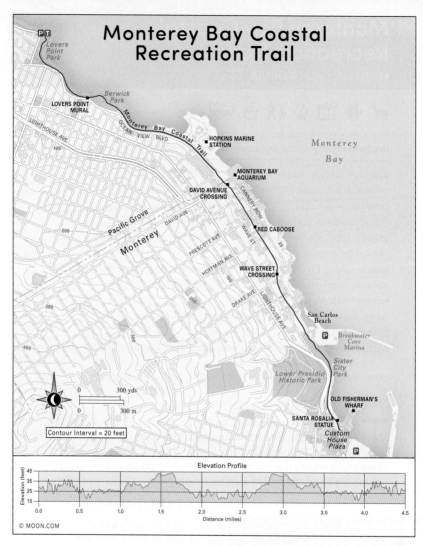

Monterey Bay Coastal Recreation Trail

the trail. The panels depict the native Rumsen Ohlone and Esselen people, Chinese fishermen, and early Japanese settlers, among others. At this point is **Berwick Park,** where there's a bronze sculpture of a sea otter and its pup and a large sculpture of two breaching humpback whales, made from cypress tree stumps.

▶ **MILE 0.4–1.2: Berwick Park to Start of City of Monterey Section**
The trail leads to a high fence blocking public access to **Hopkins Marine Station** of Stanford University and the **Marine Life Refuge.** On the other side of the fence is a sandy cove, where species of concern like harbor seals and black oystercatchers are protected.

Soon the trail takes you past an interpretative sign with China Point history—this area was once one of the largest Chinese fishing villages on the West Coast. Across Ocean View Boulevard, American Tin Cannery

▲ MONTEREY BAY COASTAL RECREATION TRAIL

Outlets represents the transition of past to present as you enter Cannery Row, today full of retail stores.

The Monterey Bay Coastal Recreation Trail then transitions from the City of Pacific Grove section to the start of the **City of Monterey section** at 1.2 miles (1.9 km).

▶ **MILE 1.2-1.9: Start of City of Monterey Section to San Carlos Beach**
Look for the blue wave-painted crosswalks as you cross several streets on this section of the trail. Where the sidewalk curves northeast toward the Monterey Bay Aquarium, stay on the trail by crossing **David Avenue.** Before reaching Hoffman Avenue at 1.5 miles (2.4 km), you can't miss the **red caboose,** built in 1916 as an outside braced boxcar and converted into a caboose circa 1940. It stands as a nod to the era when the Southern Pacific Railroad ran along this portion of the trail.

At the intersection after **Hoffman Avenue,** head right (southwest) across **Wave Street** and then straight (south) across **Drake Avenue.** The trail passes murals by Monterey resident John Cerney, depicting life on Cannery Row, before entering the **San Carlos Beach** area at 1.9 miles (3.1 km).

▶ **MILE 1.9-2.2: San Carlos Beach to Custom**
  House Plaza-Old Fisherman's Wharf
Pass the entrance for the **Breakwater Cove Marina** and continue on Monterey Bay Coastal Recreation Trail through a grove of cypress trees, past small picnic tables, to **Sister City Park,** with a sign noting Monterey's sister cities around the world, at 2 miles (3.2 km). Continue along the marina. On the barrier to the right (west) that separates the trail from **Lighthouse Avenue** are planted a rainbow of colorful flowers, including California poppies and Pride of Madeira. The trail then approaches an interpretive sign

Lerida, Spain
Distance in Miles 5,924
Distance in Kilometers 9,533

Dubrovnik, Croatia
Distance in Miles 6,406
Distance in Kilometers 10,???

Lankaran, Azerbaijan
Distance in Miles 7,193
Distance in Kilometers 11,576

Kusadasi, Turkey
Distance in Miles 6,924
Distance in Kilometers 11,143

Isola delle Femmine, Italy
Distance in Miles 6,526
Distance in Kilometers 10,502

SISTER CITY PARK ▲

explaining the Vizcaino-Serra Oak Mural ahead, which depicts the founding of Monterey.

Just before you reach Fisherman's Wharf, pass a memorial rock commemorating the first sardine cannery in Monterey and a **statue of Santa Rosalia,** the patron saint of the Italian fishermen in Monterey. At 2.2 miles (3.5 km), you arrive at the **Custom House Plaza and Old Fisherman's Wharf.** When you have completed your exploration of this area, return the way you came.

DIRECTIONS

From Monterey city center, head north on Lighthouse Avenue. Continue onto Central Avenue, and then turn right on 3rd Street. Turn left on Ocean View Boulevard and continue for 0.8 mile (1.3 km). Look for street parking, being mindful posted signs.

GPS COORDINATES: 36.6265, −121.9162; 36°37′35.4″ N, 121°54′58.3″ W

BEST NEARBY BITES

Less than 2 miles (3.2 km) from Lovers Point, the casual **Sea Harvest Restaurant and Fish Market** (598 Foam St., Monterey, 831/646-0547, 11am-7pm daily, $17-29), owned by a fishing family, puts the freshest local seafood on your plate. Try the fish-and-chips, Cajun-style grilled salmon, or a warm cup of clam chowder on a cold day. You can also purchase from the fish counter to cook at home.

3

Fort Ord National Monument Loop

FORT ORD NATIONAL MONUMENT

🦌 ❀ 🐾 🚶

This hike takes you to panoramic views of the area's rolling hills and peaks from Monterey Bay to the Gabilan Mountains on the monument's ancient sand dunes.

DISTANCE: 4 miles (6.4 km) round-trip
DURATION: 2 hours
ELEVATION GAIN: 510 feet (155 m)
EFFORT: Easy
TRAIL: Dirt fire road, gravel fire road, single-track, sand
USERS: Hikers, mountain bikers, horseback riders, leashed dogs
SEASON: Year-round
PASSES/FEES: None
MAPS: On the park website, at the trailhead
PARK HOURS: 30 minutes before sunrise to 30 minutes after sunset daily
TRAILHEAD: Trailer Parking Area
FACILITIES: Vault toilets and drinking fountain at the trailhead
CONTACT: Bureau of Land Management, 831/582-2200, www.blm.gov

The U.S. Army purchased this land in 1917 as a training ground for field artillery and cavalry troops stationed at the nearby Presidio of Monterey. The post formally closed in 1994 and today provides more than 86 miles (138 km) of trails through rolling hills, chaparral, oak woodlands, and grasslands.

START THE HIKE

Stay on the trail—hazardous military munitions may still be near some public areas. Nonhazardous military relics and objects in the national monument can't be removed.

▶ MILE 0-1.2: Trailer Parking Area to Oilwell Road Junction

At the northeast end of the **Trailer Parking Area,** look for the trail marker for Trail 1, East Perimeter Road, and Station One Road on the sandy path near the restrooms. The trail ascends into oak woodlands, curving right (south) in parallel

◀ FORT ORD NATIONAL MONUMENT LOOP

Fort Ord National Monument Loop

MONTEREY & BIG SUR

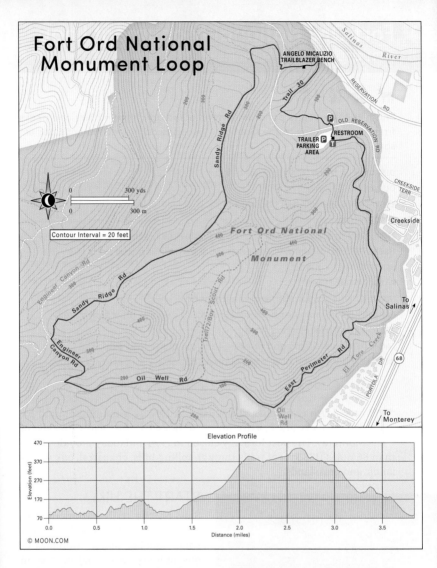

Fort Ord National Monument Loop

Elevation Profile

Contour Interval = 20 feet

© MOON.COM

with Old Reservation Road. Below you to the left (east) is El Toro Creek, and beyond it, some agricultural land. To the right (west), the hillside grasslands are green in spring and yellow in summer.

The trail begins a climb at 0.7 mile (1.1 km) with intermittent shade. To the southeast, look for the hills of Toro County Park and try to spot **Pinyon Peak** (2,247 ft/685 m) and **Saddle Mountain** (1,139 ft/347 m), as the wide service road continues to follow the curve of the hillside toward the southwest. Because of the variety of terrain in the park, hikers are likely to see blooms during any given month, including baby blue-eyes, ceanothus blue blossom, Hickman's popcorn flower, buttercups, and lupine in late winter-early spring, and sticky monkey flower, nightshade, chaparral current, and California goldenrod in the summer-autumn.

At 1.2 miles (1.9 km), Trail 1 intersects at **Oilwell Road** at an interpretive sign.

▶ MILE 1.2–2.1: Oilwell Road Junction to Sandy Ridge Road

Turn right (northwest) onto Oilwell Road and watch for mountain bikers along this straight and wide section. In about 0.5 mile (0.8 km), continue straight on Oilwell Road past a **junction** with Trail 72-Boy Scout Road. At 1.8 miles (2.9 km), an interpretative sign provides some history about the indigenous Ohlone people and the traditional practice of Ohlone basketry. Just beyond the sign is a **junction** with Engineer Canyon Road.

Turn right (northeast) onto **Engineer Canyon Road.** From here, the trail steeply ascends, curving left (northwest) at 2 miles (3.2 km), past the **junction** with Trail 28/Jack's Road. Five hundred feet (152 m) later, pass Trail 27 (on some maps also labeled as Engineer Canyon Road), and then take **Sandy Ridge Road** to the right (northeast) at 2.1 miles (3.4 km).

▶ MILE 2.1–4: Sandy Ridge Road to Trailer Parking Area

Complete the ascent in another 0.1 mile (0.2 km). Atop Sandy Ridge Road are the best panoramic views of the hike. In the sky, look for vultures, red-tailed hawks, and kestrels. Lichen-covered boulders, manzanitas, and warrior blooms surround you. Lizards often dash across the path, and you may spot quail or rabbits doing the same.

There are several single-track trails off Sandy Ridge Road, most of which are well marked but used by mountain bikers, so pay attention. At 2.9 miles (4.7 km), just after a **junction** with Trail 33, you reach the highest point of the hike and can see agricultural lands ahead and the Gabilan Mountains to the east.

Begin the descent down loose gravel. Cross Old Reservation Road at 3.5 miles (5.6 km). Continue straight (east) onto **Trail 30** and arrive at the

Angelo Micalizio Trailblazer bench. The path changes from gravel to sand, and a massive collection of sandstone spires are visible ahead. Where Trail 30 splits at 3.7 mile (6 km), go right (south). The path takes you around, behind, and then below the eroding sandy bluffs. Pass two benches just before you reach a small parking area. Enter the parking area and head south to cross Old Reservation Road where you drove in, and continue to the Trailer Parking Area and restrooms to conclude the hike where it began.

DIRECTIONS

From Monterey, follow Highway 68 (Salinas Hwy.) east to exit 20, for River Road. Turn left onto River Road, and after 0.1 mile (0.2 km), turn left onto Portola Drive for 0.2 mile (0.3 km) to Creekside Terrace, which turns into Old Reservation Road. Turn left into the Trailer Parking Area.

GPS COORDINATES: 36.6261, –121.6911; 36°37'34" N, 121°41'28" W

BEST NEARBY BITES

Just five minutes from the trailhead is local favorite **Angelina's Pizzeria** (22736 Portola Dr., Salinas, 831/484-1164, www.angelinaspizzeria. org, $15-32), where more than four generations bring you craft beer, local wine, or soda while kids of all ages enjoy the arcade and everyone loves the pizza, from the classics to their Gilroy Special, made with garlic sauce, chicken, cheese, Canadian bacon, mushrooms, fresh garlic, and green onions.

Hike over a series of exposed peaks to take in Salinas Valley and the expanse of Monterey Bay at a bird's-eye view from Valley View.

DISTANCE: 7.8 miles (12.6 km) round-trip

DURATION: 4.5 hours

ELEVATION GAIN: 2,000 feet (610 m)

EFFORT: Moderate

TRAIL: Paved road, dirt fire road, dirt, gravel, single-track

USERS: Hikers, mountain bikers, horseback riders

SEASON: Year-round

PASSES/FEES: None

MAPS: On the park website

PARK HOURS: 8am-5pm daily

TRAILHEAD: Quail Meadows Day-Use Area

FACILITIES: Restrooms and drinking fountain at Quail Meadows Day-Use Area

CONTACT: Monterey County Parks Department, 888/588-2267, www. co.monterey.ca.us

START THE HIKE

This hike is almost entirely exposed and not recommended for summer. Have a map or GPS tracking with you—poor signage increases the likelihood of hiking more miles than anticipated.

▶ **MILE 0-2.2: Quail Meadows Day-Use Area to Eagle Peak**

From the **Quail Meadows Day-Use Area,** pass the restrooms and cross the meadow's playground, heading east onto **Ollason Road.** Head right (south) on Ollason Road for 0.3 mile (0.5 km). Where the road splits, turn left (southeast) onto **Cougar Ridge Road.**

Look for a Cougar Ridge Trail sign indicating passage to the Youth Overnight Camp Area to the left (east), across from the bus parking area. Take the single-track trail as it ascends to a clearing just before the pond at the **Youth Overnight Camp Area.** Make a tight turn

Ollason Peak and Valley View

MONTEREY & BIG SUR

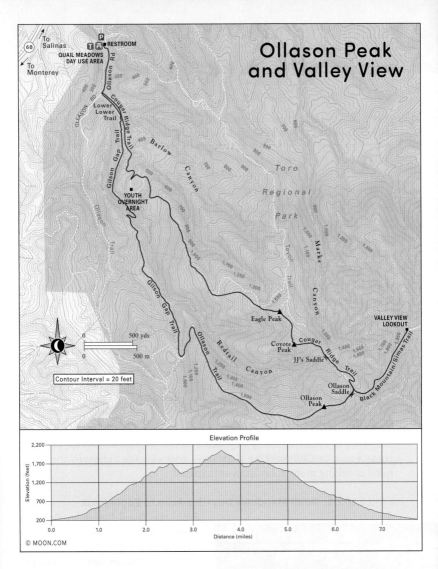

Ollason Peak and Valley View

Elevation Profile

left (east) up the gravel Cougar Ridge Road. At 1.1 miles (1.8 km), you pass a water tank, and shortly after that, a trail marker for Cougar Loop Trail. Keep right (south). The path will continue to climb for the next 1.5 miles (2.4 km).

At 2.2 miles (3.2 km), at a Cougar Ridge sign, again stay right (south) to hike up the steep hill toward the sky and arrive at **Eagle Peak** (1,607 ft/490 m).

▶ **MILE 2.2-3.6: Eagle Peak to Valley View**

Upon Eagle Peak is a **junction** with Toyon Trail, which heads left (north). Stay on Cougar Ridge Trail by continuing right (southeast). At this elevation you can see Salinas Valley and may start to see Monterey Bay, depending on the fog. The first descent of the hike comes after reaching

▲ OLLASON PEAK AND VALLEY VIEW

Coyote Peak (1,710 ft/521 m), taking you steeply downhill at 2.5 miles (4 km). Shortly following are multiple trail crossings, at 2.8 miles (4.5 km), with limited markers, an area known as **JJ's Saddle.** This is a frequented junction for mountain bikers, so be aware that they may come flying down any of the paths. Continue on Cougar Ridge Trail by following the trail as it bends right (southeast), with Coyote Spring flowing along the trail to the right (southwest) as the wide path leads through an oak grove to another crossing of multiple trails at **Ollason Saddle.**

At the **3-way split,** stay left (east) and follow Cougar Ridge Trail as it snakes along to a knoll that junctions with the unmarked Black Mountain Trail at 3.1 miles (5 km). From here, take **Black Mountain Trail** (bikers often refer to it as "Simas Skinny") as it curves in a U shape to the northwest, toward the highest ridge in your sight. In 0.5 mile (0.8 km), work your way up the ridge, gaining over 400 feet (122 m) in elevation. Look for the wooden post for **Valley View** (2,030 ft/619 m) at 3.6 miles (5.8 km).

▶ **MILE 3.6-7.8: Valley View to Quail Meadows Day-Use Area**
Take in the sights of this panoramic view of the entire Monterey Bay. When you're ready to proceed to Ollason Peak, descend back down the ridge to the Ollason saddle and head left (southwest) onto **Ollason Trail** at 4.1 miles (6.6 km). Make your way up the slope to **Ollason Peak** (1,800 ft/549 m) at 4.4 miles (7.1 km).

From here, the remainder of the hike is downhill, taking Ollason Trail into some scattered shade of oak trees to the **junction** with Gilson Gap Trail. Proceed right (southwest) onto **Gilson Gap Trail** as the trail makes a U-turn and continues north, along the east side of Gilson Canyon. Enjoy the gradual descent, passing old fencing with barbed wire and, in spring, wildflower blooms. Deer, quail, ducks, egrets, herons, and wild turkeys are commonly seen as you approach the left (west) side of the Youth

OLLASON PEAK AND VALLEY VIEW ▲

Overnight Camp Area at 6.8 miles (10.9 km). In less than 0.25 mile (0.4 km), you will see the trail is running parallel to Cougar Ridge Road and joins with Pipeline to become **Lower Lower Trail** at 7 miles (11.3 km).

The path connects to Ollason Road just southwest of Cougar Ridge Road at 7.4 miles (11.9 km). Turn right (northeast) onto Ollason Road and return to the Quail Meadows Day-Use Area the way you came.

DIRECTIONS

From Salinas, take Highway 68 west for 2.4 miles (3.9 km) and follow exit 19, for Portola Drive. Turn right onto Portola Drive and continue onto Ollason Road.

GPS COORDINATES: 36.5971, −121.6923; 36°35'49.6" N, 121°41'32.3" W

BEST NEARBY BREWS

Less than 7 miles (11.3 km) from the trailhead, **Alvarado Street Brewery's Production Taproom** (1315 Dayton St., Suite 5, Salinas, 831/800-3332, www.asb.beer, 3:30pm-8pm Tues.-Thurs., 3:30pm-9pm Fri., noon-8pm Sat., noon-6pm Sun.) is where most of the brewery's beer is produced. Grab a seat and try the Mai Tai PA, a tropical IPA with aromas of passion fruit, guava, and lychee.

Carmel Meadows
CARMEL RIVER STATE BEACH

🦌 ❀ 🏛 🐾 🚶 🚌

Grab Fido and his leash for a gentle family-friendly hike with fantastic bird-watching, river wading, and coastal views.

BEST: Kid-Friendly Hikes
DISTANCE: 1.8 miles (2.9 km) round-trip
DURATION: 1 hour
ELEVATION GAIN: 130 feet (40 m)
EFFORT: Easy
TRAIL: Dirt, gravel, sand, single-track, wooden stairs
USERS: Hikers, leashed dogs
SEASON: Year-round
PASSES/FEES: None
MAPS: Avenza Maps, Monastery Beach and Carmel River State Park
PARK HOURS: 8am to 30 minutes after sunset daily
TRAILHEAD: Carmel Meadows Trailhead
FACILITIES: None
CONTACT: California State Parks, 831/649-2836, www.parks.ca.gov

START THE HIKE

Never swim or wade at any of the beaches on this cove. The undertow and rip currents are extremely dangerous.

▶ **MILE 0-0.6: Carmel Meadows Trailhead to Carmel River State Beach**

From the trailhead, head right (west) down the wooden staircase built into the hillside, past cypress trees and costal scrub, toward the ocean. At the south end of Carmel Bay, you can see Point Lobos State Natural Reserve across the water. At the base of the stairs, turn right (north) onto the dirt trail, and enter the **Ohlone Coastal Cultural Preserve** of Carmel River State Beach.

The trail here straddles the land between the bay waters and the community of Carmel Meadows, with ice plant dominating the landscape to the left (west) and beautiful homes on the slope to the right (east). At 0.2 mile (0.3 km), a bench

◀ CARMEL MEADOWS TRAIL

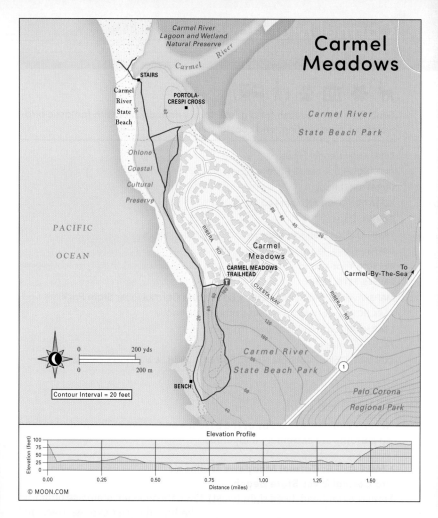

Elevation Profile

© MOON.COM

on the bluff provides an opportunity to sit and watch the waves. Shortly beyond the bench, the trail splits. Stay right (east) to continue along below the homes. Particularly on this section of the hike there is an abundance of poison oak, so stay near the inside of the wide path.

The trail meets another access point trail at 0.4 mile (0.6 km)—continue straight (north) onto a small knoll to view the **Portola Crespi Cross** historical marker, a wooden cross and rock monument memorializing the 1769 Portola Crespi Expedition from Mexico.

Return to the path and turn right (west) toward the ocean. At 0.6 mile (1 km), turn right (north) at the trail junction at the water's edge, which leads to wooden stairs down to the **Carmel River State Beach.**

▶ **MILE 0.6-1.8: Carmel River State Beach**
  to Carmel Meadows Trailhead

If the Carmel River is flowing heavily into the bay, do not cross it. When the river is a trickle or doesn't quite meet the bay, you can easily walk over

▲ CARMEL MEADOWS TRAIL

it or along its rocky south bank. Following the south bank's trail line will lead to the Carmel Lagoon, or you can stay alongside the beach shoreline. If it's safe, venture to the river and the ocean and look for the vast diversity of birds that are drawn to the bird sanctuary. Herons, pelicans, gulls, egrets, and terns are just a few.

When you are ready, return back to the wooden stairs and proceed south past the junction on your left (east) that brought you from the Portola Crespi Cross. A variety of wildflowers mix with the ice plants, and you may see lupine, California poppy, wild radish, orange bush monkey flower, and Monterey paintbrush. At 1 mile (1.6 km), rejoin the main trail where you originally stayed east and follow it back to the base of the wooden staircase where you began.

Continue straight (south) and observe the turquoise-hued water of the bay and weathered boulders. Depending on the tide level, you can walk on the sand and rocks and search the tide pools for marine life like crabs, anemones, barnacles, and mussels. At 1.4 miles (2.3 km), wooden stairs lead up the bluff to a bench and down to the beach. Another bench soon follows, and then a spur trail toward the water leads to a rocky outcrop. Pass one final bench by the water, the last spot on this hike to sit near the sparkling Carmel Bay.

At 1.5 miles (2.4 km), Highway 1 and Monastery Beach are ahead and you arrive at a **junction** with a trail that leads northeast up the hill. Turn right onto the trail, which can be dusty or muddy. Beginning here, deer and rabbits often dart across the path as you steadily walk uphill. Continue straight (northeast) past a couple of side trails, though they all ultimately end at the same place. To the east, you can see cars driving along Highway 1. The trail rounds to the left (north), presenting a higher view of the bay. Pass a viewpoint bench and then a rocky outcrop perfect to sit on

CARMEL MEADOWS TRAIL ▲

or take photos of the winding trail and waves below. The path brings you back to the neighborhood to return to the trailhead.

DIRECTIONS

From Carmel, take Highway 1 south, just past the Carmel Mission, to turn right onto Ribera Road. Continue for 0.7 mile (1.1 km), and park where Ribera Road ends at Custa Way, at 2575 Ribera Road.

GPS COORDINATES: 36.5306, −121.9243; 36°31′50.2″ N, 121°55′27.5″ W

BEST NEARBY BITES

Carmel Valley Coffee Roasting Company (Ocean Ave. and Lincoln St., Carmel-by-the-Sea, 831/626-2913, www.carmelcoffeeroasters.com, 6:30am-5:30pm daily, $4-7) brews the most fantastic espresso drinks. In addition to coffee and tea, you can grab breakfast, lunch, or a pastry at this local gem. Grab a Fog Breaker Latte (double shot, steamed whole milk, vanilla syrup, honey, and a dash of cinnamon) and a burrito, and leave a happily fed and caffeinated hiker.

This scenic trail provides incredible views of Carmel Bay, a rare Monterey cypress grove, tide pools, unique geological formations, and a chance to see a spectrum of land and marine wildlife.

BEST: Summer Hikes
DISTANCE: 5.2 miles (8.4 km) round-trip
DURATION: 3 hours
ELEVATION GAIN: 550 feet (168 m)
EFFORT: Easy-moderate
TRAIL: Dirt, gravel, sand, rocks, wooden boardwalk, single-track
USERS: Hikers, wheelchair users on part of the trail
SEASON: Year-round
PASSES/FEES: $10 day-use fee per vehicle, or California State Parks Pass
MAPS: At the park entrance
PARK HOURS: 8am–5pm daily, last entry 4:30pm
TRAILHEAD: Bird Island Parking Area
FACILITIES: Restrooms at the trailhead and at Cypress Grove Trail Junction
CONTACT: Point Lobos State Natural Reserve, 831/624-4909, www.parks. ca.gov

START THE HIKE

This hike is not ADA-compliant, but some sections of the trail are. Several wheelchairs are available for loan to visitors, and Easy Access Adventures are offered twice monthly for those with limited mobility. Contact the reserve for more information.

▶ **MILE 0-1.3: Bird Island Parking Area to Cypress Grove Trail**
Begin this hike on the **South Shore Trail** at the northwest end of the **Bird Island Parking Area.** At 0.1 mile (0.2 km), the path passes a bench and beach access to **Hidden Beach** as it follows the coast northwest. Continuing, you approach **Weston Beach,** the perfect place for tide pooling, at 0.3 mile (0.5 km).

At 0.5 mile (0.8 km) and a few other times along the hike, the trail passes along a small oceanside parking area just off Point Lobos

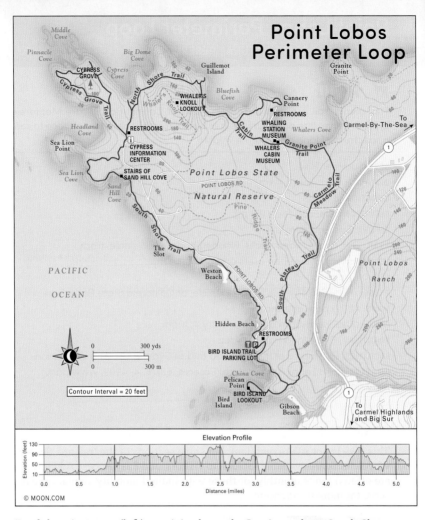

Point Lobos Perimeter Loop

Elevation Profile

© MOON.COM

Road, keeping west (left) to rejoin the path. Continue along South Shore Trail as it meanders between the coast and the road. Around 0.7 mile (1.1 km), you reach a coastal formation known as **The Slot,** where the ocean jets into a narrow open slot of the coast. From here, head up a series of sandy wooden stairs toward **Sand Hill Cove.** You reach a bench at 0.9 mile (1.4 km) before the first significant climb of the hike, up a staircase skirting the cove. At the top of the stairs, turn left (west) onto **Sand Hill Trail** and look back toward the jagged coast; anywhere along the wooden railing is an ideal photo spot.

Follow the path as it curves northwest toward **Sea Lion Cove.** Enjoy a break on a bench as you look out to **Sea Lion Point** and listen for sea lions barking. At 1.1 miles (1.8 km), the trail becomes **Sea Lion Point Trail** for a short distance. Where the trail splits, continue left (north) toward the parking area, then follow signs to the **Cypress Grove Trail** at 1.3 miles (2.1 km).

▲ POINT LOBOS PERIMETER LOOP

▶ **MILE 1.3-2.1: Allan Memorial Grove Loop via Cypress Grove Trail**
Taking the lollipop loop upon Cypress Grove Trail's peninsula is a high-light of the hike. The path rounds **Pinnacle Cove** and **Middle Cove,** and then runs alongside **Cypress Cove** through the trees and rock. All along the coastal sections of this hike, take the short spur trails to take in more magnificent views.

▶ **MILE 2.1-3.5: Cypress Grove Trail Junction to Whaler's Cabin**
Back at the junction where you turned onto Cypress Grove Trail, continue left (north) along the coast and onto **North Shore Trail** at 2.1 miles (3.4 km). The path drops through a brushy meadow and then ascends wooden stairs into a pine forest. Hike past a **junction** with Whalers Knoll Trail at 2.3 miles (3.7 km), staying left as the trail curves east past **Big Dome Cove.** At the next spur trail, look out onto **Guillemot Island,** where guillemots, western gulls, and cormorants nest. The trail follows around **Bluefish Cove,** passing another **junction** with Whalers Knoll Trail (stay left) and a **junction** with Cabin Trail at 2.8 miles (4.5 km). Continue on North Shore Trail out to the short loop at **Cannery Point.**

Return the way you came to the junction with Cabin Trail and turn left (southeast) to descend to the **Whaler's Cabin** at 3.5 miles (5.6 km). Built by Chinese fishermen in the 1850s, it's now a museum archiving hundreds of years of Indigenous peoples, Chinese fishermen, Japanese abalone fishermen, and Portuguese whalers. The adjacent **Whaling Station Museum** is the only on-site whaling museum on the West Coast, containing several interpretive panels about whales, as well as a collection of artifacts from the whaling industry.

‣ **MILE 3.5-5.2: Whaler's Cabin to Bird Island Parking Area**

Continue east by crossing **Point Lobos Road** onto **Granite Point Trail,** following the bluffs above **Whalers Cove.** At 3.6 miles (5.8 km), turn right (southeast) away from the cove onto **Carmelo Meadow Trail.** The short trail takes hikers through a Monterey pine forest to the **Point Lobos Entrance Station** area, most likely the busiest spot of the reserve. Be excessively cautious crossing Point Lobos Road here. On the south side of the station, restrooms are available before you proceed onto **South Plateau Trail.** The trail rises and falls around **Rat Hill** (144 ft/44 m) and **Vierras Knoll** (164 ft/50 m), in between passing a **junction** with Pine Ridge Trail at 4.2 miles (6.8 km).

At 4.6 miles (7.4 km), the South Plateau Trail passes a staircase down to **Gibson Beach** and arrives at **Bird Island Trail,** back at the water's edge. Continue left (southwest) onto Bird Island Trail out to **Pelican Point** and **Bird Island Overlook.** Complete the short loop, and when you return to the junction with South Plateau Trail, turn left (northwest) to continue on Bird Island Trail, rounding **China Cove.** This final stop of the hike rewards with the most stunning emerald-green water set against a white-sand beach.

Where Bird Island Trail splits at 5.1 miles (8.2 km), take the stairs to the left (northwest) or the accessible ramp to the right (northeast) back to the Bird Island Parking Area.

DIRECTIONS

From Carmel-By-The-Sea, take Highway 1 south for 3.4 miles (5.5 km) and turn west (right) into the reserve. Follow Point Lobos Road through the park until it ends at the Bird Island Parking Area. When parking is full in the reserve, or as an alternative, parking is available on the shoulder of the highway, and visitors may walk in. If you choose this option, begin the hike clockwise from the Point Lobos Entrance Station.

GPS COORDINATES: 36.5095, −121.9416; 36°30'34.2" N, 121°56'29.8" W

BEST NEARBY BREWS

After your hike, head 16 minutes north on Highway 1 to **Peter B's Brew Pub** (2 Portola Plaza, Monterey, 831/649-2699, 4pm-10pm Wed.-Sat.) for award-winning in-house brews such as Soul Sacrifice (a chili pepper beer) and Disco Biscuit (local-terroir barrel-soured Kolsch beer).

Get a stunning bird's-eye view of Carmel Valley, starting in an oak woodland forest and hiking over multiple creek crossings and through a redwood forest in Redwood Canyon.

DISTANCE: 3.6 miles (5.8 km) round-trip

DURATION: 2 hours

ELEVATION GAIN: 770 feet (235 m)

EFFORT: Easy-moderate

TRAIL: Dirt, single-track, creek crossings

USERS: Hikers, mountain bikers, horseback riders, leashed dogs

SEASON: April-November

PASSES/FEES: None

MAPS: On park website select "Garland Trail Map"

PARK HOURS: Dawn-dusk daily

TRAILHEAD: Roadside parking on East Garazas Road

FACILITIES: None

CONTACT: Monterey Peninsula Regional Park District, 831/372-3196, www. mprpd.org

START THE HIKE

This hike has multiple seasonal footbridges to assist hikers over Las Garzas Creek. It is recommended that you do this hike while the bridges are in place, from April-November. Check the park website for dates.

▶ **MILE 0-1.5: East Garzas Road Trailhead to Redwood Canyon**

At a dirt path entry at the second wooden fence along the southwest side of **East Garzas Road,** begin this hike on **Garzas Canyon Trail.** Immediately on starting the trail, you reach a **junction** with an interpretive panel with a map; continue straight (southwest).

As the trail gradually ascends, you'll catch glimpses of the Santa Lucia Mountains ridgeline through the treetops to the right (north). Pass Veeter Trail to the left (south) at 0.4 mile (0.6 km) to continue straight before dipping to a **junction** with Terrace Trail and an **"Enjoy"**

◀ REDWOOD CANYON-TERRACE LOOP

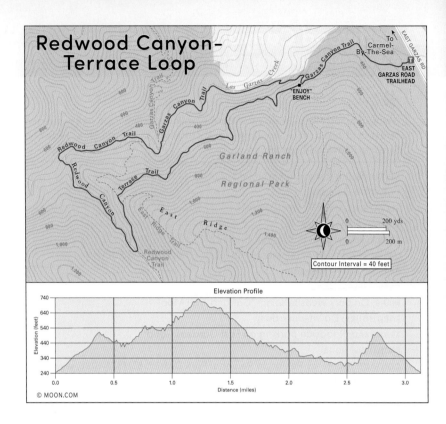

Redwood Canyon–Terrace Loop

bench. Remain on Garzas Canyon Trail by following the wooden sign directing hikers to descend northwest down a couple of switchbacks toward Las Garzas Creek.

At 0.6 mile (1 km), you can see a spot where there may be a water crossing in early spring as the trail continues southwest along Las Garzas Creek. In about 0.25 mile (0.4 km), you arrive at the first **bridge** of the hike to cross to the northwest side of the creek. Farther along, the **"Peace" bench** invites you to sit before reaching the **junction** with East Ridge Trail to Redwood Canyon at 1.1 miles (1.8 km). Go left (south) onto **East Ridge Trail** and cross a **wooden bridge** over the rocky creek. Soon thereafter, stay right (north) to take **Redwood Canyon Trail.** Rocky steps drop down to the first seasonal wooden board crossing. Look for the post with the warning sign of low branches ahead, where you may have to duck. Listen to the creek babble as you cross it on three additional seasonal bridges as you reach **Redwood Canyon.**

▶ **MILE 1.5–3.6: Redwood Canyon to East Garzas Road Trailhead**
At 1.5 miles (2.4 km), hike up the single-track into a redwood forest tucked into the canyon. Continue to ascend to the **memorial bench** for Kevin Dummer at 2.1 miles (3.4 km), where the trail leaves Redwood Canyon but remains on Redwood Canyon Trail. Follow the trail sign that directs hikers toward Las Garzas Creek, crossing the bridge and continuing to climb northwest.

▲ REDWOOD CANYON-TERRACE LOOP

When the trail reaches its highest point at 2.3 miles (3.7 km), pass East Ridge Trail by staying left (west) and begin the descent. Take a moment to sit under the shade at the **"Listen" bench** and enjoy the northwest view out to Pinyon Peak (2,247 ft/685 m) before proceeding down **Terrace Trail.** The initial downward slope is steep but provides excellent views of Garzas Creek Canyon and Carmel Valley. At 3.1 miles (5 km), Terrace Trail connects to Garzas Canyon Trail at the "Enjoy" bench. From here, return to the trailhead the way you came.

DIRECTIONS

From Carmel-by-the-Sea, take Highway 1 south to Carmel Valley Road and turn left. Proceed for 10.2 miles (16.4 km) and turn right onto Boronda Road. Continue for 0.6 mile (1 km), then turn left onto East Garazas Road for 0.2 mile (0.3 km) and park on the street.

GPS COORDINATES: 36.4868, −121.7484; 36°29'12.5" N, 121°44'54.2" W

BEST NEARBY BITES

The **Earthbound Farm Stand** (DD 7250 Carmel Valley Rd., Carmel-by-the-Sea, 831/625-6219, www.earthboundfarm.com, 8am-5pm Mon.-Sat., 9am-5pm Sun., $14-16) is about 10 minutes from the trailhead, and just down the road from the farm's original 2.5-acre farm. The organic café has hot meals, sandwiches, coffee, ice cream, smoothies, and delicious salads. You can also pick up fresh organic produce, groceries, and flowers as well as wander the property. Take a seat in a giant-size Adirondack chair and let the kids run through the Kids' Alphabet Garden, walk the labyrinth, or pick herbs from the Herb Garden.

8 | Soberanes Canyon Trail

GARRAPATA STATE PARK

✱

Hike up a hillside of hundreds of nonnative prickly pear cacti through ferns and redwoods, crisscrossing Soberanes Creek up to a peaceful creek bank deep in the canyon.

DISTANCE: 2.8 miles (4.5 km) round-trip
DURATION: 1.5 hours
ELEVATION GAIN: 490 feet (149 m)
EFFORT: Easy-moderate
TRAIL: Dirt fire road, dirt, single-track
USERS: Hikers
SEASON: Year-round
PASSES/FEES: None
MAPS: On the park website select "Brochures" and "Park Brochure"
PARK HOURS: 8am to 30 minutes after sunset daily
TRAILHEAD: Highway 1
FACILITIES: Portable toilets near the barn at the start of the hike
CONTACT: California State Parks, 831/649-2836, www.parks.ca.gov

START THE HIKE

The Soberanes Trail once safely connected to Rocky Ridge Trail, which is now closed. Do not pass the park barrier to the unmaintained and dangerously unstable ridge. This trail has some very narrow sections with steep drop-offs into a canyon. Take care passing on the trail.

▸ **MILE 0-0.5: Highway 1 Trailhead to Redwood Forest**

Start at the gate on the east side of **Highway 1,** across from gate 8 for the Garrapata Coast Trail, at a covered interpretative sign with a map of the state park. Pass through the wooden fence at the gate, where the trail starts as a dirt service road that leads to an abandoned tin barn on the left (north), with portable toilets and trash and recycling bins.

Turn left (north) around the barn and head through coastal scrub down wooden steps to a **footbridge** to cross Soberanes Creek, the first crossing of the hike. Views into the lush canyon open as you begin

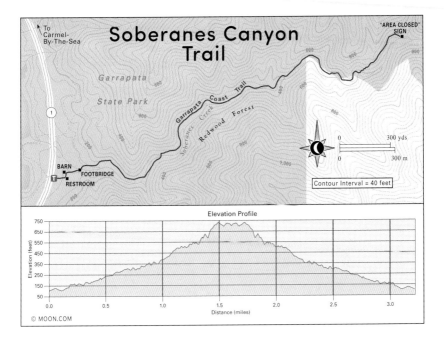

Soberanes Canyon Trail

© MOON.COM

your ascent. On both sides of the narrow trail, you see prickly pear cacti, thought to have been brought north from Mexico by Spanish missionaries.

This section of the hike is entirely exposed as it heads east, just north of Soberanes Creek. Coast morning glories, California asters, bush lupines, and poison oak mix in with the cacti until the cacti are left behind and the scrub vegetation continues.

At 0.4 mile (0.6 km), the trail passes under brief shade and crosses the creek a second time, requiring a rock hop or stream ford when there is a greater volume of water. Here, California poppies, speckled clarkia, orange bush monkey flower, and common yarrow join the brush alongside the trail. The third creek crossing leads you into the shade of a **redwood forest** at 0.5 mile (0.8 km).

▶ MILE 0.5–1.4: Redwood Forest to Trail End

Along the trail in the forest, ferns, sorrel, and ivy creep into the landscape, and coastal redwoods grow in number as the trail takes you to the fourth creek crossing. The redwoods here are not as broad or tall as those farther north, or even in other parts of Big Sur, but they are beautiful all the same as the path takes you farther into the canyon.

It becomes easy to lose count of the stream crossings as the trail continues to gain in elevation, at first alongside the flow of Soberanes Creek and gradually rising from it with increasingly steep drop-offs. At 1 mile (1.6 km), look for a patch of hummingbird sage that blooms with rose-lilac-colored flowers in spring. Steps built into the terrain carry hikers up and down the path, with a preview of the trail to the east (right), where the trail curves around.

When the trail comes to a large downed redwood at the creek's edge, and an **"Area Closed" sign,** you have reached the end of Soberanes Trail.

SOBERANES CANYON TRAIL ▲

The tree makes for a nice resting spot to sit and enjoy the sounds of the forest.

▶ **MILE 1.4-2.8: Trail End to Highway 1 Trailhead**
When it's time to leave the lush canyon, return the way you came, back to the trailhead.

DIRECTIONS

From Carmel-by-the-Sea, take Highway 1 south for 8 miles (12.9 km) and look for a row of cypress trees by a service gate on the east side of Highway 1, across from gate 8 of the Garrapata Coastal Trail. A large pullout area under the trees allows enough room for a few dozen vehicles to park.

GPS COORDINATES: 36.4546, −121.9241; 36°27'16.6" N, 121°55'26.8" W

BEST NEARBY SIGHTS

In late winter and early spring, Doud Creek, on the ocean side of Highway 1 fills with hundreds of calla lilies, giving it the name **Calla Lily Valley.** There are no signs indicating where it is, and the only indication you've reached it is the cars that line the road. To find it, go 2.6 miles (4.2 km) south on Highway 1 from Garrapata State Park Bluff Trailhead. If you pass over Garrapata Creek Bridge, you are too far south. Once you park on the west side of Highway 1, several trails lead down into the ravine and lead to the flowers. This is a great spot to explore and follow the creek toward the ocean to play on **Garrapata Beach.**

For the perfect introduction at Northern California's entrance to Big Sur, this hike gives you panoramic mountain and Pacific Ocean views, a few redwoods, some elevation, wildflowers, passage across Big Sur River, and beach access.

DISTANCE: 8 miles (12.9 km) round-trip

DURATION: 4 hours

ELEVATION GAIN: 1,440 feet (439 m)

EFFORT: Moderate

TRAIL: Dirt fire road, dirt, gravel, single-track, river crossing

USERS: Hikers, mountain bikers on part of the trail

SEASON: Spring-fall

PASSES/FEES: $10 day-use fee per vehicle, or California State Parks Pass

MAPS: National Geographic Maps "814. Big Sur, Ventana Wilderness (Los Padres National Forest)"

PARK HOURS: 8am-sunset daily

TRAILHEAD: Andrew Molera State Park Parking Area

FACILITIES: Vault toilets and drinking fountain at the trailhead

CONTACT: California State Parks, 831/667-1112, www.parks.ca.gov

START THE HIKE

The state park borders a working cattle grazing operation. Do not climb, cut, or pass through the fences, and stay on the trail.

▶ **MILE 0-0.9: Parking Area to Ridge Trail**

Start at the entrance station where you entered the **parking area,** watching for vehicles. Turn right (south) onto the "Authorized Vehicles Only" dirt road that runs along the east side of Big Sur River until you arrive at the fire road gate on the right (west), after just 0.1 mile (0.2 km). In front of you is the **Big Sur River.** Its width, depth, and current here varies depending on seasonal rainfall. Each spring, a seasonal bridge is erected for hikers to cross, but if you come too early,

Andrew Molera State Park Loop

MONTEREY & BIG SUR

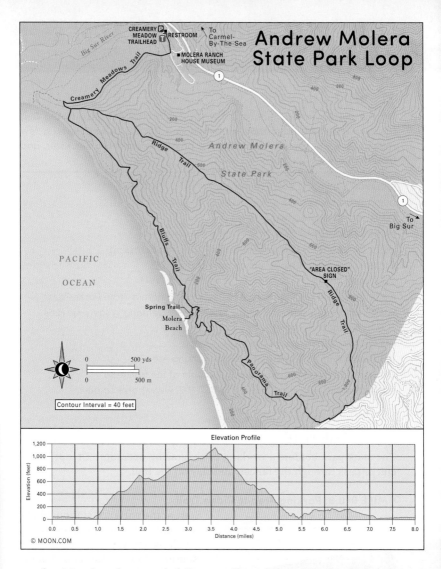

or after it's taken down each fall, you will need to decide if it feels safe enough to cross.

Once on the other side of the river, follow the **Creamery Meadows Trail** straight (southwest). The trail is flat, wide, and bordered with plantlife, including coastal bush lupines, woodland strawberries, fiesta flowers, and blackberries. The foot traffic here is the busiest of the hike. At 0.9 mile (1.4 km), turn left (south) off the path and onto the **Ridge Trail.**

▶ **MILE 0.9-3.6: Ridge Trail to Panorama Trail Junction**

Follow the trail as it heads straight up the ridge. Below you to the north is **Highway 1,** with northeastern views spanning from **Pico Blanco** (3,694 ft/1,126 m) to **Manual Peak** (3,524 ft/1,074 m). The coastline eventually comes into view to the south. Around 2 miles (3.2 km) into the hike, oak

▲ ANDREW MOLERA STATE PARK LOOP

trees provide a bit of welcome shade, and colorful blooms of Douglas iris, coast paintbrush, yellow mariposa lily, and pink honeysuckle dot the wide trail.

The trail splits at 2.8 miles (4.5 km) at an **"Area Closed" sign.** Stay right (south) to remain on the Ridge Trail. You reach the top of the long climb at 3.6 miles (5.8 km), at the park's border and **junction** with Panorama Trail.

▶ MILE 3.6-5.5: Panorama Trail Junction to Bluffs Trail

Turn right (southwest) onto **Panorama Trail.** The path descends steeply through coastal scrub as it makes a gradual U-turn southwest and then northwest toward the ocean, narrowing through often overgrown grassy vegetation, with poison oak threatening uncovered ankles. After 0.25 mile (0.4 km) going downhill, and where the trail turns northwest, ocean winds can pick up, and ropes line the path to keep you on the trail. From this height, the stunning picture-perfect Big Sur coastal landscape is just waiting to be captured—printed and placed in a frame or featured on your social media.

Continuing along, the trail snakes down to a **junction** with **Spring Trail.** This short spur trail, 0.1 mile (0.2 km) each way, leads down a gully to **Molera Beach.** Take the spur out and back, and return to the main trail, where it transitions to **Bluffs Trail** as you turn left (northwest) from the spur at 5.5 miles (8.9 km).

ANDREW MOLERA STATE PARK LOOP ▲

▶ MILE 5.5-8: Bluffs Trail to Parking Area

The wide and mostly flat trail follows the bluffs along the coast with gorgeous views of the ocean and wildflowers. At 7 miles (11.3 km), take the **junction** right (north) to briefly connect back to the Ridge Trail. After 500 feet (152 m), turn left (northwest) to retrace your steps back to Creamery Meadows Trail, over Big Sur River, and back to the parking area.

DIRECTIONS

From Carmel-by-the-Sea, take Highway 1 south for 23 miles (37 km) to the entrance to Andrew Molera State Park, on the southwest (right) side of Highway 1.

GPS COORDINATES: 36.2870, −121.8437; 36°17'13.2" N, 121°50'37.3" W

BEST NEARBY BITES AND BREWS

Twenty minutes south of the trailhead on Highway 1 is **Big Sur Taphouse** (47520 Hwy. 1, Big Sur, 831/667-2197, www.bigsurtaphouse. com, noon-9pm Mon.-Fri., 11am-9pm Sat.-Sun., $10-20), featuring Alvarado Street Brewing and Russian River Brewing beers on tap while serving tasty burgers and other food to help you refuel after your hike.

Streaming down 60 feet (18 m) of rock face, Pfeiffer Falls is a must-see quintessential Big Sur redwood forest hike on any trip to Big Sur.

DISTANCE: 1.6 miles (2.6 km) round-trip

DURATION: 1 hour

ELEVATION GAIN: 430 feet (131 m)

EFFORT: Easy

TRAIL: Dirt, gravel, single-track, wooden boardwalk

USERS: Hikers

SEASON: Year-round

PASSES/FEES: $10 day-use fee per vehicle, or California State Park Pass

MAPS: On park website select "Brochures" and "Park Brochure"

PARK HOURS: 8am-sunset daily

TRAILHEAD: Big Sur Lodge

FACILITIES: Restrooms and drinking fountain at Big Sur Lodge

CONTACT: California State Parks, 831/667-1112, www.parks.ca.gov

START THE HIKE

▶ **MILE 0-0.7: Big Sur Lodge to Valley View Spur**

From **Big Sur Lodge,** cross the main access road with the lodge to your back. You will soon see signs for Pfeiffer Falls and Valley View Trail. Proceed on the relatively flat path to a **junction** with an interpretive sign about Save the Redwoods League, where you turn right (west) and climb a **tall wooden staircase** into the forest of tan oaks, California bays, and redwoods. At the top, the gravel path leads to another road crossing at 0.2 mile (0.3 km).

To the left (east) is a **picnic area** with trash and recycling bins. Ahead, a covered interpretive panel includes a map and information about redwood trees, in front of a trail sign for Pfeiffer Falls and Valley View. Follow the fence-lined path as it gradually ascends. Listen to the soothing sounds of Pfeiffer-Redwood Creek to the left (west), and then arrive at a split in the trail. A trail marker points right to Pfeiffer Falls and left to Valley View. Turn left (west) onto Valley

MONTEREY & BIG SUR

Pfeiffer Falls

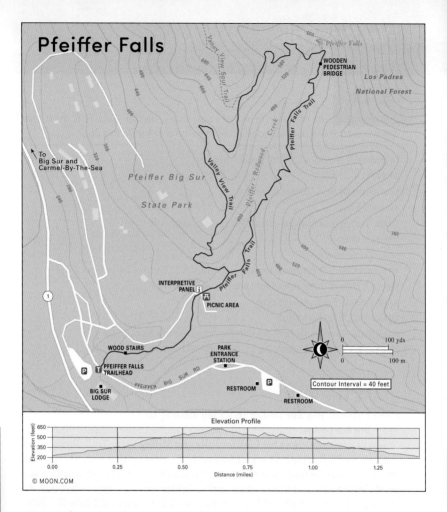

Pfeiffer Falls

Pfeiffer Falls

WOODEN
PEDESTRIAN
BRIDGE

Los Padres
National Forest

To
Big Sur and
Carmel-By-The-Sea

Pfeiffer Big Sur

State Park

Valley View Spur Trail

Valley View Trail

Pfeiffer Falls Trail

Pfeiffer–Redwood Creek

Pfeiffer Falls Trail

INTERPRETIVE
PANEL

PICNIC AREA

1

WOOD STAIRS

PFEIFFER FALLS
TRAILHEAD

PARK
ENTRANCE
STATION

P

BIG SUR
LODGE

PFEIFFER BIG SUR RD

RESTROOM

P

RESTROOM

0   100 yds

0   100 m

Contour Interval = 40 feet

Elevation Profile

Elevation (feet)

650
500
350
200

0.00   0.25   0.50   0.75   1.00   1.25

Distance (miles)

© MOON.COM

View, and cross to the west side of the creek. You will return to the trailhead from the east.

When you come to an area of large downed trees, you can see across the ravine to the return hike on the other side. Some trees here still bear burn scars from the 2008 Basin Complex Fire.

Continue up a dozen stairs, taking care as the trail becomes rocky between sets of stairs. As you gain elevation, the path provides views of the tree-covered ridgeline to the east, and at 0.7 mile (1.1 km) you come to a **spur trail** for Valley View Overlook.

▶ MILE 0.7-1.6: Valley View Spur to Big Sur Lodge

The left trail climbs another 300 feet (91 m) to dead-end at the overlook. Turn right (northeast), following the Pfeiffer Falls trail marker. The trail descends for the first time, with a steep drop-off down to the right (east) side. The path curves east, down a few zigzags, and onto back-to-back **wooden bridges** over the creek, where you can catch a glimpse of the falls through the forest to the left (west) about halfway down the second bridge.

You briefly walk on dirt before the trail takes you up a **tall wooden staircase** to an interpretive panel explaining the Big Sur Watershed. Likely, though, instead of reading the panel you are gazing up at the view of **Pfeiffer Falls**. Continue on the trail to the bench viewing area at 0.9 mile (1.4 km) to sit and enjoy watching the narrow water stream down the 60-foot (18-m) rock face.

From here, the trail follows the contour of the hillside to switchbacks made of wooden staircases that lead to a **70-foot (21-m) wooden pedestrian bridge** above the canyon floor, and down more wooden stairs. An interpretive sign explains the local fire history and its impact on the forest here before the trail descends another cascade of stairs.

The path reconnects to Valley View at 1.3 miles (2.1 km). Turn left (south) and return to Big Sur Lodge the way you came.

DIRECTIONS

From Carmel, travel 26 miles (42 km) south on Highway 1 to the entrance to the park, near mile marker 47.2. In Pfeiffer Big Sur State Park, park in Day-Use Parking Lot 1, where you take the River Path to Big Sur Lodge. Alternatively, park on the shoulder of Highway 1 and walk up the road toward Big Sur Lodge.

GPS COORDINATES: 36.2510, −121.7865; 36°15′3.6″ N, 121°47′11.4″ W

BEST NEARBY SIGHTS

Nestled between the Big Sur Ranger Station and the post office, Sycamore Canyon Road, on the west side of Highway 1, leads to the stunning **Pfeiffer Beach Day-Use Area** (GPS coordinates: 36.2383, −121.8154; 36°14′17.9″ N, 121°48′55.4″ W). The road is unmarked and drops from the highway without warning. It has narrow curves, so proceed cautiously. This spot is world-famous for the **Keyhole Arch,** a natural rock-arch formation that waves crash through, with pleasant tide pools and beautifully filtered light. The beach, with purple sand at the north end, gets very windy, so bring sun and wind protection.

Pay the $12 day-use fee at the entry kiosk or get a Parks Management Company (PMC) Annual Pass ($50). California State Park and National Park Passes are not valid for entry, as the beach is on National Forest land. Dogs are permitted and must wear a collar with current tags and be kept on a leash no longer than 6 feet (1.8 m).

Buzzards Roost Trail

PFEIFFER BIG SUR STATE PARK

Climb through a redwood forest to mountain views out to the Pacific Ocean from atop Pfeiffer Ridge.

DISTANCE: 3 miles (4.8 km) round-trip
DURATION: 1.5 hours
ELEVATION GAIN: 820 feet (250 m)
EFFORT: Easy-moderate
TRAIL: Dirt fire road, dirt, gravel, rock, roots, single-track
USERS: Hikers
SEASON: Year-round
PASSES/FEES: None
MAPS: On park website select "Brochures" and "Park Brochure"
PARK HOURS: 8am-sunset daily
TRAILHEAD: Roadside parking on Highway 1
FACILITIES: None
CONTACT: California State Parks, 831/667-1112, www.parks.ca.gov

START THE HIKE

▶ **MILE 0-0.6: Highway 1 Trailhead to Loop Split Start**
Begin at the dirt fire road entrance just off the southwest side of **Highway 1,** south of the Big Sur River crossing. Immediately entering a redwood forest, you'll easily spot ferns, sorrels, and mushrooms as the road takes you along the left (southwest) side of Big Sur River. The trail soon comes to a junction; follow the wooden trail marker straight for **Buzzards Roost Trail.**

The trail becomes sandy as you near the water's edge, but soon fills with rocks and roots and begins an ascent up single-track switchbacks from the fire road, starting by a small boulder. Thick vegetation borders the trail, and it can be muddy in spots where water runs down the mountainside. Above, you can see where the trail is reinforced with a wooden wall on a switchback you'll shortly hike. At 0.2 mile (0.3 km), the trail splits at a **wooden sign.** The sign indicates that the trail to Group Camping continues

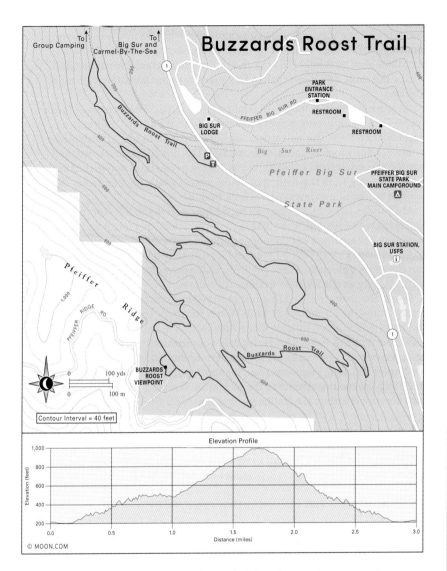

Elevation Profile

Elevation (feet): 1,000 / 800 / 600 / 400 / 200

Distance (miles): 0.0 / 0.5 / 1.0 / 1.5 / 2.0 / 2.5 / 3.0

right (north), while directing hikers left (southeast) along a wooden fence line to stay on Buzzards Roost Trail.

Head left to continue on Buzzards Roost Trail. Notably steep drop-offs begin past the fence, and evidence of past fire damage becomes more prevalent along the trail. As you ascend, the trail leads past the upper branches of the redwoods growing by the river, and higher trees tower above. There's even a giant redwood with a hollowed-by-fire base that can fit multiple people—a nice photo op—before the narrow trail gently rolls up to a **trail split** at 0.6 mile (1 km).

▶ **MILE 0.6-3: Loop Split Start to Loop Split End**
Take the trail left (east) at the signpost. The tree canopy opens to the sky, and the ridge views become more impressive as the path gently rounds

the curve of the mountainside. It's particularly impressive when warm morning light brings contrast to the sculptured slopes of the Santa Lucia Mountains. At 1 mile (1.6 km), the trail turns to zigzag westward and climbs the ridge at a more challenging grade for approximately 0.25 mile (0.4 km).

On reaching **Pfeiffer Ridge** at 1.5 miles (2.4 km), you'll find views of Sycamore Canyon and some power lines below, and the sunny habitat is noticeably drier. Here, the trail enters Big Sur chaparral, bordered with manzanita, California yerba santa, and chamise. The dirt path appears washed out, with wooden steps to assist. While nearby power lines and their poles may take away from the feeling of being remote that's so common in Big Sur, the outstanding views remain breathtaking.

At 1.7 miles (2.7 km), you reach a roped **spur trail** to the left (southwest) that leads to the **summit** of the hike, a rocky viewpoint at a tower and shed. Here you are rewarded with panoramic views of the mountains all around and the Pacific Ocean beyond Pfeiffer Ridge Road below. Summertime fog can sometimes block the view, but if you wait a moment, the scenery often shifts quickly as the fog rolls through the valleys.

Rejoin the main trail heading left (northwest) from the spur and reenter the forest at 1.8 miles (2.9 km). Watch for roots and tree stumps on the path, which isn't difficult since this section of initial descent lacks views beyond the trees. The path takes you downhill relatively quickly, with views once again opening to the east, similar to the start of the hike. At 2 miles (3.2 km), Highway 1 can be spotted intermittently, and at 2.2 miles (3.2 km) you reconnect to the loop split. Turn left (northwest) to return down the path to the trailhead.

DIRECTIONS

From Carmel, travel 26 miles (42 km) south on Highway 1, to just past the entrance to the Pfeiffer Big Sur State Park, near mile marker 47.2. Park in the highway-side parking after passing over Big Sur River.

GPS COORDINATES: 36.2493, −121.7855; 36°14'57.5" N, 121°47'7.8" W

BEST NEARBY BITES

Three miles (4.8 km) south on Highway 1, **Café Kevah** (48510 Hwy. 1, Big Sur, 831/667-2344, www.nepenthe.com, 9am-3pm daily, weather-permitting, $11-32) sits perched atop the rocky coastline of Big Sur. Part of the Nepenthe property, which includes the more upscale Nepenthe restaurant and the Phoenix Shop, the café's patio (outdoor seating only) is a lovely place to enjoy breakfast, salads, sandwiches, pastries, espresso drinks, or adult beverages while taking in spectacular views of over 60 miles (97 km) of the coast.

12 McWay Falls Overlook

JULIA PFEIFFER BURNS BIG SUR STATE PARK

❋ 🛁 🏛 🚶

This short hike awards with the iconic Big Sur view of the 80-foot (24-m) waterfall that plunges over rocky cliffs onto an inaccessible sandy beach.

DISTANCE: 0.7 mile (1.1 km) round-trip

DURATION: 30 minutes

ELEVATION CHANGE: 39 feet (12 m)

EFFORT: Easy

TRAIL: Gravel fire road, gravel, dirt, tunnel

USERS: Hikers

SEASON: Year-round

PASSES/FEES: $10 day-use fee per vehicle, or California State Parks pass

MAPS: On park website select "Brochures" and "Park Brochure"

PARK HOURS: 8am-sunset daily

TRAILHEAD: Julia Pfeiffer Burns Big Sur State Park south parking lot

FACILITIES: None

CONTACT: California State Parks, 831/667-1112, www.parks.ca.gov

START THE HIKE

There is no beach access on this hike. Attempting to get to the beach is both dangerous and a citable offense.

▸ **MILE 0-0.3: Parking Lot to McWay Falls Overlook**

Start the trail from the northeast end of the park's south **parking lot** by going down and under the drive into the lot. Follow the path as it turns left (southwest), with McWay Creek on your left (southwest).

The trail continues by passing under **Highway 1** through a tunnel and arriving at **McWay Cove,** where the ocean meets the sand. Follow the path as it turns right (northwest) around the cove. The trail ends abruptly at a metal fence at a **viewing bench overlooking McWay Falls.** The trail once continued to curve north, away from the cove

◂ McWAY FALLS OVERLOOK

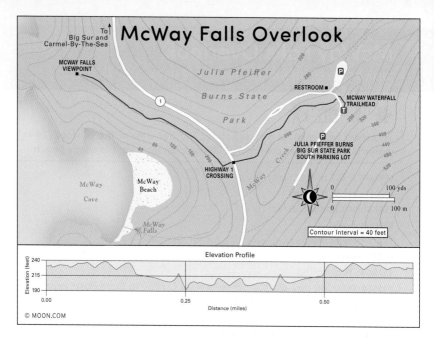

and above the crashing waves, but it is permanently closed due to dangerous conditions.

The stunning waterfall streaming down from the rocky cliffs directly to the sandy beach was created by a 1983 landslide. Different seasons and times of day impact the light, tide, and waterfall flow, highlighting varying features of the rock wall behind the falls, the color of the ocean, and the abundance of water and waves.

From the overlook, return to the trailhead the way you came.

DIRECTIONS

From Carmel-by-the-Sea, travel south on Highway 1 for 38 miles (61 km). Look for the sign on the left for the Julia Pfeiffer Burns State Park entrance. Enter and park in the south parking lot.

GPS COORDINATES: 36.1601, −121.6686; 36°9'36.4" N, 121°40'7" W

BEST NEARBY BITES

For a unique dining, gallery, and architecture experience (the structure partially comprises three redwood water tanks), snag one of the coveted parking spots and eat at **COAST Big Sur** (49901 Hwy. 1, Big Sur, 831/667-2301, 11am-4pm Thurs.-Mon., www.coastbigsur.com, $18-21). Just 3 miles (4.8 km) north of Partington Cove on Highway 1, you can get beer, boozy drinks, soft-serve concoctions, prepared food, or picnic provisions with patio views over the highway and out to the sea.

NEARBY CAMPGROUNDS

NAME	DESCRIPTION	FACILITIES	SEASON	FEE
Pfeiffer Big Sur State Park	Forest cover, river access, hiking trails within walking distance, on-site restaurant	189 RV and tent sites, showers, flush toilets, fire pits, picnic tables, potable water	year-round	$35, riverfront sites $50

Highway 1, 26 miles (42 km) south of Carmel-by-the-Sea, www.ReserveCalifornia.com

NAME	DESCRIPTION	FACILITIES	SEASON	FEE
Andrew Molera State Park	Hike-in only	22 tent sites, 2 hike-and-bike campsites, fire pits, picnic tables, food storage containers	spring-fall	$30

Highway 1, 21 miles (34 km) south of Carmel-by-the-Sea, www.ReserveCalifornia.com

NAME	DESCRIPTION	FACILITIES	SEASON	FEE
Veteran's Memorial Park	First come, first served basis	Showers, food storage containers, gas grills, potable water, flush toilets	year-round	$44

Due west on Jefferson Street (up the hill) from the center of Old Monterey

PINNACLES NATIONAL PARK

As California's newest national park, Pinnacles is just starting to get the attention it deserves. Many visitors come to climb through the talus cave homes of bat colonies; to try to spot the rare California condor; or to challenge themselves on the Steep and Narrow section of the High Peaks Trail. With its otherworldly landscape of towering rock spires, Pinnacles can also reach unbearable and dangerous temperatures in the summer; it is best enjoyed in other seasons. The park is divided into the east and west sides, with no roads connecting them. Make sure to plan your visit carefully, as it can take an hour or more to get from one gate to the other.

▲ BALCONIES CAVE TRAIL

▲ CONDOR GULCH AND HIGH PEAKS LOOP

◄ MOSES SPRING-RIM TRAIL LOOP WITH BEAR GULCH CAVE

1 Balconies Cave
DISTANCE: 2.4 miles (3.9 km) round-trip
DURATION: 1.5 hours
EFFORT: Easy

2 Condor Gulch and High Peaks Loop
DISTANCE: 5.3 miles (8.5 km) round-trip
DURATION: 3 hours
EFFORT: Moderate

3 Moses Spring-Rim Trail Loop with Bear Gulch Cave
DISTANCE: 1.7 miles (2.7 km) round-trip
DURATION: 1.5 hours
EFFORT: Easy

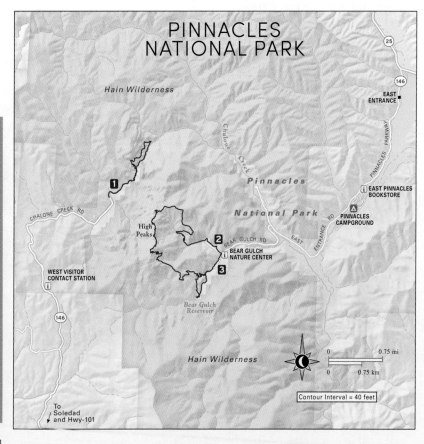

▲ BALCONIES CAVE TRAIL

This hike makes a trip up the canyon cliffs before climbing down through the shadows of the talus cave.

DISTANCE: 2.4 miles (3.9 km) round-trip
DURATION: 1.5 hours
ELEVATION GAIN: 400 feet (122 m)
EFFORT: Easy
TRAIL: Dirt, gravel, rock
USERS: Hikers
SEASON: Year-round
PASSES/FEES: $30 per vehicle, valid for 7 days
MAPS: On the park website select "Maps"
PARK HOURS: Day-use only; West Side entry gate 7:30am–8pm daily
FACILITIES: Vault toilets and drinking fountain at the trailhead
TRAILHEAD: Chaparral Trailhead parking lot
CONTACT: Pinnacles National Park, West Pinnacles Visitor Contact Station, 831/389-4427, ext. 4487, www.nps.gov/pinn

START THE HIKE

Particularly in the summer, the rocks of this hike get hot even early in the day. Before the cave, the trail is primarily exposed. Once in the cave, a headlamp is useful so your hands can be kept free. Do not attempt this hike if you are claustrophobic, afraid of dark spaces, or unable to climb over boulders within the cave. Do not attempt it without a headlamp or a flashlight. In winter or after heavy rains, creek wading may be required in the cave. Check the park's website and call ahead to confirm the status of the cave.

▶ **MILE 0-1.7: Chaparral Trailhead Parking Lot to Balconies Cave**
From the northeast end of the **parking lot,** pass the left (west) side of the restrooms and head through the picnic area. Follow the fence line to a wooden post just before a small hill with a trail marker for "Balconies Trail." At 0.2 mile (0.3 km), keep heading left (northeast); otherwise, the trail will loop back to the parking lot.

The trail meanders through chaparral toward the giant rock formations, most notably the sheer rockface of **Machete Ridge** and the Balconies jutting toward the sky. Ignore spur trails to climbing areas, indicated by brown trail signs marked with a carabiner; continue on **Balconies Trail** along the West Fork of the Chalone Creek. At 0.4 mile (0.6 km), cross the first of three short **footbridges,** followed by a dozen or so rocky stairs over and around the first boulders of the hike as the canyon narrows, followed by the second and third footbridges over the often-dry creek bed.

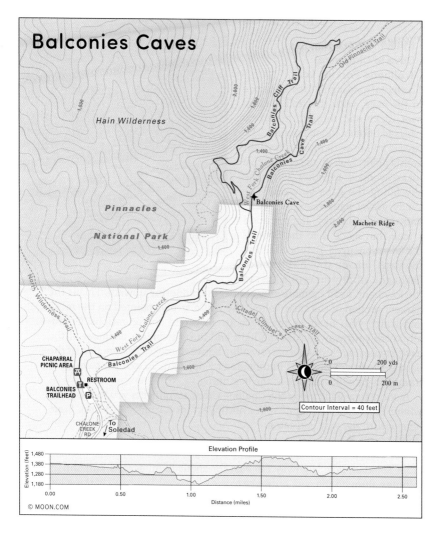

Balconies Caves

Hain Wilderness

Pinnacles

National Park

Balconies Cave

Machete Ridge

CHAPARRAL
PICNIC AREA

RESTROOM

BALCONIES
TRAILHEAD

CHALONE
CREEK
RD

To
Soledad

Contour Interval = 40 feet

200 yds

200 m

Elevation Profile

Elevation (feet)

© MOON.COM

After the final footbridge, at 0.8 mile (1.3 km) you reach a **junction** with **Balconies Cliff Trail.** Go left (northwest) and head steadily up the ridge. At 1.2 miles (1.9 km), the trail has reached its highest point, 1,500 feet (457 m) elevation, where you can see out to the broader valley and the clearest view of the spires of the Balconies to the west. The trail then descends 300 feet (91 m) over the next 0.5 mile (0.8 km), to the lowest point of the hike, where Balconies Cliff Trail **intersects** with the Old Pinnacles Trail, heading northeast along Chalone Creek. Following Old Pinnacles will take you to the east side of the park, so stay on Balconies Cliff Trail to continue southwest. Shortly thereafter a trail marker indicates the trail ahead connects to the **Balconies Cave Trail.** Take Balconies Cave Trail south along the creek, over rocks and through boulder passages, and approach **Balconies Cave** at 1.7 miles (2.7 km).

► **MILE 1.7-2.4: Balconies Cave to Chaparral Trailhead Parking Lot**

The metal gate signals the entrance to the cave, with the trail leading over rocks and through a narrow passage under a fallen boulder. The cave is still lit with filtered daylight at this point; look up to see massive rocks wedged together with the sky filling the gaps between. The sandy gravel path veers left (east) and up a few rocky steps around a rock that made it to the floor of the narrow canyon. Before climbing the steps, turn on your headlamp or flashlight. After your eyes adjust to

the low light, head up more steps to begin bouldering upward. This is the darkest section of the cave. Follow the white arrows painted on the rocks and watch your head, as the rocks are in varied configurations. Gradually work your way back to the light and into the bigger chamber of the cave, squeezing through a narrow alley between rocks. This section of the path is sandy gravel and is illuminated by daylight. To exit the cave, pass through a gate like the one at the beginning.

A short easy walk along the Chalone Creek reconnects you to the point where Balconies Cliff Trail splits northwest, at 2.1 miles (3.4 km). From here, return the way you came.

DIRECTIONS

From Soledad, take Highway 146 east for about 12 miles (19.3 km) and 25 minutes, through the park entrance to the Chaparral Trailhead parking lot.

GPS COORDINATES: 36.4920, −121.2096; 36°29'31.2" N, 121°12'34.6" W

PINNACLES NATIONAL PARK

Watch for the soaring condors as you hike, climb, and duck through the heart of the park's rock spires.

DISTANCE: 5.3 miles (8.5 km) round-trip

DURATION: 3 hours

ELEVATION GAIN: 1,300 feet (396 m)

EFFORT: Moderate

TRAIL: Dirt, rock, gravel, single-track, carved-in rock footholds

USERS: Hikers

SEASON: Year-round

PASSES/FEES: $30 per vehicle, valid for 7 days

MAPS: On the park website select "Maps," at the visitor center

PARK HOURS: East Gate open 24 hours daily

TRAILHEAD: Bear Gulch Day-Use Area Parking Lot

FACILITIES: Restrooms at the trailhead

CONTACT: Pinnacles National Park, 831/389-4486, www.nps.gov/pinn

START THE HIKE

This hike is extremely exposed, and parts of it are dangerous for young children. Be mindful of the fencing that blocks various paths and potential viewpoints that stray from the designated trail. These are in place for safety and to preserve the ecosystem.

▶ **MILE 0-1.7: Bear Gulch Day-Use Area Parking Lot to High Peaks Trail**

Look for the small wooden bridge that leads over a creek bed to the **Condor Gulch Trail,** just right (east) of the interpretive trail signs across the street from the **parking lot.** Once over the little bridge, a trail marker indicates that the Condor Gulch Viewpoint is in 1 mile (1.6 km). Over the course of that mile, the trail gradually gains 550 feet (168 m) elevation and bring you closer to the rock formations for which the park is named. Rock climbers have coined names for the formations that begin to present themselves—as you approach 1 mile (1.6 km), see if you can identify the Hippopotamus.

At 1 mile (1.6 km), take time to explore the **Condor Gulch Viewpoint** area. Carefully walk along the metal railing and look down on the gulch. Take in the High Peaks and look up into the sky to search for condors among the 160 species of birds documented in the park.

Continue on the well-marked Condor Gulch Trail as it becomes rockier and more exposed. The path temporarily turns right (east), winding around a ridge and turning north at 1.2 miles (1.9 km), with rolling eastern views and jagged rock formations to the left (west). The Condor Gulch Trail ends at **High Peaks Trail** at 1.7 miles (2.7 km), and while there's limited

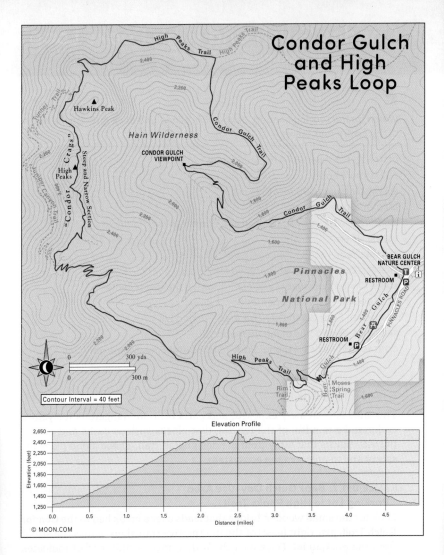

© MOON.COM

shade, it's a good point to take a break after climbing over 1,000 feet (305 m) and before continuing to ascend under the typically bright sky.

▶ **MILE 1.7–2.2: High Peaks Trail to Tunnel Trail Junction**

Turn left (west) onto High Peaks Trail, where rugged boulders and monoliths soon begin to jolt out of the landscape straight ahead. The trail then weaves among these otherworldly rock formations. At 2.2 miles (3.5 km), High Peaks Trail intersects with the **Tunnel Trail** to the right (west). For those with a fear of heights, Tunnel Trail offers a slightly longer alternative to avoid the Steep and Narrow section. To continue on to Steep and Narrow, keep left (east).

▲ CONDOR GULCH AND HIGH PEAKS LOOP

▶ **MILE 2.2–2.9: Tunnel Trail Junction to Juniper Canyon Trail Junction**
Continue toward the backbone of the pinnacles, referred to as the **Steep and Narrow** section of High Peaks Trail. A highlight of the park, you use footholds and railings to navigate over, under, and between the spires and boulders on a narrow course over steep drop-offs. At 2.5 miles (4 km), a nearly vertical climb up footholds carved into the rock provides a railing on your right to assist. Make sure no one is initiating a descent before you start up; the area at the base where you start only accommodates a couple of people.

The High Peaks are sometimes called the Condor Crags after the bird that makes its home here. Seeing a condor is definitely a fortunate occurrence, and one of the best locations to look for them is just past the obstacles of the Steep and Narrow, which is also a good place for groups to reconvene after navigating this tricky section.

Immediately following this area, at 2.6 miles (4.2 km), you begin a noticeable descent, and the trail **splits in three directions.** Take the center path to navigate over rocks to the left of a boulder, or be cautious as you take the gravel path to the right of the boulder, watching out for the drop-off on the other side.

At 2.9 miles (4.7 km) is a **junction** with Juniper Canyon Trail, where you'll find a bench and a pit toilet. Remain on High Peaks Trail, heading left (east) down the switchbacks just pass the restroom.

▶ **MILE 2.9–5.3: Juniper Canyon Trail Junction to**
   Bear Gulch Day-Use Area Parking Lot
After a series of switchbacks, the trail straightens as it descends east. The path no longer features the pinnacles (now behind you) and hugs a side

canyon of Condor Gulch for 0.5 mile (0.8 km). Continue on High Peaks Trail, pass the intersection with Rim Trail at 4.3 miles (6.9 km), and merge with **Moses Spring Trail** at 4.6 miles (7.4 km). Stay left (north) to continue down. Here the crowds tend to increase, and at 5.1 miles (8.2 km) is the **Moses Spring Parking Area.** Watch out for traffic and use the pedestrian crossing to the wooded trail ahead. For the next 0.2-mile (0.3-km) the trail passes picnic tables alongside a creek bed, then arrives back at the Bear Gulch Day-Use Area parking lot.

DIRECTIONS

From Monterey, take Highway 1 north for 13 miles (20.9 km) and keep right to continue on Highway 156. Continue for 6.2 miles (10 km), then keep left to stay on Highway 156, following signs for U.S. 101. Merge onto U.S. 101 via the ramp marked for Hollister and San Francisco, and continue for 8.3 miles (13.4 km). Take exit 345 for Highway 156 toward San Juan Bautista and Hollister, and keep right at the fork to merge onto Highway 156. Continue on Highway 156 for 7.2 miles (11.6 km). Turn right onto Union Road and continue for 4.2 miles (6.8 km). Turn right onto Highway 25 for 27 miles (43 km). Make a slight right onto Highway 146 into Pinnacles National Park, and continue for 4.4 miles (7.1 km), past the camp store, following signs for Bear Gulch Day-Use Area.

GPS COORDINATES: 36.4812, –121.1814; 36°28'52.3" N, 121°10'53" W

BEST NEARBY BITES

Nothing satisfies like a boozy beverage and a full meal after a hike like this one. Forty minutes from the trailhead, 27 miles (43 km) north on Highway 25, is **19th Hole** (7071 Airline Hwy., Tres Pinos, 831/628-0100, 4pm-8pm Wed.-Thurs., 4pm-9pm Fri.-Sun., from $14). The steak dinner comes with a baked potato, sautéed vegetables, Caesar salad, and garlic bread, but you can always opt for lighter fare.

3 Moses Spring-Rim Trail Loop with Bear Gulch Cave

PINNACLES NATIONAL PARK

This hike takes you through the tumbled-down boulders of Bear Gulch Cave and to the desert oasis of the Bear Gulch Reservoir before looping back on the Rim Trail.

DISTANCE: 1.7 miles (2.7 km) round-trip
DURATION: 1.5 hours
ELEVATION GAIN: 390 feet (119 m)
EFFORT: Easy
TRAIL: Dirt, gravel, rock, stairs
USERS: Hikers
SEASON: Year-round; check the park website for cave status
PASSES/FEES: $30 per vehicle, valid for 7 days
MAPS: On the park website select "Maps"
PARK HOURS: 24 hours daily; no overnight parking outside the campground area
TRAILHEAD: Bear Gulch Day-Use Area Parking Lot
FACILITIES: Restrooms at the trailhead
CONTACT: Pinnacles National Park, 831/389-4486, www.nps.gov/pinn

START THE HIKE

Do not attempt the cave section of this hike if you are claustrophobic, afraid of dark spaces, or have difficulty with stairs. To do the hike and avoid the cave section, or to hike the area when the cave is closed, Moses Spring Trail offers an alternate route around the cave.

Check the park's website or call ahead to confirm the status of the cave. Do not attempt the hike without a headlamp or a flashlight. Scheduled closures of Bear Gulch Cave include the entire cave for bat pupping season, typically mid-May through mid-July. The main lower section of the cave is open most of the year, while the upper section is rarely open for more than a few weeks each year to protect the endangered bats.

▶ **MILE 0-0.6: Bear Gulch Day-Use Area Parking Lot to Bear Gulch Cave**
At the west end of the **parking lot,** walk toward the restrooms and follow the path left (south) toward the **Bear Creek Picnic Area.** Cross the road at the **Moses Spring Parking Area,** watching for traffic, and continue south at the trail marker for Moses Spring Trail at 0.2 mile (0.3 km). The trail splits

Moses Spring-Rim Trail Loop with Bear Gulch Cave

PINNACLES RD

RESTROOM ▪

T **P**

i

BEAR GULCH
NATURE CENTER

Bear Gulch

Sycamore Trail

Pinnacles

BEAR CREEK
PICNIC AREA 🏕

National Park

Hain

Wilderness

PINNACLES RD

RESTROOM ▪

P

MOSES SPRING
PARKING AREA

High Peaks Trail

High Peaks Trail

High Peaks Trail

Moses Spring Trail

Rim Trail

Bear Gulch

Moses Spring Trail

◆ Bear Gulch Cave

Bear Gulch Cave Trail

Hain

Wilderness

Rim Trail

Moses Spring Trail

▪ DAM WALL

Bear Gulch Reservoir

| 0 | 100 yds |
| 0 | 100 m |

Contour Interval = 40 feet

Elevation Profile

Elevation (feet)

1,750
1,500
1,250

0.00   0.20   0.40   0.60   0.80   1.00   1.20   1.40   1.60   1.80

Distance (miles)

▲ BEAR GULCH CAVE

0.1 mile (0.2 km) later. Continue left on **Moses Spring Trail,** up the eastern side of Bear Gulch.

Pass through a **short rock tunnel,** taking care to watch for hikers coming the other direction. At 0.5 mile (0.8 km) is the Moses Spring Trail-Bear Gulch Cave Trail **split.** Continue straight (south) onto **Bear Gulch Cave Trail.** Just before arriving at the entrance of **Bear Gulch Cave,** follow the trail through a narrow slot between massive rocks to a caution sign, noting "Flashlights required, low ceilings, slippery when wet."

▶ **MILE 0.6-0.8: Bear Gulch Cave to Bear Gulch Reservoir**
With your headlamp or flashlight on, pass under the tilted boulder entrance to the cave. Here, the light illuminates the green lichen growing on the rocks with an otherworldly glow. The walkway over the often dry Bear Creek provides a great base for a vertical photo of the massive rocks and daylight filtering into the cave.

A short metal bridge and white arrows painted on the rock leads you through the first dark section of the trail, into an opening with a high ceiling of fallen boulders. Shortly following is the first staircase, with just a single spotlight from the sky showing where to begin. The trail through the talus cave is shared with the creek as you make your way through the narrow passage to the next staircase, this time in complete darkness. The stairs lead to a split at 0.7 mile (1.1 km); continue right (south) to the upper section of the cave or left (east) up toward daylight and across another short metal bridge, either of which will take you to the reservoir.

Turning left, follow the railings, rocky stairs, and trail signs toward the reservoir, but don't put away your headlamp or flashlight. The trail passes through more boulders and across a short and narrow rock bridge over the creek and to the final staircase of the hike. At the top of the stairs is the dam wall for the **Bear Gulch Reservoir.** The variety of rock colors and formations, chaparral, and bright lake vegetation reflected in the glassy artificial lake make it a beautiful spot to sit and take a break.

▶ **MILE 0.8-1.7: Bear Gulch Reservoir to Bear Gulch Day-Use Area Parking Lot**
North of the stairs leading up to the reservoir, find a trail marker for the Rim Trail. The exposed trail leads north, now with a view of the eastern Bear Gulch. At 1 mile (1.6 km), the hike has reached its highest elevation. Be on the look for the **junction** with High Peaks Trail at 1.2 miles (1.9 km). Make a sharp U-turn to the right (east) to follow **High Peaks Trail.** In less than 0.1 mile (0.2 km) is another **split.** Turn left (northwest) to avoid returning to the cave and remain on High Peaks Trail. At 1.4 miles (2.3 km), the trail connects back to Moses Spring Trail. Go left (northeast) to return the way you came.

DIRECTIONS

From Hollister, take Highway 25 south for 28.8 miles (46 km) and make a slight right onto Highway 146. Continue for 3.8 miles (6.1 km) and turn south (left) toward the Bear Gulch Day-Use Area, and continue for 1.2 miles (1.9 km) to the parking lot. If the timing works perfectly, you can try for a spot in the Moses Spring Parking Area, just a bit farther southwest, past the Bear Gulch Day-Use Area parking. The lot is very small, so don't pass up an available spot at Bear Gulch Day-Use Area if parking is filling up fast.

GPS COORDINATES: 36.4812, −121.1814; 36°28'52.3" N, 121°10'53" W

BEST NEARBY SIGHT
For a refreshing post-hike dip in a swimming pool, look no farther than the **Pinnacles Campground.** Typically open mid-April through the end of September, get access by booking a campsite, and then grab your favorite snack from the Campground Store and enjoy some down time at the lively pool.

NEARBY CAMPGROUNDS

NAME	DESCRIPTION	FACILITIES	SEASON	FEE
Pinnacles	Proximity to trails on the east side of the national park	95 campsites, 25 full-hookup sites, restrooms, showers, piped drinking water, dump station, camp store, swimming pool	year-round	from $39; separate National Park entrance fee ($35 per vehicle) required

Highway 146, Paicines, 831/200-1722, www.recreation.gov

HIKING TIPS

Safety

HIKING ESSENTIALS

It doesn't take a lot of equipment to have a safe and fun day hike. Lace up a good pair of hiking shoes and a lot of your prep work is done—but not all of it. Far too many day hikers set out carrying too little and get themselves into bad situations that could easily have been prevented. A few extra minutes spent loading your day-pack with these essentials can spare you a lot of discomfort:

Water

Having enough water can make or break your hike. Many day hikers carry a couple of 32-ounce (1-liter) wide-mouth water bottles, such as refillable Nalgene bottles, and that's often more than adequate for one person. But if the weather is especially hot or the trail is particularly steep, 64 ounces (2 liters) won't be enough.

That's where a purifier or filtering device comes in handy, allowing you to obtain water from streams, rivers, springs, or lakes without suffering any unpleasant consequences. Filtering or purifying is a critically important step—never drink water from a natural source as you find it. The microscopic organisms *Giardia lamblia* and cryptosporidium live in many backcountry water sources, and they can cause a litany of terrible gastrointestinal problems. Only purifying or boiling water from natural sources will wipe out these nasty bugs.

Fortunately, many simple lightweight devices can make backcountry water safe to drink. These include water bottle-style filters made by companies like Bota, Grayl, Aquamira, or Katadyn that eliminate the need to carry both a filter and a bottle. You simply dip the bottle in the stream, screw on the top—which contains a filter—and squeeze the bottle to drink. The water is filtered on its way out of the squeeze top.

There's even a "straw" that purifies water so you can drink right out of creeks and lakes (if you don't mind lying on your belly to get close enough). The LifeStraw Personal Water Filter costs about $20, fits in your pocket, and weighs almost nothing. Carry the LifeStraw plus an empty water bottle and you don't even have to lie on the ground. Just fill your empty bottle with water, then insert the LifeStraw and drink.

Another popular option is the SteriPEN, which uses ultraviolet light rays to purify water. It's small, light, runs on batteries, and purifies 32 ounces (1 liter) of water in about 90 seconds.

Of course, in extremely arid parts of Northern California, there may not be natural water sources to filter from, so carrying extra water may be your only option. Sure, water is heavy, but if you're hot and thirsty, it's worth its weight in gold.

One note for hikers traveling in groups: Each person should carry their own supply of water and snacks. That will save a lot of disagreements and help to keep everyone hydrated and happy.

Food

It's always unwise to get caught without a picnic or at least some snacks for emergencies, so don't forget to pack some food to eat on the trail. There are no hard-and-fast rules about what makes a great hiking snack. Any kind of food that packs well and doesn't require refrigeration can do the trick. Some hikers go gourmet and carry all the delicacies to make a show-piece charcuterie plate. Others want the lightest, simplest, high-energy snacks, so they choose nutrition bars, nuts, dried fruit, jerky, and the like. There's no right or wrong here.

We prefer to carry a mix of salty and sweet foods to be prepared for any possible craving we have. Our cardinal rule is always to bring more than we think we need. When you're carrying more than you need, you can always give it away to others and make their day.

Trail Map

Carrying a map of the park or public land you're visiting is essential. Whether it's a digital or paper map, it should be recently updated and easy to read. Many hikers think printed maps are a thing of the past, but modern GPS technology is only as good as the device it's running on. Batteries can die and cell phones and GPS devices can malfunction (try dropping your cell phone on a hunk of granite to see what happens).

Technology finds myriad ways to fail us, but paper maps are remarkably reliable. It's not a bad idea to carry both a digital map and a paper map.

The most reliable source for trail maps—digital or paper—is the managing agency of the park you're visiting. At many national, state, and regional parks, you can pick up a paper map at the park entrance station or visitor center. The vast majority of California parks and preserves have online maps that you can download for free, but always download maps before you drive to the trailhead—there's no guarantee you'll have Wi-Fi or cell service once you enter the park.

You can also get detailed maps of anywhere in the United States from the U.S. Geological Survey. Order their highly detailed topographic maps in paper format for a fee or download free digital maps at www.usgs.gov.

Full-color printed maps of popular hiking destinations like national parks, Lake Tahoe, and Mount Shasta are available from private mapping companies like Tom Harrison Maps, Green Trails, National Geographic/Trails Illustrated, and Wilderness Press. You can also download digital or print maps from apps like AllTrails, GaiaGPS, and CalTopo—and CalTopo even lets you build your own maps.

If you're traveling to any of California's national parks, consider downloading maps and other trip planning tools from the National Park Service mobile app. Again, don't forget to download before you travel because many national parks don't have cell service or Wi-Fi.

Extra Clothing Layers

On the trail, conditions can change at any time. Not only can the weather suddenly turn windy, foggy, or rainy, but your own body conditions also change: You'll perspire as you hike up a sunny hill and then get chilled at the top of a windy ridge or when heading into a shady stretch. That's why cotton fabrics don't function well outdoors. Once cotton gets wet, it stays wet. Generally, polyester, silk, or synthetic-blend fabrics dry faster. Many high-tech fabrics actually wick moisture away from your skin. Invest in a few items of clothing made from these fabrics, and you'll be more comfortable when you hike.

Additionally, always carry a lightweight jacket with you, preferably one that is waterproof and also wind-resistant. Put it in your backpack or tie it around your waist. If your jacket isn't waterproof, pack one of the inexpensive, single-use rain ponchos that come in a package the size of a deck of cards (they're available at most drugstores and outdoor retailers, and they're large enough to layer over whatever jacket you're wearing).

It doesn't hurt to carry a pair of lightweight gloves and a hat too. You never know when you might need them, especially if that notorious San Francisco Bay Area fog rolls in or a surprise hailstorm hits the Sierra; that can happen even in August.

Sunglasses and Sunscreen

We don't need to remind you of the dangers of the sun. Wear sunglasses to protect your eyes and sunscreen with a high SPF rating on any exposed skin. Put on your sunscreen 30 minutes before you go outdoors so it has time to take effect. Reapply your sunscreen every two hours or after swimming in a lake or stream. In addition, protect the skin on your face and neck by wearing a wide-brimmed hat, and don't forget about your lips, which burn easily. Wear lip balm that has a high SPF rating.

Insect Repellent

Some hikers aren't bothered much by mosquitoes; for others, the little pests can ruin the day. You can eliminate most mosquito encounters by simply carrying insect repellent in your pack and applying it when needed. Some repellents are made of natural substances, such as lemon or eucalyptus oil. Others have a chemical ingredient called DEET, which is extremely effective but also quite toxic. Children should not use repellent with high levels of DEET, although it's supposed to be safe for adults.

What bug spray works best? Every hiker has their opinion. If you visit the High Sierra in the middle of a major mosquito hatch, it will seem like nothing works except running as fast as you can. But for most buggy situations, we apply a brand called Natrapel, which is DEET-free and available in various-size spray bottles. It contains a 20 percent picaridin formula, which is recommended by the U.S. Centers for Disease Control and the World Health Organization for insect bite protection.

Flashlight or Headlamp

Just in case your hike takes a little longer than you planned and darkness falls, bring at least one flashlight or headlamp, and preferably two—in case you lose one in the darkness or your batteries fail. Never plan to rely on your cell phone flashlight. The batteries in cell phones run out fast, and in a serious emergency, you'll want to save your phone battery for an SOS call.

Small flashlights tend to be sturdier than headlamps and can handle more abuse, but headlamps are great for predawn starts, hiking after dark, or setting up camp. Choose whichever light source you like best, but be proactive and carry a spare, or at least an extra set of batteries.

First-Aid Kit

Unless you're certified in wilderness first aid, you don't need to carry a complicated medical kit on a day hike. But a few small, lightweight essentials can come in handy for minor scrapes and accidents. We recommend carrying a few large and small adhesive bandages, antibiotic ointment such as Neosporin, ibuprofen or aspirin, Spenco 2nd Skin for blisters, and an ACE bandage. And of course, if you or anyone in your party is allergic to bee stings or anything else in the outdoors, carry the appropriate medication.

Swiss Army-Style Pocket Knife

Be sure to carry one with several blades, a can opener, scissors, and tweezers. The latter is useful for removing splinters or ticks.

Personal Hygiene Needs

Just in case you or someone in your group needs to heed the call of nature, carry toilet paper and a zip-top plastic bag to carry out both the used paper and human waste. Never leave toilet paper behind—it takes many years to decay, and it's extremely unpleasant for other hikers to find.

Emergency Supplies

Ask yourself this question: "What would I need to have if I had to spend the night outdoors?" Aside from food, water, and other items previously listed, here are some basic emergency supplies that will get you through an unplanned night in the wilderness:

1. Lightweight tarp or sleeping bag. Purchase one made of foil-like Mylar film, designed to reflect radiating body heat. These weigh almost nothing and make a great emergency shelter. The nonreflective side can even be used to signal a helicopter, should the need ever arise.

2. Fire-starting kit. A couple of packs of matches, a lighter, a candle, and some cotton balls soaked in Vaseline. Keep these in a waterproof container or sealable plastic bag, just in case you ever need to build a fire in a serious emergency. No matter how dire the emergency, be extremely careful not to let your emergency fire become a forest fire.

3. Whistle. A plastic whistle is a cheap investment that can save your life. If you need help, you can blow a whistle for a lot longer than you can shout. Voices don't carry well in high winds or near a running stream.

4. Small signal mirror. This old-school safety item could get you found if you ever get lost. A tiny mirror can reflect sunlight with life-saving accuracy, drawing attention to your location. Use it properly and you may be able to help a search-and-rescue helicopter find you. If a mirror seems a bit rudimentary, consider purchasing its modern high-tech replacement, the personal locator beacon (PLB). If you wind up injured and your cell phone doesn't work, a PLB will let you signal for help using GPS technology.

Hiking or Trekking Poles

Hiking poles aren't essential, but they're incredibly useful, and many hikers refuse to go anywhere without them. In terms of biomechanics, hiking poles transform you from a somewhat awkward two-legged human to an ultra-efficient four-legged mountain goat. Research shows that hiking poles improve your speed and efficiency when walking, so if you're traveling a long distance, they'll get you where you want to go faster and with less fatigue.

We've had enough injuries to know that a pair of ultra-lightweight hiking poles can save the day on rough, rocky mountain trails where balance and grip are especially important. Not only that, but poles are incredibly useful when you need to ford a creek or river (plant your poles in the streambed and they provide stability, so you have less chance of going for a swim) or when you're hiking steeply downhill on loose shale (plant your poles ahead of you so you don't topple forward).

Today's hiking poles are extremely lightweight and fold up into small sections, so if you don't want to use them for your entire trek, you can always strap them to your pack's exterior or stuff them inside.

On the Trail

WEATHER

It's simply irresponsible to set out for a long day hike without first checking the weather. Is there a chance of afternoon thunderstorms? Is the fog going to roll out or roll in? What are the predicted temperatures for the day? These are the questions you want answered before you step foot on a trail. The answers will dictate not just how you dress and what you carry with you, but also whether you go at all. If lightning is in the forecast, alter your plans to bag a superhigh peak. Instead, pick a forested hike where you won't be a sitting duck on a high granite ridge.

WILDFIRES

Anyone who plans to hike in the West should understand that wildfires are an all-too-common hazard. In Northern California, wildfire season typically runs July through October, when the weather is especially warm and dry. If you're traveling far to visit a park or preserve during the summer or fall months, do some pre-trip research to see if fire or smoke may affect your hike.

Before you leave your house, check websites and apps that track active fires, like https://fire.airnow.gov or www.fireweatheravalanche.org. See what's happening where you're going: If there's a fire burning in the region, specific trails or even entire parks or forests may be closed. But even when a wildfire is far away—100 miles or more—drifting smoke can spoil your hike. Not only is wildfire smoke unhealthy for your lungs, it also obscures vistas and puts a damper on your fun.

That's why it's always smart to check the air quality index for your destination. If the index is higher than 100, consider heading somewhere else. Dozens of apps and websites report on air quality, but one excellent source is the National Oceanic and Atmospheric Administration's smoke-monitoring website, https://airquality.weather.gov.

As you hike this book's trails, you'll find some that pass through recently burned areas. When hiking these trails, employ extra vigilance. Always pay attention to signs and respect all closures in burn areas. Trails may remain choked with fallen trees or burned debris long after the flames have passed through. Scorched tree limbs and trunks can break and fall at any time, and they're especially vulnerable on windy days or after periods of heavy rain.

Walking through a burned forest can be a jarring experience, but there is an upside. Even severely burned landscapes can and do regenerate, and hikers get to witness the fascinating process of renewal.

TROUBLESOME CRITTERS, INSECTS, AND PLANTS
Bears

The only bears found in California are black bears, even though they are usually brown in color. Black bears weigh 250 to 400 pounds (113-181 kg), can run up to 30 miles per hour (48 km/h), and are powerful swimmers and climbers. California's black bears are mostly harmless and almost never harm human beings—although you should never approach or feed a bear, or get between a bear and its cubs or its food. If provoked, a bear could cause serious injury.

There's only one important fact to remember about bears: They love snacks. The average black bear has to eat as much as 30,000 calories a day, and since their natural diet is made up of berries, fruits, plants, fish, insects, and the like, the high-calorie food of human beings is very appealing. Unfortunately, too many people have trained California's bears to crave the taste of corn chips, trail bars, and all other human food.

The best thing you can do help California's bears—and protect yourself and your belongings—is to keep your food away from them. In regions where bears live, including Yosemite, Tahoe, the Eastern Sierra, Shasta, Lassen, and other mountainous areas, always store your food safely in bear-proof storage lockers. You'll find these brown metal boxes at almost every car campground and most trailheads. If at all possible, do not leave food in your vehicle—a bear can smell food from 0.5 mile (0.8 km) away and break into a car in about three seconds. Additionally, at national parks like Yosemite and Sequoia, rangers will give you a ticket if they look in your car window and see a cooler or bag of groceries.

Bears visit campgrounds and trailheads fairly often, but you're much less likely to encounter a bear on a trail. If you're hiking, bears will most likely hear you coming and avoid you. If a bear approaches you—either on the trail or in camp—yell loudly, throw small rocks or pine cones in the vicinity, and try to frighten the bear away. A bear that is afraid of humans is a bear that will stay wild and stay alive.

Mountain Lions

Mountain lions are almost everywhere in California, but they are very shy and secretive animals and, as a result, are rarely seen. When they do show themselves, they get a lot of media attention. If you're hiking in an area where mountain lions or their tracks have been spotted, remember to keep your children close to you on the trail and your dog leashed. If you see a mountain lion, it will most likely vanish into the landscape as soon as it notices you. If it doesn't, make yourself appear as large and aggressive as possible. Raise your arms, open your jacket, wave a big stick, and shout. If you have children with you, pick them up off the ground, but try to do so without crouching down or leaning over. Crouching makes you appear smaller and more submissive, like prey. Don't turn your back on the cat or run from it; instead, back away slowly and deliberately, always keeping an aggressive pose and speaking loudly and firmly.

Ticks

Ticks are a common problem in California's coastal and foothill areas, especially in the spring months. In fact, ticks are found almost everywhere except in high mountainous areas above 7,000 feet (2,134 m).

The easiest way to stay clear of ticks is to wear long pants and long sleeves when you hike, stay on the cleared trail, and tuck your pant legs into your socks. But this system isn't foolproof—the pests sometimes find their way onto your skin anyway. Always check yourself thoroughly when you finish your hike, looking carefully for anything that might be crawling on you. Check your clothes and also your skin underneath. A good friend can be a useful assistant in this endeavor.

A very small percentage of California ticks carry Lyme disease; it's much more common in East Coast ticks. Most tick bites cause a sharp sting that will get your attention. But on rare occasions, you may not notice that a tick has bitten you. If you've been out hiking and then a few days or a week later start to experience flu-like symptoms, such as headaches, fever, muscle soreness, neck stiffness, or nausea, see a doctor immediately. Tell the doctor you are concerned about possible exposure to ticks and Lyme disease.

Another early telltale symptom is a slowly expanding red rash near the tick bite, which appears a week to a month after the bite. Caught in its early stages, Lyme disease is easily treated with antibiotics, but left untreated, it can be severely debilitating.

Rattlesnakes

Eight rattlesnake species live throughout California. These members of the pit viper family have wide triangular heads, narrow necks, and rattles on their tails. Rattlesnakes may be found anywhere it's warm, usually at elevations below 7,000 feet (2,134 m). If you're hiking on a warm day, when rattlesnakes may be out sunning themselves on trails and rocks, keep on the lookout so you don't step on one or accidentally place your hand on it. Be extra vigilant in the spring months, when the snakes leave their winter burrows to warm up in the sun. Morning is the most common time to see them, as the midday sun is usually too hot. If you happen to come across a rattlesnake, give it plenty of space to get away without feeling threatened.

Although rattlesnake bites are painful, they are very rarely fatal. Each year, about 230 people in California are bitten by rattlesnakes, with only one or two fatalities on average. About 25 percent of rattlesnake bites are dry, with no venom injected. Symptoms of venomous bites usually include tingling around the mouth, nausea and vomiting, dizziness, weakness, sweating, and chills.

If you get bitten by a rattlesnake, your car key—and the nearest telephone—are your best first-aid tools. Call 911 as soon as you can, or have someone drive you to the nearest hospital. Don't panic or run, which can speed the circulation of venom through your system.

Poison Oak

Poison oak is the bane of hikers in lower elevations and coastal areas, but you can avoid it with a little common sense. Learn to recognize and avoid *Toxicodendron diversilobum,* which produces an itching rash that can last for weeks. If you can't readily identify poison oak, at least remember the old Boy Scout motto: Leaves of three, let them be. But also remember that poison oak disguises itself in different seasons. In spring and summer when it is in full leaf, it looks somewhat like wild blackberry bushes. In late summer, its leaves turn bright red. But in winter, the plant loses all or most of its leaves and resembles clusters of bare sticks. Poison oak is poisonous year-round.

To avoid poison oak, stay on the trail and watch what you brush up against. If you know you have a bad reaction to poison oak, wear long pants and long sleeves, and remove and wash your clothes immediately after hiking.

If you have been exposed to poison oak, you can often prevent a rash from developing by washing the area thoroughly with soap and water, or with an oil-removing product like Tecnu Extreme, as soon as possible. If you develop a poison oak rash, a product called Zanfel can help you get rid of it. It's available at pharmacies without a prescription. Simply pour it on the rash and the rash vanishes—or at least greatly diminishes. If these over-the-counter products don't work for you, the only recourse is a trip to the doctor for prednisone pills, and there's nothing fun about that.

TRAIL ETIQUETTE

Hiking is a great way to get out of the concrete jungle and into the woods and the wild to explore places of natural beauty. Unfortunately, this manner of thinking is shared by millions of people. Following some basic rules of etiquette will ensure that we all get along and keep the outdoors as a place we can enjoy together.

1. Enjoy the silence and let nature's sounds prevail. Keep your voice low and avoid making loud noises. This will increase your chance of encountering wildlife and help others enjoy their quiet time in the outdoors.

2. Be aware of other trail users and yield appropriately. If you hear someone coming up behind you who clearly is hiking faster than you, stand aside and let that hiker pass. On narrow trails, hikers going downhill should always yield to hikers going uphill. Get out of their way so uphill hikers can keep their momentum as they climb. Also, large groups of hikers should always yield to smaller groups or solo travelers.

HIKING WITH DOGS

Dogs are allowed on many trails in Northern California, but not all. Check the information listing under each trail write-up in this book to determine whether dogs are permitted on the specific trail you're planning to hike, and then double-check by phoning the park or checking its website—especially if you and your dog are making a long drive to the trailhead.

Here are a few general rules for dog owners headed to California's parklands: National and state parks are known for having a strict no-dogs-on-trails policy, although they usually permit dogs in campgrounds, picnic areas, and on paved roads. That means no canine hiking fun at almost any place that has "National Park," "State Park," or "State Reserve" in the title.

County and regional parks have their own rules, and they're often, but not always, more dog-friendly. Some parks will let you hike with your dog for a small extra fee.

Far and away the most reliably dog-friendly lands are those managed by the U.S. Forest Service and the Bureau of Land Management. On the vast majority of trails on USFS or BLM land, dogs are not only permitted to join you on the trail, they're often allowed to hike leash-free. But as a responsible dog owner, you need to carefully consider whether this is a good idea. If your dog isn't attached to you by a leash, he or she may get into an unwanted encounter with a coyote, mountain lion, porcupine, raccoon—or perhaps worst of all, a skunk. In places like Lake Tahoe and the San Francisco Bay Area, where human-wildlife encounters happen almost daily, coyotes prey on beloved pets far too often. If your dog is on a leash, you have a much better chance of keeping them safe from harm.

Whether you let your dog hike leash-free is also a matter of wilderness ethics, even if the park or public land permits it. Dogs are wonderful friends and great companions, but dogs and nature don't always mix well. Bless their furry little hearts, most dogs can't resist disturbing the local wildlife. Even if they don't chase or bark at squirrels or birds or other animals, dogs leave droppings that may intimidate other creatures into altering their normal routines. But a dog who is kept on a leash and picked up after can be the best hiking companion you could ask for.

Always follow each park's specific rules about dogs. Trails where dogs are prohibited are almost always noted as such at the trailhead, so simply obey the signs and you and your dog will stay happily out of trouble.

3. Be friendly and polite to other trail users. A smile or a "hello" as you pass others on the trail is always a good idea. If someone steps aside to allow you to pass, say "thank you."

4. Obey all posted signs and trail closures. Only hike where it's legal. Do not invent shortcuts or hike across private property without the express permission of the owner.

5. Hike only on established trails. As soon as you walk off a trail, you trample vegetation. Never cut switchbacks; hillside trails are built with switchbacks to keep the slope from eroding. Just a few people cutting switchbacks can destroy a hillside.

6. Yield to equestrians. Horses can be badly spooked by just about anything, so always give them plenty of room. If horses are approaching, stop alongside the trail until they pass. If horses are traveling in your direction and you need to pass them, call out politely to the riders and ask permission. If horses and riders move off the trail and the riders tell you it's okay, then pass.

PROTECT THE ENVIRONMENT

Take good care of this beautiful land you're hiking on. The basics are simple: Leave no trace of your visit. Pack out all your trash. Do your best not to disturb animals or plantlife. Don't collect specimens of plants, wildlife, or even pinecones. Never, ever carve anything into the trunks of trees. If you're following a trail, don't cut the switchbacks. Leave everything in nature exactly as you found it because each tiny piece has its place in the great scheme of things.

You can go the extra mile too. Pick up any litter that you see on the trail. Teach your children to do this as well. Carry an extra bag to hold the litter until you get to a trash receptacle, or just keep an empty pocket for that purpose in your backpack.

If you have the extra time or energy, join a trail organization in your area or spend some time volunteering in your local park. Anything you do to help this beautiful planet will be repaid to you many times over. For more information, visit **Leave No Trace** at www.lnt.org.

GETTING LOST AND GETTING FOUND

If you're hiking with a family or group, make sure everybody knows to stay together. If anyone decides to split off from the group for any reason, make sure that person has a trail map and knows how to read it. Also, be sure that everyone in your group knows the key rules about what to do if they get lost:

1. Whistle or shout loudly at regular intervals.

2. If you can find a trail, stay on the trail. You'll be easier to find than if you wander off the trail.

3. Find a noticeable landmark like a tree or a big boulder, sit down next to it, and don't move. Stay in one place and you'll be easier to find.

4. Continue to whistle or shout loudly.

PASSES, PERMITS, AND FEES

At many California parks and public lands, there's no cost to go for a hike or park at the trailhead. But that's not true everywhere. Some parks charge

AVOIDING THE CROWDS

Many of California's better-known parks and public lands are notorious for crowds. No matter where in the state you want to hike, you don't have to subject yourself to packed parking lots and long lines of people snaking up and down switchbacks. Follow the tips outlined below and you can avoid the crowds almost anywhere, even in well-traveled parks near urban areas and in our famous national parks.

- **HIKE IN THE OFF-SEASON:** For most public lands, the off-season is any time other than summer, or any time when school is in session. October through mid-May is an excellent period for hiking trips (except around holidays like Christmas, Presidents Day, and Easter).
- **TIME YOUR TRIP FOR MIDWEEK:** Tuesday, Wednesday, and Thursday are always the quietest days of the week in any park or public land.
- **GET UP EARLY:** Even über-popular Yosemite Valley is serene and peaceful at 8am, and the long days of summer buy you plenty of early-morning solitude (dawn comes between 5:30am and 6am in June and most of July; in late August dawn arrives at 6:30am). If you arrive at trailheads before 9am at almost any California park, you'll enjoy the first few hours of your hike with very little company.
- **IF YOU CAN'T GET UP EARLY, STAY OUT LATE:** On long summer days, you can hike shorter trails from 4pm to 7:30pm or even later. You may see other hikers in the first hour or so, but they'll soon disperse. Trailhead parking lots are often packed at 1pm, then nearly empty at 5pm. Note that if you hike in the late afternoon or evening, you should always carry a flashlight with you (at least one per person), just in case it gets dark sooner than you planned.
- **GET OUT AND HIKE IN FOUL WEATHER:** Don your favorite impermeable layer and go where fair-weather hikers dare not go. Any avid hiker can tell you that some of the best memories are made on rainy days, cloudy days, foggy days, and days when the wind blows at gale force. The fact is, the vast majority of people hike only when the sun is out. Witness nature in all its varied moods, and you may be surprised at how much fun you have.

as much as $10 per day or $35 per week for vehicle parking. If you're an avid hiker, consider purchasing an annual pass that will save you money. A park pass comes with a bonus: Just like paying for a gym membership inspires you to go to the gym, owning a park pass will inspire you to get out and hike more.

NATIONAL PARKS AND FEDERAL LANDS

Almost every national park in this book requires an entrance fee. At most parks, the fee is per vehicle, not per person, and it's good for 7 consecutive days. A few examples: Yosemite as well as Sequoia and Kings Canyon charge $35 per vehicle for 7 days. Lassen Volcanic charges $30 per vehicle for 7 days. Whiskeytown charges $25 per vehicle for 7 days.

If you're planning to visit two or more national parks in a 12-month period—and this applies to every national park in the country, not just in

California—consider purchasing an **America the Beautiful** pass to save money. These passes cover entry fees on lands managed by six federal agencies: the National Park Service (national parks), U.S. Forest Service (national forests and grasslands), U.S. Fish and Wildlife Service (national wildlife refuges), Bureau of Land Management, Bureau of Reclamation, and U.S. Army Corps of Engineers.

Passes are good for one year from the date of purchase. Most people are only eligible for the $80 annual America the Beautiful pass, but seniors, U.S. military members, people with permanent disabilities, and fourth-grade students and teachers have other options:

Annual Pass: Buy this $80 pass at any national park, by phone at 888/275-8747, option 2, or online at https://store.usgs.gov/pass.

Annual Senior or Lifetime Senior Pass: U.S. citizens and permanent residents 62 and older may buy a lifetime interagency pass for $80 or an annual pass for $20. Passes may be purchased online at www.store.usgs.gov/pass, through the mail, or, to avoid a $10 processing fee, in person at a federal recreation site.

Military Pass: This pass is free for current U.S. military members and dependents; obtain a pass by showing a Common Access Card or military ID at a federal recreation site.

4th Grade Pass: Kids and their families get free access to federal recreation lands during the student's fourth-grade year. Fourth-grade teachers and those at organizations serving fourth-graders (youth group leaders, camp directors, and so on) are also eligible. Visit https://everykidoutdoors.gov for details.

Access Pass: This pass if free for U.S. citizens and permanent residents with permanent disabilities. Documentation of permanent disability is required. Passes are available at federal recreation sites and by mail; ordering by mail requires a $10 processing fee.

Volunteer Pass: Once you volunteer 250 hours with federal agencies participating in the Interagency Pass Program, you're eligible for a free pass. Contact your local federal recreation site for specifics. Find volunteer opportunities at www.volunteer.gov.

NATIONAL FORESTS

Hikers have free access to most national forests managed by the U.S. Forest Service, but there are a few Northern California exceptions: Some popular trailheads and beaches near Lake Tahoe and Carson Pass charge $5-10 per vehicle for parking. If you don't see a human being collecting fees, there will be an "iron ranger" or metal collection box where you deposit your fee. If you possess an America the Beautiful pass (see above), you can simply place it on your dashboard in lieu of paying for day-use.

CALIFORNIA STATE PARKS

Most state parks charge $8-10 per vehicle per day for entrance and parking, and these fees can add up fast. If you're planning to visit several state parks during the course of a year, take a look at California State Parks' annual pass offerings (passes can be purchased online at https://store.parks.ca.gov or at any state park entrance station):

California Explorer Vehicle Day-Use Annual Pass: This $195 pass is good at all California state park units.

Golden Poppy Vehicle Day-Use Annual Pass: This $125 pass is good at most, but not all, Northern California parks, beaches, and reservoirs.

Tahoe Regional Vehicle Day-Use Annual Pass: This $75 pass is good only at Lake Tahoe state parks.

4th Grade State Parks Adventure Pass: Kids and their families get free access to 19 California state park lands during the student's fourth-grade year.

California State Parks Library Pass: Every public library in California has annual passes that any library patron can check out (free). These passes grant vehicle day-use access to parks across the state.

COUNTY AND REGIONAL PARKS

Several county and regional parks also offer discounted annual passes. If you plan to hike frequently in one specific county or region—for example, within the Mount Tamalpais Watershed or San Mateo County Parks—check to see if an annual pass is available, and if it's a more affordable option for you.

RESOURCES

CALIFORNIA STATE PARKS

JUG HANDLE STATE NATURAL RESERVE
15700 Hwy. 1
Caspar, CA 95420
707/937-5804
parks.ca.gov

POINT CABRILLO LIGHT STATION STATE HISTORIC PARK
13800 Point Cabrillo Dr.
Mendocino, CA 95460
707/937-6123
parks.ca.gov

RUSSIAN GULCH STATE PARK
(no street address) Hwy. 1
Mendocino, CA 95460
707/937-5804
parks.ca.gov

VAN DAMME STATE PARK
8001 Hwy. 1
Little River, CA 95456
707/937-5804
parks.ca.gov

HENDY WOODS STATE PARK
18599 Philo Greenwood Rd.
Philo, CA 95466
707/895-3141
parks.ca.gov

**JEDEDIAH SMITH REDWOODS STATE PARK,
DEL NORTE COAST REDWOODS STATE PARK,
AND PRAIRIE CREEK REDWOODS STATE PARK**
1111 2nd St.
Crescent City, CA 95531
707/464-6101
parks.ca.gov

SUE-MEG STATE PARK
4150 Patricks Point Dr.
Trinidad, CA 95570
707/677-3570
parks.ca.gov

CASTLE CRAGS STATE PARK
20022 Castle Creek Rd.
Castella, CA 96017
530/235-2684
parks.ca.gov

MCARTHUR-BURNEY FALLS MEMORIAL STATE PARK
24898 Hwy. 89
Burney, CA 96013
530/335-2777
parks.ca.gov

EMERALD BAY STATE PARK
138 Emerald Bay Rd.
South Lake Tahoe, CA 96154
530/541-3030
parks.ca.gov

NATIONAL PARKS, MONUMENTS, & RECREATION AREAS

REDWOOD NATIONAL PARK
1111 2nd St.
Crescent City, CA 95531
707/464-6101
www.nps.gov/redw

WHISKEYTOWN NATIONAL RECREATION AREA
P.O. Box 188
Whiskeytown, CA 96095
530/242-3400
www.nps.gov/whis

LASSEN VOLCANIC NATIONAL PARK
P.O. Box 100
Mineral, CA 96063
530/595-4480
www.nps.gov/lavo

YOSEMITE NATIONAL PARK
P.O. Box 577
Yosemite, CA 95389
209/372-0200
www.nps.gov/yose

DEVILS POSTPILE NATIONAL MONUMENT
P.O. Box 3999
Mammoth Lakes, CA 93546
760/934-2289
www.nps.gov/depo

SEQUOIA & KINGS CANYON NATIONAL PARKS
47050 Generals Hwy.
Three Rivers, CA 93271
559/565-3341
www.nps.gov/seki

NATIONAL FORESTS & WILDERNESS AREAS

SHASTA-TRINITY NATIONAL FOREST
3644 Avtech Pkwy.
Redding, CA 96002
530/226-2500
www.fs.usda.gov/stnf

PLUMAS NATIONAL FOREST
159 Lawrence St.
Quincy, CA 95971-6025
530/283-2050
www.fs.usda.gov/plumas

TAHOE NATIONAL FOREST
631 Coyote St.
Nevada City, CA 95959
530/265-4531
www.fs.usda.gov/tahoe

ELDORADO NATIONAL FOREST
100 Forni Rd.
Placerville, CA 95667
530/622-5061
www.fs.usda.gov/eldorado

HUMBOLDT-TOIYABE NATIONAL FOREST
75694 U.S. 395
HC 62 Box 1000
Bridgeport, CA 93517
760/932-7070
www.fs.usda.gov/htnf

INYO NATIONAL FOREST
351 Pacu Lane Suite 200
Bishop, CA 93514
760/873-2500
www.fs.usda.gov/inyo

INDEX

PHOTO CREDITS

Explore Near and Far with Moon Travel Guides

MOON
Alaska
Lisa Maloney

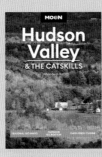

MOON
Hudson Valley
& THE CATSKILLS
Nikki Goth Itoi

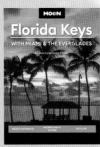

MOON
Florida Keys
WITH MIAMI & THE EVERGLADES
Joshua Lawrence Kinser

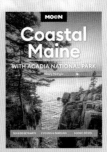

MOON
Coastal Maine
WITH ACADIA NATIONAL PARK
Hilary Nangle

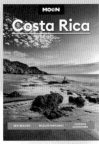

MOON
Costa Rica

MOON
Greek Islands
& ATHENS

MOON
Japan
Jonathan DeHart

MOON
Maui
Greg Archer

MOON
Morocco
Lucas Peters

MOON
Puerto Rico
Suzanne Van Atten

MOON
Idaho
James Brailey Kaufman

MOON
Portugal
WITH MADEIRA & THE AZORES

Victoria
& VANCOUVER ISLAND
Andrew Hempstead

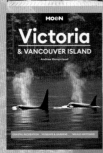

MOON
Scotland

MOON
Tahiti
& FRENCH POLYNESIA
Chantae Reden

MOON
Colorado

MOON.COM | @MOONGUIDES

National Parks Travel Guides from Moon

MOON

ACADIA
NATIONAL PARK

SEASIDE TOWNS · FALL FOLIAGE
CYCLING & PADDLING

HILARY NANGLE

MOON

ARCHES &
CANYONLANDS
NATIONAL PARKS

HIKING · BIKING
SCENIC DRIVES

JUDY JEWELL & W. C. McRAE

MOON

BANFF
NATIONAL PARK

HIKE · CAMP
SEE WILDLIFE

ANDREW HEMPSTEAD

MOON

CANADIAN
ROCKIES

WITH BANFF & JASPER NATIONAL PARKS

SCENIC DRIVES · WILDLIFE
HIKING & SKIING

ANDREW HEMPSTEAD

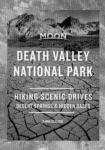

DEATH VALLEY
NATIONAL PARK

HIKING · SCENIC DRIVES
DESERT SPRINGS & HIDDEN OASES

JENNA BLOUGH

MOON

GLACIER
NATIONAL PARK

HIKING · CAMPING
LAKES & PEAKS

BECKY LOMAX

MOON

GRAND
CANYON

HIKE · CAMP
RAFT THE
COLORADO RIVER

TIM HULL

MOON

GREAT SMOKY
MOUNTAINS
NATIONAL PARK

HIKING · CAMPING
SCENIC DRIVES

JASON FRYE

MOON

JOSHUA TREE
& PALM SPRINGS

HIKING · SCENIC DRIVES
DESERT GETAWAYS

JENNA BLOUGH

MOON

ROCKY
MOUNTAIN
NATIONAL PARK

HIKE · CAMP
SEE WILDLIFE

ERIN ENGLISH

MOON

SEQUOIA &
KINGS CANYON

HIKING · CAMPING
WATERFALLS & BIG TREES

LEIGH BERNACCHI

MOON

YELLOWSTONE
& GRAND TETON

HIKE · CAMP
SEE WILDLIFE

BECKY LOMAX

MOON

YOSEMITE
SEQUOIA &
KINGS CANYON

HIKING · CAMPING
WATERFALLS & BIG TREES

ANN MARIE BROWN

MOON

ZION &
BRYCE

WITH ARCHES, CANYONLANDS, CAPITOL REEF,
GRAND STAIRCASE-ESCALANTE & MOAB

HIKING & BIKING
STARGAZING · SCENIC DRIVES

MAE DRIVER

Get the bestselling all-parks guide, or check out Moon's new Best Of Parks series to make the most of a 1-3 day visit to top parks.

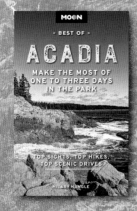

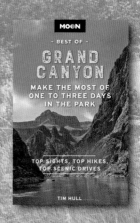

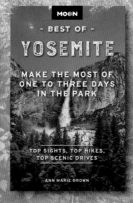

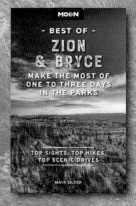

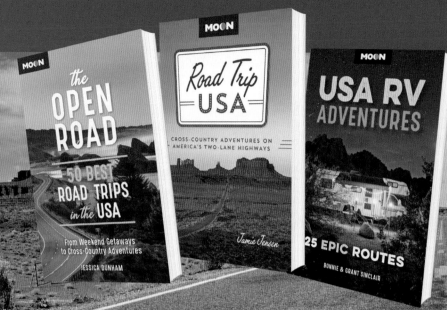

MOON

the OPEN ROAD

50 BEST ROAD TRIPS in the USA

From Weekend Getaways to Cross-Country Adventures

JESSICA DUNHAM

MOON

Road Trip USA

CROSS-COUNTRY ADVENTURES ON AMERICA'S TWO-LANE HIGHWAYS

Jamie Jensen

MOON

USA RV ADVENTURES

25 EPIC ROUTES

BONNIE & GRANT SINCLAIR

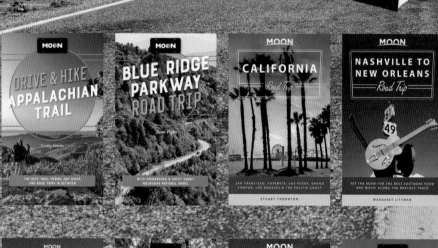

MOON

DRIVE & HIKE APPALACHIAN TRAIL

Timothy Malcolm

THE BEST TRAIL TOWNS, DAY HIKES, AND ROAD TRIPS IN BETWEEN

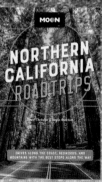

MOON

BLUE RIDGE PARKWAY ROAD TRIP

Jason Frye

WITH SHENANDOAH & GREAT SMOKY MOUNTAINS NATIONAL PARKS

MOON

CALIFORNIA Road Trip

SAN FRANCISCO, YOSEMITE, LAS VEGAS, GRAND CANYON, LOS ANGELES & THE PACIFIC COAST

STUART THORNTON

MOON

NASHVILLE TO NEW ORLEANS Road Trip

HIT THE ROAD FOR THE BEST SOUTHERN FOOD AND MUSIC ALONG THE NATCHEZ TRACE

MARGARET LITTMAN

MOON

NEW ENGLAND Road Trip

SEASIDE SPOTS, MAJESTIC MOUNTAINS & FALL FOLIAGE, COZY GETAWAYS

MILES HOWARD

MOON

NORTHERN CALIFORNIA ROAD TRIPS

Stuart Thornton & Jenna Anderson

DRIVES ALONG THE COAST, REDWOODS, AND MOUNTAINS WITH THE BEST STOPS ALONG THE WAY

MOON

OREGON TRAIL Road Trip

HISTORIC SITES, SMALL TOWNS, AND SCENIC LANDSCAPES ALONG THE LEGENDARY WESTWARD ROUTE

KATRINA EMERY

MOON

PACIFIC COAST HIGHWAY ROAD TRIP

CALIFORNIA, OREGON & WASHINGTON

MOON.COM | @MOONGUIDES

ROAD TRIP GUIDES FROM MOON

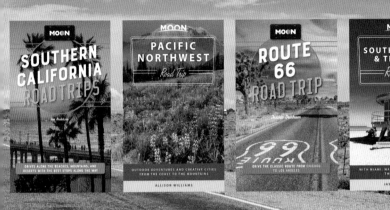
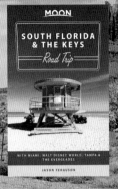

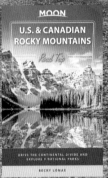

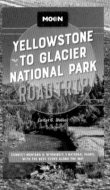
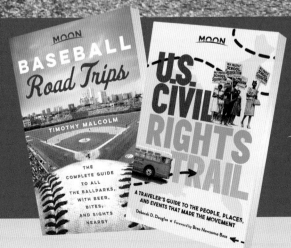

Explore the U.S. with expert authors like baseball writer Timothy Malcolm and journalist Deborah D. Douglas!

TRAILS AT A GLANCE

PAGE	HIKE NAME	DISTANCE	DURATION
San Francisco			
32	Lands End	3.3 mi rt	1.5 hr
35	Presidio Tunnel Tops and Promenade Tour	1.9 mi rt	1 hr
38	Ecology Trail and Lovers' Lane Loop	2.2 mi rt	1 hr
41	Mount Sutro Loop	2.5 mi rt	1 hr
Peninsula & South Bay			
48	Mori Point and Sweeney Ridge	6.8 mi rt	3.5 hr
52	Purisima Loop	8.8 mi rt	4.5 hr
55	Russian Ridge Loop	3.4 mi rt	1.5 hr
58	Año Nuevo Point Trail	4.3 mi rt	2 hr
61	Hunter's Point Loop	2.9 mi rt	1 hr
64	Eagle Rock	2.7 mi rt	1.5 hr
67	Almaden Quicksilver Loop	5.9 mi rt	3 hr
70	Uvas Canyon Waterfall Loop	3.5 mi rt	1.5 hr
East Bay			
78	Stream-East Ridge Loop	3.2 mi rt	1.5 hr
81	Briones Loop	5 mi rt	2 hr
84	Mount Diablo Waterfalls Loop	5.8 mi rt	3 hr
87	Rocky Ridge View–Elderberry Loop	5.2 mi rt	2.5 hr
90	Mission Peak	7.3 mi rt	3.5 hr
93	Little Yosemite	3.1 mi rt	1.5 hr
Muir Woods & Mount Tamalpais			
104	Angel Island	5.5 mi rt	3 hr
107	Tennessee Valley Trail	4 mi rt	1.5 hr
111	Dias Ridge	7.2 mi rt	4 hr
115	Canopy View Loop	3.8 mi rt	2 hr

DIFFICULTY	SEASONAL ACCESS	WILDLIFE	WATERFALLS	DOG-FRIENDLY
Easy	Year-round	x		x
Easy	Year-round			
Easy	Year-round	x		x
Easy	Year-round			x
Moderate-strenuous	Year-round	x		x
Moderate	Year-round	x		
Easy-moderate	Year-round	x		
Easy	Year-round	x		
Easy	Year-round	x		x
Easy	Year-round			
Easy-moderate	Year-round			x
Easy-moderate	Year-round		x	x
Easy	Year-round	x		x
Easy-moderate	Year-round			x
Moderate	Year-round		x	
Easy-moderate	Year-round			
Moderate-strenuous	Year-round	x		x
Easy	Year-round		x	x
Moderate	Year-round	x		
Easy	Year-round	x		
Moderate	Year-round	x		
Easy-moderate	Year-round	x	x	

TRAILS AT A GLANCE

PAGE	HIKE NAME	DISTANCE	DURATION
119	Dipsea–Matt Davis Loop	9 mi rt	5 hr
123	Mount Tamalpais West Point Loop	4.2 mi rt	2.5 hr
126	East Peak Summit Lookout Loop	1.7 mi rt	1 hr
129	Cataract Falls	3 mi rt	2 hr
133	Carson Falls	4.6 mi rt	2 hr
136	Bay View Loop	3.7 mi rt	1.5 hr
Point Reyes National Seashore			
146	Tomales Point	9.4 mi rt	5 hr
150	Abbotts Lagoon	3.3 mi rt	1.5 hr
153	Chimney Rock Trail	1.9 mi rt	1 hr
156	Secret Beach	7.6 mi rt	4 hr
159	Inverness Ridge Loop	5.2 mi rt	2.5 hr
163	Mount Wittenberg	5.2 mi rt	2.5 hr
166	Stairstep Falls	2.3 mi rt	1 hr
169	Alamere Falls	13.4 mi rt	7 hr
Napa & Sonoma			
178	Salt Point Trail	3.3 mi rt	1.5 hr
181	Fort Ross Reef Trail	2.7 mi rt	1.5 hr
184	Pomo Canyon Red Hill	5.2 mi rt	2.5 hr
187	Pioneer Nature Trail Loop	1.2 mi rt	30 min
190	Table Rock	4.2 mi rt	3 hr
193	Homestead–Blue Ridge	5.3 mi rt	3 hr
Mendocino			
204	Ecological Staircase Nature Trail	5.1 mi rt	2.5 hr
207	Point Cabrillo Light Station	1–2.3 mi rt	30 min–1 hr
210	Fern Canyon Trail to Russian Gulch Falls	6.3 mi rt	3 hr
213	Spring Ranch Trail	3.6 mi rt	2 hr

DIFFICULTY	SEASONAL ACCESS	WILDLIFE	WATERFALLS	DOG-FRIENDLY
Moderate-strenuous	Year-round	x	x	
Easy-moderate	Year-round	x		
Easy	Year-round	x		x
Easy-moderate	Year-round		x	x
Easy-moderate	Year-round	x	x	x
Easy	Year-round	x		
Moderate	Year-round	x		
Easy	Year-round	x		
Easy-moderate	Year-round	x		
Moderate	Year-round	x		
Easy-moderate	Year-round			
Moderate	Year-round			
Easy	Year-round	x	x	
Strenuous	Year-round	x	x	
Easy	Year-round	x		
Easy	Year-round	x		
Easy-moderate	Year-round			
Easy	Year-round			
Moderate	Year-round			
Moderate-strenuous	Year-round	x		
Easy-moderate	Year-round			
Easy	Year-round	x		x
Easy-moderate	Year-round	x	x	
Easy	Year-round	x		x

TRAILS AT A GLANCE

PAGE	HIKE NAME	DISTANCE	DURATION
216	Fern Canyon and 20 Bridges Loop	8.2 mi rt	4 hr
219	Big Hendy Grove and Hermit Huts	3.8 mi rt	2 hr
222	Point Arena-Stornetta Trails	5.2 mi rt	2.5 hr
226	Bowling Ball Beach	1.2 mi rt	1 hr
North Coast & Redwood Empire			
236	Boy Scout Tree Trail to Fern Falls	5.6 mi rt	3 hr
239	Damnation Creek Trail	4 mi rt	2-3 hr
242	Yurok Loop and Coastal Trail to Hidden Beach	2.3 mi rt	1 hr
245	Brown Creek, Rhododendron, and South Fork Loop	3.6 mi rt	2 hr
248	James Irvine and Miners Ridge Loop to Fern Canyon	11.4 mi rt	6-7 hr
252	Skunk Cabbage Creek and Coastal Trail	7.6 mi rt	4 hr
256	Tall Trees Grove	3.6 mi rt	2-3 hr
259	Rim Trail	5 mi rt	2.5 hr
Shasta-Trinity National Forest			
270	Deadfall Lakes and Mount Eddy	10.4 mi rt	6-7 hr
273	Bunny Flat to Alpine Lodge/Hidden Valley	5.8 mi rt	4 hr
277	Gray Butte	3.2 mi rt	1.5-2 hr
280	South Gate Meadows	3.6 mi rt	2 hr
283	Castle Lake to Heart Lake	2.4 mi rt	1.5 hr
286	McCloud Falls	3.8 mi rt	2 hr
289	Crags Trail to Castle Dome	5.4 mi rt	3-4 hr
292	Burney Falls, Pacific Crest Trail, and Headwaters Loop	2.7 mi rt	1.5 hr
295	James K. Carr Trail to Whiskeytown Falls	3.4 mi rt	2 hr

DIFFICULTY	SEASONAL ACCESS	WILDLIFE	WATERFALLS	DOG-FRIENDLY
Easy-moderate	Year-round	x		
Easy	Year-round			
Easy-moderate	Year-round	x		x
Easy	Year-round			x
Easy-moderate	Year-round		x	
Moderate	Year-round			
Easy	Year-round	x		
Easy-moderate	Year-round			
Moderate-strenuous	Year-round	x		
Easy-moderate	Year-round			
Easy-moderate	Year-round			
Easy-moderate	Year-round			
Moderate-strenuous	June-Nov.			
Moderate	Year-round			
Easy-moderate	May-Oct.			x
Easy-moderate	June-Oct.			
Easy-moderate	May-Nov.			
Easy	Spring-fall	x		
Moderate-strenuous	Apr.-Nov.			
Easy	Year-round	x		
Easy-moderate	Year-round	x		

TRAILS AT A GLANCE

PAGE	HIKE NAME	DISTANCE	DURATION
Lassen Volcanic National Park			
304	Chaos Crags	4.2 mi rt	2–3 hr
307	Manzanita Creek Trail	6.8 mi rt	3–4 hr
311	Paradise Meadow	2.8 mi rt	2 hr
315	Kings Creek Falls	2.5 mi rt	1.5 hr
318	Terrace, Shadow, and Cliff Lakes	3.6 mi rt	2 hr
321	Lassen Peak	4.8 mi rt	3 hr
325	Bumpass Hell	3.2 m rt	2 hr
328	Ridge Lakes	2 mi rt	1.5 hr
331	Brokeoff Mountain	6.9 mi rt	4 hr
334	Cinder Cone	3.8 mi rt	3 hr
Sacramento & Gold Country			
348	Phantom Falls Overlook	4.5 mi rt	2.5 hr
351	Fairy Falls	5 mi rt	2 hr
354	Stevens Trail	7.4 mi rt	3.5 hr
357	Hidden Falls Loop	4.4 mi rt	2 hr
361	American River Parkway (Jedidiah Smith Memorial Trail)	3 mi rt	1.5 hr
364	Cosumnes Nature Loop	4 mi rt	2 hr
Tahoe			
372	Bear, Silver, Round Lakes Loop	4.7 mi rt	2.5 hr
375	Sierra Buttes Lookout	4.6 mi rt	3 hr
378	Five Lakes	4.6 mi rt	2.5 hr
381	Vikingsholm Castle and Emerald Point	4.4 mi rt	2 hr
384	Mount Tallac	9.8 mi rt	6 hr
388	Glen Alpine Trail to Susie Lake	8.4 mi rt	5 hr
391	Echo Lakes to Tamarack and Ralston Lakes	8.1 mi rt	5 hr
394	Carson Pass to Winnemucca and Round Top Lakes	6.8 mi rt	3 hr

DIFFICULTY	SEASONAL ACCESS	WILDLIFE	WATERFALLS	DOG-FRIENDLY
Easy–moderate	June–Oct.			
Easy–moderate	June–Oct.			
Easy–moderate	June–Oct.		x	
Easy–moderate	June–Oct.		x	
Easy–moderate	June–Oct.			
Moderate	June–Oct.			
Easy	July–Oct.			
Easy–moderate	June–Oct.	x		
Moderate-strenuous	July–Oct.	x		
Moderate	June–Oct.			
Easy–moderate	Year-round		x	x
Easy	Year-round		x	x
Moderate	Year-round		x	x
Easy	Year-round		x	x
Easy	Year-round			x
Easy	Year-round	x		
Easy–moderate	June–Oct.			x
Moderate	June–Oct.			x
Easy–moderate	June–Oct.			x
Easy	Apr.–Oct.			
Strenuous	June–Oct.			x
Moderate	June–Oct.			x
Easy–moderate	June–Oct.			x
Easy–moderate	June–Oct.			x

TRAILS AT A GLANCE

PAGE	HIKE NAME	DISTANCE	DURATION
Yosemite National Park			
406	Wapama Falls and Hetch Hetchy Reservoir	5 mi rt	2.5 hr
409	May Lake and Mount Hoffmann	5.8 mi rt	4 hr
412	Cathedral Lakes	9.6 mi rt	5-6 hr
415	Lembert Dome and Dog Lake	5 mi rt	3 hr
418	Middle and Upper Gaylor Lakes	3.8 mi rt	2.5 hr
421	Mount Dana	5.6 mi rt	4 hr
424	Upper Yosemite Fall	6.4 mi rt	5 hr
427	Vernal and Nevada Falls	6 mi rt	4 hr
430	McGurk Meadow and Dewey Point	7.6 mi rt	4 hr
434	Sentinel Dome and Taft Point	4.5 mi rt	2.5 hr
437	Chilnualna Falls	7.7 mi rt	4.5 hr
Eastern Sierra			
446	Barney Lake	8 mi rt	5 hr
449	Green Creek Trail to East Lake	9 mi rt	5 hr
452	Virginia Lakes to Summit/Burro Pass	5.8 mi rt	3-4 hr
455	Lundy Canyon	3.5 mi rt	2.5 hr
458	Bennettville Mine and Fantail Lake	4.4 mi rt	2 hr
461	Parker Lake	3.8 mi rt	2 hr
464	Mammoth Consolidated Gold Mine and Heart Lake	3 mi rt	2 hr
467	Duck Pass	7.4 mi rt	4 hr
471	Devils Postpile and Rainbow Falls	5.2 mi rt	3 hr
475	Convict Lake Loop	2.5 mi rt	1.5 hr
478	Little Lakes Valley to Gem Lake	7.2 mi rt	4-5 hr
Sequoia & Kings Canyon National Parks			
488	Mist Falls	7.8-8.2 mi rt	5-5.5 hr
491	River Trail to Roaring River Falls and Zumwalt Meadow	5.3 mi rt	3 hr

DIFFICULTY	SEASONAL ACCESS	WILDLIFE	WATERFALLS	DOG-FRIENDLY
Easy-moderate	Year-round	x	x	
Moderate	July–Oct.			
Moderate	July–Oct.			
Easy-moderate	July–Oct.			
Moderate	July–Oct.			
Strenuous	July–Oct.			
Moderate-strenuous	Year-round		x	
Moderate	Year-round		x	
Moderate	June–Oct.			
Easy-moderate	June–Oct.			
Moderate	Year-round		x	
Moderate	June–Oct.			x
Moderate	June–Oct.			x
Moderate	June–Oct.			x
Easy-moderate	June–Oct.	x		x
Easy-moderate	June–Oct.			x
Easy-moderate	June–Oct.			x
Easy-moderate	June–Oct.			x
Moderate	June–Oct.			x
Easy-moderate	June–Sept.	x		x
Easy	June–Oct.			x
Moderate	June–Oct.			x
Easy-moderate	May–Oct.		x	
Easy	May–Oct.		x	

TRAILS AT A GLANCE

PAGE	HIKE NAME	DISTANCE	DURATION
494	General Grant Tree, North Grove, and Dead Giant	3.4 mi rt	2 hr
497	Mitchell Peak	6.4 mi rt	4 hr
500	Little Baldy	3.4 mi rt	1.5 hr
503	Tokopah Falls	4.2 mi rt	2 hr
506	Lakes Trail to Heather, Aster, Emerald, and Pear Lakes	8-12 mi rt	5-7 hr
509	General Sherman Tree and Congress Trail	2.9 mi rt	1.5 hr
513	Moro Rock from Giant Forest Museum	3.6 mi rt	2 hr
517	Tharp's Log and Log Meadow	4 mi rt	2 hr
Santa Cruz			
530	Saratoga Gap and Ridge Trail	4.9 mi rt	3 hr
534	Ocean View Summit	3.3 mi rt	1.5 hr
537	Quail Hollow Loop	3 mi rt	1.5 hr
540	Fall Creek Loop	3.3 mi rt	1.5 hr
543	Henry Cowell Observation Deck Loop	5.3 mi rt	2.5 hr
547	Bonny Doon Beach and Shark Fin Cove	2.4 mi rt	1 hr
550	Old Cove Landing Trail	2.4 mi rt	1 hr
553	Monarch-Moore Creek Loop	1.5 mi rt	1 hr
557	West Cliff Drive	4 mi rt	1.5 hr
560	Maple Falls	6 mi rt	2 hr
564	Aptos Creek Loop	2.9 mi rt	1.5 hr
567	South Marsh Loop	2.2 mi rt	1 hr
Monterey & Big Sur			
574	Pacific Grove Ocean View	4.4 mi rt	2.5 hr
577	Monterey Bay Coastal Recreation Trail	4.5 mi rt	1.5 hr
581	Fort Ord National Monument Loop	4 mi rt	2 hr

DIFFICULTY	SEASONAL ACCESS	WILDLIFE	WATERFALLS	DOG-FRIENDLY
Easy-moderate	Year-round			
Moderate-strenuous	May-Oct.			
Easy-moderate	Year-round	x		
Easy-moderate	Year-round	x	x	
Strenuous	Year-round			
Easy	Year-round			
Easy-moderate	Year-round			
Easy	Apr.-Oct.			
Moderate	Year-round	x	x	
Easy-moderate	Year-round			
Easy	Year-round			
Easy	Year-round	x		
Easy-moderate	Year-round	x		
Easy	Year-round	x		
Easy	Year-round	x		
Easy	Year-round	x		
Easy	Year-round	x		x
Moderate	Year-round	x	x	
Easy	Year-round			x
Easy	Year-round	x		
Easy	Year-round	x		x
Easy-moderate	Year-round	x		x
Easy	Year-round	x		x

TRAILS AT A GLANCE

PAGE	HIKE NAME	DISTANCE	DURATION
585	Ollason Peak and Valley View	7.8 mi rt	4.5 hr
589	Carmel Meadows	1.8 mi rt	1 hr
593	Point Lobos Perimeter Loop	5.2 mi rt	3 hr
597	Redwood Canyon-Terrace Loop	3.6 mi rt	2 hr
600	Soberanes Canyon Trail	2.8 mi rt	1.5 hr
603	Andrew Molera State Park Loop	8 mi rt	4 hr
607	Pfeiffer Falls	1.6 mi rt	1 hr
610	Buzzards Roost Trail	3 mi rt	1.5 hr
613	McWay Falls Overlook	0.7 mi rt	30 min
Pinnacles National Park			
620	Balconies Cave	2.4 mi rt	1.5 hr
623	Condor Gulch and High Peaks Loop	5.3 mi rt	3 hr
627	Moses Spring-Rim Trail Loop with Bear Gulch Cave	1.7 mi rt	1.5 hr

DIFFICULTY	SEASONAL ACCESS	WILDLIFE	WATERFALLS	DOG-FRIENDLY
Moderate	Year-round	x		
Easy	Year-round	x		x
Easy-moderate	Year-round	x		
Easy-moderate	Apr.-Nov.			x
Easy-moderate	Year-round			
Moderate	Spring-fall	x		
Easy	Year-round		x	
Easy-moderate	Year-round	x		
Easy	Year-round		x	
Easy	Year-round			
Moderate	Year-round	x		
Easy	Year-round			

MOON NORTHERN CALIFORNIA HIKING

Avalon Travel
Hachette Book Group
1700 Fourth Street
Berkeley, CA 94710, USA
www.moon.com

Editor: Vy Tran
Managing Editor: Hannah Brezack
Copy Editor: Christopher Church
Graphics Coordinator: Rue Flaherty
Production Coordinator: Rue Flaherty
Cover Design: Kimberly Glyder Design
Interior Design: Megan Jones Design
Map Editor: Kat Bennett
Cartographers: John Culp, Erin Greb
    Cartography, Abby Whelan
Proofreader: Callie Stoker-Graham
Indexer: Greg Jewett

ISBN-13: 978-1-64049-968-3

Printing History
1st Edition — April 2024
5 4 3 2 1

Front cover photo: Muir Woods
National Monument © mvaligursky
/ iStock / Getty Images Plus
Back cover photo: Yosemite National
Park © Cbork7 | Dreamstime.com

Printed in China by APS

ICON AND MAP SYMBOLS KEY

🧍🚶 Kid-friendly	❀ Wildflowers	🚌🚋 Public transit
🏛 Historic landmarks	🐾 Dog-friendly	♿ Wheelchair accessible
🐾 Wildlife	⚓ Water features	

Expressway	Feature Trail	♣ Grove/Significant Tree	🄿 Picnic Table/Area
Primary Road	Other Trail	✛ Natural Feature	▪ Point of Interest
Secondary Road	1,200 Index Contour Line	▲ Mountain	ⓘ Information
Unpaved Road	Contour Line	⌇ Waterfall	○ City
Paved Path	🅣 Trailhead	✛ Water Feature	○ Town/Village
Stairs	🅟 Parking Area	⛑ Camping Area	✈ Airport

 QUICK-REFERENCE CHART: TRAILS AT A GLANCE